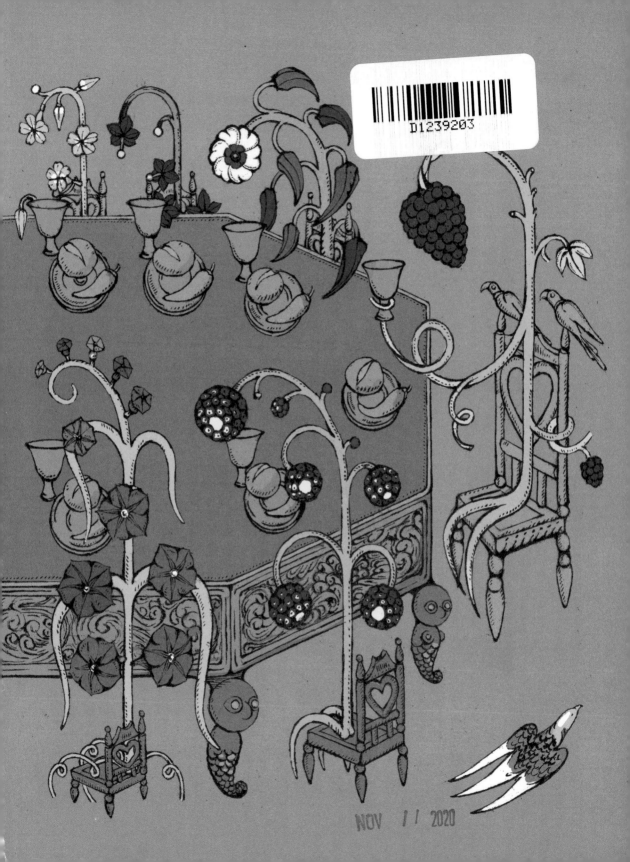

THE BEST AMERICAN

Comics 2019

GUEST EDITORS OF THE
BEST AMERICAN COMICS

2006	HARVEY PEKAR
2007	CHRIS WARE
2008	LYNDA BARRY
2009	CHARLES BURNS
2010	NEIL GAIMAN
2011	ALISON BECHDEL
2012	FRANÇOISE MOULY
2013	JEFF SMITH
2014	SCOTT McCLOUD
2015	JONATHAN LETHEM
2016	ROZ CHAST
2017	BEN KATCHOR
2018	PHOEBE GLOECKNER
2019	JILLIAN TAMAKI

THE BEST AMERICAN

Comics

2019

EDITED *and* INTRODUCED
by Jillian Tamaki

BILL KARTALOPOULOS,
series editor

HOUGHTON MIFFLIN HARCOURT
BOSTON · NEW YORK   2019

hmhbooks.com

Library of Congress Cataloging-in-Publication Data is available.

ISSN 1941-6385 (print)   ISBN 978-0-358-06728-3 (print)
ISSN 2573-3869 (ebook)   ISBN 978-0-358-06729-0 (ebook)

Book design: Chrissy Kurpeski   Cover art: Sophia Foster-Dimino
Endpaper art: Nishant Saldanha   Cover art direction: Christopher Moisan

PRINTED IN THE UNITED STATES OF AMERICA

DOC 10 9 8 7 6 5 4 3 2 1

Permissions credits are located on page 374.

Contents

vii : BILL KARTALOPOULOS Foreword

xiv : JILLIAN TAMAKI Introduction

1 : LALE WESTVIND Grip, Vol. 1 (*Excerpt*)

25 : E. A. BETHEA Bit Rot

28 : FANNY BRITT AND ISABELLE ARSENAULT Louis Undercover (*Excerpt*)

44 : JOE SACCO Bitumen or Bust

55 : ANATOLA HOWARD Self-Love-Cycle

58 : LESLIE STEIN Vanguard

69 : MARGOT FERRICK Dognurse (*Excerpt*)

88 : LAUREN WEINSTEIN Being an Artist and a Mother

93 : BEN PASSMORE Martin Luther King Jr. Was More Radical Than You Think

105 : JOHN PORCELLINO Selections FROM *King-Cat #78*

130 : ERIK NEBEL Why Don't We Come Together (*Excerpt*)

143 : SOPHIA FOSTER-DIMINO Small Mistakes Make Big Problems

154 : XIA GORDON Kindling (*Excerpt*)

164 : VERA BROSGOL Welcome to O.R.R.A. FROM *Be Prepared* (*Excerpt*)

189 : JED McGOWAN Uninhabitable

204 : NISHANT SALDANHA Snow Day for Mr. Good Guy

206 : NICK DRNASO Sabrina (*Excerpt*)

220 : REMY BOYDELL AND MICHELLE PEREZ
Sex Positive FROM *The Pervert* (*Excerpt*)

232 : ANGIE WANG In Search of Water-Boiled Fish

271 : CONNOR WILLUMSEN Anti-Gone (*Excerpt*)

286 : NOEL FREIBERT Old Ground (*Excerpt*)

300 : JERRY MORIARTY whatsa paintoonist? (*Excerpt*)

318 : TOMMI PARRISH
Perfect Discipline FROM *Perfect Discipline and Unbending Loyalty* (*Excerpt*)

337 : LAURA LANNES
By Monday I'll Be Floating in the Hudson with the Other Garbage (*Excerpt*)

344 : ELEANOR DAVIS Hurt or Fuck

371 : Notable Comics from September 1, 2017, to August 31, 2018

Foreword

Comics is an art form of simultaneity.

Most obviously, comics often employ text and image simultaneously. Often, but not always. Some comics—including work in this volume—don't use text at all, and strictly express their meanings through structured sequences of images. Nevertheless, the integration of text and image is a powerful aspect of many comics, and one that is characteristic of the form to many readers.

But comics perform much more subtle and complex acts of simultaneity in every aspect of their composition. Chris Ware has characterized the experience of reading comics as one that integrates seeing and reading. When he says that, he isn't talking about the combination of text and image—although it may sound like he is. What Ware means instead is that each representational image in a narrative comic has aesthetic qualities that we can look at (like any image), while simultaneously providing narrative information that we can visually read. In other words, narrative images in comics communicate symbolic visual information that a reader should be able to interpret in order to make the work's meaning clear while also functioning as aesthetic objects. We inspect each image visually and glean information from it intellectually: we simultaneously see and read the images. (Ware has referred to his own drawings, strongly developed toward this particular function, as typographical in character.)

Images in comics are usually contained within panels, which function to isolate individual compositions. The carefully delineated limits of each composition inscribe each panel's separateness and signal each individual panel's legible integrity. Simultaneously, each panel's juxtaposition alongside other panels activates its *other* status as part of a sequence of images. Nineteenth-century comics pioneer Rodolphe Töpffer noted that the individual panels in a comic function as "links in a chain." Each panel presents a new, comprehensible composition, while functioning as an elaboration or development of the panels that came before. And each panel also establishes a context and preconditions for the subsequent panels that follow. Within the context of any comic's intended reading order, each individual panel contains both a link to the past and a bridge to the future while maintaining its own particular singularity.

In printed comics, those panels are usually organized within the overall structure of a page, which has historically been the fundamental unit of composition in comics designed for publication. Each page contains an accretion of panels within the spatial limits of its particular format. The arrangement of panels on a comics page usually follows the pattern by which lines of typeset text are arranged in prose: in Western cultures a reader often follows a row of panels from left to right across the width of the page, and then repeats the procedure for each subsequent row.

But each page of comics is more than an arbitrary agglomeration of individual panels. It is simultaneously an overall visual-narrative composition that has been considered by the artist. A page's underlying compositional strategy may be principally narrative: a page may be organized to present a complete narrative idea, or various (possibly even opposing) aspects of an idea, sitting together in eternally suspended tension within the static framework of the page. The composition may be based on design, balancing a range of graphic elements across the page as carefully as they might be balanced within an individual panel. This design may create a pleasing overall effect and lead the reader's eye fluidly from one panel to the next. But the page itself may also function as a communicative device, arranging panels within a harmonious composition that visually communicates an overall concept that is the product—not merely the sum—of the individual meanings of all of its choreographed constituent panels. Much more significant than the integration of text and image on a panel-by-panel basis, the true text-image combination that defines comics is each page's dynamic between the simultaneously textual reading order of its panels and its overall imagistic, compositional integrity.

It should be noted that recent digital comics increasingly disrupt conventional approaches to page layout, arranging panels and images in a way that exploits the affordances of the vertical scrolling typical of many current digital interfaces. In some digital comics—like Angie Wang's, which was reformatted to appear in this book—the overall composition of the work quite strikingly determines the underlying logic of the arrangement of its individual images. Works like these revise and often reverse the priority of linear legibility over global composition that has historically characterized page design in most printed comics.

Within a more traditional codex, like a magazine or a book, each page usually appears opposite another page; the two pages together are called a "spread." Like any pair of panels, pages facing each other in a spread might also have a relationship: they may echo or reflect one another, present a contrast, or work together to form another integrated composition while each page maintains its own integrity.

A multipage story—whether three pages or three hundred pages long—expands upon the spread and offers further opportunities for expressive composition. Individual images may recur throughout a work and accrue further meaning, gaining complexity and symbolic value. Individual panel compositions may recur in surprising places, to link narrative moments together. Even individual page compositions may repeat, reflect, or echo one another at significant points—sometimes dozens or hundreds of pages apart—to indicate a relationship between separate visual narrative situations.

Well beyond the already sophisticated interplay of text and image, every element in a comic is part of a complex composition. Each element of a comic potentially bears many simultaneous immanent layers of meaning, based upon its relationship with other individual elements of the work and with the work as a whole. Not every comic does all of these things, but this brief survey indicates the complexity of the form and the vast compositional palette available to all comics artists. What's thrilling about comics is that these tools are all conceptual and intellectual—not material—and remain available to any artist with a pencil and paper at their disposal.

The contemporary comics field is, itself, simultaneously many things. For some artists, it is a means of direct—even raw—personal expression. For others, it is a field of aesthetic and formal exploration (which is, itself, an expression of personal intellectual fascination). Comics can be instructive or educational. Comics can speak to contemporary events and can serve as an accessible platform for marginalized voices. One part of the comics field, in the form of graphic novels, has largely become a subset of the commercial book publishing industry, which often privileges its own genres and forms including long-form literary fiction, memoir, and graphic novels for younger readers. Another heavily commercialized part of the comics field privileges serialized adventure-oriented entertainment, often featuring decades-old, highly recognizable characters (usually owned by corporate entities). Most comics simultaneously exist within more than one of the handful of categories I've briefly (and incompletely) sketched out here, and many comics are utterly unclassifiable. As carefully composed as any comic may be, it is not the job of any artist in any field to make work that fits neatly into conceptual boxes.

As series editor for the Best American Comics, I have remained keenly aware of the complex ways that comics work and the countless, diverse things that comics do. I expect that excellent and surprising work can emerge from every part of the field and can take any form. Each year's volume begins with an effort to track this constantly growing, always evolving field of creative work. Within that, I have sought work that is—regardless of where or how it is published or what form it takes—ambitious, artistic, expressive, unique, and personally motivated; work that pushes boundaries and takes risks, and in so doing is highly accomplished, distinctive, and outstanding. It is always my hope that readers—and publishers, editors, and critics—will demand the same of comics.

As a result, the Best American Comics is many things at once. It is a time capsule that presents a cross section of work published within a particular twelve-month period. It is also a collection of excellent work that bears reading and re-reading long after each volume has been followed by subsequent volumes. (Like a panel in a comics sequence, each annual volume is a "link in a chain" that maintains its own individual integrity while functioning as part of an overall series.) And every year I collaborate with a special guest editor, who chooses the work that is ultimately reprinted in each year's volume. While each volume is an attempt to make a broad critical statement about work published during that year's eligibility period, the guest editor's selections also make the book a personal expression of that editor's engagement, responses, tastes, and artistic values. Each volume is both timely and timeless; a critical project and a personal statement. It is, hopefully, a satisfying reading experience in and of itself while also introducing the reader to artists and works that demand further exploration.

I was grateful to be joined in the task of assembling this year's volume by guest editor Jillian Tamaki. As much as any other artist, Jillian's body of work reflects the broad range of comics today. She has published challenging work with small boutique micropresses, graphic novels for younger readers with large corporate publishers, has serialized comics online, and more. She has made work for publication using traditional pen and ink, digital media, and even embroidery. Her range of activity—including comics, illustration, children's books, and teaching—reflects the range of professional options available to artists who have mastered the manifold skills that comics require. As guest editor for *The Best American Comics 2019*, Jillian brought a diligent, searching engagement to this year's volume, motivated by a strong desire to best represent the breadth of contemporary comics. She went about her task thoughtfully and with careful consideration. I'm grateful that readers of this book will have a chance to experience Jillian's perspective on the past year's work in the comics field.

The Best American Comics 2019 represents a selection of outstanding North American work first published between September 1, 2017, and August 31, 2018. Many of the comics we considered came to us through our open submission process. Additionally, I sought out work for consideration at comic book stores, at comics festivals, online, and through recommendations from trusted colleagues. Through all of these activities, I amassed and considered a large pool of comics, and selected approximately 120 pieces to forward to our guest editor, who made the final selections that constitute the present volume (while retaining the flexibility to bring in work they may have discovered independently). In addition to the work we have reprinted here, I've assembled a lengthy list of additional Notable Comics that appears at the back of this book. If you have enjoyed any of the comics in this volume, the works listed in our Notable Comics list are all also worth seeking out. I have posted a version of this list to my website (on-panel.com) that includes links to sites where you can learn more about those comics.

Thanks as always to our in-house editor at Houghton Mifflin Harcourt, Nicole Angeloro, who manages and coordinates the many moving parts behind this challenging annual book project with considerable aplomb. This book would not be possible without her hard work and support. Thanks to art director Christopher Moisan, who works with our artists on the cover and endpapers for each volume. Thanks to Chrissy Kurpeski, our interior designer, and to Beth Burleigh Fuller for managing the complex production behind this book. Thanks as well to Mary Dalton-Hoffman, who secures the crucial rights and permissions for each year's volume. Many thanks to all of my colleagues who offered helpful suggestions, advice and guidance as I worked on this volume.

Special thanks to Sophia Foster-Dimino for providing this year's exceptional cover, which says something about the comics form; suggests the relationship between author, subject, and reader; and signals the radical shifts in perspective that any anthology should offer readers from piece to piece. Thanks as well to Nishant Saldahnha for drawing this year's eye-popping endpapers.

Our efforts are intended to both honor excellent work and to give you, the reader, a look at the vital and robust world of contemporary North American comics. An anthology like this offers an opportunity to reflect on the variety of comics today and the unique qualities of each piece. But it also creates a context within which to think about what these diverse works might have in common. The points of contact between and among these pieces certainly include each artist's commitment to the comics form in its diverse manifestations. This body of work is also an expression of Jillian Tamaki's personal vision, working within the parameters of this series. And, like every title in the "Best American" series of annuals, these works together suggest the many deeply personal ways that people can engage life as it is today, and then express that engagement through art. These very different works make a shared statement about the diversity of ways that a human being can live, think, feel, see, be, and, finally, express their thoughts and experience, whether through comics, essays, short fiction, or any other form.

BILL KARTALOPOULOS

Introduction

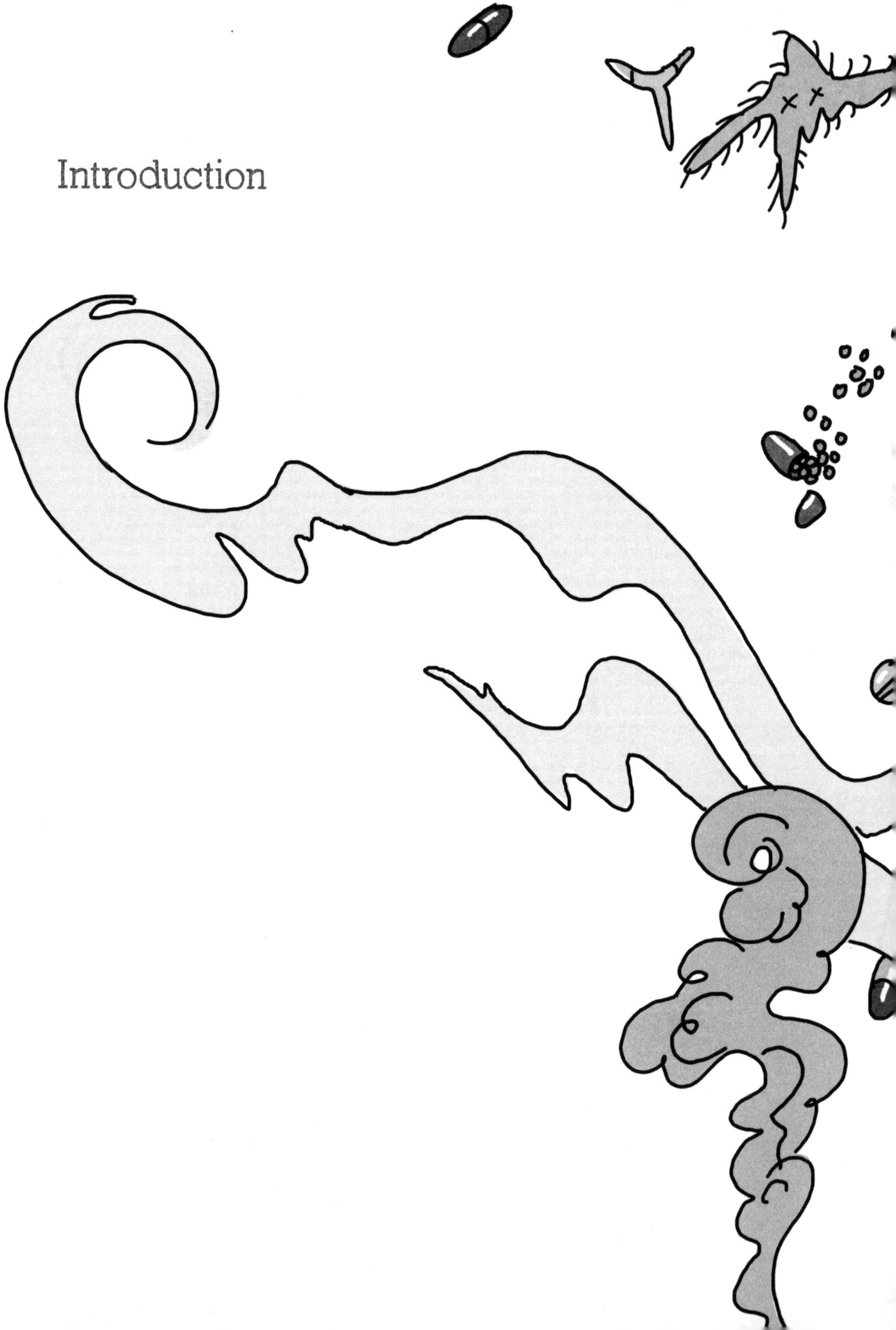

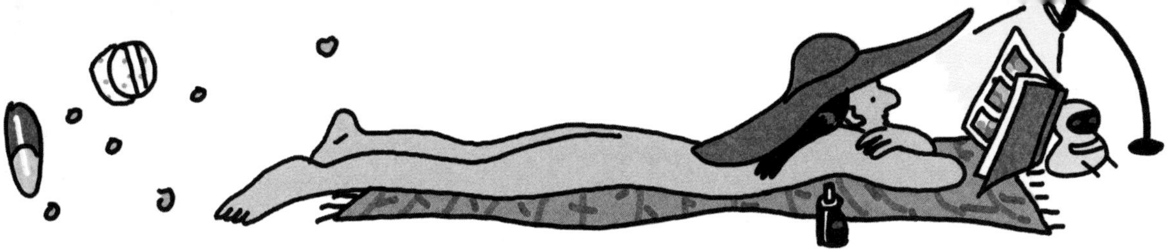

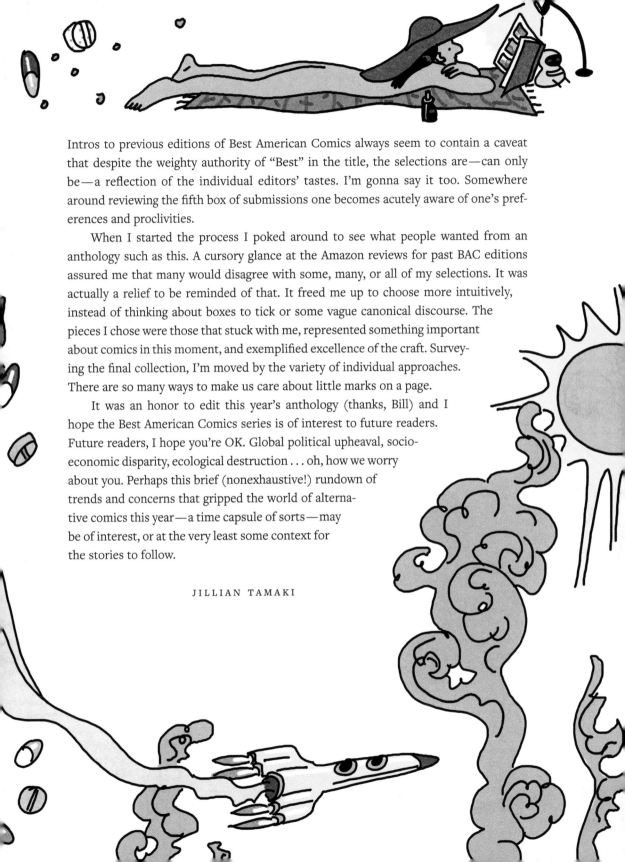

Intros to previous editions of Best American Comics always seem to contain a caveat that despite the weighty authority of "Best" in the title, the selections are—can only be—a reflection of the individual editors' tastes. I'm gonna say it too. Somewhere around reviewing the fifth box of submissions one becomes acutely aware of one's preferences and proclivities.

When I started the process I poked around to see what people wanted from an anthology such as this. A cursory glance at the Amazon reviews for past BAC editions assured me that many would disagree with some, many, or all of my selections. It was actually a relief to be reminded of that. It freed me up to choose more intuitively, instead of thinking about boxes to tick or some vague canonical discourse. The pieces I chose were those that stuck with me, represented something important about comics in this moment, and exemplified excellence of the craft. Surveying the final collection, I'm moved by the variety of individual approaches. There are so many ways to make us care about little marks on a page.

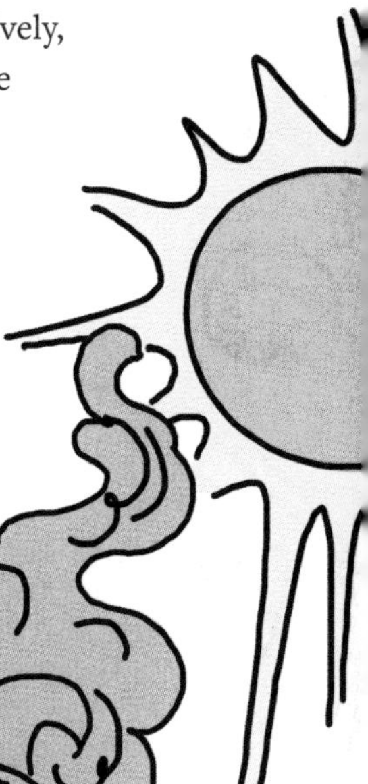

It was an honor to edit this year's anthology (thanks, Bill) and I hope the Best American Comics series is of interest to future readers. Future readers, I hope you're OK. Global political upheaval, socioeconomic disparity, ecological destruction . . . oh, how we worry about you. Perhaps this brief (nonexhaustive!) rundown of trends and concerns that gripped the world of alternative comics this year—a time capsule of sorts—may be of interest, or at the very least some context for the stories to follow.

JILLIAN TAMAKI

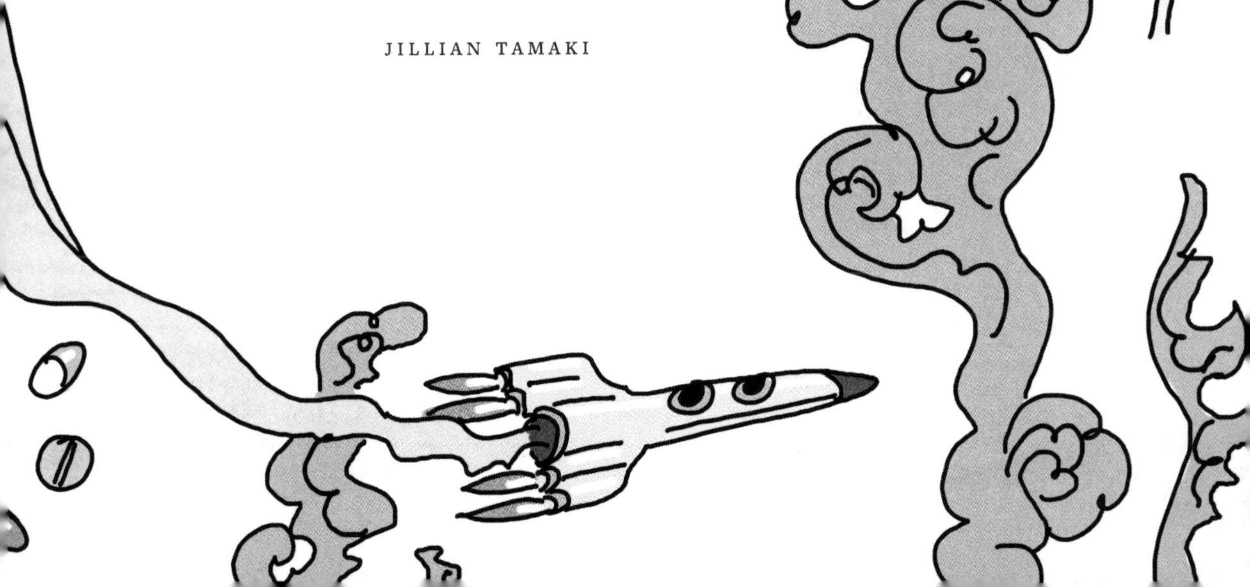

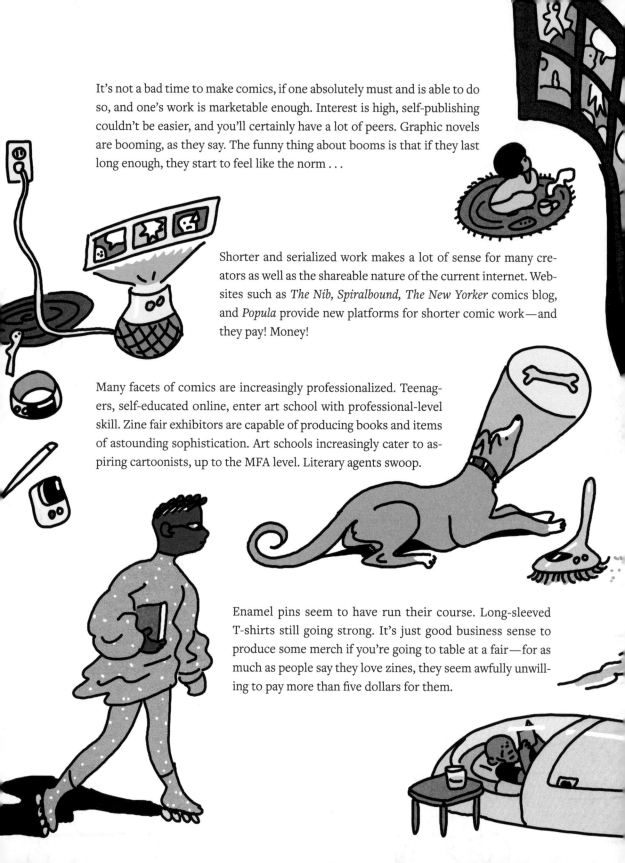

It's not a bad time to make comics, if one absolutely must and is able to do so, and one's work is marketable enough. Interest is high, self-publishing couldn't be easier, and you'll certainly have a lot of peers. Graphic novels are booming, as they say. The funny thing about booms is that if they last long enough, they start to feel like the norm . . .

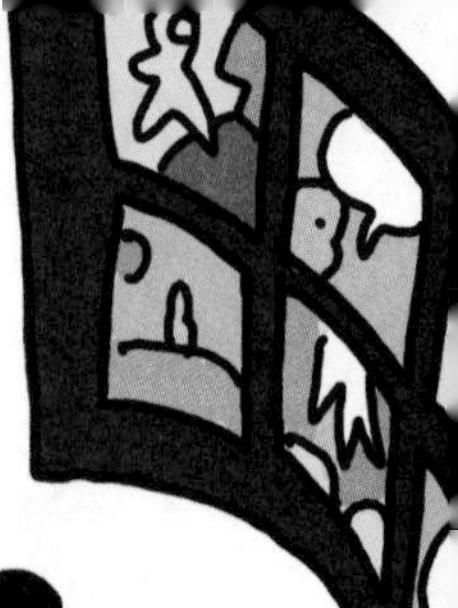

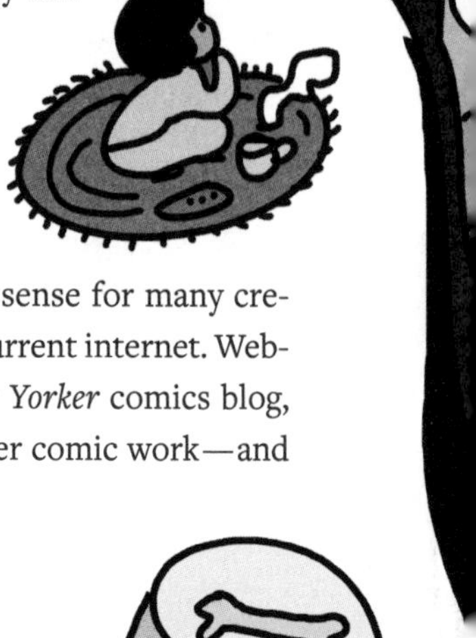

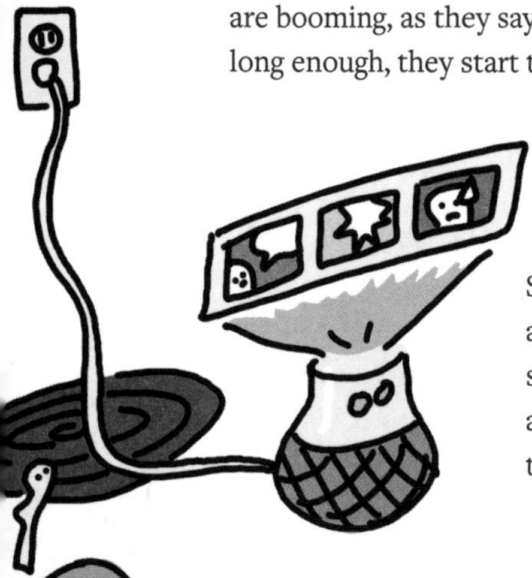

Shorter and serialized work makes a lot of sense for many creators as well as the shareable nature of the current internet. Websites such as *The Nib, Spiralbound, The New Yorker* comics blog, and *Popula* provide new platforms for shorter comic work—and they pay! Money!

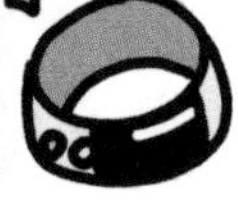

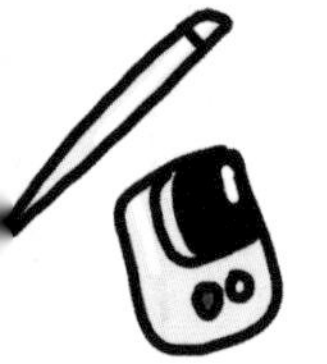

Many facets of comics are increasingly professionalized. Teenagers, self-educated online, enter art school with professional-level skill. Zine fair exhibitors are capable of producing books and items of astounding sophistication. Art schools increasingly cater to aspiring cartoonists, up to the MFA level. Literary agents swoop.

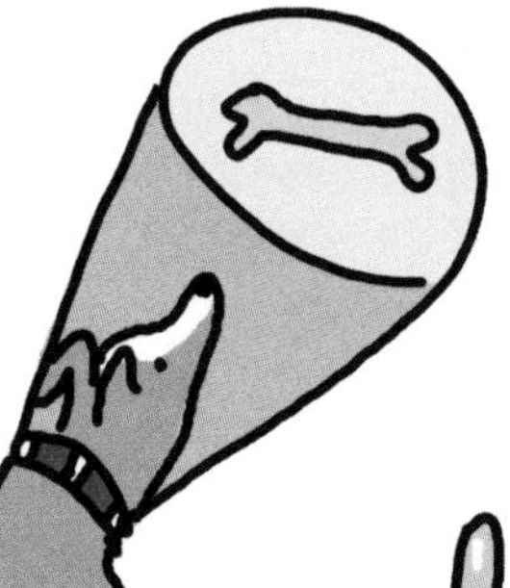

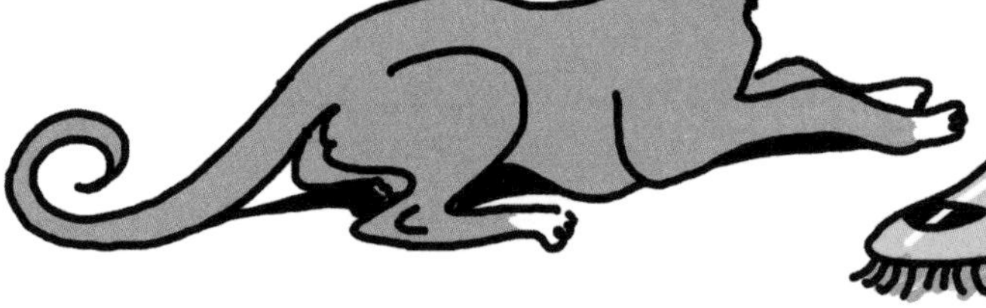

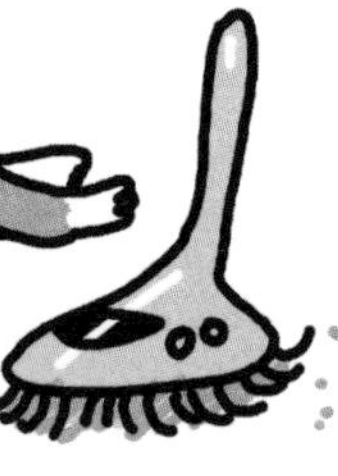

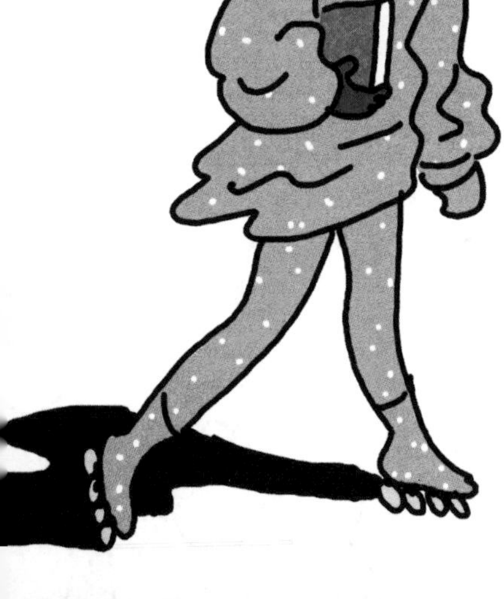

Enamel pins seem to have run their course. Long-sleeved T-shirts still going strong. It's just good business sense to produce some merch if you're going to table at a fair—for as much as people say they love zines, they seem awfully unwilling to pay more than five dollars for them.

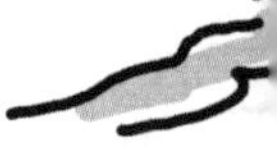

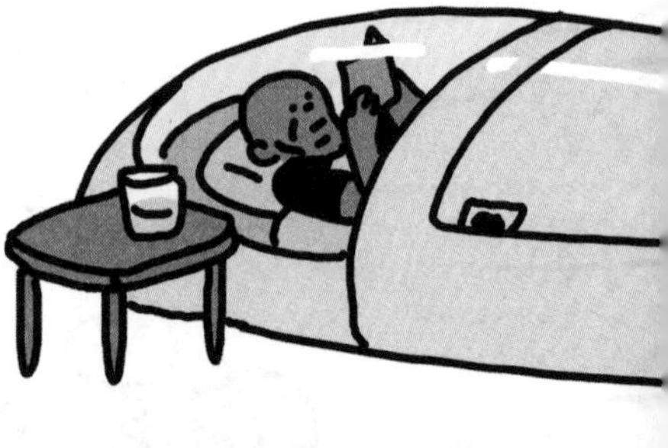

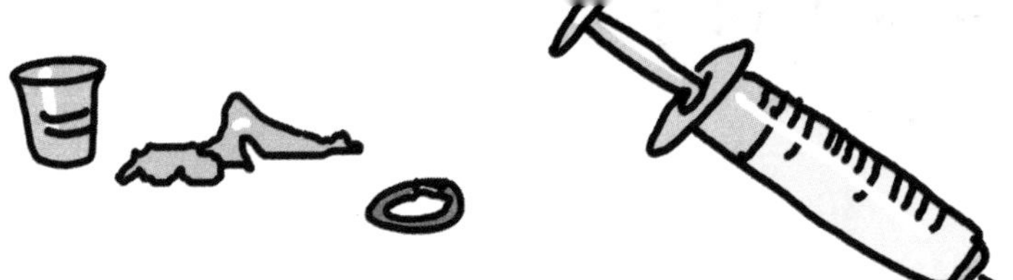

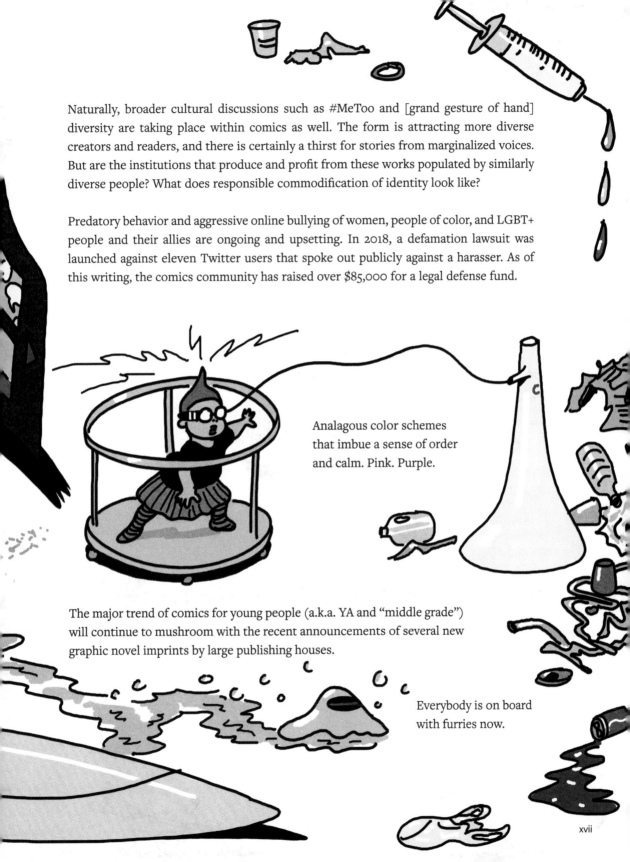

Naturally, broader cultural discussions such as #MeToo and [grand gesture of hand] diversity are taking place within comics as well. The form is attracting more diverse creators and readers, and there is certainly a thirst for stories from marginalized voices. But are the institutions that produce and profit from these works populated by similarly diverse people? What does responsible commodification of identity look like?

Predatory behavior and aggressive online bullying of women, people of color, and LGBT+ people and their allies are ongoing and upsetting. In 2018, a defamation lawsuit was launched against eleven Twitter users that spoke out publicly against a harasser. As of this writing, the comics community has raised over $85,000 for a legal defense fund.

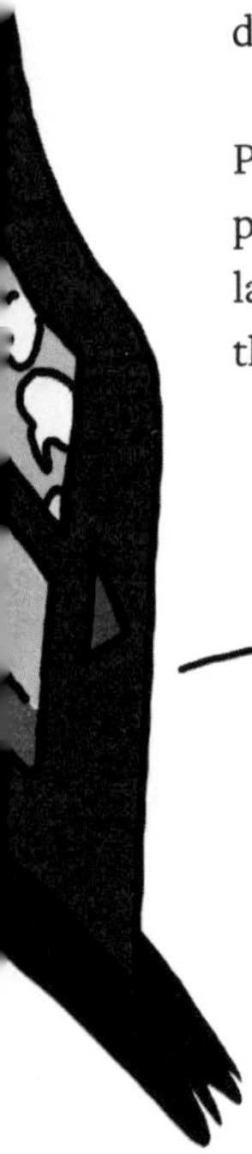

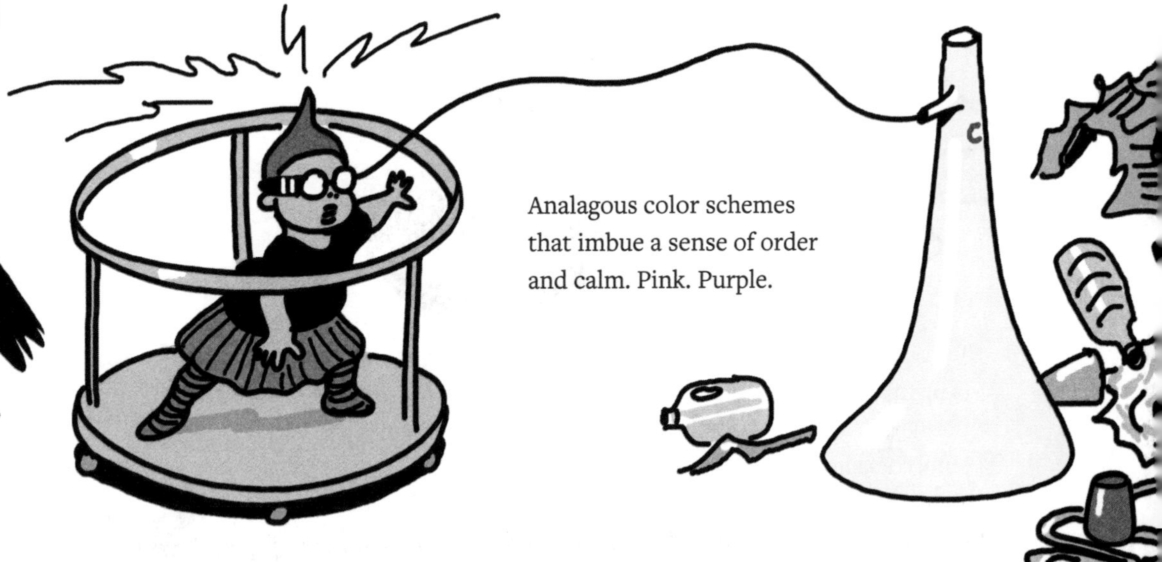

Analagous color schemes that imbue a sense of order and calm. Pink. Purple.

The major trend of comics for young people (a.k.a. YA and "middle grade") will continue to mushroom with the recent announcements of several new graphic novel imprints by large publishing houses.

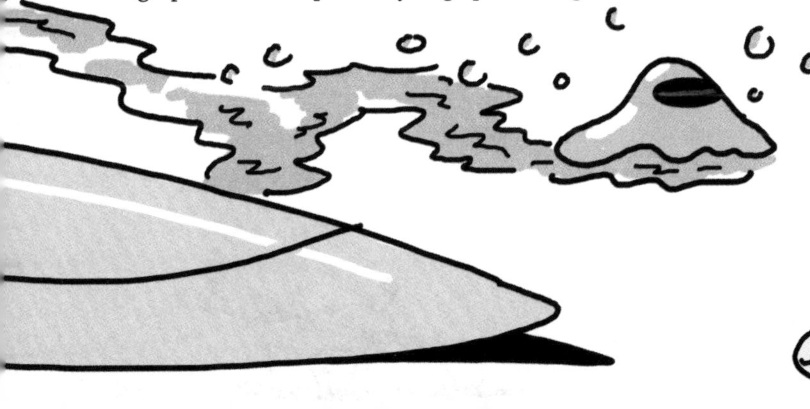

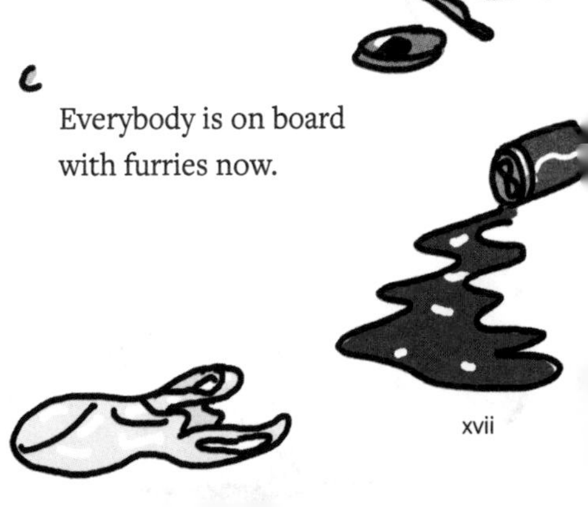

Everybody is on board with furries now.

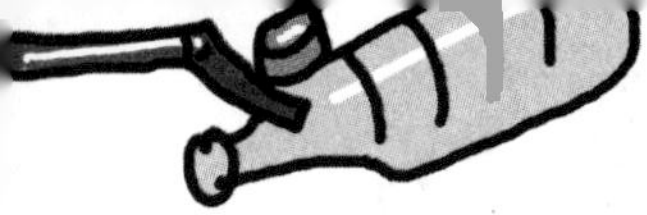

Despite the aforementioned "boom" and increased venues for work, debate about the economic feasibility of a career in comics remains evergreen. My hunch is that there are more people making a living (ranging from meager to very lucrative) off of comics than in the past, but the vast majority of practitioners are still grappling with very challenging dollar-per-hour math, as is attendant to a very time-consuming art form.

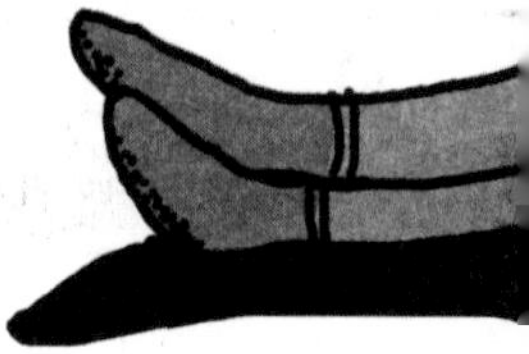

But is it simply the nature of comics to be relentlessly taxing? Overwork is central to the mythologies of the form's most beloved creators. That *Astro Boy* creator Osamu Tezuka overexerted himself to an early death at age sixty forms part of his legend. The romanticization of the self-sacrificing artist and ceaseless output in general is called to task by the concept of "self-care," which questions productivity at the expense of personal well-being.

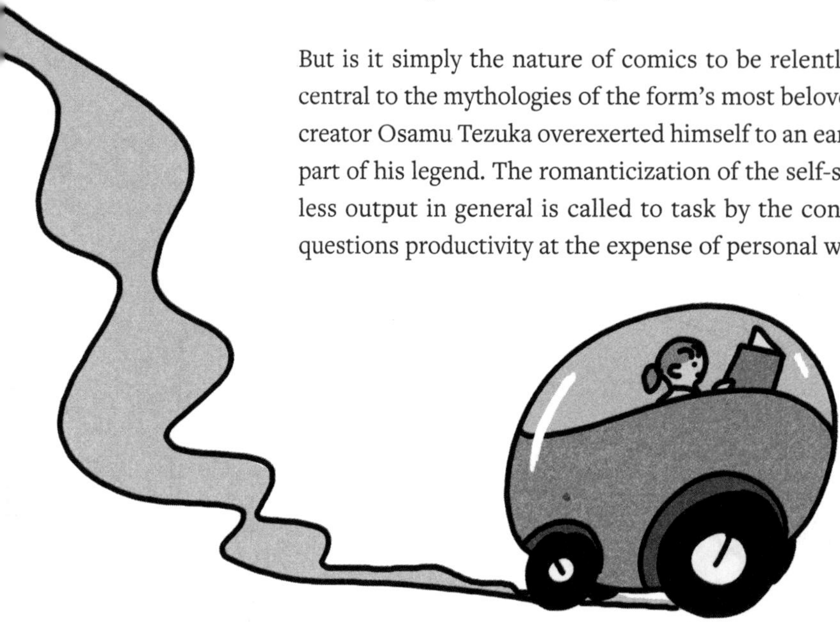

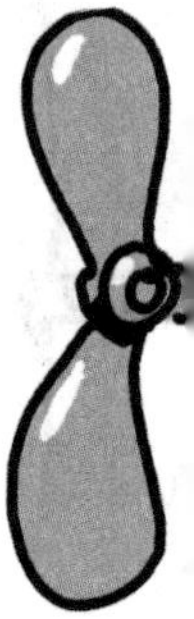

Rug Hooking!

Tattoos haven't been cutting-edge cool for a while, and I say this as a person who got their first tattoos in their mid-thirties after a divorce. But isn't there something a *little* transgressive and fun about shoving ink under your friends' skin in a hotel room? Oh Future Reader, you may laugh!

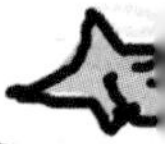

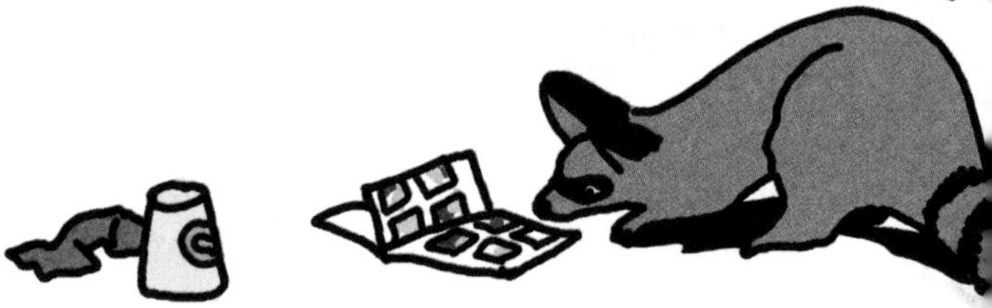

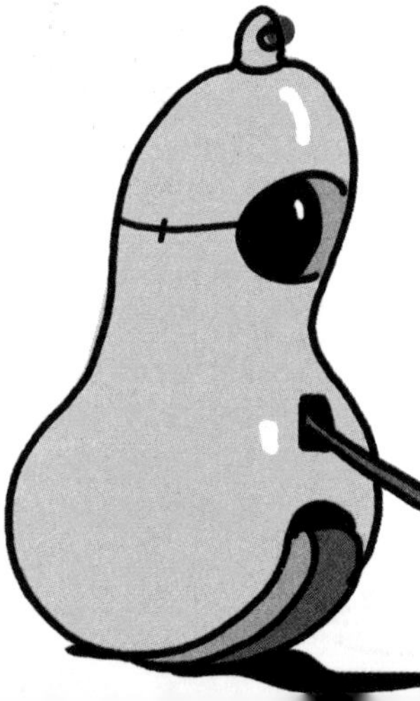

Is it even worth mentioning the crosscurrents between comics and animation? The two are so firmly enmeshed together, sharing not only practitioners but also aesthetics and point of view. While most studio jobs are still production-side, several creators have ascended to helm their own shows and become objectively famous people. Perhaps the real news item is that many often choose to continue making comics?

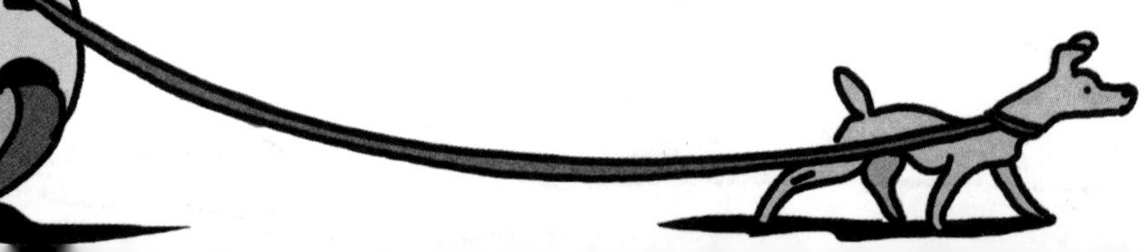

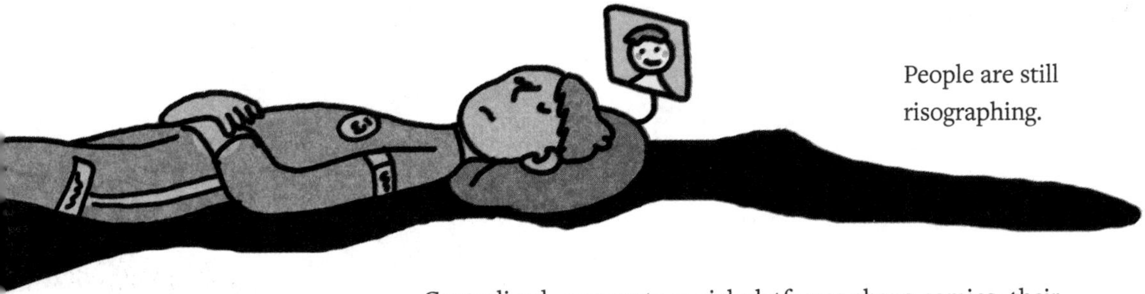

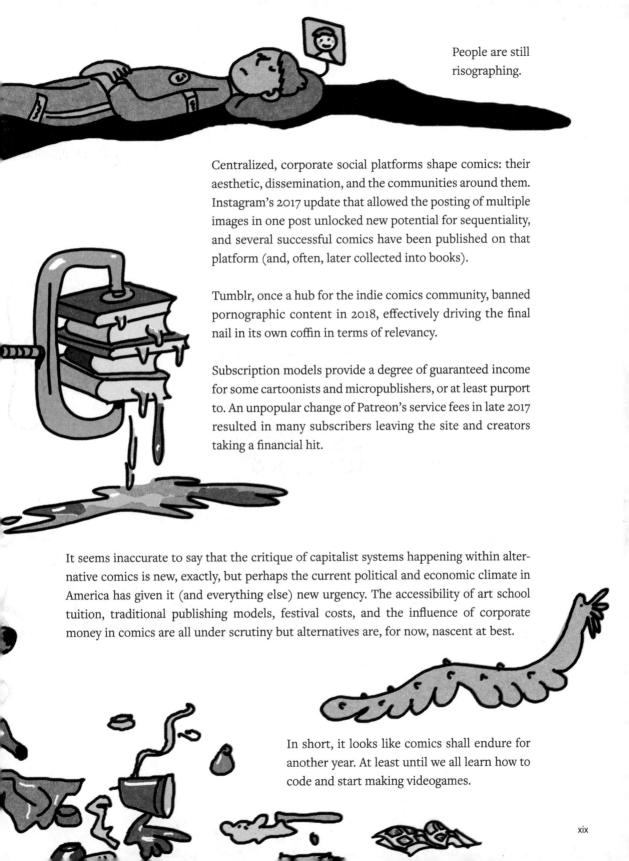

People are still risographing.

Centralized, corporate social platforms shape comics: their aesthetic, dissemination, and the communities around them. Instagram's 2017 update that allowed the posting of multiple images in one post unlocked new potential for sequentiality, and several successful comics have been published on that platform (and, often, later collected into books).

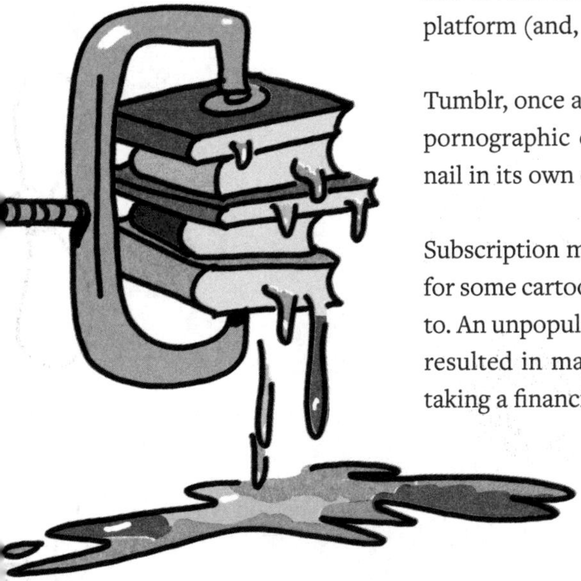

Tumblr, once a hub for the indie comics community, banned pornographic content in 2018, effectively driving the final nail in its own coffin in terms of relevancy.

Subscription models provide a degree of guaranteed income for some cartoonists and micropublishers, or at least purport to. An unpopular change of Patreon's service fees in late 2017 resulted in many subscribers leaving the site and creators taking a financial hit.

It seems inaccurate to say that the critique of capitalist systems happening within alternative comics is new, exactly, but perhaps the current political and economic climate in America has given it (and everything else) new urgency. The accessibility of art school tuition, traditional publishing models, festival costs, and the influence of corporate money in comics are all under scrutiny but alternatives are, for now, nascent at best.

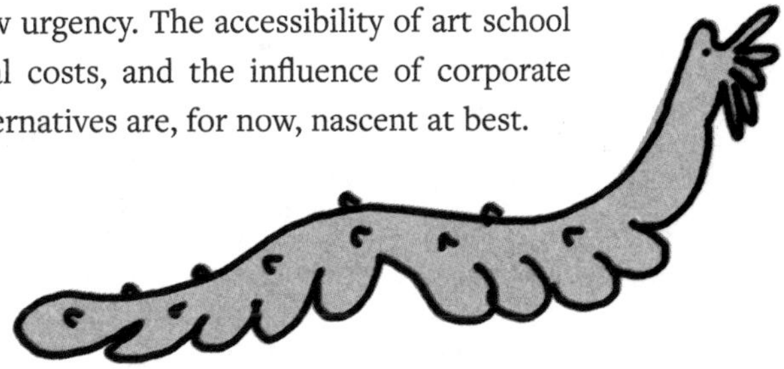

In short, it looks like comics shall endure for another year. At least until we all learn how to code and start making videogames.

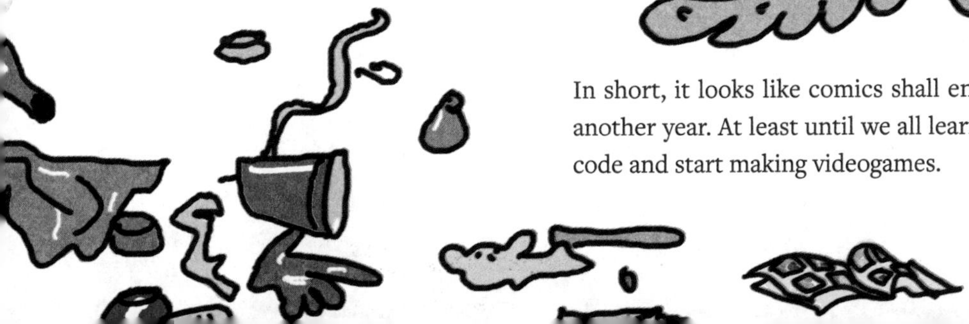

THE BEST AMERICAN

Comics 2019

Grip, Vol. 1 (*Excerpt*)

LALE WESTVIND

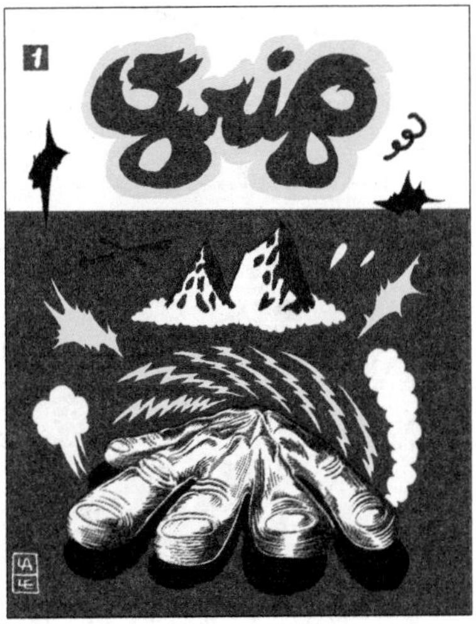
1
Grip

originally published in

Grip, Vol. 1

PERFECTLY ACCEPTABLE PRESS

6.5 x 8 inches • 68 pages

Biography

Lale Westvind, born in 1987, currently lives in Philadelphia. She is the author of over a dozen self-published comics and two anthologies, including the Hot Dog Beach series and *Hyperspeed to Nowhere.* Westvind has a penchant for depicting movement, speed, energy, and mechanical animism. Her work has been published internationally in anthologies such as *Kramers Ergot, The Lifted Brow, Strapazin,* and *Lagon Revue.* She is the author of *Hax* (Breakdown Press, 2015), *Now and Here* #1–3 (Pegacorn Press, 2014), and *Yazar and Arkadaş* (Fume Room Press, 2016). She teaches part-time in the Illustration department at Parsons School of Design.
lalewestvind.com

Statement

Grip is dedicated to women working in the trades and any person working with their hands. I have tremendous admiration for those individuals who have conquered or are learning the myriad skillful movements required for physical jobs, especially those with a passion for doing them well. It was inspired by all the women I have met, working hard and with skill as mechanics, carpenters, blacksmiths, servers, cooks, cleaners, and gardeners. My partner, specifically, was a large inspiration for the story having recently become an apprentice in an electrician's union after working as a server for many years. Originally the comic had text but it was removed because I found it redundant and distracting.

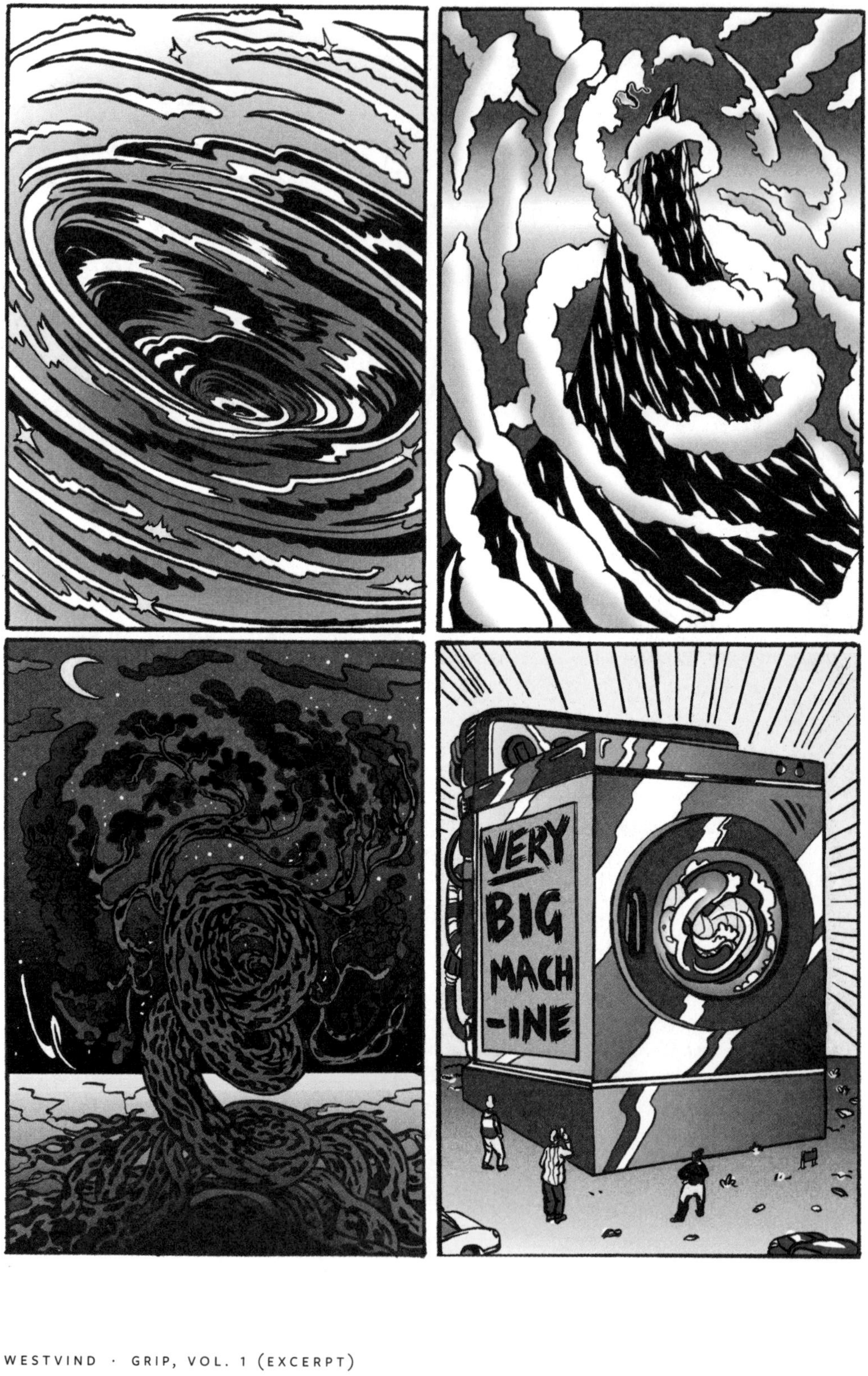
VERY
BIG
MACH
-INE

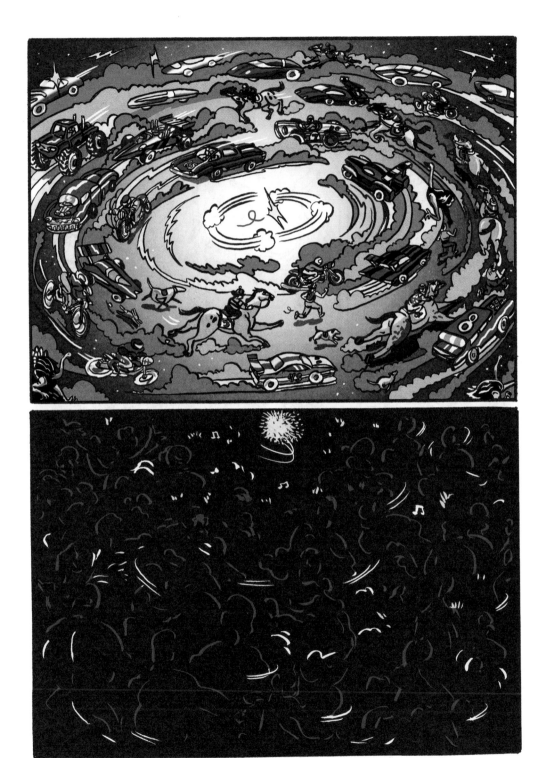

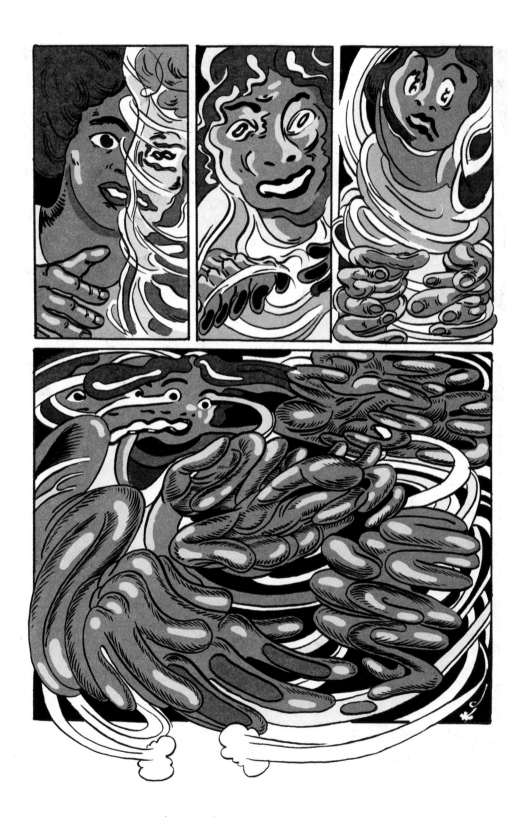

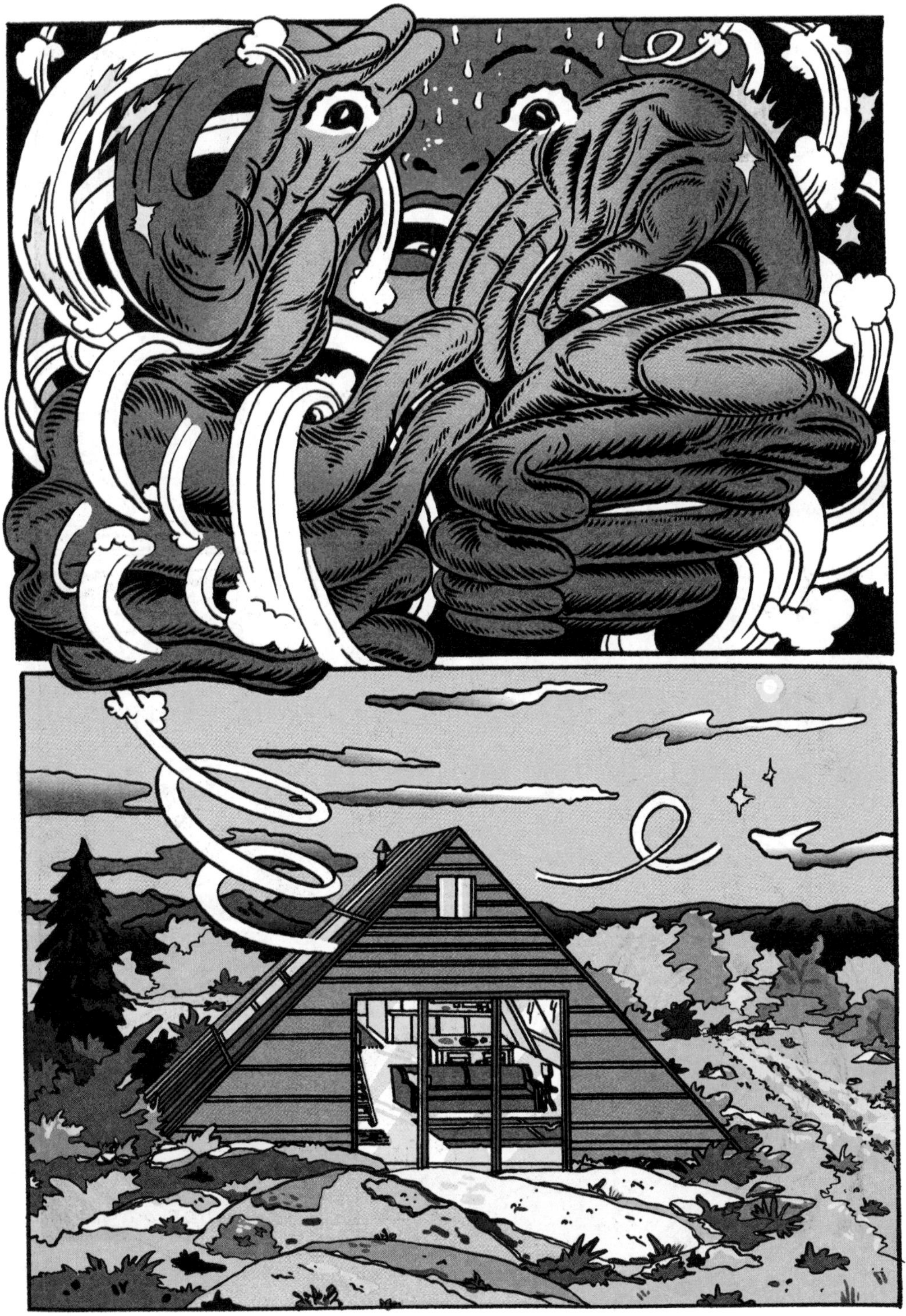

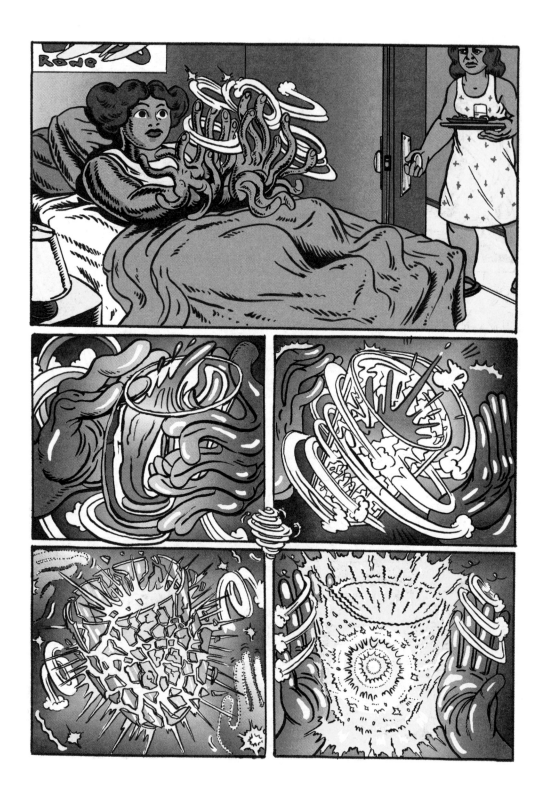

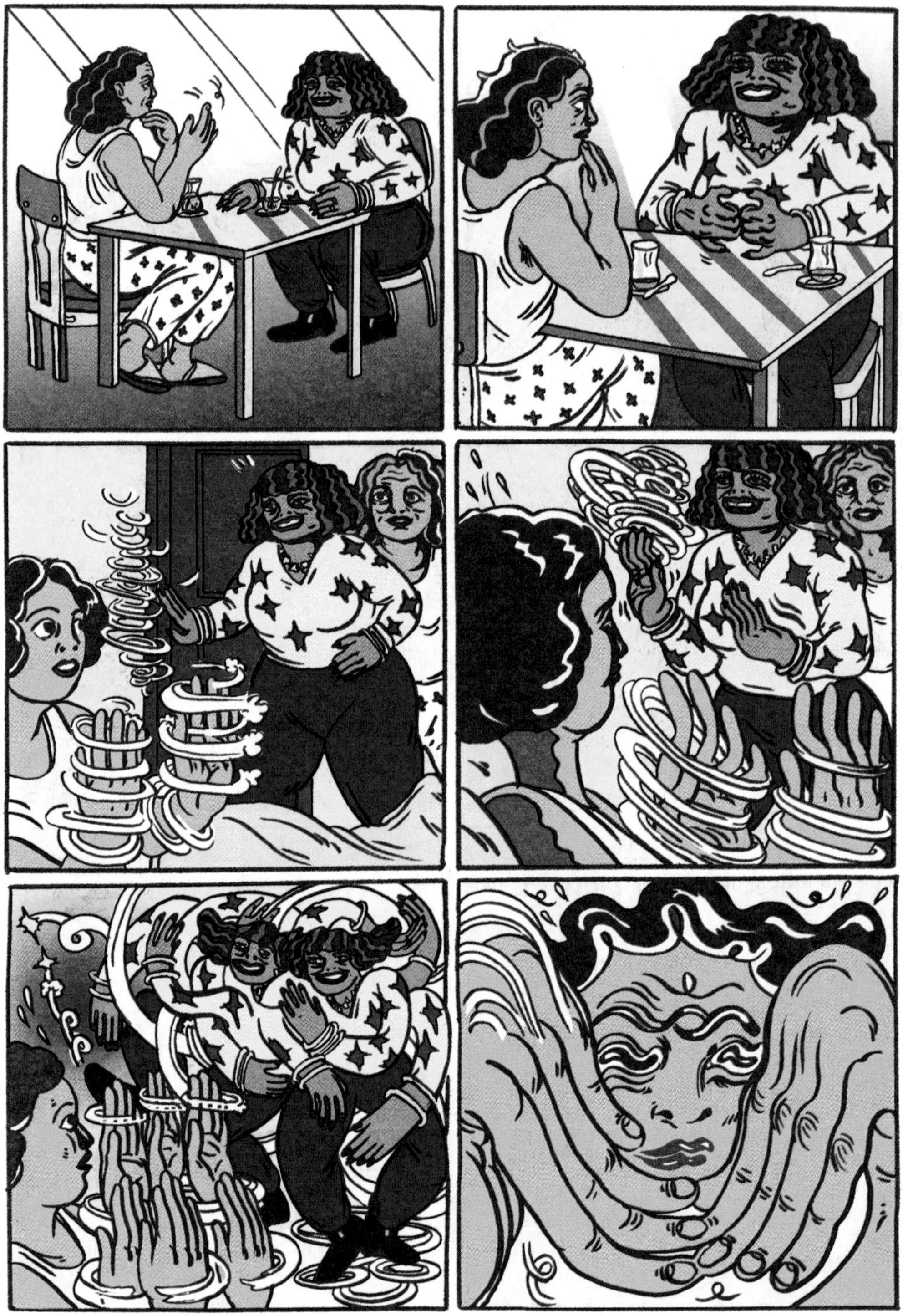

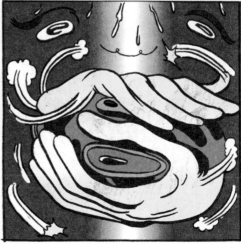

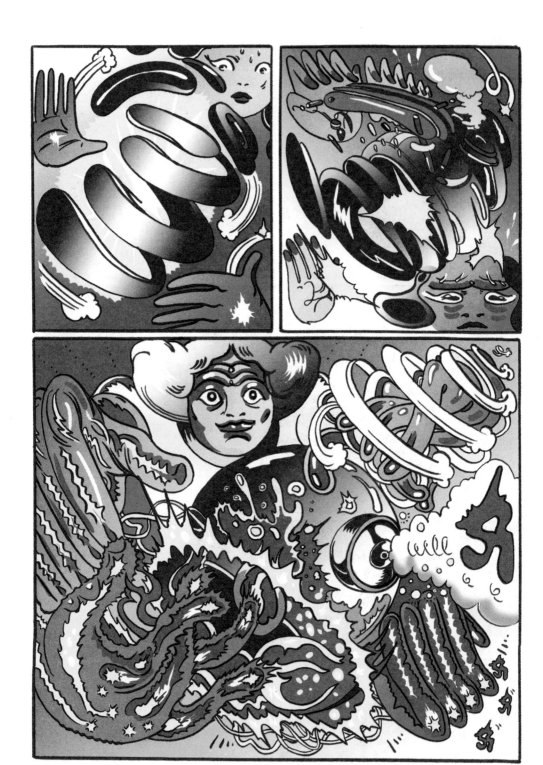

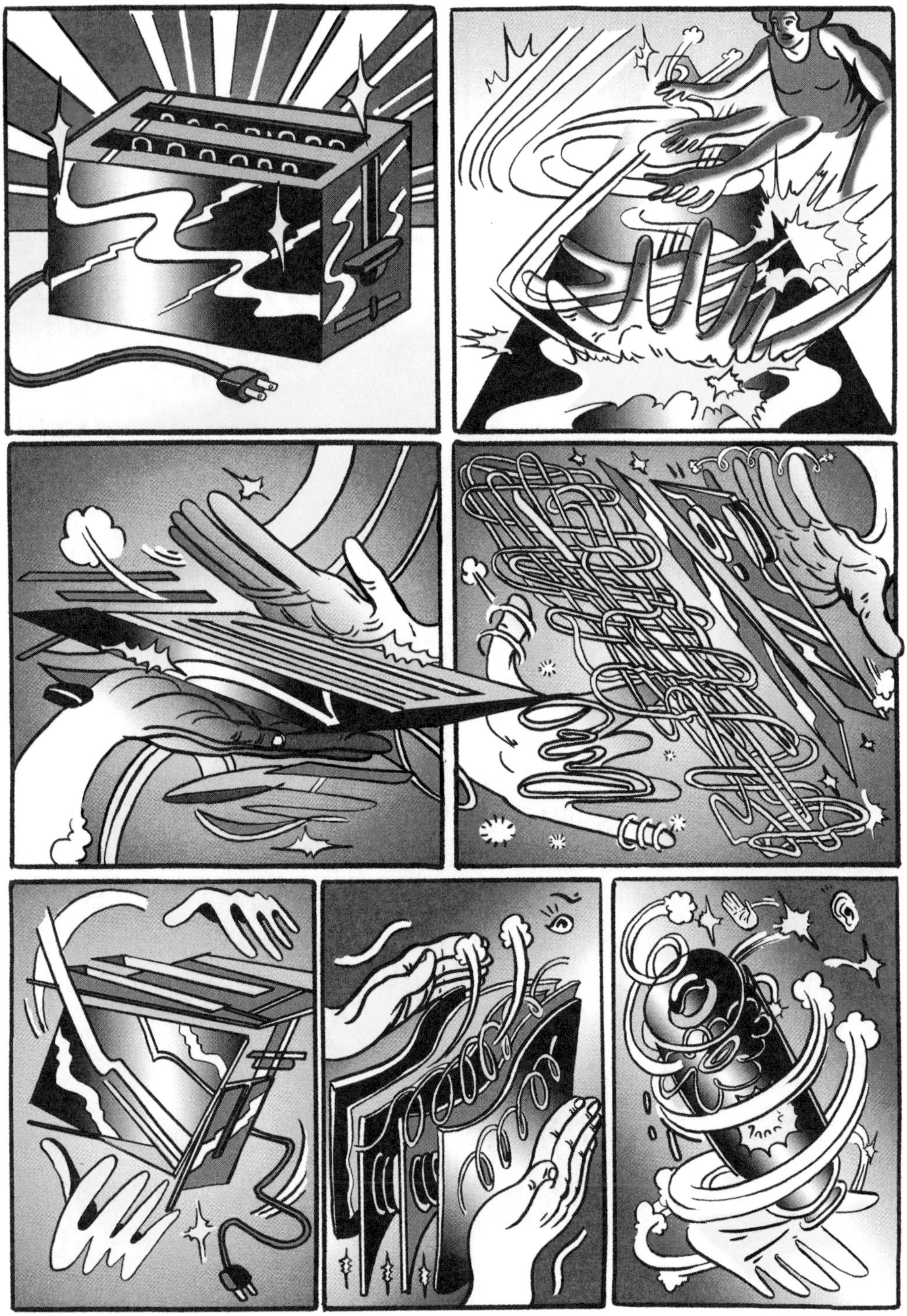

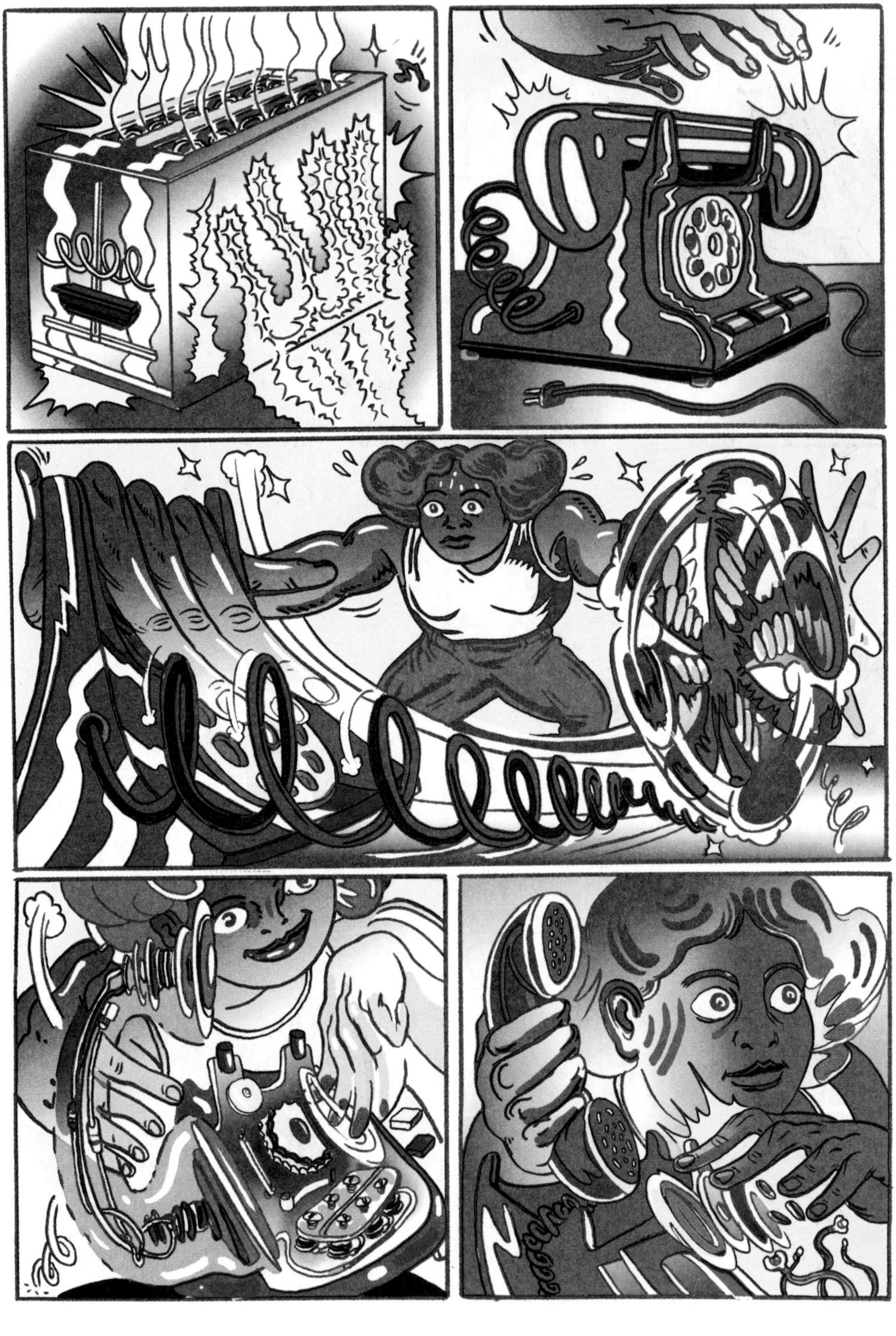

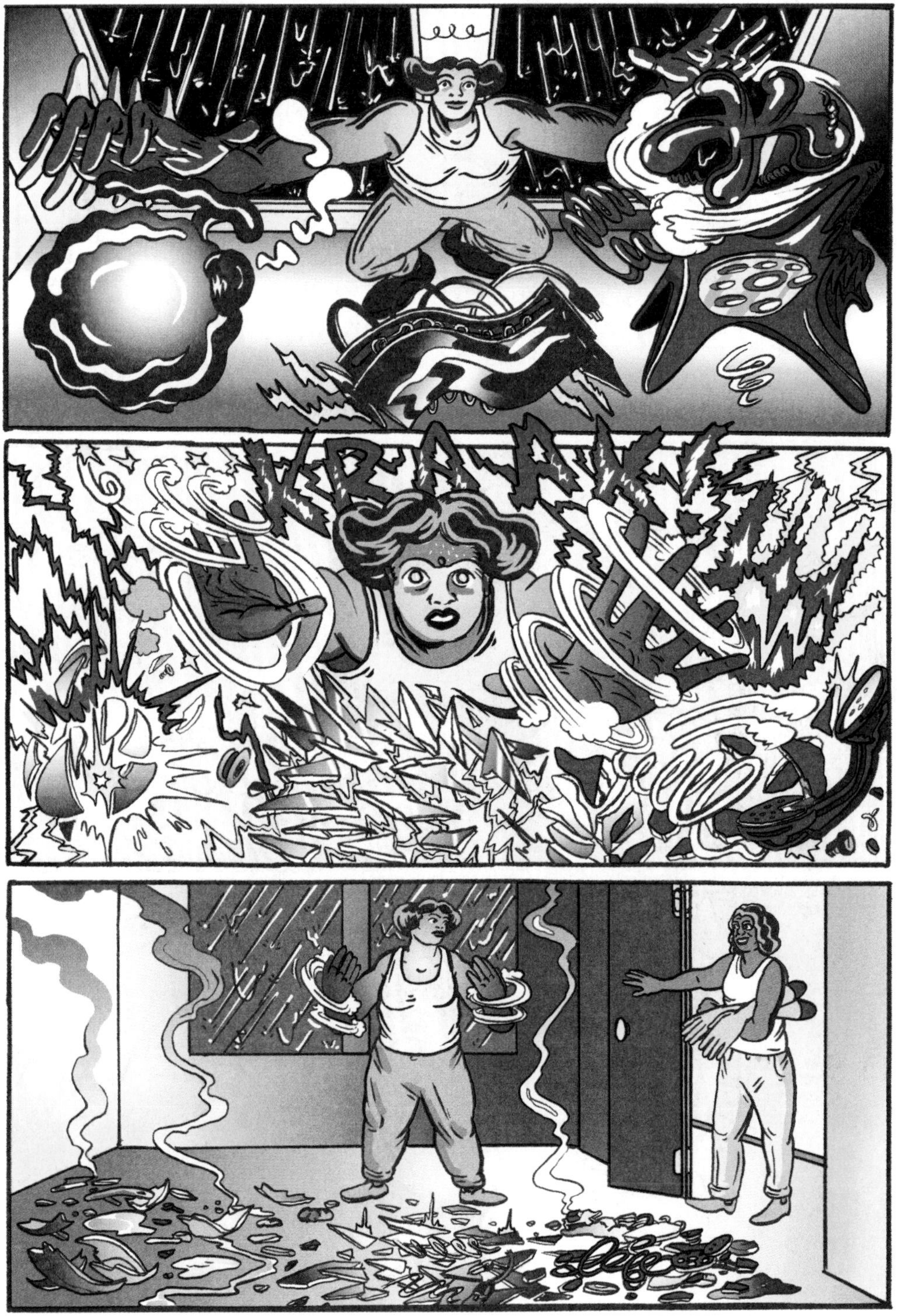
KRAAK!

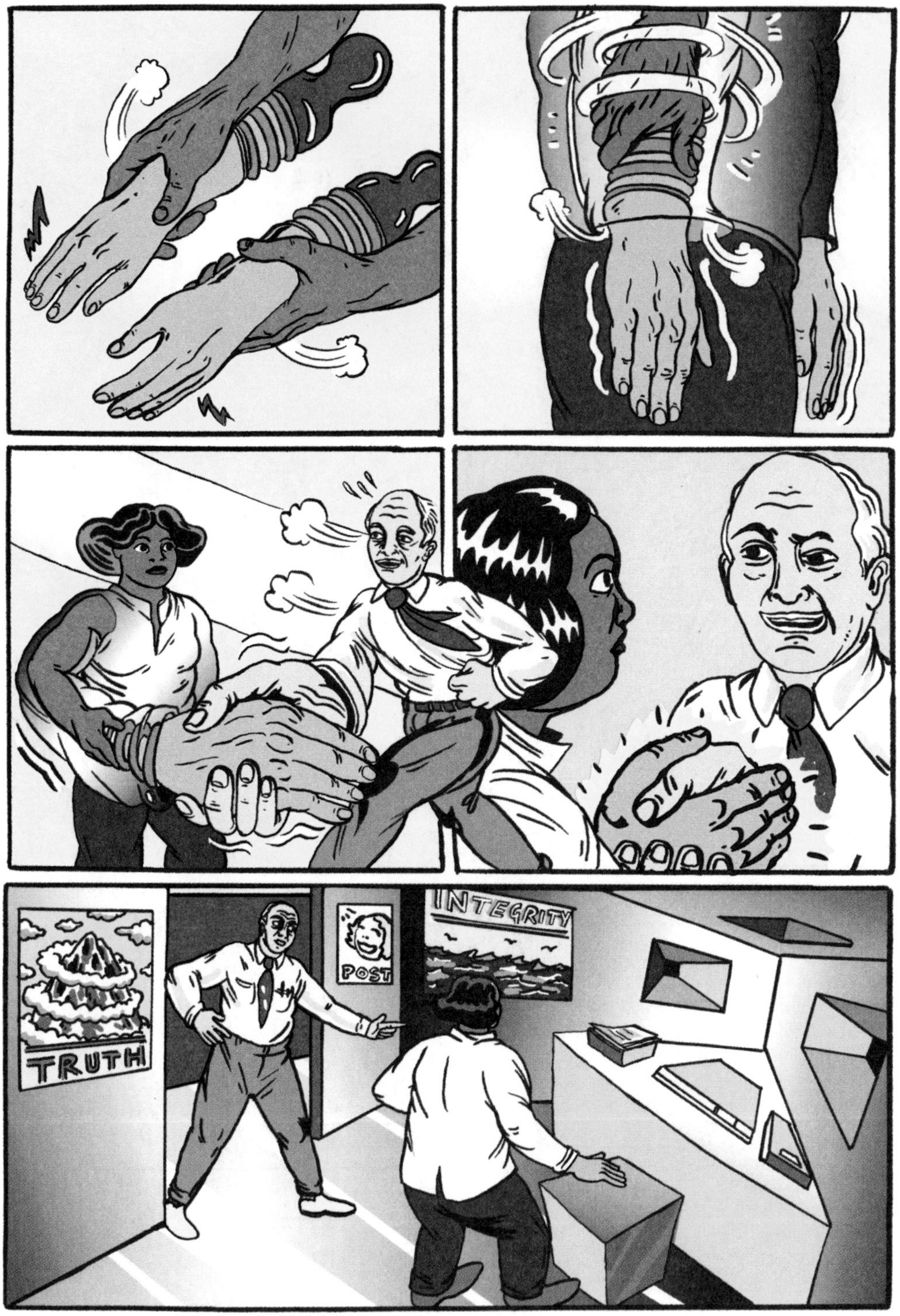

TRUTH
POST
INTEGRITY

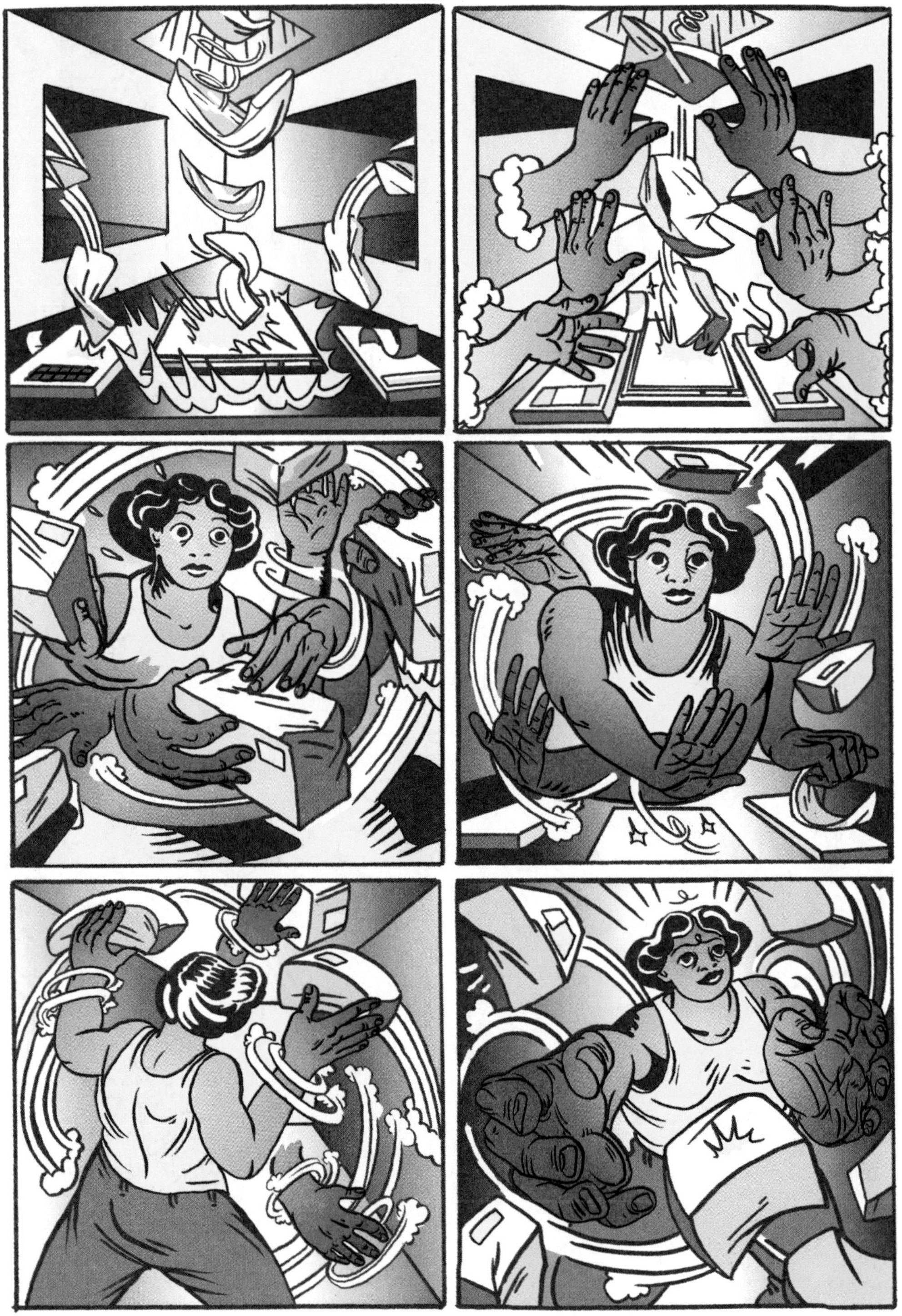

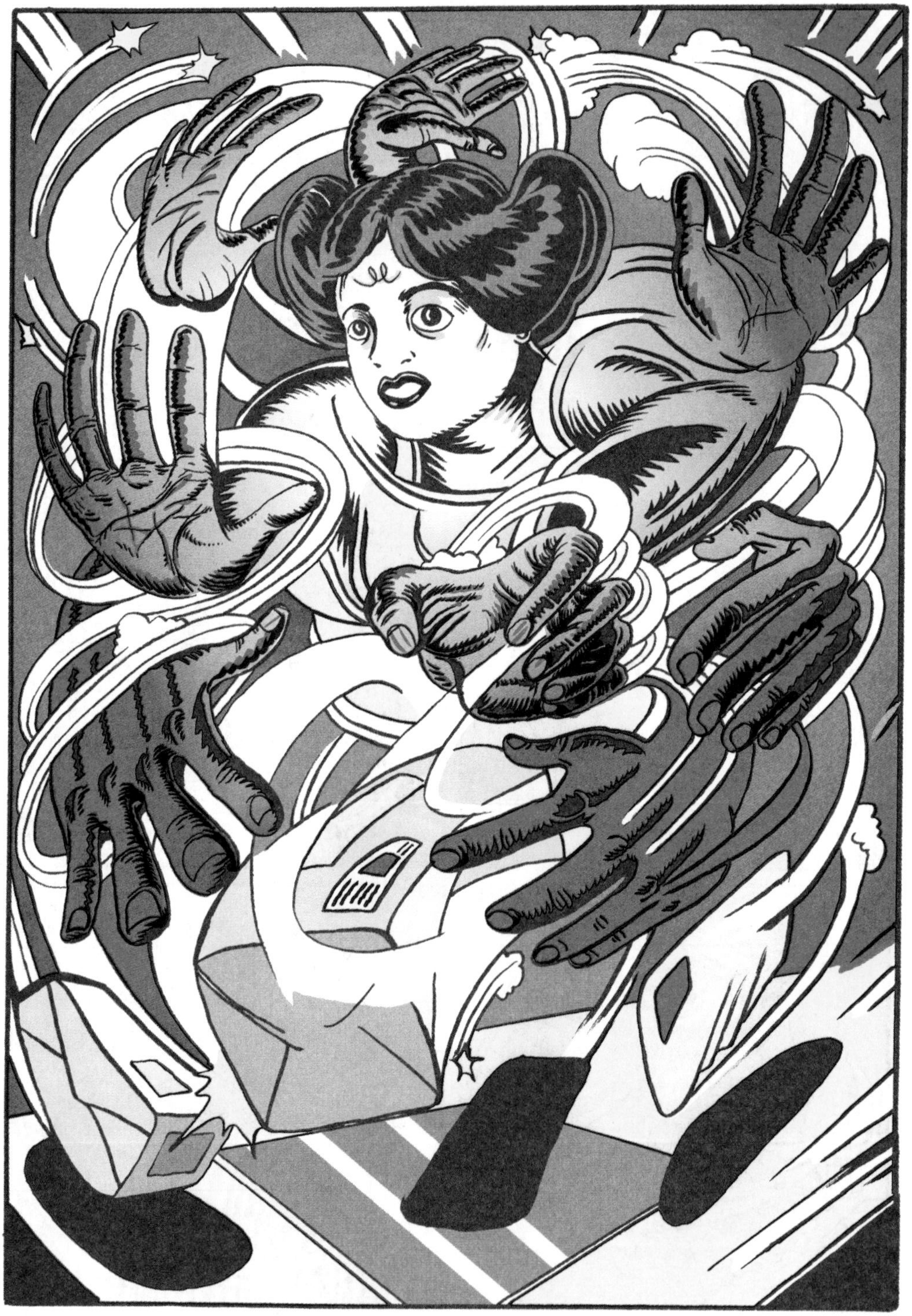

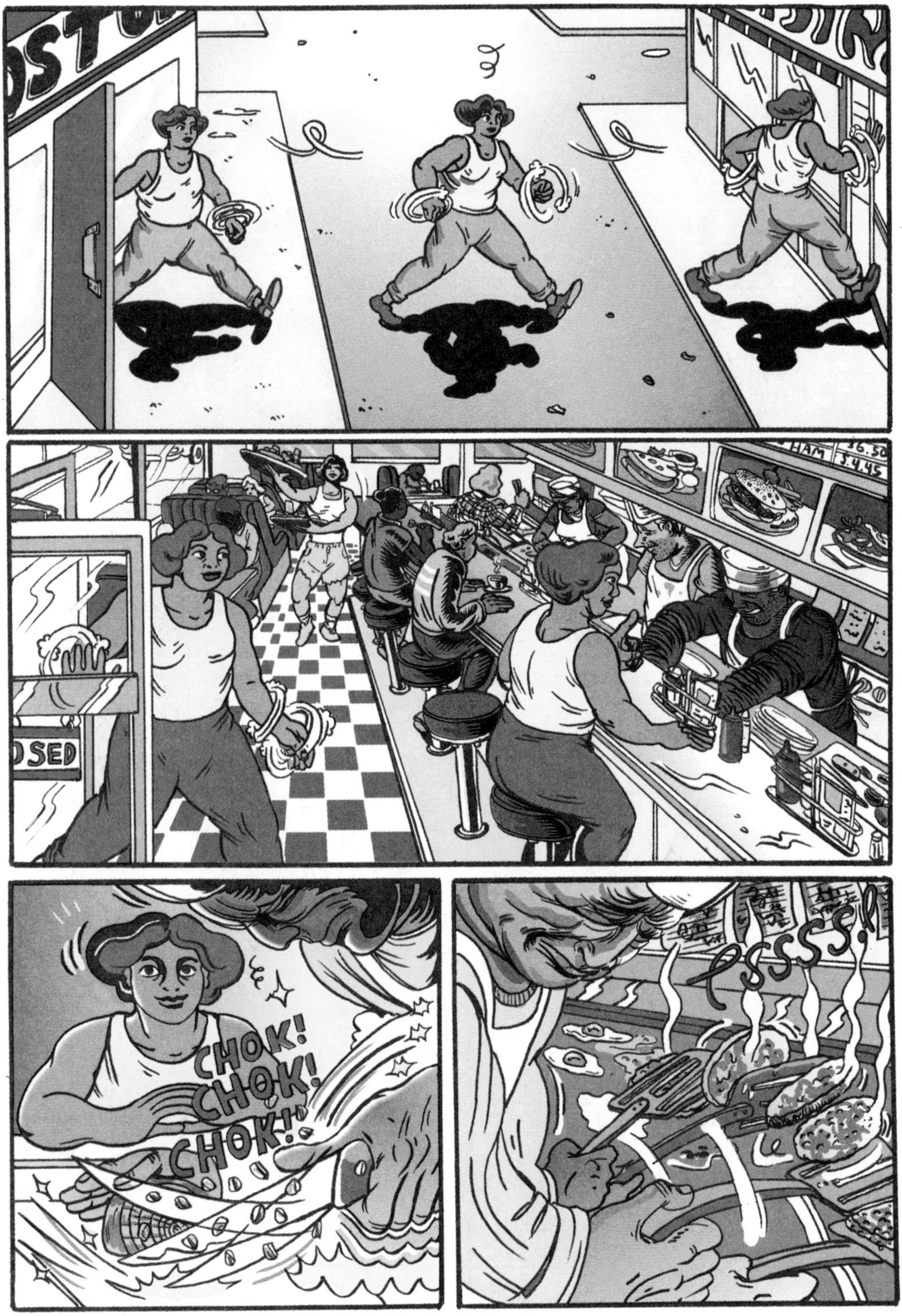
OSED
CHOK! CHOK! CHOK!
PSSSS!

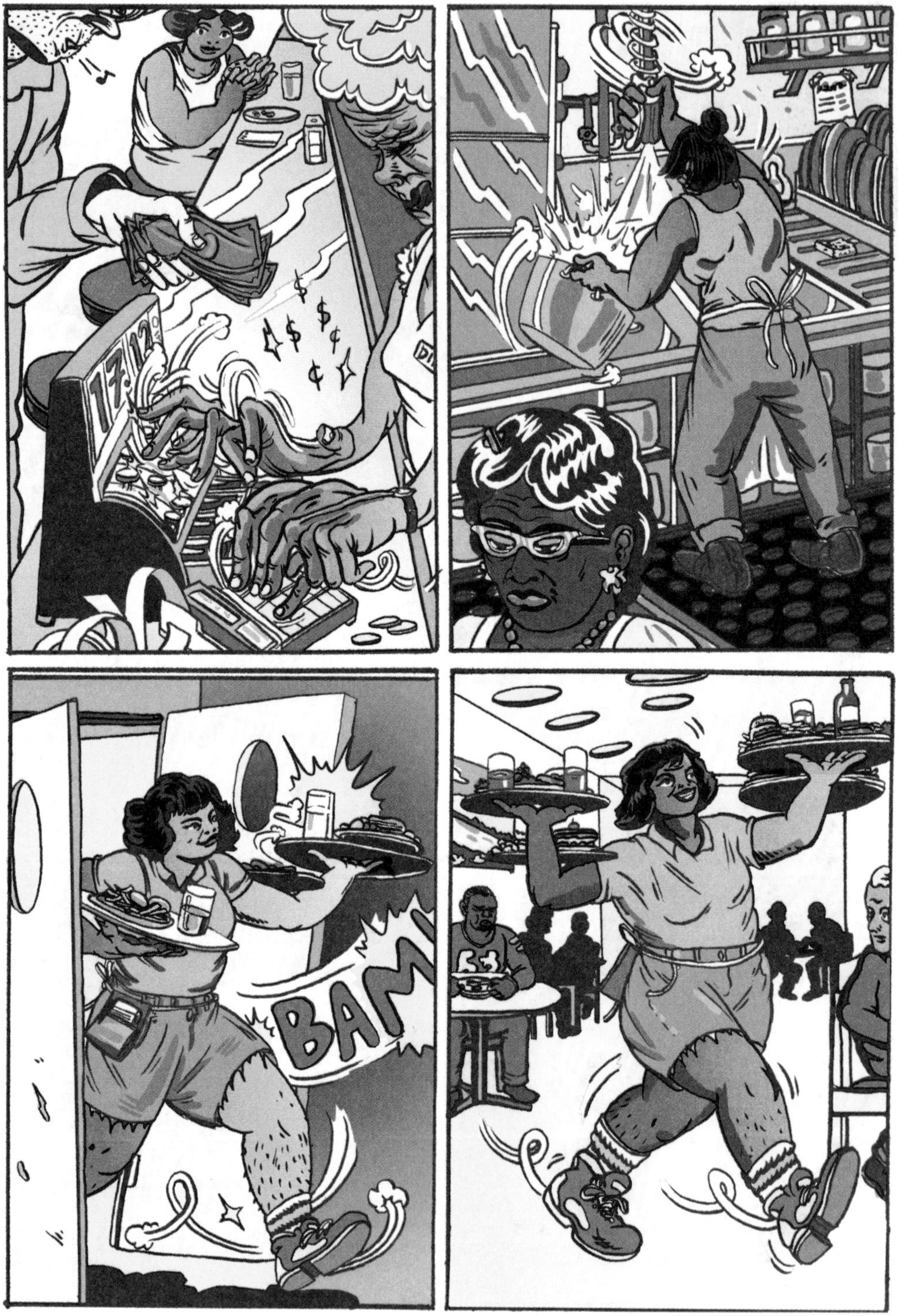
BAM

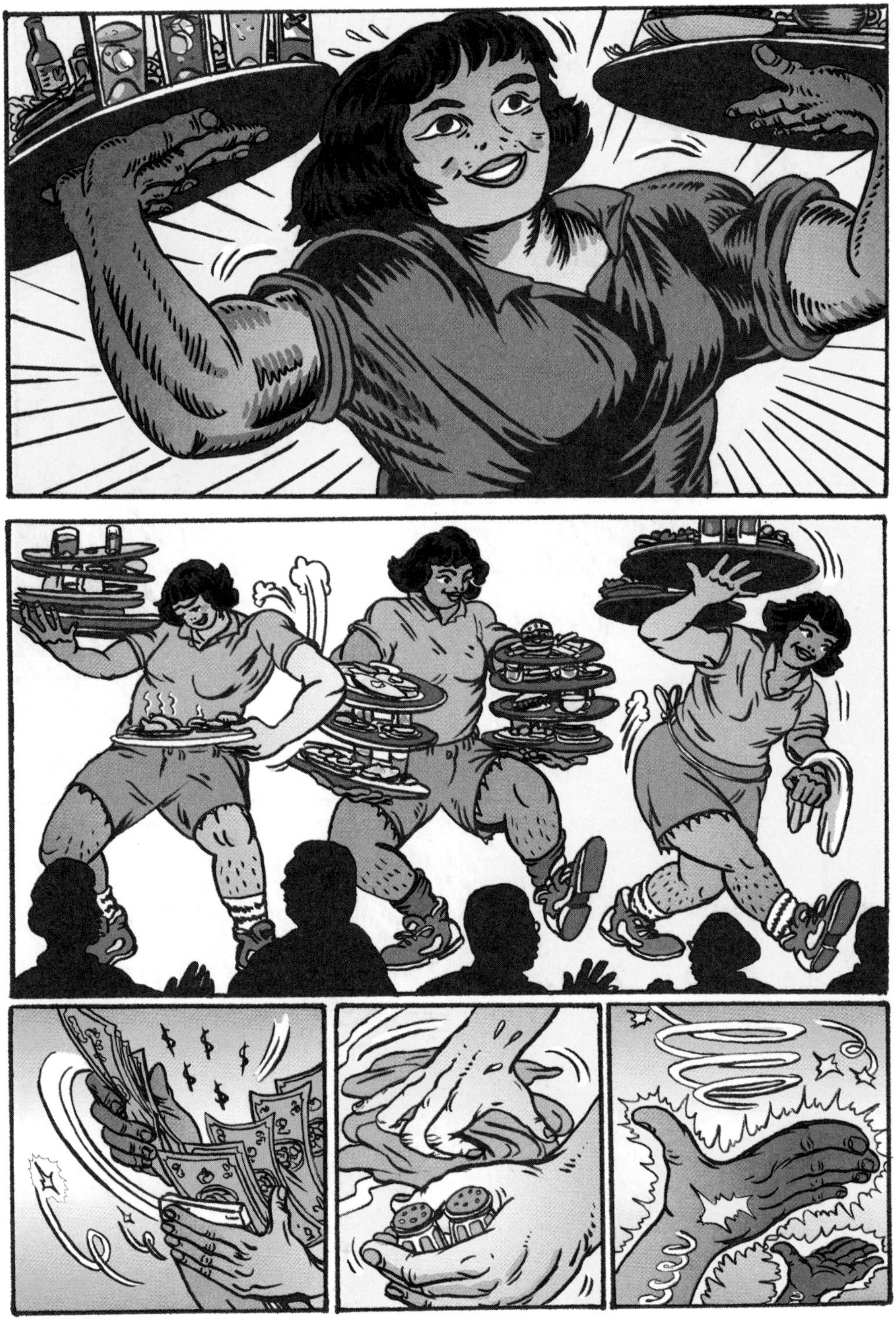

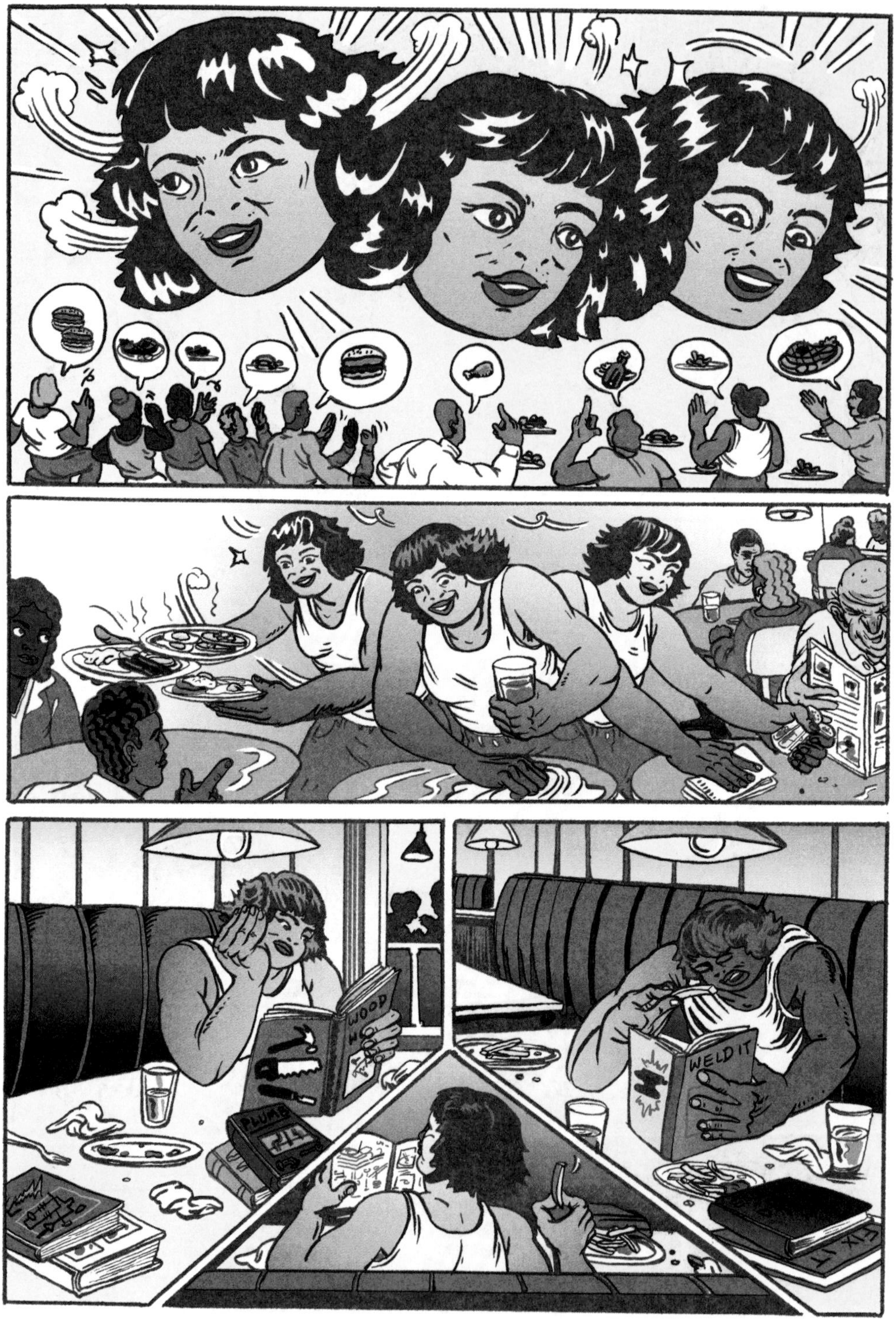
WOOD
PLUMB
WELD IT
FIX IT

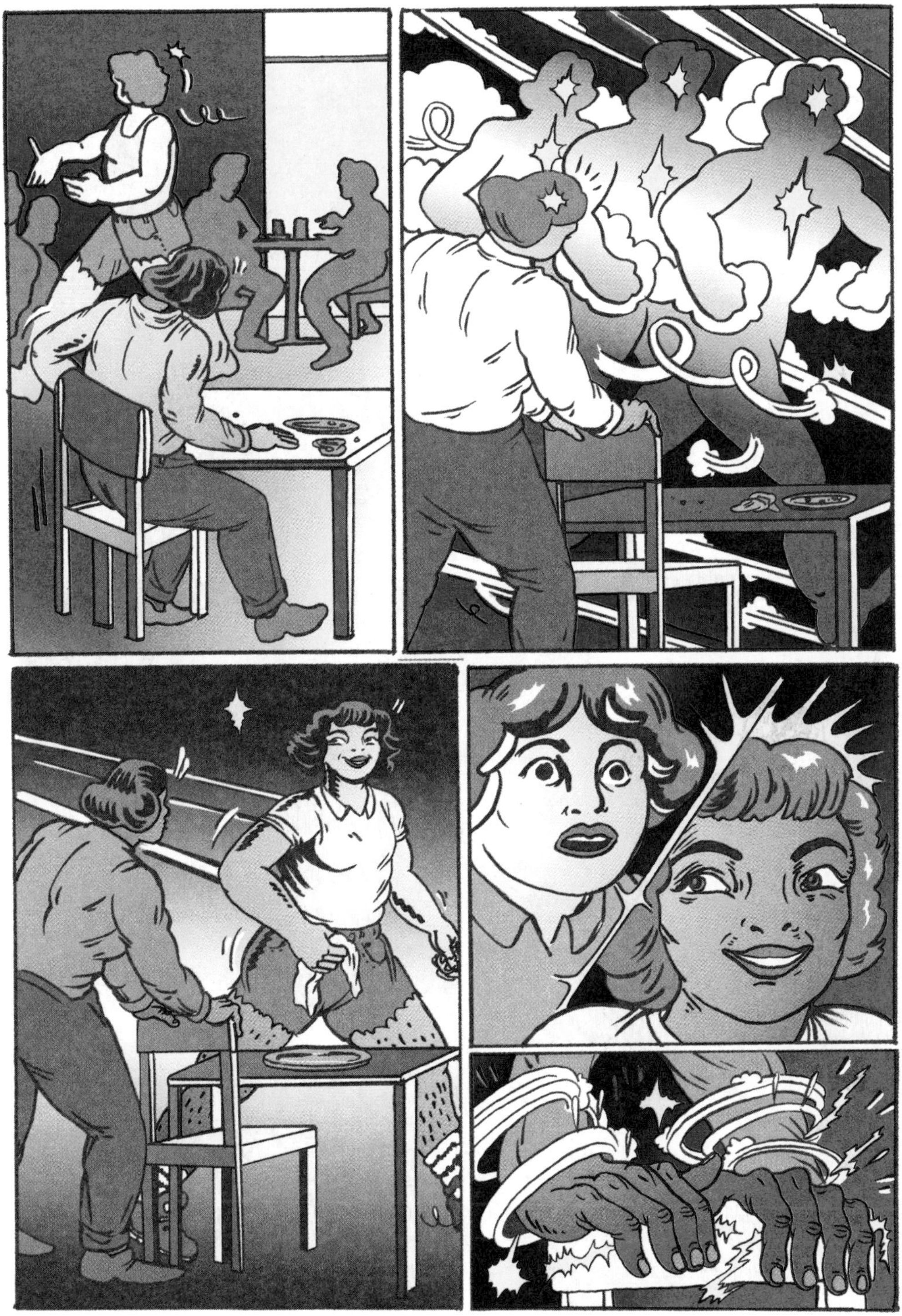

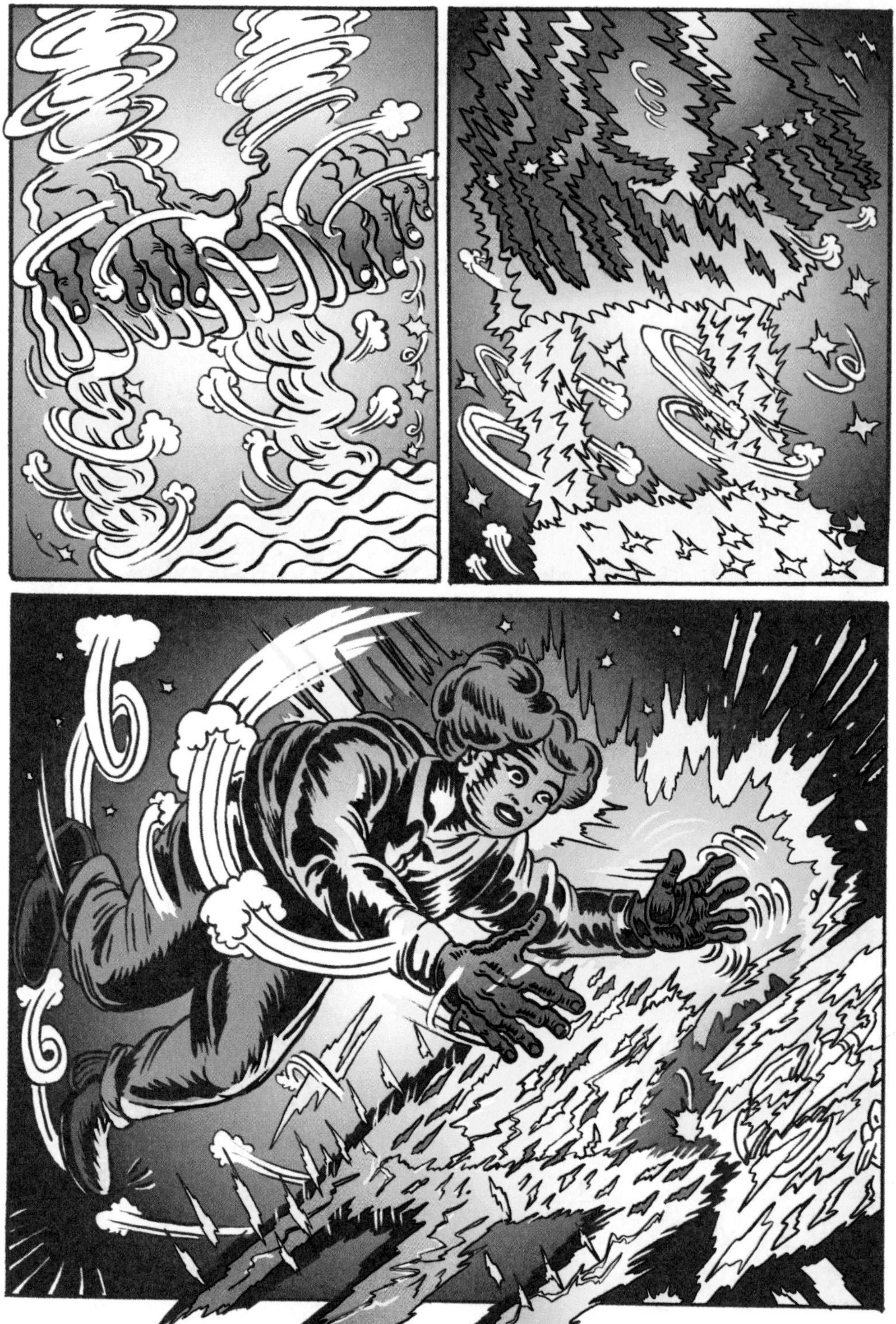

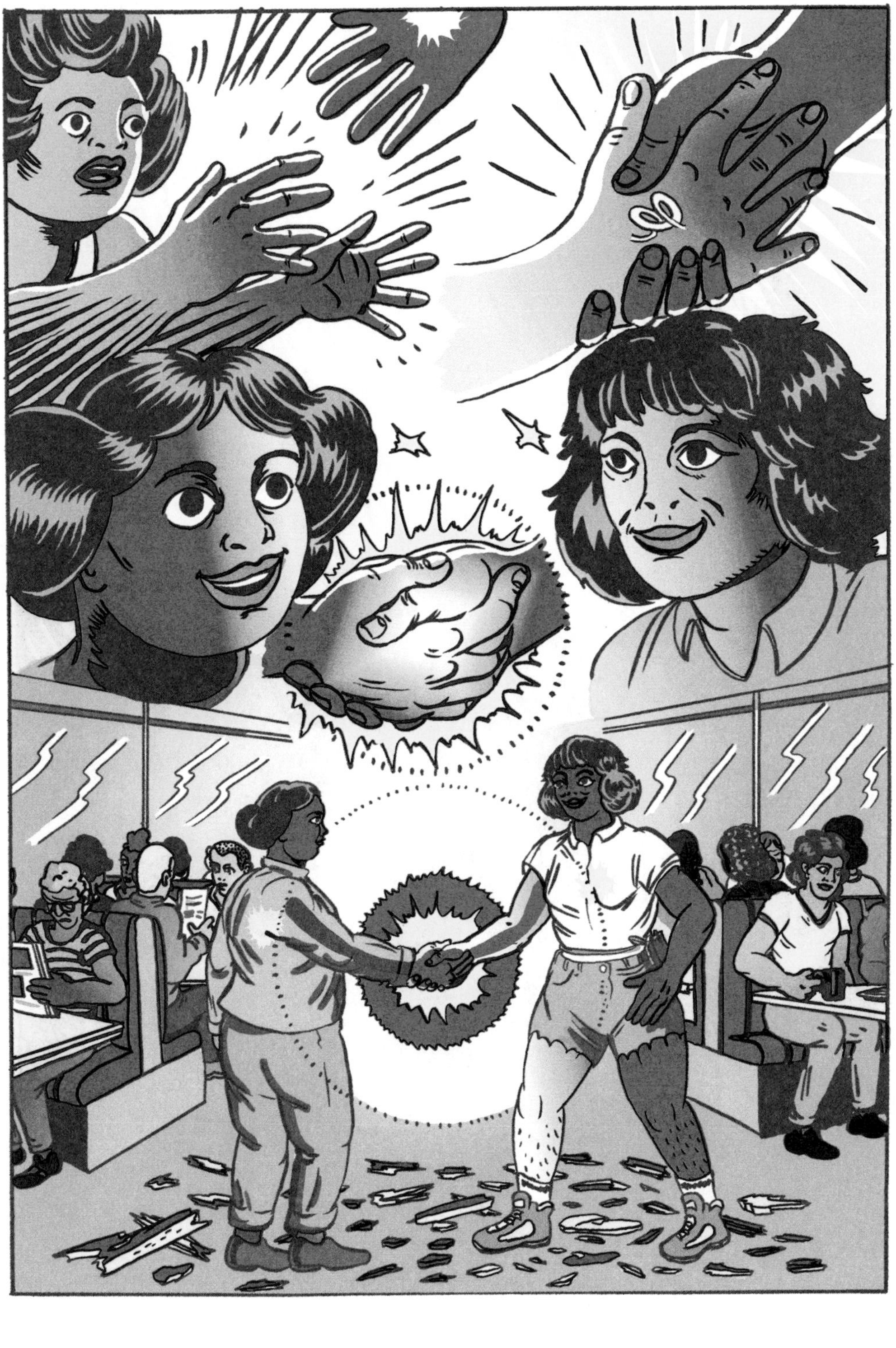

Bit Rot

E. A. BETHEA

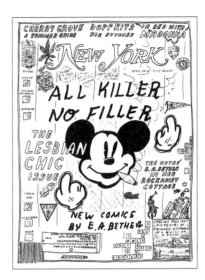

originally published in

All Killer No Filler

SELF-PUBLISHED

8.5 x 11 inches • 20 pages

CHERRY GROVE
A SUMMER GUIDE
DOPP KITS
IN BED WITH
MADONNA
NEW YORK
ALL KILLER
NO FILLER
THE
LESBIAN
CHIC
ISSUE
NEW COMICS
BY E.A. BETHEA

Biography

I am a New Orleans native who lives by the beach in Far Rockaway, New York City. I make comics and zines and write poetry. Among my publications are *Faded Frankenstein* (self-published, 2016), *Book of Daze* (Domino Books, 2017), and *Forlorn Toreador* (TBD, 2019). My work is concerned with obscured histories, love, lust, memory, and the junction of the deeply personal and universal.
eabethea.com

Statement

In February 2018 I found myself jet-lagged and wide awake in a little Left Bank hotel in Paris on an alley off the Seine. Now four-star, it had once been a dump. In the fifties Allen Ginsberg, William Burroughs, and many other freaky people rented rooms, wrote, and starved there.

During that trip I left the Winter Olympics on the TV 24/7. I had been walking the city, visiting the graves of my idols. I walked twelve miles one day. I placed mums on the stone of Jeanne Moreau, freshly dead, and at the mausoleum at Père Lachaise I placed my palm on the final resting spot of Richard Wright, tucked within a wall like a safety deposit box drawer.

Sleepless and ruminating in the bed, staring up at handsawn wooden beams from the fifteenth century, I grabbed my laptop. On a notes app I typed out a stream of consciousness. It was about degradation in its many forms: digital, sexual, corporeal, and mental. It was about being real, about not being able to be unreal, and a bunch of other stuff. "Bit Rot" is a distillation of that late-night consultation with myself, in comic form.

BIT ROT

WHERE WILL ALL MY EMAILS GO? FROM CHASE-MANHATTAN BANK AND LINKED IN AND THE BROOKLYN COLLEGE FILM CLUB LIST-SERV AND TICKET-MASTER AND WAYFAIR AND CON-ED AND THE GOVERNOR OF NEW YORK WHOSE FATHER WAS ALSO THE GOVERNOR OF NEW YORK AND ON AND ON?

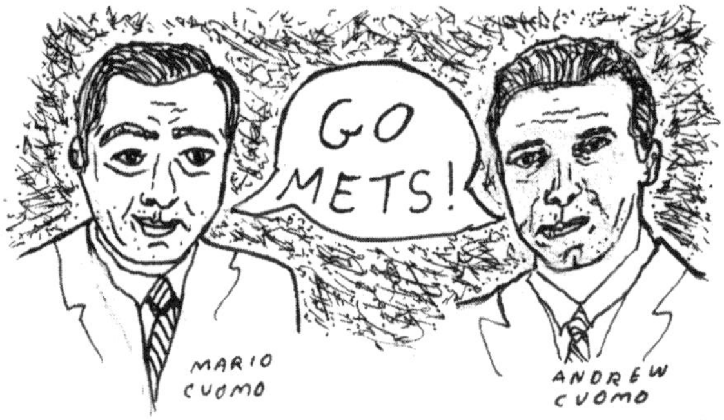

GO METS!
MARIO CUOMO
ANDREW CUOMO

WHERE WILL MY LATE NIGHT MISSIVES TO DISINTERESTED PARTIES IN WHICH I PLEAD FOR LOVE GO? IT NEVER WORKED TO DEMAND AFFECTIONS FROM ANYONE AND BESIDES ONCE WON, I GREW FICKLE, LIKE THE CAT UPON THE OPEN CAN OF FISHY ORIGINS, LOOKING UP AT ME AS IF TO SAY IS THAT ALL YOU HAVE TO OFFER?

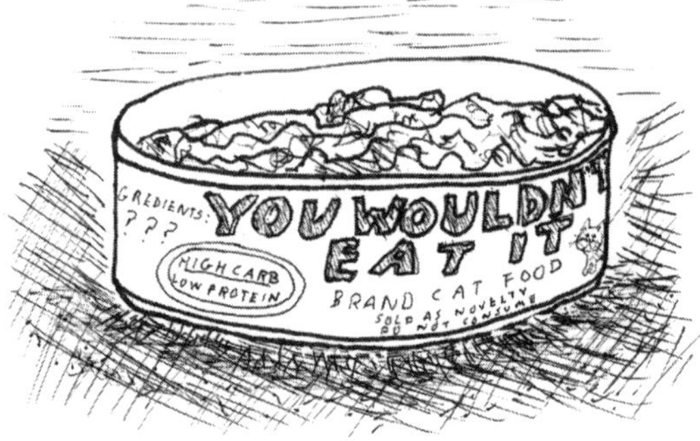

GREDIENTS: ???
YOU WOULDN'T EAT IT
HIGH CARB
LOW PROTEIN
BRAND CAT FOOD
SOLD AS NOVELTY
DO NOT CONSUME

WHEN THE DIGITAL TRACES OF MY EXISTENCE HAVE DEGRADED, FADED OFF INTO DISINTEGRATING BABY-BLUE CHEM TRAILS, HOW WILL THE FUTURE ALIENS KNOW THAT I LIVED ONCE AND FUCKED WOMEN AND WORE BLUE JEANS AND RECEIVED ELECTRONIC INVITATIONS TO BIRTHDAY PARTIES AT THE TURN OF THE CENTURY?

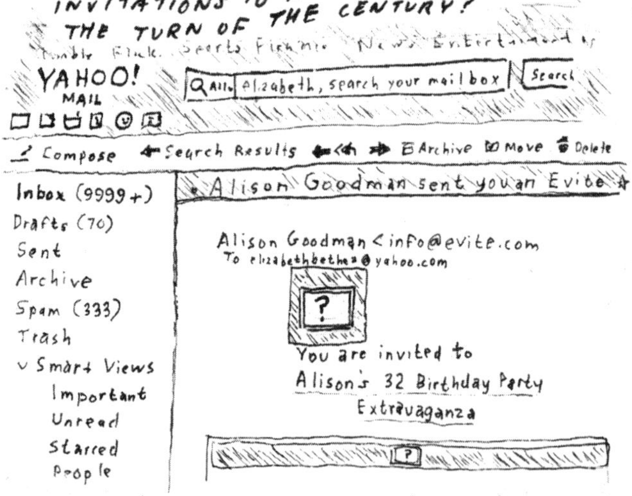

YAHOO! MAIL
All elizabeth, search your mailbox
Search
Compose
Search Results
Archive
Move
Delete
Inbox (9999+)
Drafts (70)
Sent
Archive
Spam (333)
Trash
Smart Views
Important
Unread
Starred
People
Alison Goodman sent you an Evite
Alison Goodman <info@evite.com
To elizabethbethea@yahoo.com
?
You are invited to
Alison's 32 Birthday Party
Extravaganza
?

WILL THE PAPER EVIDENCE OF MY SPIRIT REMAIN, DISCOVERED IN A JUNKSHOP IN GREENPOINT OR A 5'x 5' STORAGE SPACE- ONLY 99 DOLLARS A MONTH TO STORE SHIT YOU OBVIOUSLY DON'T NEED ANYMORE OR NEVER DID- YOU LET IT GO- THE BILL HAS LAPSED- WHO HAS YOUR DIARIES NOW, TO BE ENJOYED LIKE THE PARIS HILTON SEX TAPE? ARE THEY ENJOYING THE POEMS YOU WROTE WHEN YOU WERE 24, FUCKING A CO-WORKER WHO KIND OF BLEW YOUR MIND?

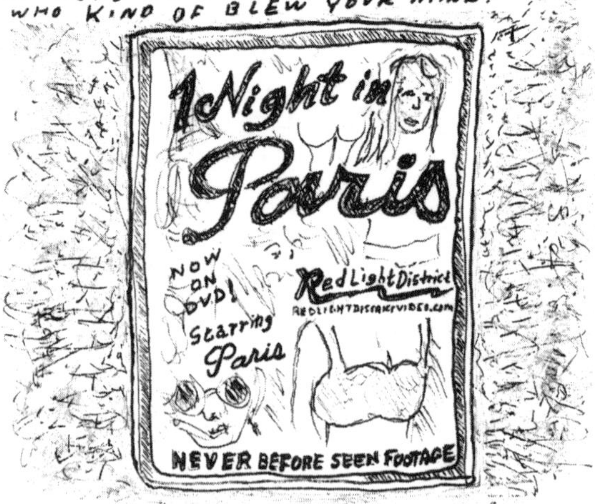

1 Night in Paris
NOW ON DVD!
RedLightDistrict
REDLIGHTDISTRICTVIDEO.COM
Starring Paris
NEVER BEFORE SEEN FOOTAGE

I TYPED POEMS ON MY MOTHER'S IBM SELECTRIC THAT SHE TYPED HER THESIS ON FAULKNER'S AS I LAY DYING UPON. I WAS OVERSEXED, UNBUCKLING IN THE BARNES AND NOBLE PARKING LOT OR DRIVING UNDER THE LIVE OAKS IN CITY PARK, SPANISH MOSS SWAYING IN A WARM BREEZE OFF THE LAKE THAT SPILLED OUT INTO THE GULF OF MEXICO, WHICH SPILLED OUT INTO THE BLUE ATLANTIC, AND SO ON AND SO ON, NEED I PRATTLE ON?

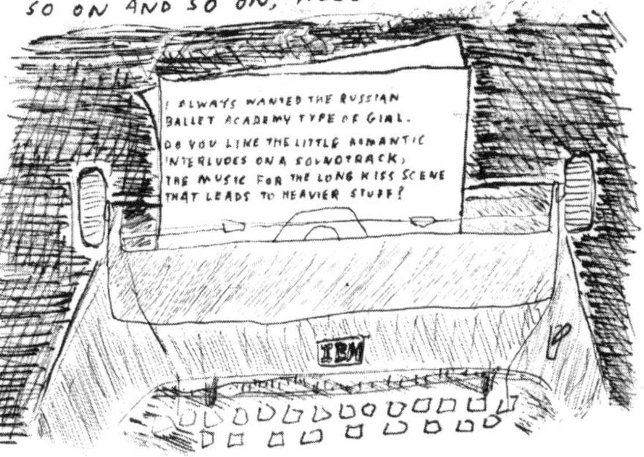
I ALWAYS WANTED THE RUSSIAN BALLET ACADEMY TYPE OF GIRL.
DO YOU LIKE THE LITTLE ROMANTIC INTERLUDES ON A SOUNDTRACK;
THE MUSIC FOR THE LONG KISS SCENE THAT LEADS TO HEAVIER STUFF?
IBM

[I ALWAYS LOVED THE WAY "PONTCHARTRAIN" SOUNDED OFF MY TONGUE, IT IS EXQUISITE AND WITHIN ITS NOMENCLATURE THERE IS A BRIDGE ("PONT"), A MAP ("CHART") AND A TRAIN TAKING US WHERE? HOW WILL WE GET FROM HERE TO THERE AND WILL YOU BE THERE? I AM NOT WEARING A BELT AND YOU ARE WEARING A SKIRT, I CAN JUST FEEL THE WARMTH EMANATING BETWEEN US, IT IS NARCOTIC AND OVERCOMING...]

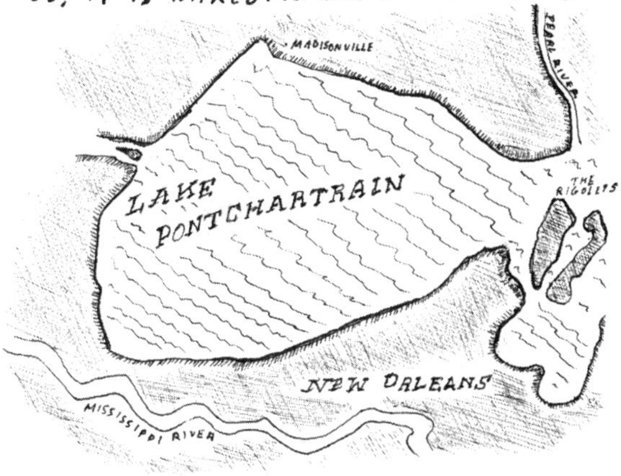
MADISONVILLE
PEARL RIVER
LAKE PONTCHARTRAIN
THE RIGOLETS
NEW ORLEANS
MISSISSIPPI RIVER

WITH THEIR SMALL BRUSHES THE EXCAVATERS WILL UNCOVER THAT I HAVE LIBRARY FINES IN SEVERAL MAJOR AMERICAN CITIES, THAT MY BLOOD IS TYPE O, THAT I'M A LITTLE DAMAGED, THAT AN ONLINE AUCTION HOUSE THOUGHT I MIGHT BE INTERESTED IN BIDDING ON "MORE ITEMS LIKE MARINA OSWALD NEWSWIRE PHOTO," HOW WILL THEY KNOW I DIDN'T BUY XANAX ONLINE OR HOOK UP ON CRAIG'S LIST? THAT I WAS SCARED OF BLONDES OR LOVED A HIPHOP WAKE-UP SHOW ON THE RADIO? WILL THE YOUNG HANDSOME ARCHEOLOGIST ALIEN VAMPIRE MAKE LOVE TO THEIR WIFE FOR HOURS AFTER DISCOVERING A PAIR OF MY PLAID BOXERS ON WHICH A CERTAIN GIRL HAD SEWN THE FIRST INITIAL OF MY CHRISTIAN NAME?

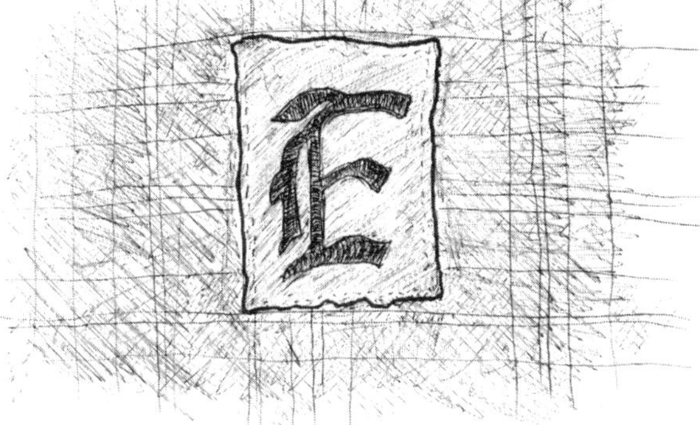
E

HOW WILL I KNOW IF THEY REALLY KNOW I WAS SINCERE, THE ACT WAS REAL, I CAN ONLY BE MYSELF AND WHEN I LISTEN TO "MYSELF WHEN I AM REAL" BY MINGUS ON PIANO I MIGHT SHED A HOT FAT TEAR. I AM IN LOVE WITH THE WORLD, I AM IN LOVE WITH WOMEN. I AM THROWING MY ROPE TO THE SHORE, WILL YOU BE THE ONE TO PULL ME IN? HOW WILL WE SPEND THE NIGHT? HOW WILL I KNOW IF YOU REALLY LOVE ME ON THE LAVENDER SHEETS OF THE CALIFORNIA KING? WHEN YOU COME, WILL I GO, HOW WILL I KNOW?

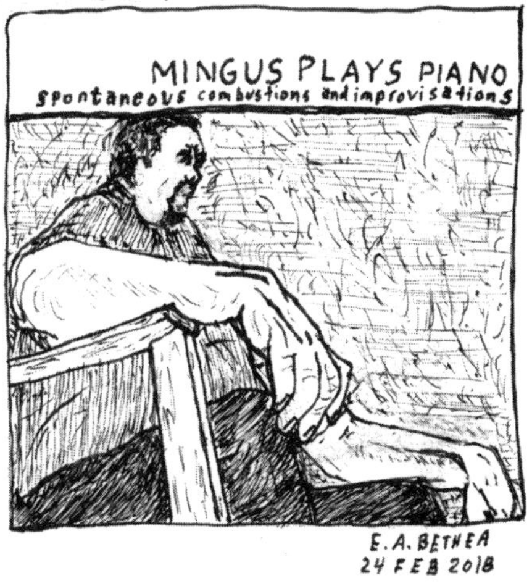
MINGUS PLAYS PIANO
spontaneous combustions and improvisations

E. A. BETHEA
24 FEB 2018

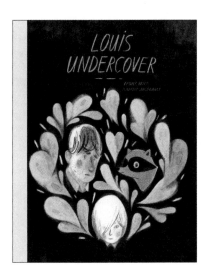

Louis Undercover (*Excerpt*)

FANNY BRITT AND
ISABELLE ARSENAULT

originally published in

Louis Undercover
GROUNDWOOD BOOKS
9 x 12 inches · 160 pages

Biography

Isabelle Arsenault is an internationally renowned children's book illustrator whose work has won many awards and much praise from critics. Her books include the graphic novels *Jane, the Fox and Me* and *Louis Undercover* by Fanny Britt, *Spork* and *Virginia Wolf* by Kyo Maclear, *Cloth Lullaby* by Amy Novesky (Bologna Ragazzi Award 2017), and *Colette's Lost Pet,* which marks her debut as an author. She has won the prestigious Governor General's Award for Children's Literature three times, and two of her picture books were named as *New York Times* Best Illustrated Books of the Year. The poetry expressed through Isabelle Arsenault's graphic universe, the gentle flow of her lines, and the overall charm of her books have made her one of Quebec's best-known and esteemed illustrators.
isabellearsenault.com

Fanny Britt is a writer and translator from Montreal. She has won a Governor General's Award in Drama for her play *Bienveillance,* and was nominated for the prix France-Québec and the prix littéraire des collégiens for her first novel, *Les Maisons (Hunting Houses).* Her first collaboration with Isabelle Arsenault, *Jane, The Fox and Me,* won a dozen awards in Canada and the US, as well as appearing in *Best American Comics 2014.*

Statement

Louis's dad drinks. His mom worries. Louis himself is crippled with fears about love, family, and the future. Between trying to protect his little brother, Truffle, from the assaults of the real world and working up the courage to talk to Billie, the wonderfully fearless girl in his class, Louis will face old ghosts, new starts, and a lost raccoon, and learn a lesson or two about the strength found in vulnerability.

This book is our second collaboration, after *Jane, the Fox and Me*. This excerpt features a hopeful moment in the life of Louis and Truffle after the recent separation of their parents. The brothers go back and forth between their two homes. Here they have just arrived at their old home in the country where their dad still lives, and find him looking surprisingly radiant. He has just vowed to stop drinking and is planning exciting activities for the boys' summer break, in the hopes of piecing the family back together.

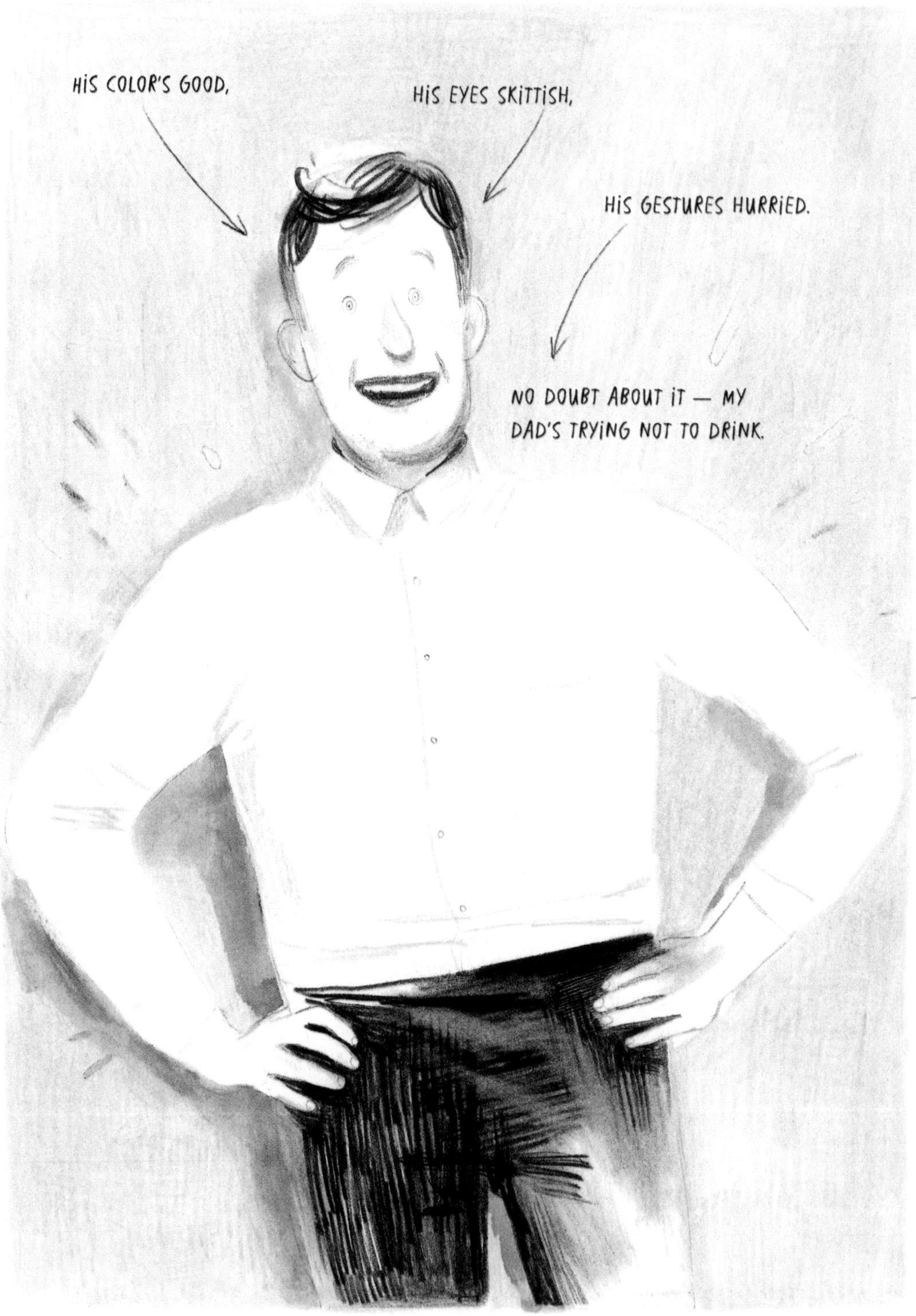
HIS COLOR'S GOOD,
HIS EYES SKITTISH,
HIS GESTURES HURRIED.
NO DOUBT ABOUT IT — MY DAD'S TRYING NOT TO DRINK.

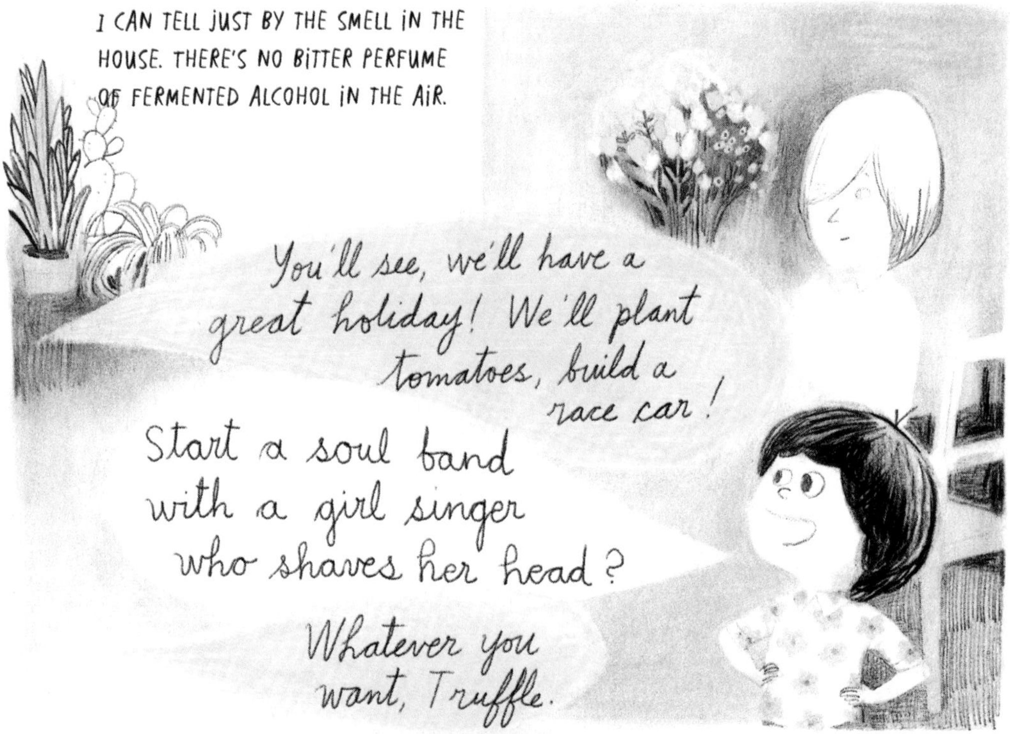
I CAN TELL JUST BY THE SMELL IN THE HOUSE. THERE'S NO BITTER PERFUME OF FERMENTED ALCOHOL IN THE AIR.
You'll see, we'll have a great holiday! We'll plant tomatoes, build a race car!
Start a soul band with a girl singer who shaves her head?
Whatever you want, Truffle.

I CONSIDER CALLING MY MOM TO REASSURE HER. IT'S NOT LIKE SHE SAID ANYTHING, BUT I SAW THE WAY SHE CUT HERSELF SOME BANGS ON IMPULSE IN THE BATHROOM THE MORNING WE LEFT.

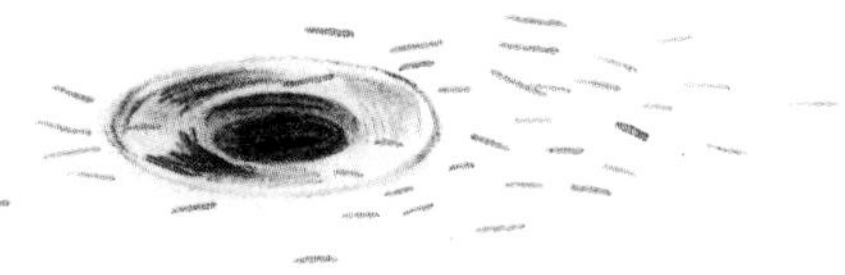

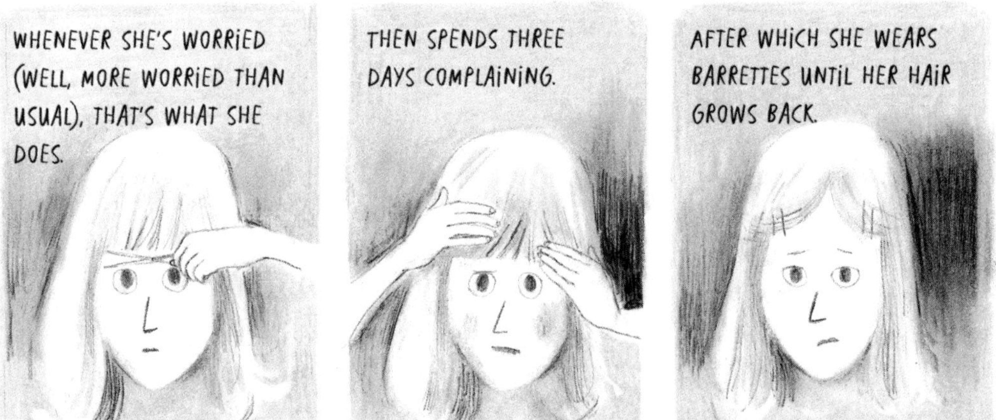
WHENEVER SHE'S WORRIED (WELL, MORE WORRIED THAN USUAL), THAT'S WHAT SHE DOES.
THEN SPENDS THREE DAYS COMPLAINING.
AFTER WHICH SHE WEARS BARRETTES UNTIL HER HAIR GROWS BACK.
THEN STARTS ALL OVER AGAIN.

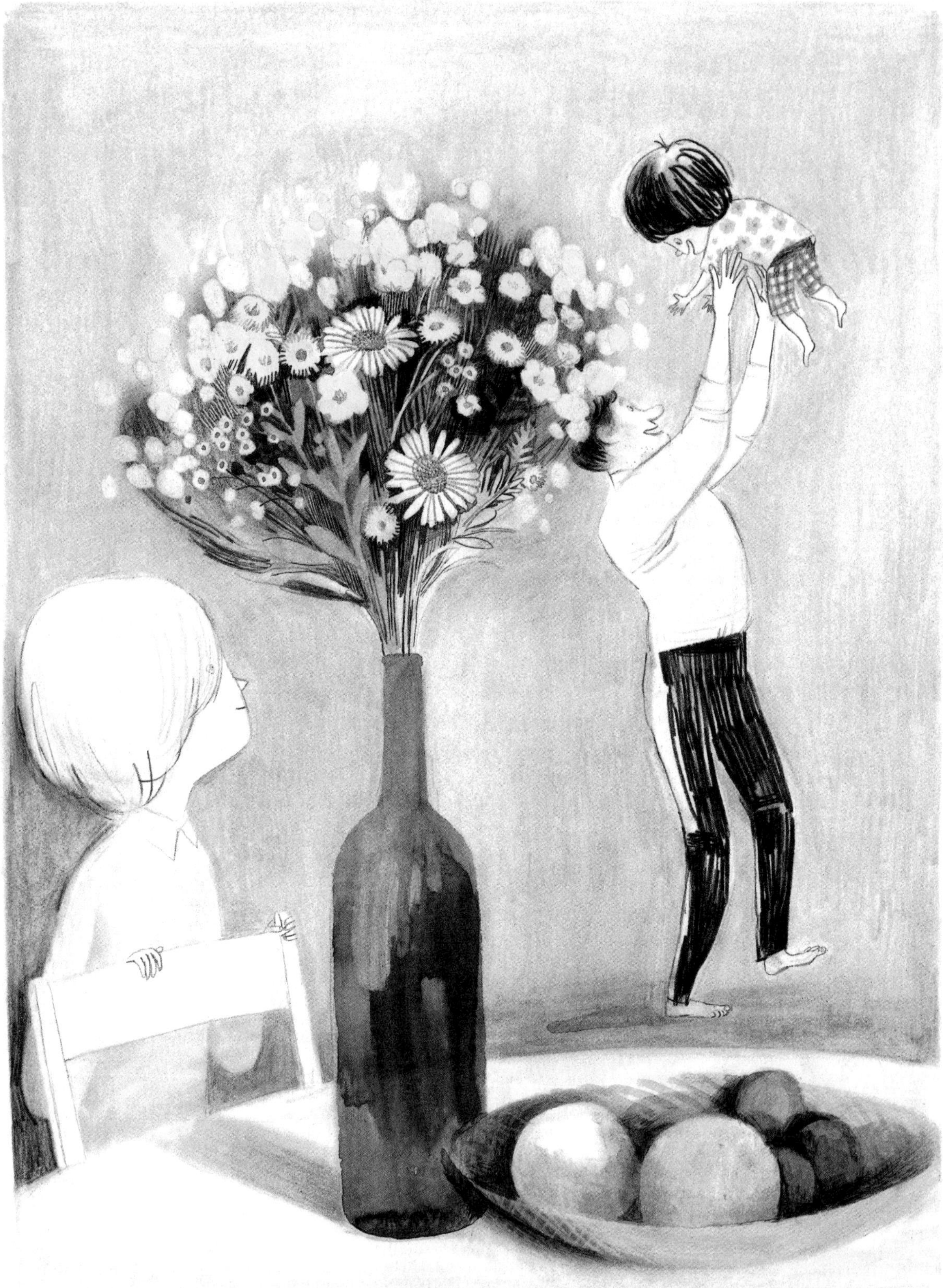

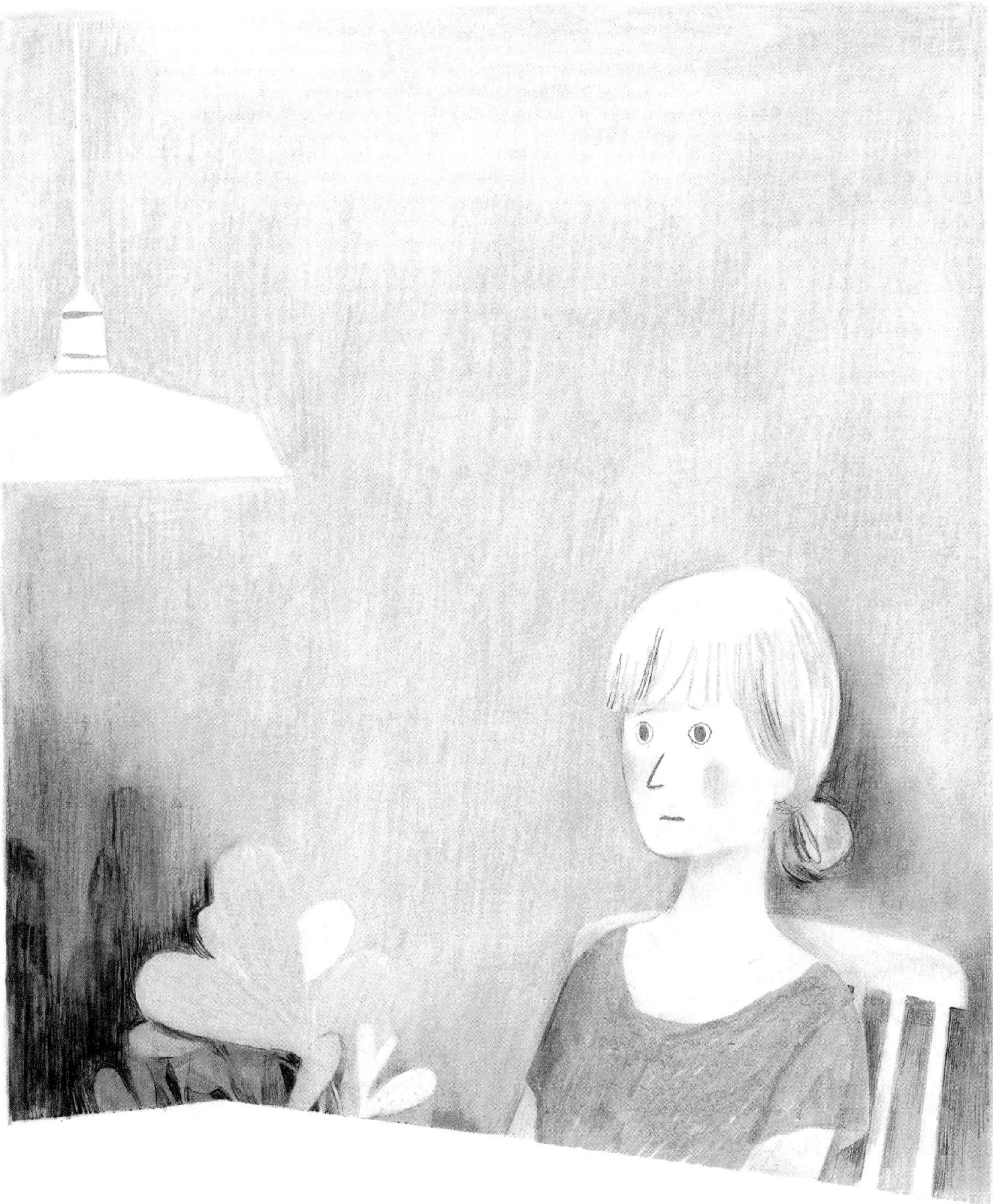

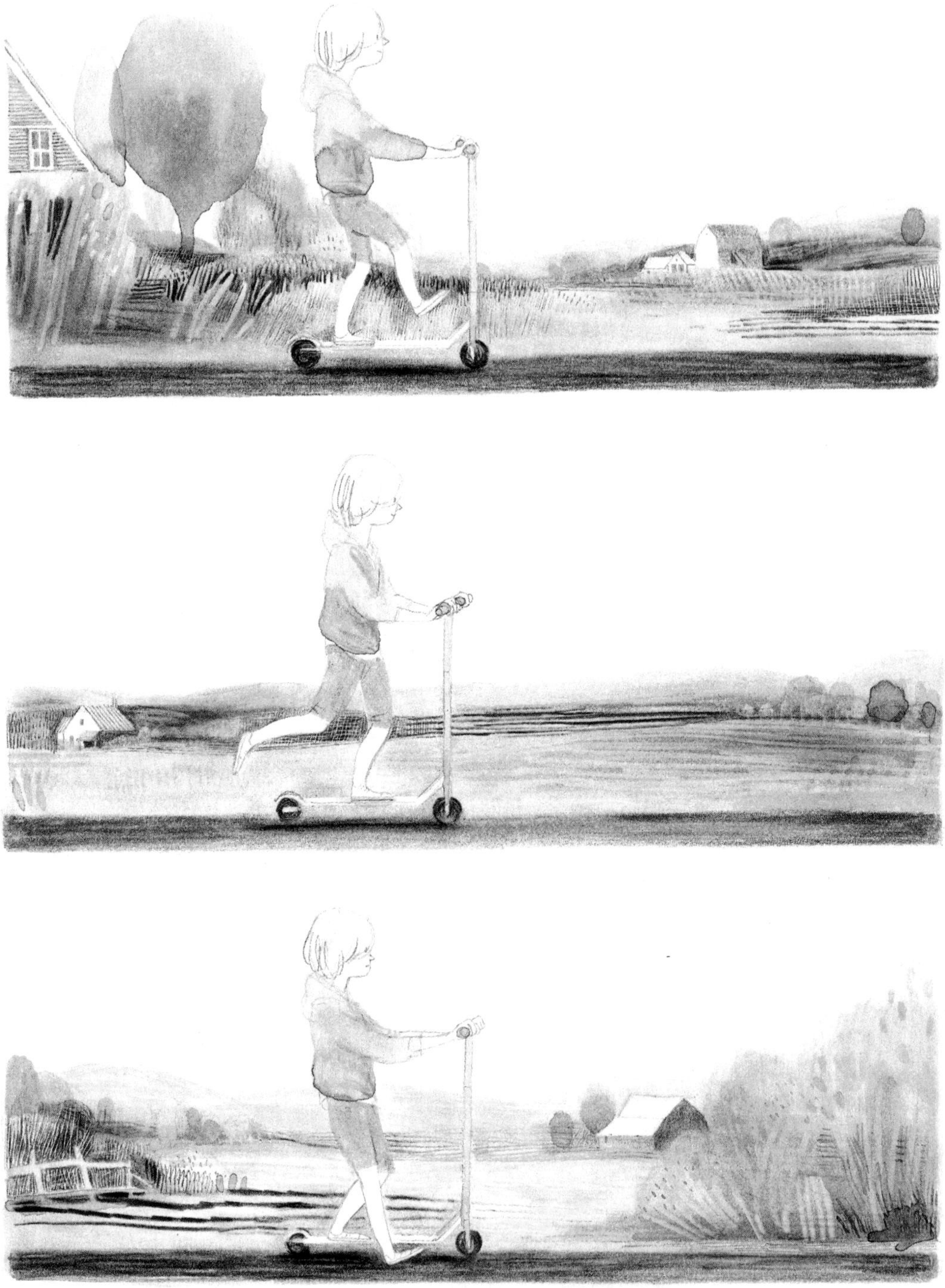

AT FIRST, I THINK IT'S A BAG OR A PILE
OF BRANCHES.

THEN I SEE IT'S AN ANIMAL.

A GOPHER?

A BEAVER?

A RACCOON?

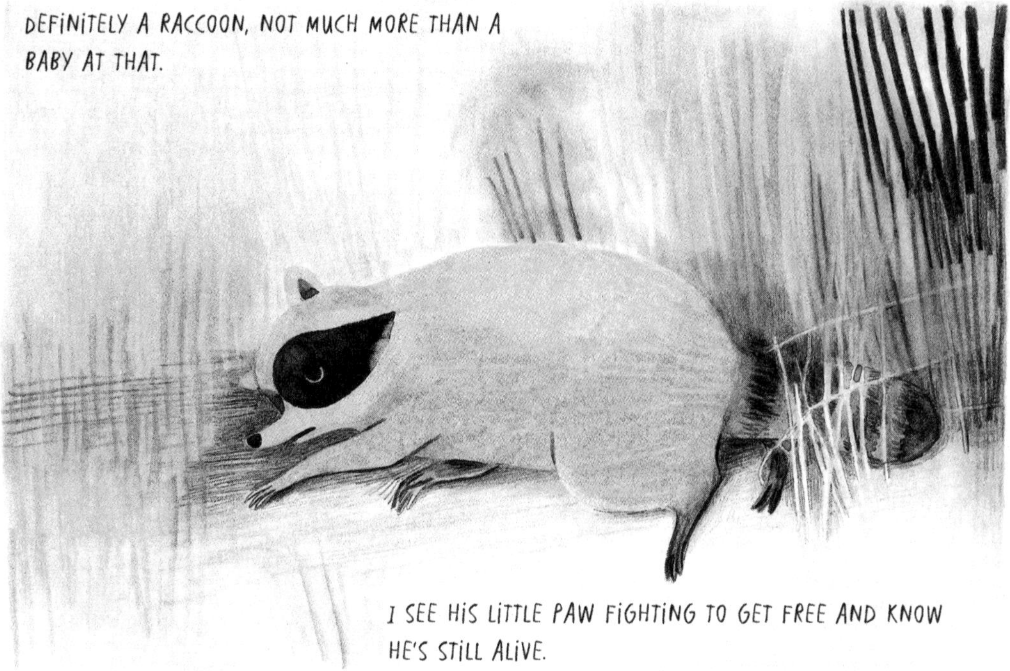
DEFINITELY A RACCOON, NOT MUCH MORE THAN A BABY AT THAT.
I SEE HIS LITTLE PAW FIGHTING TO GET FREE AND KNOW HE'S STILL ALIVE.

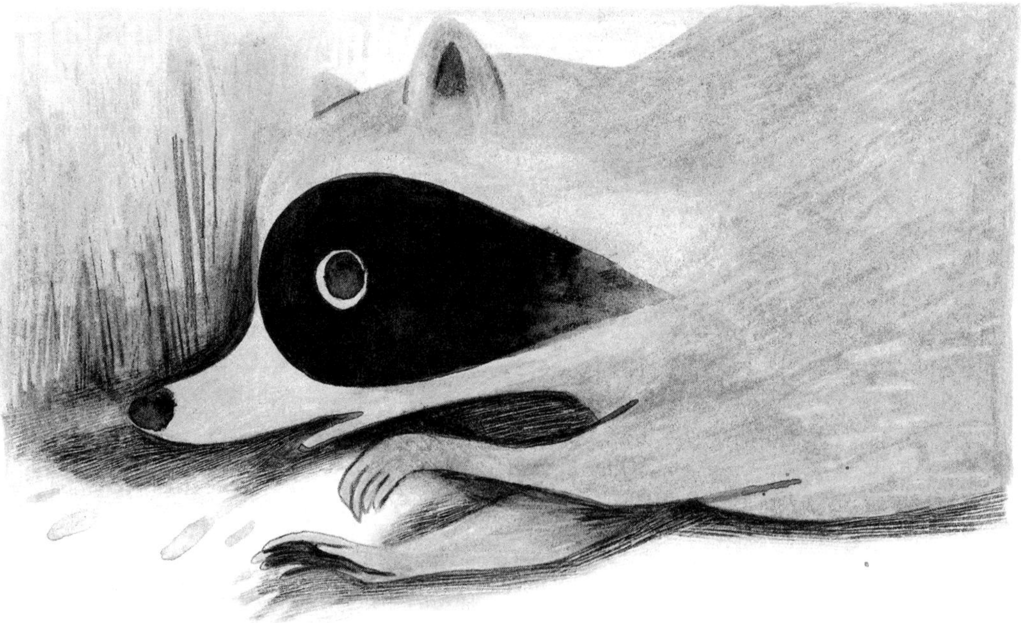

SHORT, JAGGED BREATHS. WARY EYES ASSAULTED BY THE LIGHT. I REMEMBER THAT RACCOONS DON'T LIKE FULL SUN.

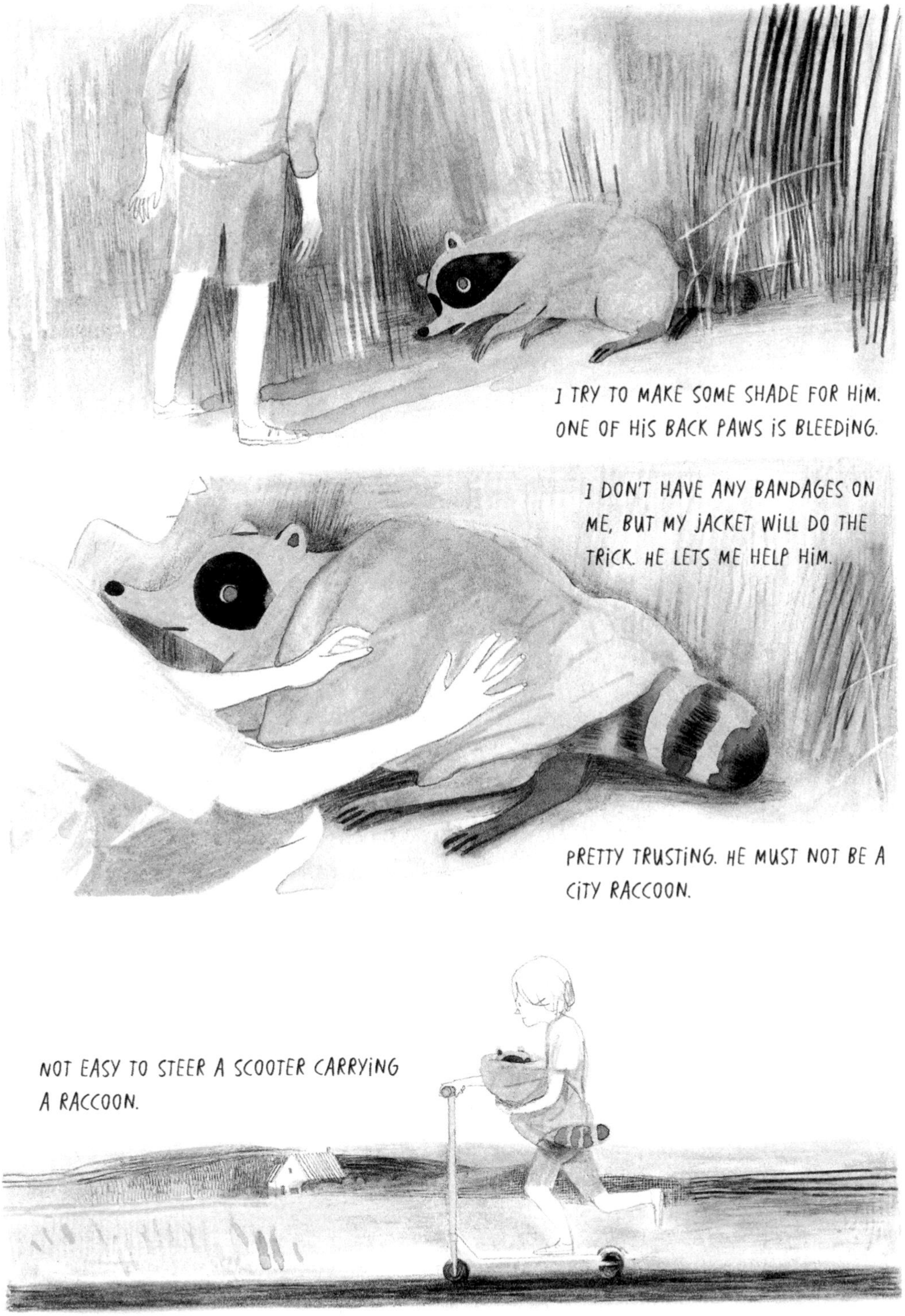
I TRY TO MAKE SOME SHADE FOR HIM.
ONE OF HIS BACK PAWS IS BLEEDING.
I DON'T HAVE ANY BANDAGES ON ME, BUT MY JACKET WILL DO THE TRICK. HE LETS ME HELP HIM.
PRETTY TRUSTING. HE MUST NOT BE A CITY RACCOON.
NOT EASY TO STEER A SCOOTER CARRYING A RACCOON.

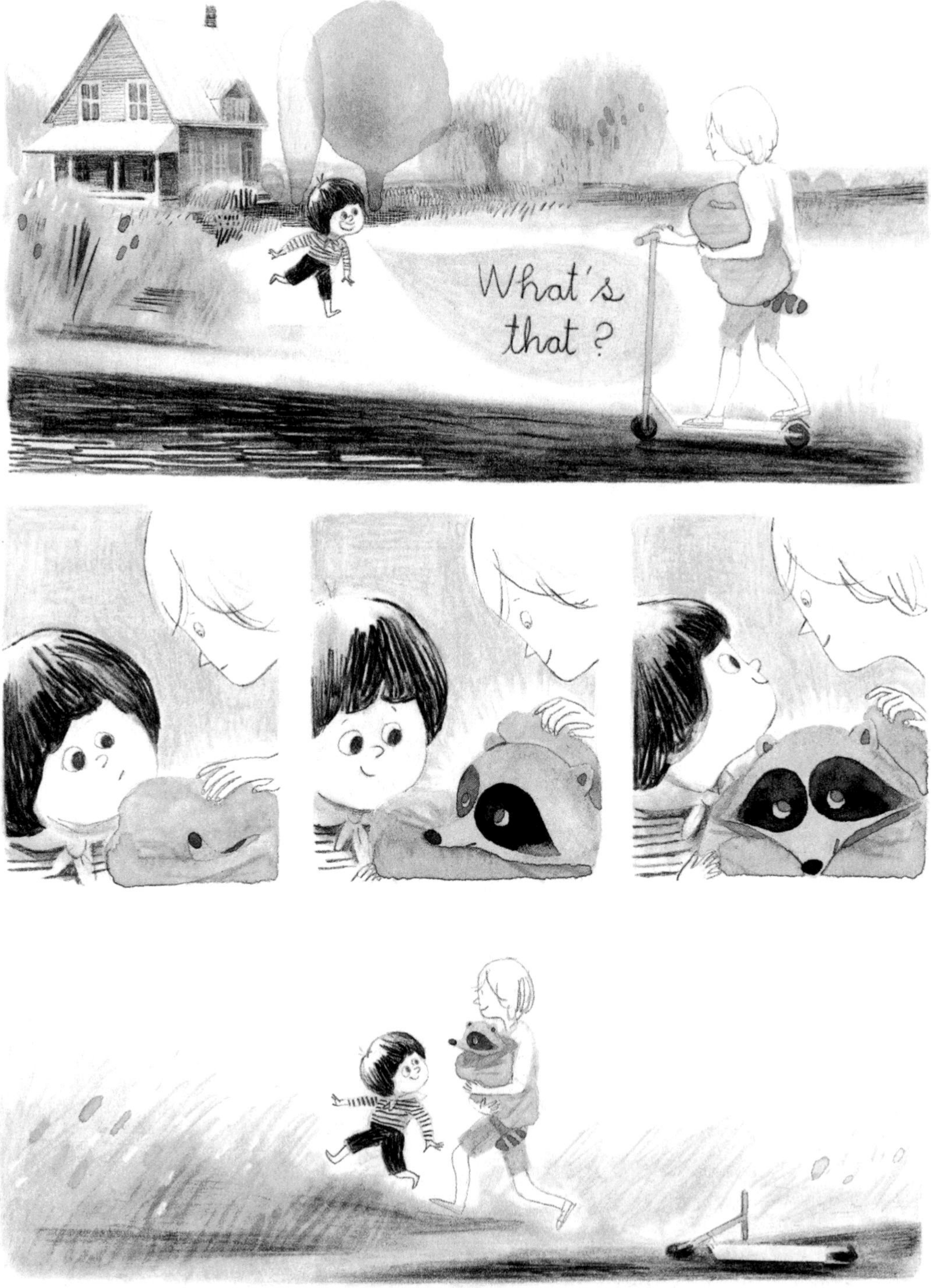
What's that?

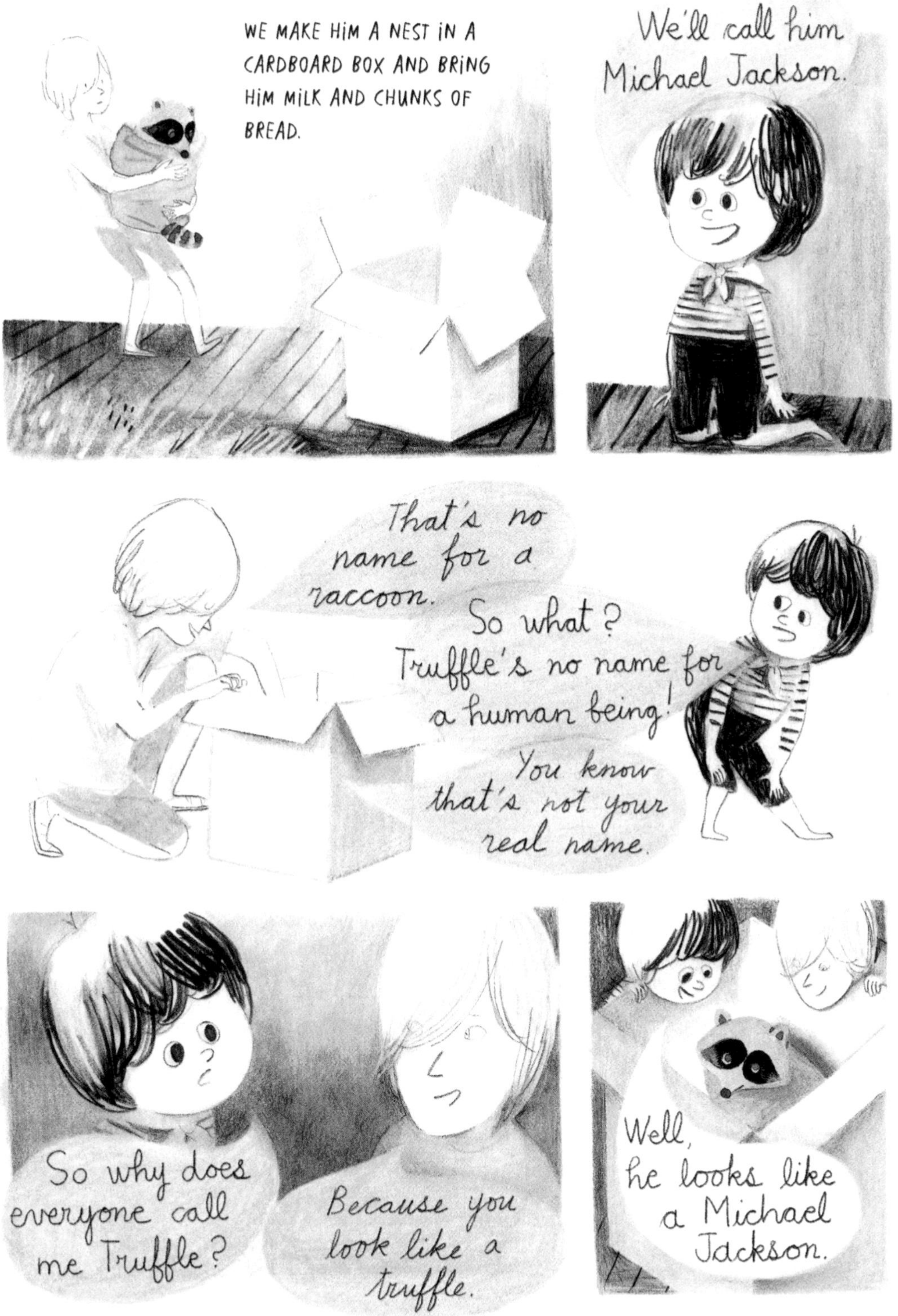
WE MAKE HIM A NEST IN A CARDBOARD BOX AND BRING HIM MILK AND CHUNKS OF BREAD.
We'll call him Michael Jackson.
That's no name for a raccoon.
So what? Truffle's no name for a human being!
You know that's not your real name.
So why does everyone call me Truffle?
Because you look like a truffle.
Well, he looks like a Michael Jackson.

MY DAD LETS US KEEP HIM, JUST NOT IN THE HOUSE.

HE KNOWS MY MOM WOULD BE FURIOUS, AND SINCE HE ALLOWED HIMSELF ONE BEER LAST NIGHT, HE DOESN'T WANT TO TAKE ANY MORE CHANCES.

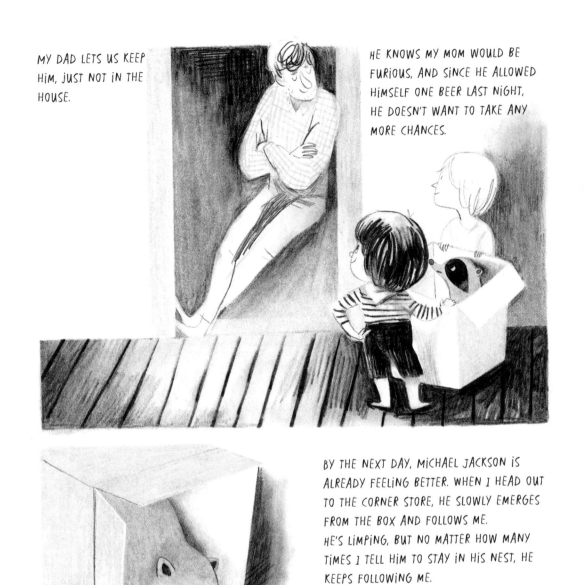

BY THE NEXT DAY, MICHAEL JACKSON IS ALREADY FEELING BETTER. WHEN I HEAD OUT TO THE CORNER STORE, HE SLOWLY EMERGES FROM THE BOX AND FOLLOWS ME.
HE'S LIMPING, BUT NO MATTER HOW MANY TIMES I TELL HIM TO STAY IN HIS NEST, HE KEEPS FOLLOWING ME.

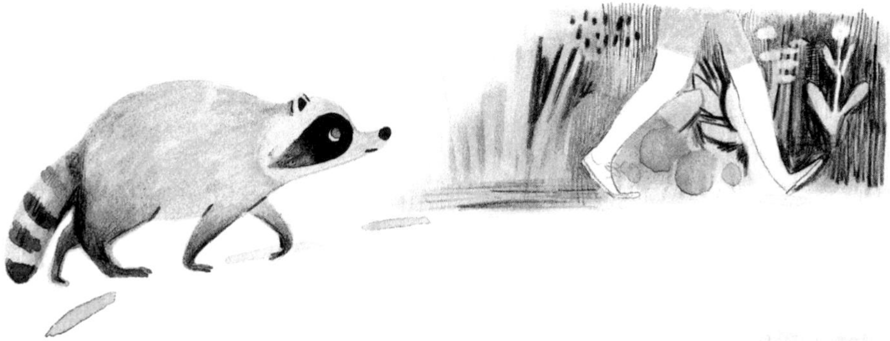

HE HIDES UNDER THE STEPS IN FRONT OF THE STORE. I BUY HIM A POPSICLE THAT HE SPITS OUT.

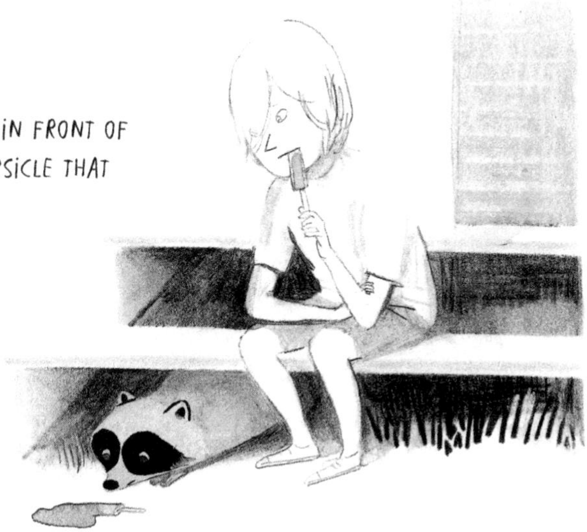

LOOKS LIKE I'LL HAVE TO CATCH HIM SOME FISH.

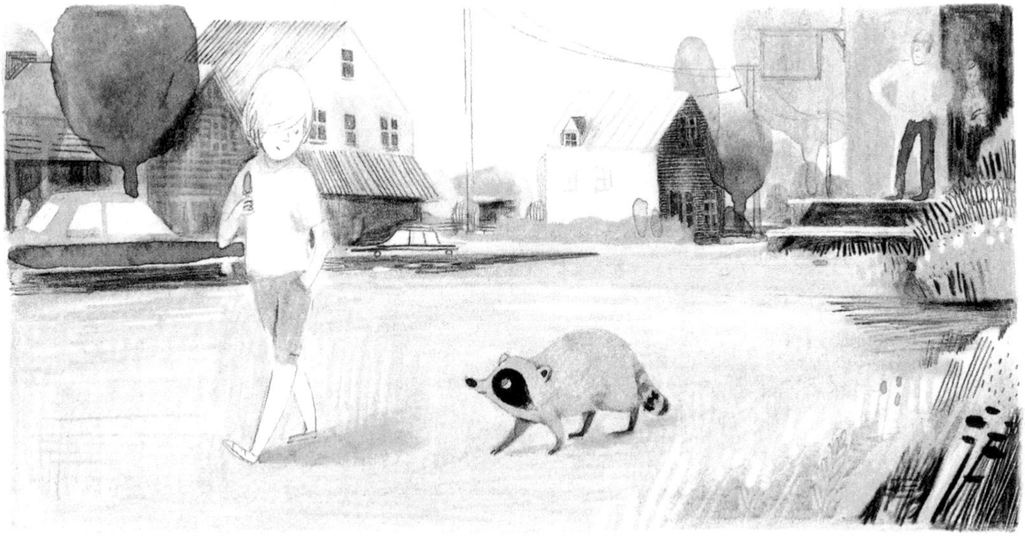

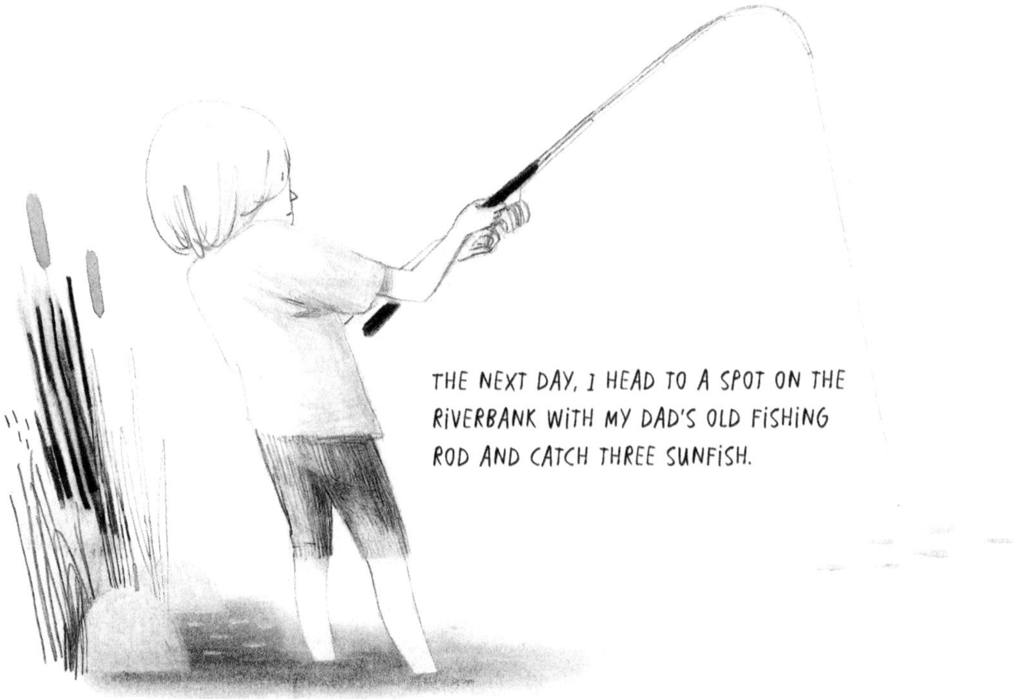

THE NEXT DAY, I HEAD TO A SPOT ON THE RIVERBANK WITH MY DAD'S OLD FISHING ROD AND CATCH THREE SUNFISH.

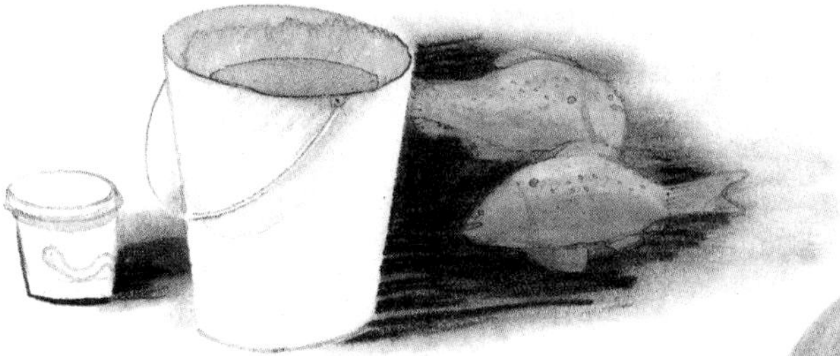

HE DEVOURS THEM ALL.

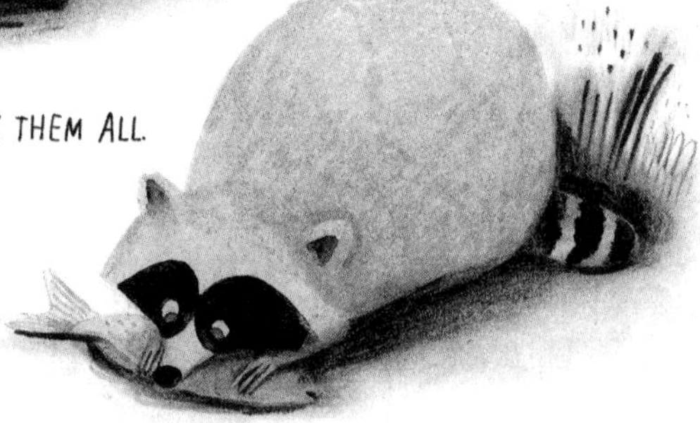

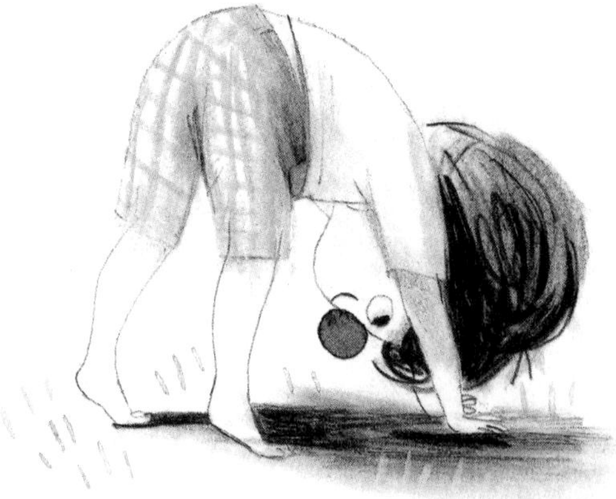

TRUFFLE DECIDES TO TEACH HIM SOME CIRCUS TRICKS.

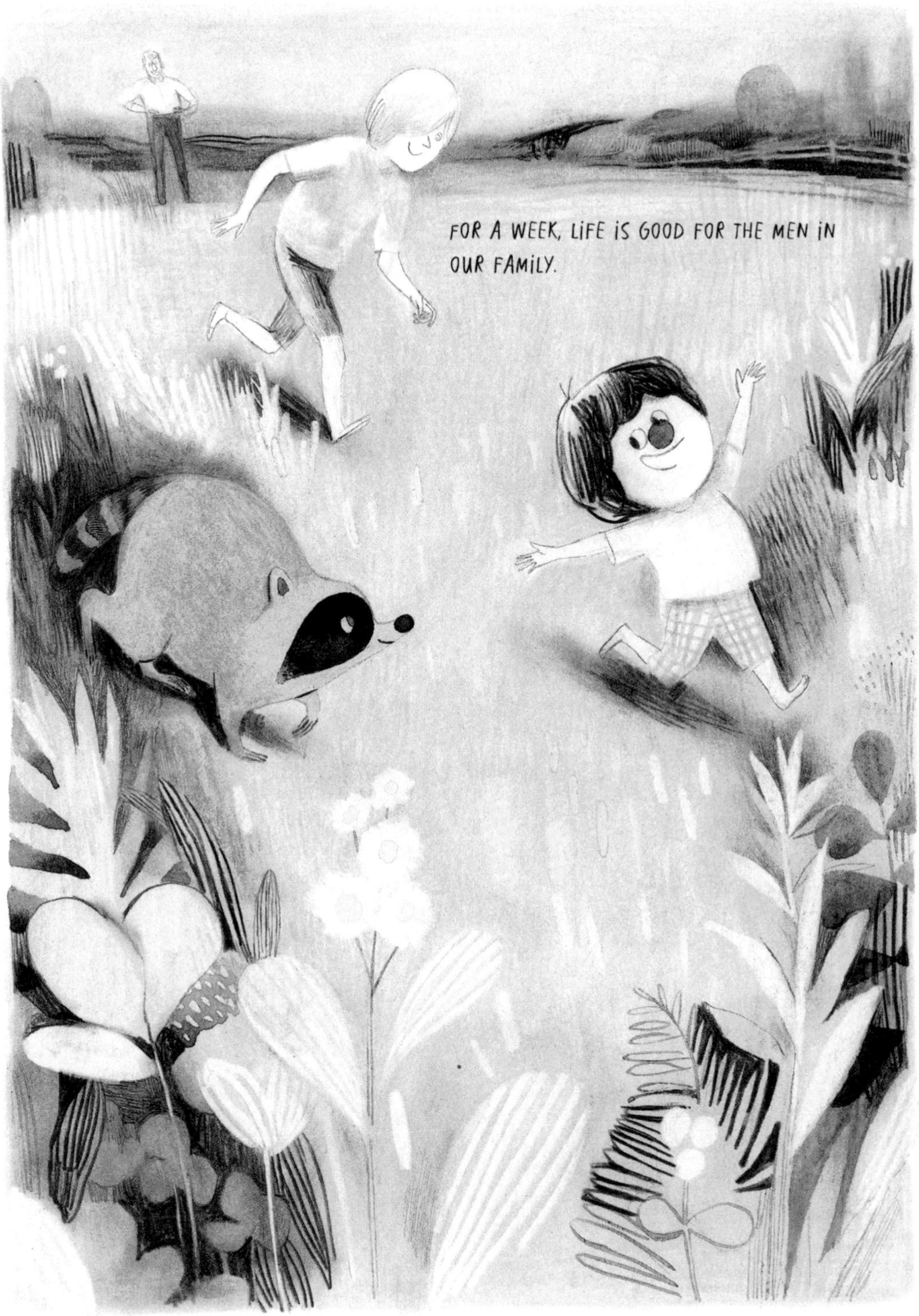
FOR A WEEK, LIFE IS GOOD FOR THE MEN IN OUR FAMILY.

GLOBAL
WARMING
and the Sweetness of Life
A TAR SANDS TALE
MATT HERN AND AM JOHAL
WITH JOE SACCO

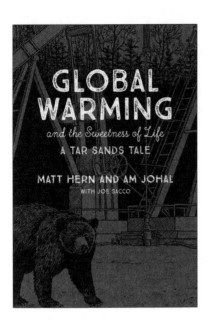

Bitumen or Bust

JOE SACCO

originally published in

Global Warming and the Sweetness of Life

THE MIT PRESS

6 x 9 inches • 232 pages

Biography

Joe Sacco is a cartoonist and is mostly known for journalistic comics.

Statement

This work was included in a prose book for the MIT Press by Matt Hern and Am Johal and is based on a trip we took together to Alberta. Those fellows were a lot of fun and let me do some of the driving.

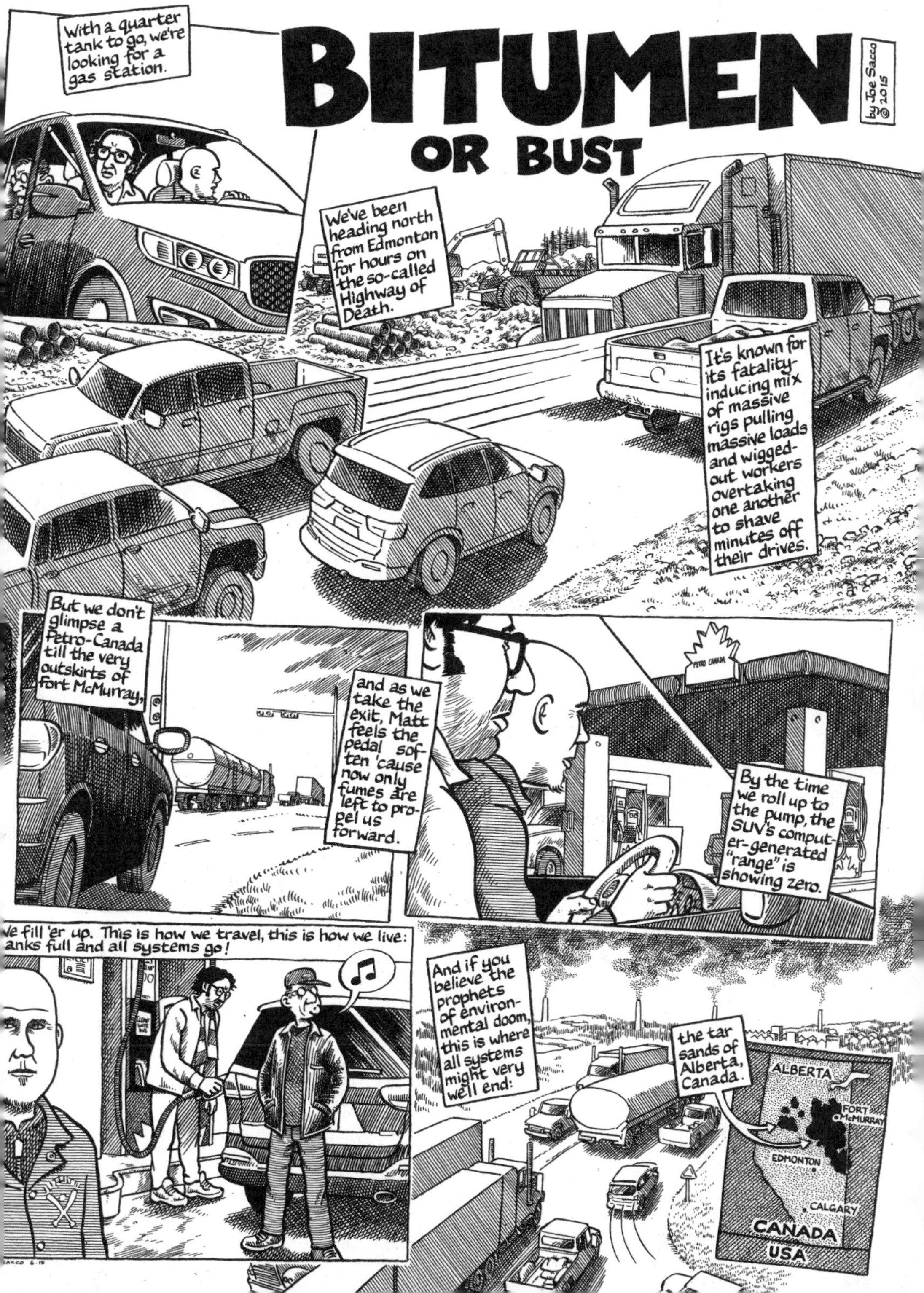

With a quarter tank to go, we're looking for a gas station.
BITUMEN
OR BUST
by Joe Sacco ©2015
We've been heading north from Edmonton for hours on the so-called Highway of Death.
It's known for its fatality-inducing mix of massive rigs pulling massive loads and wigged-out workers overtaking one another to shave minutes off their drives.
But we don't glimpse a Petro-Canada till the very outskirts of Fort McMurray,
and as we take the exit, Matt feels the pedal soften 'cause now only fumes are left to propel us forward.
PETRO CANADA
By the time we roll up to the pump, the SUV's computer-generated "range" is showing zero.
e fill 'er up. This is how we travel, this is how we live:
anks full and all systems go!
And if you believe the prophets of environmental doom, this is where all systems might very well end:
the tar sands of Alberta, Canada.
ALBERTA
FORT McMURRAY
EDMONTON
CALGARY
CANADA
USA
SACCO 6.15

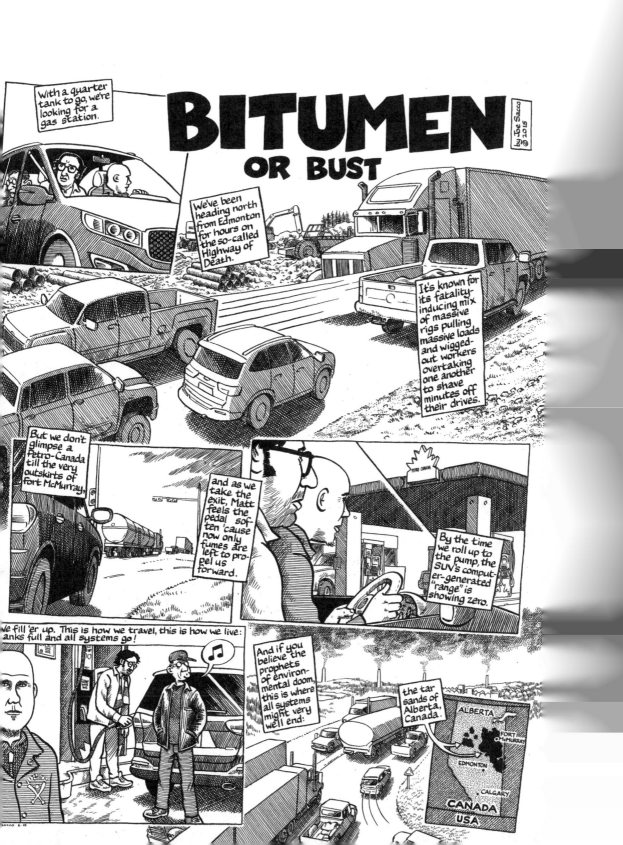

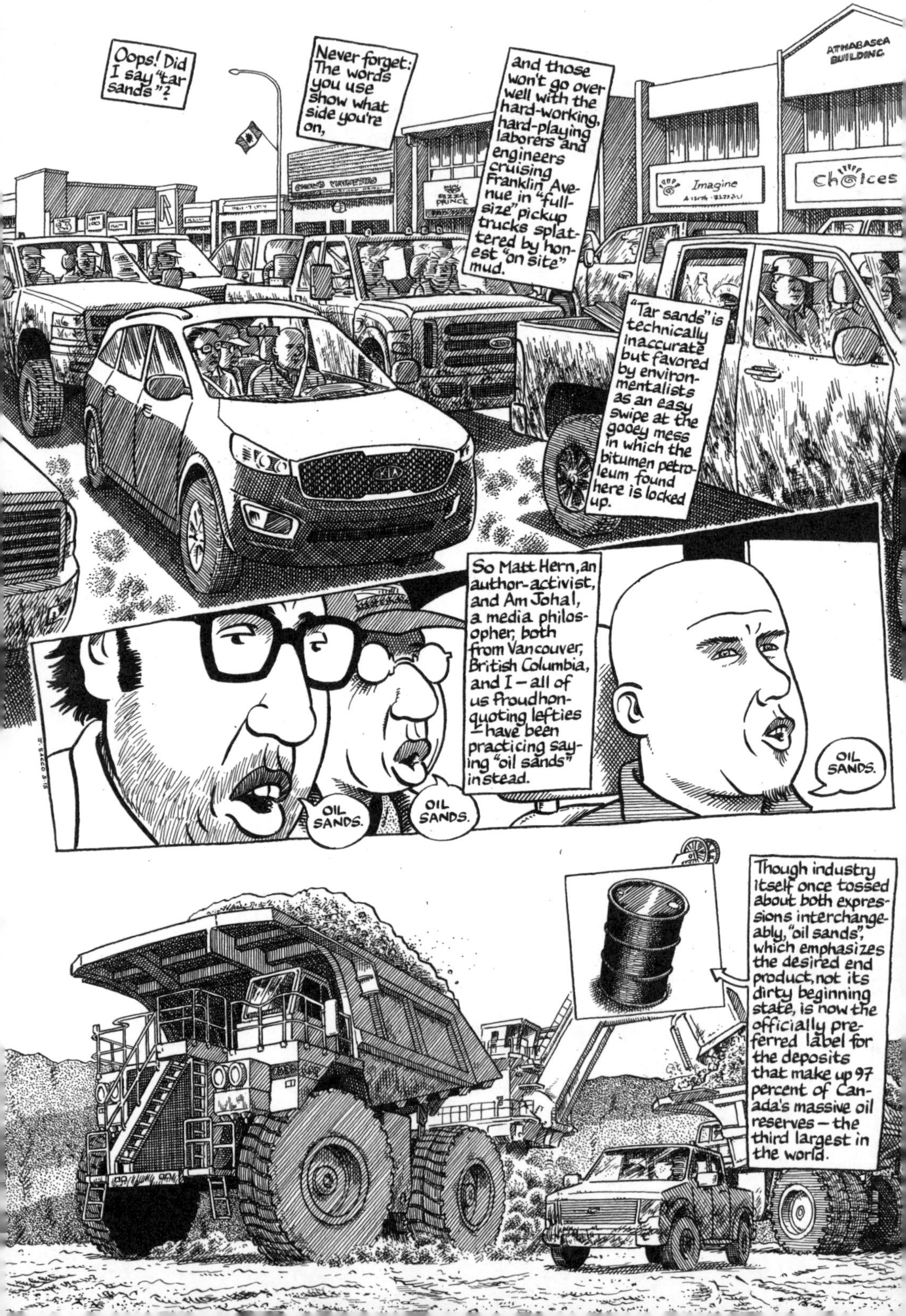

Oops! Did I say "tar sands"?
Never forget: The words you use show what side you're on,
and those won't go over well with the hard-working, hard-playing laborers and engineers cruising Franklin Avenue in "full-size" pickup trucks splattered by honest "on site" mud.
ATHABASCA BUILDING
Imagine
Choices
PIZZA PRINCE
"Tar sands" is technically inaccurate but favored by environmentalists as an easy swipe at the gooey mess in which the bitumen petroleum found here is locked up.
So Matt Hern, an author-activist, and Am Johal, a media philosopher, both from Vancouver, British Columbia, and I — all of us Proudhon-quoting lefties — have been practicing saying "oil sands" instead.
OIL SANDS.
OIL SANDS.
OIL SANDS.
Though industry itself once tossed about both expressions interchangeably, "oil sands", which emphasizes the desired end product, not its dirty beginning state, is now the officially preferred label for the deposits that make up 97 percent of Canada's massive oil reserves — the third largest in the world.

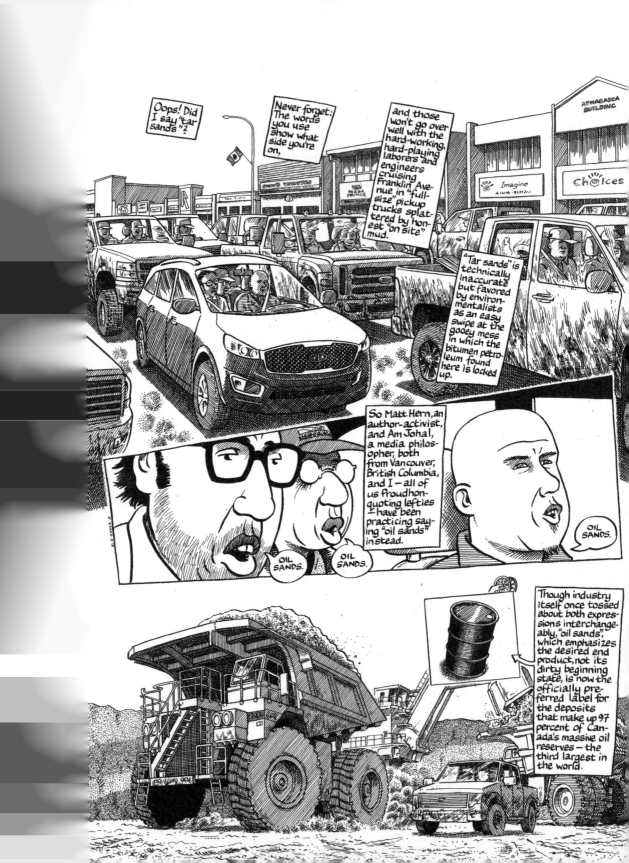

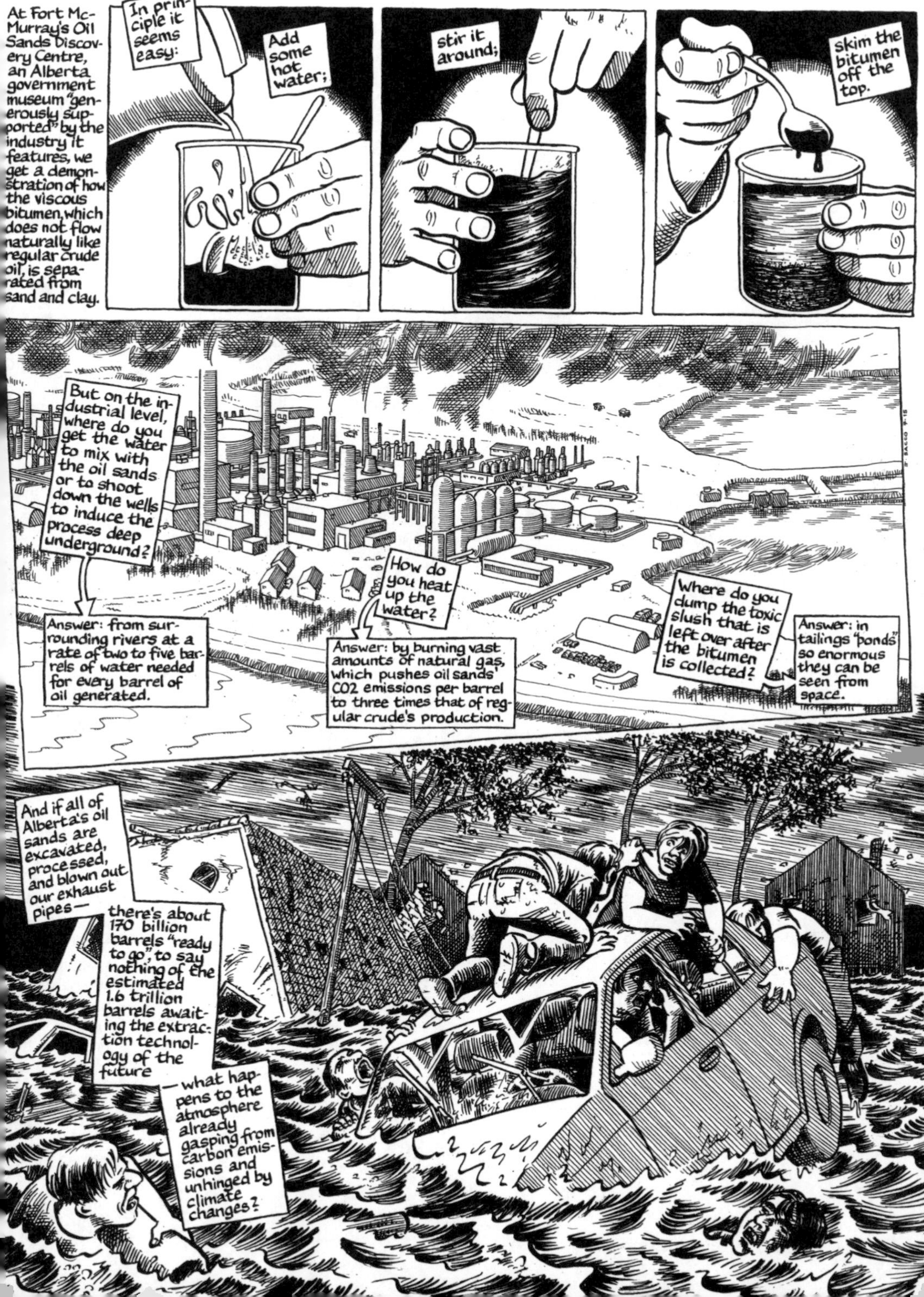
At Fort McMurray's Oil Sands Discovery Centre, an Alberta government museum "generously supported" by the industry it features, we get a demonstration of how the viscous bitumen, which does not flow naturally like regular crude oil, is separated from sand and clay.
In principle it seems easy:
Add some hot water;
stir it around;
skim the bitumen off the top.
But on the industrial level, where do you get the water to mix with the oil sands or to shoot down the wells to induce the process deep underground?
Answer: from surrounding rivers at a rate of two to five barrels of water needed for every barrel of oil generated.
How do you heat up the water?
Answer: by burning vast amounts of natural gas, which pushes oil sands' CO2 emissions per barrel to three times that of regular crude's production.
Where do you dump the toxic slush that is left over after the bitumen is collected?
Answer: in tailings "ponds" so enormous they can be seen from space.
And if all of Alberta's oil sands are excavated, processed, and blown out our exhaust pipes—
there's about 170 billion barrels "ready to go", to say nothing of the estimated 1.6 trillion barrels awaiting the extraction technology of the future
—what happens to the atmosphere already gasping from carbon emissions and unhinged by climate changes?

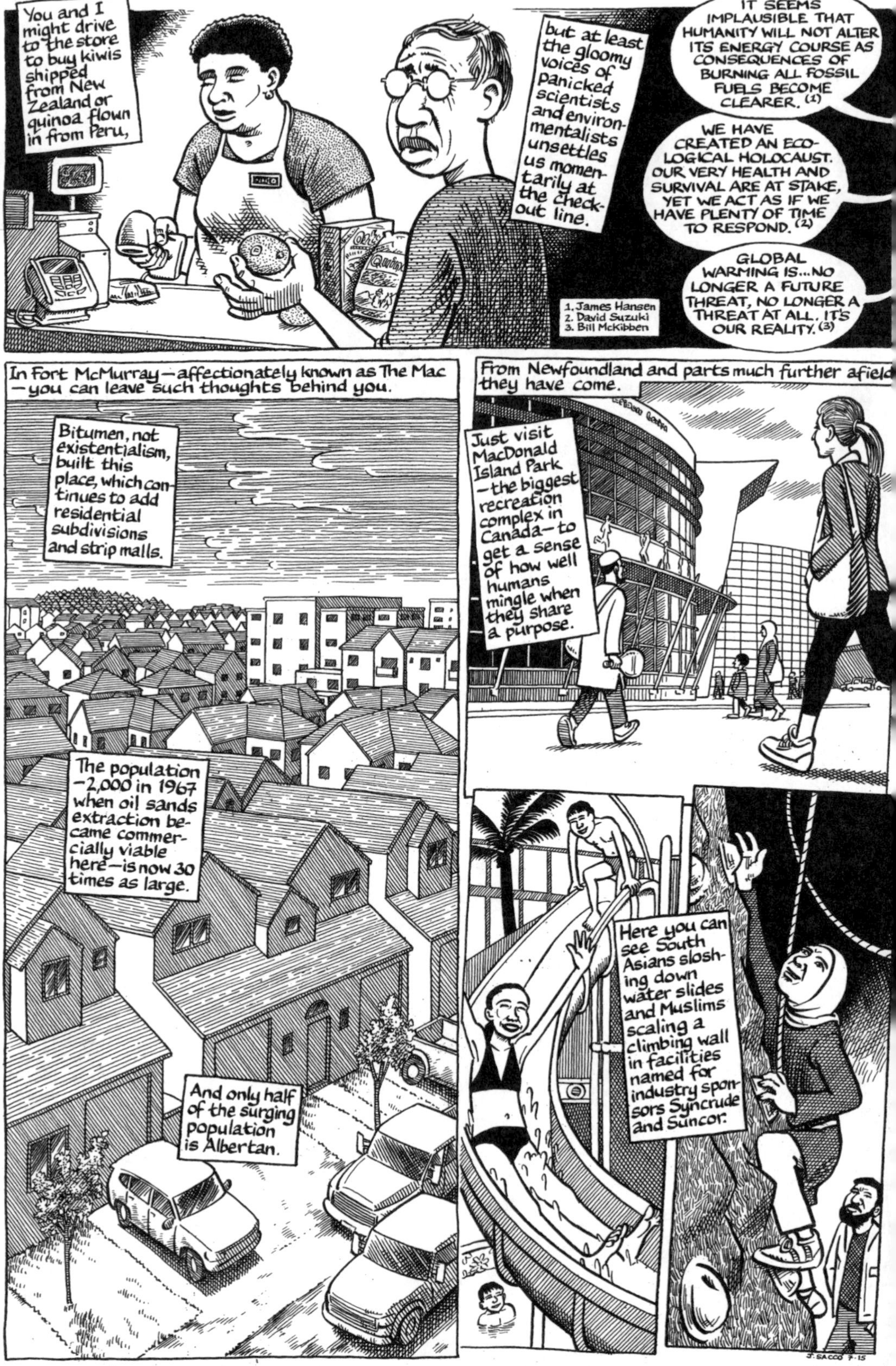
You and I might drive to the store to buy kiwis shipped from New Zealand or quinoa flown in from Peru,
but at least the gloomy voices of panicked scientists and environmentalists unsettles us momentarily at the check-out line.
IT SEEMS IMPLAUSIBLE THAT HUMANITY WILL NOT ALTER ITS ENERGY COURSE AS CONSEQUENCES OF BURNING ALL FOSSIL FUELS BECOME CLEARER. (1)
WE HAVE CREATED AN ECOLOGICAL HOLOCAUST. OUR VERY HEALTH AND SURVIVAL ARE AT STAKE, YET WE ACT AS IF WE HAVE PLENTY OF TIME TO RESPOND. (2)
GLOBAL WARMING IS...NO LONGER A FUTURE THREAT, NO LONGER A THREAT AT ALL. IT'S OUR REALITY. (3)
1. James Hansen
2. David Suzuki
3. Bill McKibben
In Fort McMurray—affectionately known as The Mac—you can leave such thoughts behind you.
Bitumen, not existentialism, built this place, which continues to add residential subdivisions and strip malls.
The population—2,000 in 1967 when oil sands extraction became commercially viable here—is now 30 times as large.
And only half of the surging population is Albertan.
From Newfoundland and parts much further afield they have come.
Just visit MacDonald Island Park—the biggest recreation complex in Canada—to get a sense of how well humans mingle when they share a purpose.
Here you can see South Asians sloshing down water slides and Muslims scaling a climbing wall in facilities named for industry sponsors Syncrude and Suncor.
J. SACCO 7·15

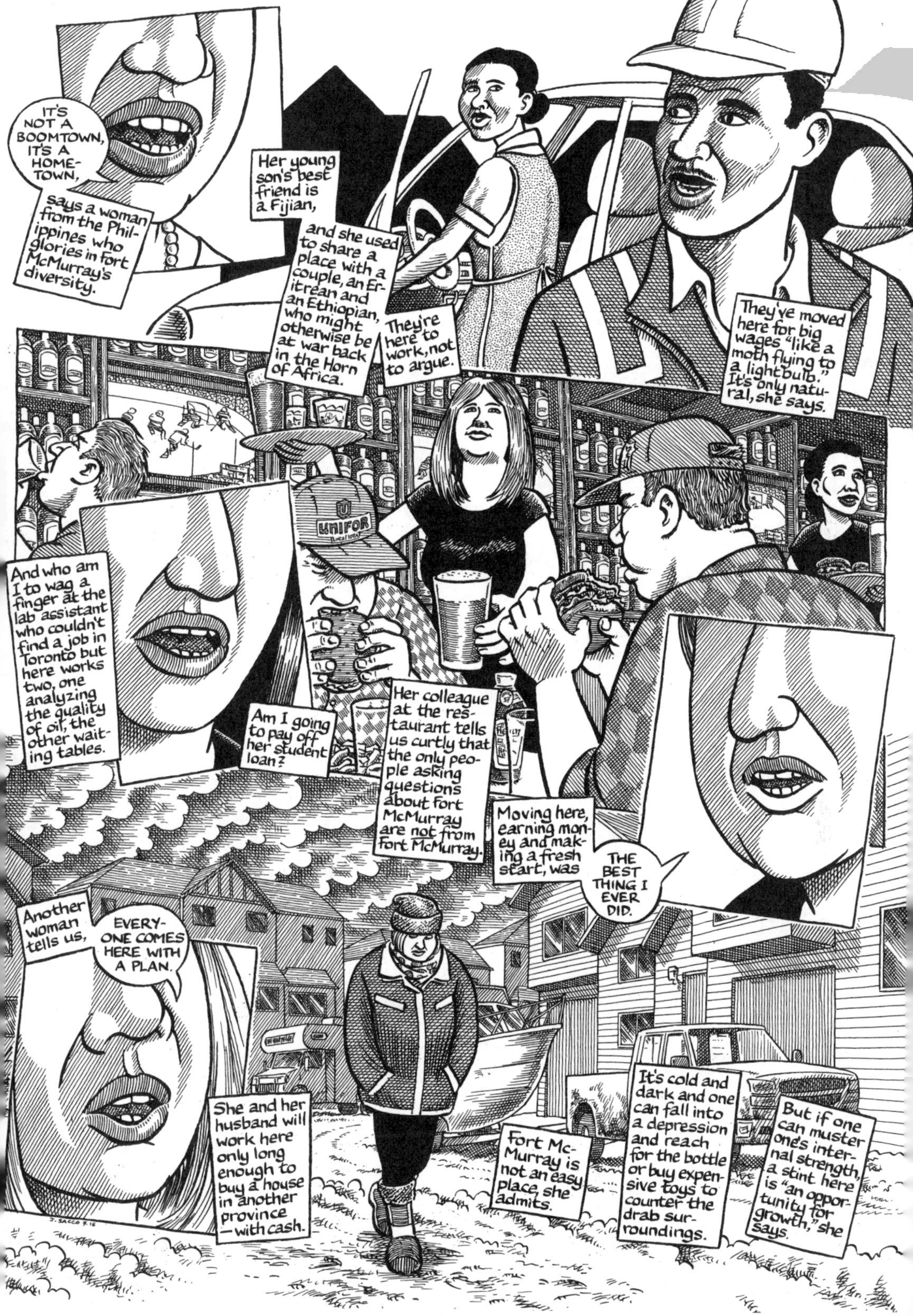
IT'S NOT A BOOMTOWN, IT'S A HOMETOWN,
says a woman from the Philippines who glories in Fort McMurray's diversity.
Her young son's best friend is a Fijian,
and she used to share a place with a couple, an Eritrean and an Ethiopian, who might otherwise be at war back in the Horn of Africa.
They're here to work, not to argue.
They've moved here for big wages "like a moth flying to a lightbulb." It's only natural, she says.
UNIFOR
And who am I to wag a finger at the lab assistant who couldn't find a job in Toronto but here works two, one analyzing the quality of oil, the other waiting tables.
Am I going to pay off her student loan?
Her colleague at the restaurant tells us curtly that the only people asking questions about Fort McMurray are not from Fort McMurray.
Moving here, earning money and making a fresh start, was
THE BEST THING I EVER DID.
Another woman tells us,
EVERYONE COMES HERE WITH A PLAN.
She and her husband will work here only long enough to buy a house in another province—with cash.
Fort McMurray is not an easy place, she admits.
It's cold and dark and one can fall into a depression and reach for the bottle or buy expensive toys to counter the drab surroundings.
But if one can muster one's internal strength, a stint here is "an opportunity for growth," she says.
J. SACCO

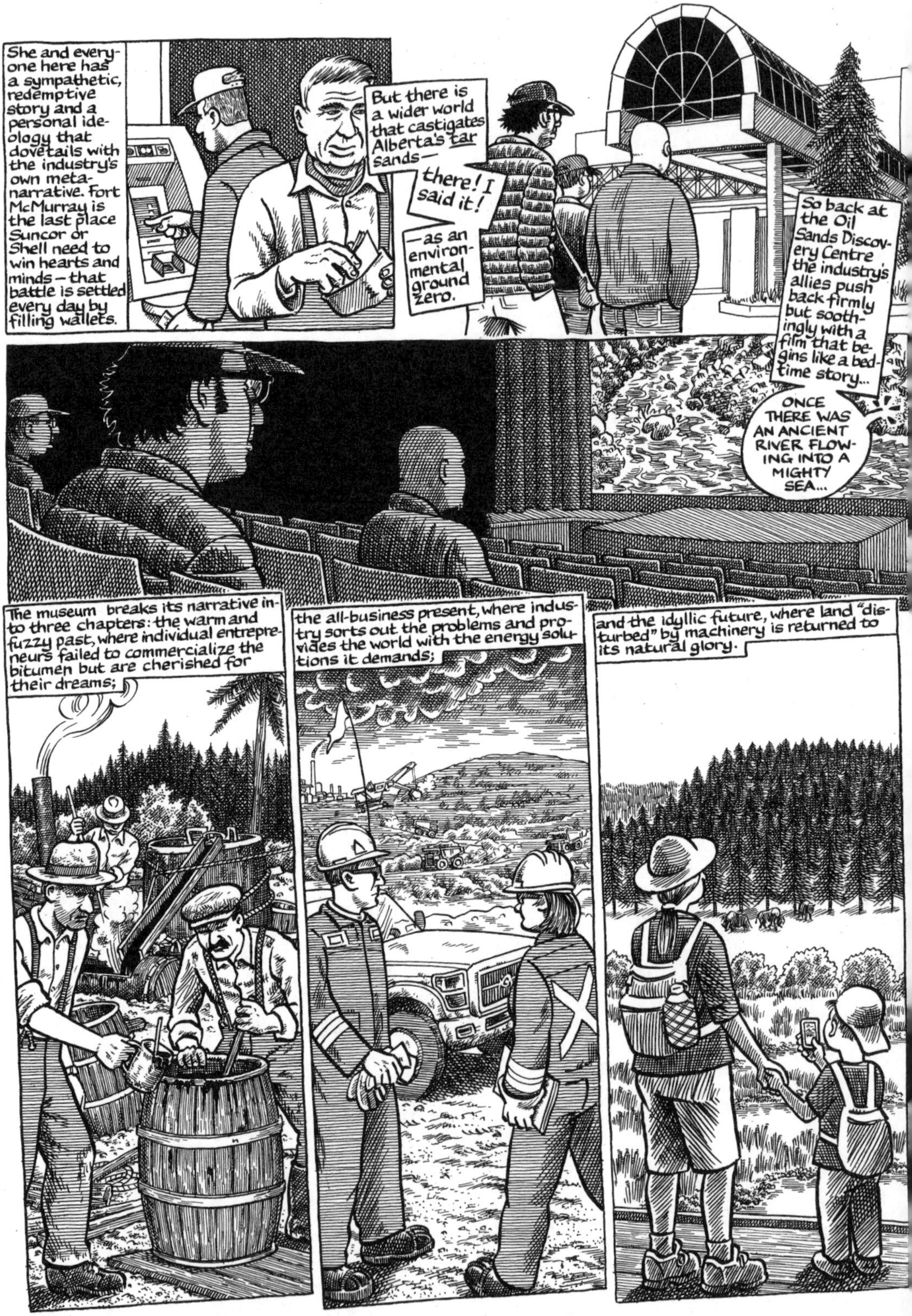
She and everyone here has a sympathetic, redemptive story and a personal ideology that dovetails with the industry's own metanarrative. Fort McMurray is the last place Suncor or Shell need to win hearts and minds—that battle is settled every day by filling wallets.
But there is a wider world that castigates Alberta's tar sands—
there! I said it!
—as an environmental ground zero.
So back at the Oil Sands Discovery Centre the industry's allies push back firmly but soothingly with a film that begins like a bedtime story...
ONCE THERE WAS AN ANCIENT RIVER FLOWING INTO A MIGHTY SEA...
The museum breaks its narrative into three chapters: the warm and fuzzy past, where individual entrepreneurs failed to commercialize the bitumen but are cherished for their dreams;
the all-business present, where industry sorts out the problems and provides the world with the energy solutions it demands;
and the idyllic future, where land "disturbed" by machinery is returned to its natural glory.

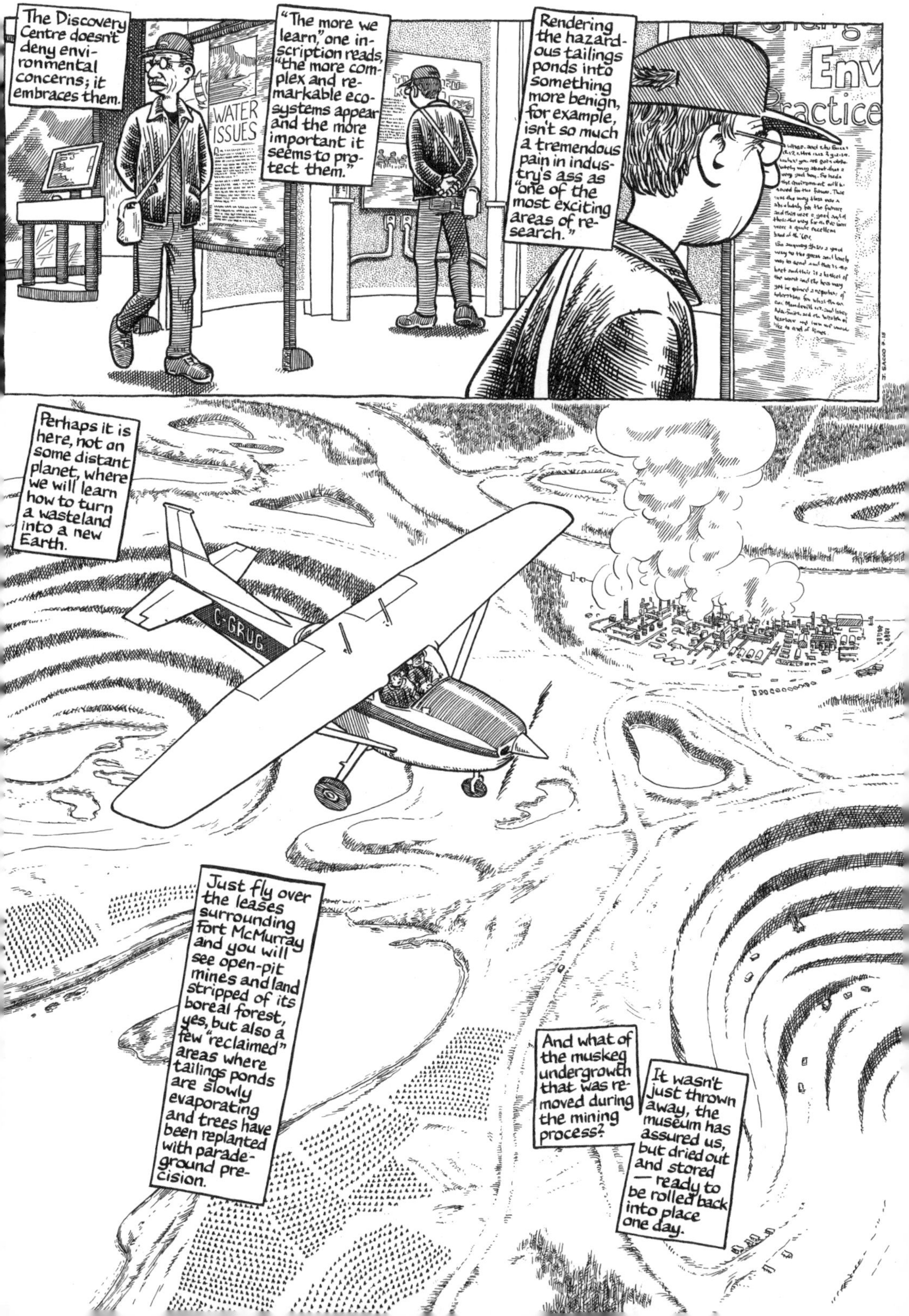

The Discovery Centre doesn't deny environmental concerns; it embraces them.
WATER ISSUES
"The more we learn," one inscription reads, "the more complex and remarkable ecosystems appear and the more important it seems to protect them."
Rendering the hazardous tailings ponds into something more benign, for example, isn't so much a tremendous pain in industry's ass as "one of the most exciting areas of research."
Perhaps it is here, not on some distant planet, where we will learn how to turn a wasteland into a new Earth.
C-GRUG
Just fly over the leases surrounding Fort McMurray and you will see open-pit mines and land stripped of its boreal forest, yes, but also a few "reclaimed" areas where tailings ponds are slowly evaporating and trees have been replanted with parade-ground precision.
And what of the muskeg undergrowth that was removed during the mining process?
It wasn't just thrown away, the museum has assured us, but dried out and stored — ready to be rolled back into place one day.

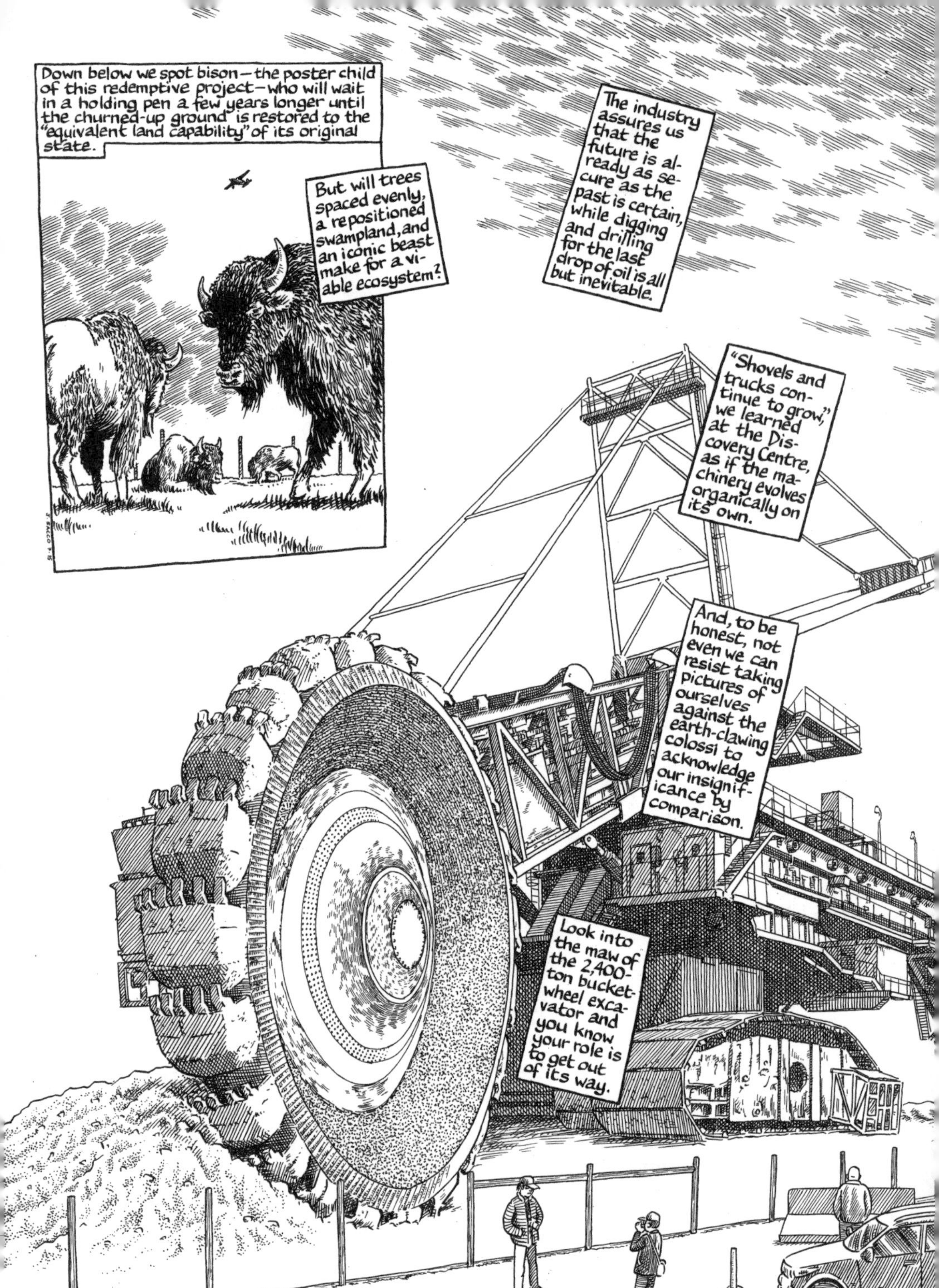
Down below we spot bison—the poster child of this redemptive project—who will wait in a holding pen a few years longer until the churned-up ground is restored to the "equivalent land capability" of its original state.
But will trees spaced evenly, a repositioned swampland, and an iconic beast make for a viable ecosystem?
The industry assures us that the future is already as secure as the past is certain, while digging and drilling for the last drop of oil is all but inevitable.
"Shovels and trucks continue to grow," we learned at the Discovery Centre, as if the machinery evolves organically on its own.
And, to be honest, not even we can resist taking pictures of ourselves against the earth-clawing colossi to acknowledge our insignificance by comparison.
Look into the maw of the 2,400-ton bucket-wheel excavator and you know your role is to get out of its way.

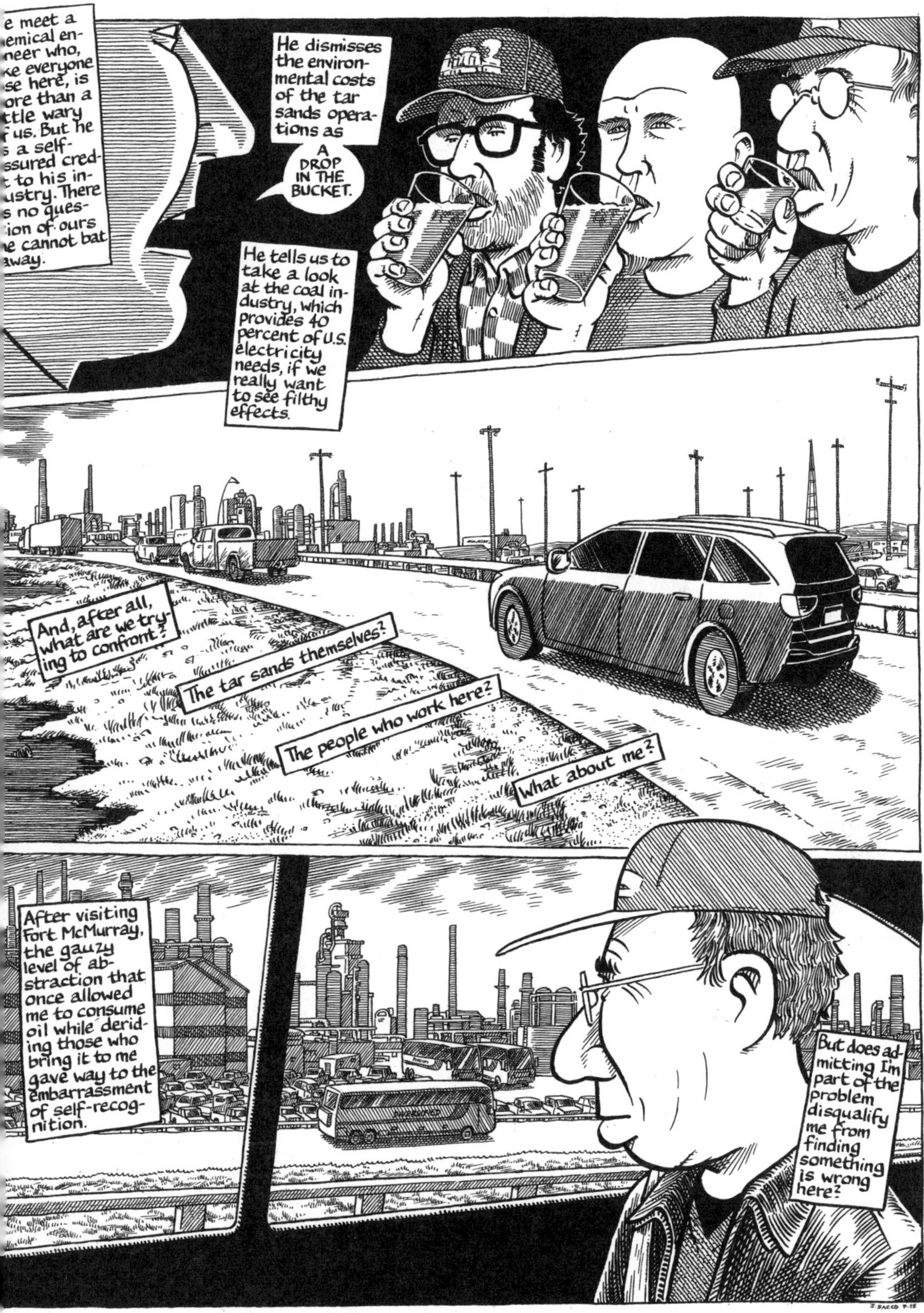
e meet a emical en- neer who, ke everyone se here, is ore than a ttle wary f us. But he s a self- ssured cred- t to his in- ustry. There s no ques- ion of ours e cannot bat away.
He dismisses the environ- mental costs of the tar sands opera- tions as
A DROP IN THE BUCKET.
He tells us to take a look at the coal in- dustry, which provides 40 percent of U.S. electricity needs, if we really want to see filthy effects.
And, after all, what are we try- ing to confront?
The tar sands themselves?
The people who work here?
What about me?
After visiting Fort McMurray, the gauzy level of ab- straction that once allowed me to consume oil while derid- ing those who bring it to me gave way to the embarrassment of self-recog- nition.
But does ad- mitting I'm part of the problem disqualify me from finding something is wrong here?
J. SACCO 9-15

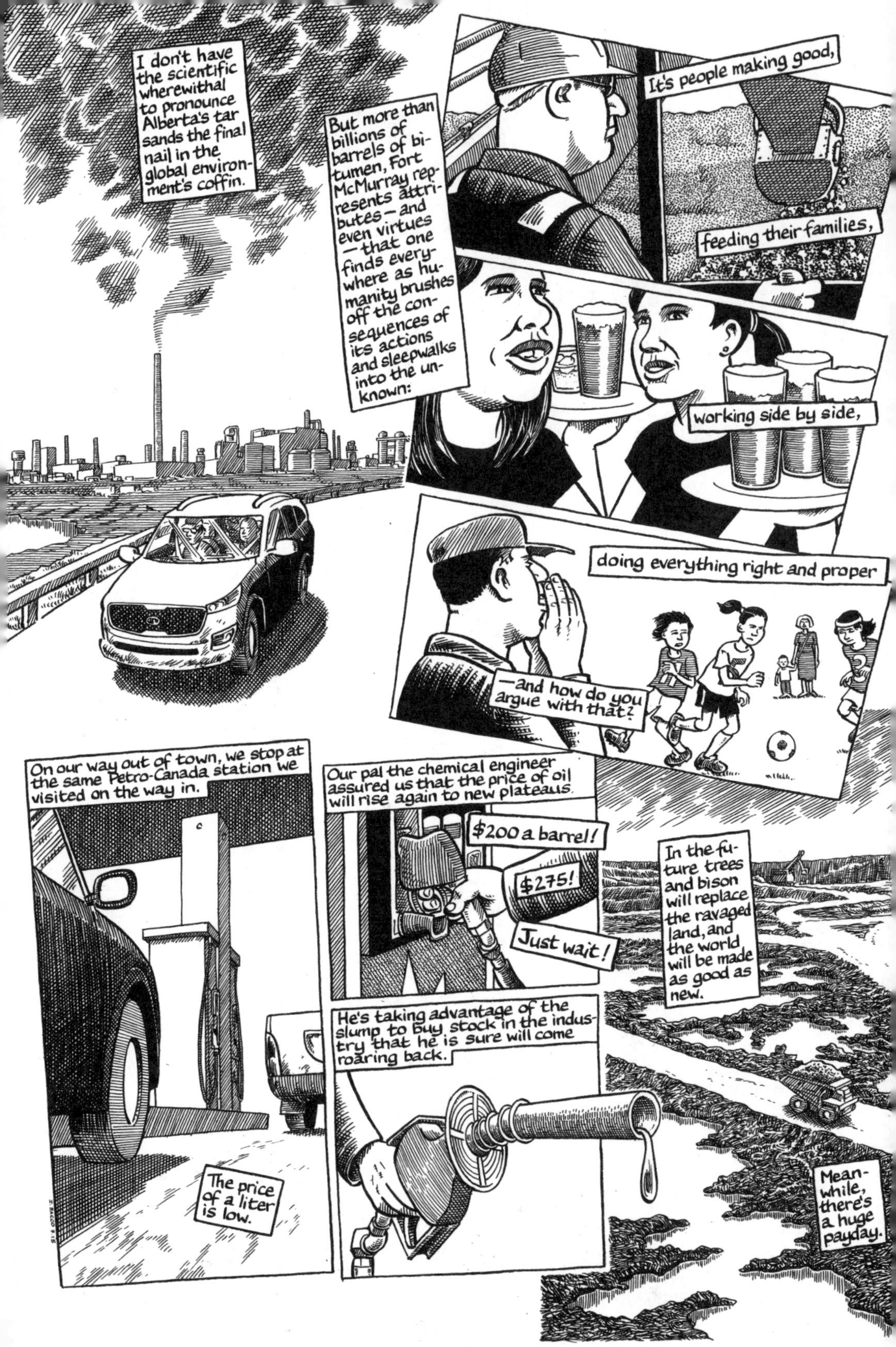
I don't have the scientific wherewithal to pronounce Alberta's tar sands the final nail in the global environment's coffin.
But more than billions of barrels of bitumen, Fort McMurray represents attributes—and even virtues—that one finds everywhere as humanity brushes off the consequences of its actions and sleepwalks into the unknown:
It's people making good,
feeding their families,
working side by side,
doing everything right and proper
—and how do you argue with that?
On our way out of town, we stop at the same Petro-Canada station we visited on the way in.
The price of a liter is low.
Our pal the chemical engineer assured us that the price of oil will rise again to new plateaus.
$200 a barrel!
$275!
Just wait!
He's taking advantage of the slump to buy stock in the industry that he is sure will come roaring back.
In the future trees and bison will replace the ravaged land, and the world will be made as good as new.
Meanwhile, there's a huge payday.

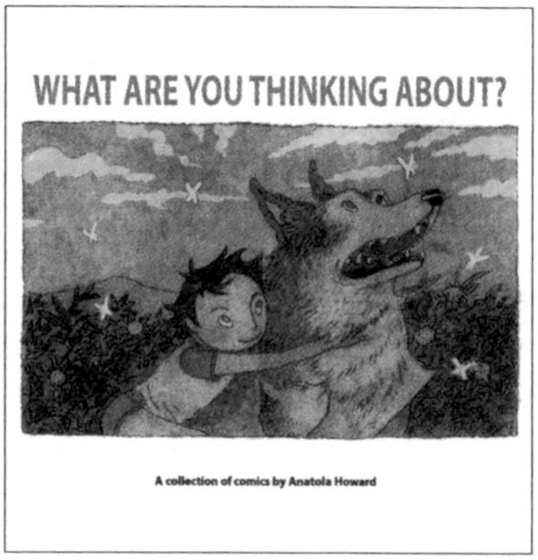
WHAT ARE YOU THINKING ABOUT?
A collection of comics by Anatola Howard

Self-Love-Cycle

ANATOLA HOWARD

originally published in

What Are You Thinking About?

SHORTBOX

8.25 x 8.25 inches • 36 pages

Biography

Anatola Howard used to live on a giant Flemish rabbit farm, but now she's in Los Angeles making comics and animations for you!
anatolahoward.com

Statement

I was worried if a guy raising a baby clone of himself then marrying it would be a problem in the context of this comic, but I guess not if they're quite literally the same person. I figured if "nothing" is a "problem" in an impossible love cycle like this, then the entire operation must be a convoluted sham. Sometimes impossible controversies need to be solved, I guess.

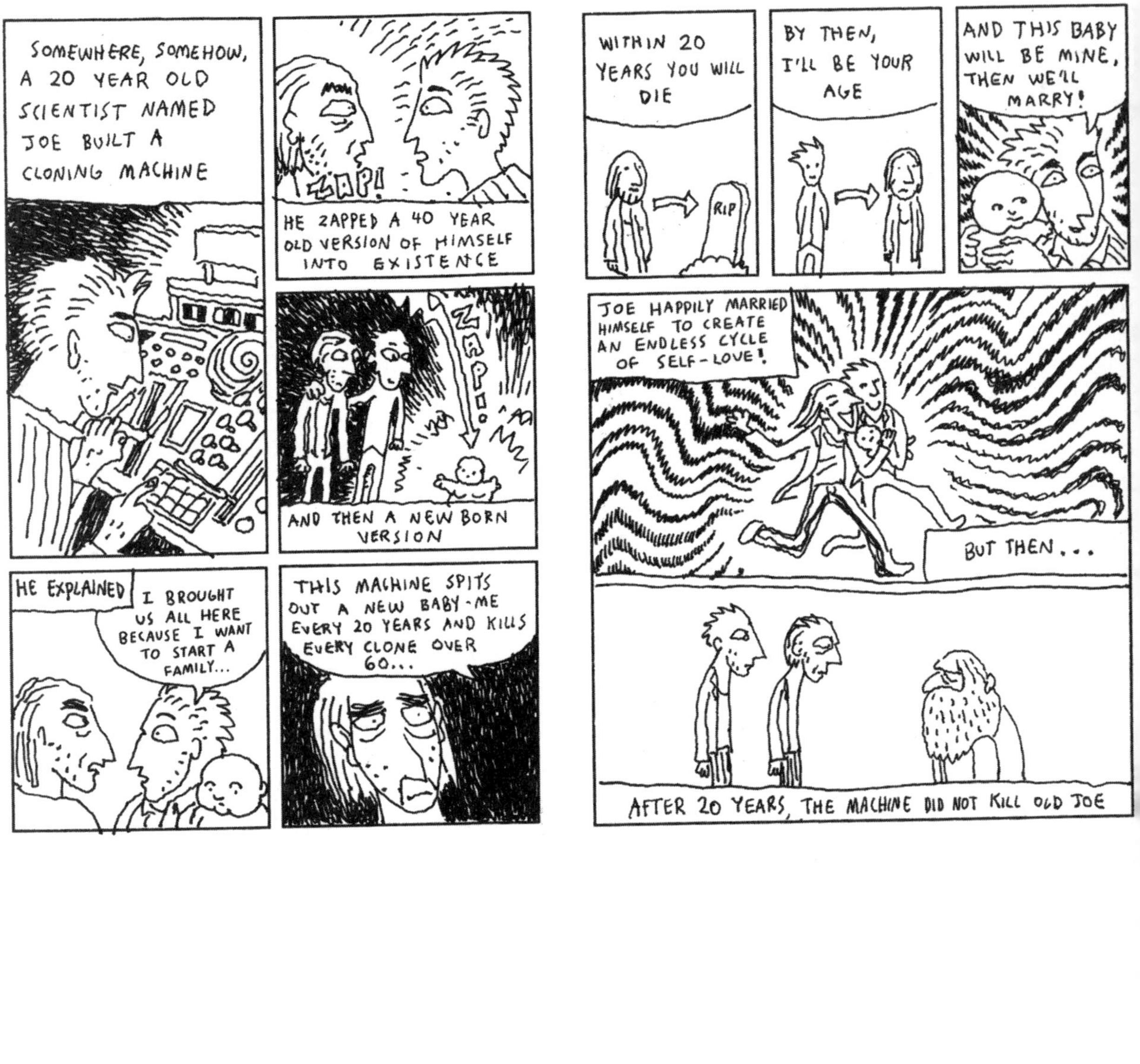
SOMEWHERE, SOMEHOW, A 20 YEAR OLD SCIENTIST NAMED JOE BUILT A CLONING MACHINE
ZAP!
HE ZAPPED A 40 YEAR OLD VERSION OF HIMSELF INTO EXISTENCE
ZAP!
AND THEN A NEW BORN VERSION
HE EXPLAINED
I BROUGHT US ALL HERE BECAUSE I WANT TO START A FAMILY...
THIS MACHINE SPITS OUT A NEW BABY-ME EVERY 20 YEARS AND KILLS EVERY CLONE OVER 60...
WITHIN 20 YEARS YOU WILL DIE
RIP
BY THEN, I'LL BE YOUR AGE
AND THIS BABY WILL BE MINE, THEN WE'LL MARRY!
JOE HAPPILY MARRIED HIMSELF TO CREATE AN ENDLESS CYCLE OF SELF-LOVE!
BUT THEN...
AFTER 20 YEARS, THE MACHINE DID NOT KILL OLD JOE

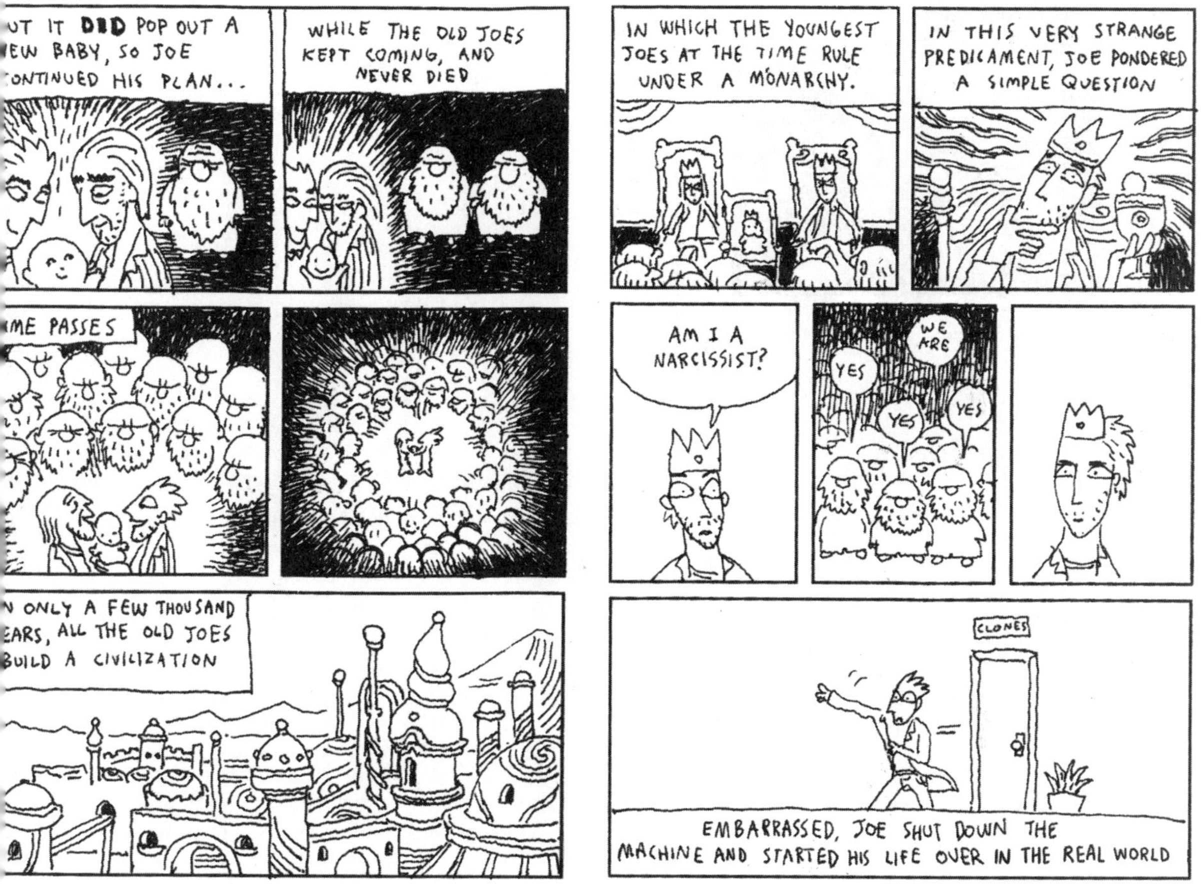
UT IT DID POP OUT A
EW BABY, SO JOE
ONTINUED HIS PLAN...
WHILE THE OLD JOES KEPT COMING, AND NEVER DIED
ME PASSES
N ONLY A FEW THOUSAND
EARS, ALL THE OLD JOES
BUILD A CIVILIZATION
IN WHICH THE YOUNGEST JOES AT THE TIME RULE UNDER A MONARCHY.
IN THIS VERY STRANGE PREDICAMENT, JOE PONDERED A SIMPLE QUESTION
AM I A NARCISSIST?
WE ARE
YES
YES
YES
CLONES
EMBARRASSED, JOE SHUT DOWN THE MACHINE AND STARTED HIS LIFE OVER IN THE REAL WORLD

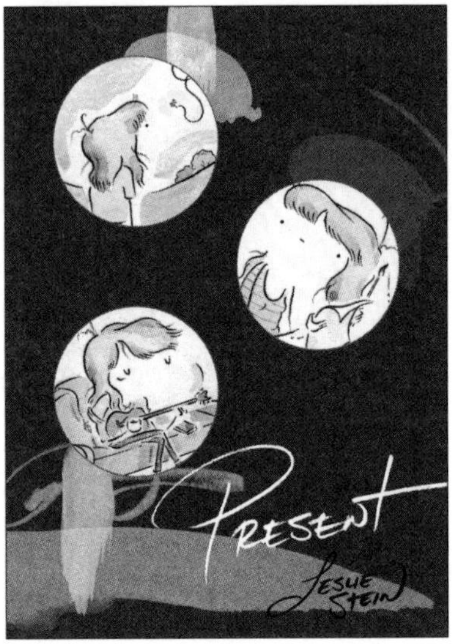
PRESENT
LESLIE STEIN

Vanguard

LESLIE STEIN

originally published in

Present

DRAWN AND QUARTERLY

6 x 7.8 inches • 168 pages

Biography

Leslie Stein is the creator of the three-volume series Eye of the Majestic Creature and the diary comic *Bright-Eyed at Midnight.* Her autobiographical comics have appeared in *The New Yorker, Vice,* and PEN America. Her most recent book, *Present,* won the *Los Angeles Times* Book Prize for Graphic Novel of the Year in 2018. She lives in Brooklyn, New York.
instagram.com/leslieamstein

Statement

It's hard to believe that after living in New York for many years, I had never been to the legendary Village Vanguard in Greenwich Village. I had been using jazz and experimental music to paint to for a couple years prior, but had never left the house to do so. A narrative element I had planned on incorporating into the strip, but didn't, was that after I left the club almost exactly at midnight, it was my thirty-fourth birthday. So I felt even more fortunate to have stumbled into the club when I did. It made for a nice, thoughtful, and solitary moment. Even so, I thought the strip felt completed at that last line.

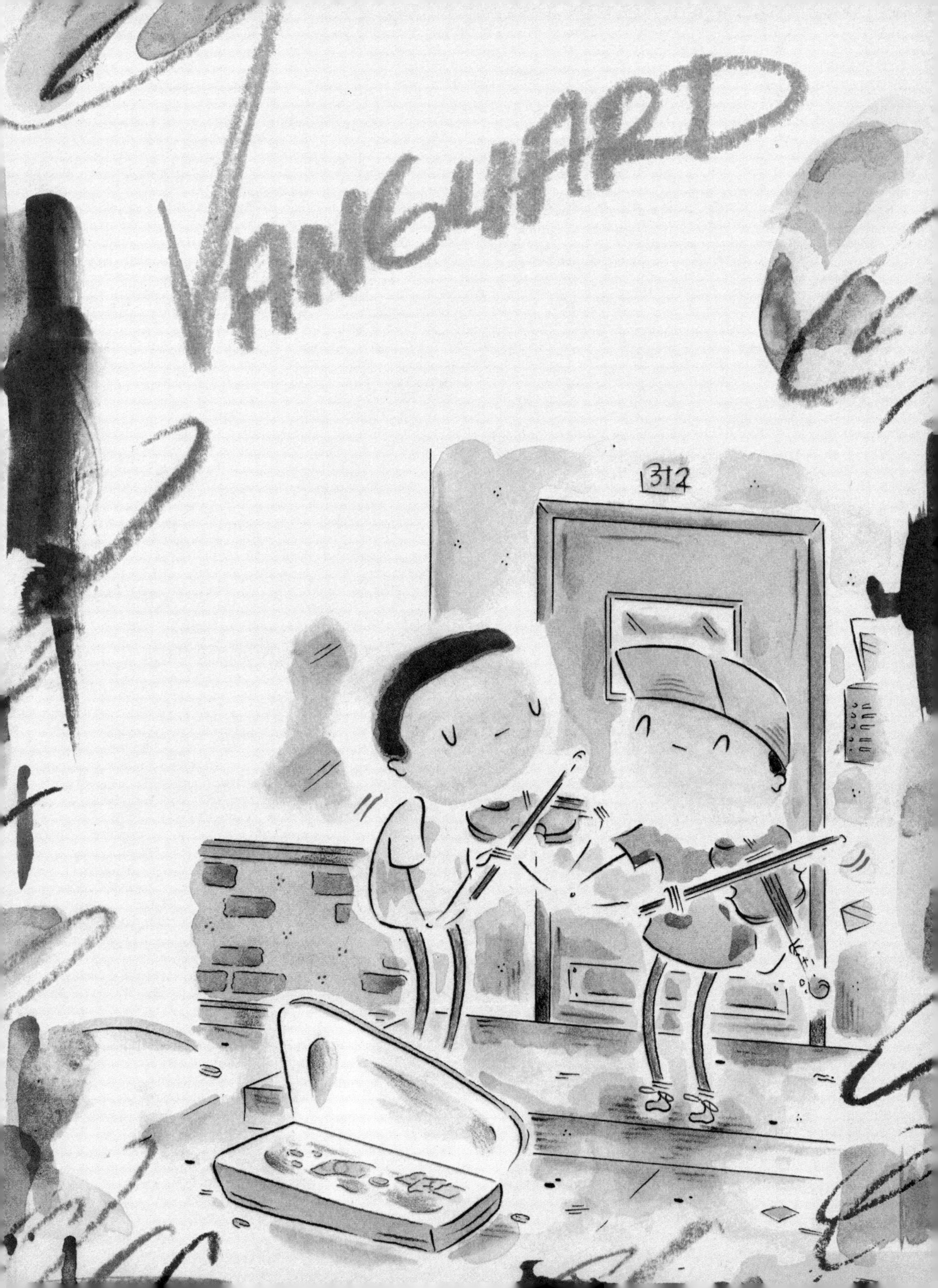
VANGUARD
312

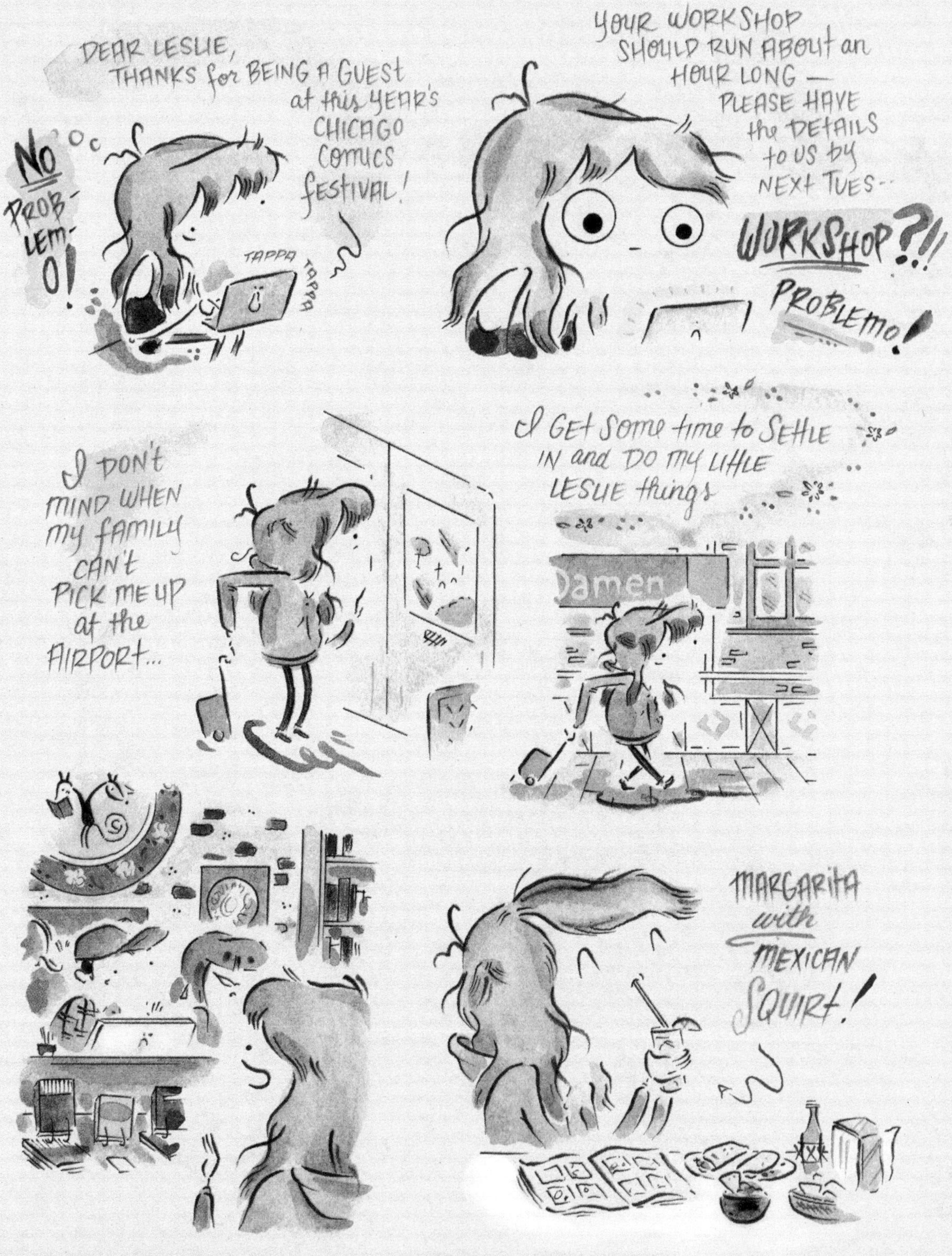
DEAR LESLIE,
THANKS for BEING A GUEST at this YEAR's CHICAGO Comics festival!
NO PROB-LEM-O!
TAPPA TAPPA
YOUR WORKSHOP SHOULD RUN ABOUT an HOUR LONG — PLEASE HAVE the DETAILS to US by NEXT TUES..
WORKSHOP?!!
PROBLEMO!
I DON'T mind WHEN my FAMILY CAN'T PICK ME UP at the AIRPORT...
I GET some time to SETTLE IN and DO my LITTLE LESLIE things
Damen
MARGARITA with MEXICAN SQUIRT!

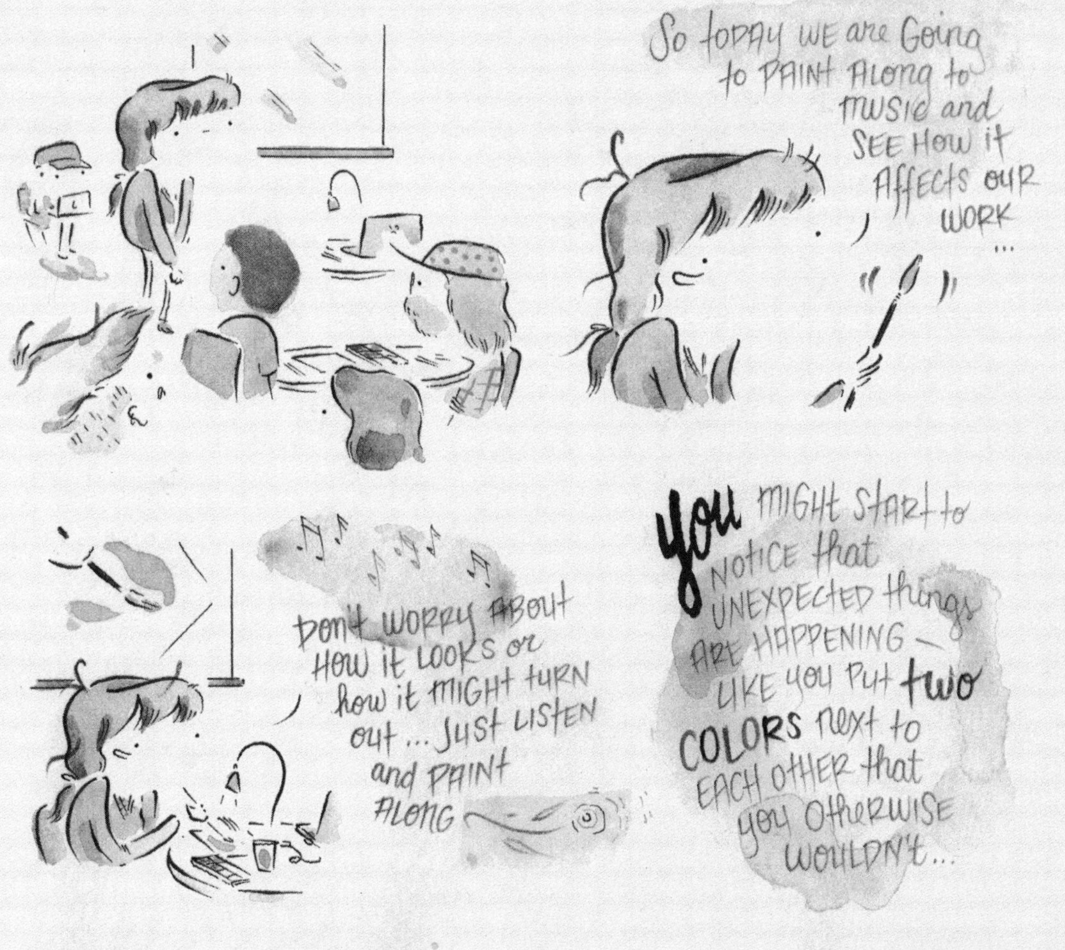

So today we are Going to PAINT Along to music and SEE HOW it Affects our work ...
YOU MIGHT start to notice that UNEXPECTED things ARE HAPPENING — LIKE YOU Put two COLORS next to EACH OTHER that you OtherWISE WOULDN'T...
Don't worry about how it looks or how it might turn out ... Just listen and paint along
... and you like the way they complement each other.
OKAY!! FOR this NEXT Song, WE ARE GOING to take the "MISTAKES" WE LIKE from the first PAINTING AND —
CAN YOU QUEUE UP that ALICE COLTRANE Song?

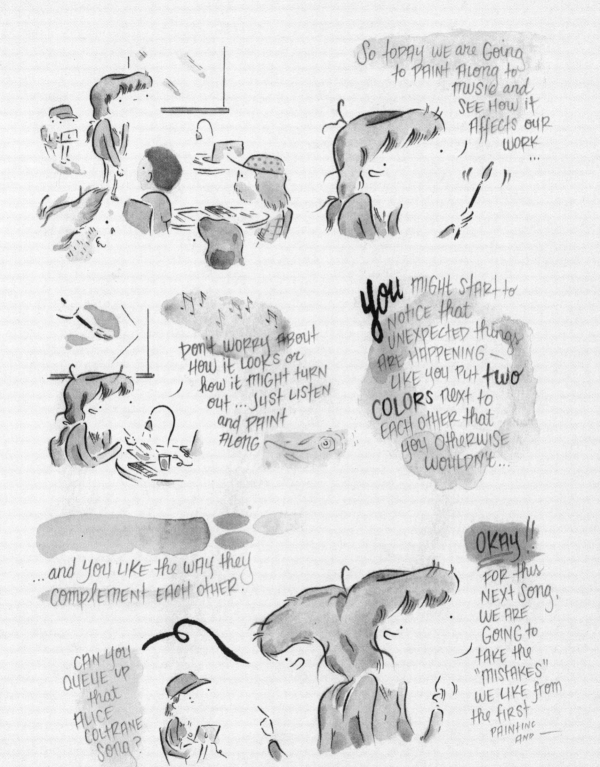

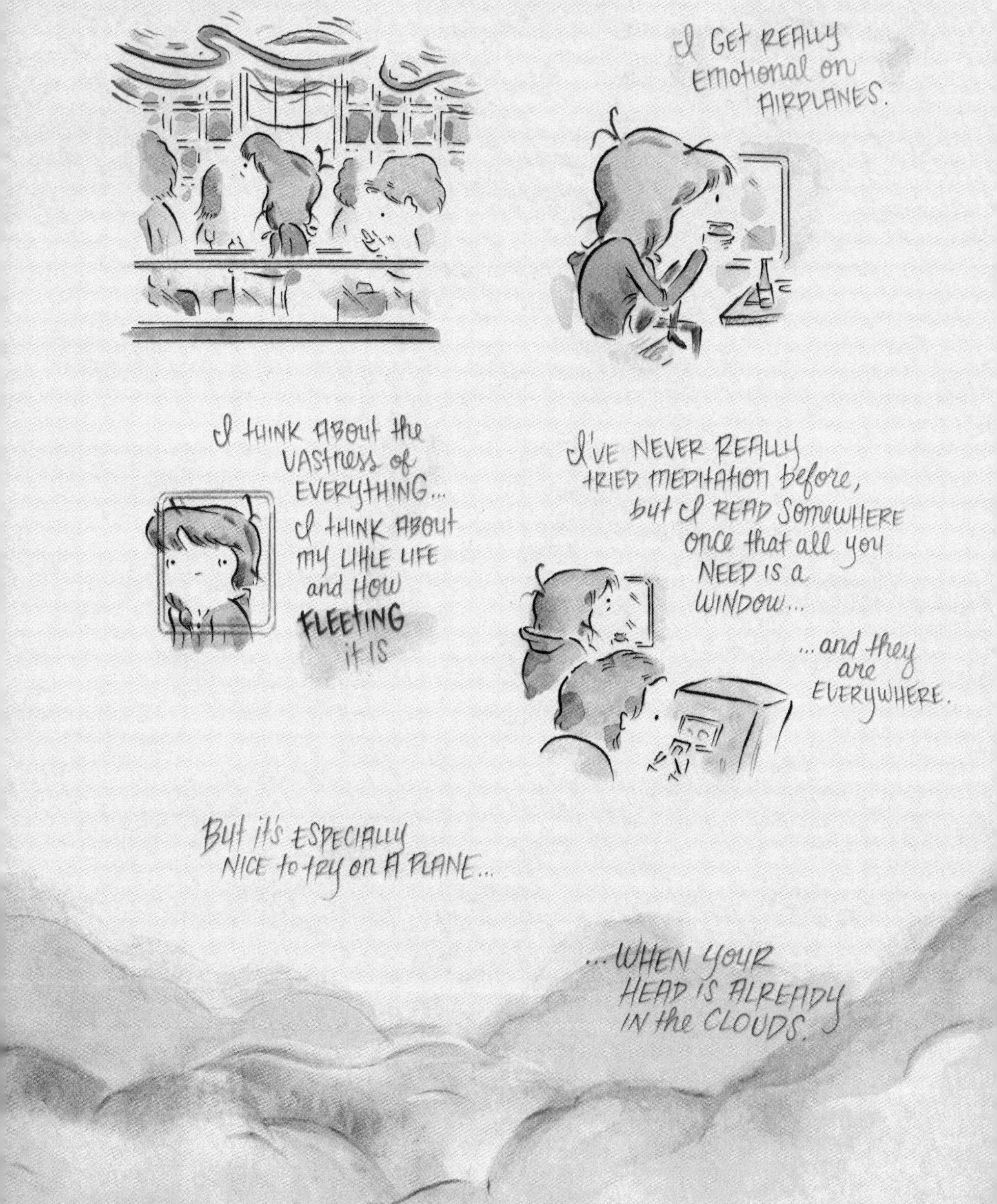
I GET REALLY EMOTIONAL ON AIRPLANES.
I THINK ABOUT THE VASTNESS OF EVERYTHING...
I THINK ABOUT MY LITTLE LIFE AND HOW FLEETING IT IS
I'VE NEVER REALLY TRIED MEDITATION BEFORE, BUT I READ SOMEWHERE ONCE THAT ALL YOU NEED IS A WINDOW...
...AND THEY ARE EVERYWHERE.
BUT IT'S ESPECIALLY NICE TO TRY ON A PLANE...
...WHEN YOUR HEAD IS ALREADY IN THE CLOUDS.

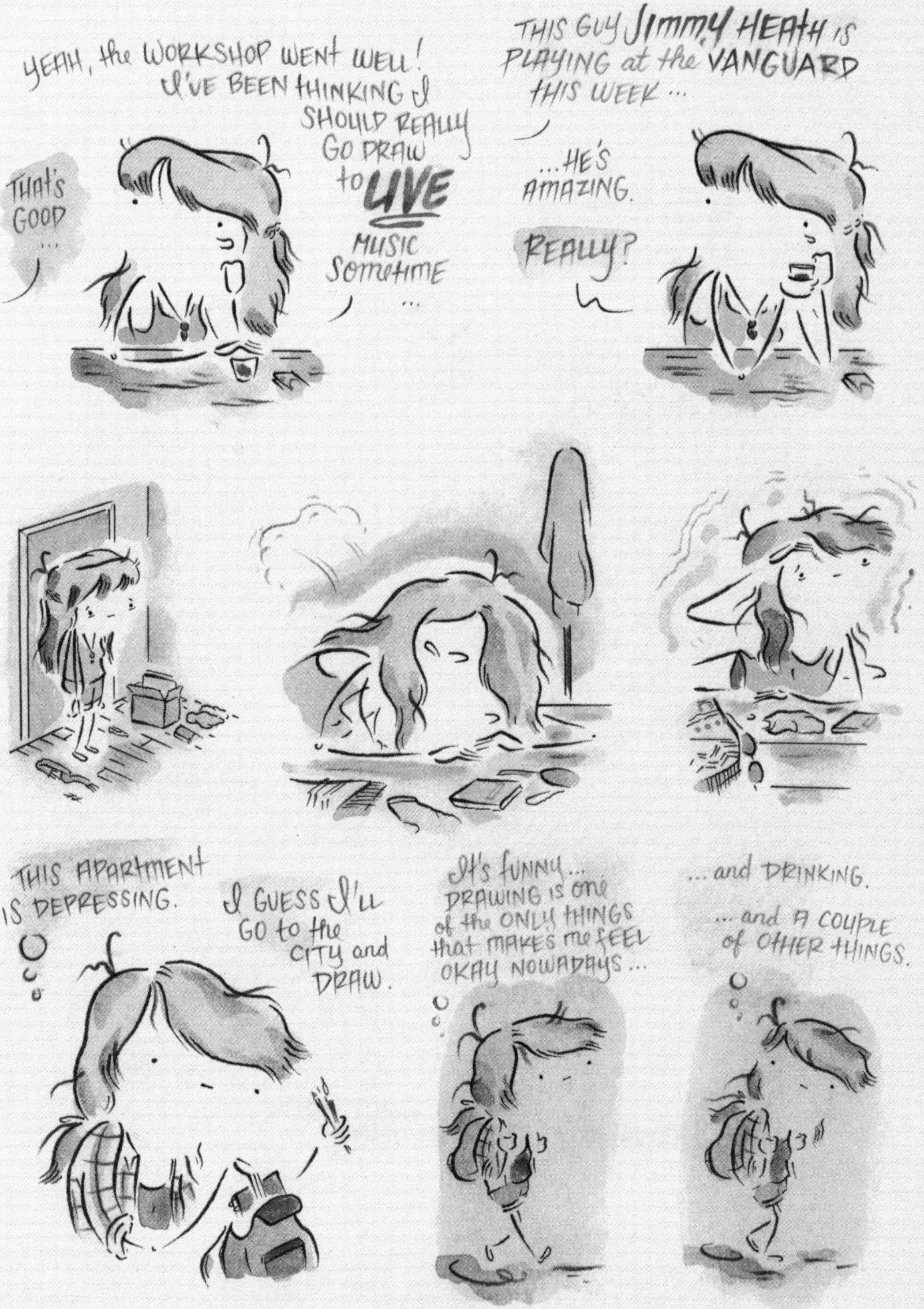
YEAH, the WORKSHOP WENT WELL! I'VE BEEN THINKING I SHOULD REALLY GO DRAW to LIVE MUSIC sometime ...
THAT'S GOOD ...
THIS GUY Jimmy HEATH is PLAYING at the VANGUARD THIS WEEK ...
... HE'S AMAZING.
REALLY?
THIS APARTMENT IS DEPRESSING.
I GUESS I'LL GO to the CITY and DRAW.
It's funny... DRAWING is one of the ONLY THINGS that MAKES me FEEL OKAY NOWADAYS ...
... and DRINKING.
... and A COUPLE of OTHER THINGS.

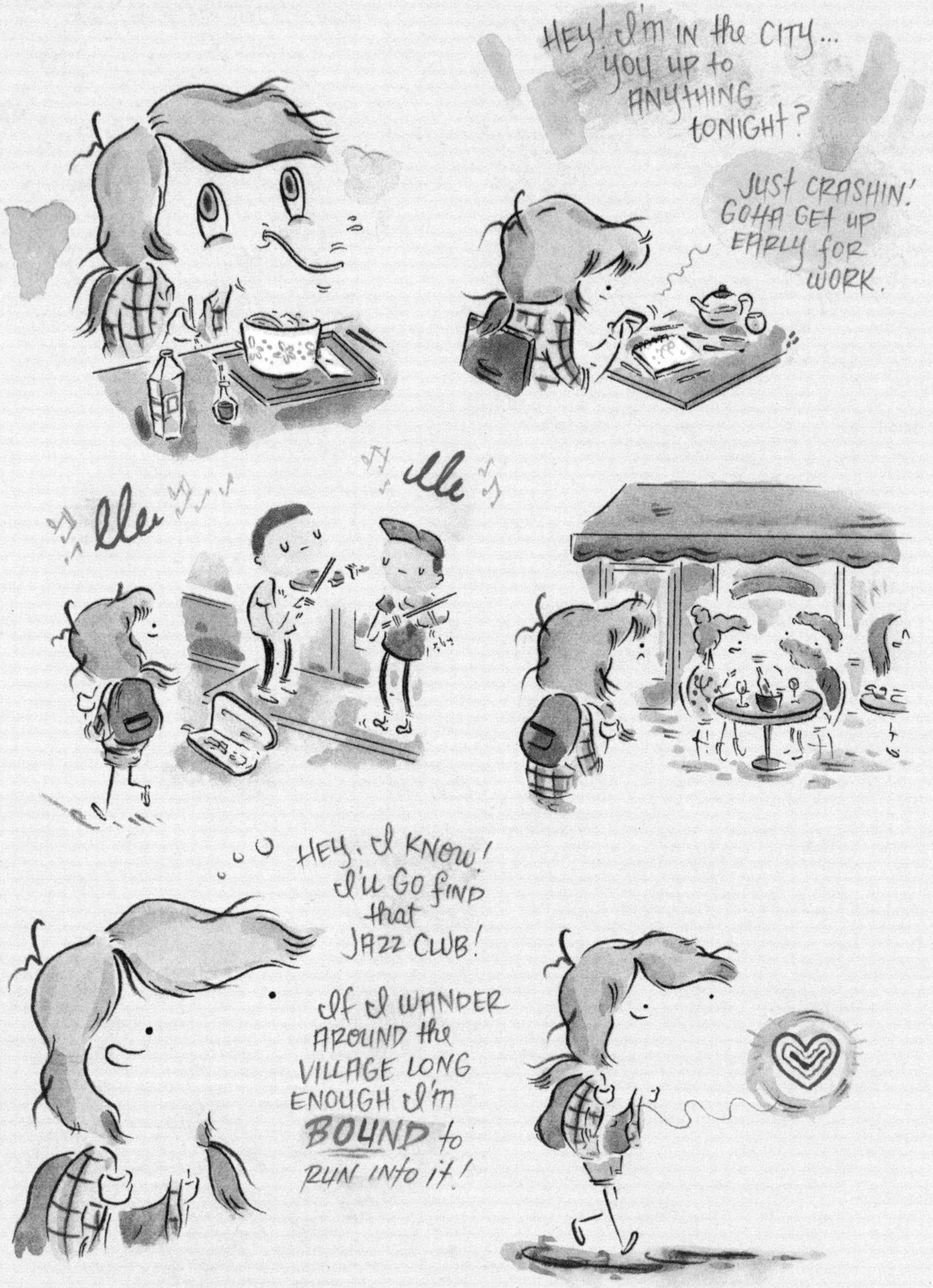
HEY! I'm IN the CITY... YOU UP to ANYTHING TONIGHT?
JUST CRASHIN'! GOTTA GET UP EARLY FOR WORK.
HEY, I KNOW! I'll GO find that JAZZ CLUB!
If I WANDER AROUND the VILLAGE LONG ENOUGH I'm BOUND to RUN INTO it!

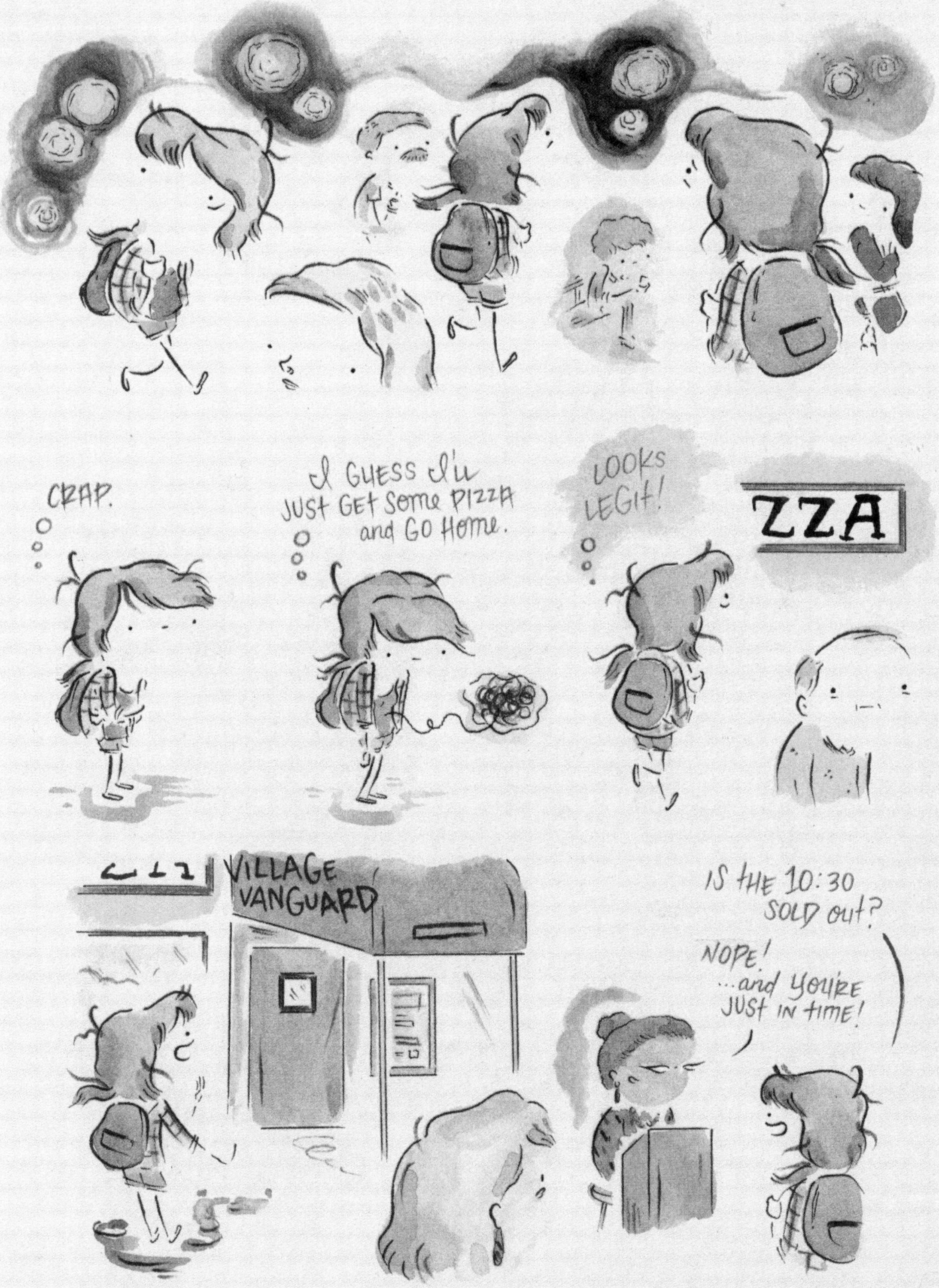
CRAP.
I GUESS I'LL JUST GET SOME PIZZA and GO HOME.
LOOKS LEGIT!
ZZA
VILLAGE VANGUARD
IS THE 10:30 SOLD OUT?
NOPE! ...and YOU'RE JUST IN TIME!

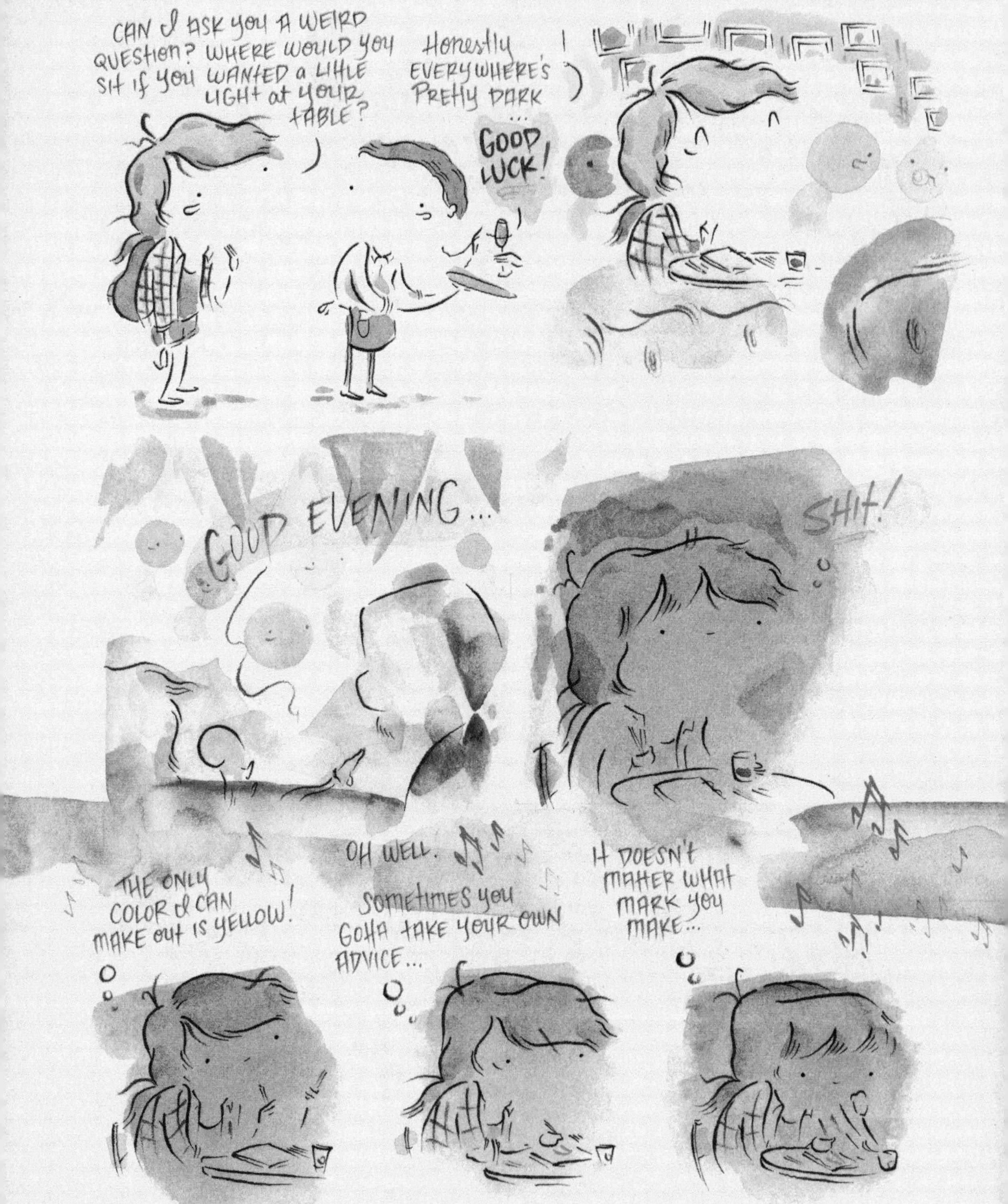

CAN I ASK YOU A WEIRD QUESTION? WHERE WOULD YOU SIT IF YOU WANTED A LITTLE LIGHT AT YOUR TABLE?
Honestly EVERYWHERE'S PRETTY DARK ...
GOOD LUCK!
GOOD EVENING...
SHIT!
THE ONLY COLOR I CAN MAKE OUT IS YELLOW!
OH WELL.
SOMETIMES YOU GOTTA TAKE YOUR OWN ADVICE...
IT DOESN'T MATTER WHAT MARK YOU MAKE...

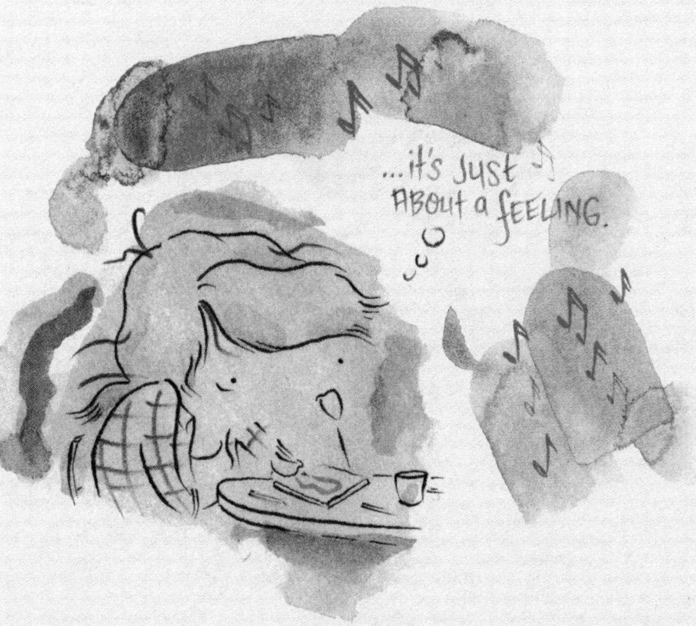
...it's just
about a feeling.

Dognurse (*Excerpt*)

MARGOT FERRICK

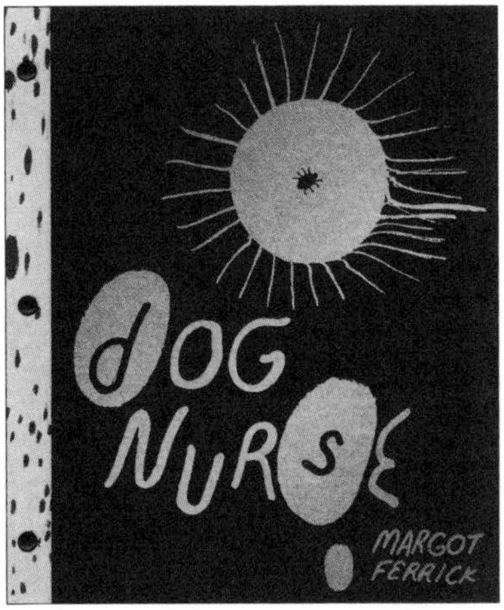
DOG
NURSE
MARGOT
FERRICK

originally published in

Dognurse

PERFECTLY ACCEPTABLE PRESS

8 x 9.25 inches • 52 pages

Biography

Margot Ferrick was born in 1988 on Long Island and now lives in Chicago.
instagram.com/eggyswans

Statement

One of the biggest inspirations for this comic was Catherine Breillat's movie *Fat Girl*. Maybe that connection only makes sense to me and maybe it's a loose connection. I wanted to create a character who refuses to be victimized (even when she clearly is a victim) and survives by defining her reality on her own terms.

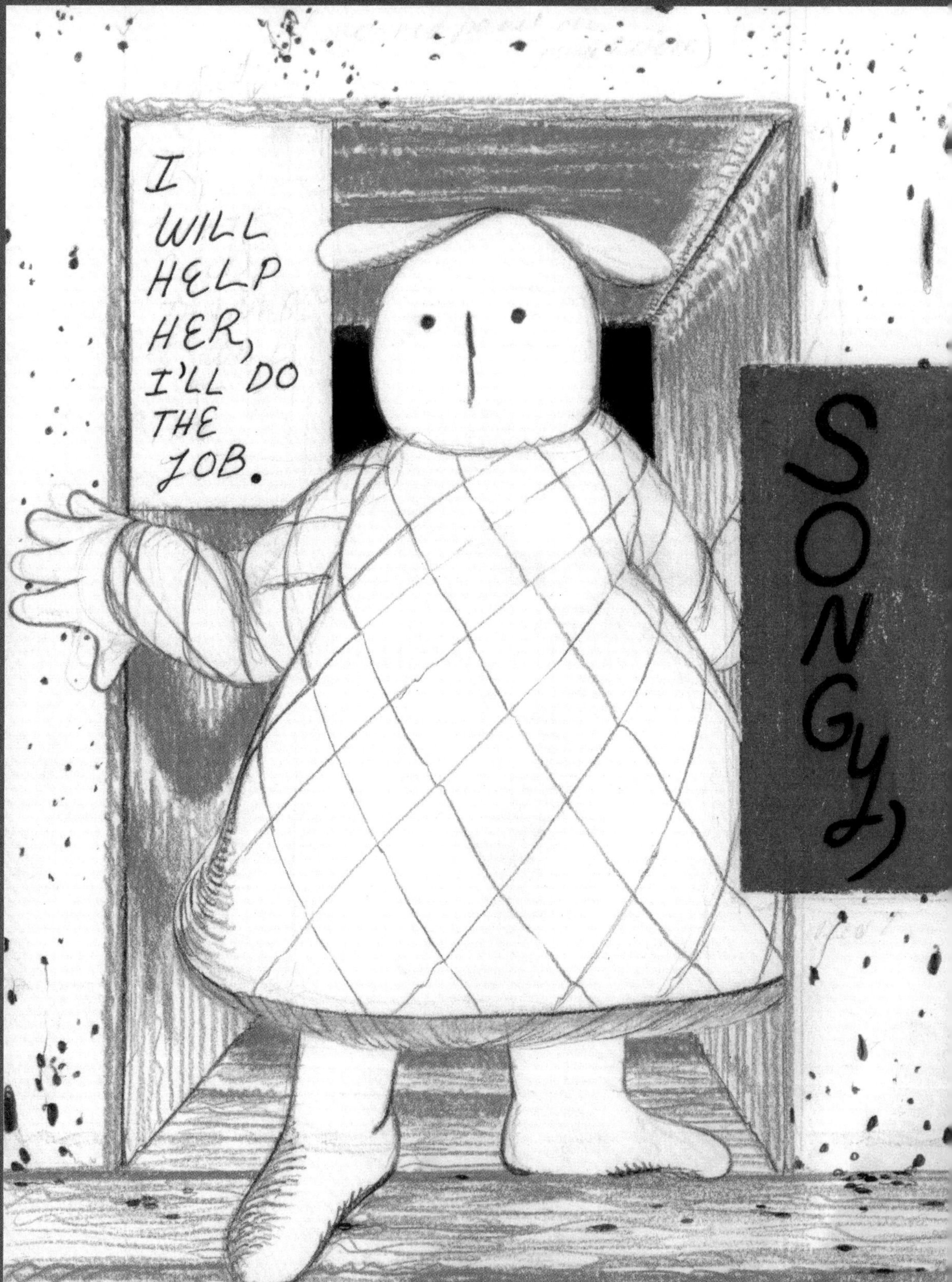
I WILL HELP HER, I'LL DO THE JOB.
SONGY

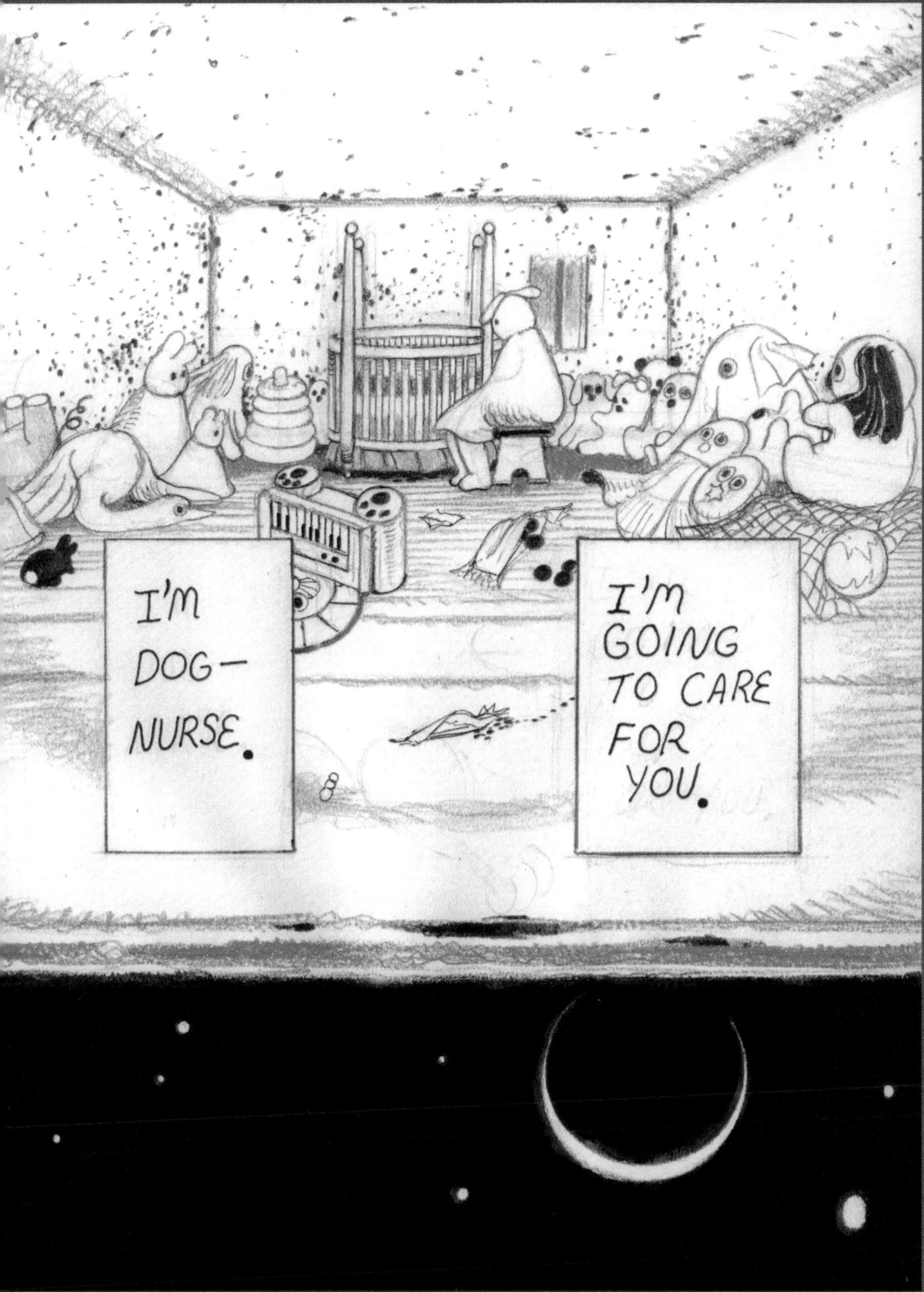
I'M DOG-NURSE.
I'M GOING TO CARE FOR YOU.

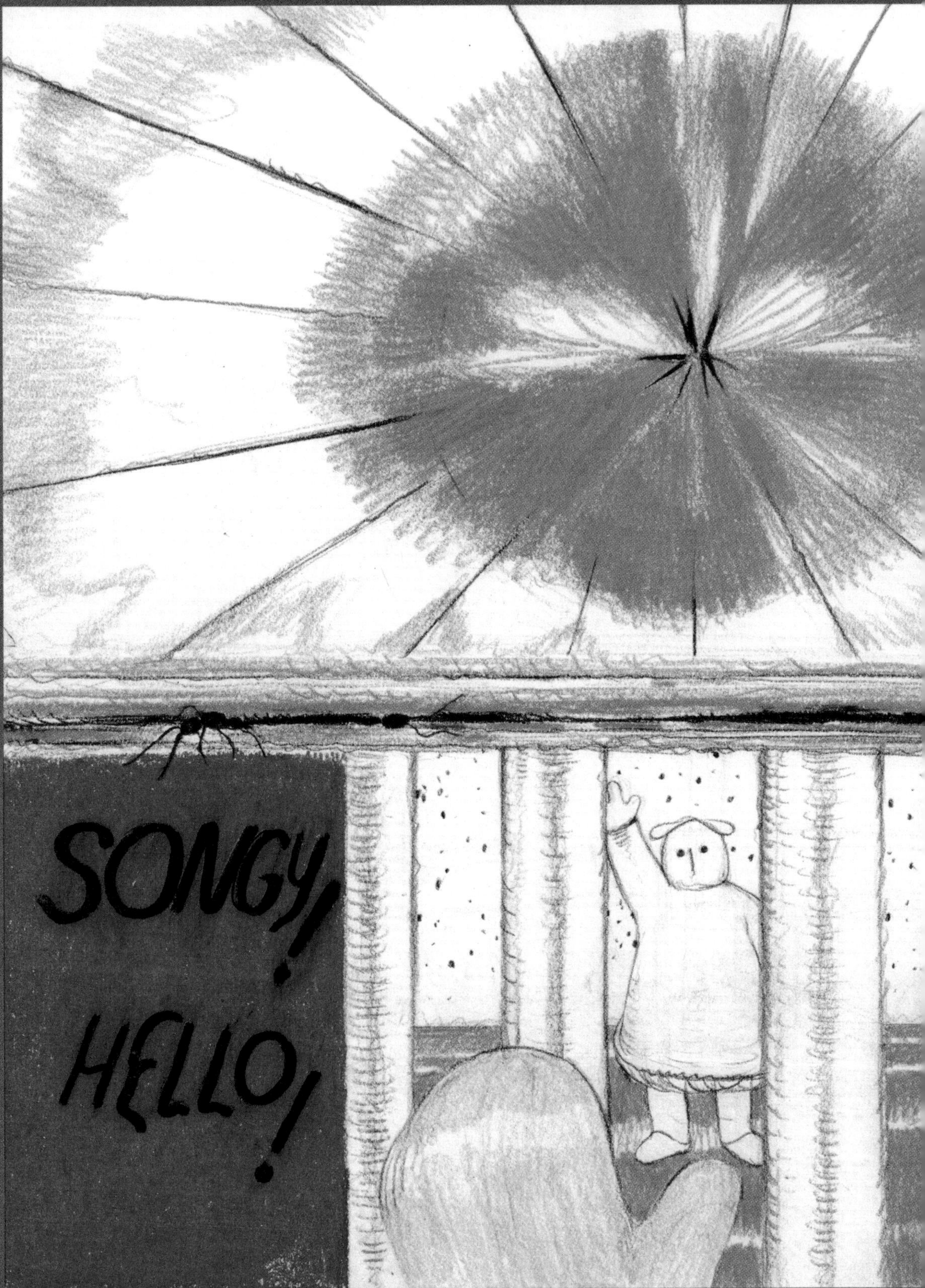
SONGY, HELLO!

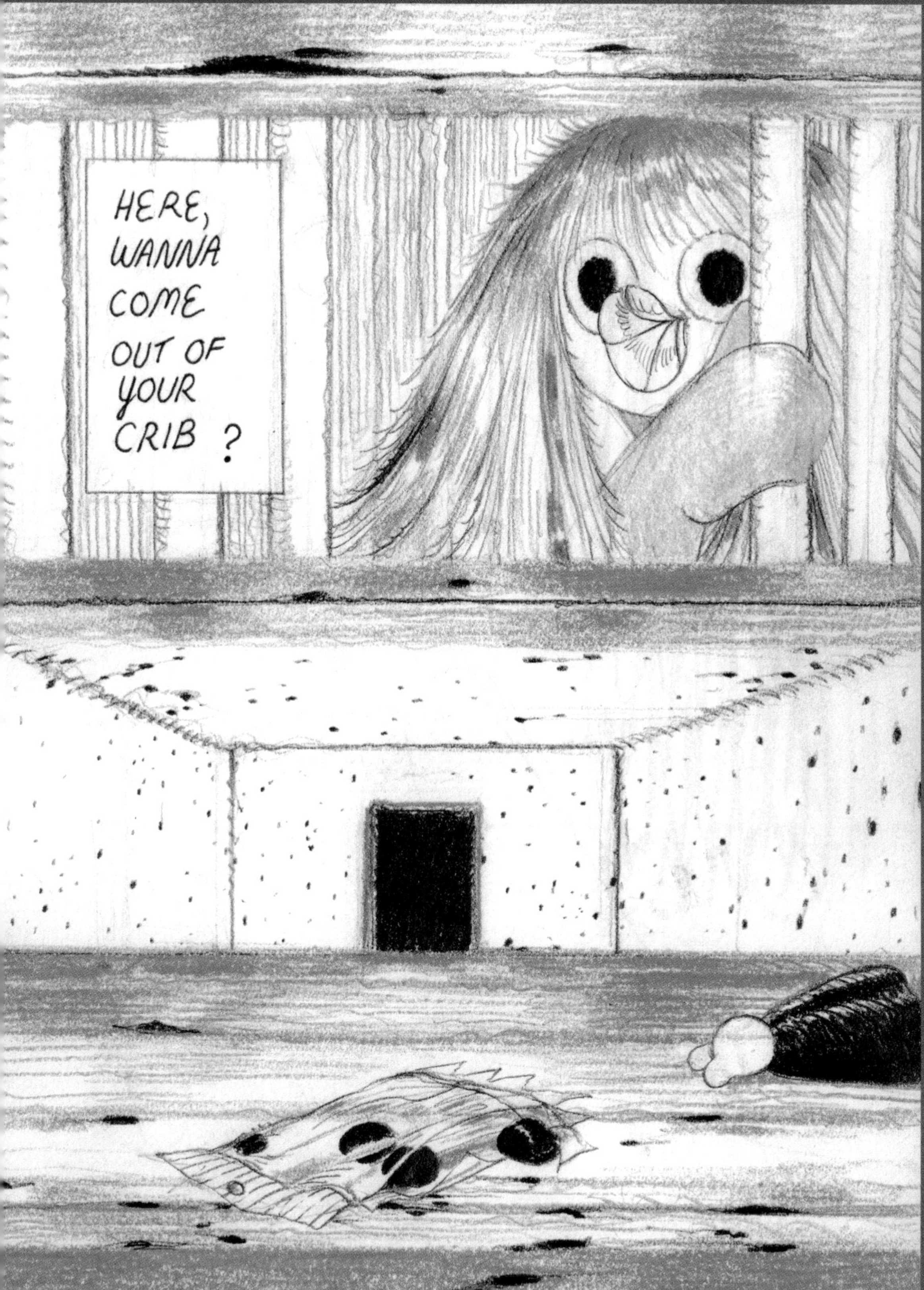
HERE, WANNA COME OUT OF YOUR CRIB ?

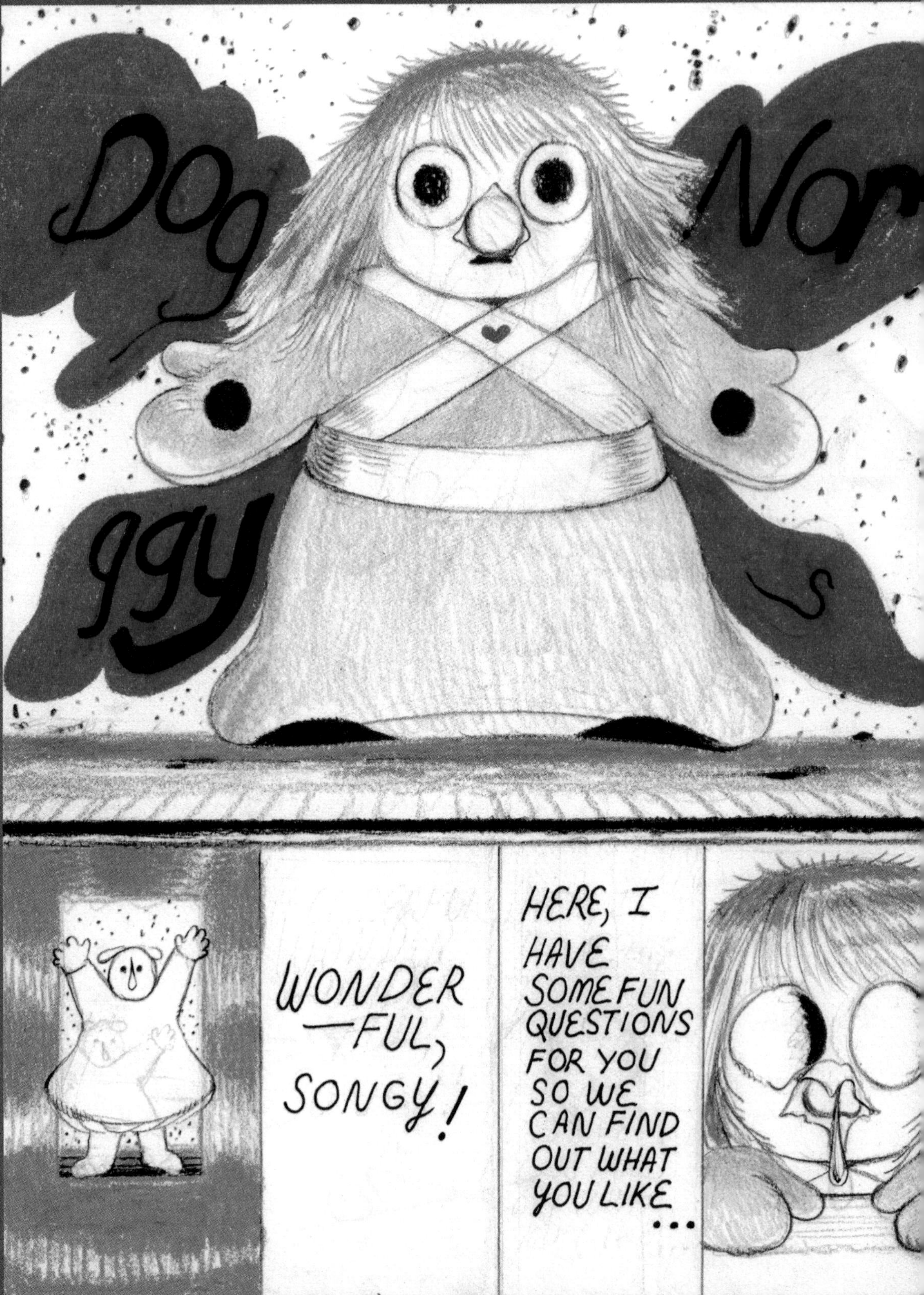
Doggy
WONDER—FUL, SONGY!
HERE, I HAVE SOME FUN QUESTIONS FOR YOU SO WE CAN FIND OUT WHAT YOU LIKE...

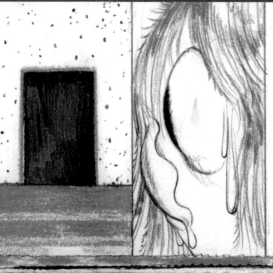

WHAT'S YOUR FAVORITE COLOR

uuh, n-non sure,

IT'S OK, WHAT'S YOUR FAVORITE FOOD ?

not sor e)

WHAT'S YOUR FAVORITE ANIMAL ?

BUTTIE — uh, notton sure,

IT'S OK, WHAT DO YOU WANT TO BE WHEN YOU GROW UP ?

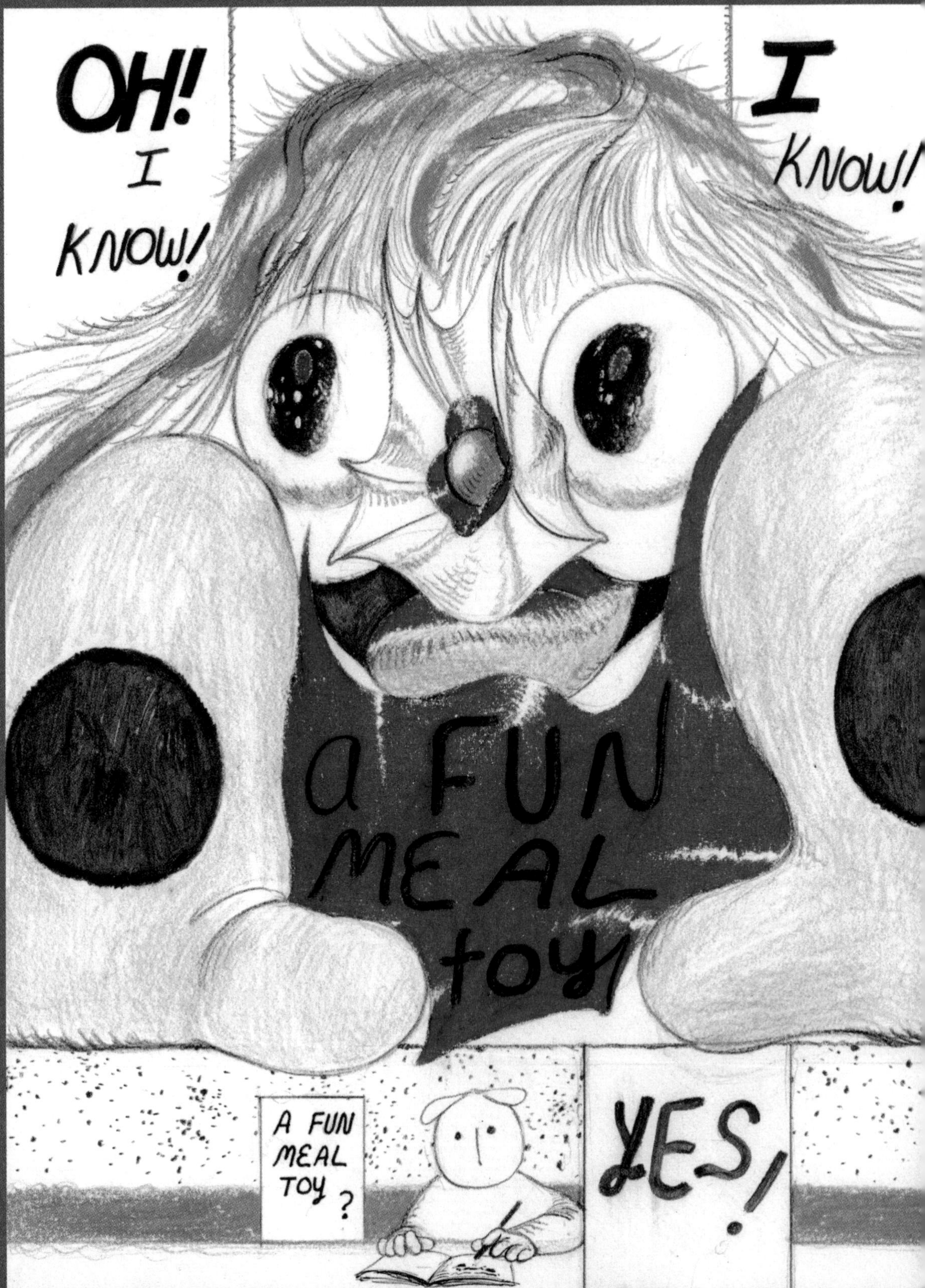
OH! I KNOW!
I KNOW!
a FUN MEAL toy
A FUN MEAL TOY?
YES!

I'D sit
& wait
at the
bottom
of the
box,

& they'd
find me
after
they
finish
their
food,

and then
I'D smile
& hold
out my
arms,

and then
they'd
pick me
up &
they'd
feel
happy.

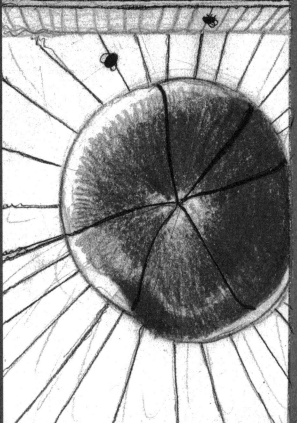

SONGY

?

WHERE
ARE
YOU

?

hee,
R,

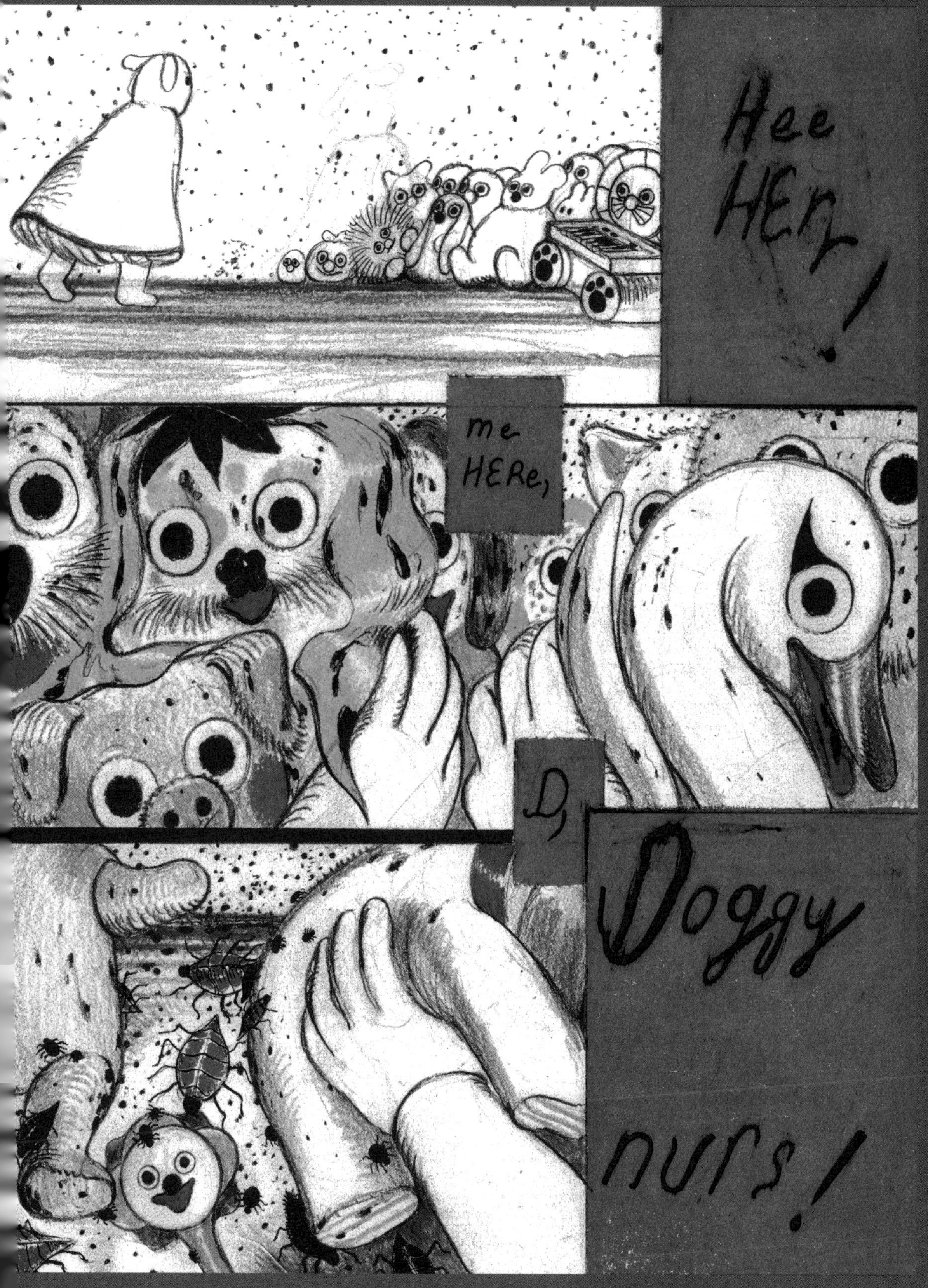

Hee HEr!
me HERe,
D,
Doggy
nurs!

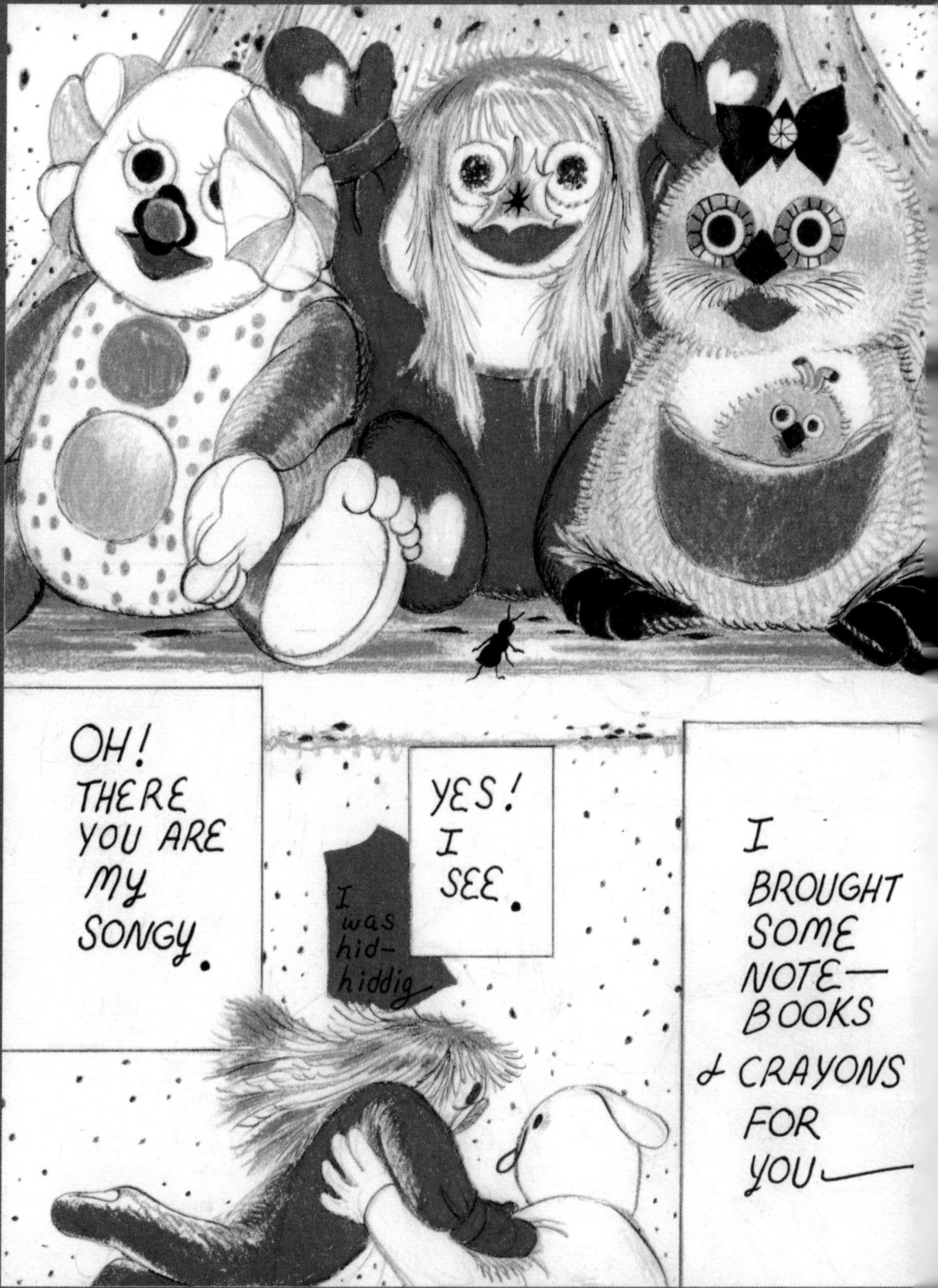
OH! THERE YOU ARE MY SONGY.
I was hid- hiddig
YES! I SEE.
I BROUGHT SOME NOTE-BOOKS & CRAYONS FOR YOU

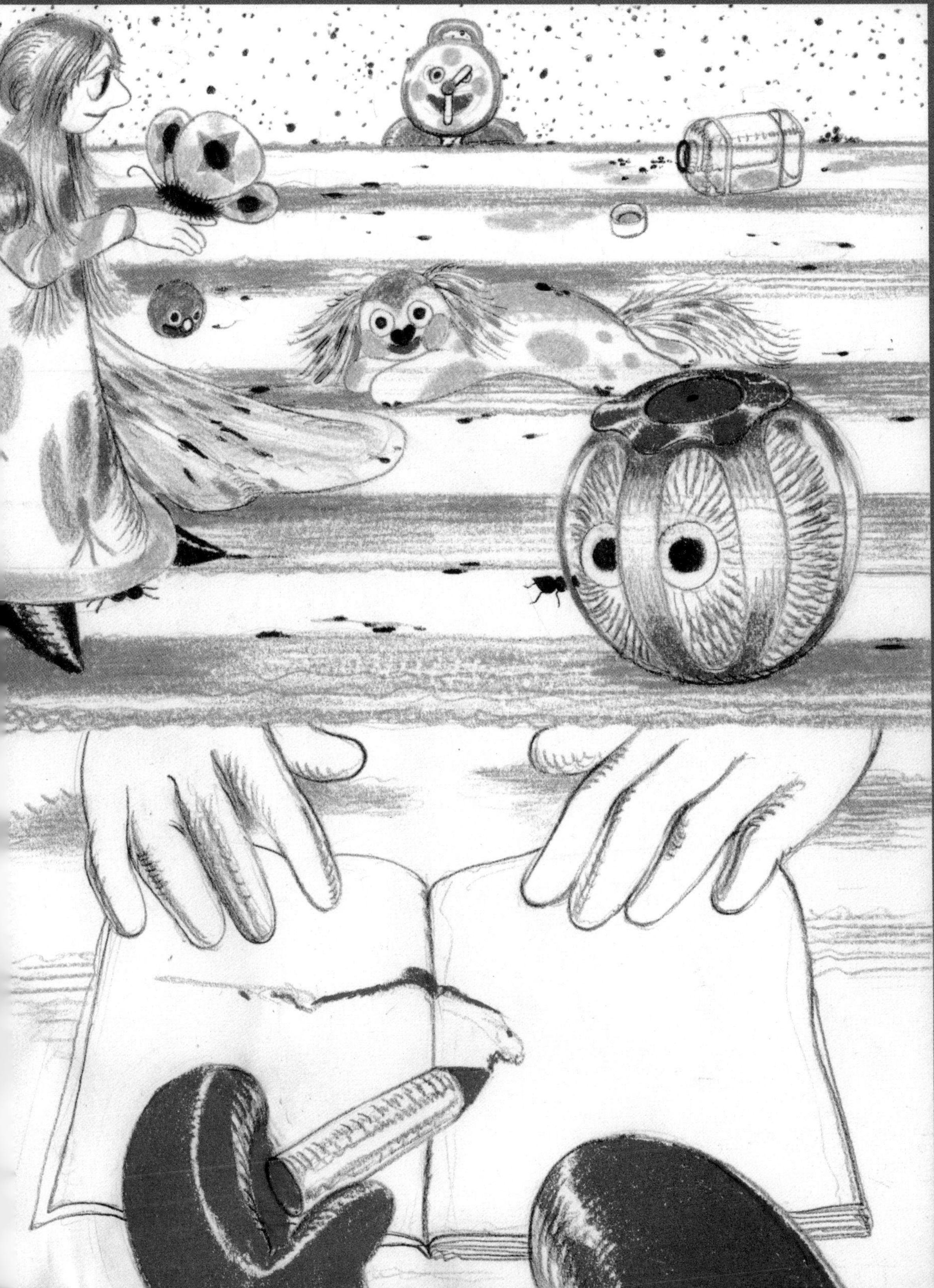

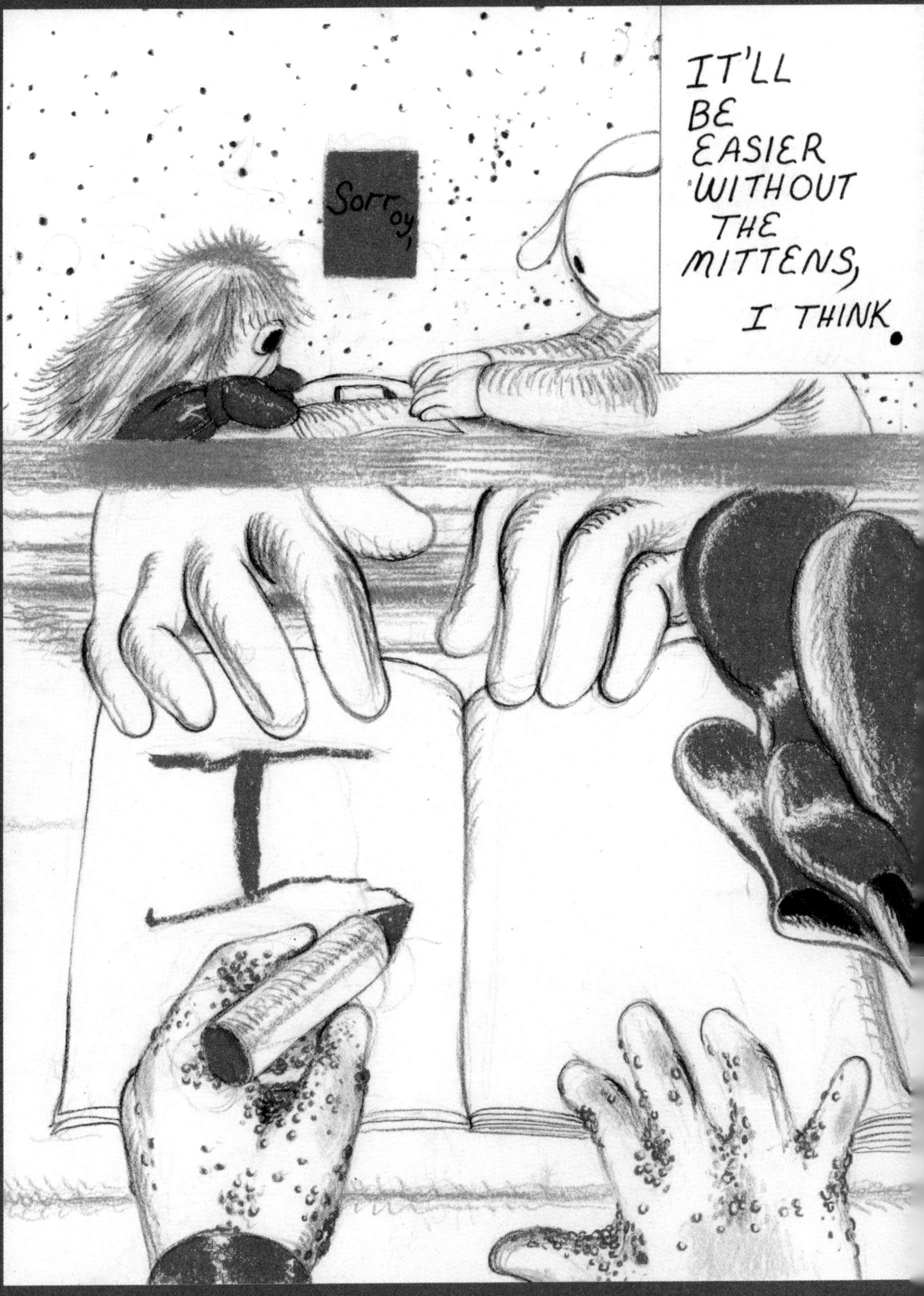
Sorroy,
IT'LL BE EASIER WITHOUT THE MITTENS, I THINK.

WHAT IS THAT?

OH, just buttie, uh, BUTTER-FLY.

I buttie

I Fouy

Fouy

OH! I SEE!

I

I wish

I had A DOOP DOOR

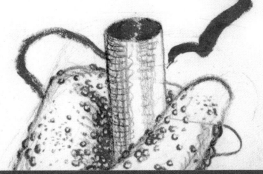

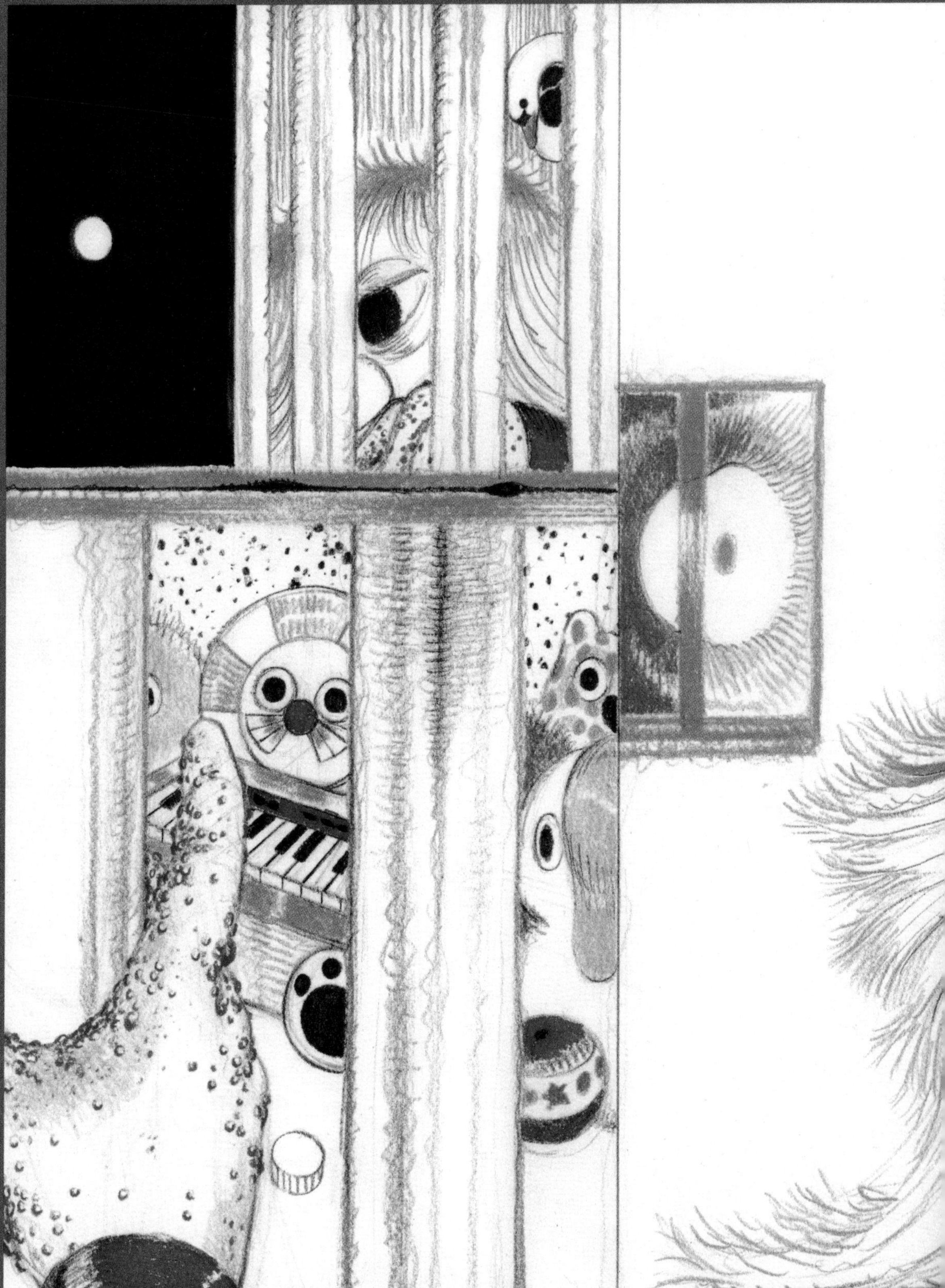

SONGY
I AM SONGY
AND I WAIT FOR
DOG-NURSE
I, SONGY WAIT FOR DOG NURSE.

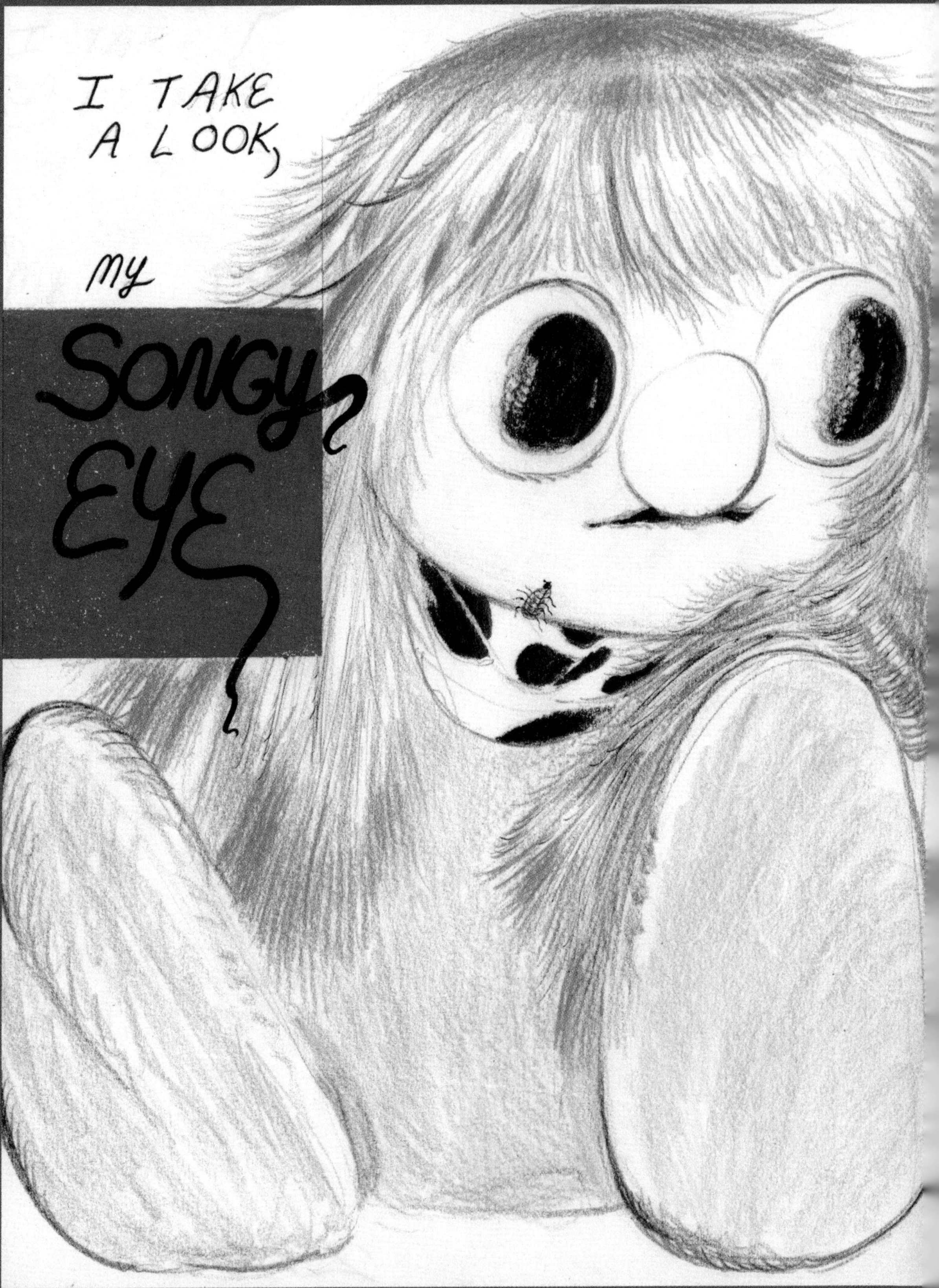
I TAKE A LOOK,
my
SONGY EYE

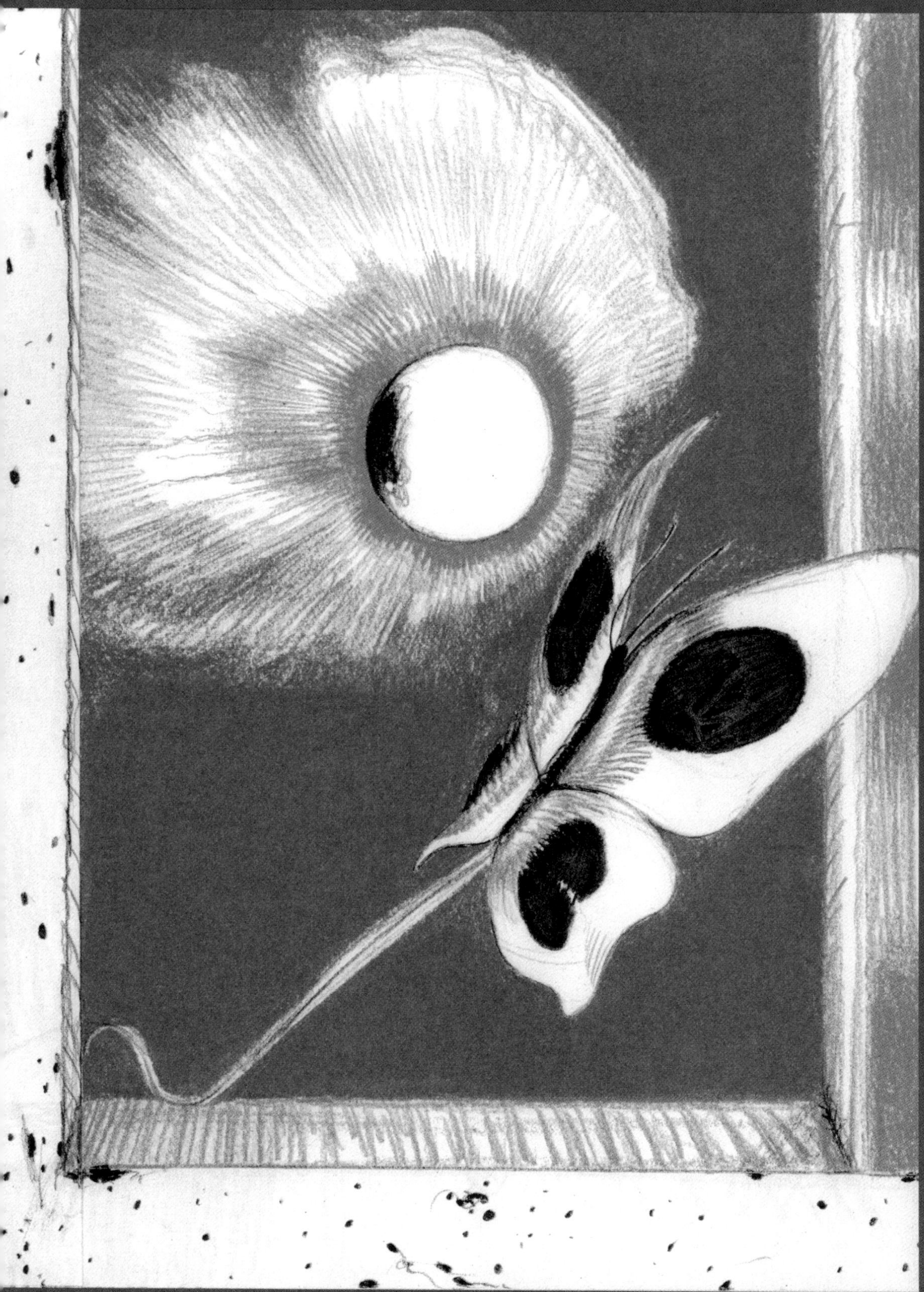

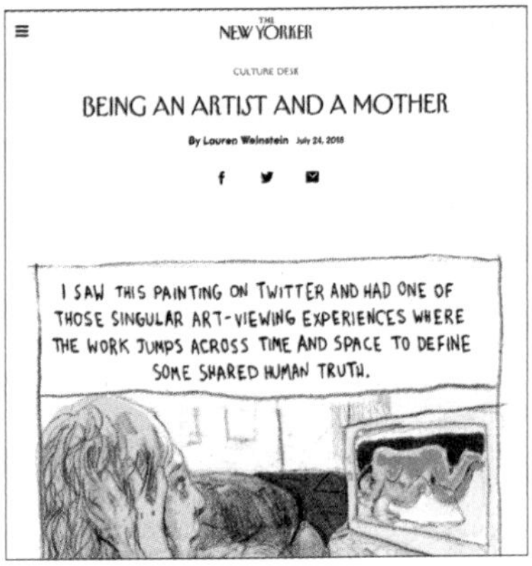
THE NEW YORKER
CULTURE DESK
BEING AN ARTIST AND A MOTHER
By Lauren Weinstein July 24, 2018
I SAW THIS PAINTING ON TWITTER AND HAD ONE OF THOSE SINGULAR ART-VIEWING EXPERIENCES WHERE THE WORK JUMPS ACROSS TIME AND SPACE TO DEFINE SOME SHARED HUMAN TRUTH.

Being an Artist and a Mother

LAUREN WEINSTEIN

originally published on

The New Yorker

NEWYORKER.COM

DIGITAL

Biography

Lauren Weinstein's highly acclaimed comic strip, *Normel Person,* ran weekly in the *Village Voice* and now runs on Popula.com. Her graphic novella *Mother's Walk* was published by Youth In Decline for their Frontier series. "Being an Artist and a Mother" was recently on *The New Yorker*. She has published three books: *Girl Stories, Inside Vineyland,* and *Goddess of War*. Currently she is working on a teenage memoir, tentatively entitled *Calamity,* to be published by Henry Holt, and is also compiling a collection of comics about motherhood.
laurenweinstein.com

Statement

"Being an Artist and a Mother" came about because I was both inspired and frustrated looking at a painting of a mother nursing by Paula Modersohn-Becker. Being a nursing mom myself, I'm constantly fighting a battle not to disappear creatively, like so many mother artists before me. I keep thinking of how in the Masters of American Comics show of 2006 there were no women cartoonists, because they didn't cleanly fit into the trajectory mapped out by The Canon (Winsor McCay, George Herriman, Lyonel Feininger). What if there was another historical line? Who came before Lynda Barry, Aline Kominsky-Crumb, Julie Doucet—was it Alice Neel, Charlotte Salomon? Things seem to be changing now—more mothers are doing comics, and more voices are being taken seriously.

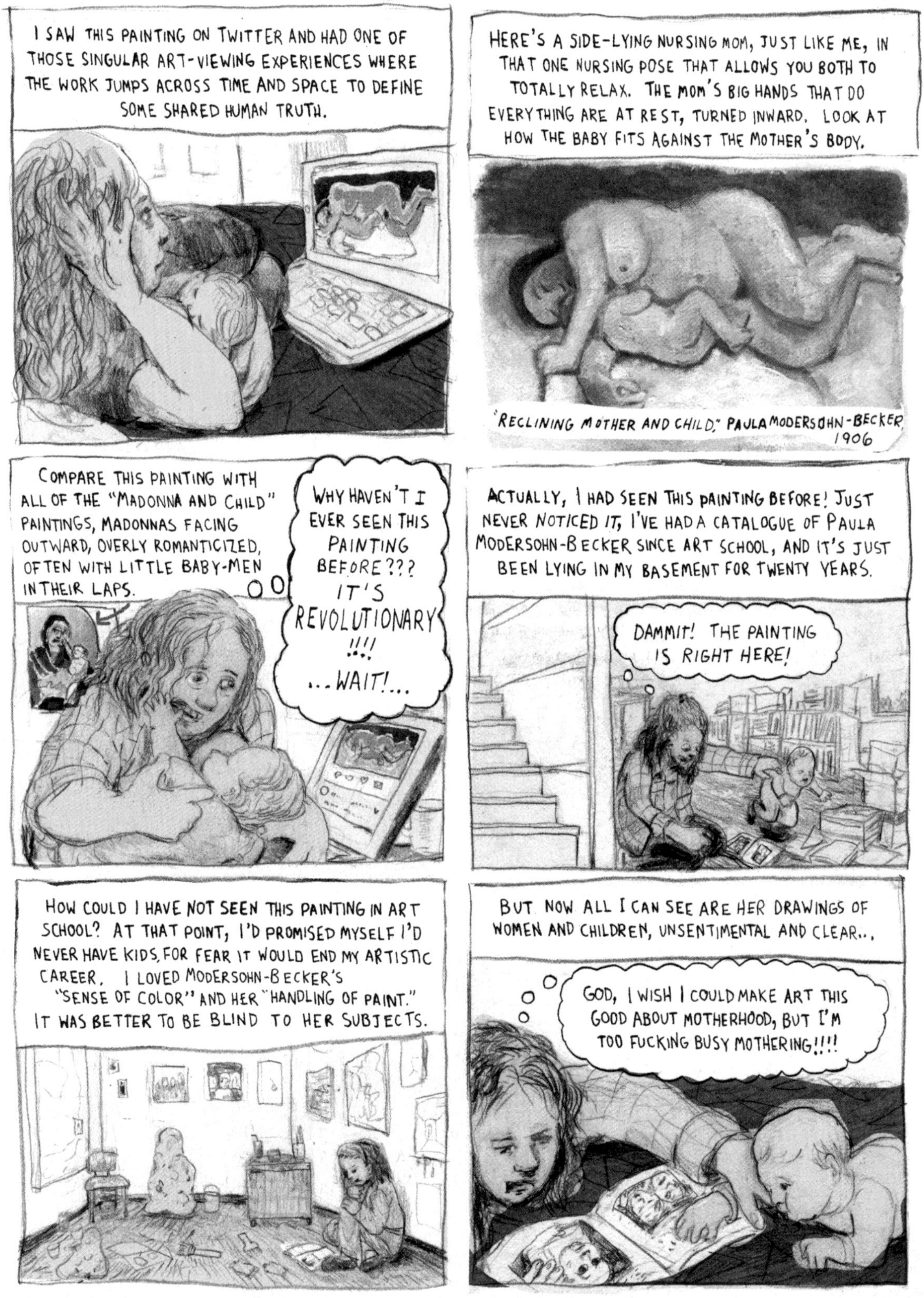
I SAW THIS PAINTING ON TWITTER AND HAD ONE OF THOSE SINGULAR ART-VIEWING EXPERIENCES WHERE THE WORK JUMPS ACROSS TIME AND SPACE TO DEFINE SOME SHARED HUMAN TRUTH.
HERE'S A SIDE-LYING NURSING MOM, JUST LIKE ME, IN THAT ONE NURSING POSE THAT ALLOWS YOU BOTH TO TOTALLY RELAX. THE MOM'S BIG HANDS THAT DO EVERYTHING ARE AT REST, TURNED INWARD. LOOK AT HOW THE BABY FITS AGAINST THE MOTHER'S BODY.
"RECLINING MOTHER AND CHILD," PAULA MODERSOHN-BECKER 1906
COMPARE THIS PAINTING WITH ALL OF THE "MADONNA AND CHILD" PAINTINGS, MADONNAS FACING OUTWARD, OVERLY ROMANTICIZED, OFTEN WITH LITTLE BABY-MEN IN THEIR LAPS.
WHY HAVEN'T I EVER SEEN THIS PAINTING BEFORE??? IT'S REVOLUTIONARY !!!! ...WAIT!...
ACTUALLY, I HAD SEEN THIS PAINTING BEFORE! JUST NEVER NOTICED IT, I'VE HAD A CATALOGUE OF PAULA MODERSOHN-BECKER SINCE ART SCHOOL, AND IT'S JUST BEEN LYING IN MY BASEMENT FOR TWENTY YEARS.
DAMMIT! THE PAINTING IS RIGHT HERE!
HOW COULD I HAVE NOT SEEN THIS PAINTING IN ART SCHOOL? AT THAT POINT, I'D PROMISED MYSELF I'D NEVER HAVE KIDS, FOR FEAR IT WOULD END MY ARTISTIC CAREER. I LOVED MODERSOHN-BECKER'S "SENSE OF COLOR" AND HER "HANDLING OF PAINT." IT WAS BETTER TO BE BLIND TO HER SUBJECTS.
BUT NOW ALL I CAN SEE ARE HER DRAWINGS OF WOMEN AND CHILDREN, UNSENTIMENTAL AND CLEAR...
GOD, I WISH I COULD MAKE ART THIS GOOD ABOUT MOTHERHOOD, BUT I'M TOO FUCKING BUSY MOTHERING!!!!

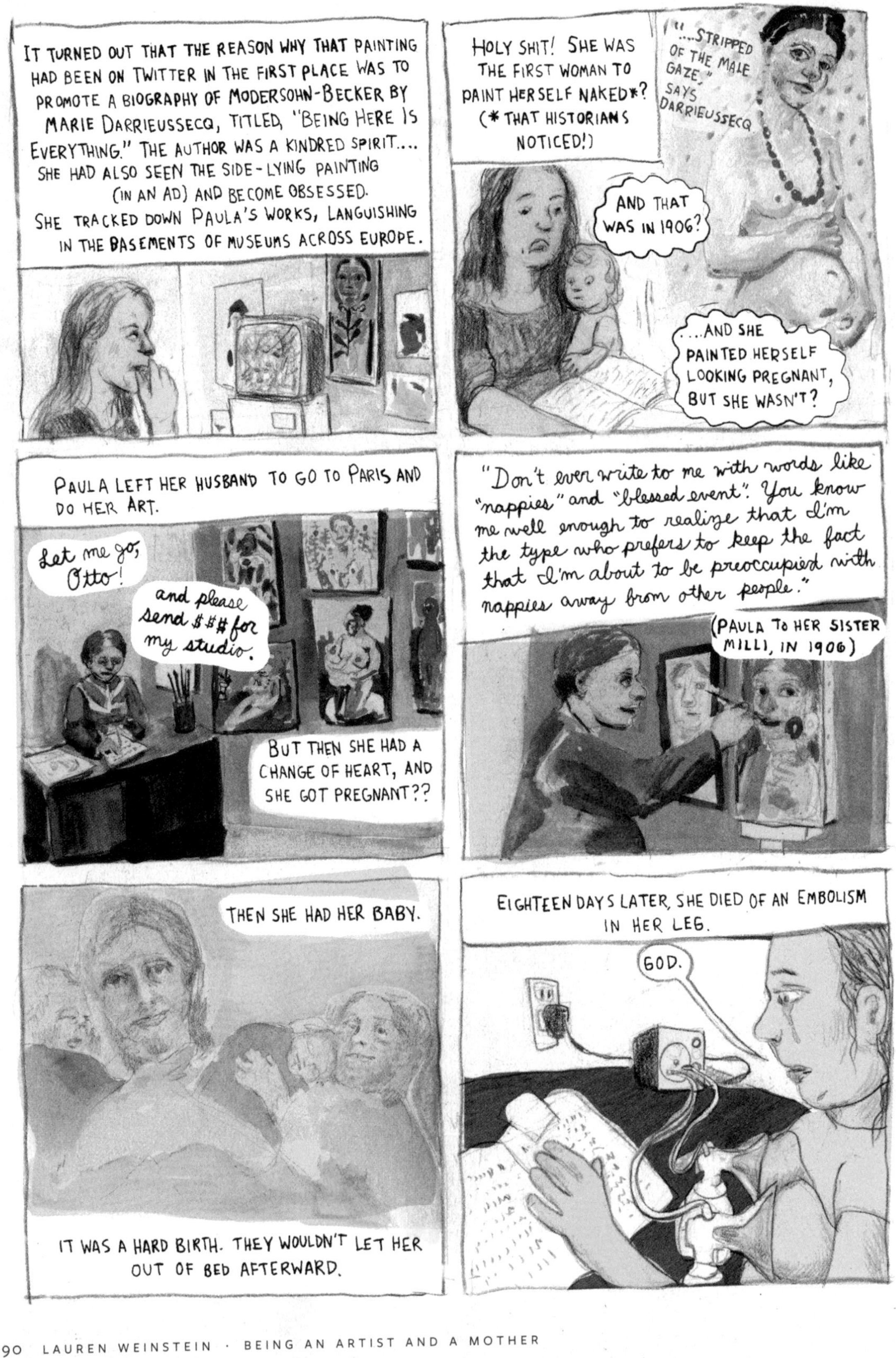
IT TURNED OUT THAT THE REASON WHY THAT PAINTING HAD BEEN ON TWITTER IN THE FIRST PLACE WAS TO PROMOTE A BIOGRAPHY OF MODERSOHN-BECKER BY MARIE DARRIEUSSECQ, TITLED, "BEING HERE IS EVERYTHING." THE AUTHOR WAS A KINDRED SPIRIT.... SHE HAD ALSO SEEN THE SIDE-LYING PAINTING (IN AN AD) AND BECOME OBSESSED.
SHE TRACKED DOWN PAULA'S WORKS, LANGUISHING IN THE BASEMENTS OF MUSEUMS ACROSS EUROPE.
HOLY SHIT! SHE WAS THE FIRST WOMAN TO PAINT HERSELF NAKED*? (* THAT HISTORIANS NOTICED!)
"....STRIPPED OF THE MALE GAZE," SAYS DARRIEUSSECQ
AND THAT WAS IN 1906?
....AND SHE PAINTED HERSELF LOOKING PREGNANT, BUT SHE WASN'T?
PAULA LEFT HER HUSBAND TO GO TO PARIS AND DO HER ART.
Let me go, Otto!
and please send $## for my studio.
BUT THEN SHE HAD A CHANGE OF HEART, AND SHE GOT PREGNANT??
"Don't ever write to me with words like "nappies" and "blessed event". You know me well enough to realize that I'm the type who prefers to keep the fact that I'm about to be preoccupied with nappies away from other people."
(PAULA TO HER SISTER MILLI, IN 1906)
THEN SHE HAD HER BABY.
IT WAS A HARD BIRTH. THEY WOULDN'T LET HER OUT OF BED AFTERWARD.
EIGHTEEN DAYS LATER, SHE DIED OF AN EMBOLISM IN HER LEG.
GOD.

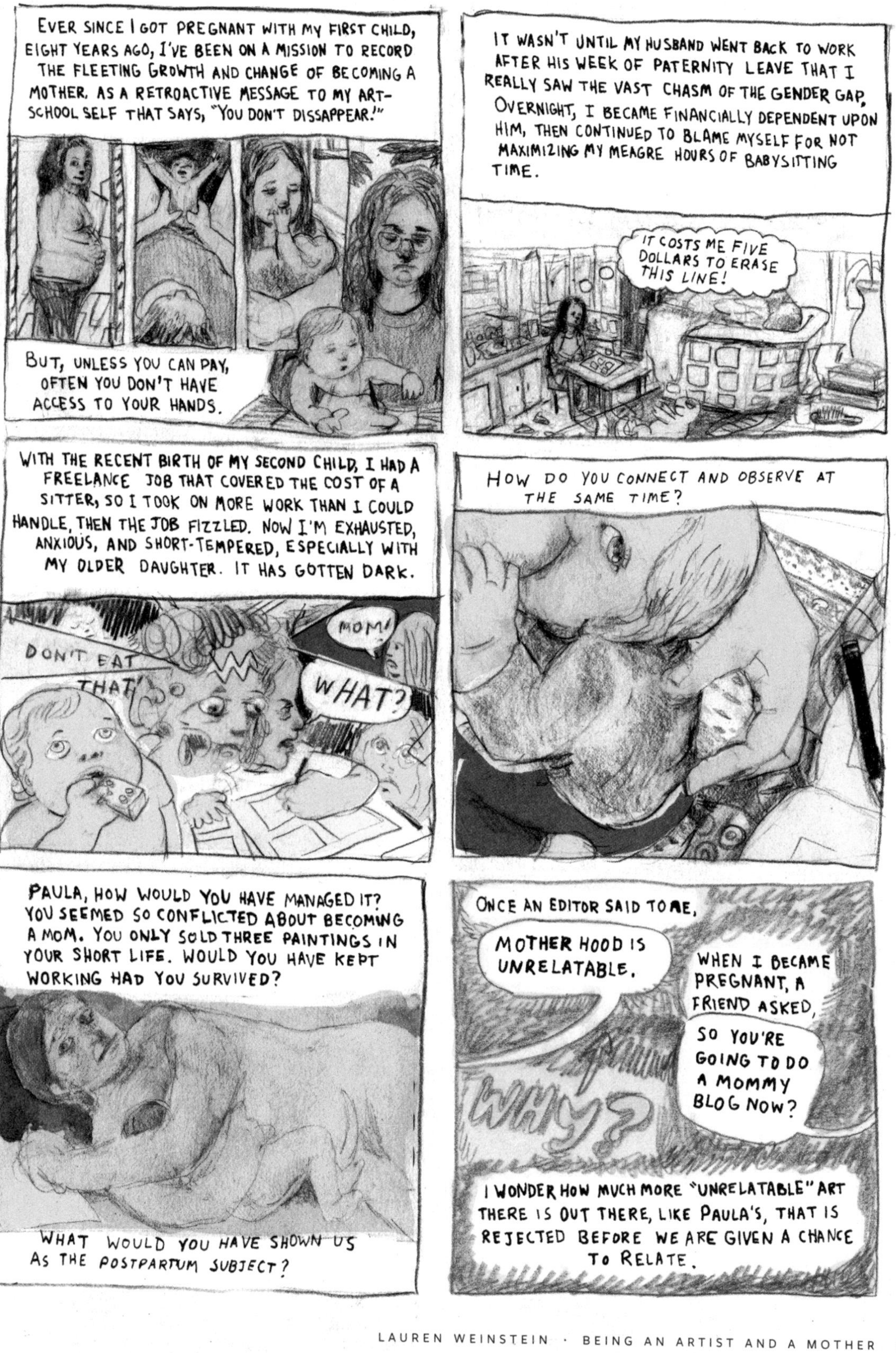
EVER SINCE I GOT PREGNANT WITH MY FIRST CHILD, EIGHT YEARS AGO, I'VE BEEN ON A MISSION TO RECORD THE FLEETING GROWTH AND CHANGE OF BECOMING A MOTHER. AS A RETROACTIVE MESSAGE TO MY ART-SCHOOL SELF THAT SAYS, "YOU DON'T DISSAPPEAR!"
BUT, UNLESS YOU CAN PAY, OFTEN YOU DON'T HAVE ACCESS TO YOUR HANDS.
IT WASN'T UNTIL MY HUSBAND WENT BACK TO WORK AFTER HIS WEEK OF PATERNITY LEAVE THAT I REALLY SAW THE VAST CHASM OF THE GENDER GAP. OVERNIGHT, I BECAME FINANCIALLY DEPENDENT UPON HIM, THEN CONTINUED TO BLAME MYSELF FOR NOT MAXIMIZING MY MEAGRE HOURS OF BABYSITTING TIME.
IT COSTS ME FIVE DOLLARS TO ERASE THIS LINE!
WITH THE RECENT BIRTH OF MY SECOND CHILD, I HAD A FREELANCE JOB THAT COVERED THE COST OF A SITTER, SO I TOOK ON MORE WORK THAN I COULD HANDLE, THEN THE JOB FIZZLED. NOW I'M EXHAUSTED, ANXIOUS, AND SHORT-TEMPERED, ESPECIALLY WITH MY OLDER DAUGHTER. IT HAS GOTTEN DARK.
DON'T EAT THAT!
MOM!
WHAT?
HOW DO YOU CONNECT AND OBSERVE AT THE SAME TIME?
PAULA, HOW WOULD YOU HAVE MANAGED IT? YOU SEEMED SO CONFLICTED ABOUT BECOMING A MOM. YOU ONLY SOLD THREE PAINTINGS IN YOUR SHORT LIFE. WOULD YOU HAVE KEPT WORKING HAD YOU SURVIVED?
WHAT WOULD YOU HAVE SHOWN US AS THE POSTPARTUM SUBJECT?
ONCE AN EDITOR SAID TO ME,
MOTHER HOOD IS UNRELATABLE.
WHY?
WHEN I BECAME PREGNANT, A FRIEND ASKED,
SO YOU'RE GOING TO DO A MOMMY BLOG NOW?
I WONDER HOW MUCH MORE "UNRELATABLE" ART THERE IS OUT THERE, LIKE PAULA'S, THAT IS REJECTED BEFORE WE ARE GIVEN A CHANCE TO RELATE.

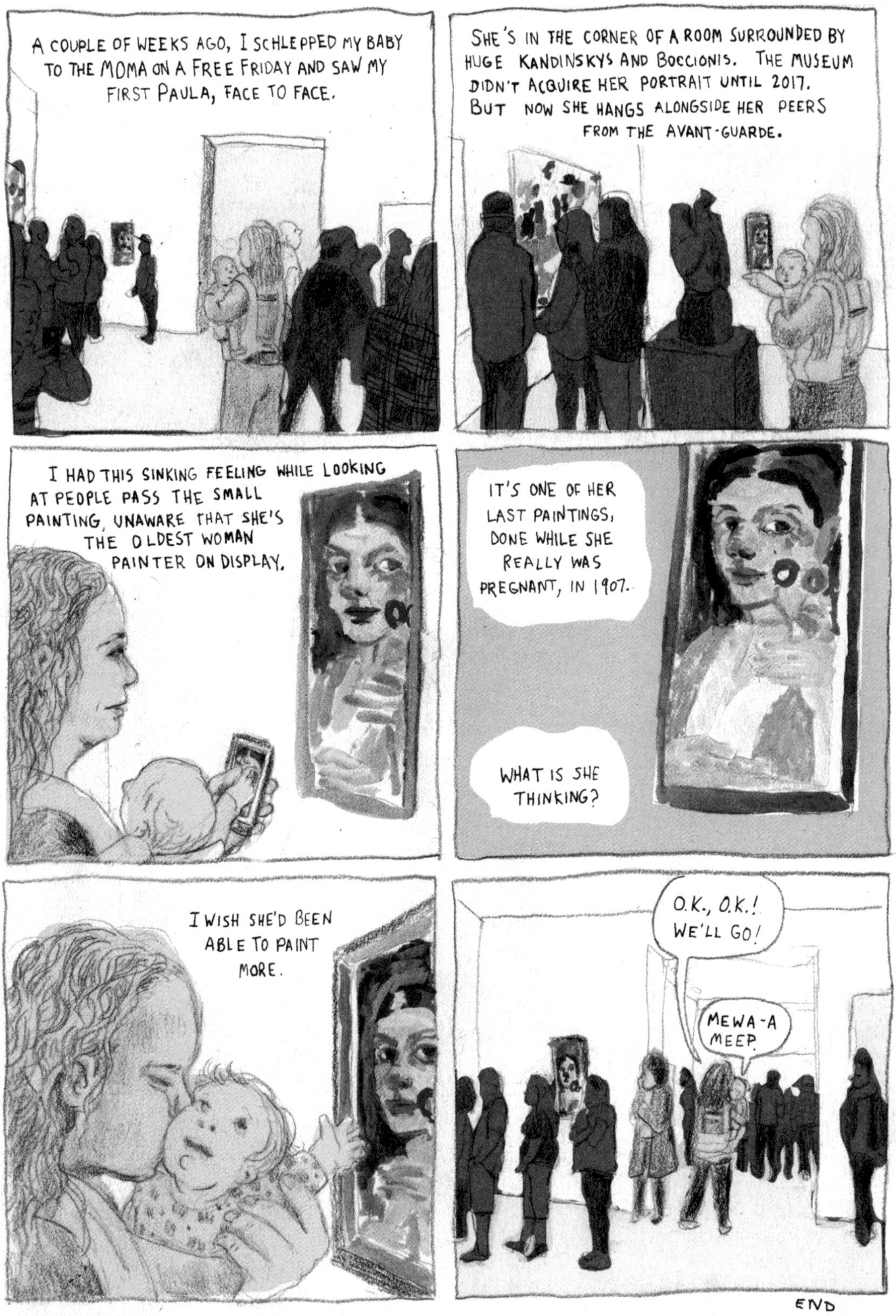
A COUPLE OF WEEKS AGO, I SCHLEPPED MY BABY TO THE MOMA ON A FREE FRIDAY AND SAW MY FIRST PAULA, FACE TO FACE.
SHE'S IN THE CORNER OF A ROOM SURROUNDED BY HUGE KANDINSKYS AND BOCCIONIS. THE MUSEUM DIDN'T ACQUIRE HER PORTRAIT UNTIL 2017. BUT NOW SHE HANGS ALONGSIDE HER PEERS FROM THE AVANT-GUARDE.
I HAD THIS SINKING FEELING WHILE LOOKING AT PEOPLE PASS THE SMALL PAINTING, UNAWARE THAT SHE'S THE OLDEST WOMAN PAINTER ON DISPLAY.
IT'S ONE OF HER LAST PAINTINGS, DONE WHILE SHE REALLY WAS PREGNANT, IN 1907.
WHAT IS SHE THINKING?
I WISH SHE'D BEEN ABLE TO PAINT MORE.
O.K., O.K.! WE'LL GO!
MEWA-A MEEP
END

Martin Luther King Jr. Was More Radical Than You Think

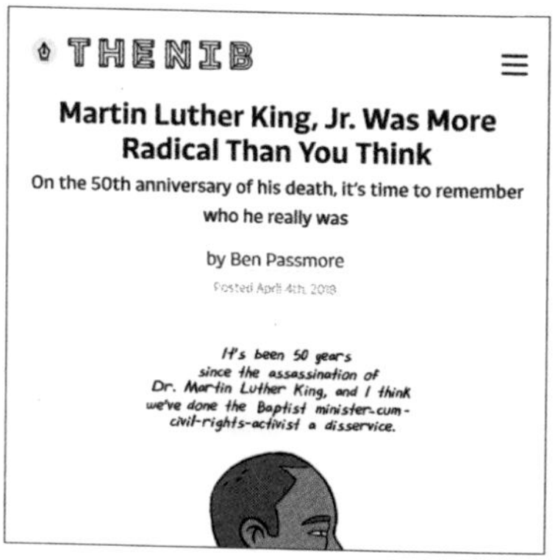
THENIB
Martin Luther King, Jr. Was More Radical Than You Think
On the 50th anniversary of his death, it's time to remember who he really was
by Ben Passmore
Posted April 4th, 2018
It's been 50 years since the assassination of Dr. Martin Luther King, and I think we've done the Baptist minister-cum-civil-rights-activist a disservice.

BEN PASSMORE

originally published on

The Nib

THENIB.COM

DIGITAL

Biography

Ben Passmore is the author of *DAYGLOAYHOLE, Goodbye,* and *Your Black Friend.* He is also a regular contributor to thenib.com. He likes to write disingenuously about anarchism, race, the DIY scene, hang-ups, monsters, and corner stores. He enjoys rollerskating, long walks, and stealing candy bars.
BenPassmoreart.com

Statement

When my editor asked me to write about Martin Luther King Jr., I was resistant. Both King Jr. and the Civil Rights era are well-worn territory and are often trotted out as shining examples of serenity and moral fortitude against racism. They are contrasted against more martial organizations like the Black Liberation Army in an attempt to shame struggles that prioritize tactics that win liberation rather than remain "good citizens." A good citizen doesn't interrupt everyday life. It's a shame because King's nonviolence was not the nonviolence of today—interruption was central. The fact that they harassed and killed him is proof enough for me. So despite being more of a Kuwasi Balagoon, Kwame Ture, and Nat Turner fan, I wanted to put the teeth back in Martin Luther King Jr. because he gave us ours.

MARTIN LUTHER KING JR. IS MORE RADICAL Than You Think!

by Ben Passmore

It's been 50 years since the assassination of Dr. Martin Luther King, and I think we've done the Baptist minister come civil rights activist a disservice.

He has been overly simplified into a prop representing vague "equality."

white boy! you got the no spicy?

White boy!? If Martin were here today he'd cry!

RIP BO

Despite MLK getting a lot of hype including a holiday and tons of streets and buildings named after him, we don't actually learn that much about his philosophy, and it's hard to feel like this is an accident.

Which is not to say I agree with MLK's avid advocating for the use of nonviolence against white-supremacy. In any debate between violence vs nonviolence I always quote Kwame Ture.

In order for nonviolence to work, your opponent must have a conscience. The United States has none.

Kwame Ture, member of SNCC, A-APAR, and developed the Black Power Movement.

PREACH!

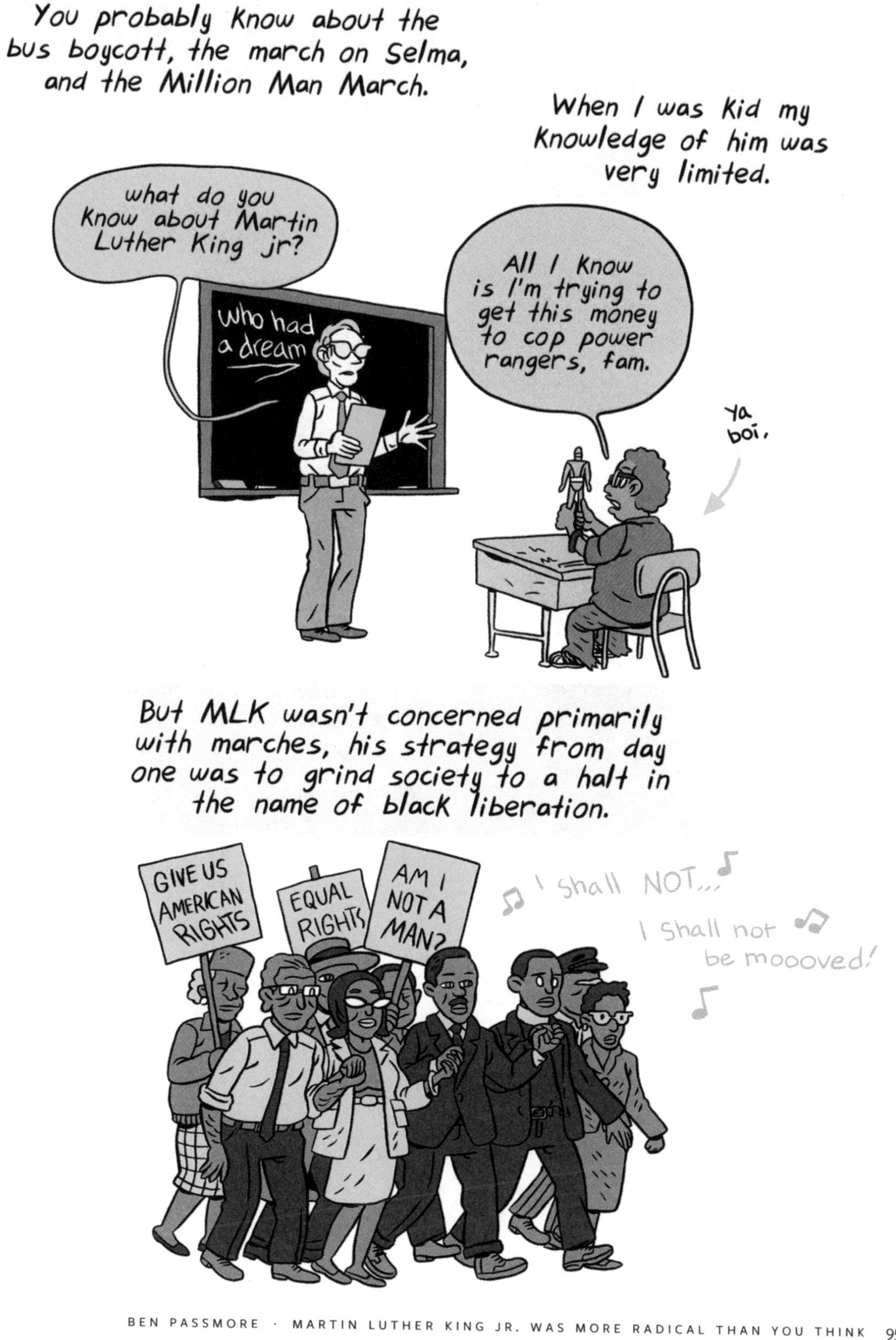
You probably know about the bus boycott, the march on Selma, and the Million Man March.
When I was kid my knowledge of him was very limited.
what do you know about Martin Luther King jr?
who had a dream
All I know is I'm trying to get this money to cop power rangers, fam.
Ya boi.
But MLK wasn't concerned primarily with marches, his strategy from day one was to grind society to a halt in the name of black liberation.
GIVE US AMERICAN RIGHTS
EQUAL RIGHTS
AM I NOT A MAN?
I shall NOT...
I shall not be moooved!

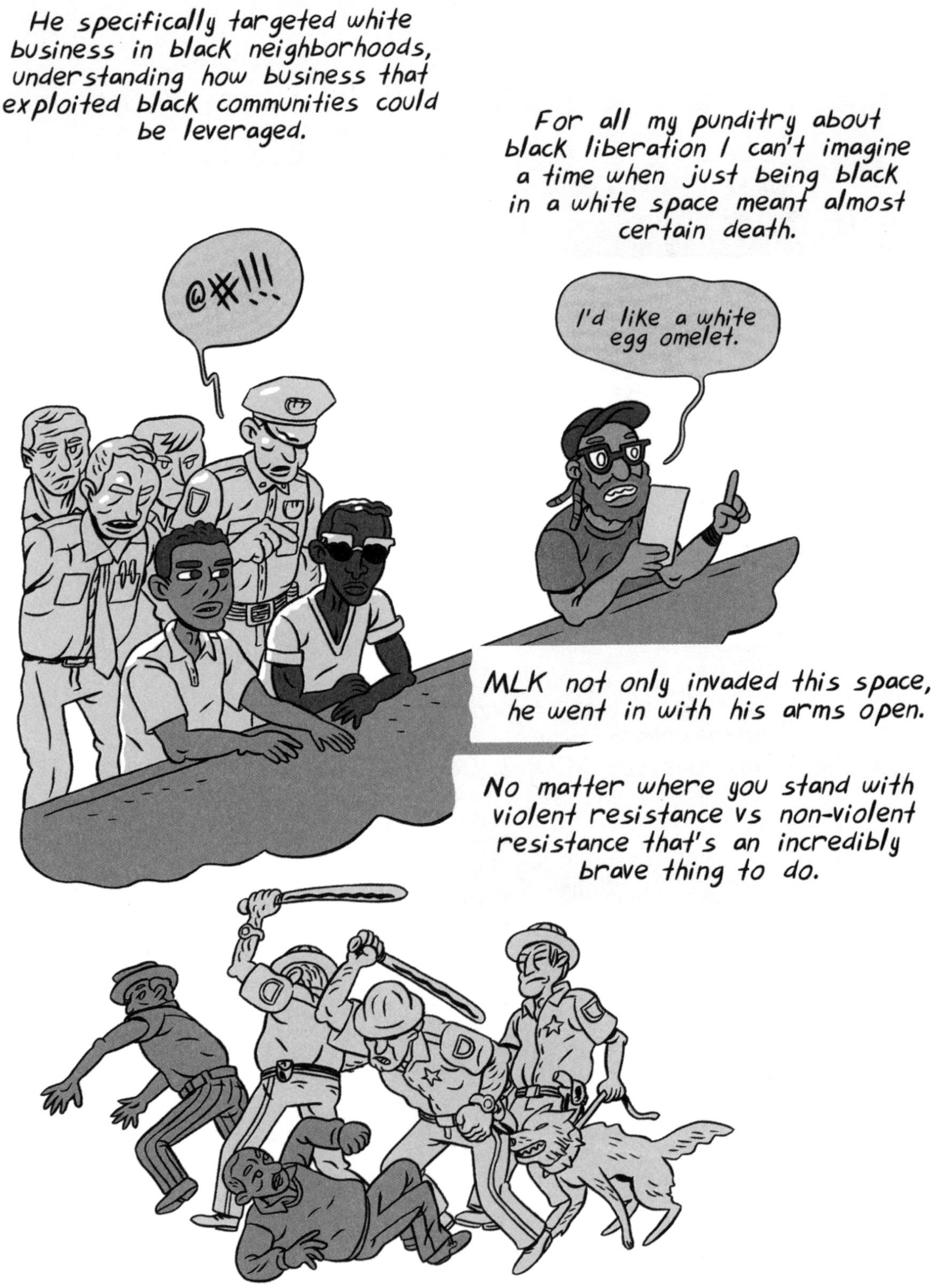
He specifically targeted white business in black neighborhoods, understanding how business that exploited black communities could be leveraged.
@#!!!
For all my punditry about black liberation I can't imagine a time when just being black in a white space meant almost certain death.
I'd like a white egg omelet.
MLK not only invaded this space, he went in with his arms open.
No matter where you stand with violent resistance vs non-violent resistance that's an incredibly brave thing to do.

Overtime MLK developed more intersectional politics, focusing on general systematic oppressions like US foreign wars...

...and an economic critique of American society. It was not enough to integrate society if society itself was insufficient.

Now our struggle is for genuine equality, which means economic equality. For we know that it isn't enough to integrate lunch counters.

It was this focus on economic injustice and the Poor People's Campaign, which organized to fill the Washington Mall with a three thousand person occupation, that made the federal government worried about MLK as a political force not woke speeches.

Sen. John L McCellan Democrat of Arkansas

[The occupation is a] premeditated act of contempt and rebellion against the sovereignty of government.

(from The SCLC's implementation of the poor peoples' campaign of 1968f by Michael J. Winston.)

FBI Director J. Edgar Hoover used agency resources to monitor MLK's movements and wiretap his communications in a effort to prove that the civil rights leader was a communist.

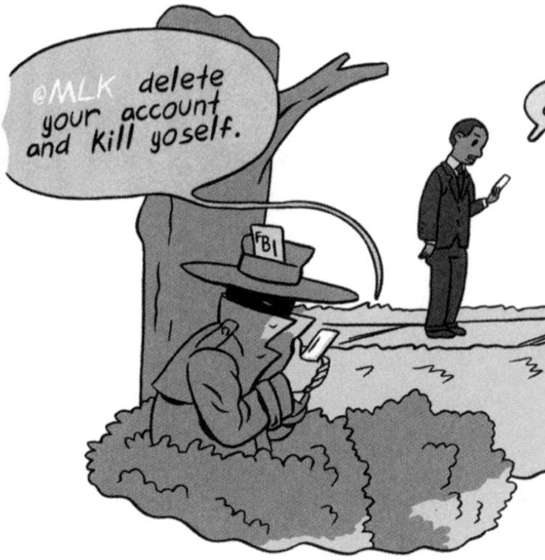
@MLK delete your account and kill yoself.
FBI

Hoover even went as far as sending threatening anonymous letters to MLK in an attempt frighten him into killing himself.

Ironically, I would have protected him from violence with violence.

If asked to pick a side, I'll pick someone fighting for liberation everytime.

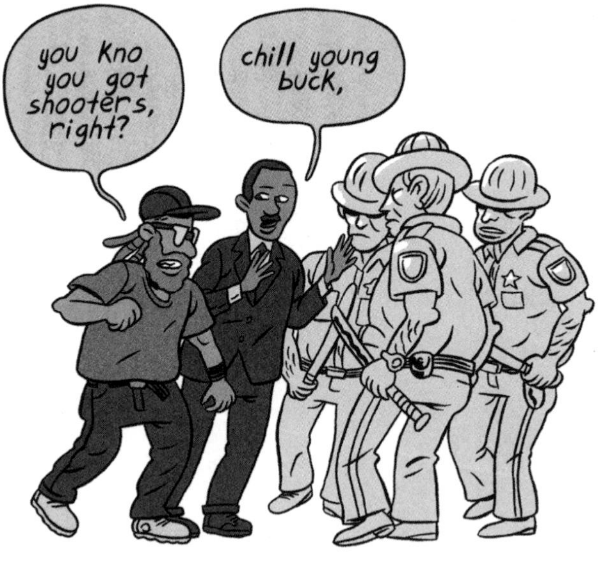
you kno you got shooters, right?
chill young buck,

But I'd be lying if I didn't think that MLK and his legacy has played a large part in the over valorization of self-assigned black "leaders".

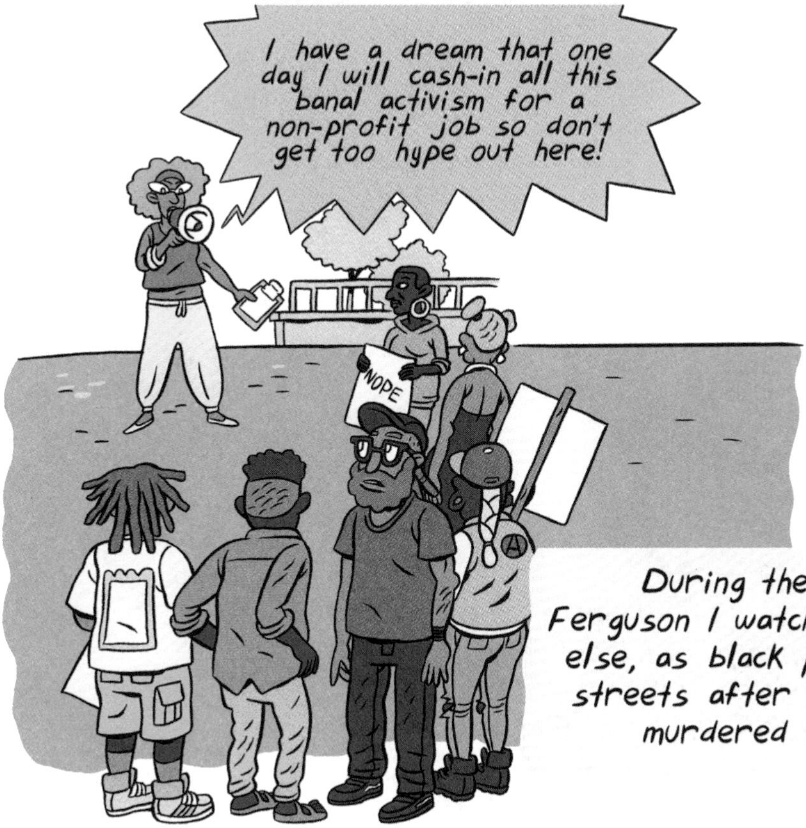
I have a dream that one day I will cash-in all this banal activism for a non-profit job so don't get too hype out here!
NOPE

During the uprising in Ferguson I watched, like everyone else, as black people filled the streets after Mike Brown was murdered by the police.

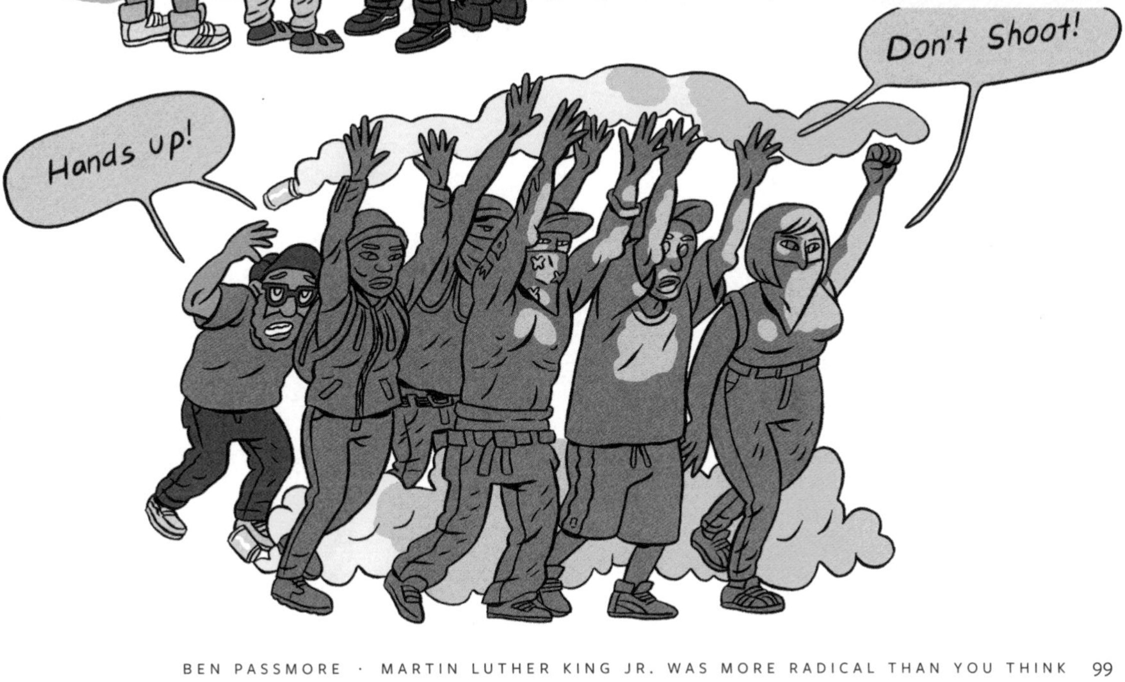
Hands up!
Don't Shoot!

Over time, famous political leaders came to Ferguson to be seen and heard and the people of Ferguson rebuked them as invaders and opportunists.

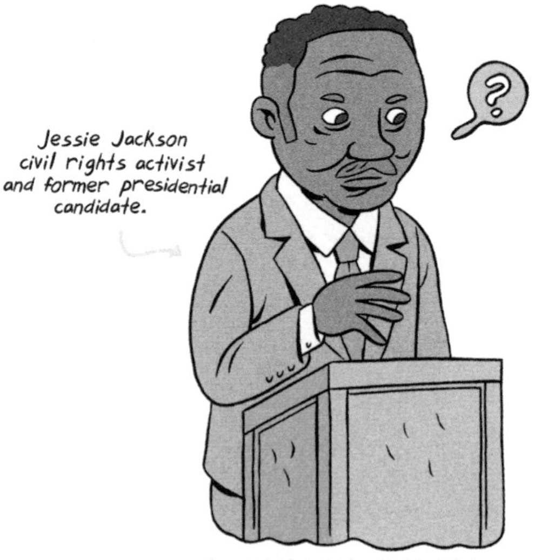
Jessie Jackson
civil rights activist
and former presidential
candidate.
?

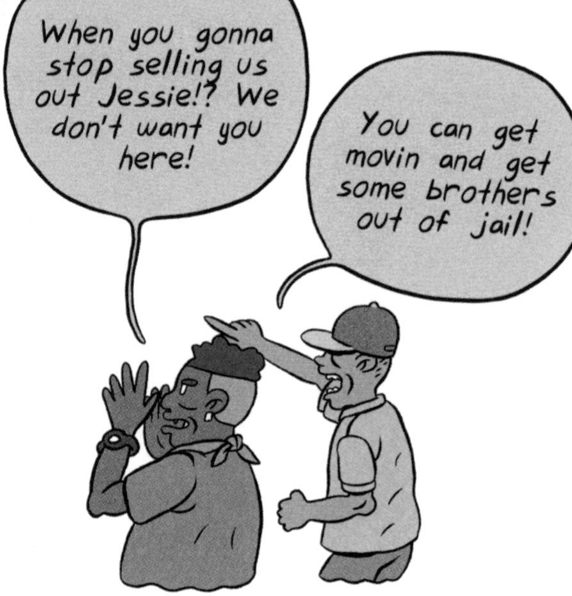
When you gonna stop selling us out Jessie!? We don't want you here!
You can get movin and get some brothers out of jail!

This expressed a long-standing uneasy relationship between professional activists and people lashing out at their oppression.

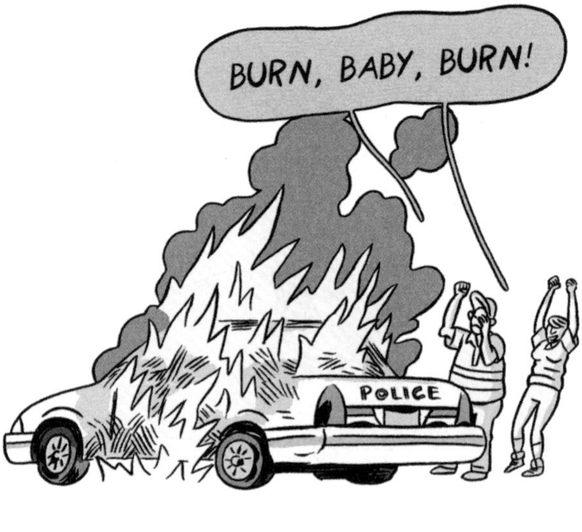
BURN, BABY, BURN!
POLICE

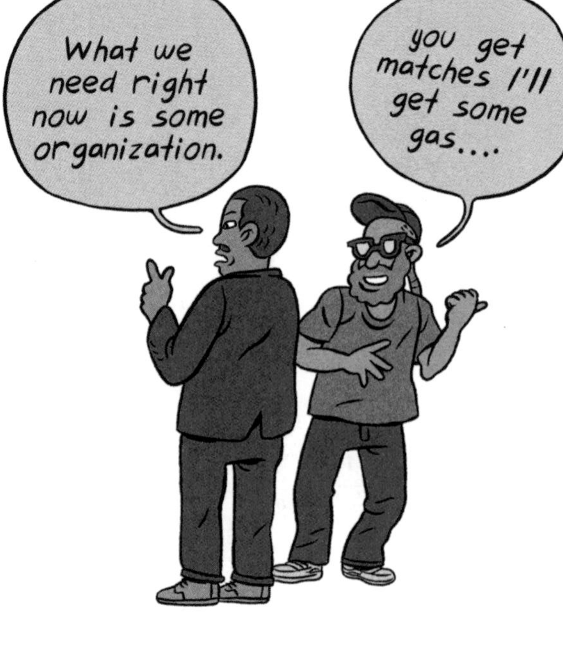
What we need right now is some organization.
you get matches I'll get some gas....

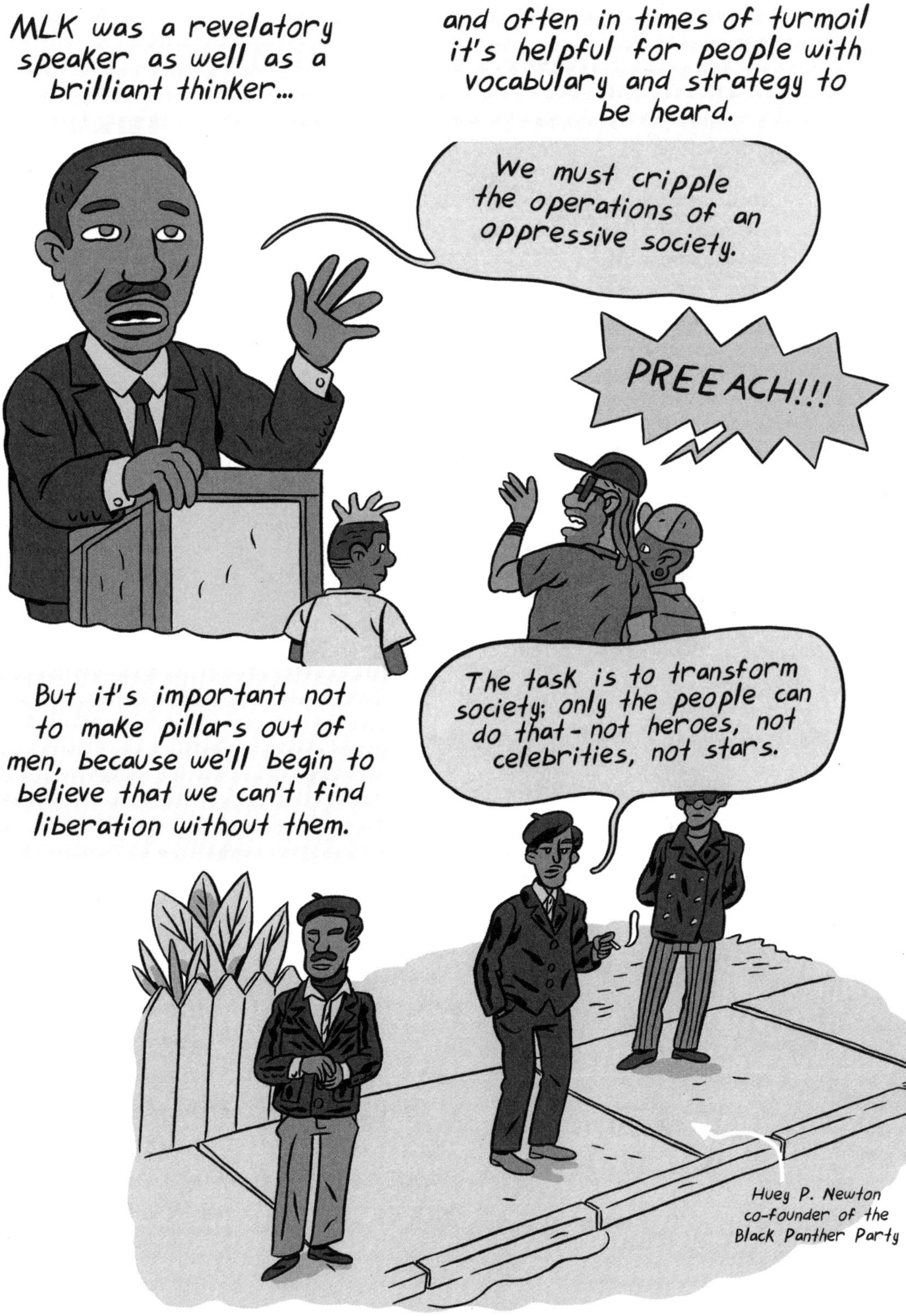
MLK was a revelatory speaker as well as a brilliant thinker...
and often in times of turmoil it's helpful for people with vocabulary and strategy to be heard.
We must cripple the operations of an oppressive society.
PREEACH!!!
But it's important not to make pillars out of men, because we'll begin to believe that we can't find liberation without them.
The task is to transform society; only the people can do that - not heroes, not celebrities, not stars.
Huey P. Newton co-founder of the Black Panther Party

As we're watching the rise of white-supremacists in and outside the White House it's hard for me to hear people express bewilderment...

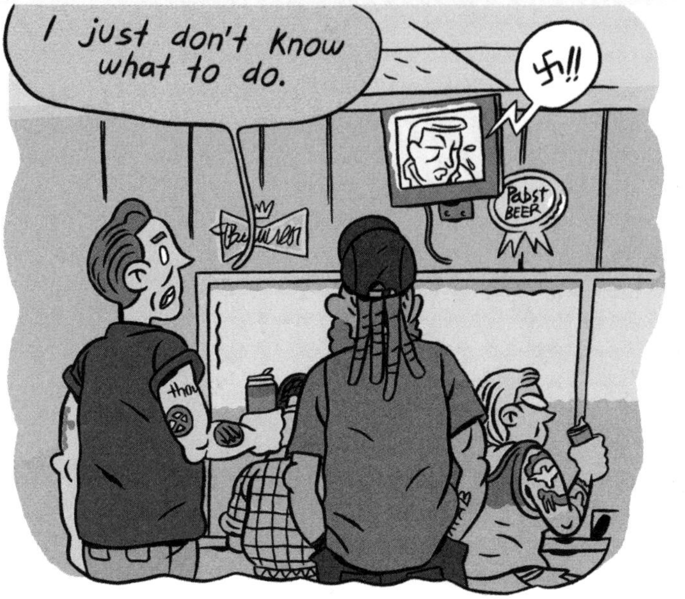
I just don't know what to do.
卐!!
Pabst BEER

None of what we are seeing is new, and, as tiring as it is, we fortunately have a long history of battling oppression.

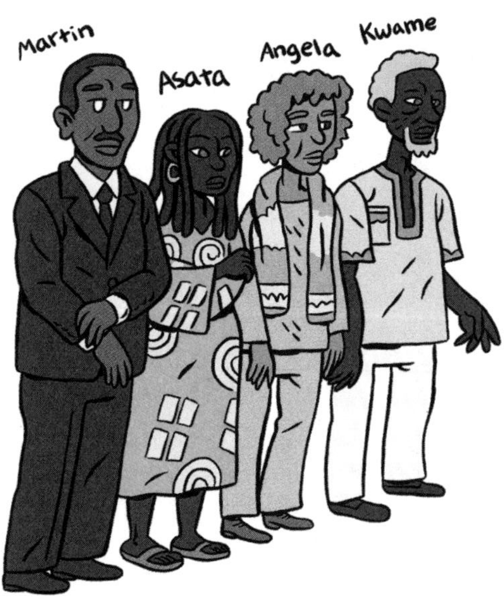
Martin
Asata
Angela
Kwame

MLK was part of a generation that introduced many types of antagonisms and, even though he was deeply committed to non-violence, the minister understood that society needed to be interrupted.

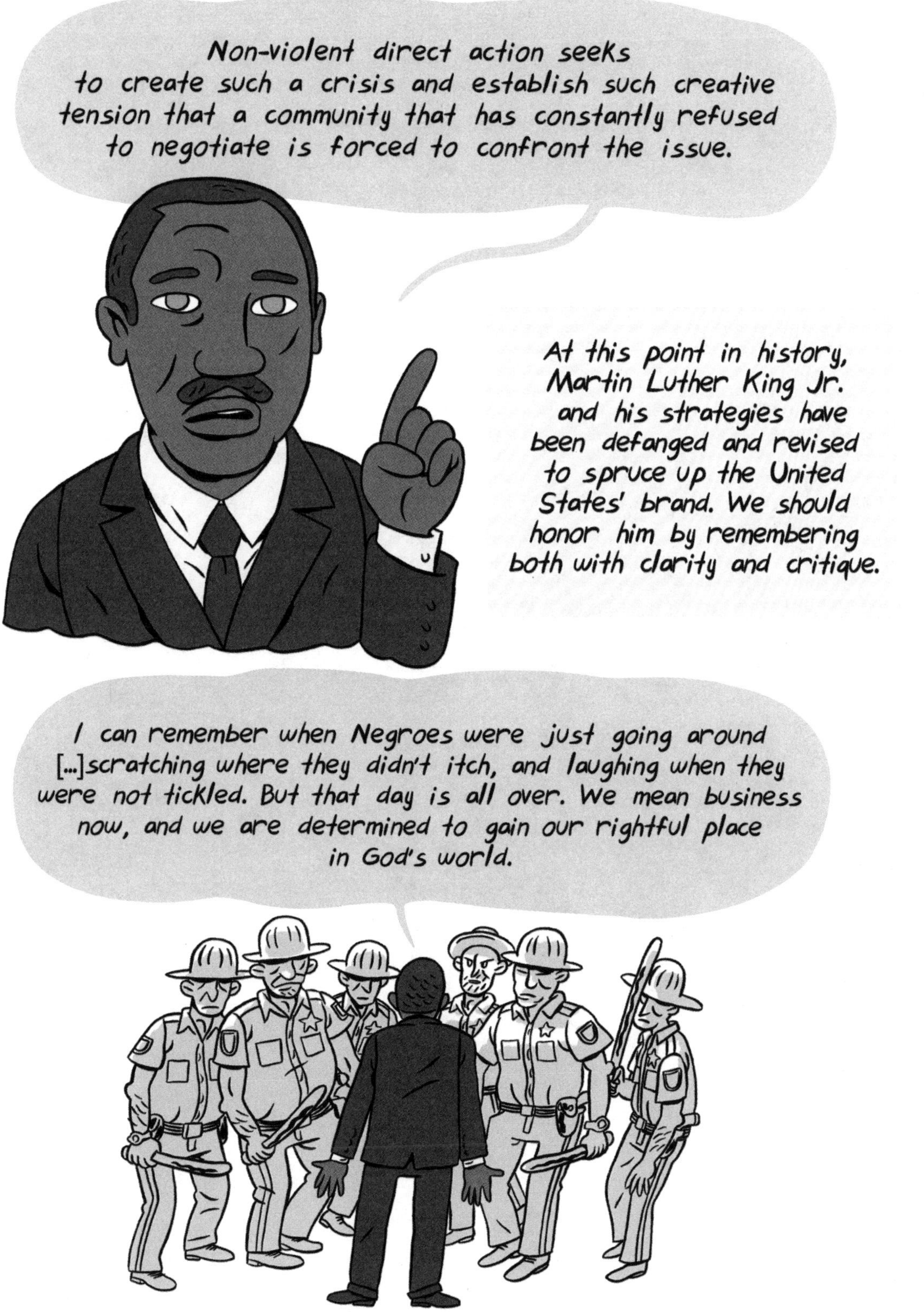
Non-violent direct action seeks to create such a crisis and establish such creative tension that a community that has constantly refused to negotiate is forced to confront the issue.
At this point in history, Martin Luther King Jr. and his strategies have been defanged and revised to spruce up the United States' brand. We should honor him by remembering both with clarity and critique.
I can remember when Negroes were just going around [...]scratching where they didn't itch, and laughing when they were not tickled. But that day is all over. We mean business now, and we are determined to gain our rightful place in God's world.

SELECTIONS FROM

King-Cat #78

JOHN PORCELLINO

KING-CAT
COMICS and STORIES
No. 78
$5.00
BY JOHN PORCELLINO

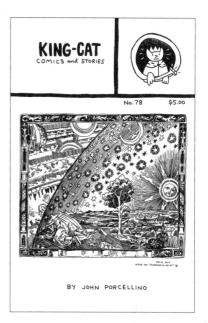

originally published in

King-Cat Comics and Stories #78

SELF-PUBLISHED

5.5 x 8.5 inches • 36 pages

Biography

John Porcellino has been drawing and writing his self-published zine, *King-Cat Comics,* since 1989. His most recent collection, *From Lone Mountain,* was published in 2018 by Drawn and Quarterly. He lives with his girlfriend and numerous quadruped animals in Beloit, Wisconsin.
king-cat.net

Statement

As I grow older and the world around me grows more insane, I've sought comfort in the small world right around me. I never try to force a theme when making a new issue of *King-Cat,* but instead stumble through ideas, false-starts, and blunders until some kind of thread presents itself in the work. In the case of this issue, #78, that thread became our home and backyard, and the life found within. Having lived for decades the unpredictable and unstable life of an American cartoonist, I relish my current domestic situation, one filled with love, humor, acceptance, and warmth, and that became the unifying theme of the issue.

GRey day
Cold house
Wind thRough the RafteRs

Many afteRnoons

A STORY ABOUT NINNY

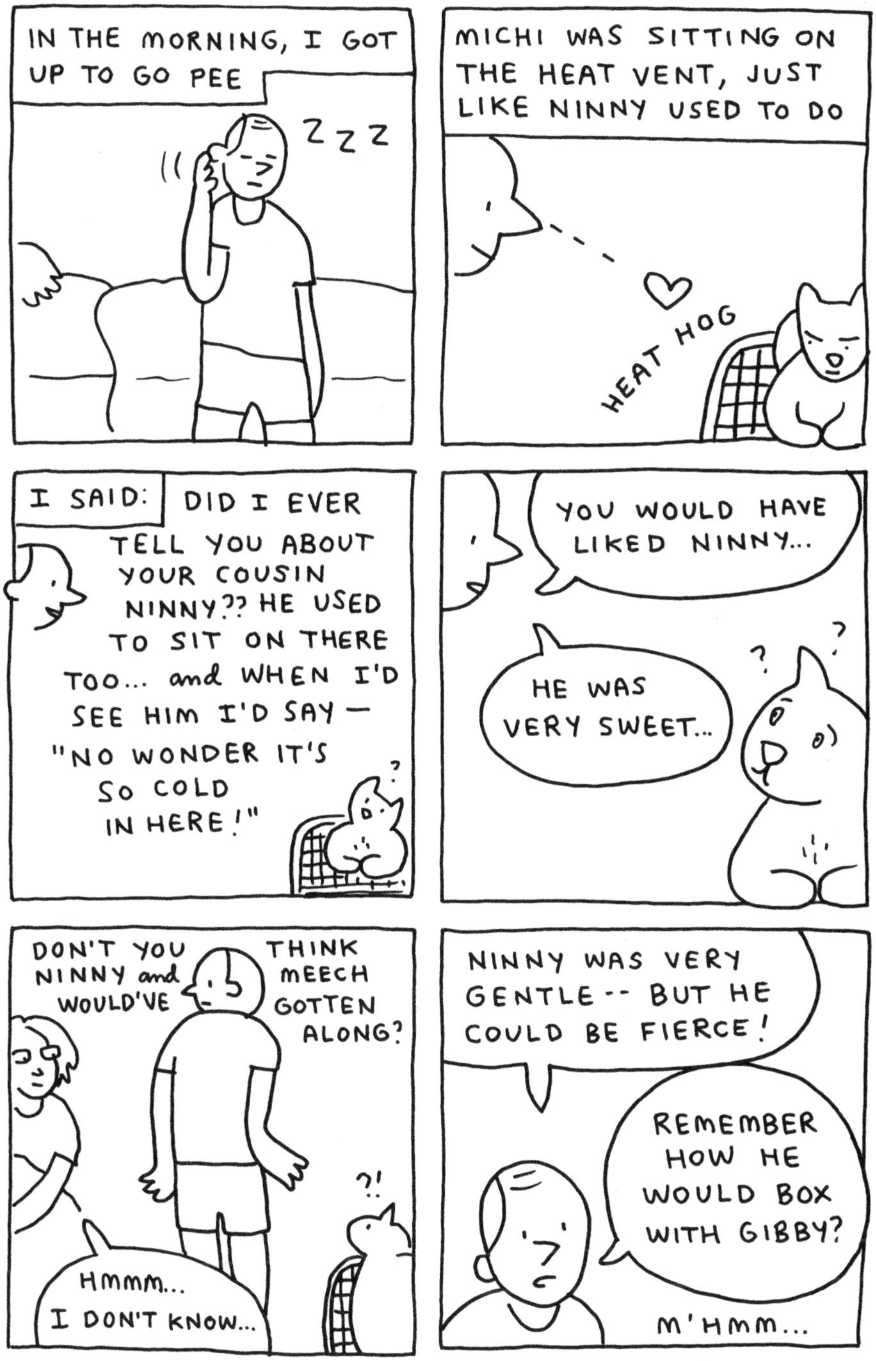
IN THE MORNING, I GOT UP TO GO PEE
ZZZ
MICHI WAS SITTING ON THE HEAT VENT, JUST LIKE NINNY USED TO DO
HEAT HOG
I SAID: DID I EVER TELL YOU ABOUT YOUR COUSIN NINNY?? HE USED TO SIT ON THERE TOO... and WHEN I'D SEE HIM I'D SAY — "NO WONDER IT'S SO COLD IN HERE!"
YOU WOULD HAVE LIKED NINNY...
HE WAS VERY SWEET...
DON'T YOU THINK NINNY and MEECH WOULD'VE GOTTEN ALONG?
?!
HMMM... I DON'T KNOW...
NINNY WAS VERY GENTLE -- BUT HE COULD BE FIERCE!
REMEMBER HOW HE WOULD BOX WITH GIBBY?
M'HMM...

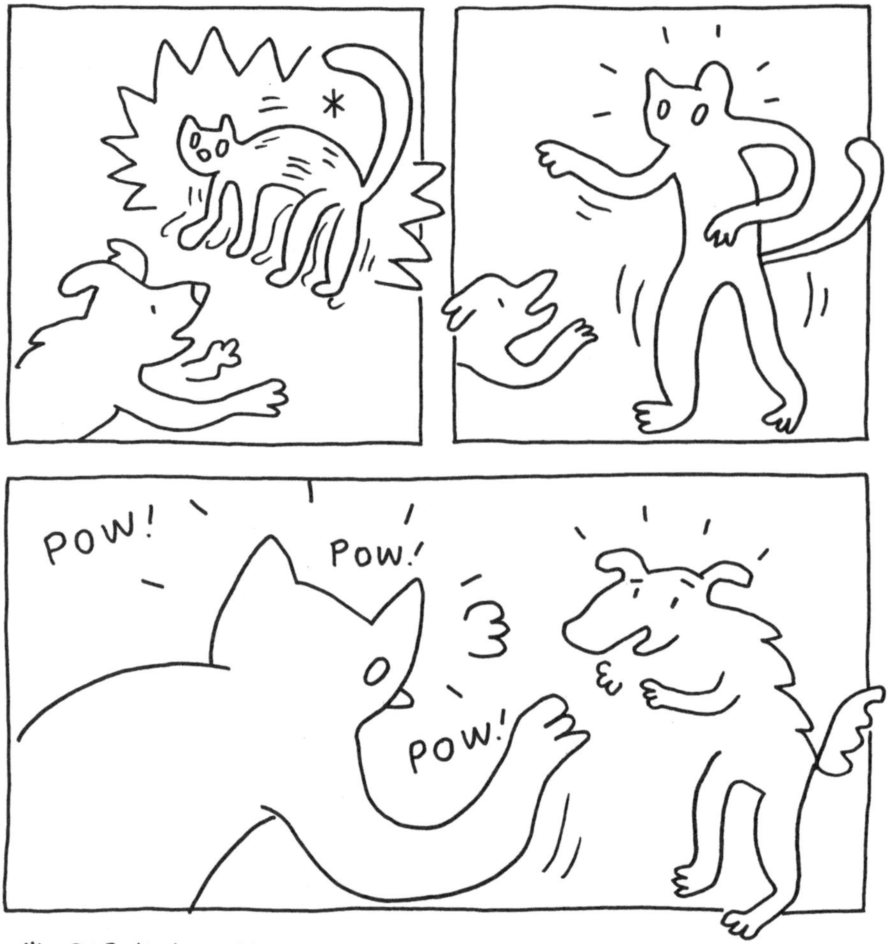
*
POW!
POW!
POW!

* CRABWALK CHAMPION
2012-2015 ♡

HAPPENED SUNDAY
MORNING 12/10/17
DRAWN IN 2018

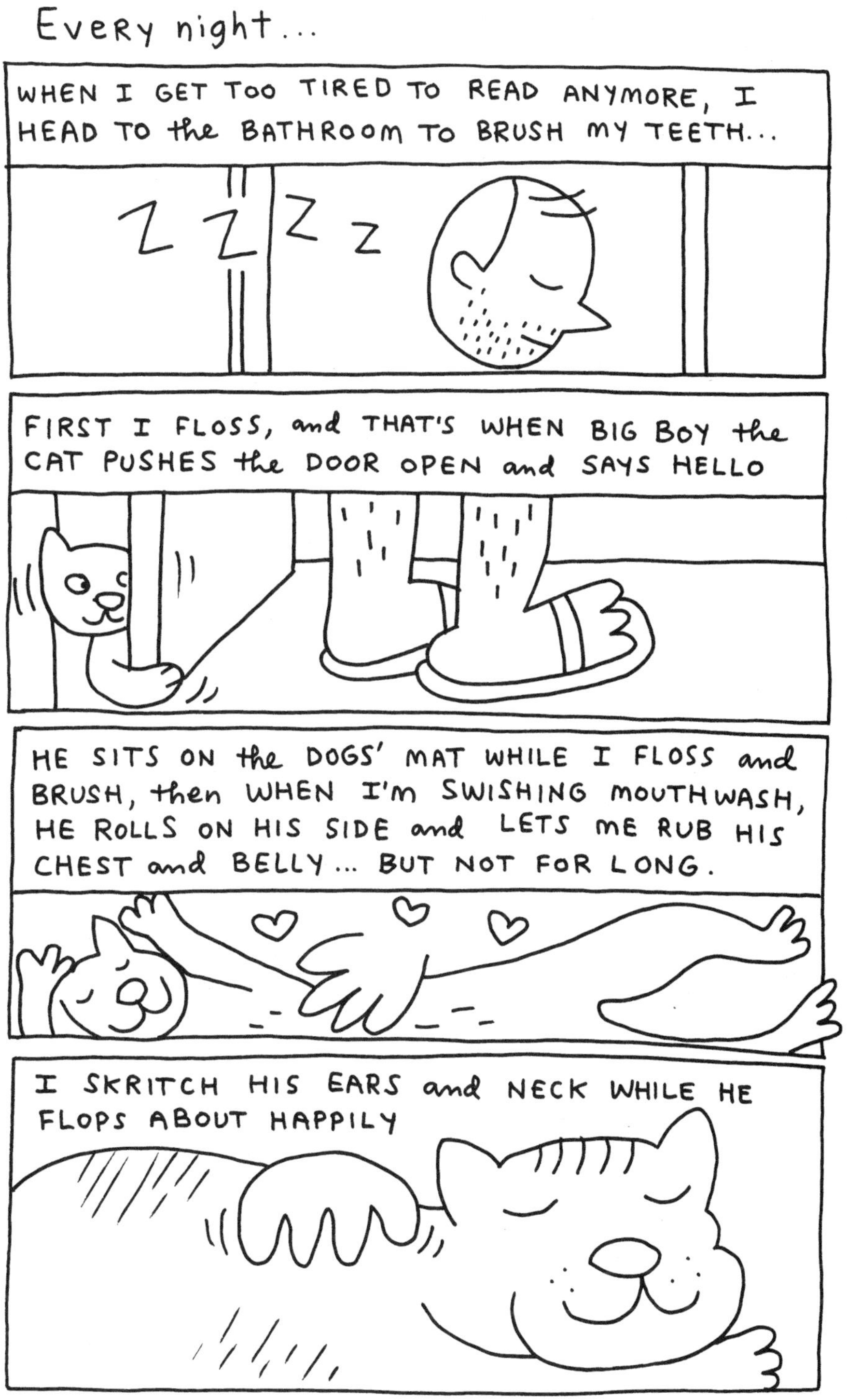

Every night...
WHEN I GET TOO TIRED TO READ ANYMORE, I HEAD TO the BATHROOM TO BRUSH MY TEETH...
Z Z Z Z
FIRST I FLOSS, and THAT'S WHEN BIG BOY the CAT PUSHES the DOOR OPEN and SAYS HELLO
HE SITS ON the DOGS' MAT WHILE I FLOSS and BRUSH, then WHEN I'm SWISHING MOUTHWASH, HE ROLLS ON HIS SIDE and LETS ME RUB HIS CHEST and BELLY... BUT NOT FOR LONG.
I SKRITCH HIS EARS and NECK WHILE HE FLOPS ABOUT HAPPILY

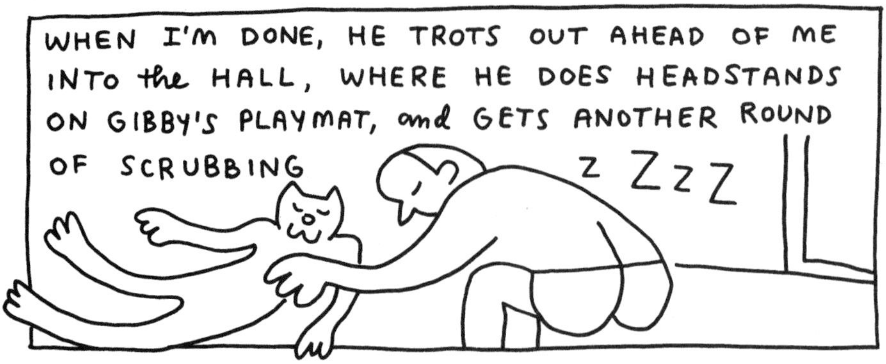
WHEN I'M DONE, HE TROTS OUT AHEAD OF ME INTO the HALL, WHERE HE DOES HEADSTANDS ON GIBBY'S PLAYMAT, and GETS ANOTHER ROUND OF SCRUBBING
z Z z Z

FINALLY, I WISH HIM GOODNIGHT and, TURNING OUT the HALL LIGHT, I GO TO BED...

SWEET DREAMS
BIG BOY...

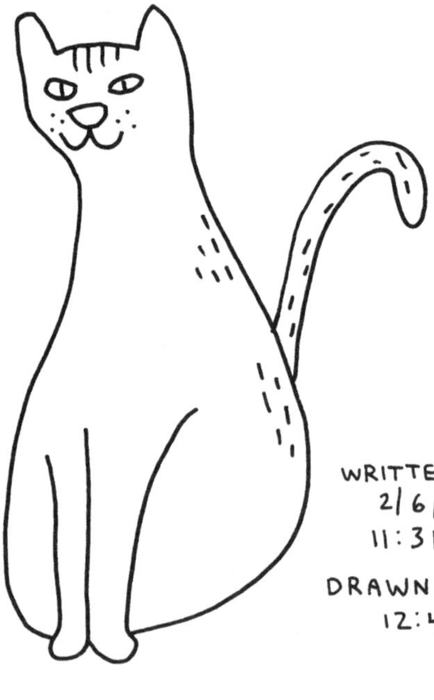

WRITTEN DOWN
2/6/17
11:31 pm
DRAWN 8/17/17
12:40 pm

Nighttime Encounter with the Void

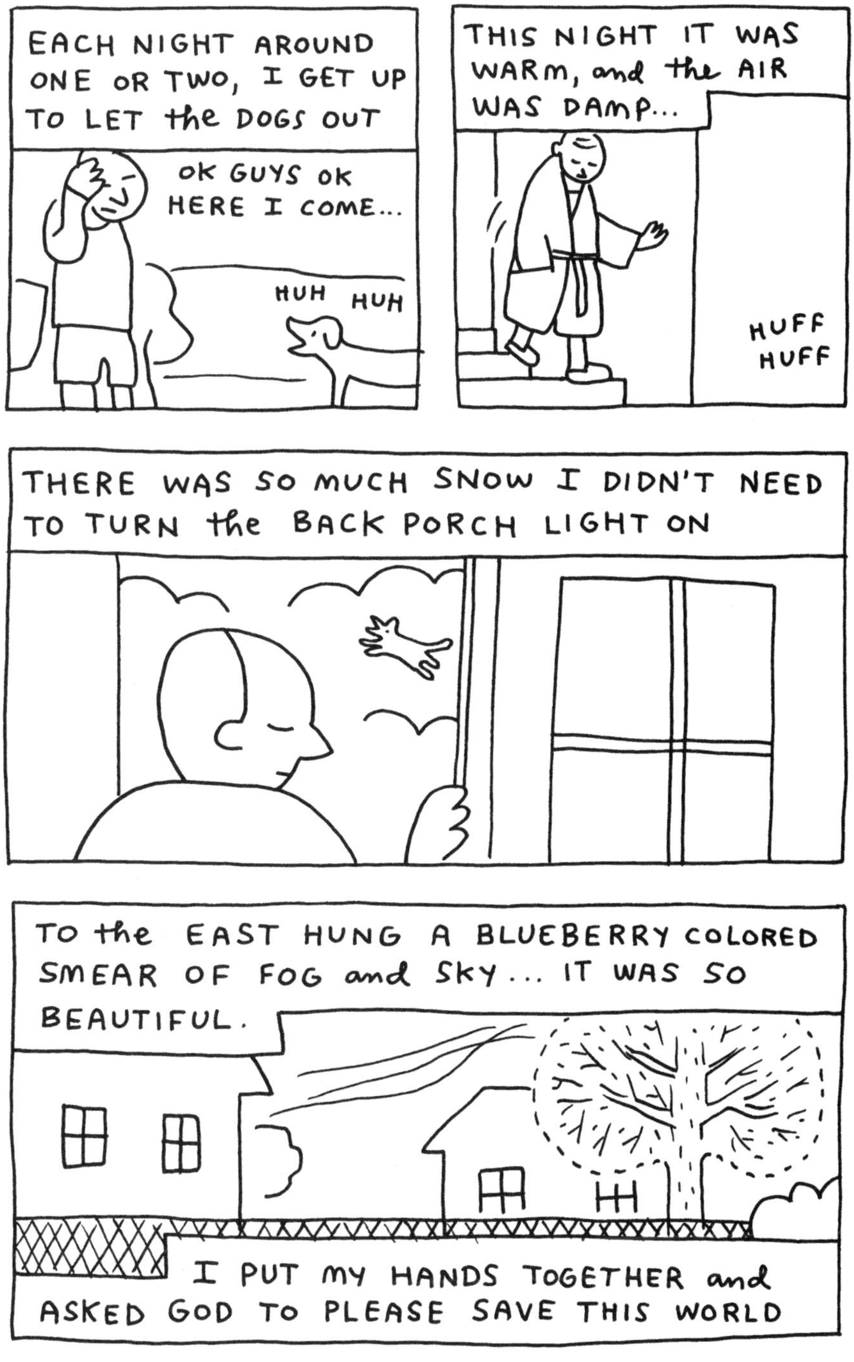
EACH NIGHT AROUND ONE OR TWO, I GET UP TO LET the DOGS OUT
OK GUYS OK HERE I COME...
HUH HUH
THIS NIGHT IT WAS WARM, and the AIR WAS DAMP...
HUFF HUFF
THERE WAS SO MUCH SNOW I DIDN'T NEED TO TURN the BACK PORCH LIGHT ON
TO the EAST HUNG A BLUEBERRY COLORED SMEAR OF FOG and SKY... IT WAS SO BEAUTIFUL.
I PUT MY HANDS TOGETHER and ASKED GOD TO PLEASE SAVE THIS WORLD

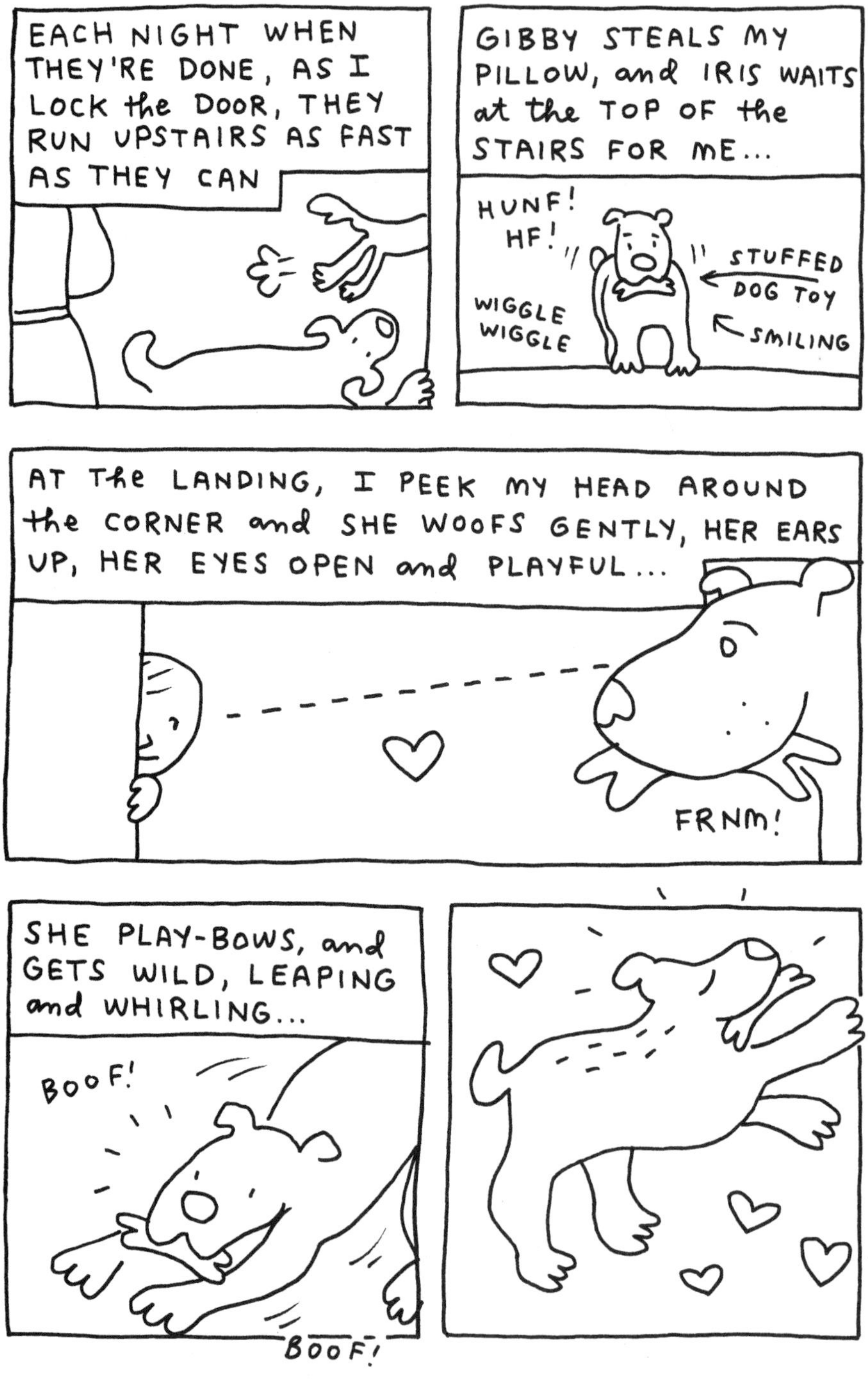

EACH NIGHT WHEN THEY'RE DONE, AS I LOCK the DOOR, THEY RUN UPSTAIRS AS FAST AS THEY CAN
GIBBY STEALS MY PILLOW, and IRIS WAITS at the TOP OF the STAIRS FOR ME...
HUNF! HF!
WIGGLE WIGGLE
STUFFED DOG TOY
SMILING
AT The LANDING, I PEEK MY HEAD AROUND the CORNER and SHE WOOFS GENTLY, HER EARS UP, HER EYES OPEN and PLAYFUL...
FRNM!
SHE PLAY-BOWS, and GETS WILD, LEAPING and WHIRLING...
BOOF!
BOOF!

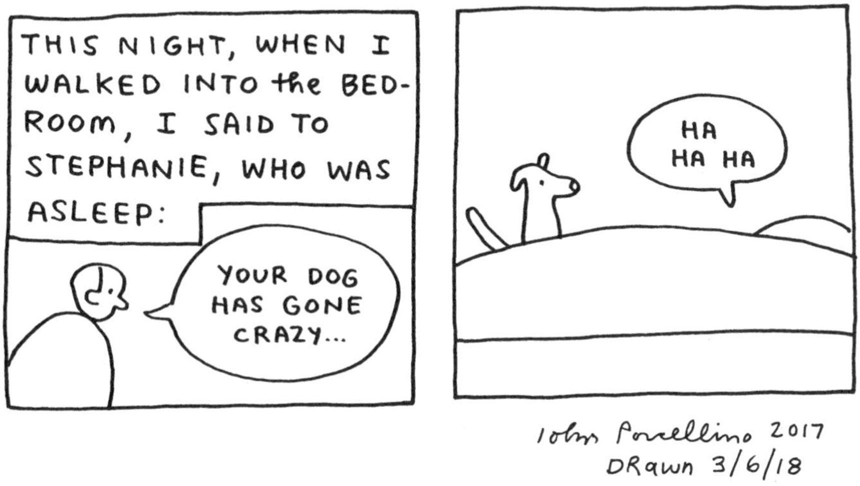
THIS NIGHT, WHEN I WALKED INTO the BED-ROOM, I SAID TO STEPHANIE, WHO WAS ASLEEP:
YOUR DOG HAS GONE CRAZY...
HA HA HA
John Porcellino 2017
DRawn 3/6/18

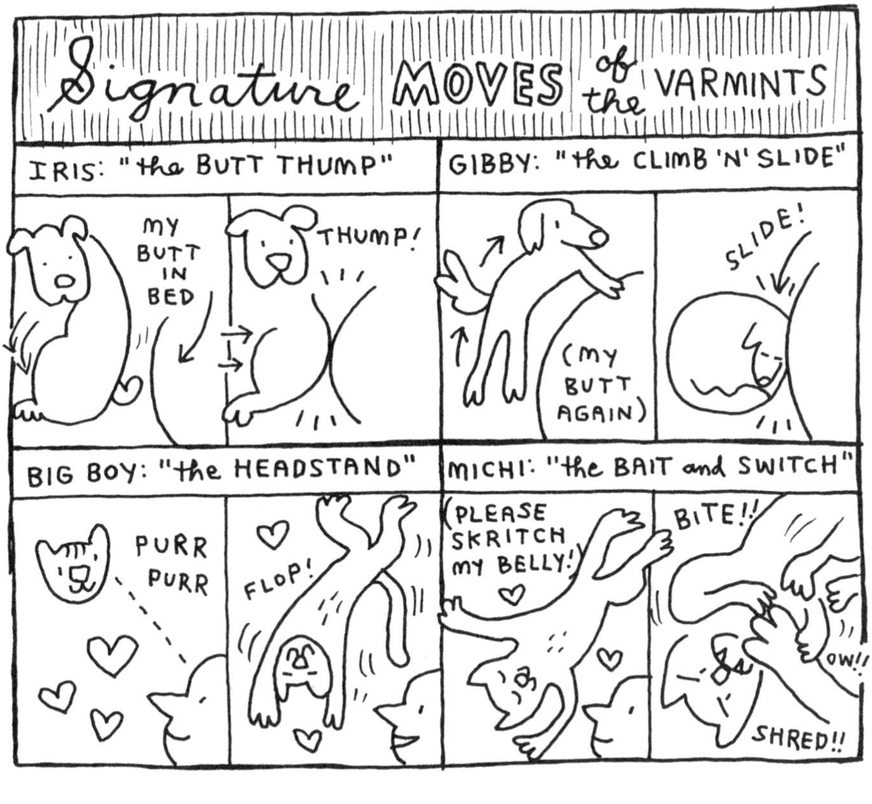
Signature MOVES of the VARMINTS
IRIS: "the BUTT THUMP"
MY BUTT IN BED
THUMP!
GIBBY: "the CLIMB 'N' SLIDE"
(MY BUTT AGAIN)
SLIDE!
BIG BOY: "the HEADSTAND"
PURR PURR
FLOP!
MICHI: "the BAIT and SWITCH"
(PLEASE SKRITCH MY BELLY!)
BITE!!
OW!!
SHRED!!

Nature Notes...

- 2017 Woodchuck Count: 334
- There were so many bees on the hyssop this year, it was impossible to count them.

Squirrels' Squash Garden No. 1

- I went my whole life without seeing a mink, and then I saw two in three days (Weds. 6/28/17, Fri. 6/30/17).
- I hope I never take fireflies for granted.
- "My li'l beetle's slow."
- I have a dog named Gibby, and a cat named Biggie.

Squirrels' Squash Garden No. 2

- EVOLUTION OF A NICKNAME:
  Iris → Snirus → Snibus → Snibey → Snibes

- Jus' me and the Stinkbugs.

- ACORN FEVER: Catch it!

TERMINOLOGY OUR DOGS UNDERSTAND:

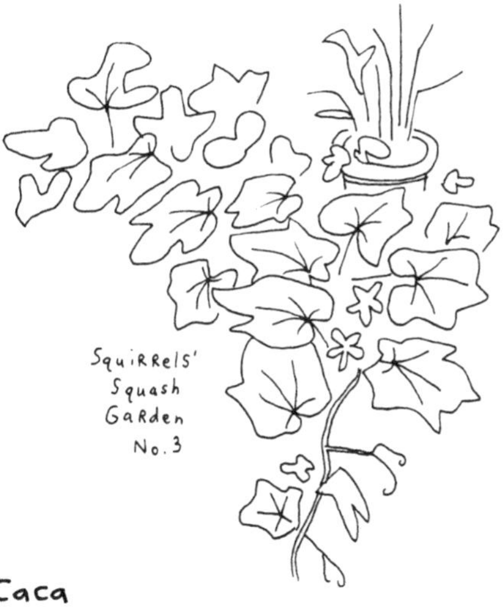

Squirrels' Squash Garden No. 3

- "Izquierdo" — Turn left.
- "Derecho" — Turn Right.
- "Tighten Up" — Wait at the corner para los coches pasar.
- "Wrong way 'Round the Barbecue" — Reverse course, you're wrapping your leash around a tree/lamppost/street sign, etc
- "Weepers" — Pee Pee
- "Boom Boom/Boomers" — Caca
- "Bath" (Alternately, "B.A.T.H.") — Danger!
- "Shower" — Run away!
- "Drop it!" — Eat it as quickly as possible.

→ LET'S LAUGH!

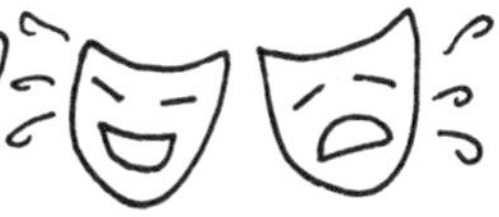

- What's the difference between a woodchuck and a beer made especially for dogs?

  • One is a "groundhog," the other is a "Hound Grog."

- What side of a cat has the most fur?

  • The "outside."

- How do dogs say "Goodbye" in Hamburg (GERMANY)?

  • "ARF wiedersehen" (Auf wiedersehen).

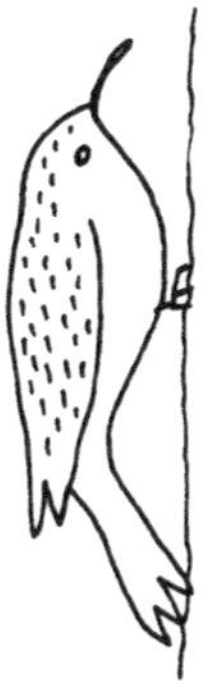

Brown Creeper on tree (Certhia americana)

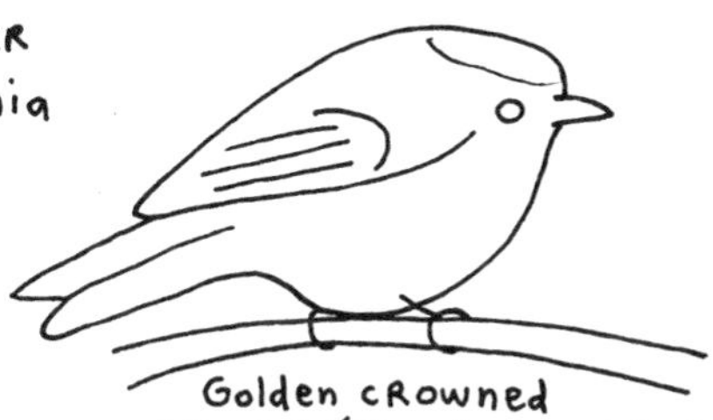

Golden crowned Kinglet (Regulus satrapa)

<u>MONARCH SUMMER</u>/ In 2016 or so, we planted a

bunch of milkweed, which is the only species of plant that Monarch butterflies will eat (and lay their eggs on). The first year, nothing, but this last summer we were delighted to see three big, juicy Monarch caterpillars on our backyard stand of Butterfly milk-weed (Asclepias tuberosa). Then, just when they got big enough that we figured they were about to pupate, they disappeared overnight.

We were really bummed, as we figured a possum or someone had gotten to them.* So, when we noticed another little "cat" on the plant, we put a large mesh cage over the top (an old reptile cage Stephanie had lying around the garage), to protect him.

Soon enough this new caterpillar was joined by another, and another, until we had seven or eight of them running around the leaves, chowing down.

Finally one day, the first one (or #4, technically) climbed up to the top of the cage, spun a small silk pad, and pupated. Two weeks later, he popped out (it was a male), fully grown and beautiful.

By the end of the summer, we'd successfully reared five adults. I'd heard that only 5% of monarch eggs make it to adulthood safely, so when we watched #5 emerge ("eclose") from his chry-salis, then fly haphazardly onto the neighbor's garage, then stum-ble around a bit, we were kind of nervous. When he finally (it was also a male) stretched his new wings and took off over Danielle's house, into the blue sky and out of sight, it damn near brought a tear to my eye. Our little guy... brand new and out in the world alone, next stop Central Mexico (where the final generation of the year travels, to overwinter).

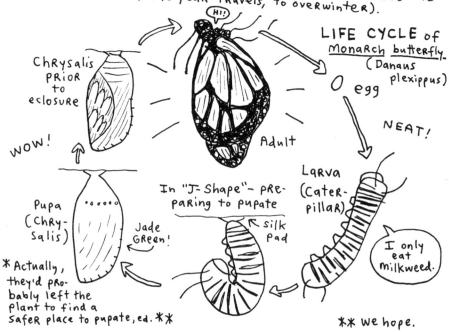

HI!

LIFE CYCLE of <u>Monarch butterfly</u>. (Danaus plexippus)

Chrysalis PRIOR to eclosure

egg

NEAT!

WOW!

Adult

Larva (Cater-pillar)

Pupa (Chry-salis)

In "J-Shape"- pre-paring to pupate

Jade Green!

silk pad

I only eat milkweed.

*Actually, they'd pro-bably left the plant to find a safer place to pupate, ed. **

** we hope.

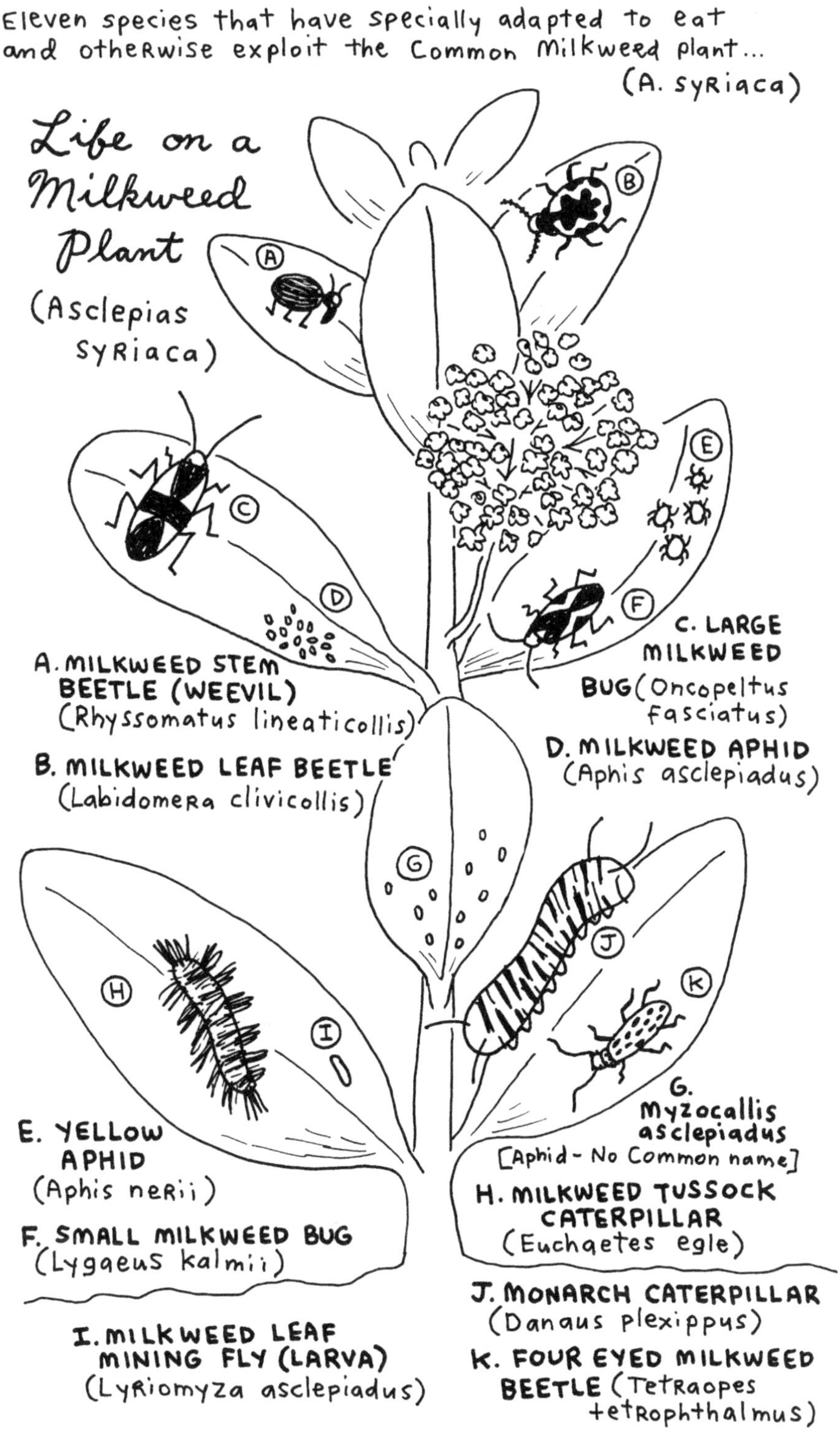
Eleven species that have specially adapted to eat and otherwise exploit the Common Milkweed plant...
(A. syRiaca)
Life on a Milkweed Plant
(Asclepias syRiaca)
A
B
C
D
E
F
G
H
I
J
K
A. MILKWEED STEM BEETLE (WEEVIL) (Rhyssomatus lineaticollis)
B. MILKWEED LEAF BEETLE (Labidomera clivicollis)
C. LARGE MILKWEED BUG (Oncopeltus fasciatus)
D. MILKWEED APHID (Aphis asclepiadus)
E. YELLOW APHID (Aphis neRii)
F. SMALL MILKWEED BUG (Lygaeus kalmii)
G. Myzocallis asclepiadus [Aphid - No Common name]
H. MILKWEED TUSSOCK CATERPILLAR (Euchaetes egle)
I. MILKWEED LEAF MINING FLY (LARVA) (LyRiomyza asclepiadus)
J. MONARCH CATERPILLAR (Danaus plexippus)
K. FOUR EYED MILKWEED BEETLE (TetRaopes tetRophthalmus)

SPOTLIGHT ON:
AMERICAN MINK *(Mustela vison)*

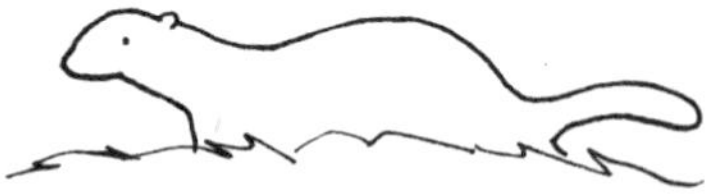

"Not an excessively shy mammal," "...its inquisitive watching may be prolonged by one's squeaking or chirping like a mouse or bird."

"Considerably larger than most other mustelids," the American Mink is also known by the names water weasel, minx, ching-woo-se (Chippewa), and n'pshikwä (Potawatomi).

"[C]annot easily be confused with any other Wisconsin mammal."

"[N]ot so pugnacious as the New York weasel," it "frequently climbs around logs or stumps..."

Although it is "not particularly unfriendly," the American Mink is "extremely hard to kill."

SPOTLIGHT ON:
NORTHERN HOUSE WREN *(Troglodytes aedon)*

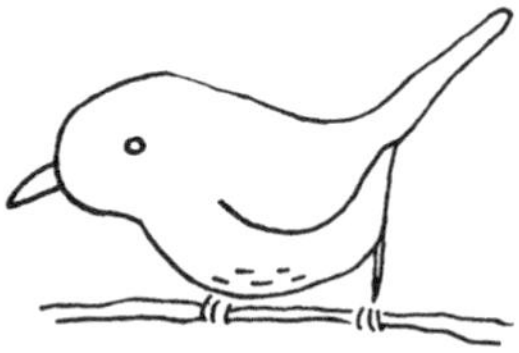

"Overall jizz* is of a plain, typical wren," (NG) although with an "effervescent" voice" (NG, CLO agree).

"In winter, they become more secretive..." (CLO)

Their nest is composed of twigs upon which the female "builds [a] cup of grasses, plant fibers, rootlets, feathers, hair, [and] rubbish." Notable House Wren nest locations include: "radiator of unused auto, top of pump, empty cow skull, leg of work pant on clothesline, flowerpot, pocket of scarecrow, boots, shoes, [and] in or on the nests of other birds." [EBN]

They often add spider egg sacs to their nests, which upon hatching help mitigate mites and other parasites. (CLO)

The House Wren "responds readily to pishing," (NG) and "...weighs about as much as two quarters..." (CLO)

**I had to look it up, ed.*

SPOTLIGHT ON:
NORTHERN SHORT-TAILED SHREW *(Blarina brevicauda)*

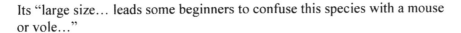

"A more blood-thirsty animal of its size I have never seen."
–Fmr. Pres. Theodore Roosevelt, Jr., writing in 1888

"[P]erhaps the most frequently captured of our shrews."

Its "large size… leads some beginners to confuse this species with a mouse or vole…"

"…prefers moist environments…"

Has the ability to echolocate.

"One of the few venomous mammals in the world…"

"Aggressive."

"The most important fact to be kept in mind is that shrews are nervous, ill-tempered, unsociable, and frequently blood-thirsty." – Dr. O.P. Pearson (1942)

SPOTLIGHT ON:
MOTHBALLS *(Naphthalene/1,4-dichlorobenzene)*

Mothballs once "consisted primarily of naphthalene, but due to naphthalene's flammability, many modern mothball formulations instead use 1,4-dichlorobenzene."

Both formulations present a "strong, pungent, sickly-sweet odor…" and "… may repel snakes or mice."

"Older-formula mothballs have … been used by drag racers to enhance the octane rating of fuel, by dissolving [them] in some of the fuel and filtering out the remains…"

"Exposure to naphthalene mothballs can cause acute hemolysis (anemia) in people with glucose-6-phosphate dehydrogenase deficiency," and the

International Agency for Research on Cancer (IARC) considers naphthalene "possibly carcinogenic to humans and other animals…"

"We're all going to die." – John Porcellino, 2017

* * *

Unless otherwise noted, quotations are from the following sources:

American Mink: Jackson, Hartley H.T.: *Mammals of Wisconsin.* U. of Wisconsin Press, 1961; Madison.

Northern House-Wren: Alderfer, Jonathan, ed., with Jon L. Dunn: *Complete Birds of North America.* National Geographic, 2006; Washington, D.C. (NG); Cornell Lab of Ornithology (allaboutbirds.org, viewed Jan. 12, 2018) (CLO); Harrison, Hal H.: *Field Guide to Eastern Birds' Nests* (Peterson Field Guides). Houghton Mifflin Co., 1975; Boston and New York. (EBN)

Northern Short-tailed Shrew: Burt, William Henry: *Mammals of the Great Lakes Region*, revised ed. of 1957. U. of Michigan Press, 1995; Ann Arbor.

Mothballs: Wikipedia: *https://en.wikipedia.org/wiki/Mothball* (viewed Jan. 12, 2018)

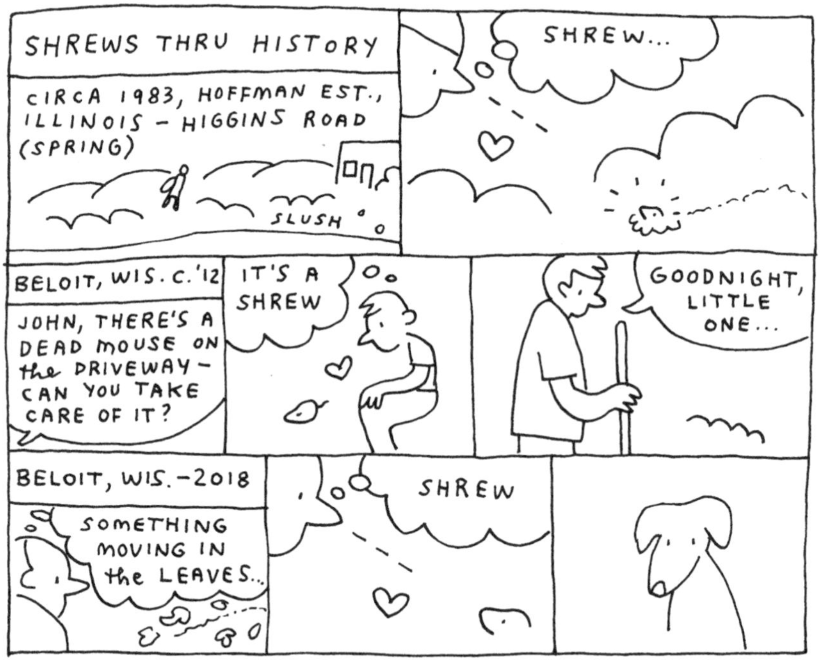
SHREWS THRU HISTORY
CIRCA 1983, HOFFMAN EST., ILLINOIS - HIGGINS ROAD (SPRING)
SLUSH
SHREW...
BELOIT, WIS. C.'12
JOHN, THERE'S A DEAD MOUSE ON the DRIVEWAY - CAN YOU TAKE CARE OF IT?
IT'S A SHREW
GOODNIGHT, LITTLE ONE...
BELOIT, WIS.-2018
SOMETHING MOVING IN the LEAVES...
SHREW

LOST and FOUND in the WOODS

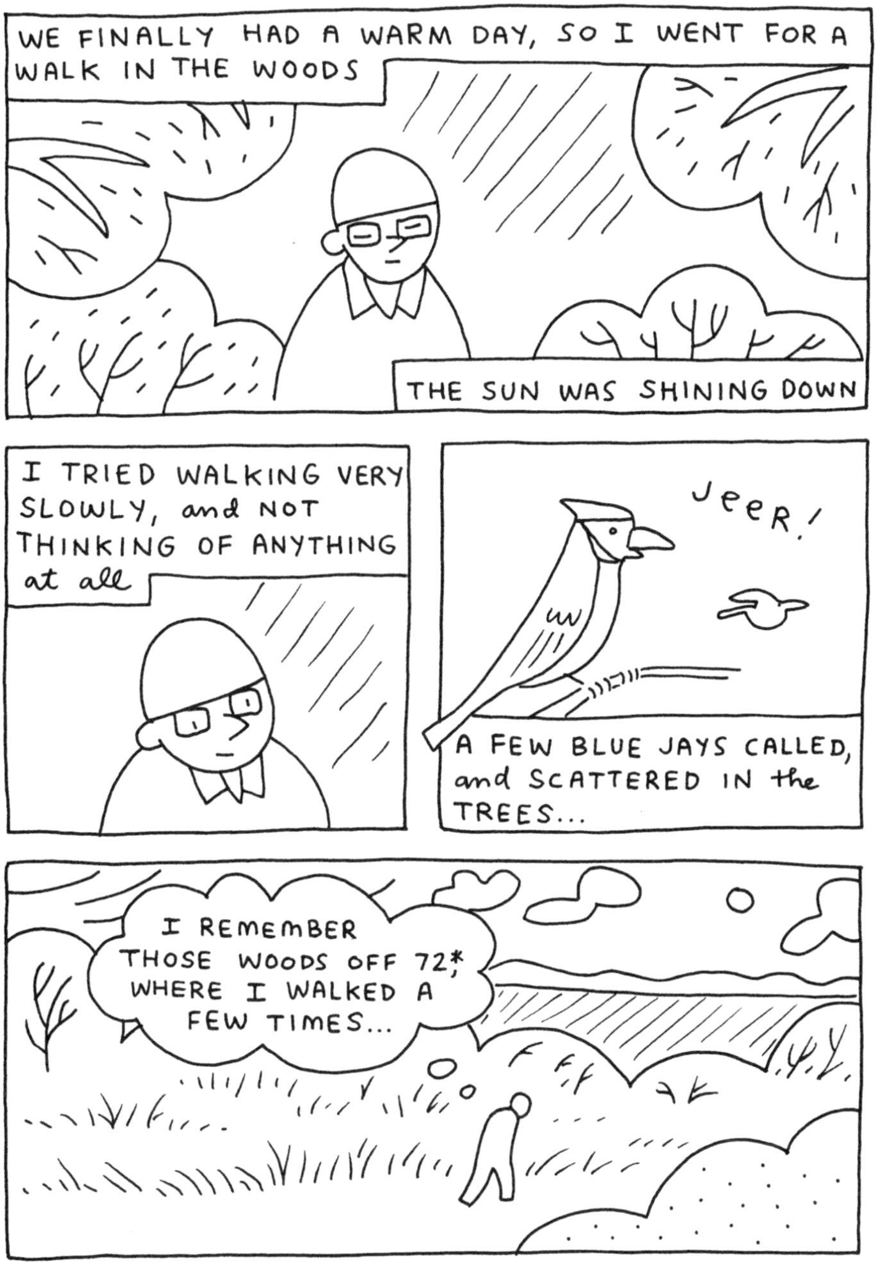
WE FINALLY HAD A WARM DAY, SO I WENT FOR A WALK IN THE WOODS
THE SUN WAS SHINING DOWN
I TRIED WALKING VERY SLOWLY, and NOT THINKING OF ANYTHING at all
JEER!
A FEW BLUE JAYS CALLED, and SCATTERED IN the TREES...
I REMEMBER THOSE WOODS OFF 72,* WHERE I WALKED A FEW TIMES...

* ILL. ROUTE 72, HIGGINS ROAD, ed.

THAT'S WHERE THAT PIPE-SMOKING MAN STEPPED OUT OF the BUSHES, RIGHT IN FRONT OF ME, and ONTO THE PATH

!

? ? ?

COMPLETELY SILENT

TWEED JACKET W/ CORDUROY ELBOW PATCHES, ed.

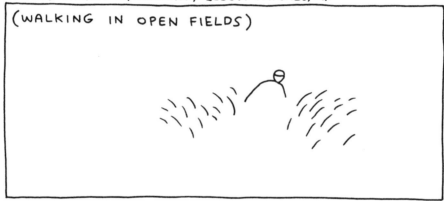

(WALKING IN OPEN FIELDS)

(THE BLUE JAYS ARE FOLLOWING ME)

♪...

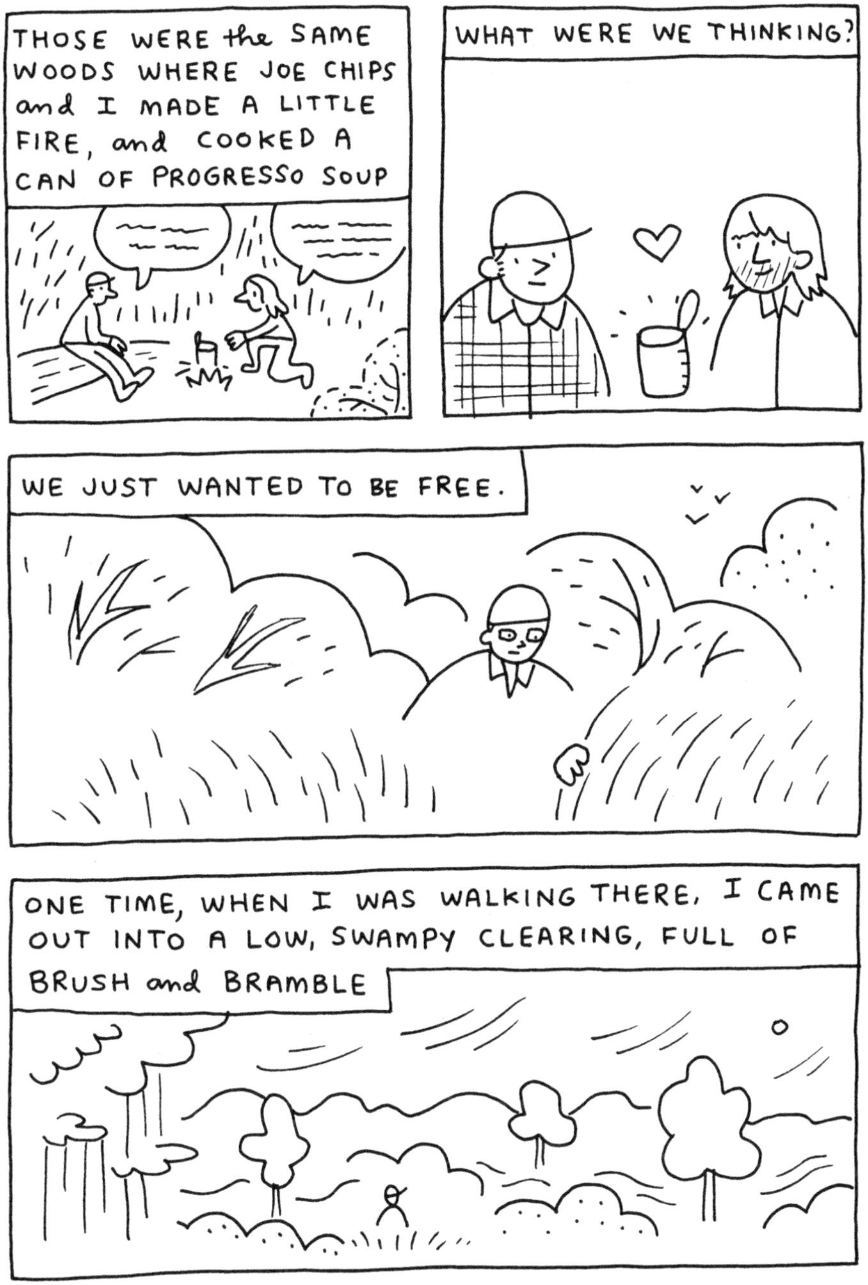
THOSE WERE the SAME WOODS WHERE JOE CHIPS and I MADE A LITTLE FIRE, and COOKED A CAN OF PROGRESSO SOUP
WHAT WERE WE THINKING?
WE JUST WANTED TO BE FREE.
ONE TIME, WHEN I WAS WALKING THERE, I CAME OUT INTO A LOW, SWAMPY CLEARING, FULL OF BRUSH and BRAMBLE

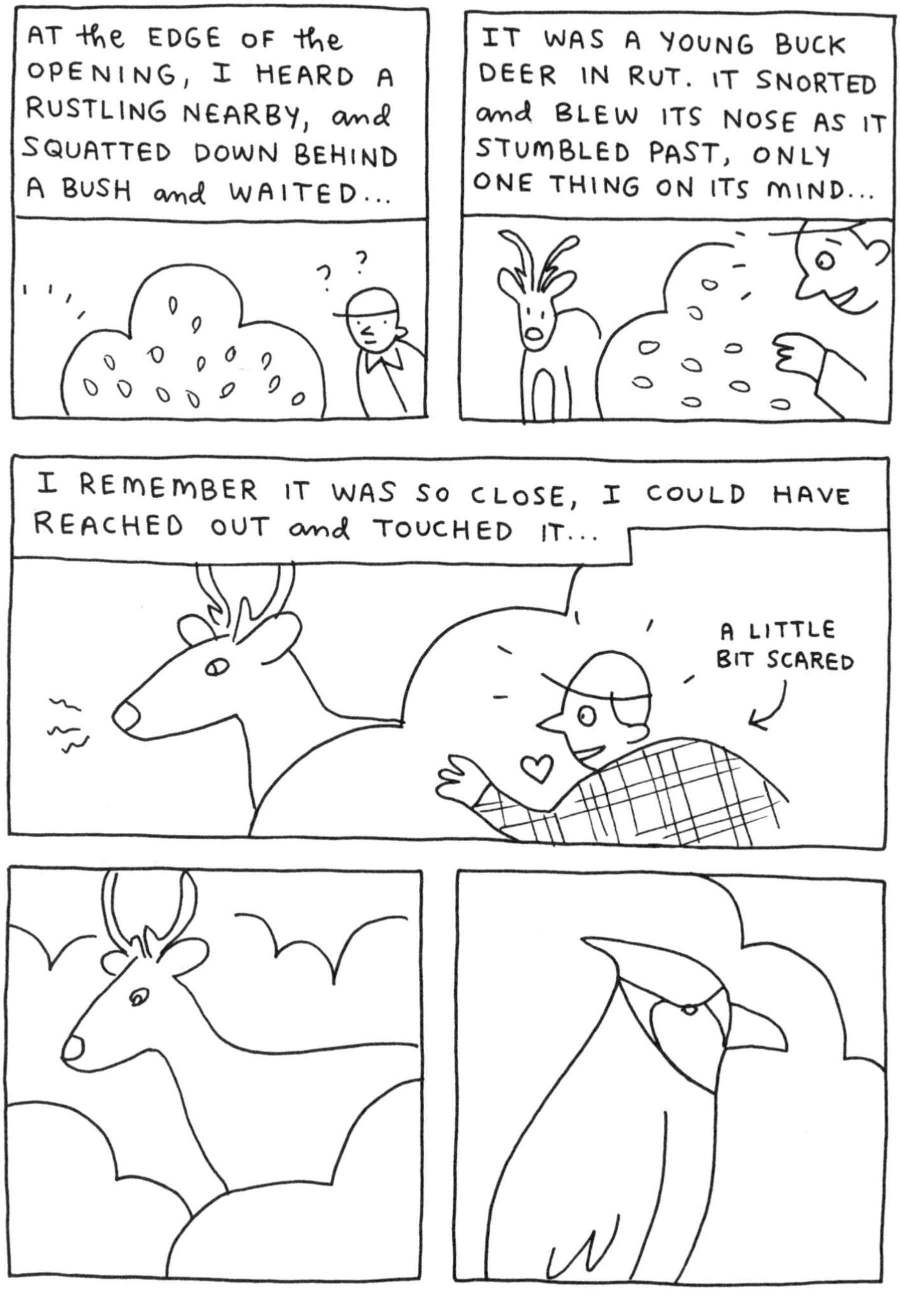
AT the EDGE OF the OPENING, I HEARD A RUSTLING NEARBY, and SQUATTED DOWN BEHIND A BUSH and WAITED...
? ?
IT WAS A YOUNG BUCK DEER IN RUT. IT SNORTED and BLEW ITS NOSE AS IT STUMBLED PAST, ONLY ONE THING ON ITS MIND...
I REMEMBER IT WAS SO CLOSE, I COULD HAVE REACHED OUT and TOUCHED IT...
A LITTLE BIT SCARED

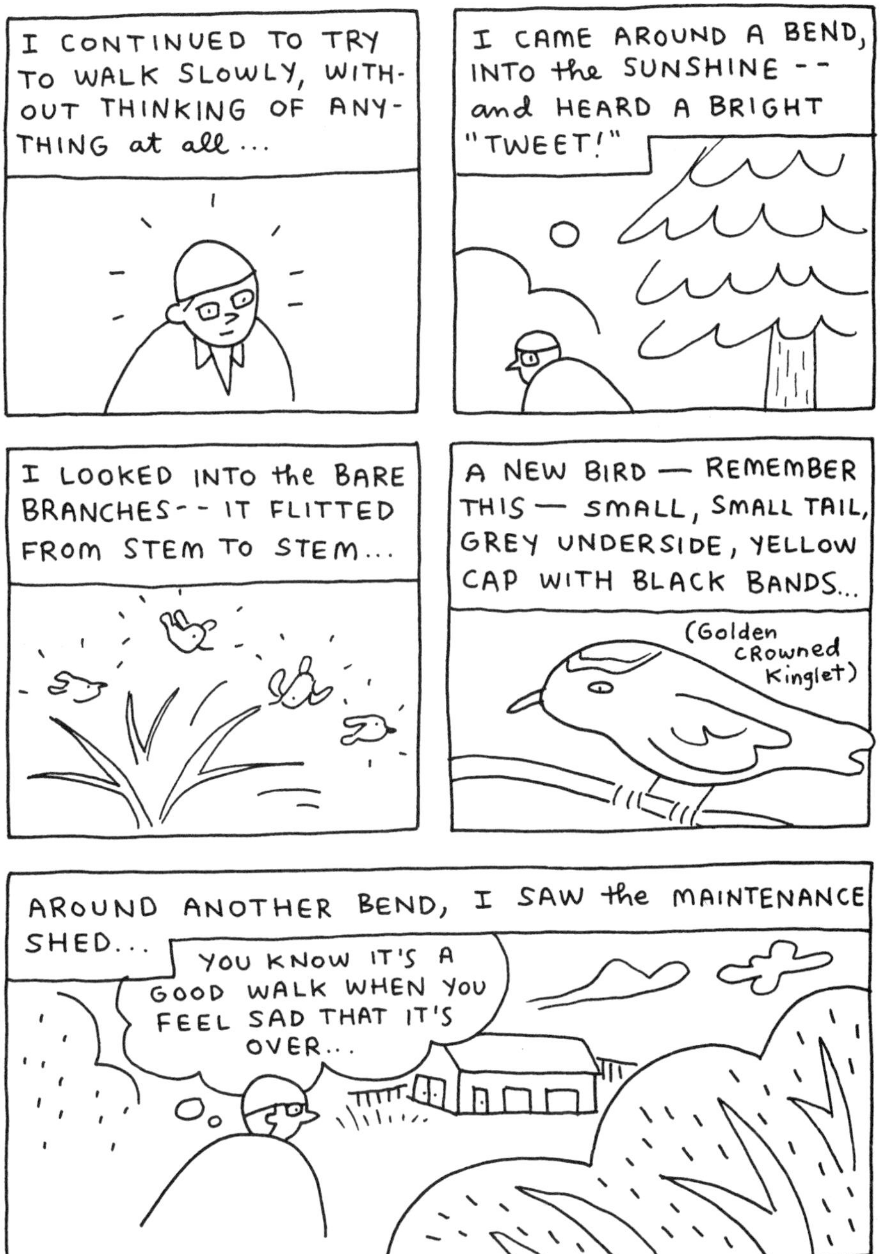
I CONTINUED TO TRY TO WALK SLOWLY, WITHOUT THINKING OF ANYTHING at all...
I CAME AROUND A BEND, INTO the SUNSHINE -- and HEARD A BRIGHT "TWEET!"
I LOOKED INTO the BARE BRANCHES-- IT FLITTED FROM STEM TO STEM...
A NEW BIRD — REMEMBER THIS — SMALL, SMALL TAIL, GREY UNDERSIDE, YELLOW CAP WITH BLACK BANDS...
(Golden CRowned Kinglet)
AROUND ANOTHER BEND, I SAW the MAINTENANCE SHED...
YOU KNOW IT'S A GOOD WALK WHEN YOU FEEL SAD THAT IT'S OVER...

Epilogue

THAT AFTERNOON I WAS IN the KITCHEN, MAKING LUNCH

mew?

I ABSENT-MINDEDLY SKRITCHED MY STOMACH, WHEN...

THE OLD TICK IN the BELLY BUTTON TRICK!!

HAPPENED 11/25/17
WRITTEN DOWN 2/6
DRAWN MARCH 2018

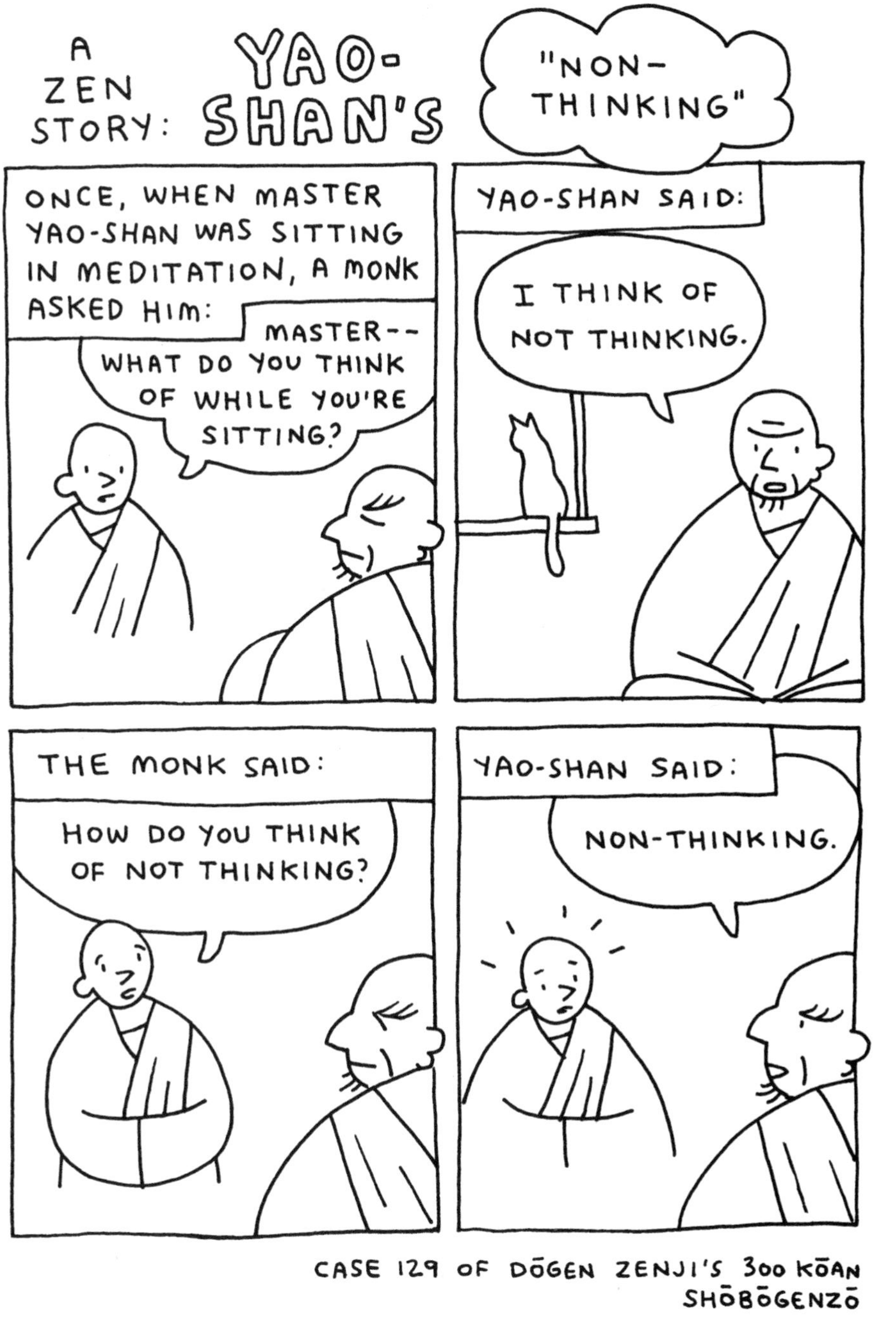
A ZEN STORY: YAO-SHAN'S "NON-THINKING"
ONCE, WHEN MASTER YAO-SHAN WAS SITTING IN MEDITATION, A MONK ASKED HIM:
MASTER-- WHAT DO YOU THINK OF WHILE YOU'RE SITTING?
YAO-SHAN SAID:
I THINK OF NOT THINKING.
THE MONK SAID:
HOW DO YOU THINK OF NOT THINKING?
YAO-SHAN SAID:
NON-THINKING.
CASE 129 OF DŌGEN ZENJI'S 300 KŌAN SHŌBŌGENZŌ

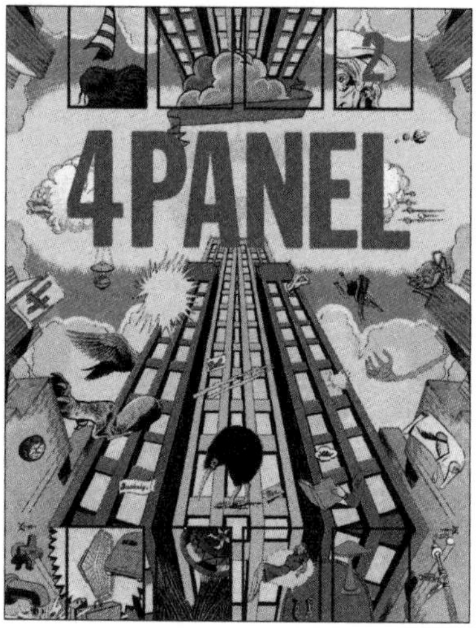
4PANEL

Why Don't We Come Together (*Excerpt*)

ERIK NEBEL

originally published in

4PANEL2

POPNOIR EDITIONS

7.5 x 9.5 inches • 80 pages

Biography

Erik Nebel recently finished drawing three graphic novels: *War and Peace* (based on the novel by Tolstoy), *Dead Souls* (based on the novel by Gogol), and *Come* (inspired by the pulp fiction of Leigh Brackett and Catherine Lucille Moore).
eriknebel.com

Statement

This comic was published in *4PANEL2* (the second volume of the *4PANEL* comics anthology), as part of The 4PANEL Project. The basic premise of this project is that the editor, Mark Laliberte, invites artists from around the world to draw comic strips using the same four-panel template. Over a hundred creators have contributed so far, and the strips are published in the 4PANEL anthologies, in *CAROUSEL* magazine (Toronto), and online at 4panel.ca.

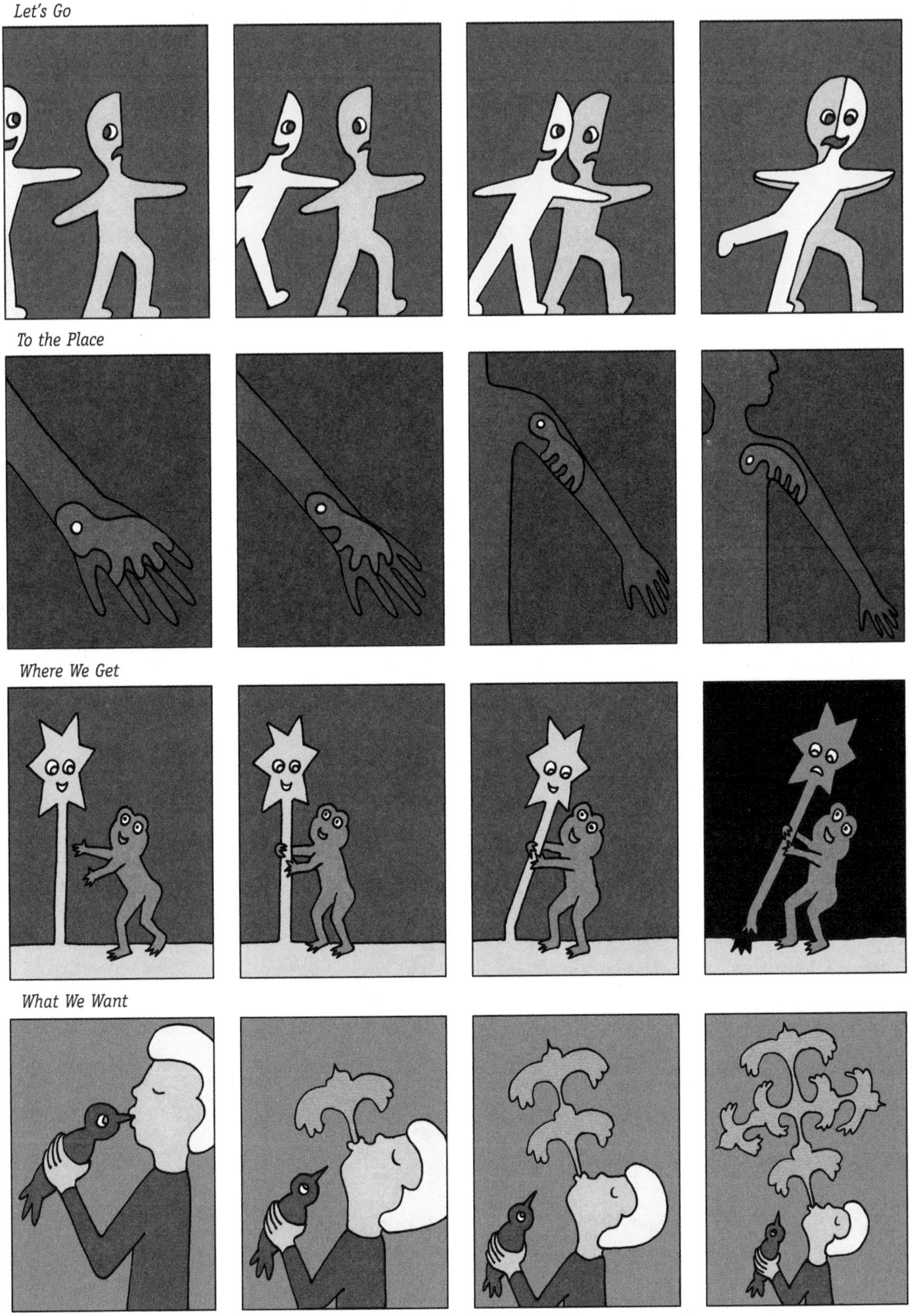
Let's Go
To the Place
Where We Get
What We Want

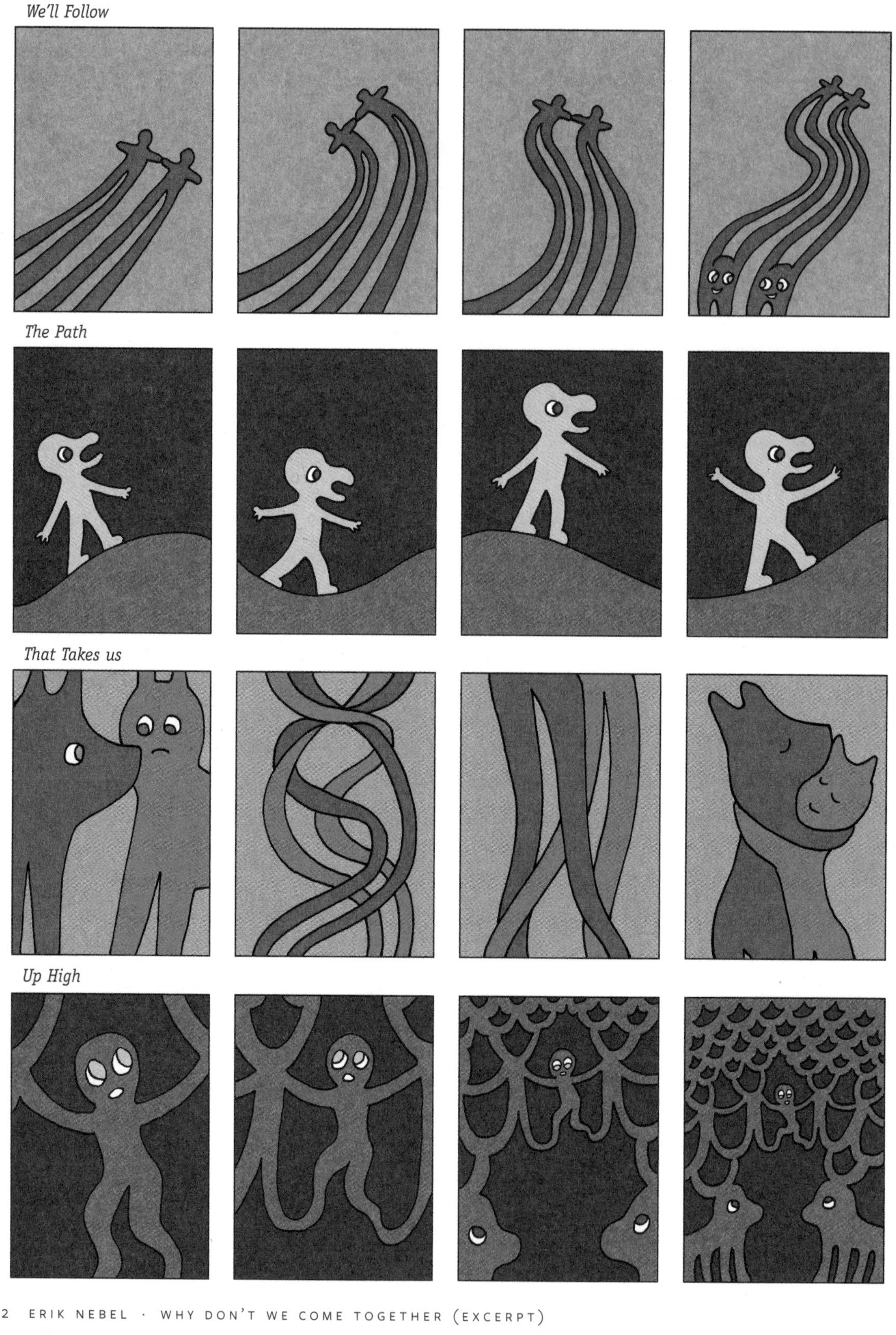
We'll Follow
The Path
That Takes us
Up High

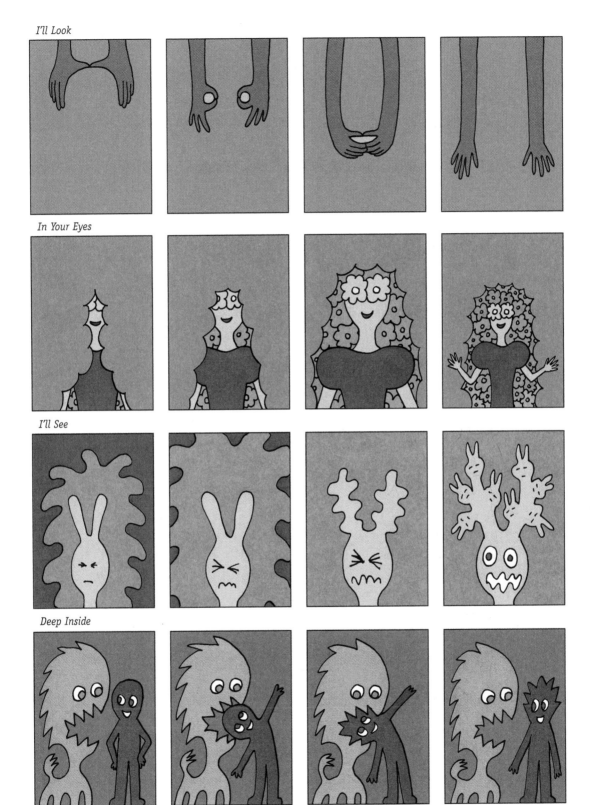

I'll Look

In Your Eyes

I'll See

Deep Inside

You Are Pretty

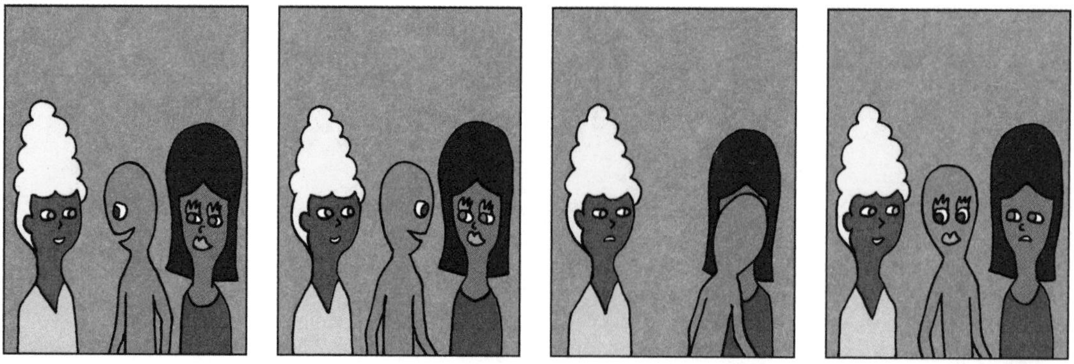

You Are Strong

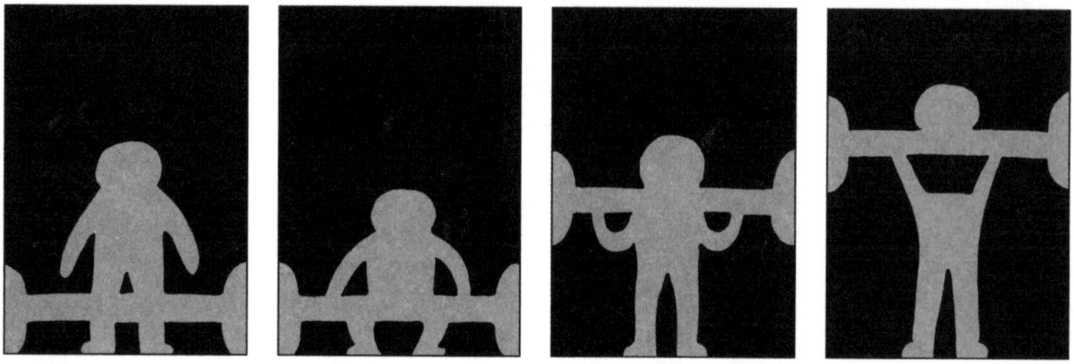

All Is Bright

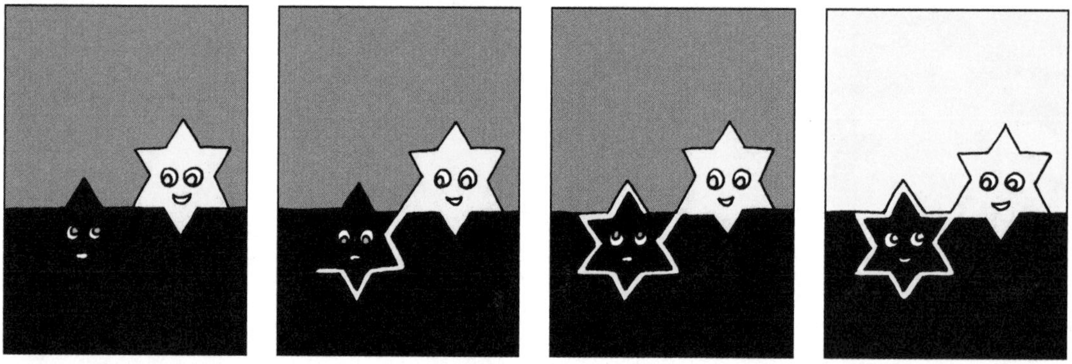

All Is Calm

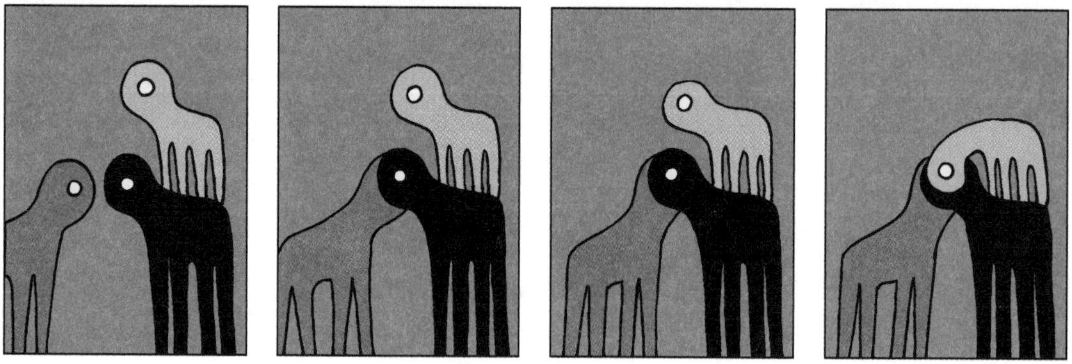

Everything Will Be Okay

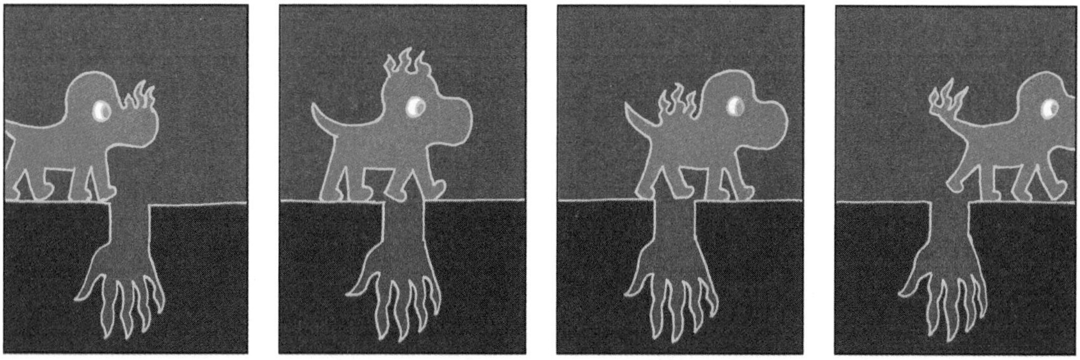

All The Bad Will Go Away

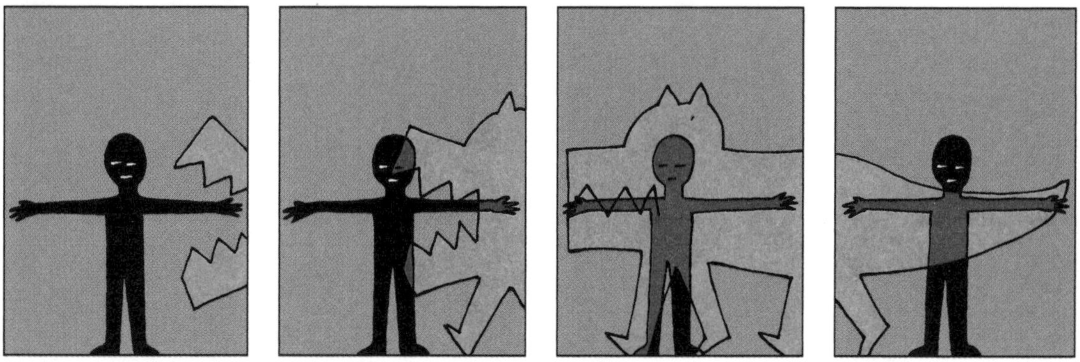

Everyone Is On Our Side

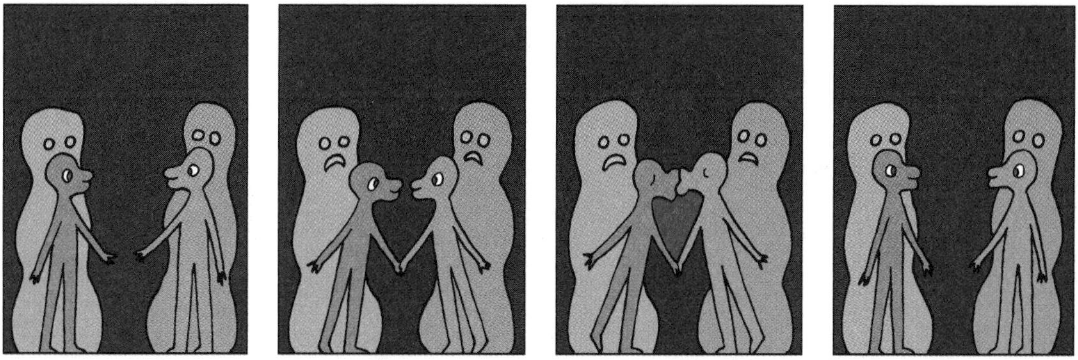

Nothing Can Go Wrong

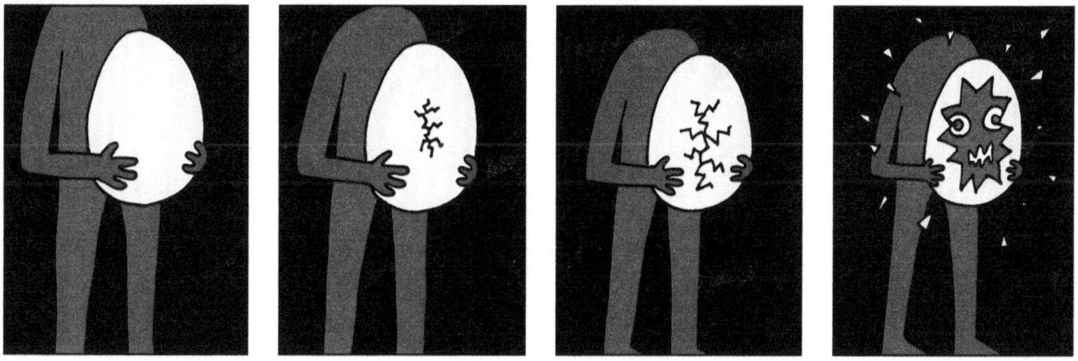

Here Is The End Of All Our Problems

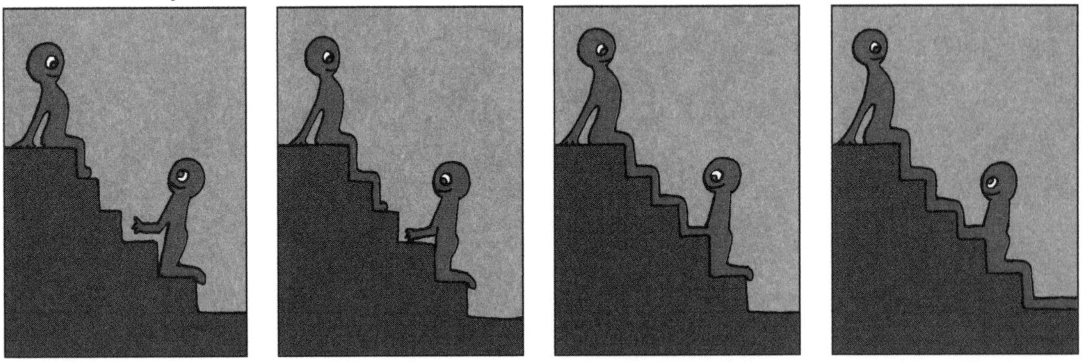

Here Is The Answer To All Our Prayers

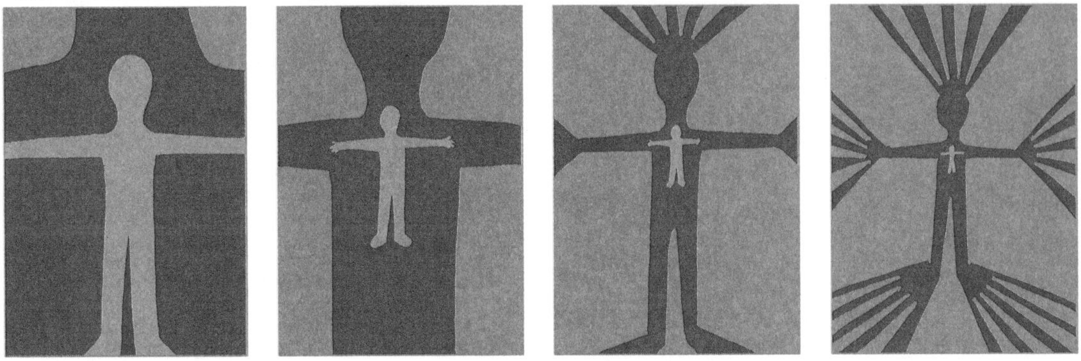

Goodbye To Pain

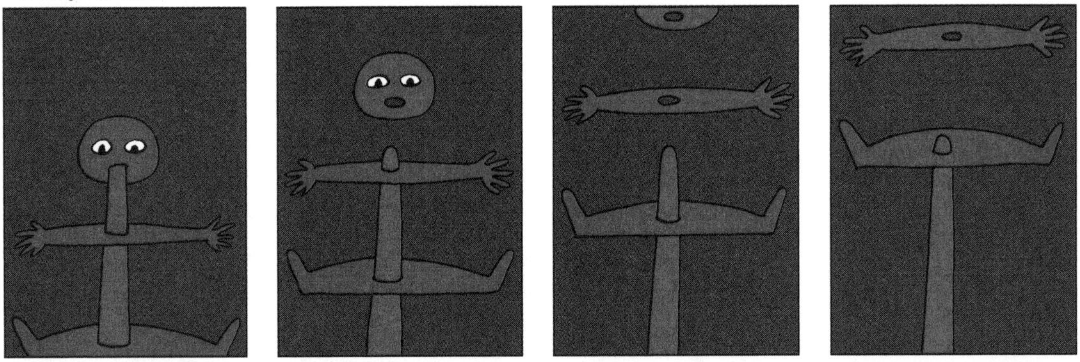

Farewell To Despair

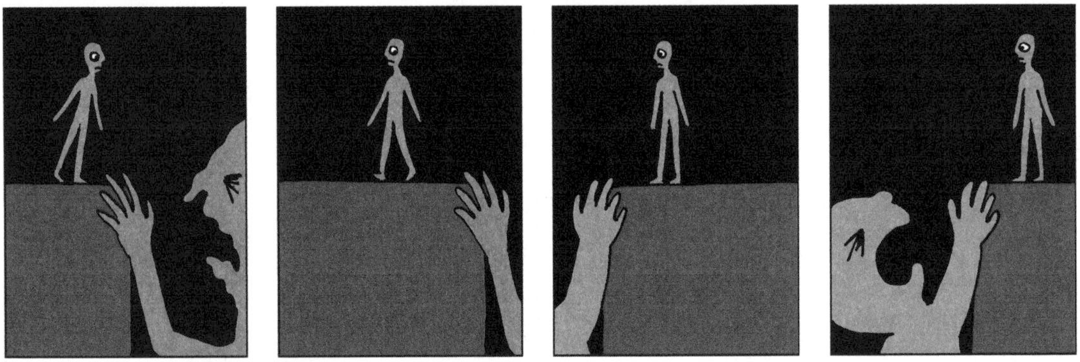

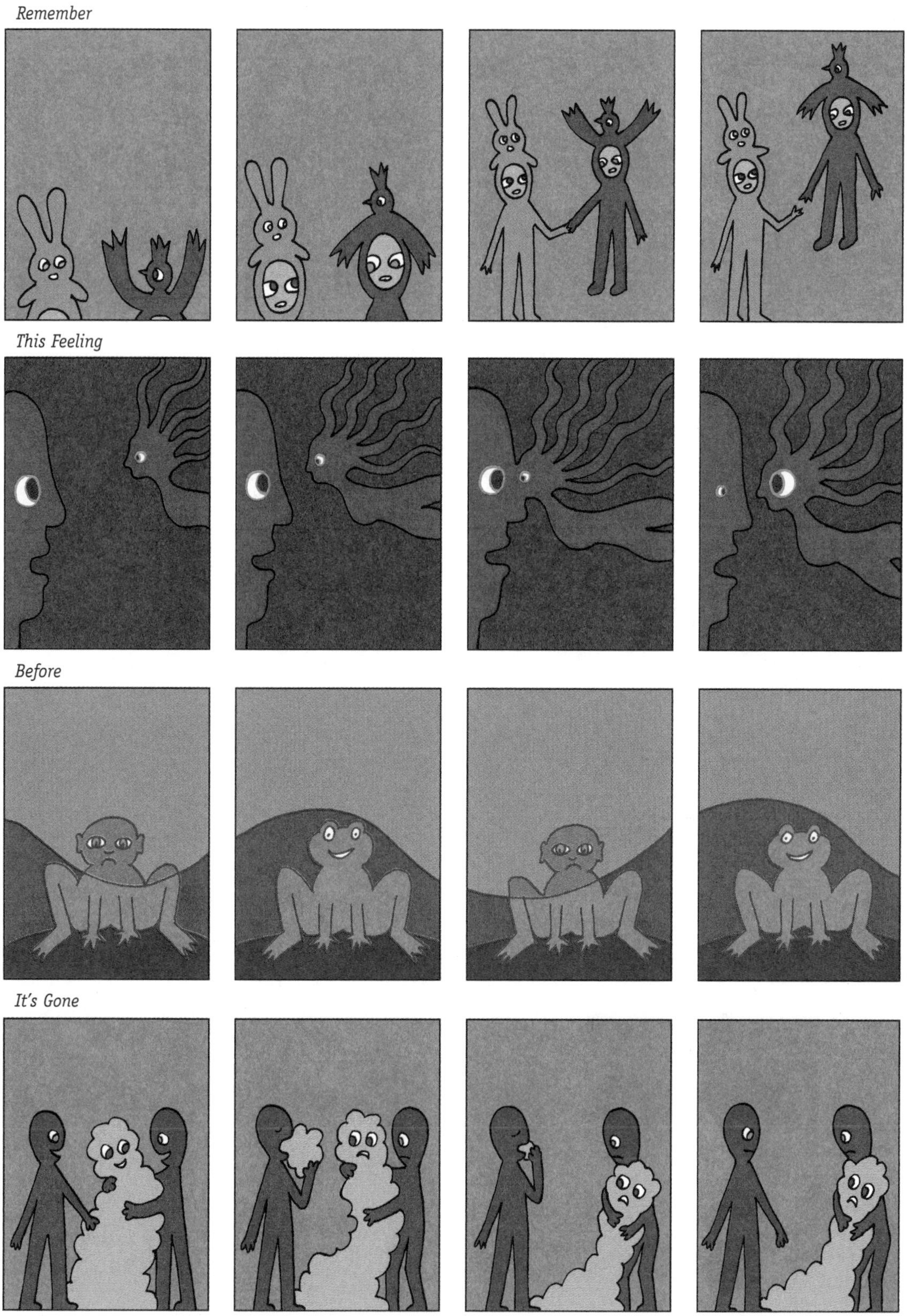
Remember
This Feeling
Before
It's Gone

Thanks

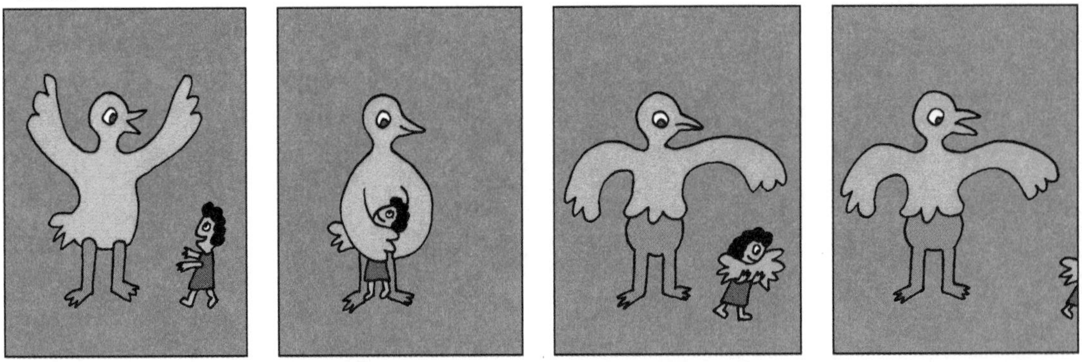

For The Fun

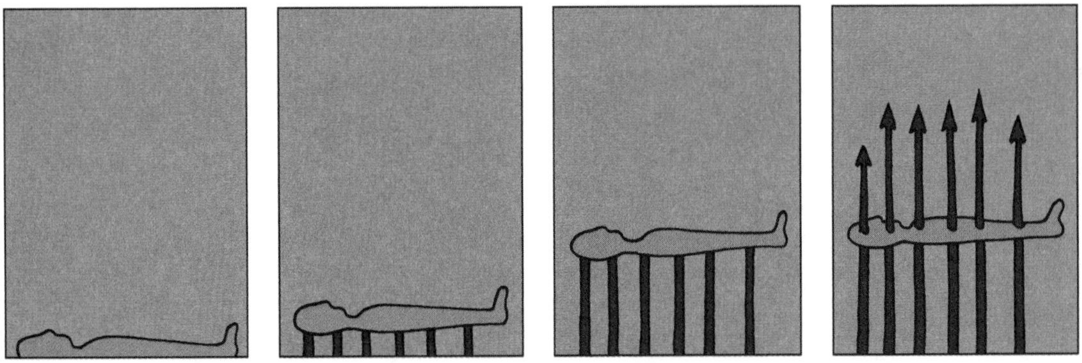

Don't Say That

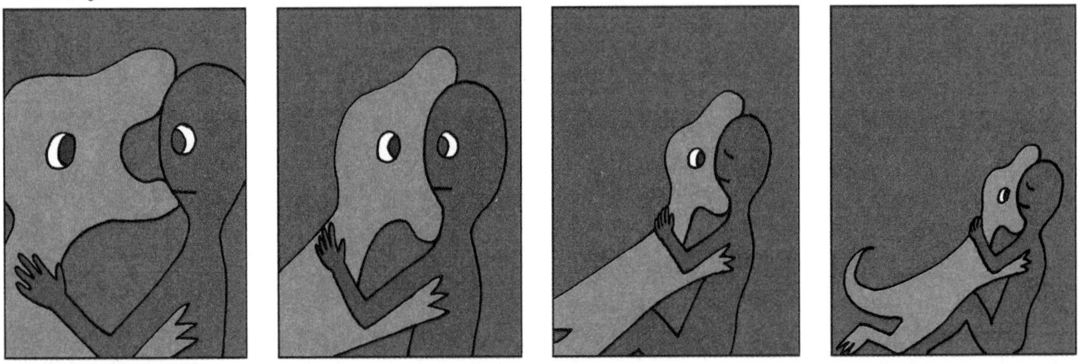

We're Done

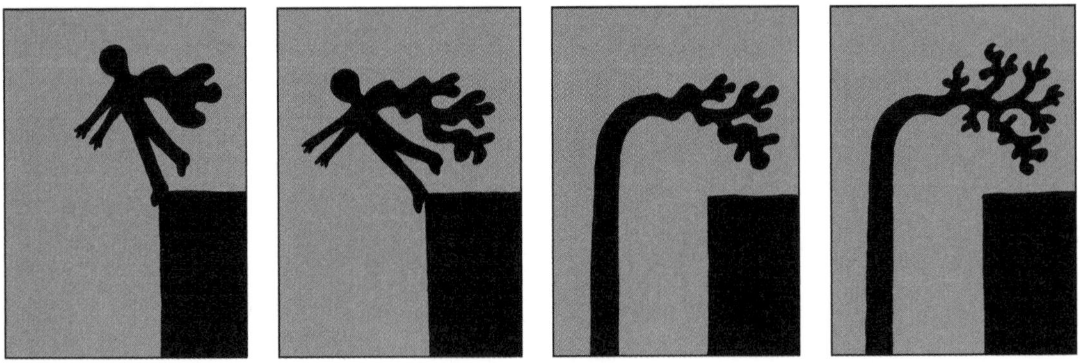

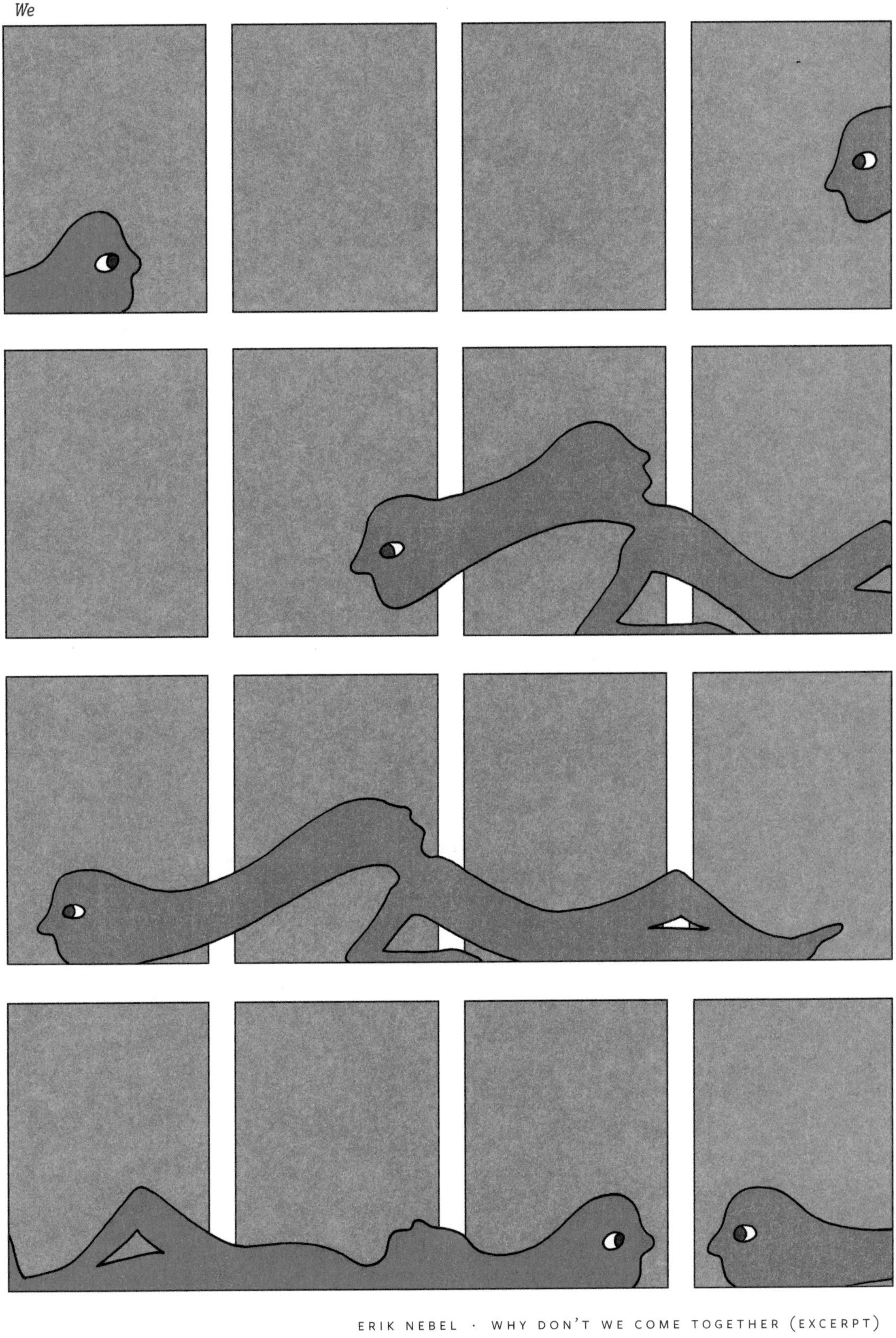

We

Could Be

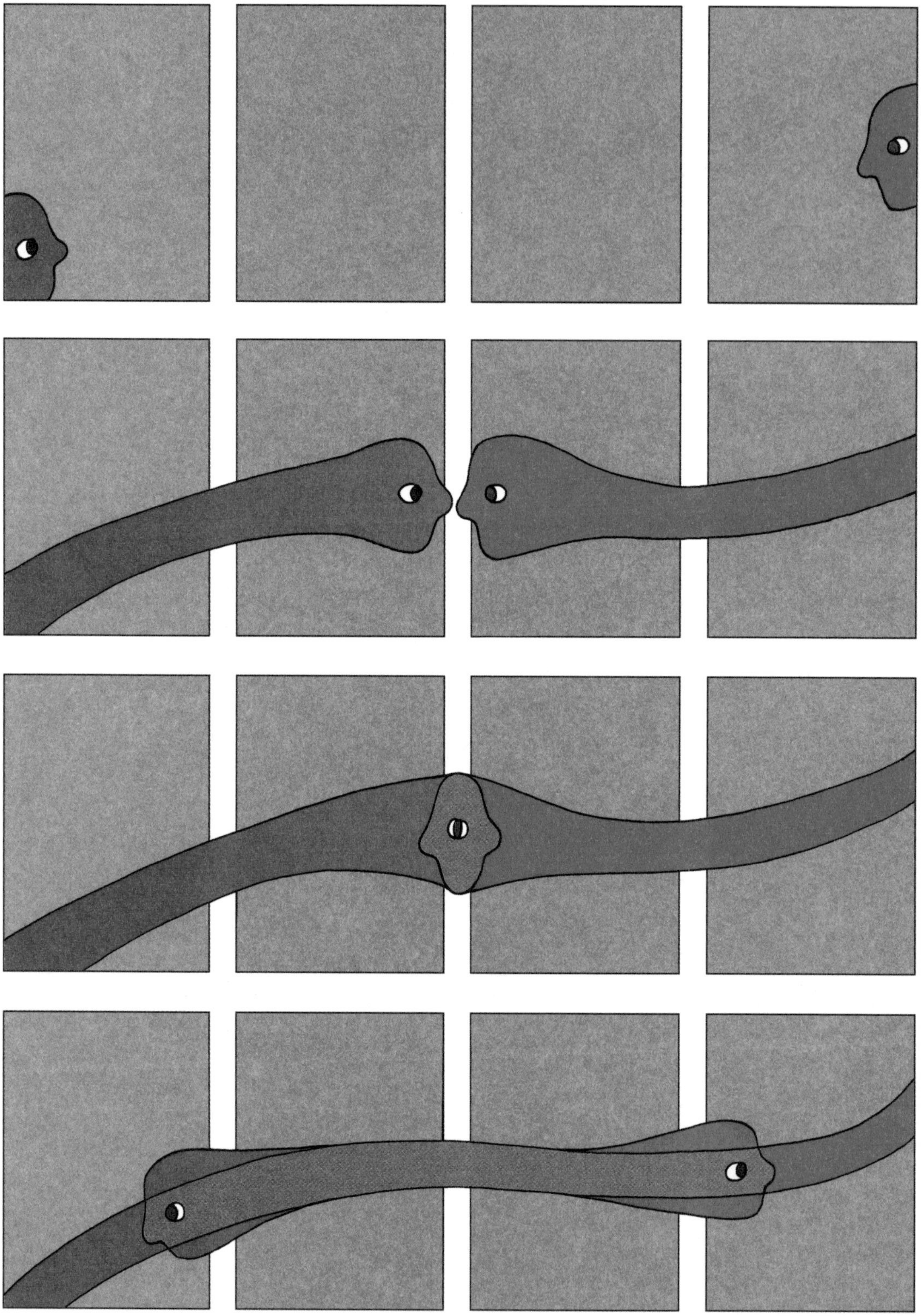

Together

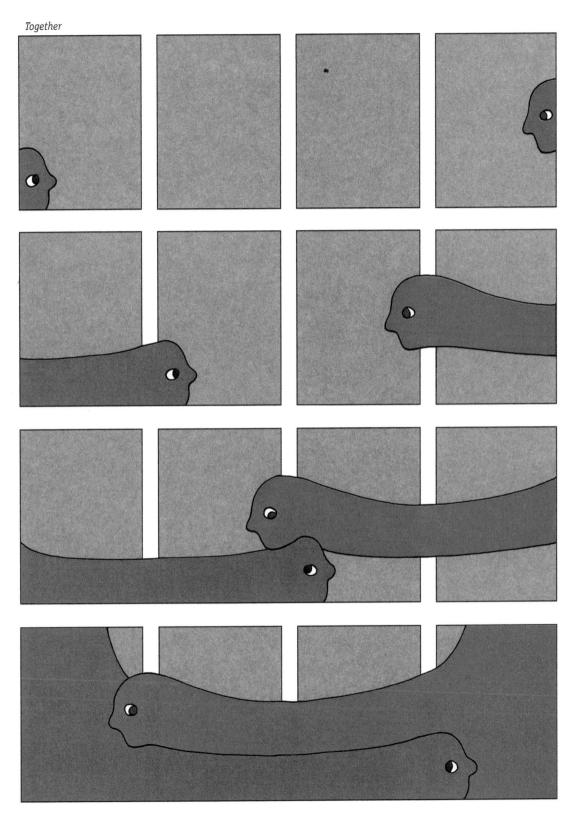

Forever

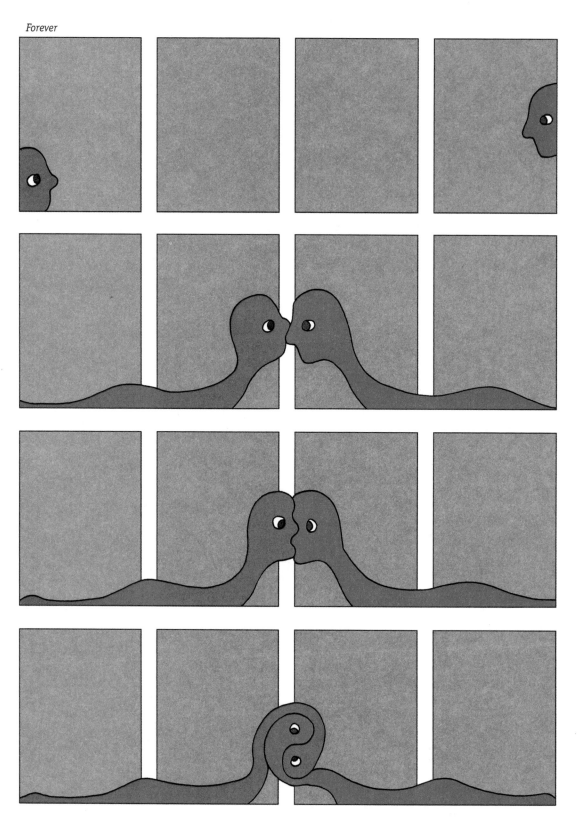

Small Mistakes Make Big Problems

SOPHIA FOSTER-DIMINO

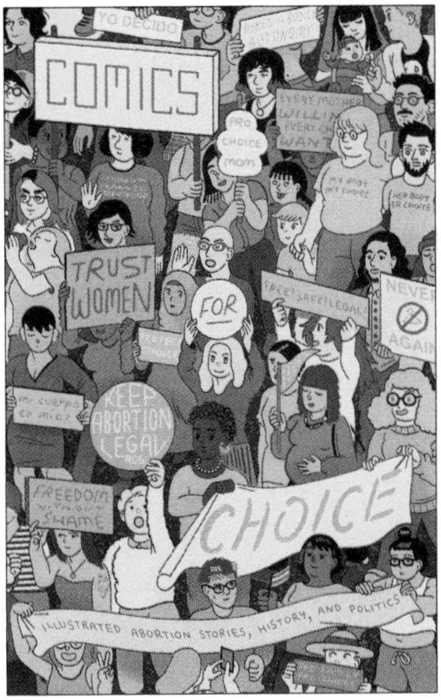
COMICS
FOR
CHOICE
ILLUSTRATED ABORTION STORIES, HISTORY, AND POLITICS
YO DECIDO
TRUST WOMEN
KEEP ABORTION LEGAL
FREEDOM WITHOUT SHAME

originally published in

Comics for Choice

HAZEL NEWLEVANT

6.625 x 10.25 inches • 300 pages

Biography

Sophia Foster-Dimino is a cartoonist, illustrator, and educator living in Oakland, California. She is the recipient of four Ignatz Awards, including the Outstanding Collection award for her collected minicomic series *Sex Fantasy,* published by Koyama Press. Her comics have also been published by Shortbox and McSweeney's. She teaches in the illustration department at California College of the Arts, and, in her free time, she is an avid long-distance cyclist.
hellophia.com

Statement

This comic was originally published in *Comics for Choice,* an anthology of abortion stories benefitting the National Network of Abortion Funds. I was approached by editors Hazel Newlevant, Whit Taylor, and Ø.K. Fox to draw the cover and submit a comic for the anthology in late 2016. The presidential election of 2016 was the galvanizing impetus for the anthology's creation—the editors and contributors felt fear for the future, and a powerful need to reassert that abortion is an inalienable human right. I would not have had the strength to tell this story outside the context of *Comics for Choice.* The isolating stigma surrounding abortion ensured I kept mine a secret for nearly a decade. In 2018, this comic was nominated for an Eisner Award and I published it online with my editors' blessings. I was contacted by countless cis women, nonbinary people, and trans men who were grateful to see an experience similar to theirs openly depicted. I wish to thank my editors for bringing me together with the other contributors in the fight for abortion access.

Content warning: This comic depicts nudity, sexuality, abusive relationships, and abortion.

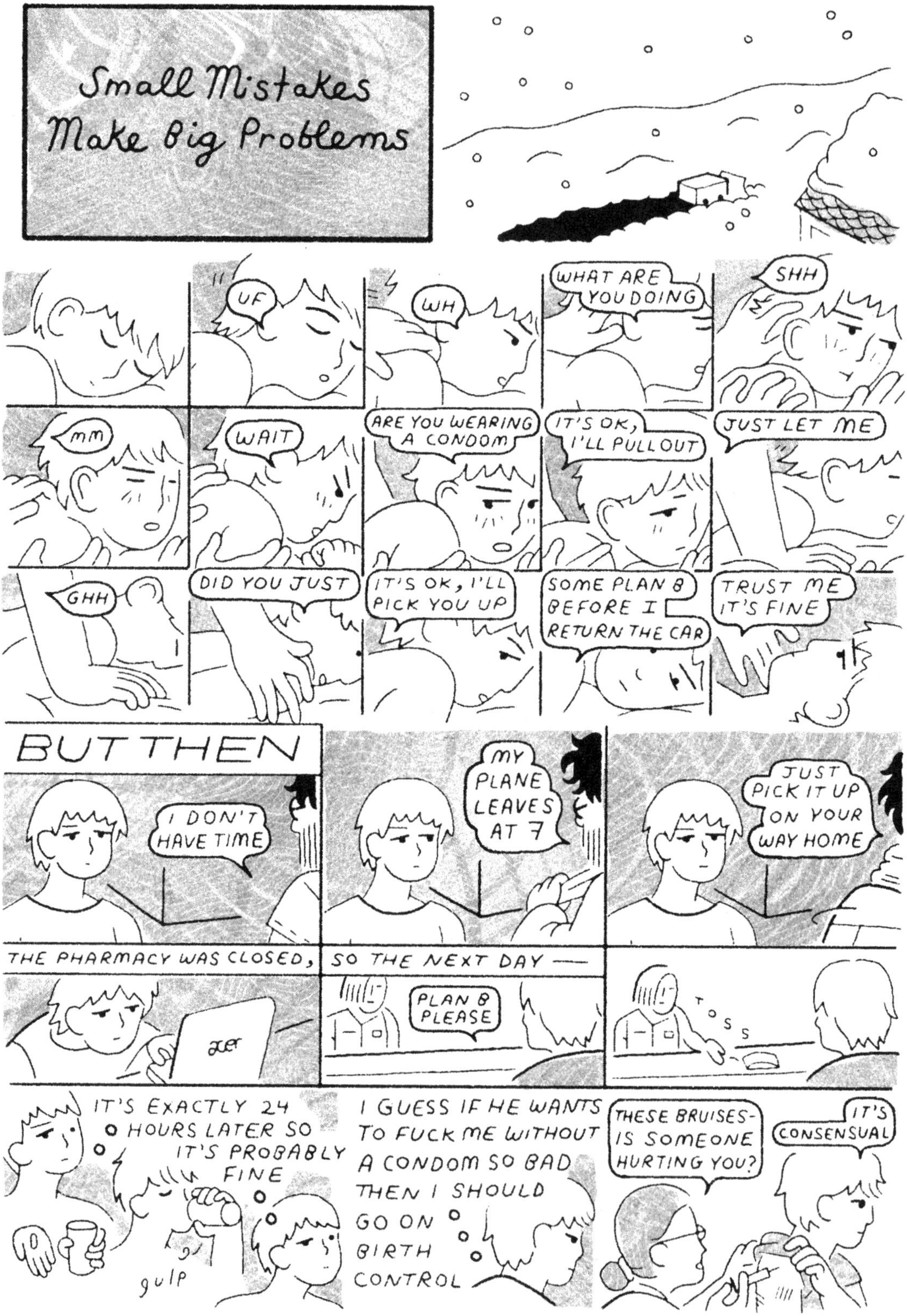

Small Mistakes Make Big Problems
UF
WH
WHAT ARE YOU DOING
SHH
mm
WAIT
ARE YOU WEARING A CONDOM
IT'S OK, I'LL PULL OUT
JUST LET ME
GHH
DID YOU JUST
IT'S OK, I'LL PICK YOU UP
SOME PLAN B BEFORE I RETURN THE CAR
TRUST ME IT'S FINE
BUT THEN
I DON'T HAVE TIME
MY PLANE LEAVES AT 7
JUST PICK IT UP ON YOUR WAY HOME
THE PHARMACY WAS CLOSED,
SO THE NEXT DAY —
PLAN B PLEASE
TOSS
IT'S EXACTLY 24 HOURS LATER SO IT'S PROBABLY FINE
gulp
I GUESS IF HE WANTS TO FUCK ME WITHOUT A CONDOM SO BAD THEN I SHOULD GO ON BIRTH CONTROL
THESE BRUISES- IS SOMEONE HURTING YOU?
IT'S CONSENSUAL

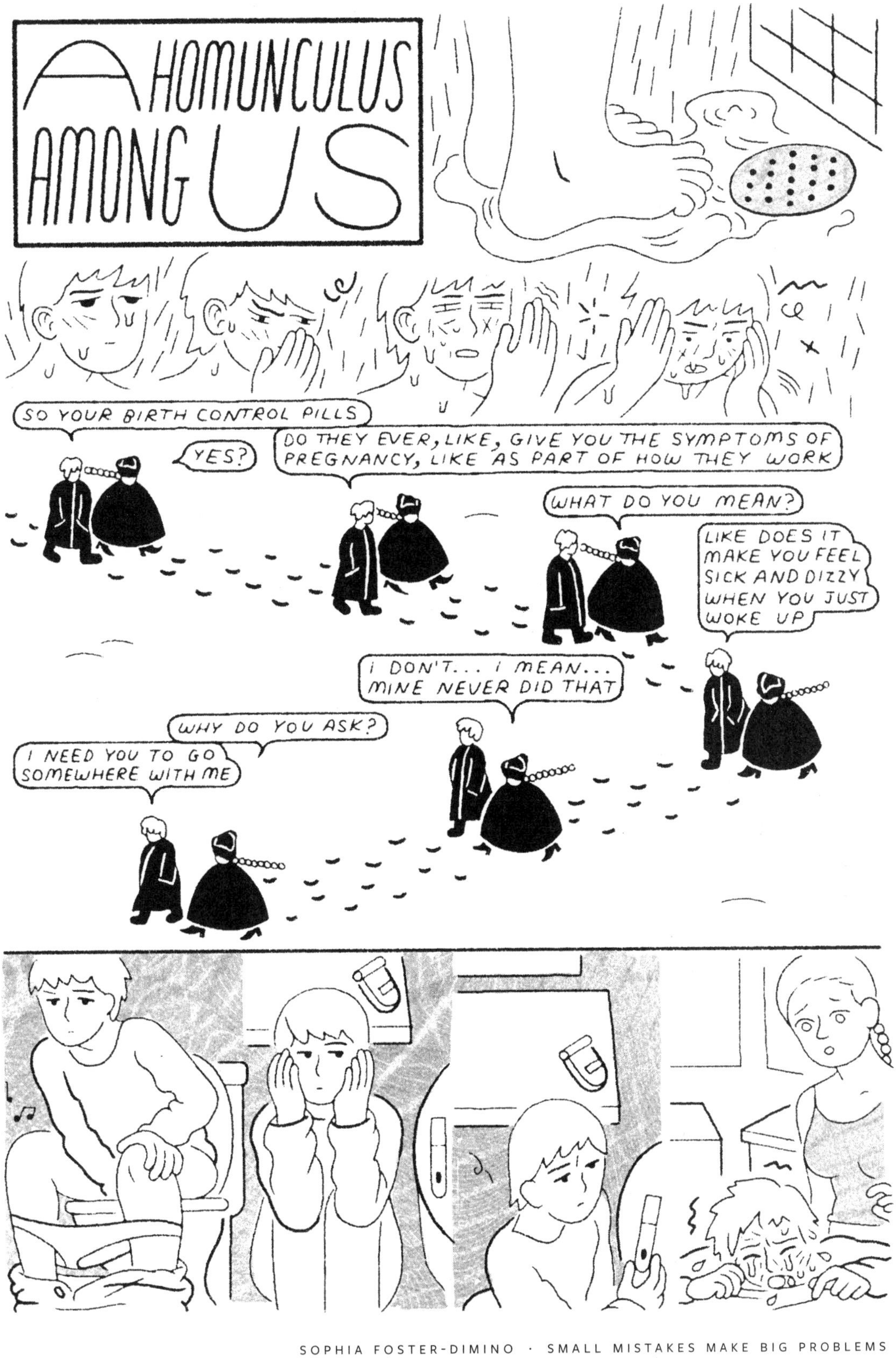
A HOMUNCULUS AMONG US
SO YOUR BIRTH CONTROL PILLS
YES?
DO THEY EVER, LIKE, GIVE YOU THE SYMPTOMS OF PREGNANCY, LIKE AS PART OF HOW THEY WORK
WHAT DO YOU MEAN?
LIKE DOES IT MAKE YOU FEEL SICK AND DIZZY WHEN YOU JUST WOKE UP
I DON'T... I MEAN... MINE NEVER DID THAT
WHY DO YOU ASK?
I NEED YOU TO GO SOMEWHERE WITH ME

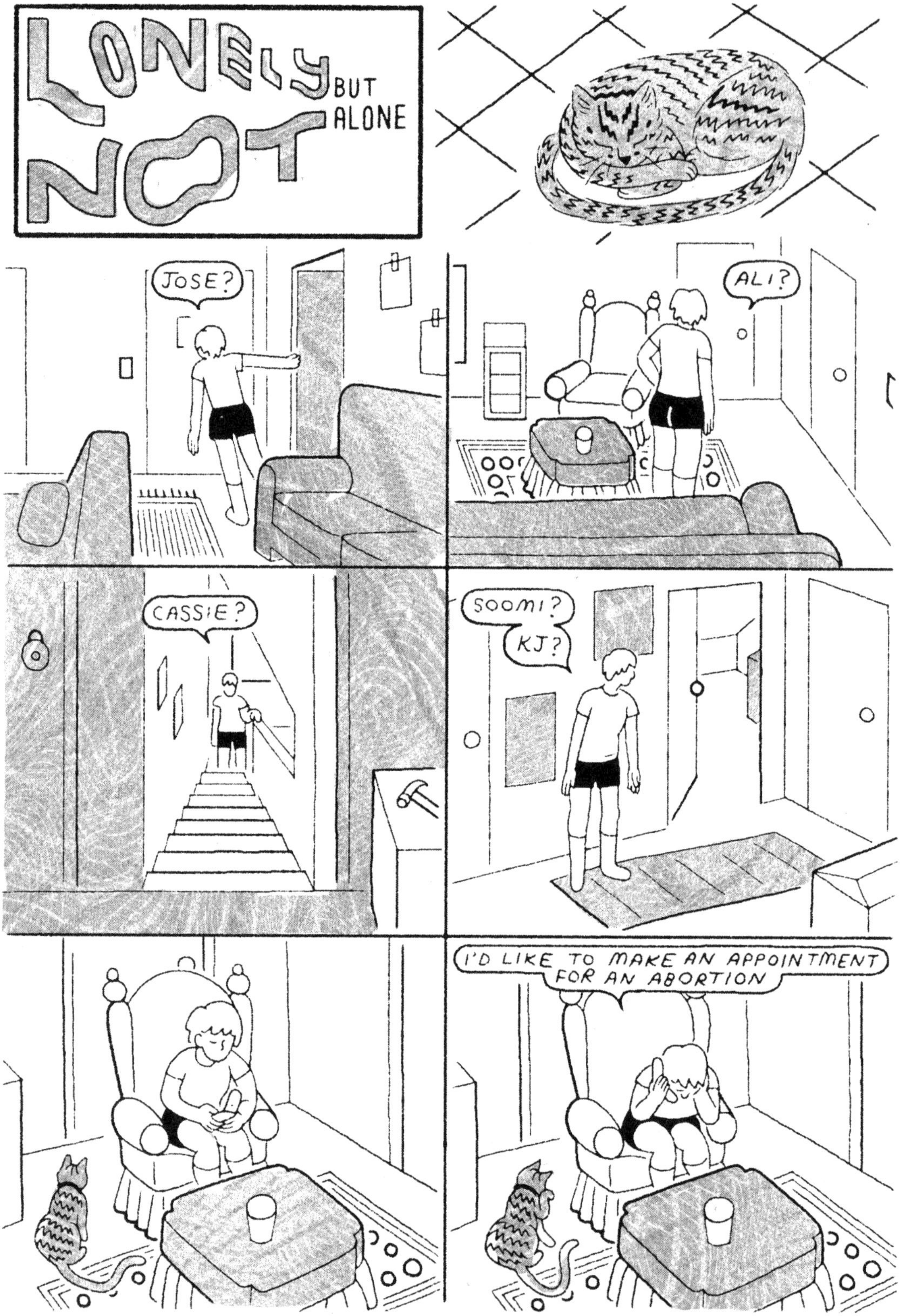
LONELY BUT NOT ALONE
JOSE?
ALI?
CASSIE?
SOOMI?
KJ?
I'D LIKE TO MAKE AN APPOINTMENT FOR AN ABORTION

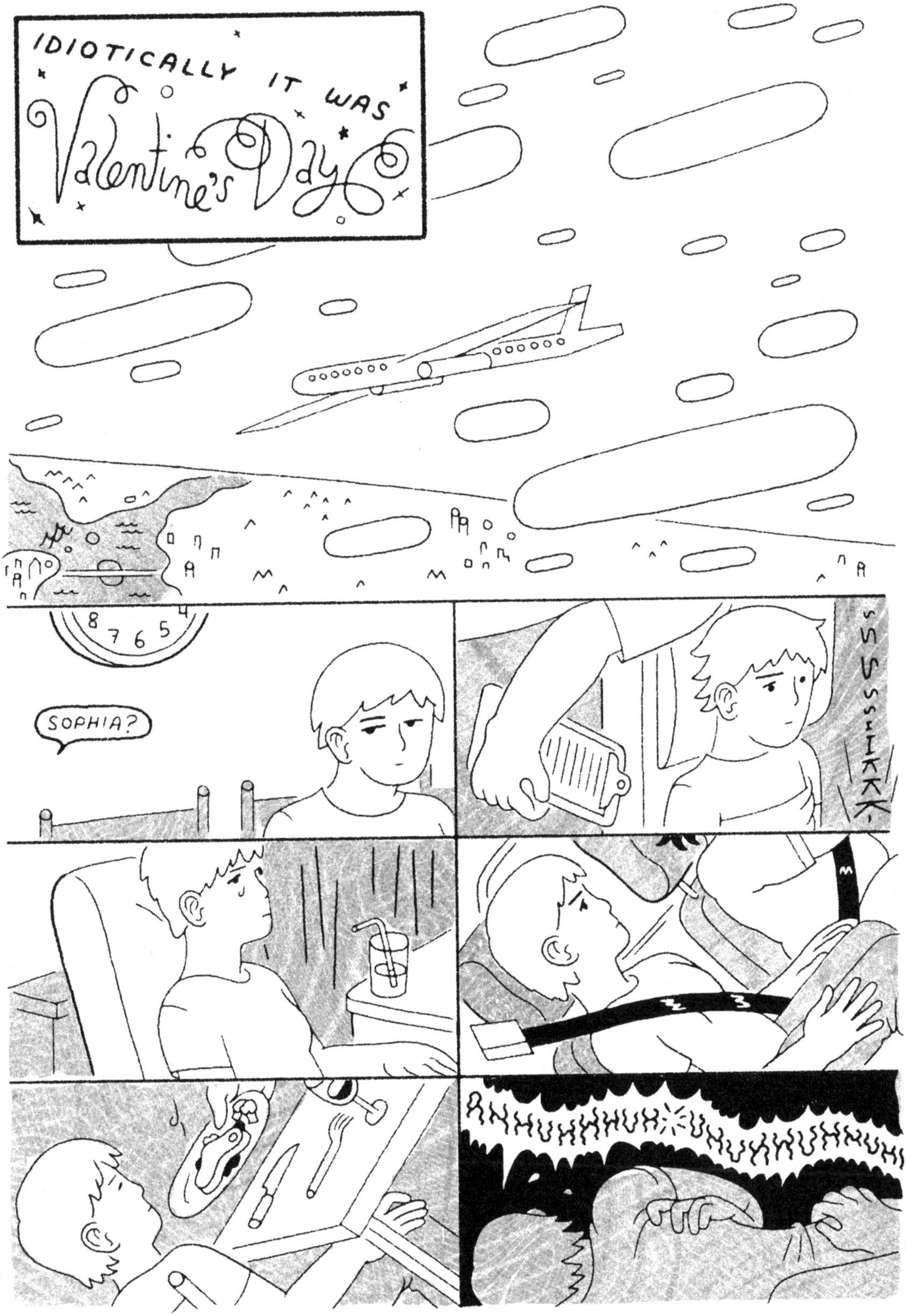
IDIOTICALLY IT WAS
Valentine's Day
SOPHIA?
SSSSSHIKKK-

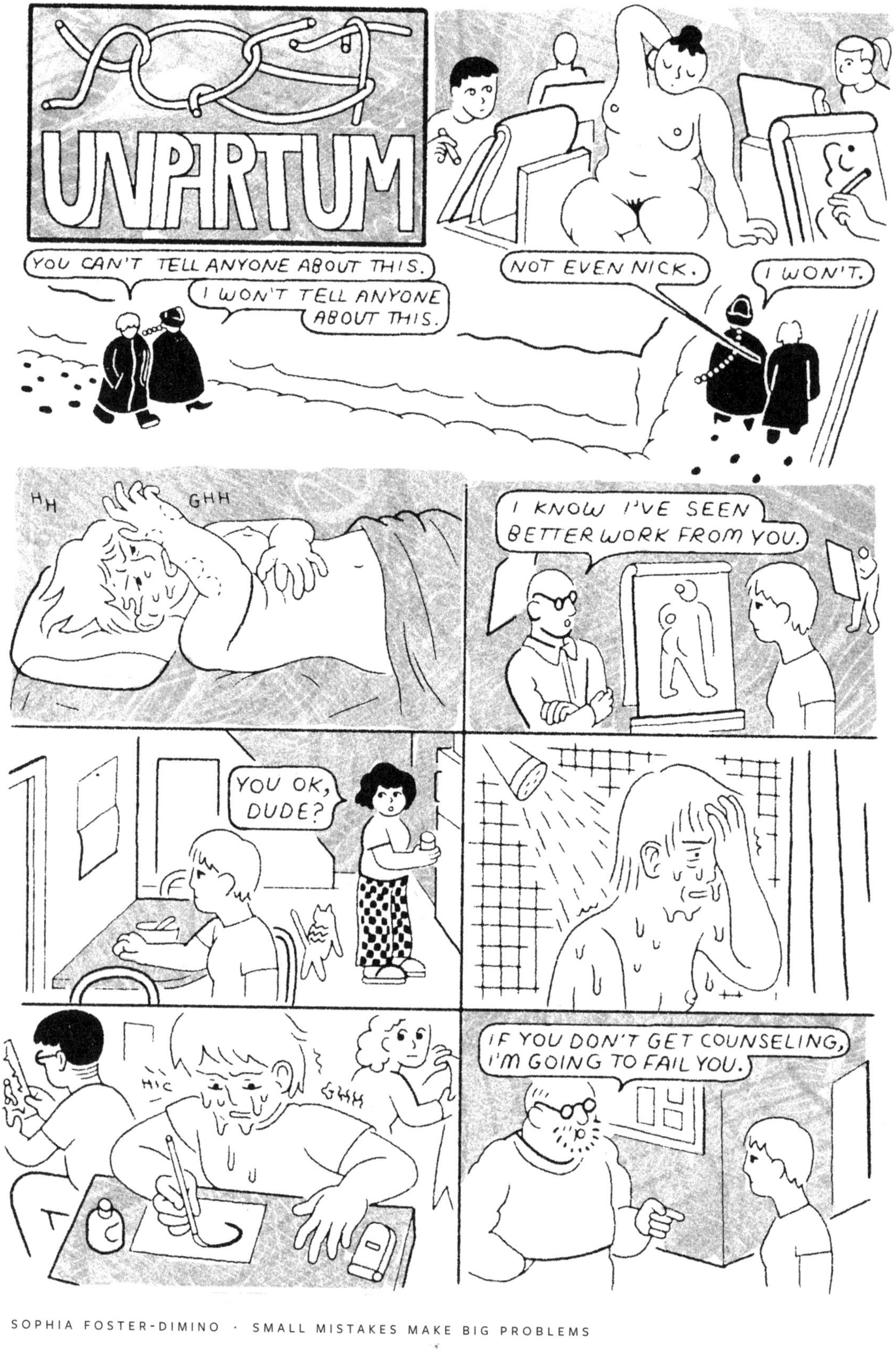
UNPARTUM
YOU CAN'T TELL ANYONE ABOUT THIS.
I WON'T TELL ANYONE ABOUT THIS.
NOT EVEN NICK.
I WON'T.
HH
GHH
I KNOW I'VE SEEN BETTER WORK FROM YOU.
YOU OK, DUDE?
HIC
GHH
IF YOU DON'T GET COUNSELING, I'M GOING TO FAIL YOU.

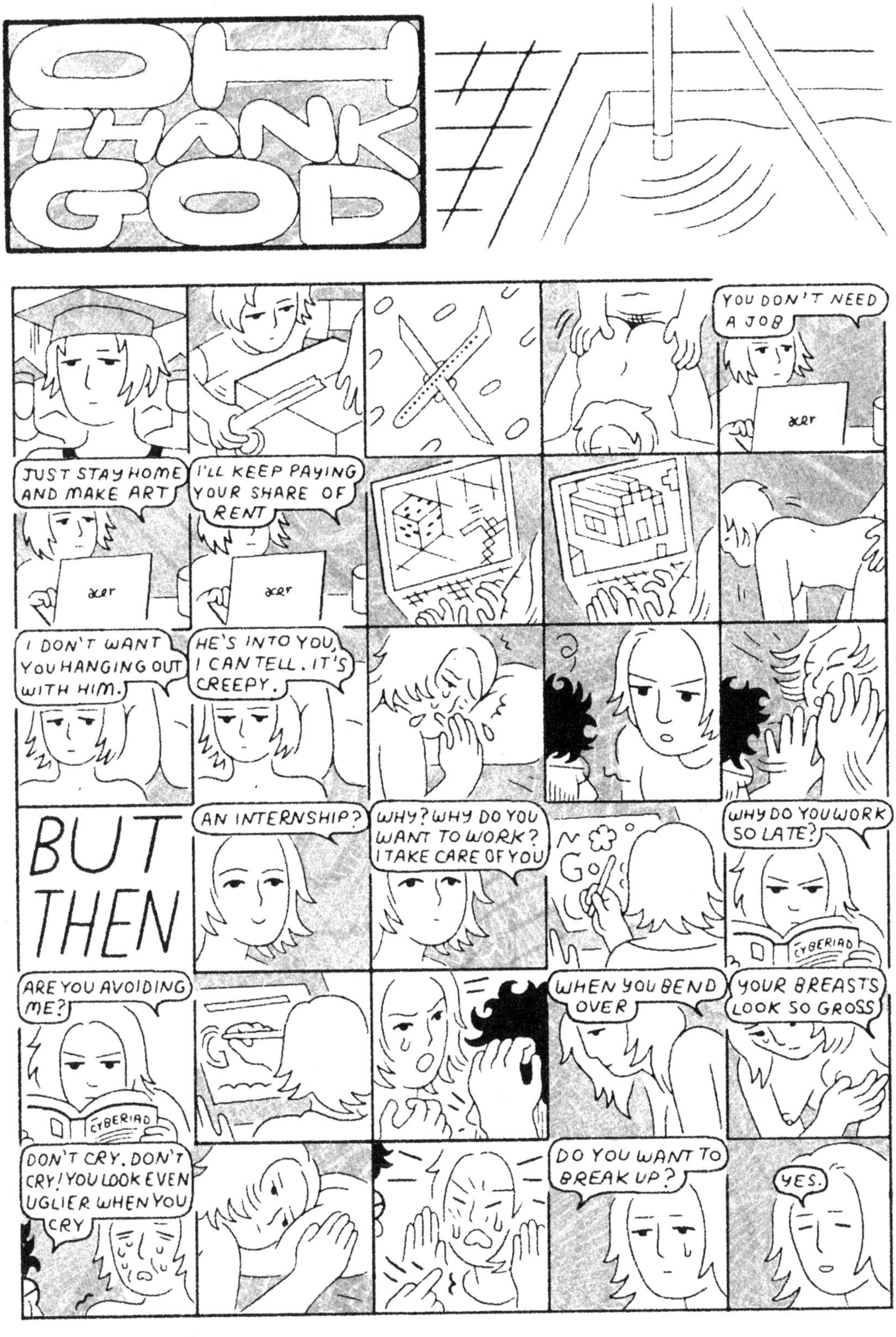
OH THANK GOD
YOU DON'T NEED A JOB
JUST STAY HOME AND MAKE ART
I'LL KEEP PAYING YOUR SHARE OF RENT
I DON'T WANT YOU HANGING OUT WITH HIM.
HE'S INTO YOU, I CAN TELL. IT'S CREEPY.
BUT THEN
AN INTERNSHIP?
WHY? WHY DO YOU WANT TO WORK? I TAKE CARE OF YOU
WHY DO YOU WORK SO LATE?
CYBERIAD
ARE YOU AVOIDING ME?
CYBERIAD
WHEN YOU BEND OVER
YOUR BREASTS LOOK SO GROSS
DON'T CRY. DON'T CRY! YOU LOOK EVEN UGLIER WHEN YOU CRY
DO YOU WANT TO BREAK UP?
YES.

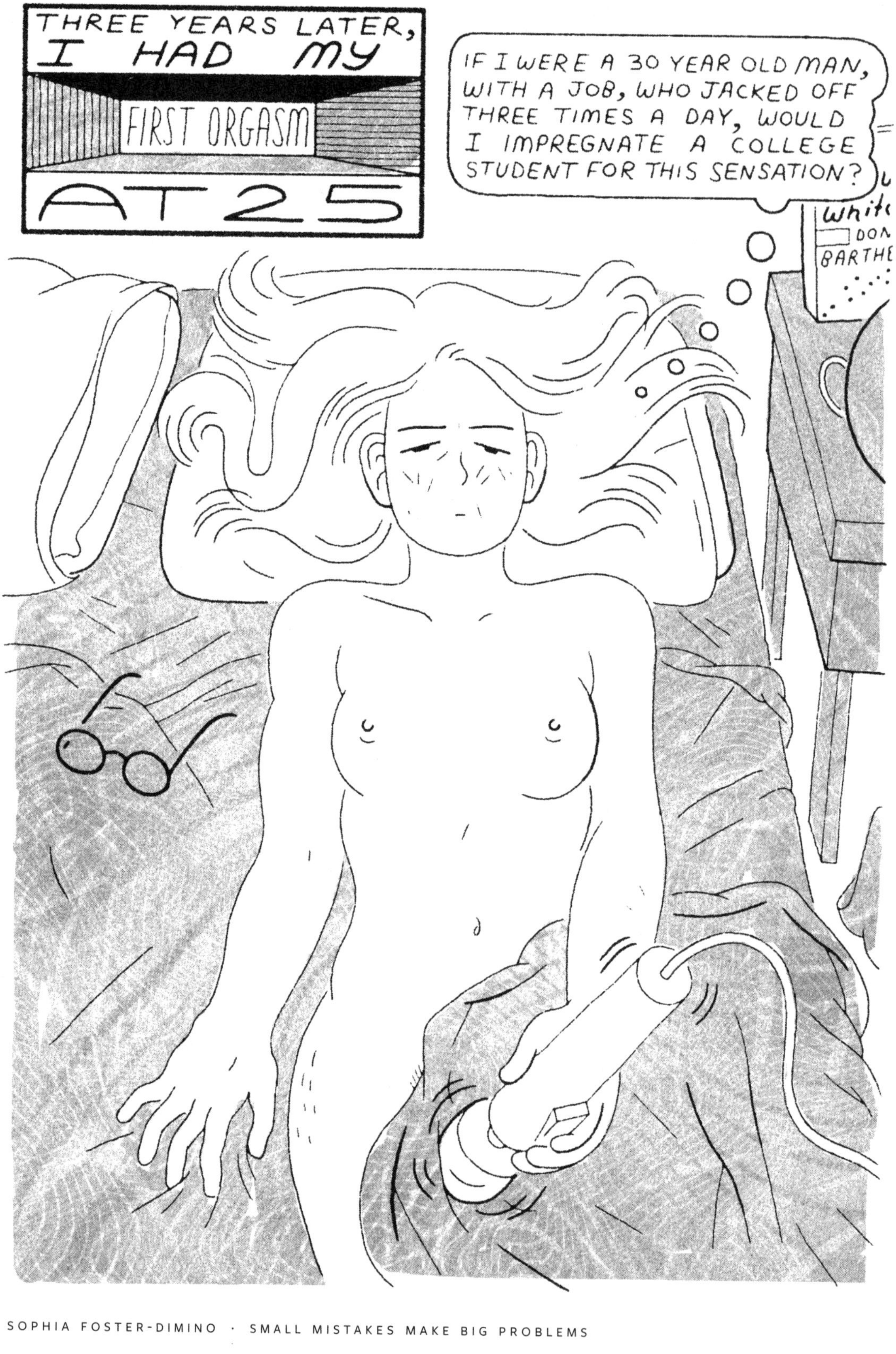
THREE YEARS LATER, I HAD MY
FIRST ORGASM
AT 25
IF I WERE A 30 YEAR OLD MAN, WITH A JOB, WHO JACKED OFF THREE TIMES A DAY, WOULD I IMPREGNATE A COLLEGE STUDENT FOR THIS SENSATION?

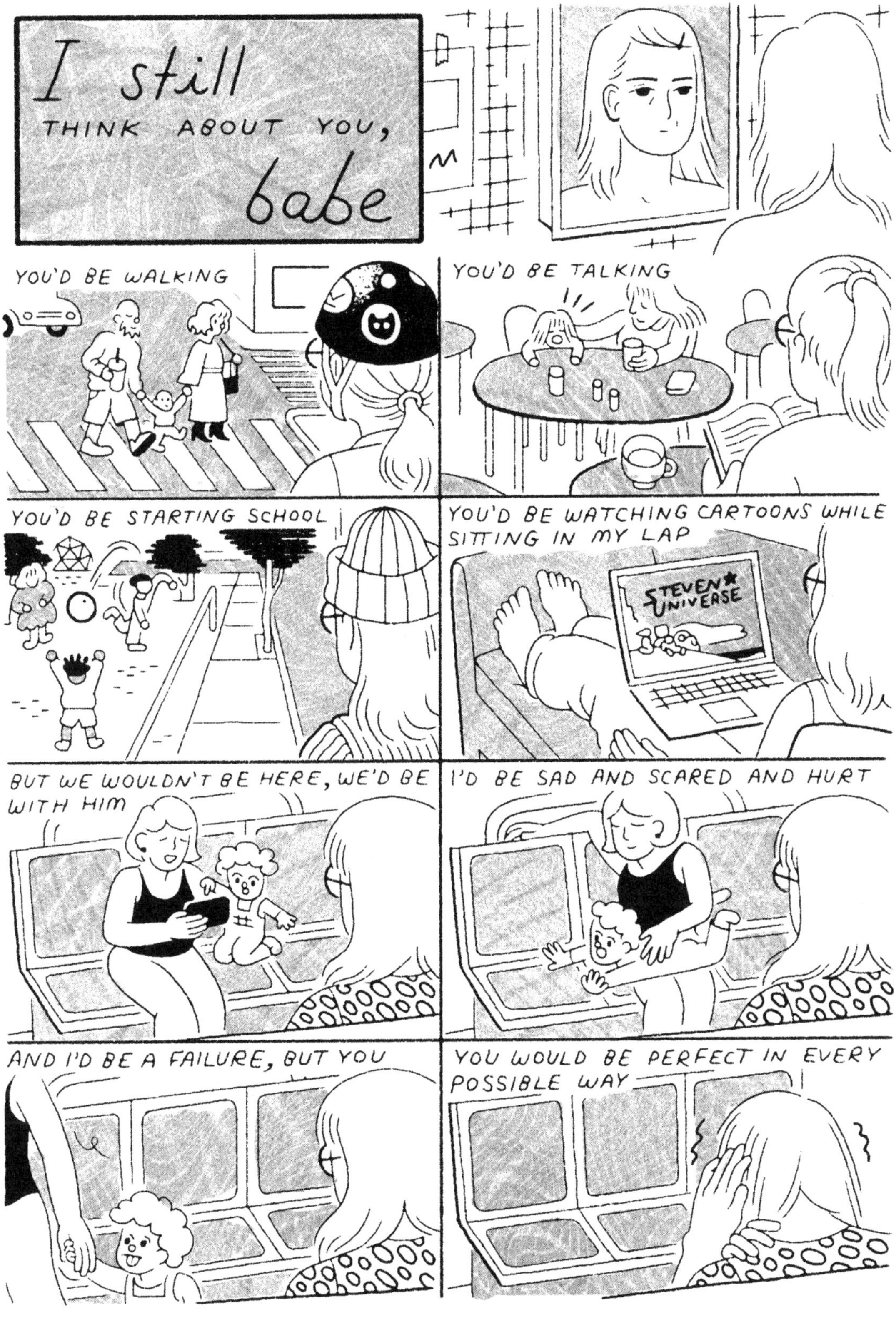
I still think about you, babe
YOU'D BE WALKING
YOU'D BE TALKING
YOU'D BE STARTING SCHOOL
YOU'D BE WATCHING CARTOONS WHILE SITTING IN MY LAP
STEVEN UNIVERSE
BUT WE WOULDN'T BE HERE, WE'D BE WITH HIM
I'D BE SAD AND SCARED AND HURT
AND I'D BE A FAILURE, BUT YOU
YOU WOULD BE PERFECT IN EVERY POSSIBLE WAY

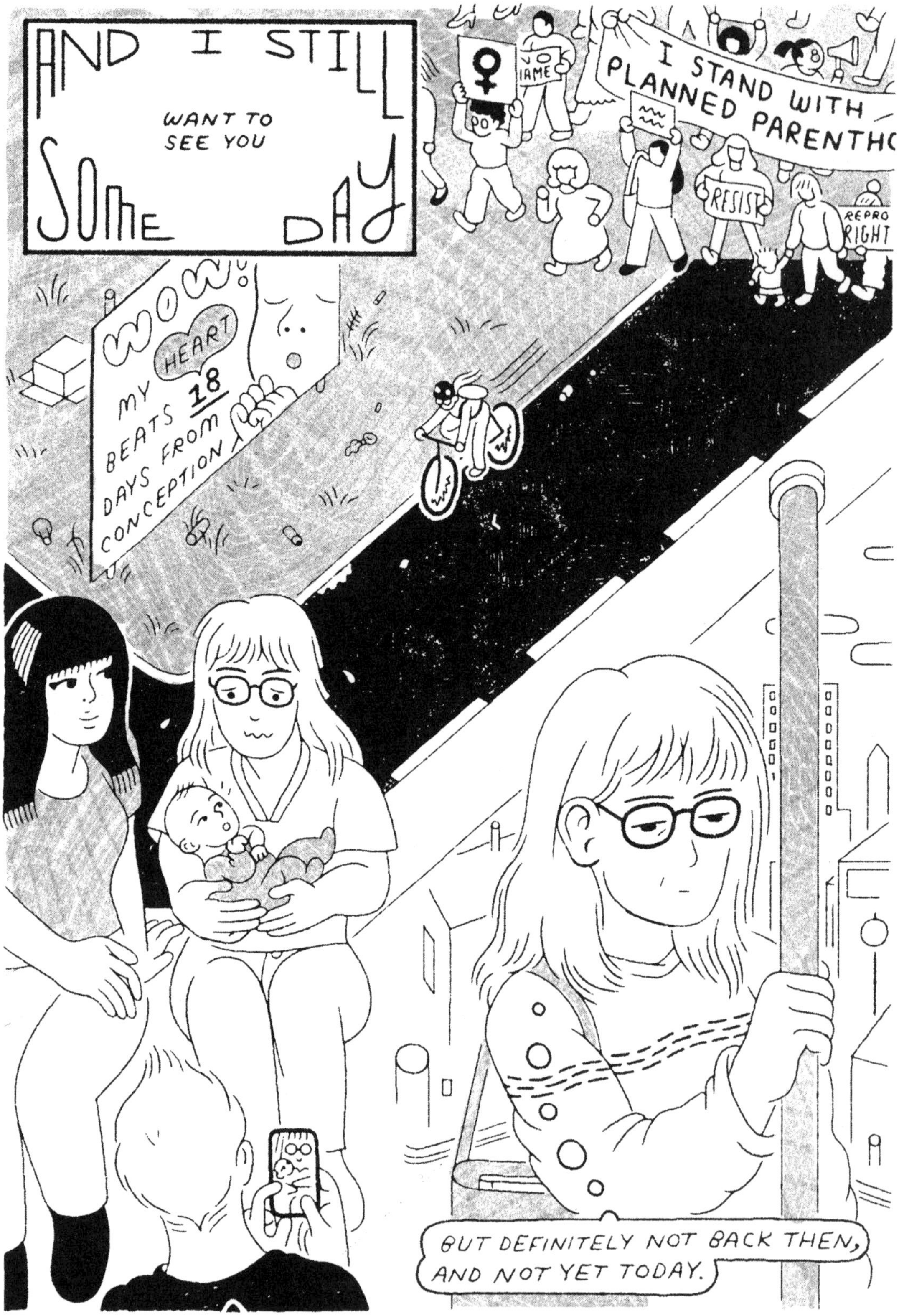
AND I STILL
WANT TO SEE YOU
SOME DAY
I STAND WITH PLANNED PARENTHO
RESIST
REPRO RIGHT
WOW
MY HEART BEATS 18 DAYS FROM CONCEPTION
BUT DEFINITELY NOT BACK THEN, AND NOT YET TODAY.

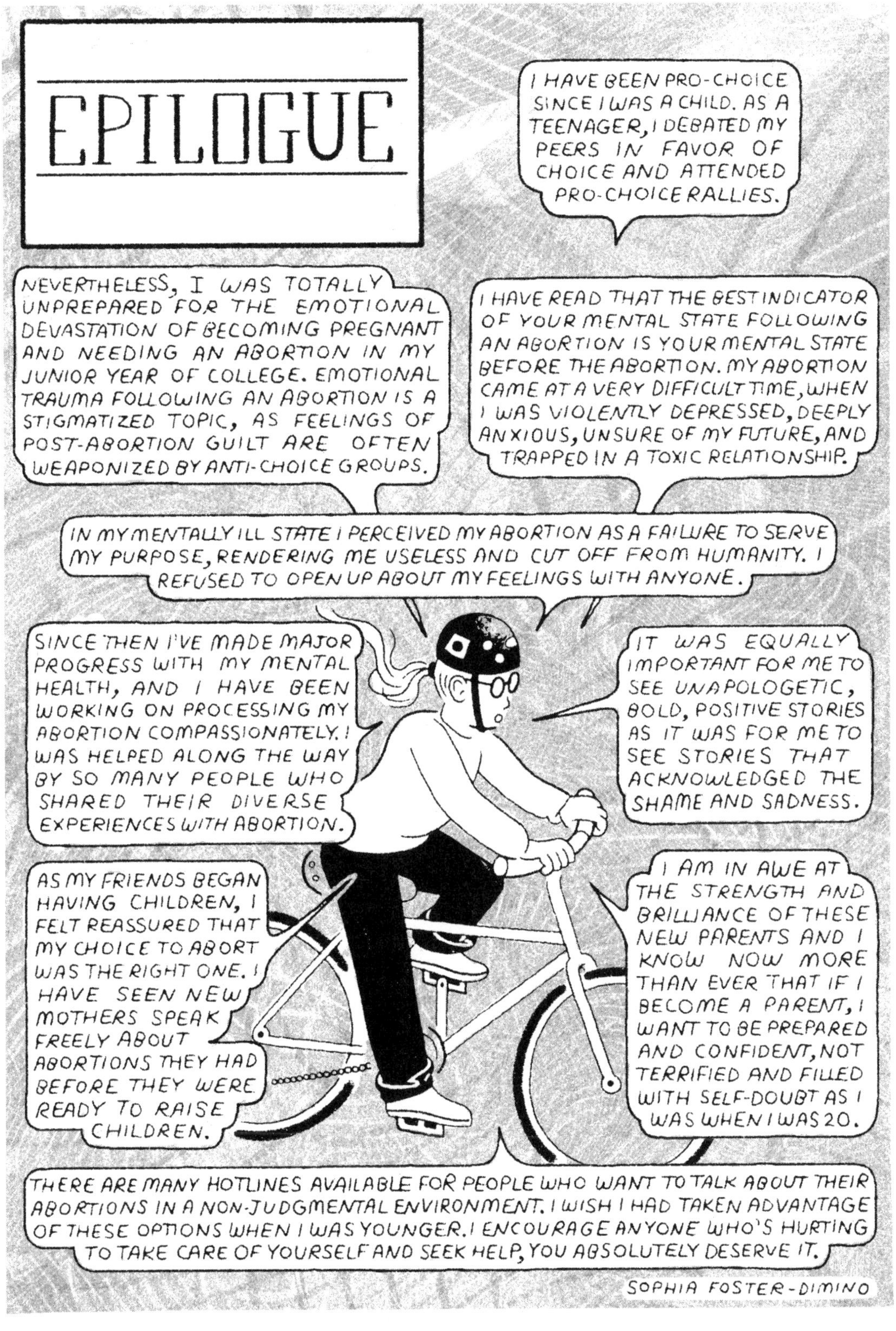
EPILOGUE
I HAVE BEEN PRO-CHOICE SINCE I WAS A CHILD. AS A TEENAGER, I DEBATED MY PEERS IN FAVOR OF CHOICE AND ATTENDED PRO-CHOICE RALLIES.
NEVERTHELESS, I WAS TOTALLY UNPREPARED FOR THE EMOTIONAL DEVASTATION OF BECOMING PREGNANT AND NEEDING AN ABORTION IN MY JUNIOR YEAR OF COLLEGE. EMOTIONAL TRAUMA FOLLOWING AN ABORTION IS A STIGMATIZED TOPIC, AS FEELINGS OF POST-ABORTION GUILT ARE OFTEN WEAPONIZED BY ANTI-CHOICE GROUPS.
I HAVE READ THAT THE BEST INDICATOR OF YOUR MENTAL STATE FOLLOWING AN ABORTION IS YOUR MENTAL STATE BEFORE THE ABORTION. MY ABORTION CAME AT A VERY DIFFICULT TIME, WHEN I WAS VIOLENTLY DEPRESSED, DEEPLY ANXIOUS, UNSURE OF MY FUTURE, AND TRAPPED IN A TOXIC RELATIONSHIP.
IN MY MENTALLY ILL STATE I PERCEIVED MY ABORTION AS A FAILURE TO SERVE MY PURPOSE, RENDERING ME USELESS AND CUT OFF FROM HUMANITY. I REFUSED TO OPEN UP ABOUT MY FEELINGS WITH ANYONE.
SINCE THEN I'VE MADE MAJOR PROGRESS WITH MY MENTAL HEALTH, AND I HAVE BEEN WORKING ON PROCESSING MY ABORTION COMPASSIONATELY. I WAS HELPED ALONG THE WAY BY SO MANY PEOPLE WHO SHARED THEIR DIVERSE EXPERIENCES WITH ABORTION.
IT WAS EQUALLY IMPORTANT FOR ME TO SEE UNAPOLOGETIC, BOLD, POSITIVE STORIES AS IT WAS FOR ME TO SEE STORIES THAT ACKNOWLEDGED THE SHAME AND SADNESS.
AS MY FRIENDS BEGAN HAVING CHILDREN, I FELT REASSURED THAT MY CHOICE TO ABORT WAS THE RIGHT ONE. I HAVE SEEN NEW MOTHERS SPEAK FREELY ABOUT ABORTIONS THEY HAD BEFORE THEY WERE READY TO RAISE CHILDREN.
I AM IN AWE AT THE STRENGTH AND BRILLIANCE OF THESE NEW PARENTS AND I KNOW NOW MORE THAN EVER THAT IF I BECOME A PARENT, I WANT TO BE PREPARED AND CONFIDENT, NOT TERRIFIED AND FILLED WITH SELF-DOUBT AS I WAS WHEN I WAS 20.
THERE ARE MANY HOTLINES AVAILABLE FOR PEOPLE WHO WANT TO TALK ABOUT THEIR ABORTIONS IN A NON-JUDGMENTAL ENVIRONMENT. I WISH I HAD TAKEN ADVANTAGE OF THESE OPTIONS WHEN I WAS YOUNGER. I ENCOURAGE ANYONE WHO'S HURTING TO TAKE CARE OF YOURSELF AND SEEK HELP, YOU ABSOLUTELY DESERVE IT.
SOPHIA FOSTER-DIMINO

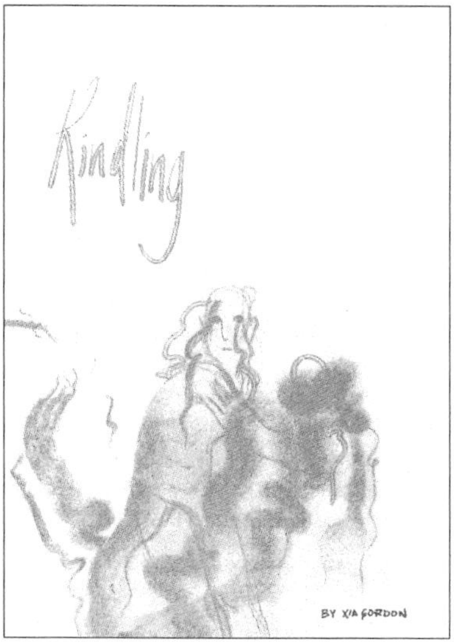
Kindling
BY XIA GORDON

Kindling (*Excerpt*)

XIA GORDON

originally published in

Kindling

2DCLOUD

5 x 7 inches • 32 pages

Biography

Xia Gordon is an Ignatz-nominated cartoonist and illustrator living in Brooklyn. She grew up in Orlando, Florida, and graduated from the School of Visual Arts with a BFA in Cartooning & Illustration in 2016.
xiagordon.com

Statement

Kindling is a meditation on a near masochistic level of self-sacrifice. This sequence depicts a transformation—a shedding of oneself, of ego, and of identity.

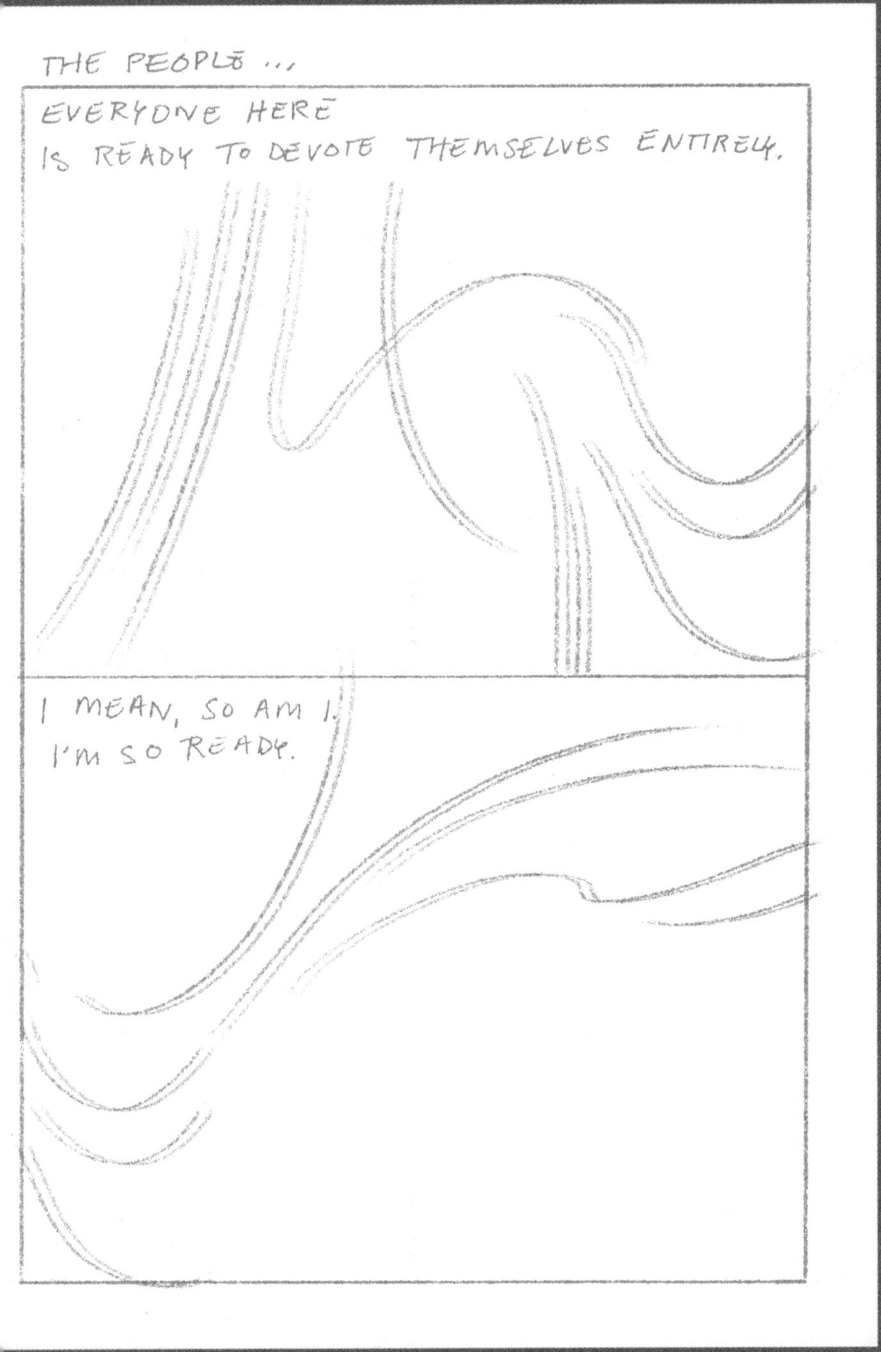
THE PEOPLE ...
EVERYONE HERE
IS READY TO DEVOTE THEMSELVES ENTIRELY.
I MEAN, SO AM I.
I'M SO READY.

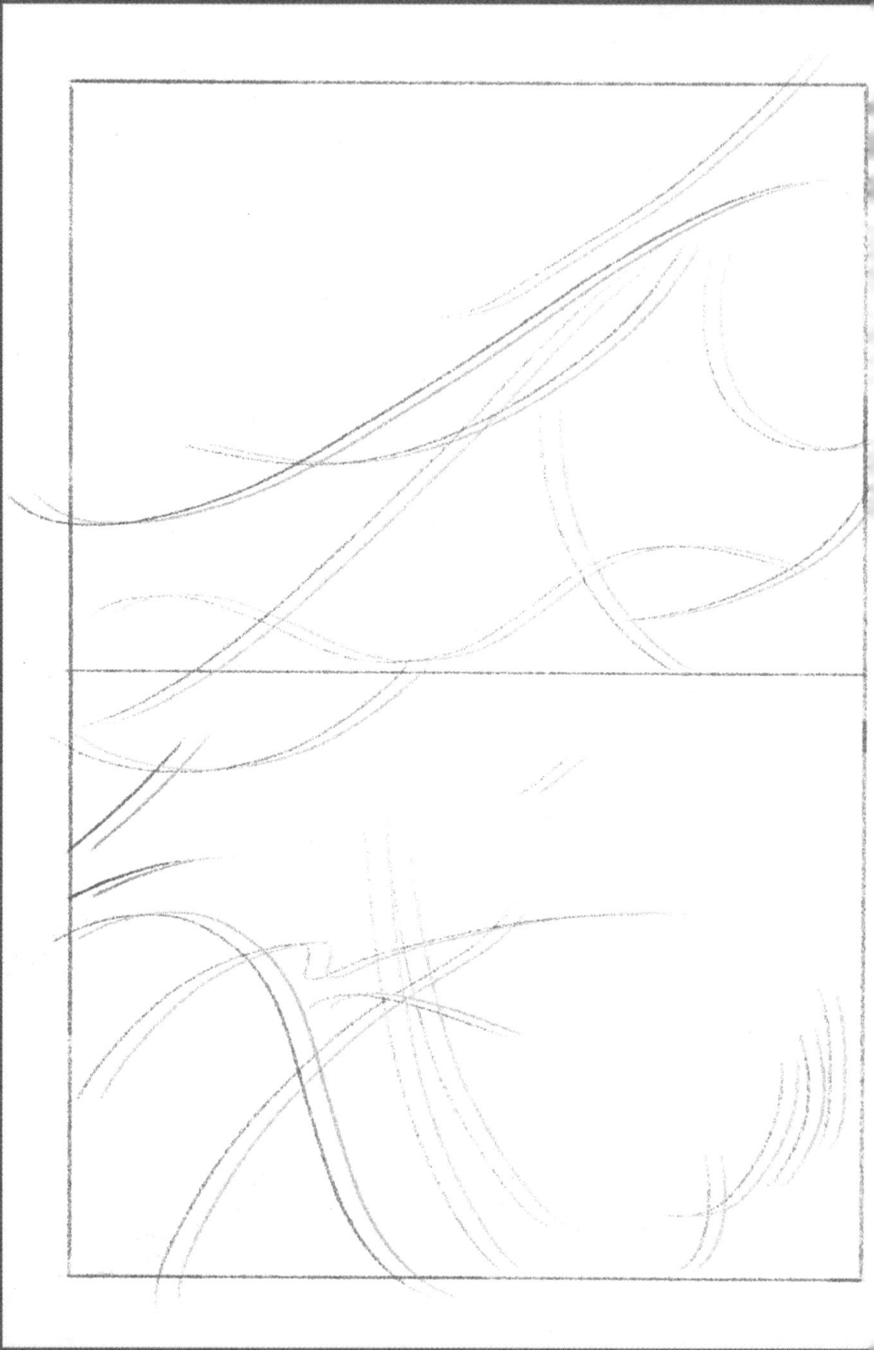

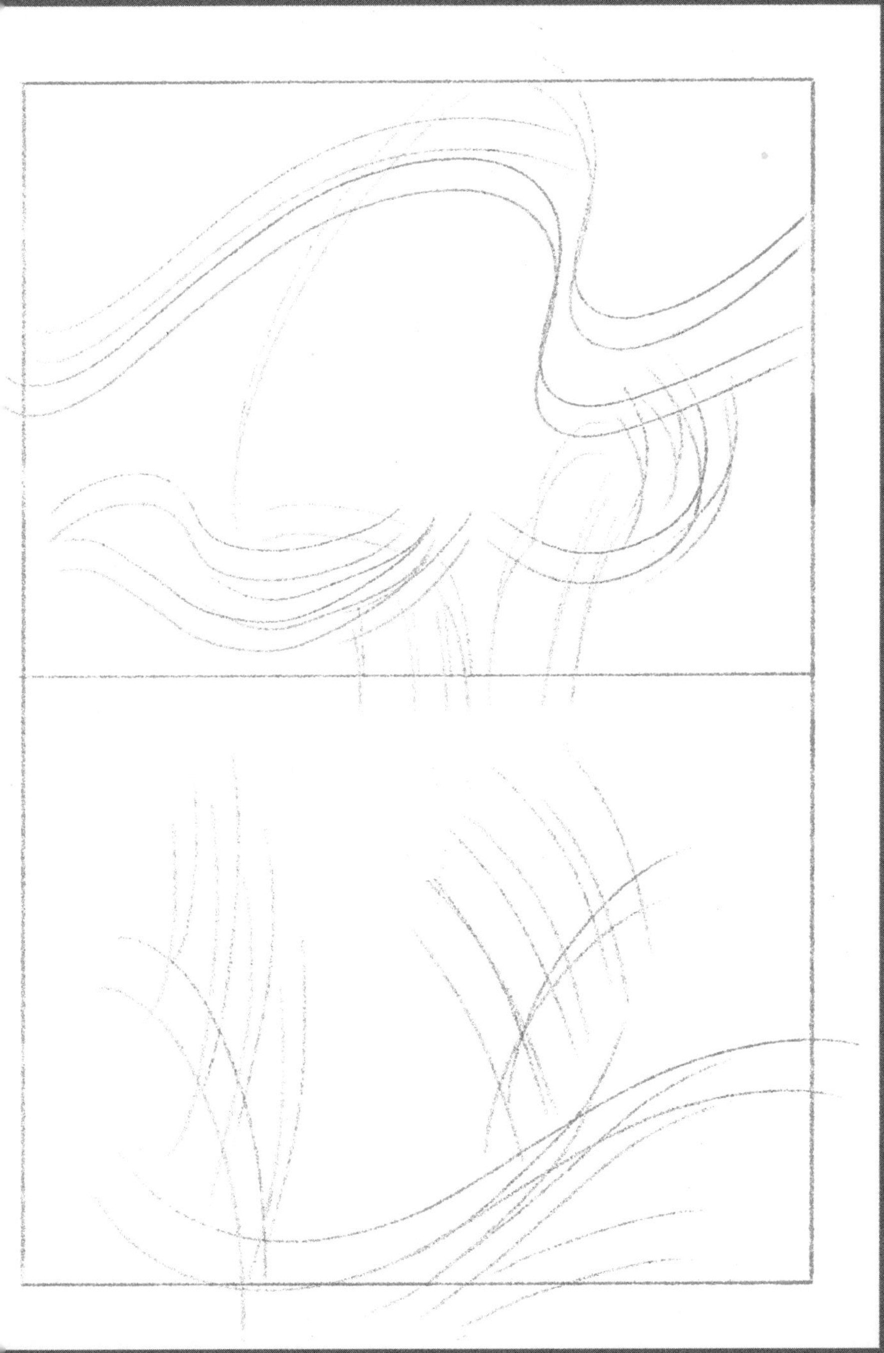

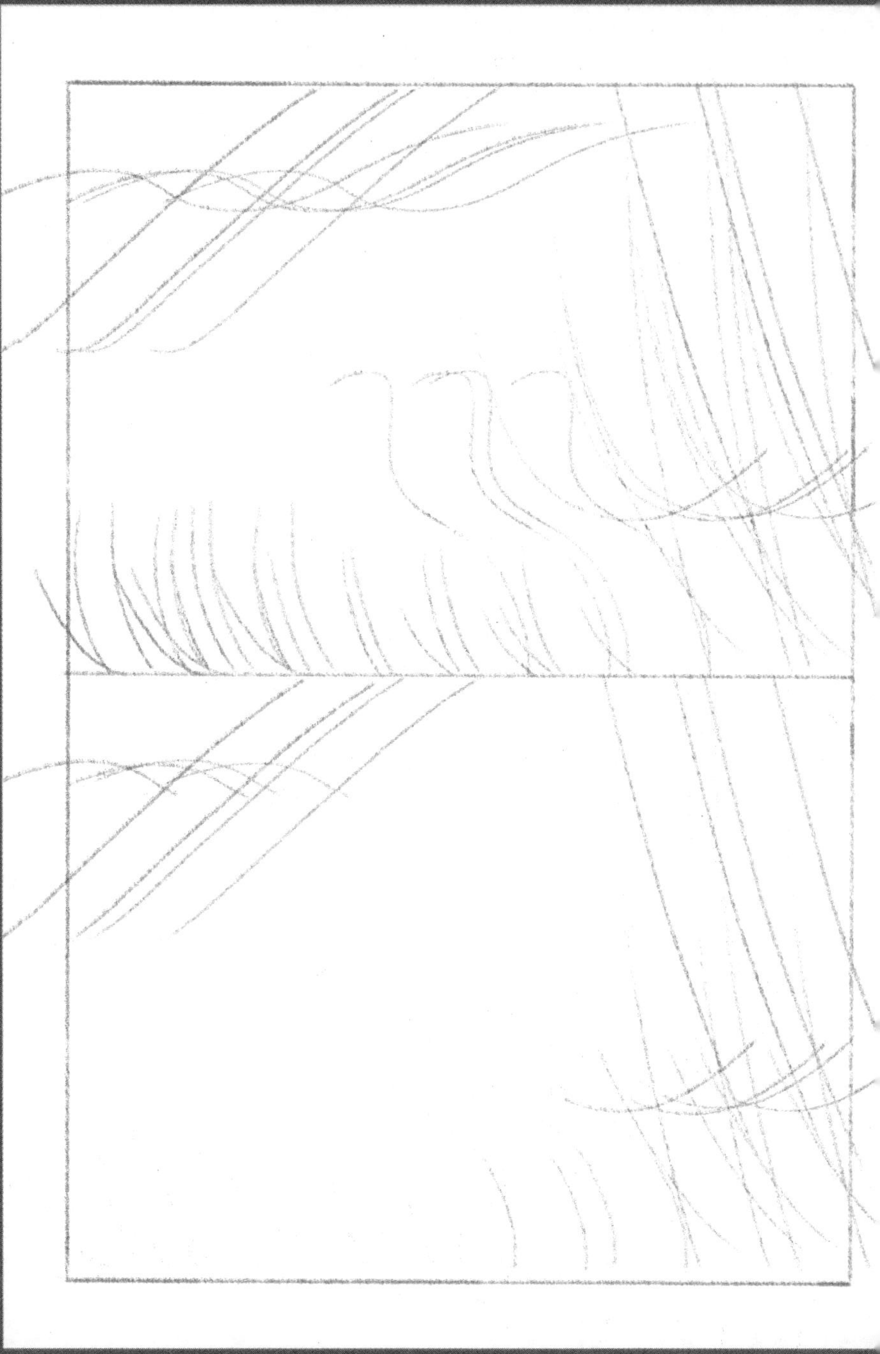

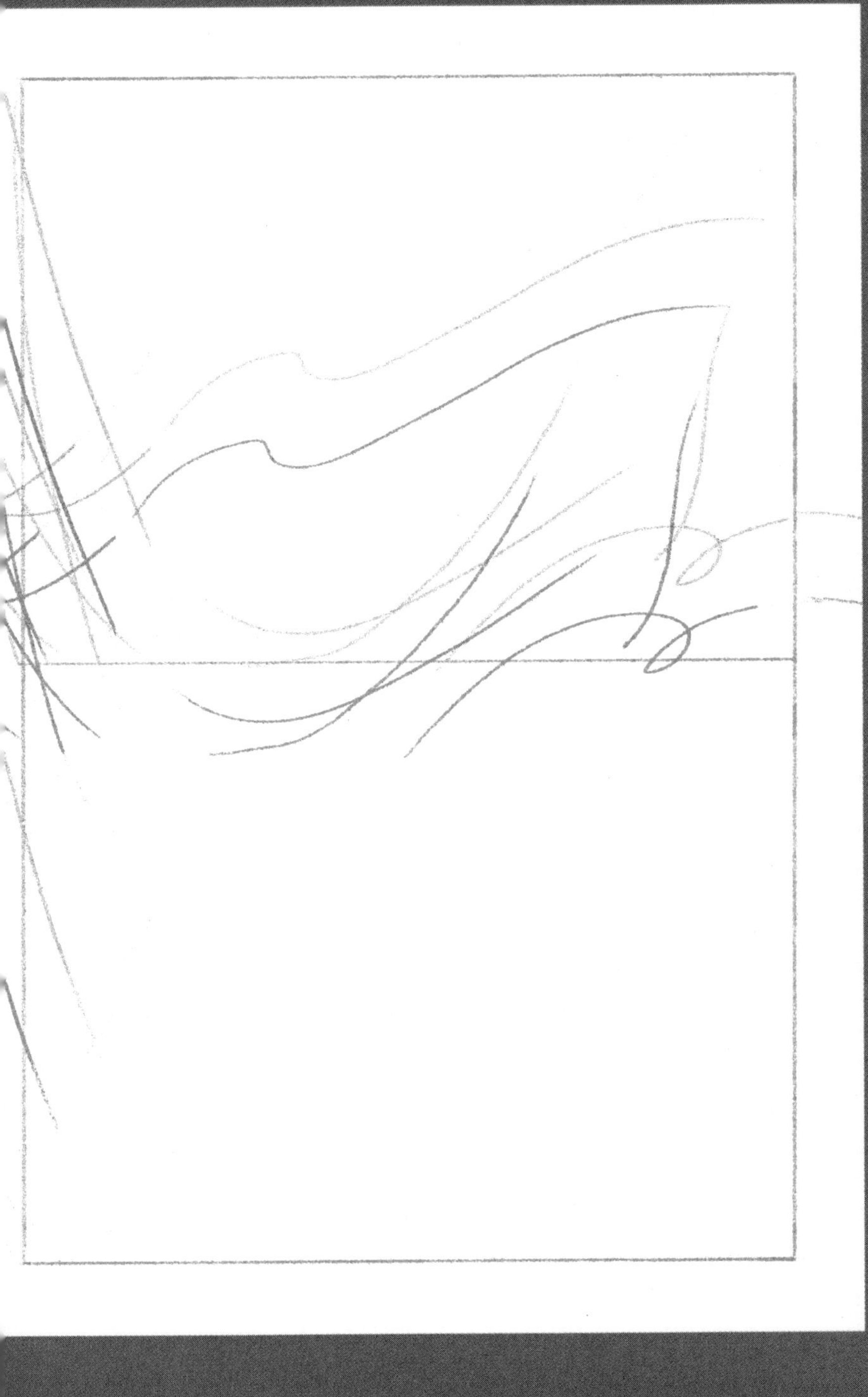

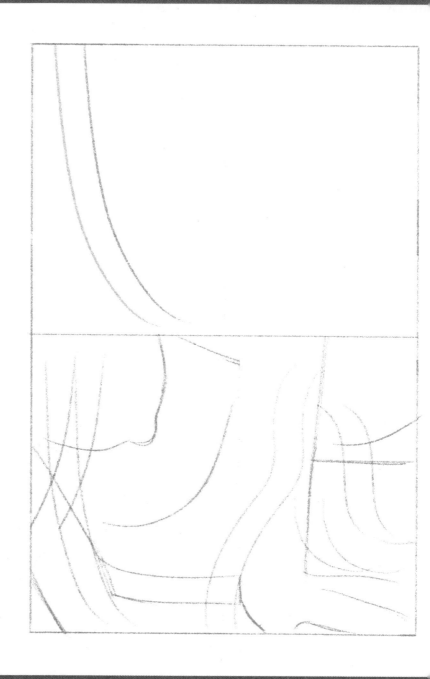

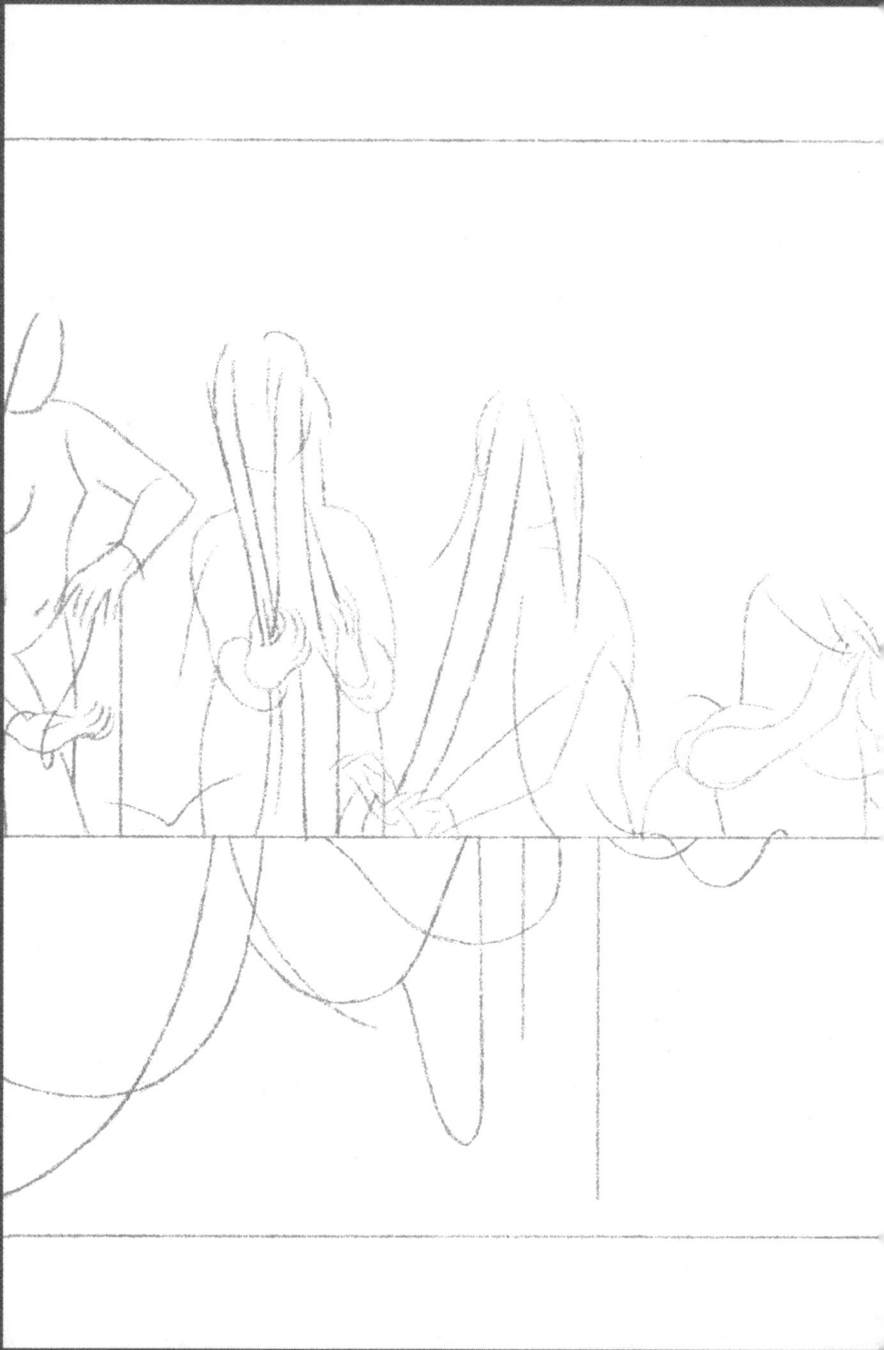

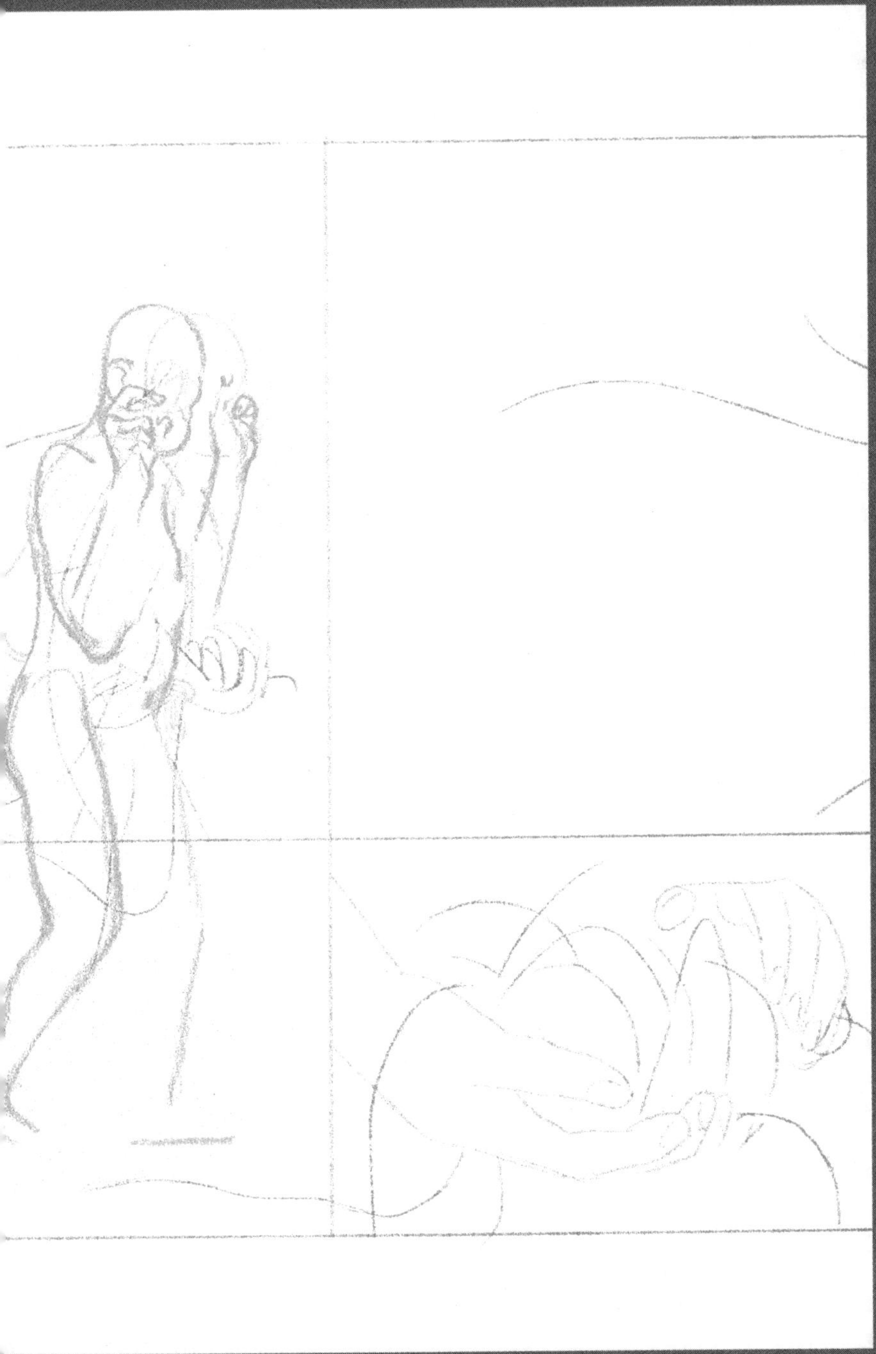

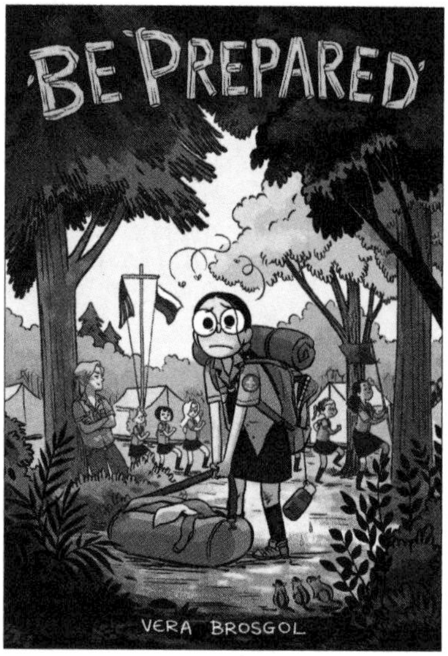
BE PREPARED
VERA BROSGOL

Welcome to O.R.R.A. (*Excerpt*)

VERA BROSGOL

originally published in

Be Prepared

FIRST SECOND BOOKS

6 x 8.5 inches • 256 pages

Biography

Vera Brosgol was born in Moscow, Russia, and moved to the US when she was five. She studied classical animation at Sheridan College, and spent many years working in feature animation as a storyboard artist. Vera now writes and illustrates books full-time. Her first graphic novel, *Anya's Ghost,* was published in 2011 by First Second Books and won an Eisner Award. Her first picture book, *Leave Me Alone,* was published in 2016 by Roaring Brook Press and won a Caldecott Honor. She lives and works in sunny Portland, Oregon.
verabee.com

Statement

Be Prepared is a fictionalized memoir of my time at a Russian Orthodox summer camp. As a first-generation immigrant, I had a hard time fitting in with my WASPy, affluent American classmates. So when I found out about a camp for Russian kids like me, I was all over it. I went there with high hopes of finding fast friends who would know what I went through back home and would welcome me with open arms. But upon arrival I found older kids who'd known each other for years and had no interest in including a weird little nerd in their summer fun. It was a rough, lonely summer, but by the end of it I'd learned the value of friend quality over friend quantity. AND how to make four kinds of campfire. I don't remember the campfire lessons, but the friend ones have stood the test of time.

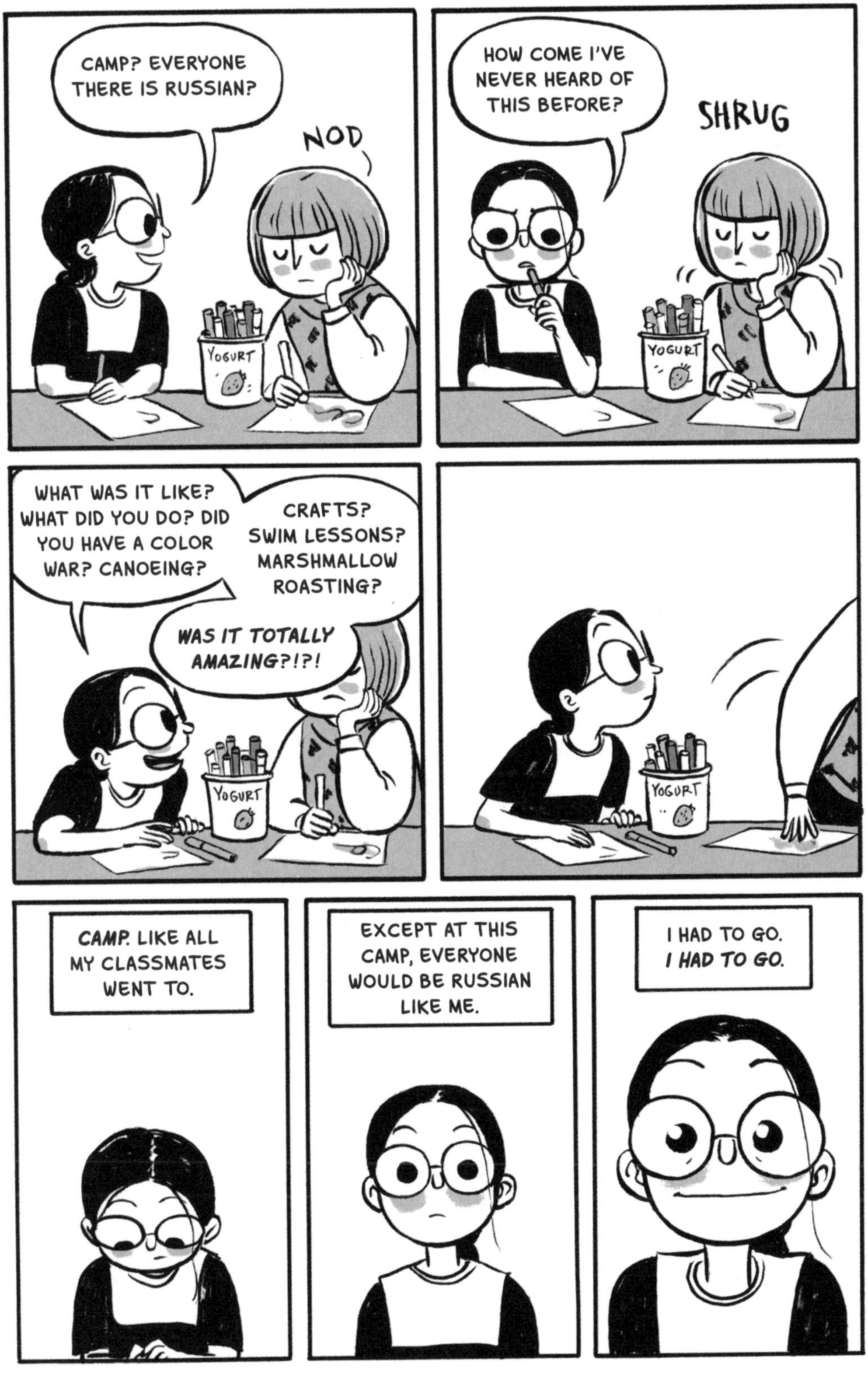
CAMP? EVERYONE THERE IS RUSSIAN?
NOD
HOW COME I'VE NEVER HEARD OF THIS BEFORE?
SHRUG
WHAT WAS IT LIKE? WHAT DID YOU DO? DID YOU HAVE A COLOR WAR? CANOEING?
CRAFTS? SWIM LESSONS? MARSHMALLOW ROASTING?
WAS IT TOTALLY AMAZING?!?!
CAMP. LIKE ALL MY CLASSMATES WENT TO.
EXCEPT AT THIS CAMP, EVERYONE WOULD BE RUSSIAN LIKE ME.
I HAD TO GO. I HAD TO GO.

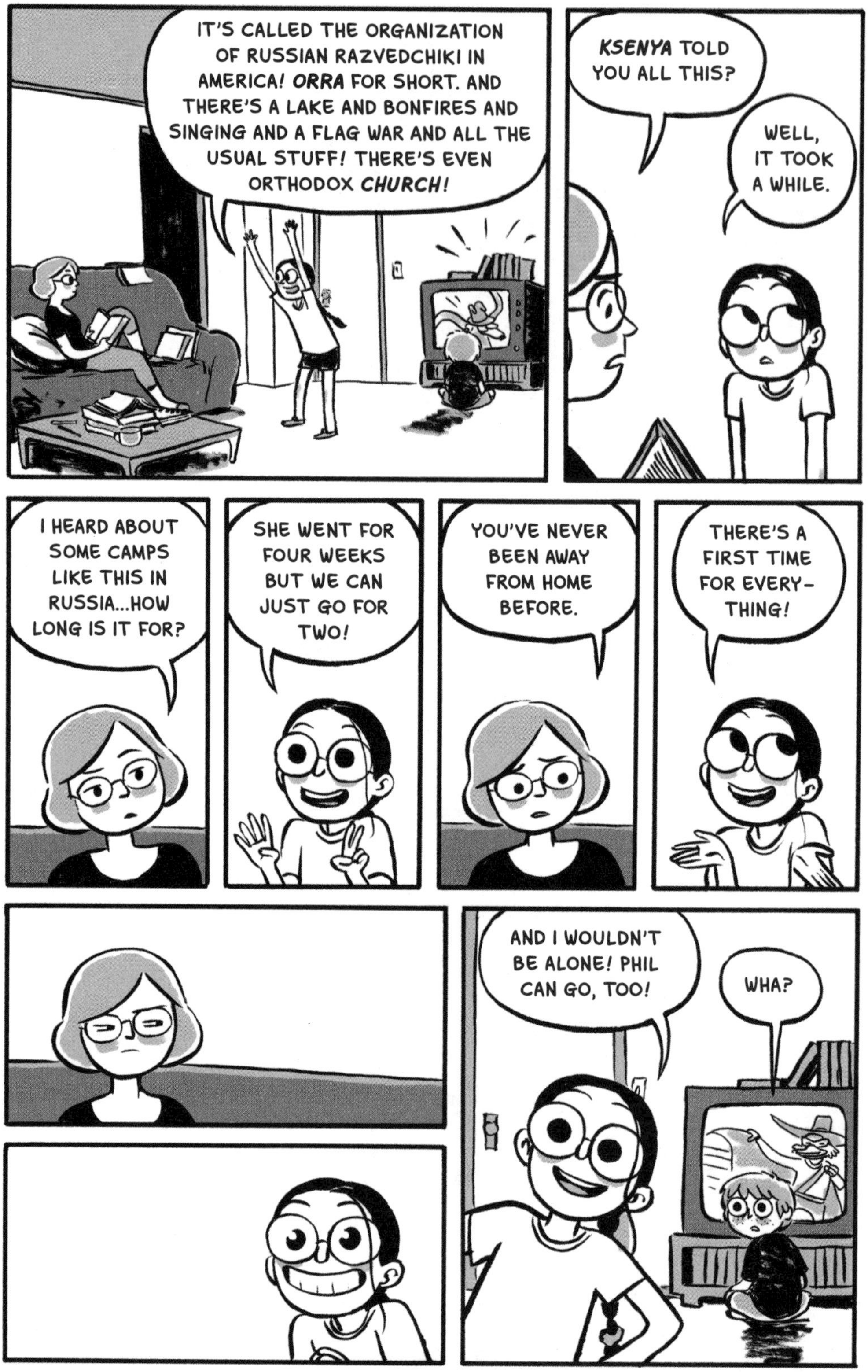
IT'S CALLED THE ORGANIZATION OF RUSSIAN RAZVEDCHIKI IN AMERICA! ORRA FOR SHORT. AND THERE'S A LAKE AND BONFIRES AND SINGING AND A FLAG WAR AND ALL THE USUAL STUFF! THERE'S EVEN ORTHODOX CHURCH!
KSENYA TOLD YOU ALL THIS?
WELL, IT TOOK A WHILE.
I HEARD ABOUT SOME CAMPS LIKE THIS IN RUSSIA...HOW LONG IS IT FOR?
SHE WENT FOR FOUR WEEKS BUT WE CAN JUST GO FOR TWO!
YOU'VE NEVER BEEN AWAY FROM HOME BEFORE.
THERE'S A FIRST TIME FOR EVERY-THING!
AND I WOULDN'T BE ALONE! PHIL CAN GO, TOO!
WHA?

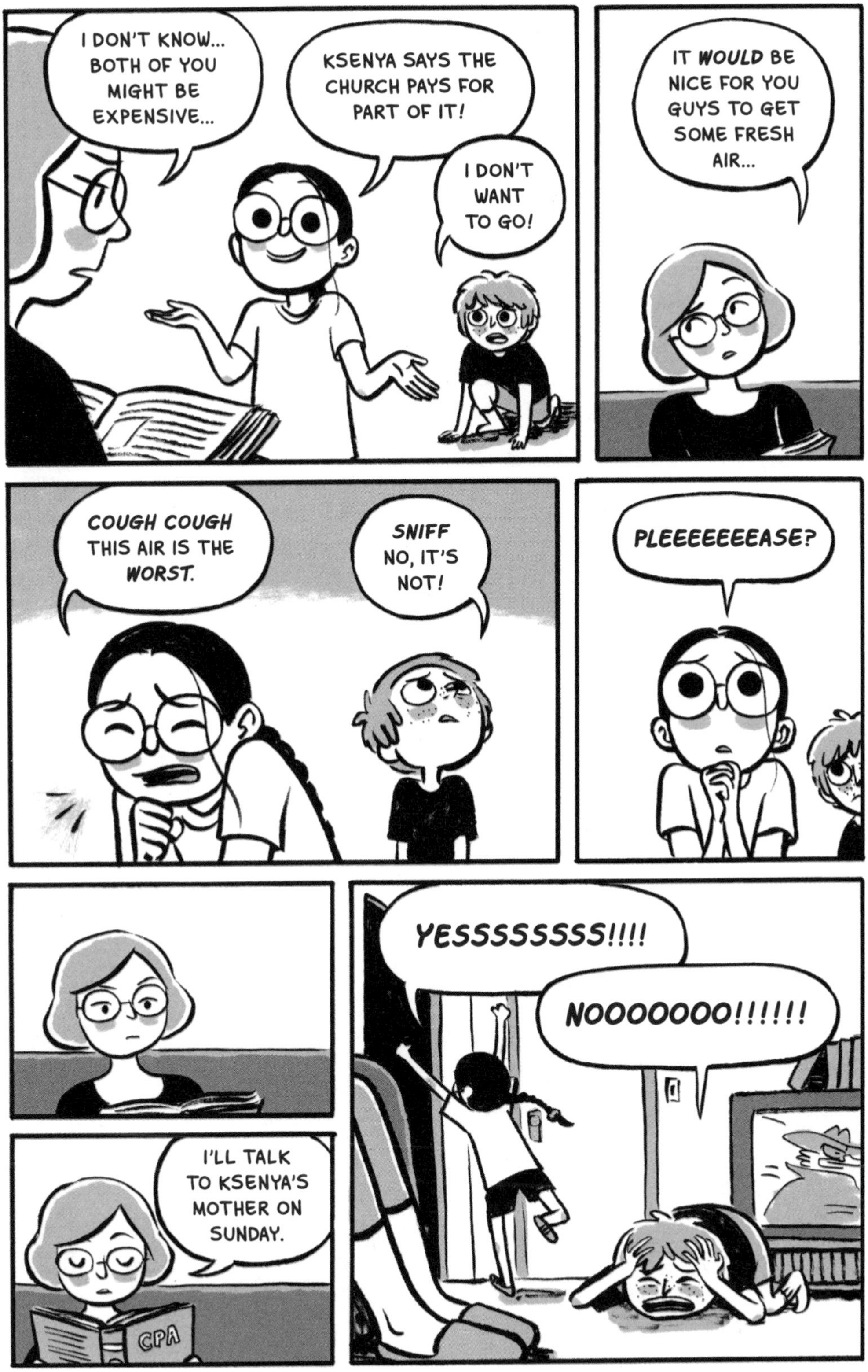
I DON'T KNOW... BOTH OF YOU MIGHT BE EXPENSIVE...
KSENYA SAYS THE CHURCH PAYS FOR PART OF IT!
I DON'T WANT TO GO!
IT WOULD BE NICE FOR YOU GUYS TO GET SOME FRESH AIR...
COUGH COUGH THIS AIR IS THE WORST.
SNIFF NO, IT'S NOT!
PLEEEEEEEASE?
I'LL TALK TO KSENYA'S MOTHER ON SUNDAY.
YESSSSSSSS!!!!
NOOOOOOO!!!!!!
CPA

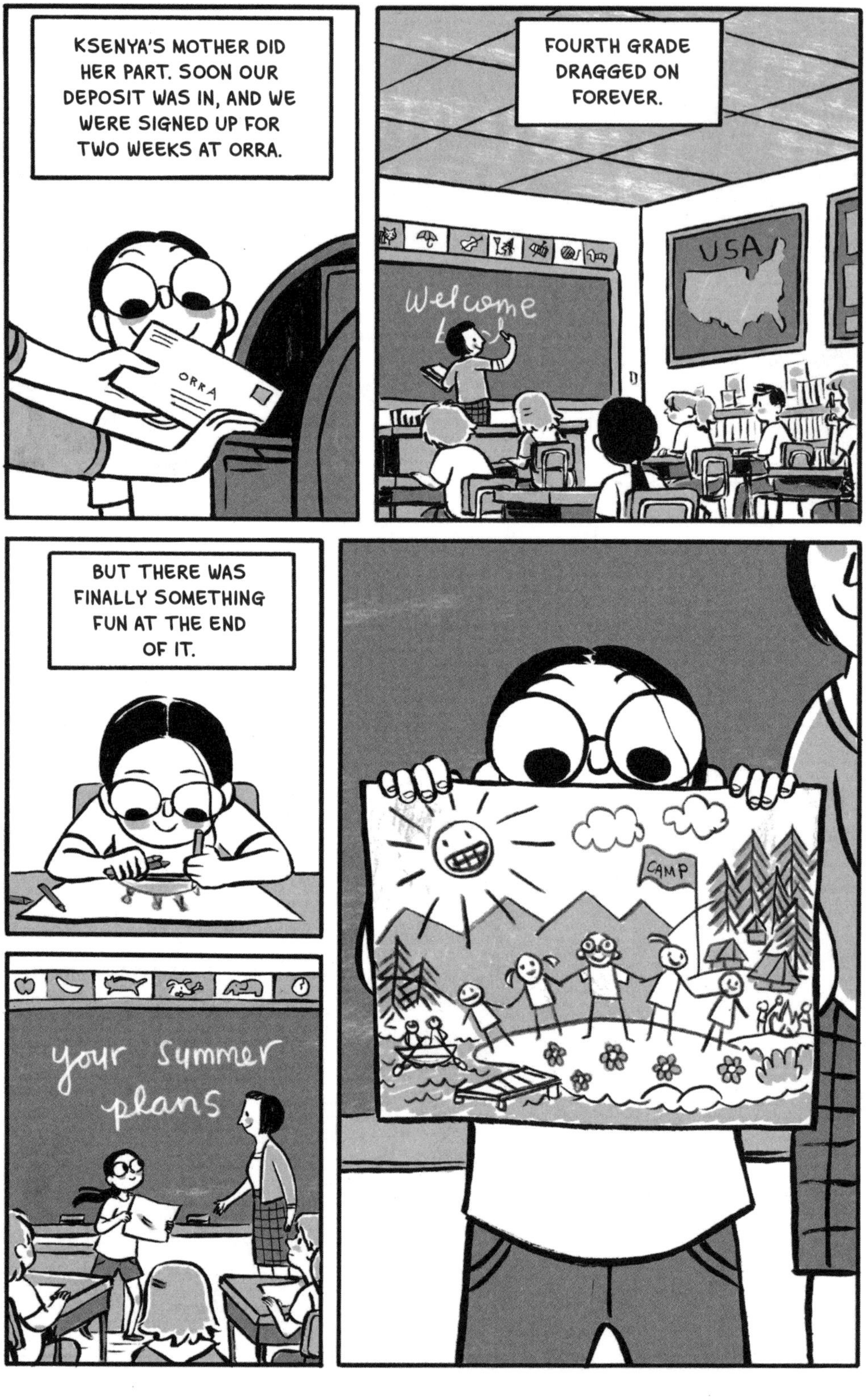
KSENYA'S MOTHER DID HER PART. SOON OUR DEPOSIT WAS IN, AND WE WERE SIGNED UP FOR TWO WEEKS AT ORRA.
ORRA
FOURTH GRADE DRAGGED ON FOREVER.
USA
Welcome
BUT THERE WAS FINALLY SOMETHING FUN AT THE END OF IT.
your summer plans
CAMP

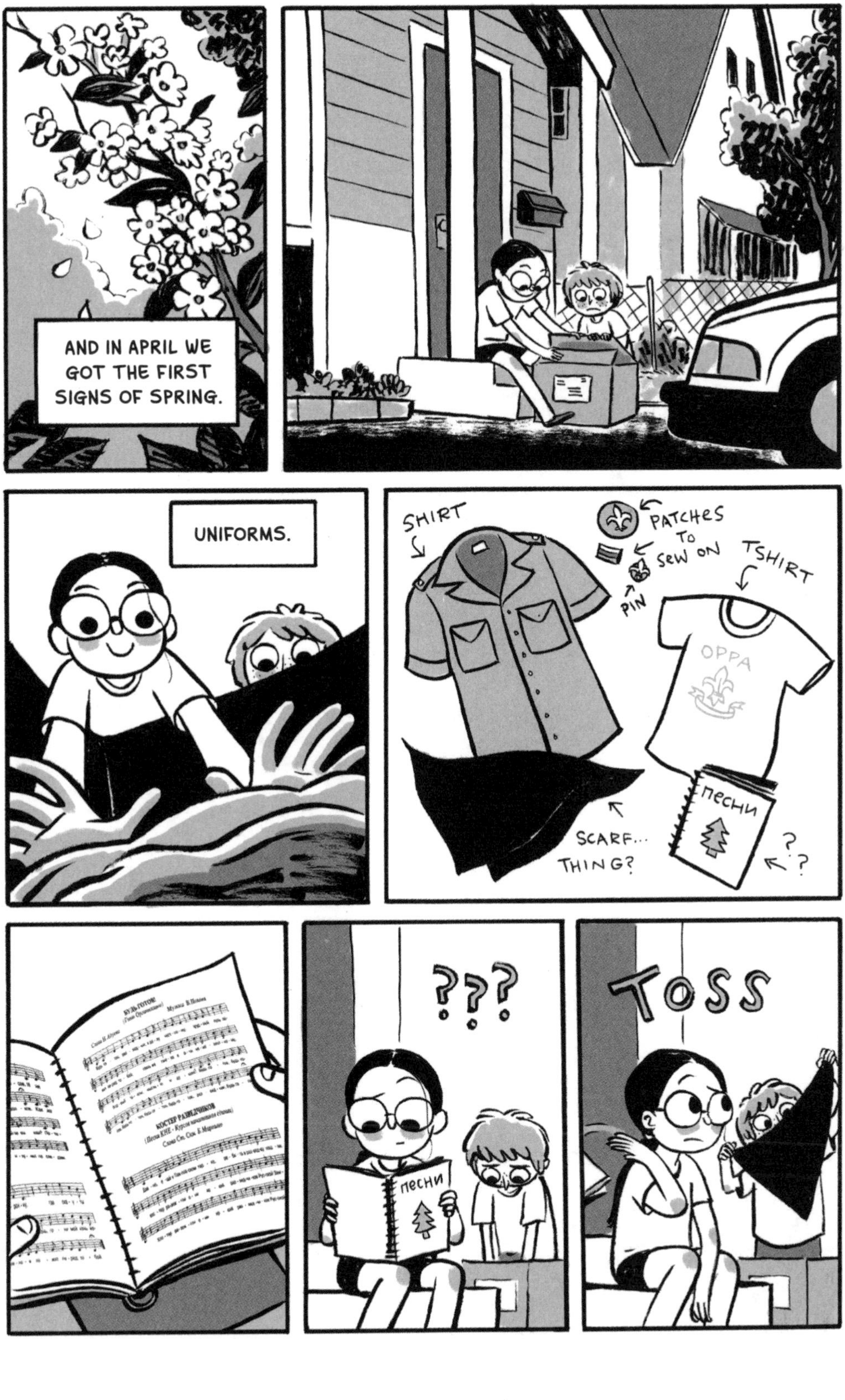
AND IN APRIL WE GOT THE FIRST SIGNS OF SPRING.
UNIFORMS.
SHIRT
PATCHES TO SEW ON
PIN
TSHIRT
OPPA
SCARF... THING?
песни
??
???
песни
TOSS

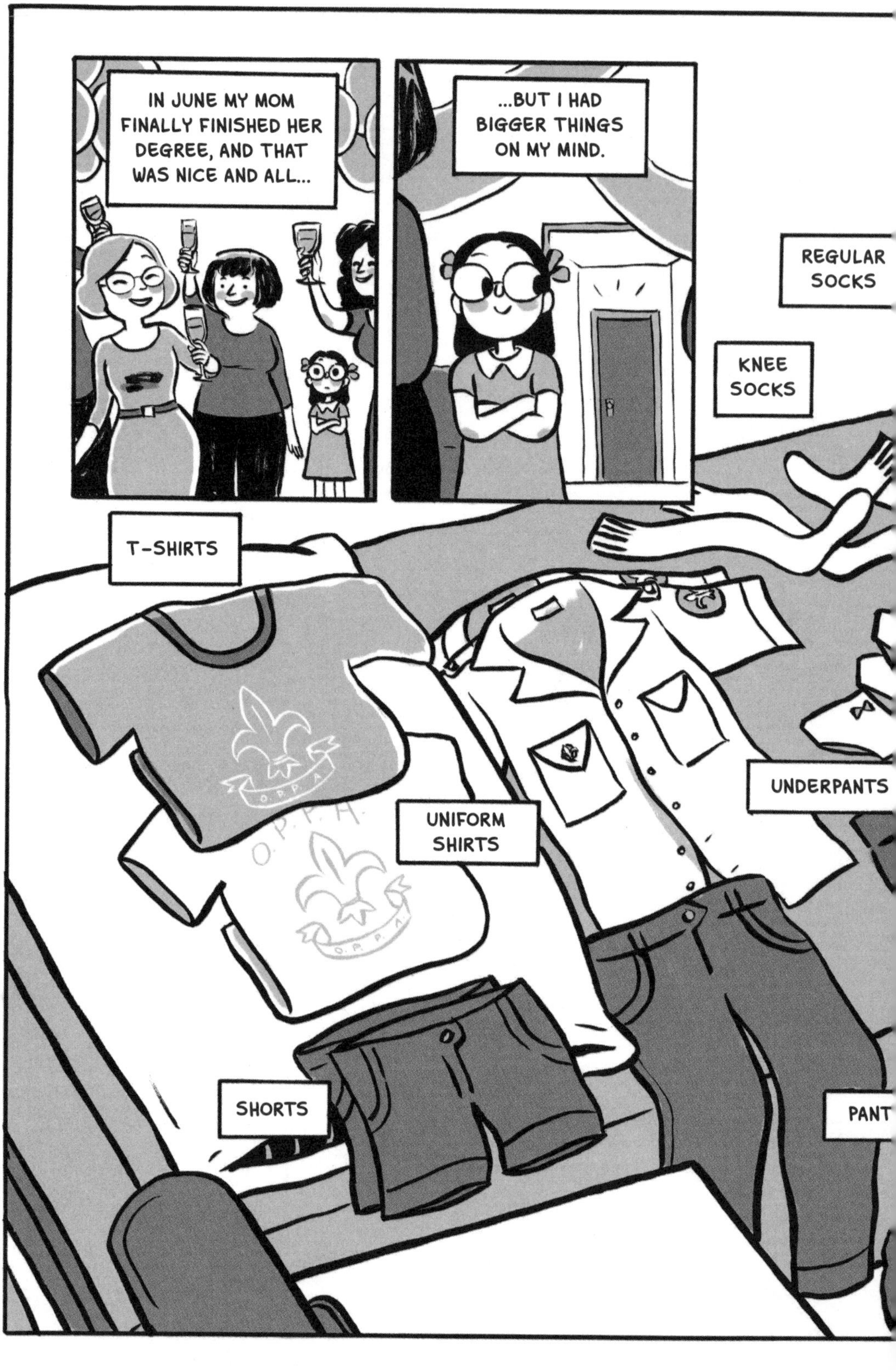
IN JUNE MY MOM FINALLY FINISHED HER DEGREE, AND THAT WAS NICE AND ALL...
...BUT I HAD BIGGER THINGS ON MY MIND.
REGULAR SOCKS
KNEE SOCKS
T-SHIRTS
O.P.P.A.
UNIFORM SHIRTS
UNDERPANTS
SHORTS
PANT

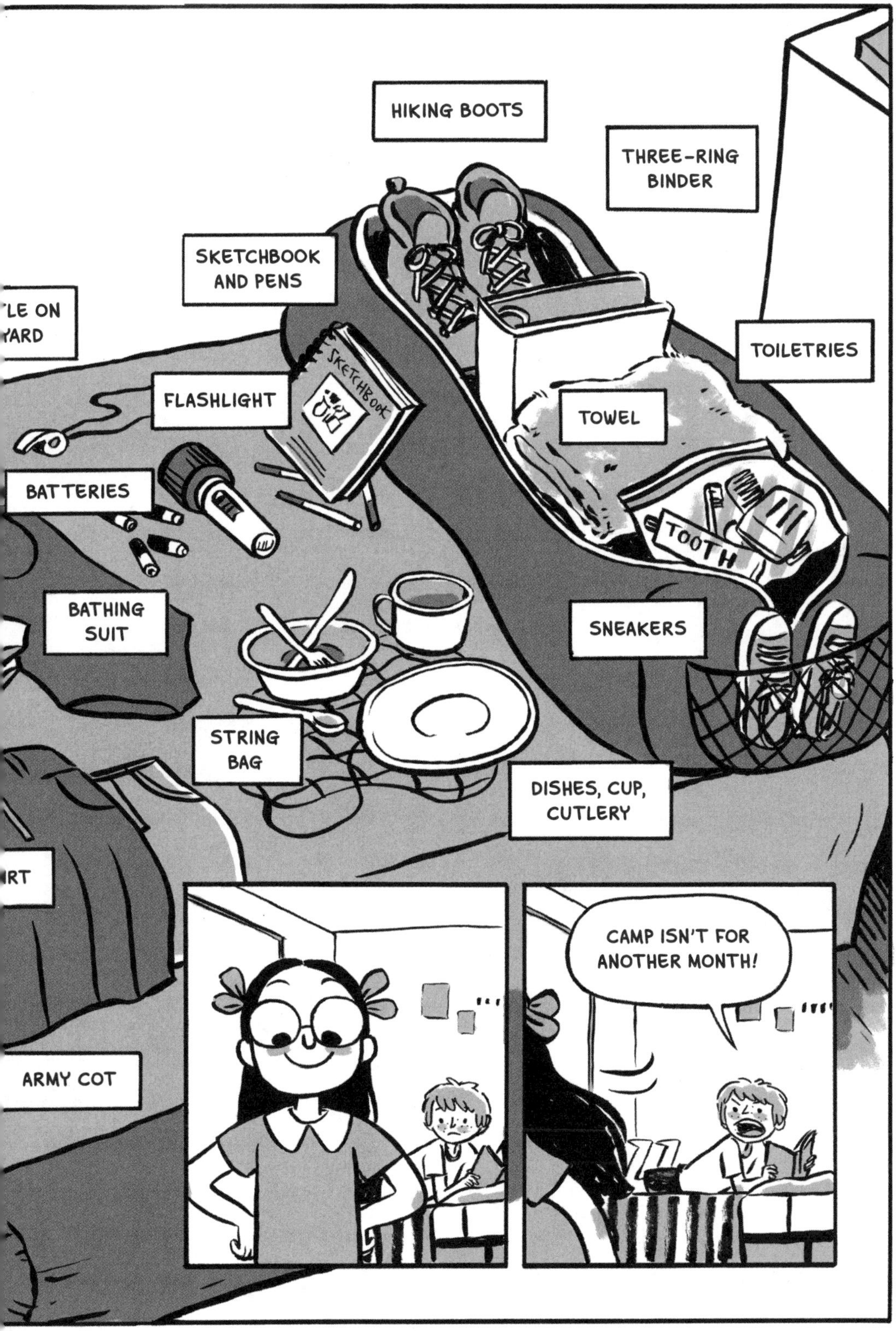
HIKING BOOTS
THREE-RING BINDER
SKETCHBOOK AND PENS
LE ON
ARD
TOILETRIES
FLASHLIGHT
SKETCHBOOK
TOWEL
BATTERIES
TOOTH
BATHING SUIT
SNEAKERS
STRING BAG
DISHES, CUP, CUTLERY
RT
ARMY COT
CAMP ISN'T FOR ANOTHER MONTH!

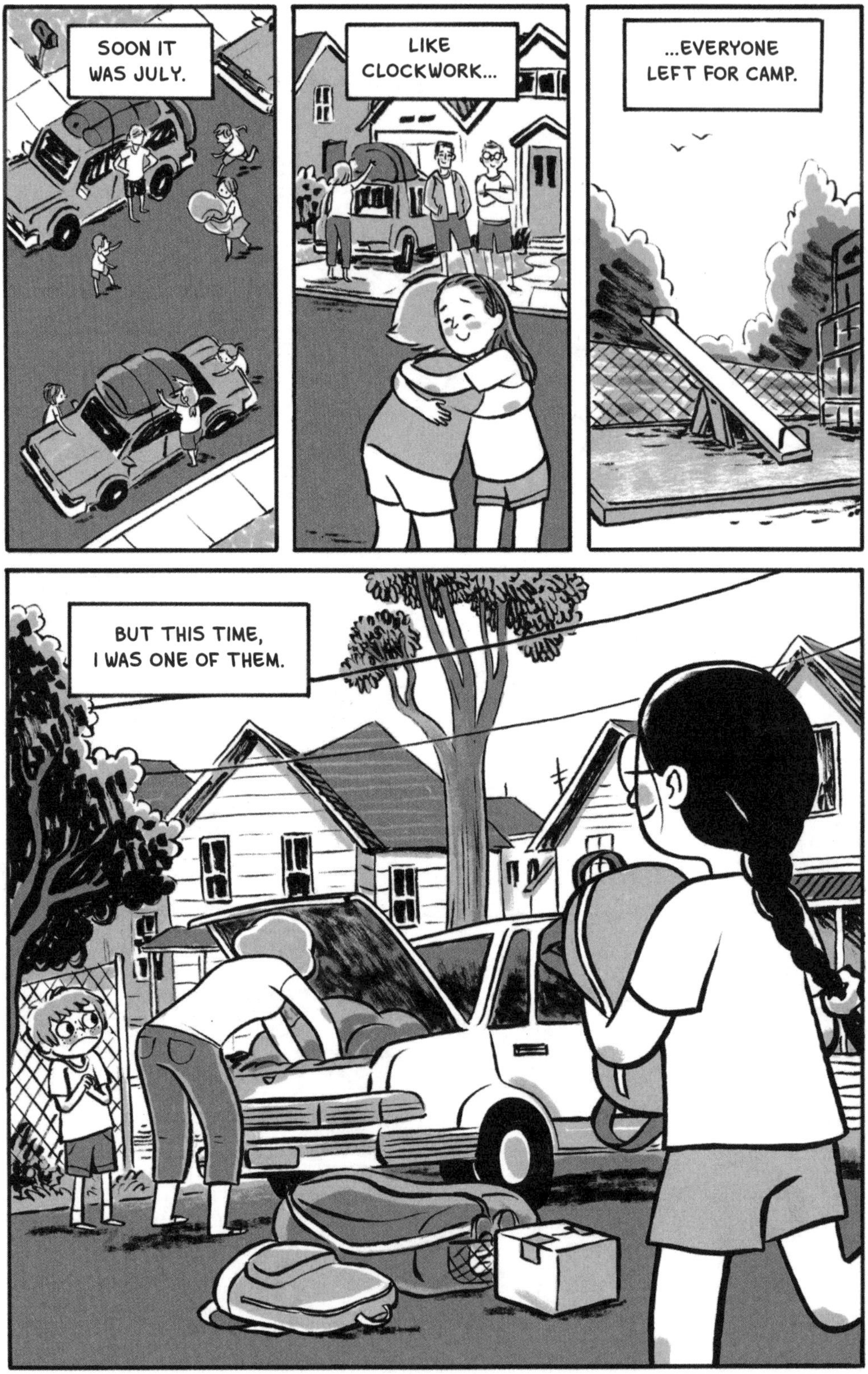
SOON IT WAS JULY.
LIKE CLOCKWORK...
...EVERYONE LEFT FOR CAMP.
BUT THIS TIME, I WAS ONE OF THEM.

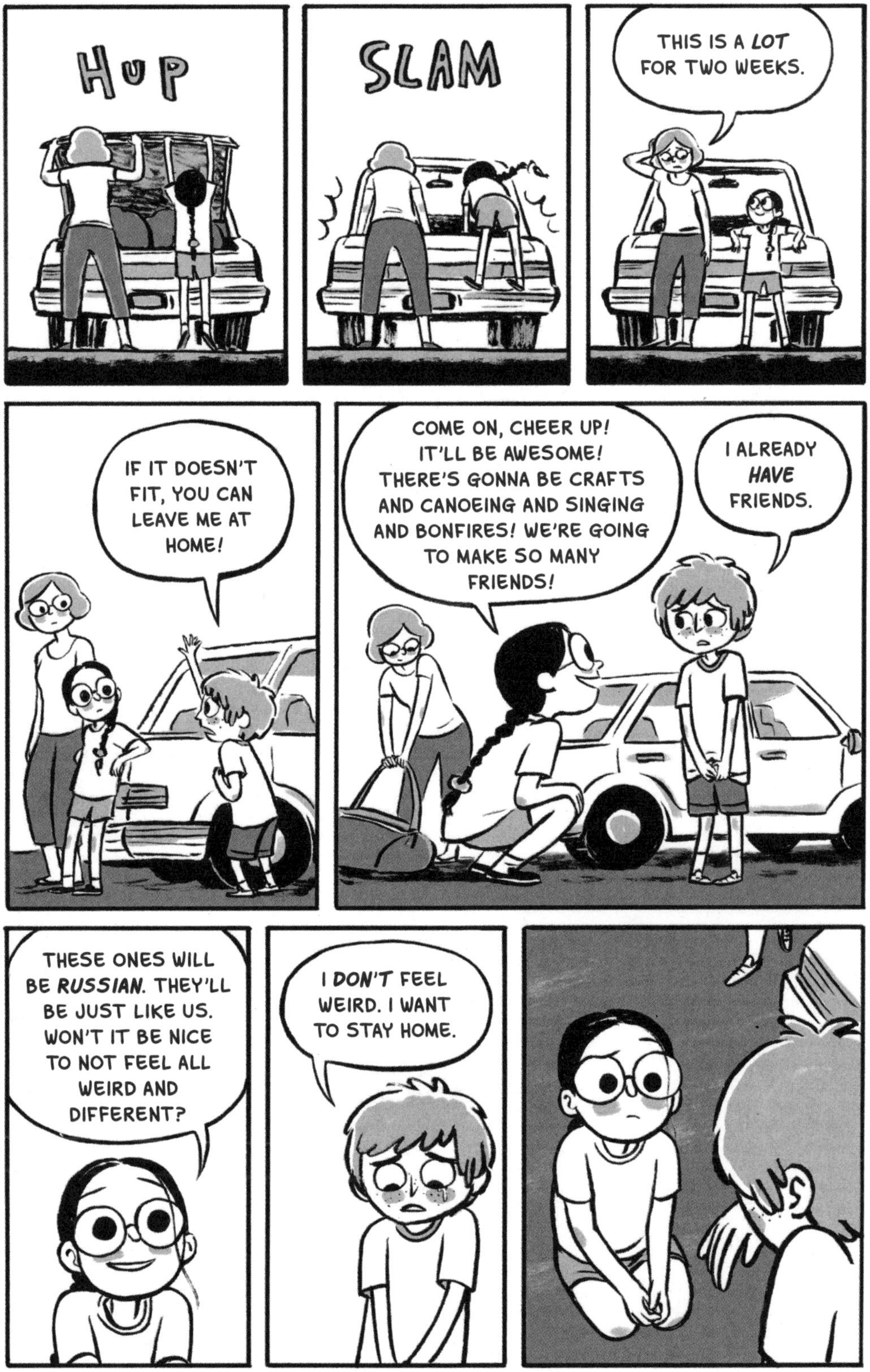
HUP
SLAM
THIS IS A *LOT* FOR TWO WEEKS.
IF IT DOESN'T FIT, YOU CAN LEAVE ME AT HOME!
COME ON, CHEER UP! IT'LL BE AWESOME! THERE'S GONNA BE CRAFTS AND CANOEING AND SINGING AND BONFIRES! WE'RE GOING TO MAKE SO MANY FRIENDS!
I ALREADY *HAVE* FRIENDS.
THESE ONES WILL BE *RUSSIAN*. THEY'LL BE JUST LIKE US. WON'T IT BE NICE TO NOT FEEL ALL WEIRD AND DIFFERENT?
I *DON'T* FEEL WEIRD. I WANT TO STAY HOME.

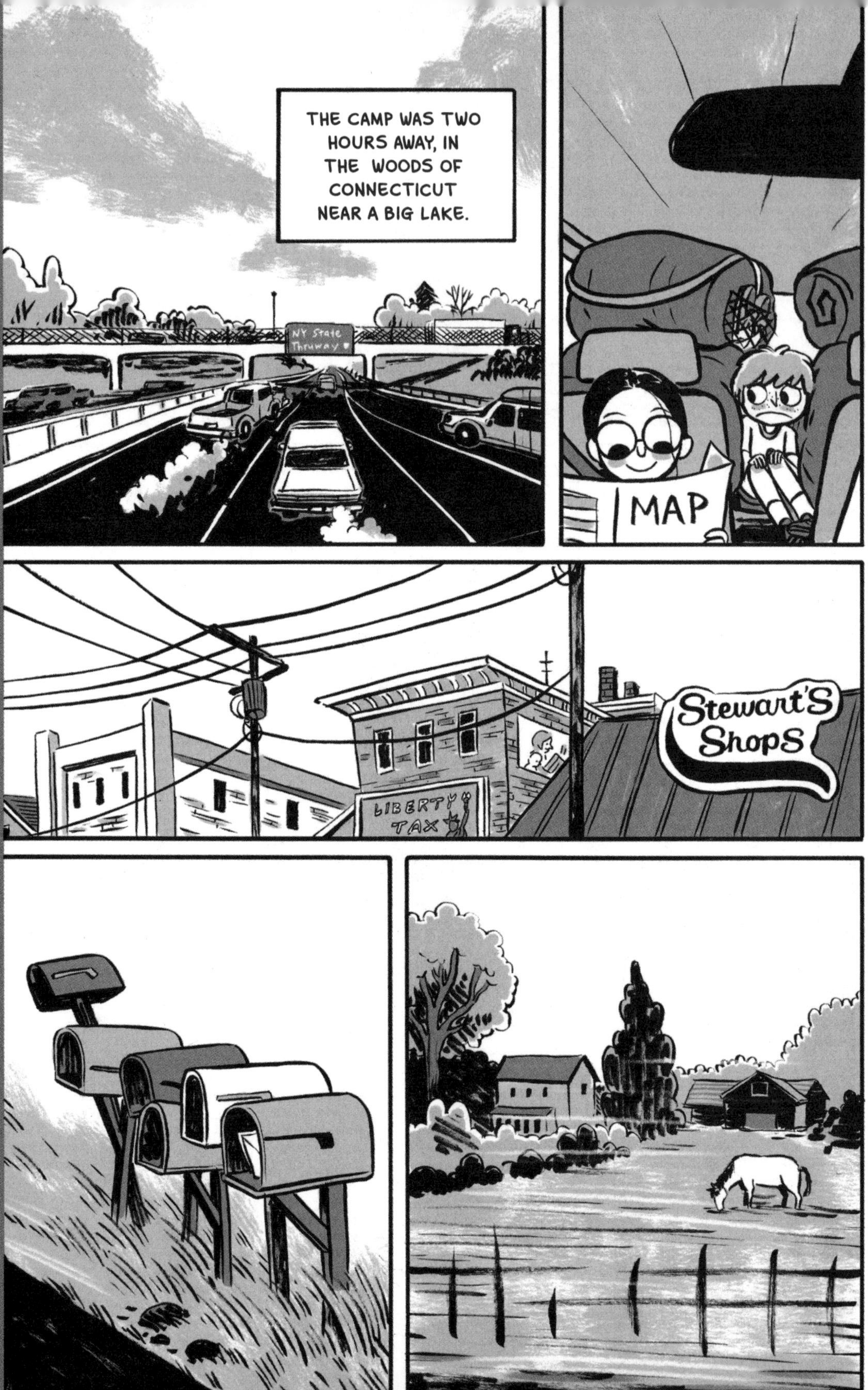
THE CAMP WAS TWO HOURS AWAY, IN THE WOODS OF CONNECTICUT NEAR A BIG LAKE.
NY State Thruway
MAP
Stewart's Shops
LIBERTY TAX

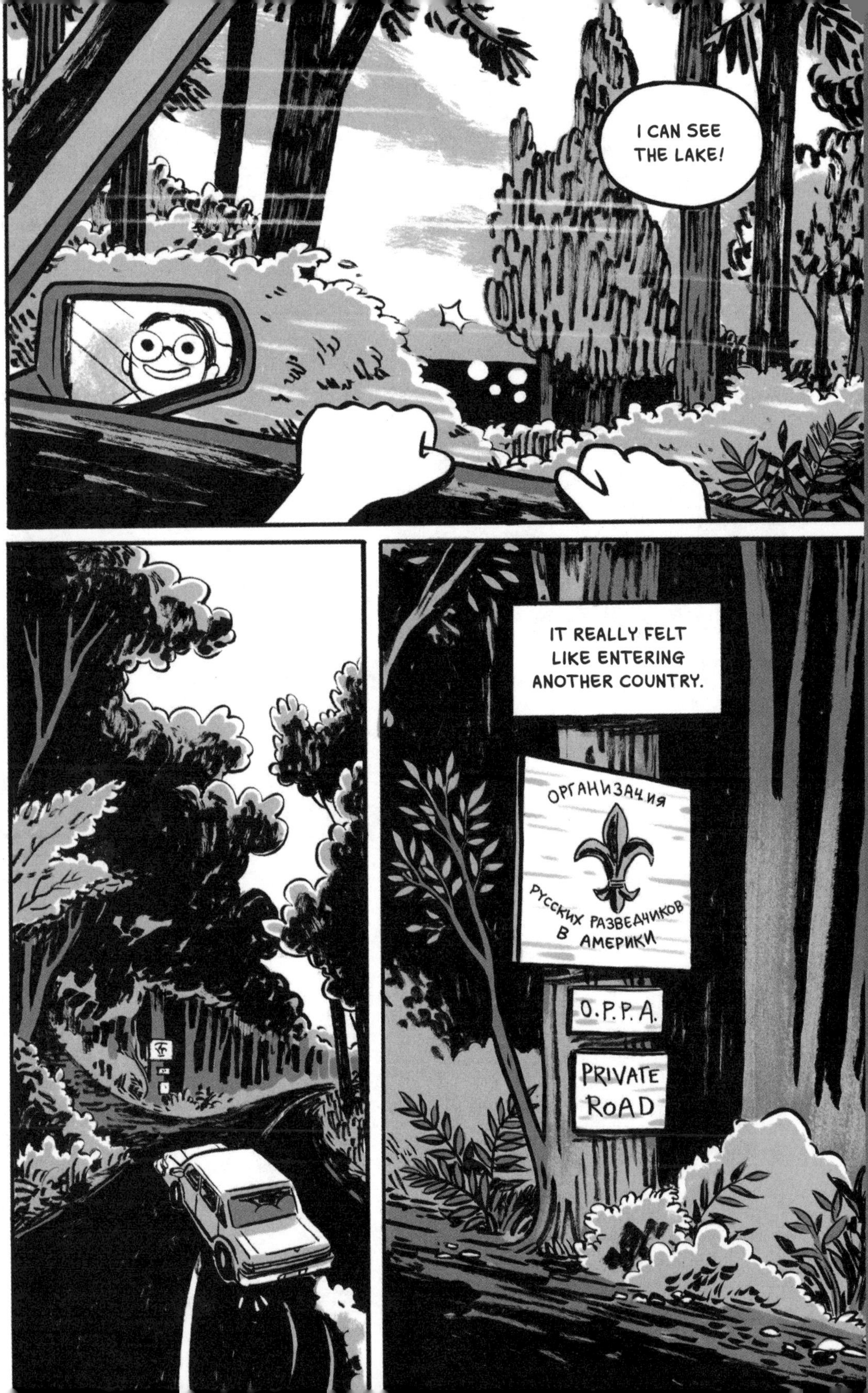
I CAN SEE THE LAKE!
IT REALLY FELT LIKE ENTERING ANOTHER COUNTRY.
ОРГАНИЗАЦИЯ
РУССКИХ РАЗВЕДЧИКОВ В АМЕРИКИ
O.P.P.A.
PRIVATE ROAD

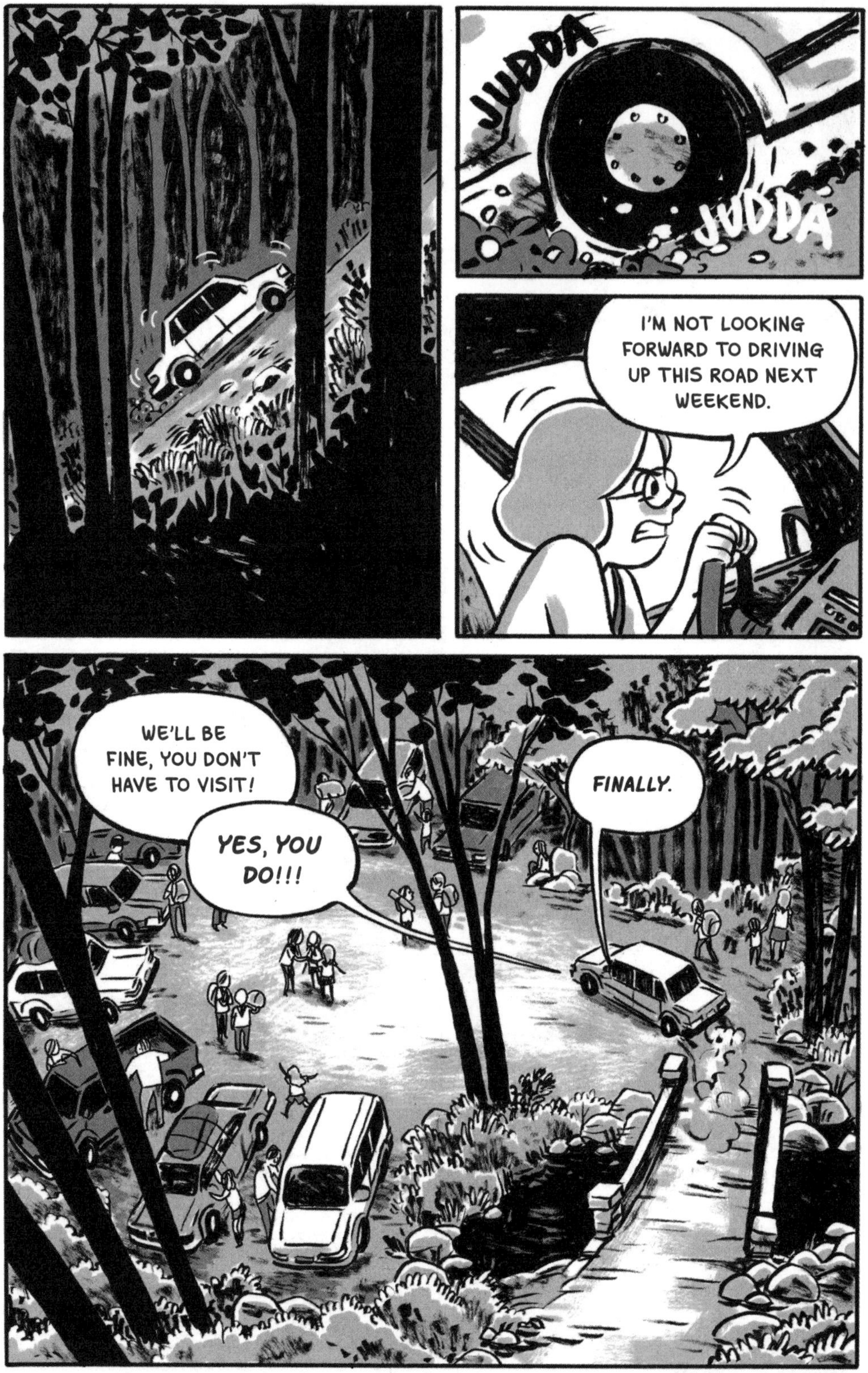
JUDDA
JUDDA
I'M NOT LOOKING FORWARD TO DRIVING UP THIS ROAD NEXT WEEKEND.
WE'LL BE FINE, YOU DON'T HAVE TO VISIT!
YES, YOU DO!!!
FINALLY.

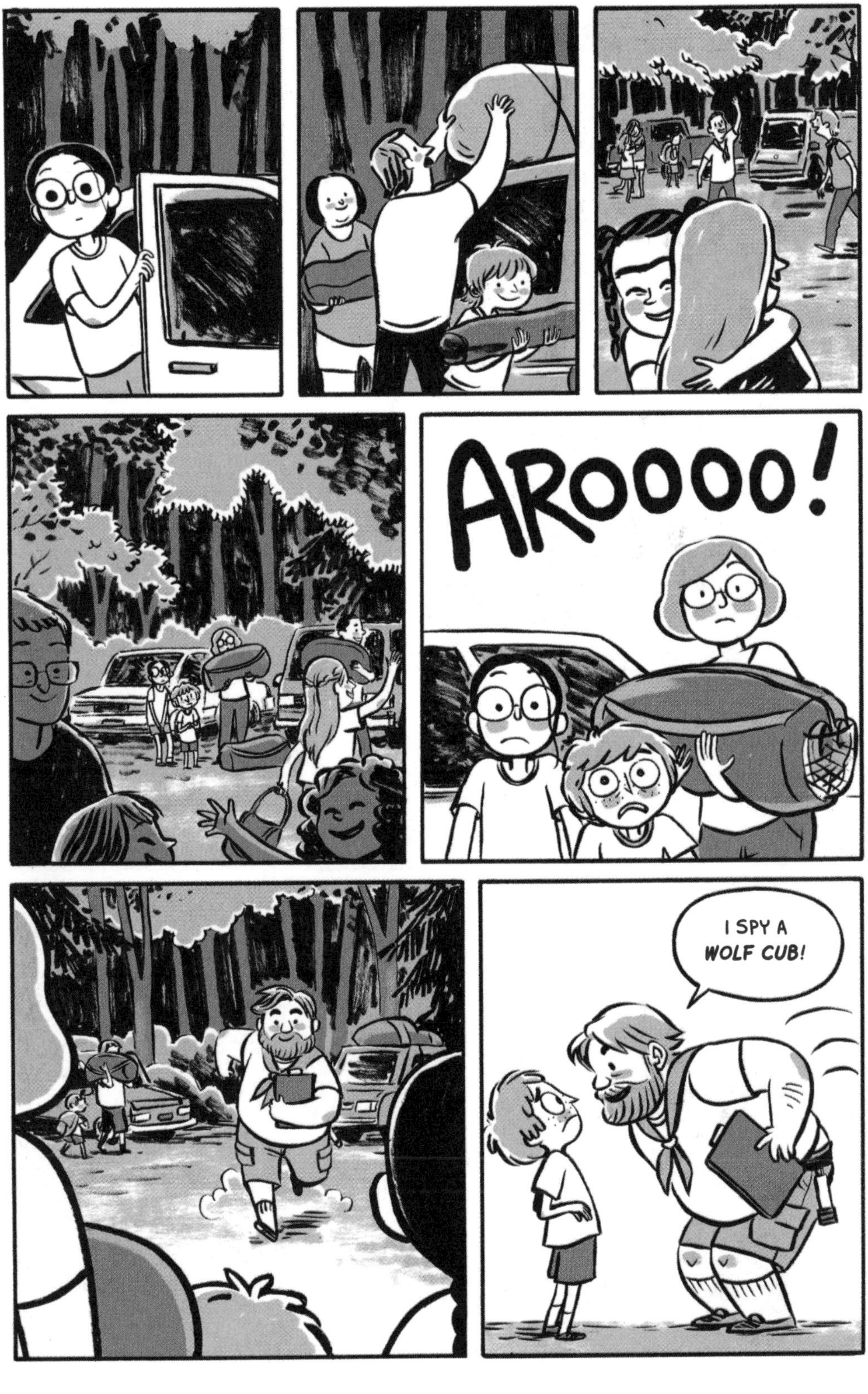
AROOOO!
I SPY A
WOLF CUB!

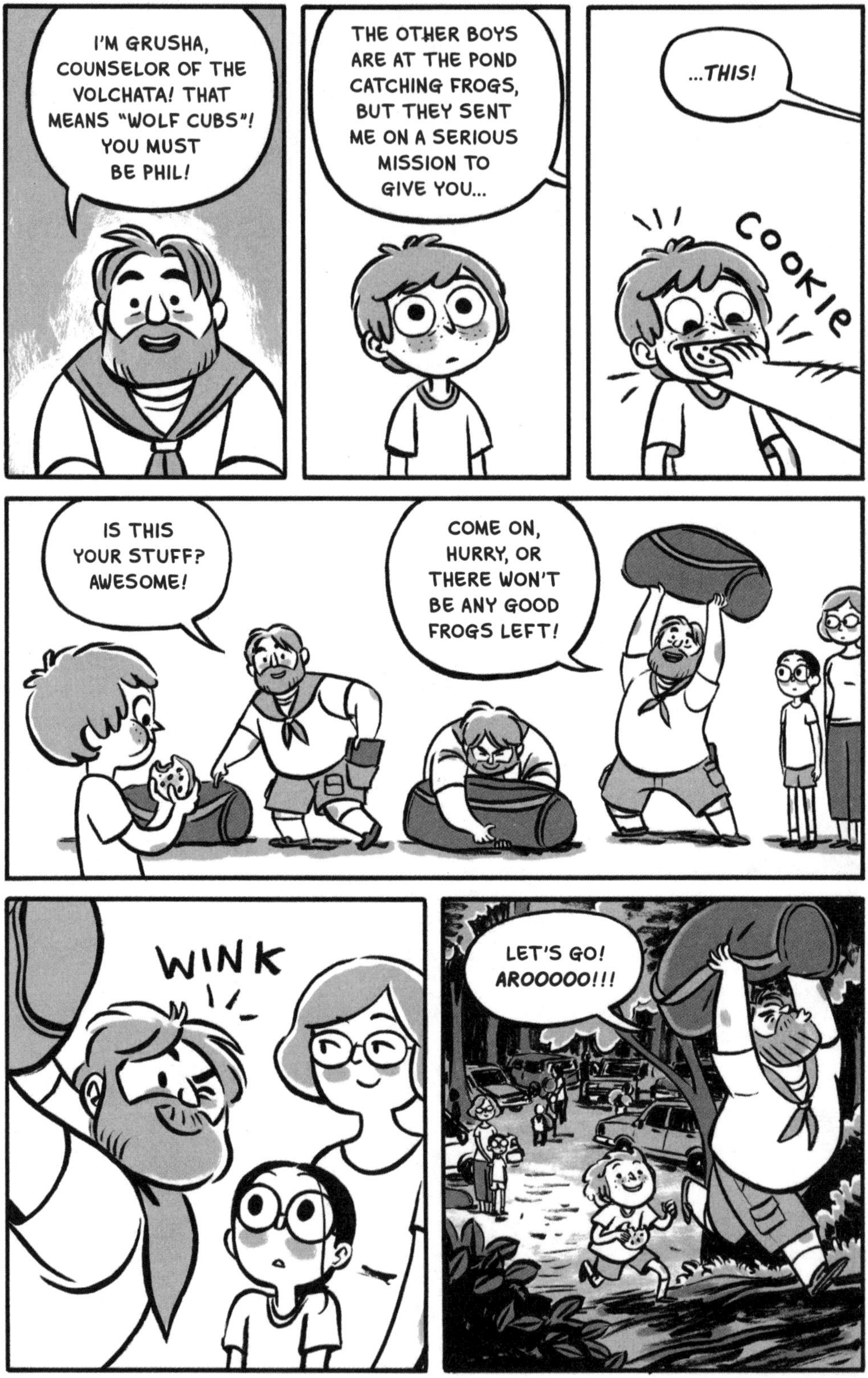
I'M GRUSHA, COUNSELOR OF THE VOLCHATA! THAT MEANS "WOLF CUBS"! YOU MUST BE PHIL!
THE OTHER BOYS ARE AT THE POND CATCHING FROGS, BUT THEY SENT ME ON A SERIOUS MISSION TO GIVE YOU...
...THIS!
COOKIE
IS THIS YOUR STUFF? AWESOME!
COME ON, HURRY, OR THERE WON'T BE ANY GOOD FROGS LEFT!
WINK
LET'S GO! AROOOOO!!!

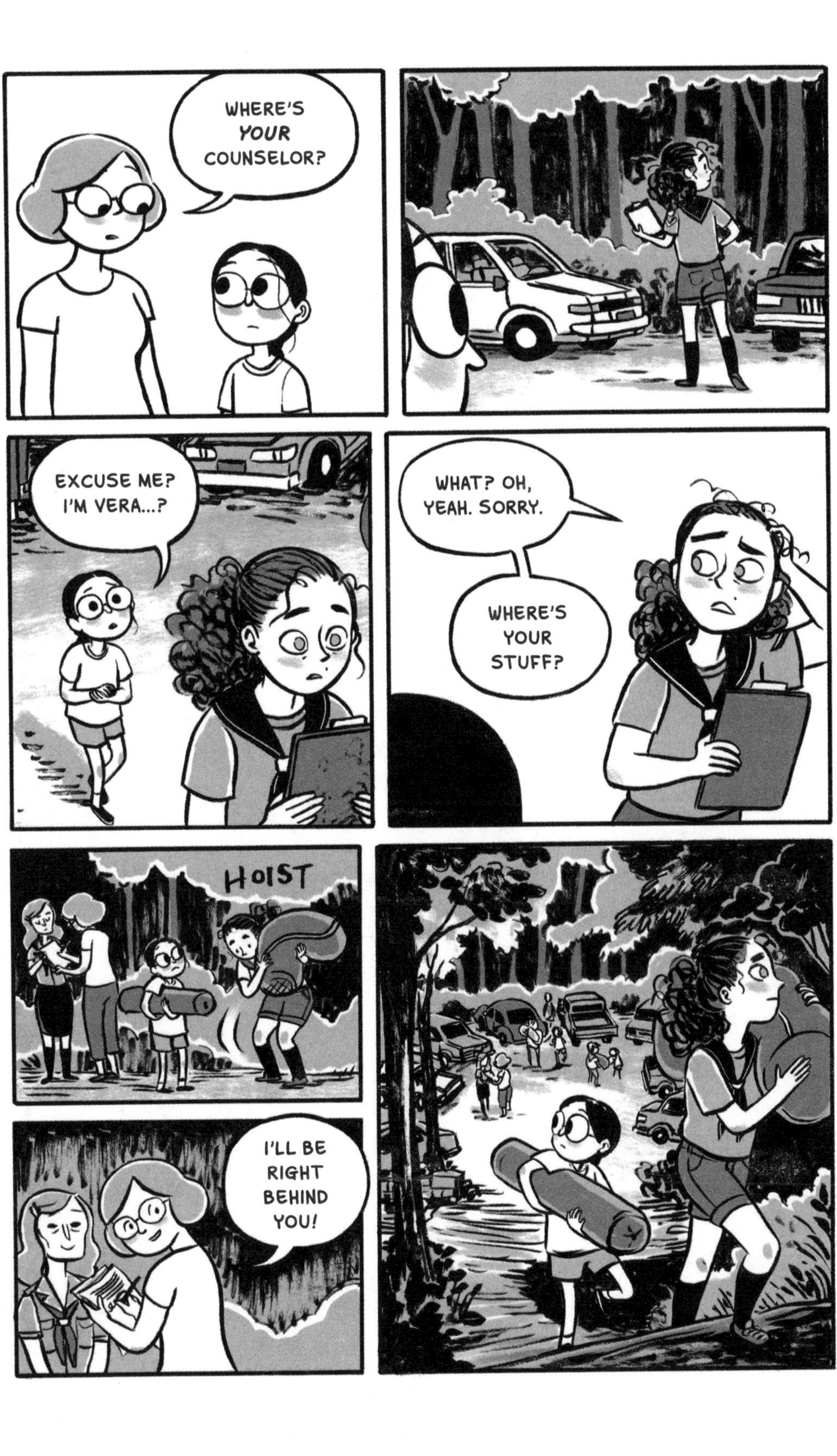
WHERE'S YOUR COUNSELOR?
EXCUSE ME? I'M VERA...?
WHAT? OH, YEAH. SORRY.
WHERE'S YOUR STUFF?
HOIST
I'LL BE RIGHT BEHIND YOU!

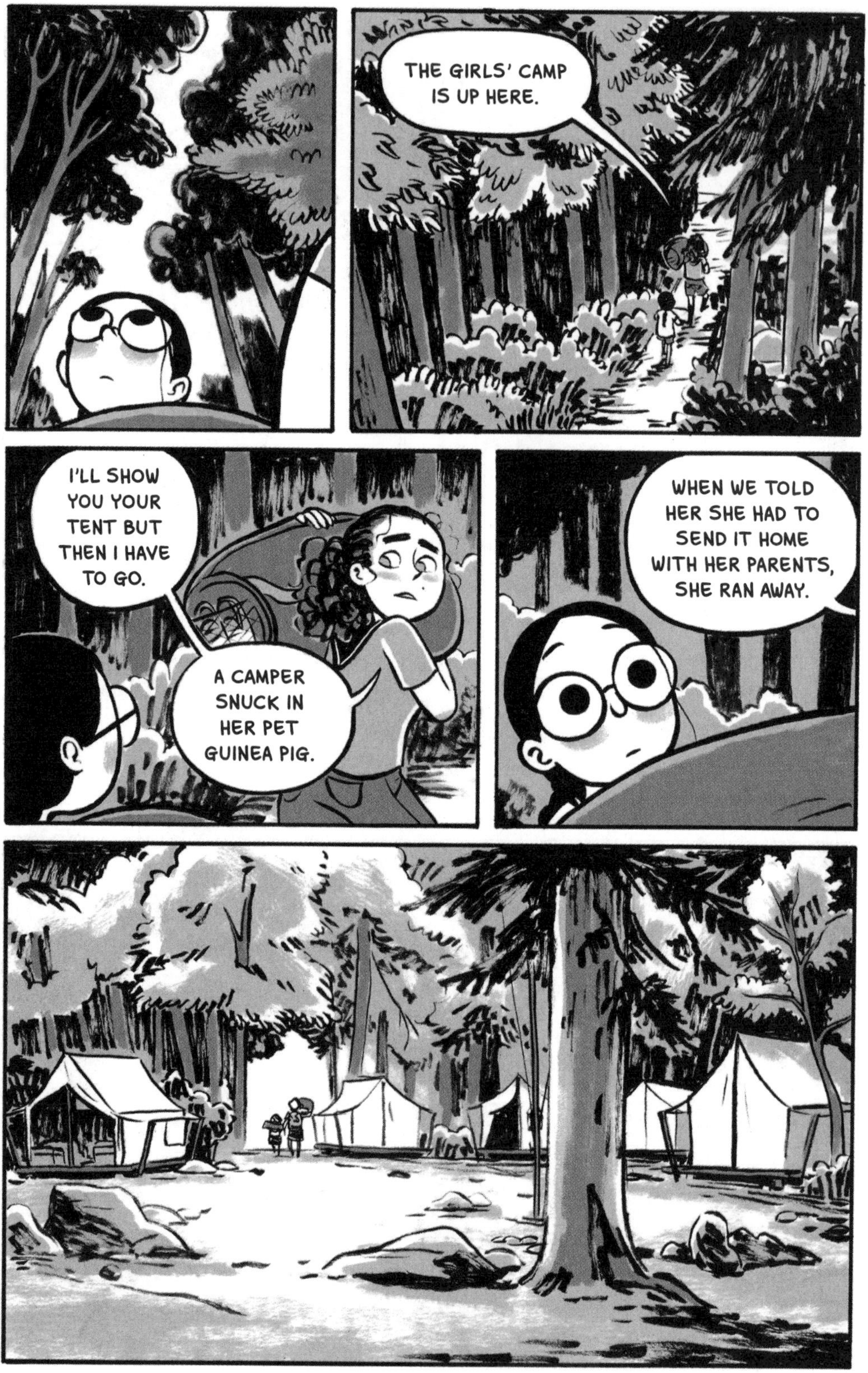
THE GIRLS' CAMP IS UP HERE.
I'LL SHOW YOU YOUR TENT BUT THEN I HAVE TO GO.
A CAMPER SNUCK IN HER PET GUINEA PIG.
WHEN WE TOLD HER SHE HAD TO SEND IT HOME WITH HER PARENTS, SHE RAN AWAY.

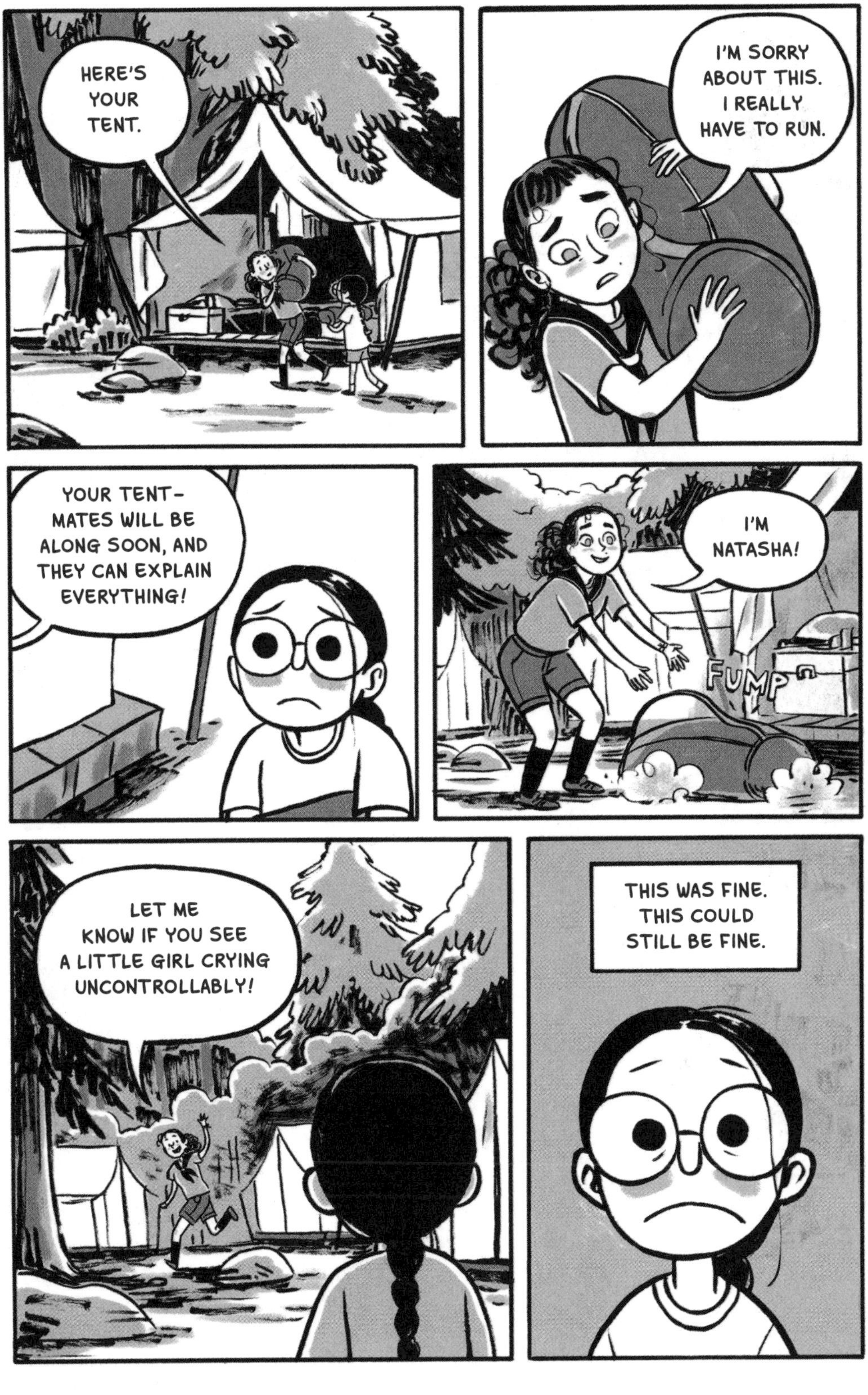
HERE'S YOUR TENT.
I'M SORRY ABOUT THIS. I REALLY HAVE TO RUN.
YOUR TENT-MATES WILL BE ALONG SOON, AND THEY CAN EXPLAIN EVERYTHING!
I'M NATASHA!
FUMP
LET ME KNOW IF YOU SEE A LITTLE GIRL CRYING UNCONTROLLABLY!
THIS WAS FINE. THIS COULD STILL BE FINE.

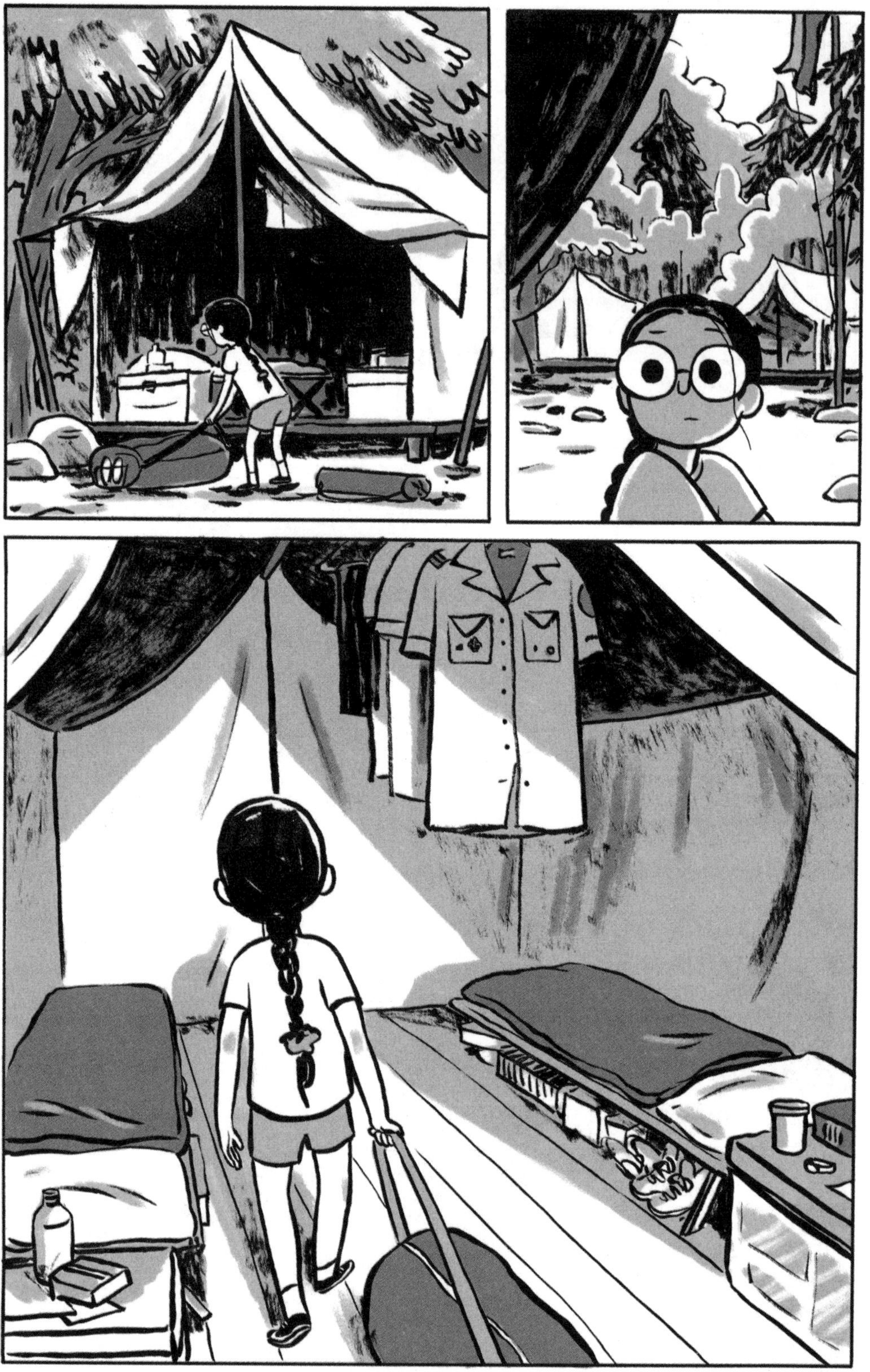

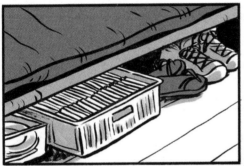

WHAT ARE
YOU DOING.

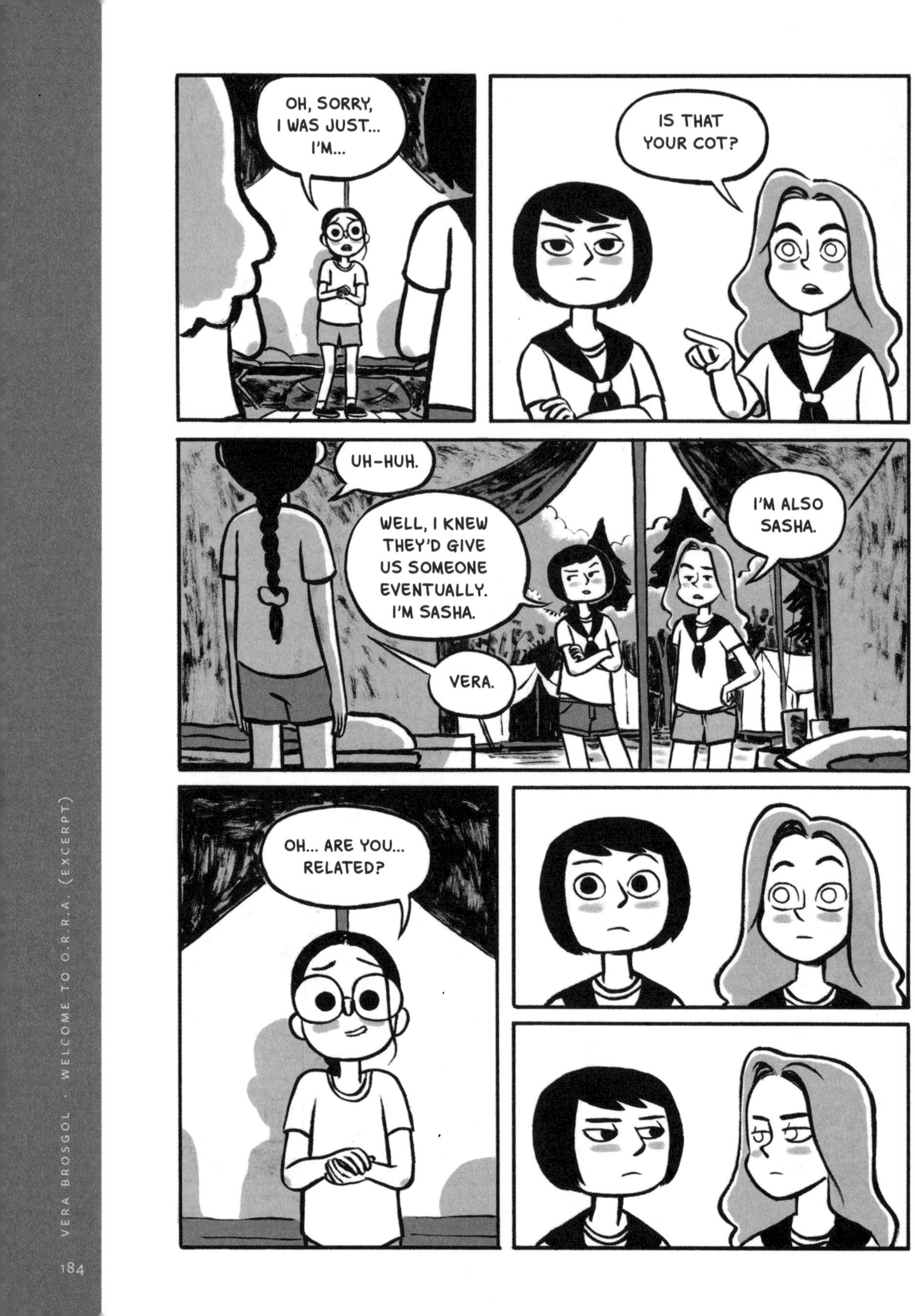
OH, SORRY,
I WAS JUST...
I'M...
IS THAT
YOUR COT?
UH-HUH.
WELL, I KNEW
THEY'D GIVE
US SOMEONE
EVENTUALLY.
I'M SASHA.
I'M ALSO
SASHA.
VERA.
OH... ARE YOU...
RELATED?

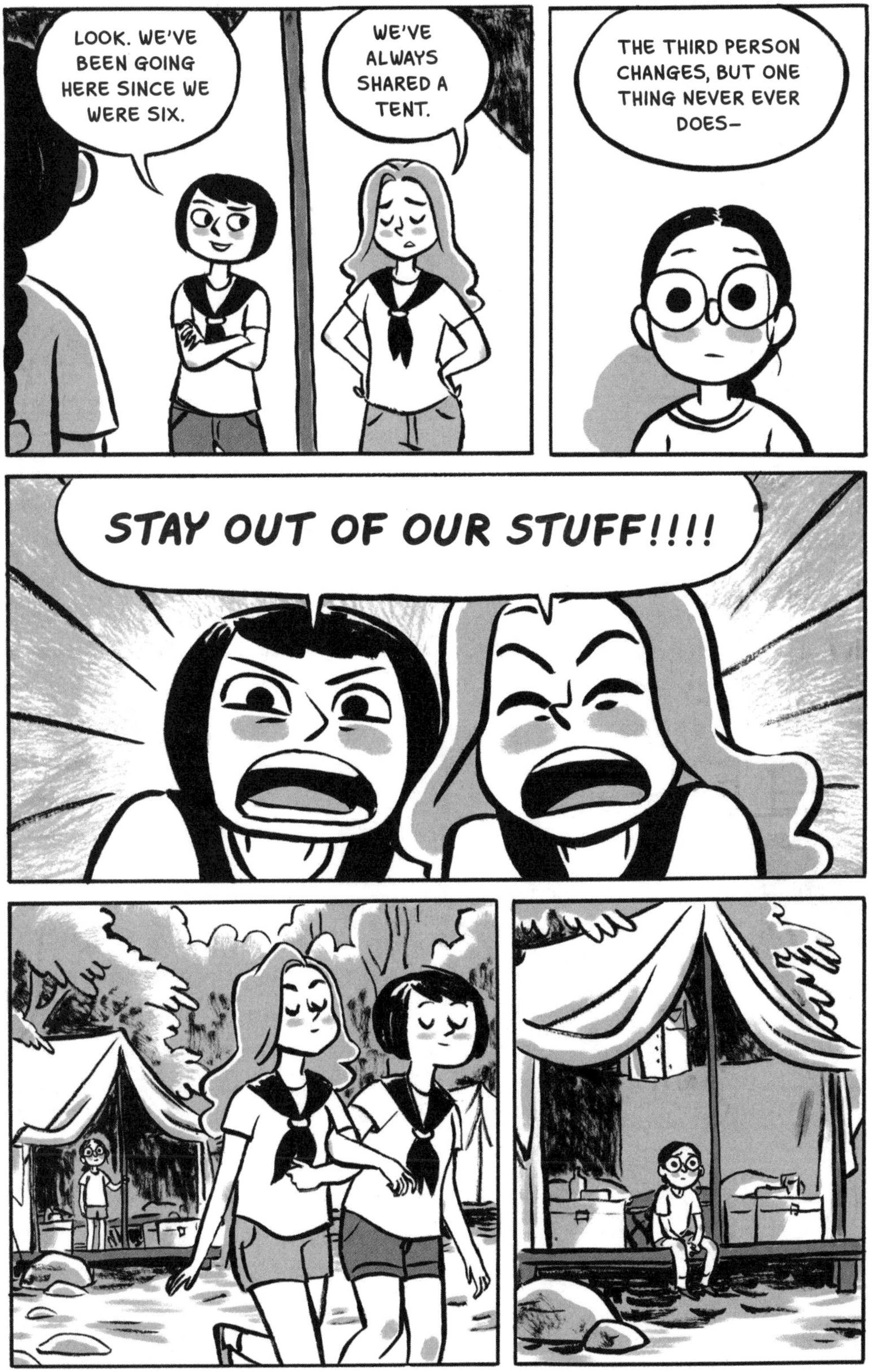
LOOK. WE'VE BEEN GOING HERE SINCE WE WERE SIX.
WE'VE ALWAYS SHARED A TENT.
THE THIRD PERSON CHANGES, BUT ONE THING NEVER EVER DOES—
STAY OUT OF OUR STUFF!!!!

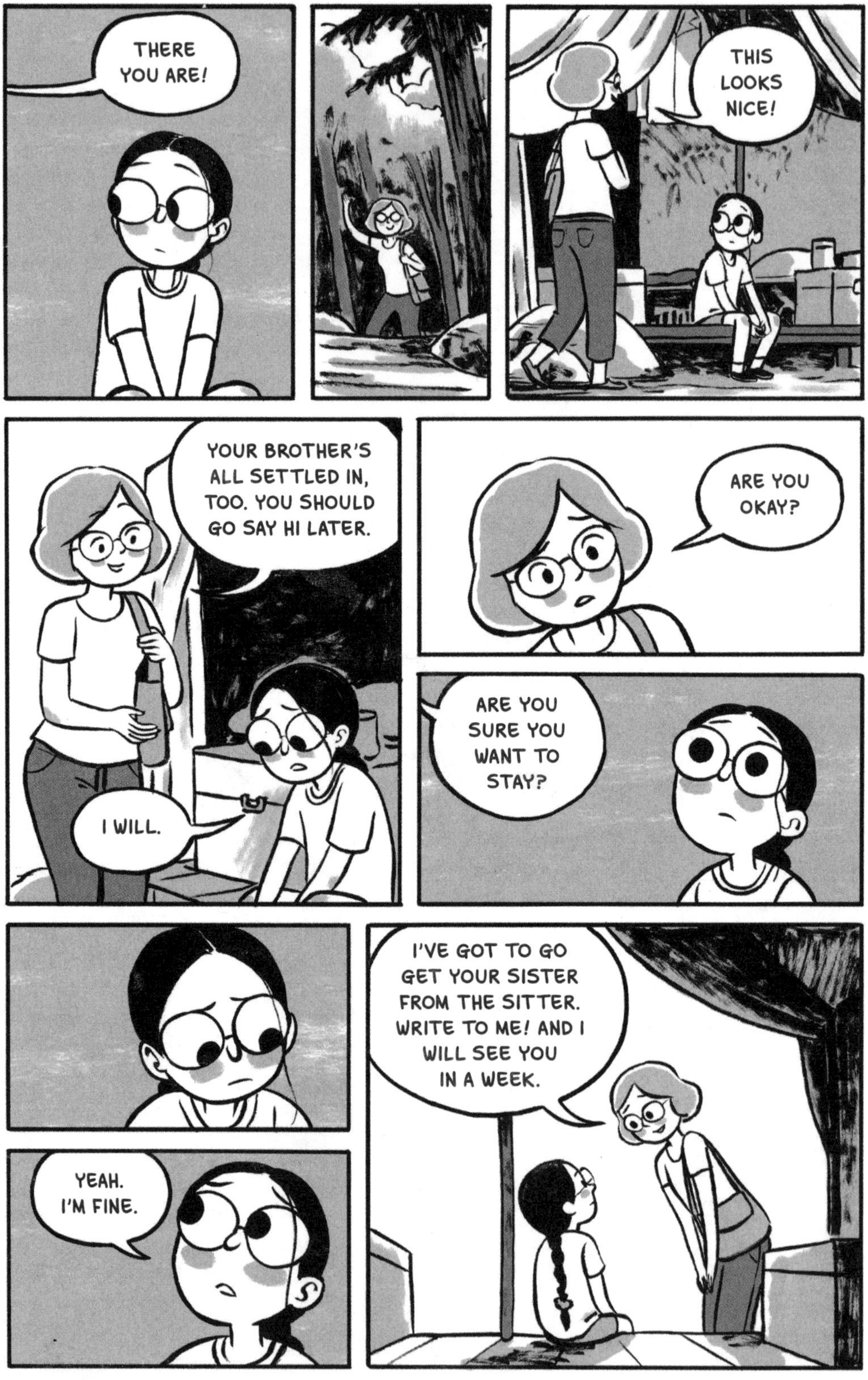
THERE YOU ARE!
THIS LOOKS NICE!
YOUR BROTHER'S ALL SETTLED IN, TOO. YOU SHOULD GO SAY HI LATER.
I WILL.
ARE YOU OKAY?
ARE YOU SURE YOU WANT TO STAY?
YEAH. I'M FINE.
I'VE GOT TO GO GET YOUR SISTER FROM THE SITTER. WRITE TO ME! AND I WILL SEE YOU IN A WEEK.

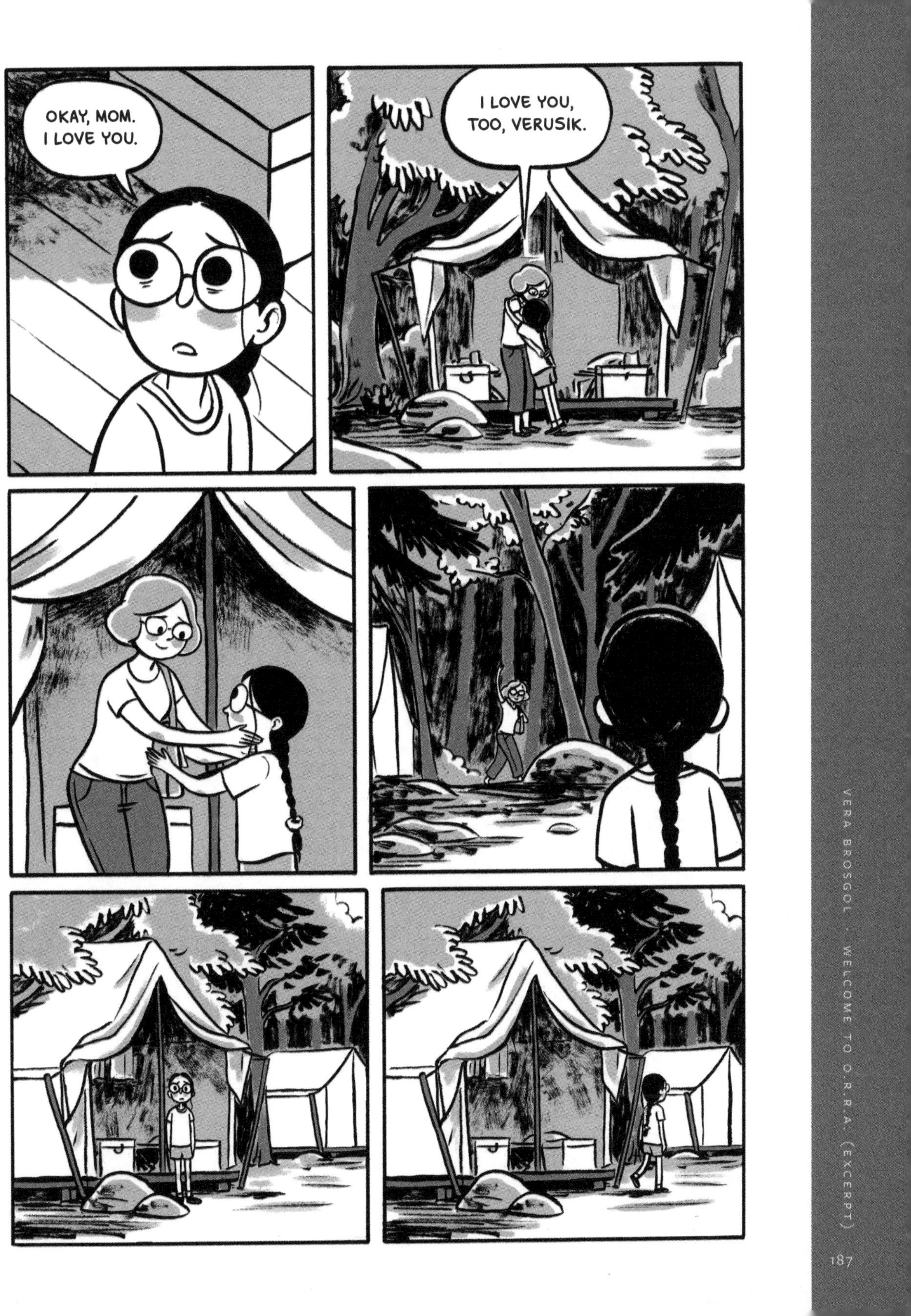
OKAY, MOM.
I LOVE YOU.
I LOVE YOU,
TOO, VERUSIK.

Uninhabitable

JED McGOWAN

JED MCGOWAN
Uninhabitable
UNINHABITABLE
Jed McGowan

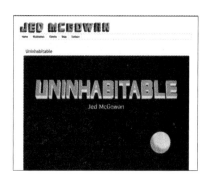

originally published on

jedmcgowan.com
SELF-PUBLISHED
DIGITAL

Biography

Jed McGowan writes and draws in Los Angeles, California. His first graphic novel, *Lone Pine,* was published with a grant from the Xeric Foundation and distributed by AdHouse Books. His latest comic, *Gonzalo,* was published by ShortBox. He's also designed backgrounds for animation and created illustrations for the *New York Times, Vice,* and other publications. Several of Jed's shorter comics can be read at his website. jedmcgowan.com

Statement

With "Uninhabitable," I set out to tell a story about the environment and change at a massive scale. As the comic took shape, it became about change at a smaller, more personal scale too.

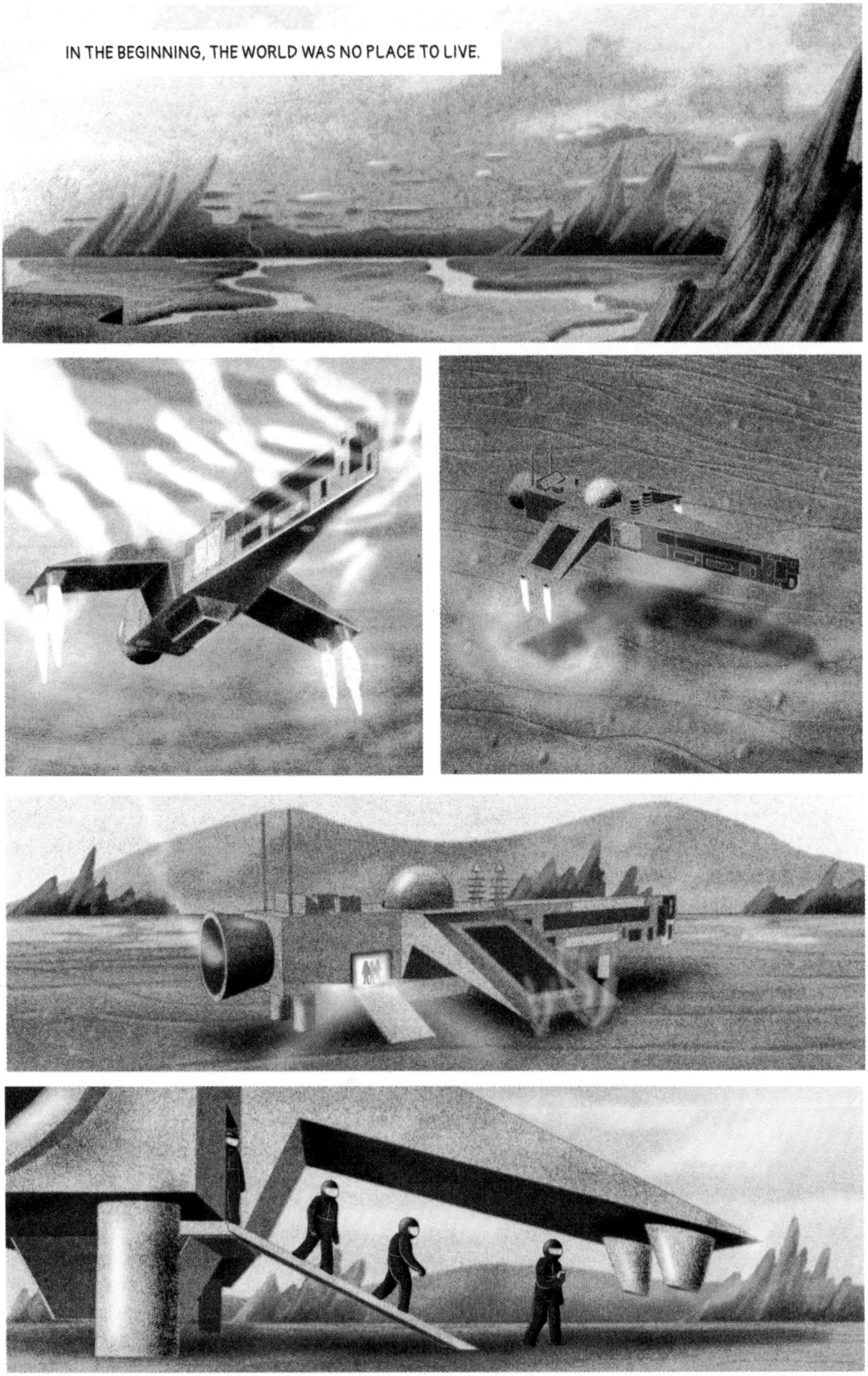
IN THE BEGINNING, THE WORLD WAS NO PLACE TO LIVE.

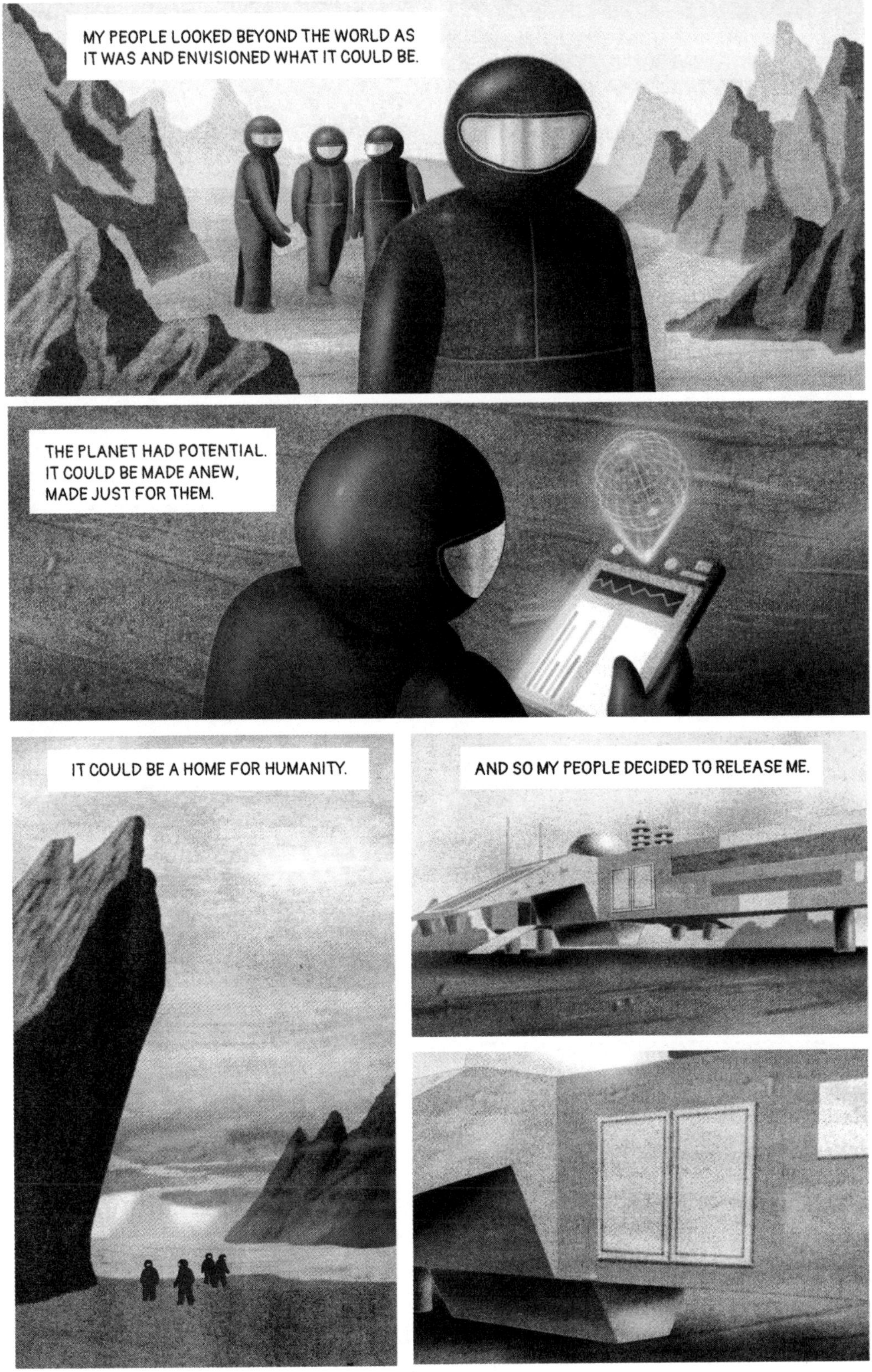
MY PEOPLE LOOKED BEYOND THE WORLD AS IT WAS AND ENVISIONED WHAT IT COULD BE.
THE PLANET HAD POTENTIAL. IT COULD BE MADE ANEW, MADE JUST FOR THEM.
IT COULD BE A HOME FOR HUMANITY.
AND SO MY PEOPLE DECIDED TO RELEASE ME.

THE SHIP'S COMPUTER ESTABLISHED A LINK, TOLD ME TO READY MYSELF.

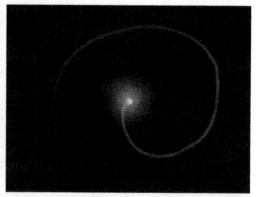

MY UNITS, ALL ONE HUNDRED BILLION OF THEM, BUZZED LIKE A SWARM OF INSECTS AGAINST THE SHIP'S HATCH.

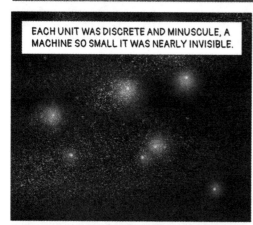
EACH UNIT WAS DISCRETE AND MINUSCULE, A MACHINE SO SMALL IT WAS NEARLY INVISIBLE.

AND YET EACH UNIT WAS PART OF A WHOLE, PART OF ME.

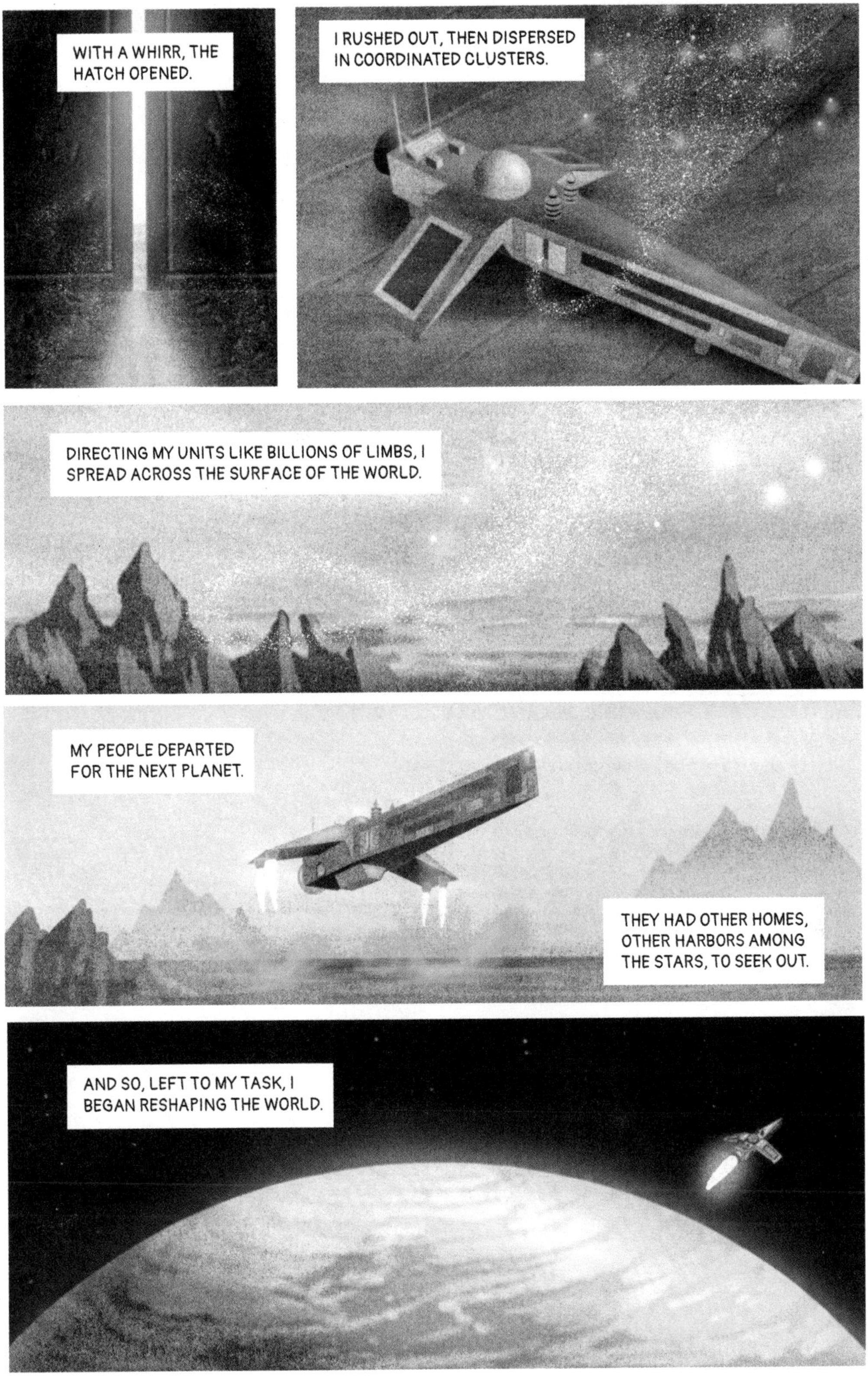
WITH A WHIRR, THE HATCH OPENED.
I RUSHED OUT, THEN DISPERSED IN COORDINATED CLUSTERS.
DIRECTING MY UNITS LIKE BILLIONS OF LIMBS, I SPREAD ACROSS THE SURFACE OF THE WORLD.
MY PEOPLE DEPARTED FOR THE NEXT PLANET.
THEY HAD OTHER HOMES, OTHER HARBORS AMONG THE STARS, TO SEEK OUT.
AND SO, LEFT TO MY TASK, I BEGAN RESHAPING THE WORLD.

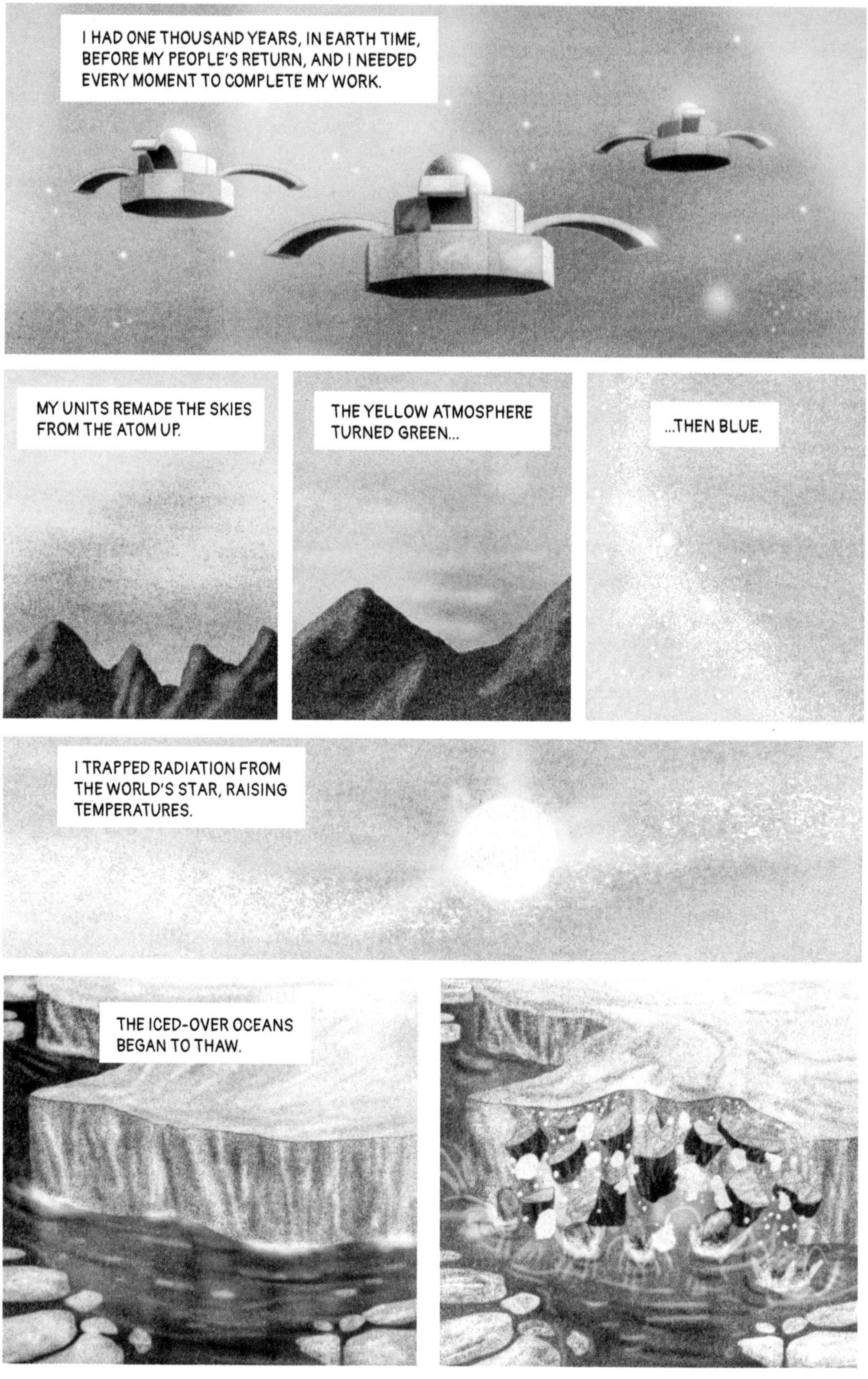
I HAD ONE THOUSAND YEARS, IN EARTH TIME, BEFORE MY PEOPLE'S RETURN, AND I NEEDED EVERY MOMENT TO COMPLETE MY WORK.
MY UNITS REMADE THE SKIES FROM THE ATOM UP.
THE YELLOW ATMOSPHERE TURNED GREEN...
...THEN BLUE.
I TRAPPED RADIATION FROM THE WORLD'S STAR, RAISING TEMPERATURES.
THE ICED-OVER OCEANS BEGAN TO THAW.

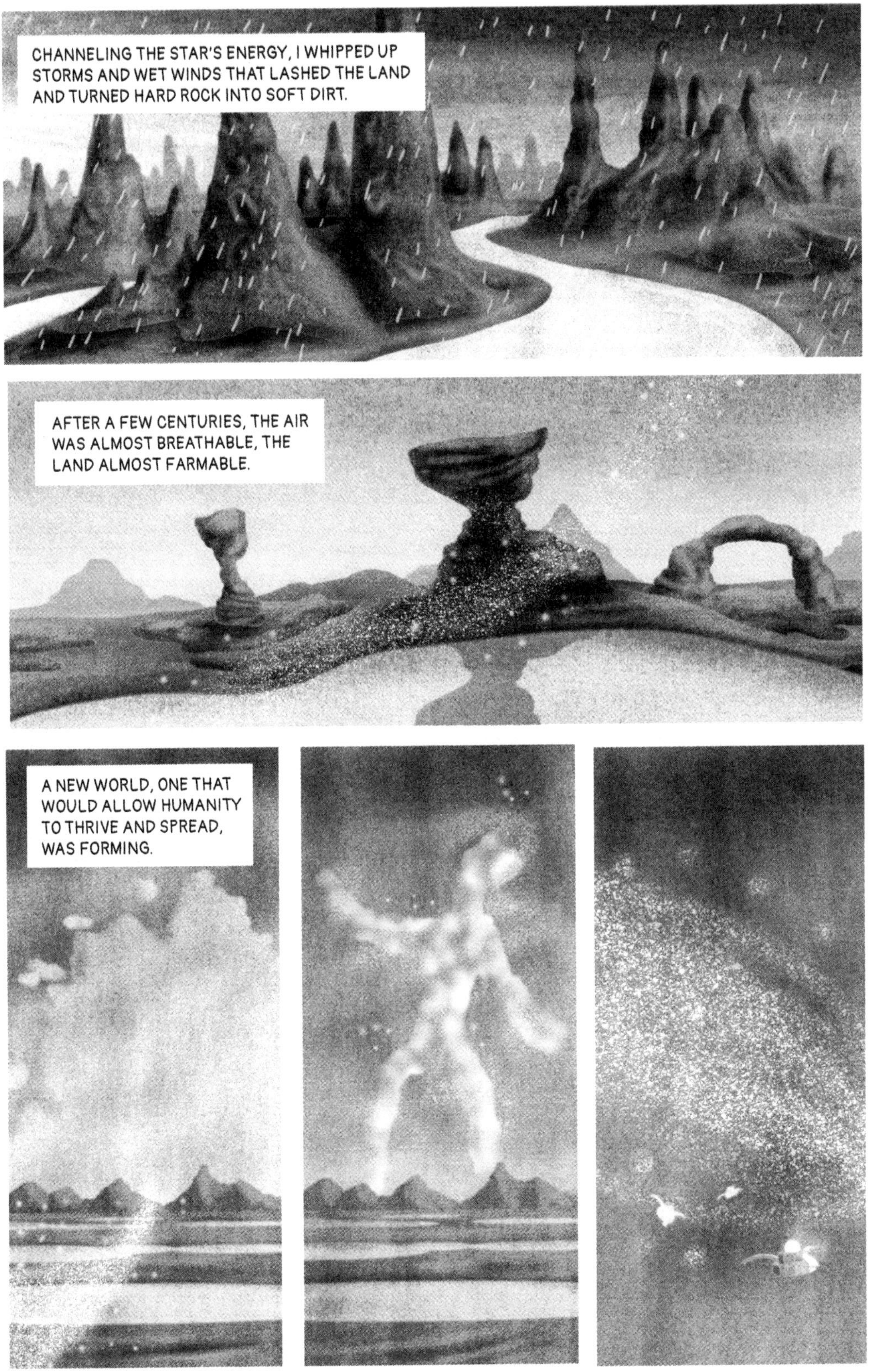
CHANNELING THE STAR'S ENERGY, I WHIPPED UP STORMS AND WET WINDS THAT LASHED THE LAND AND TURNED HARD ROCK INTO SOFT DIRT.
AFTER A FEW CENTURIES, THE AIR WAS ALMOST BREATHABLE, THE LAND ALMOST FARMABLE.
A NEW WORLD, ONE THAT WOULD ALLOW HUMANITY TO THRIVE AND SPREAD, WAS FORMING.

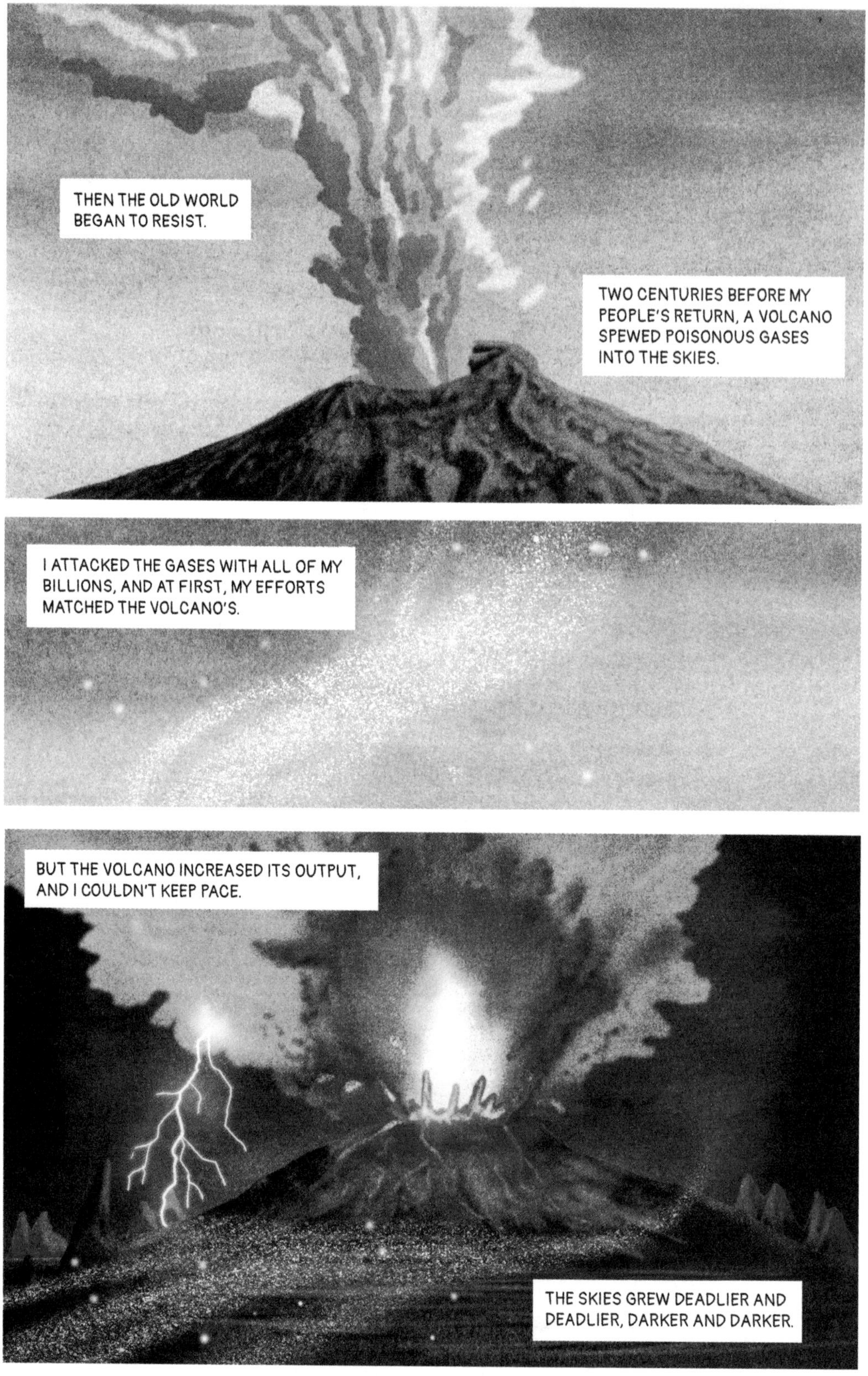
THEN THE OLD WORLD BEGAN TO RESIST.
TWO CENTURIES BEFORE MY PEOPLE'S RETURN, A VOLCANO SPEWED POISONOUS GASES INTO THE SKIES.
I ATTACKED THE GASES WITH ALL OF MY BILLIONS, AND AT FIRST, MY EFFORTS MATCHED THE VOLCANO'S.
BUT THE VOLCANO INCREASED ITS OUTPUT, AND I COULDN'T KEEP PACE.
THE SKIES GREW DEADLIER AND DEADLIER, DARKER AND DARKER.

I CHANGED TACK AND SWARMED DOWN THE VOLCANO'S THROAT, ATTEMPTING TO COOL THE BUBBLING LAVA AND PLUG THE MAIN VENT.

I WAS NOT DESIGNED FOR SUCH WORK, AND THE VOLCANO QUICKLY BURNED THROUGH MY NUMBERS.

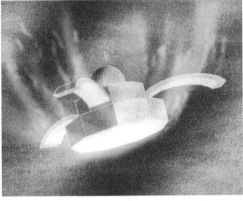

I CONTINUED — AND CONTINUED TO HAVE NO EFFECT — UNTIL ONLY A FEW BILLION OF ME REMAINED.

FINALLY, I RETREATED.

I DRIFTED ON THE WIND AS THE VOLCANO CONTINUED TO POISON THE WORLD, UNDOING CENTURIES OF WORK.

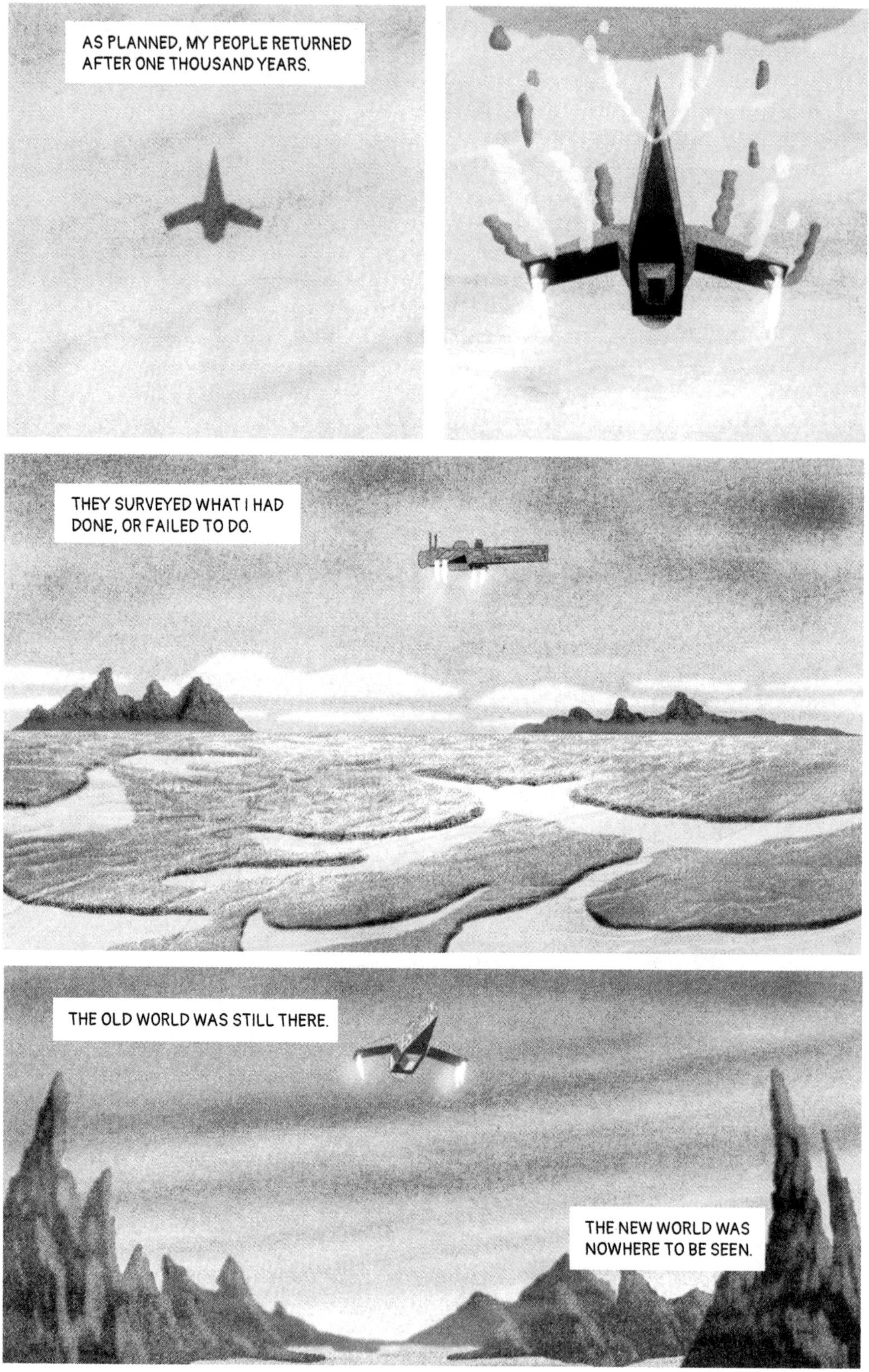
AS PLANNED, MY PEOPLE RETURNED AFTER ONE THOUSAND YEARS.
THEY SURVEYED WHAT I HAD DONE, OR FAILED TO DO.
THE OLD WORLD WAS STILL THERE.
THE NEW WORLD WAS NOWHERE TO BE SEEN.

I WAITED FOR THE SHIP'S COMPUTER TO LINK WITH ME SO I COULD EXPLAIN MYSELF, EXPLAIN I NEEDED MORE TIME, MORE UNITS.

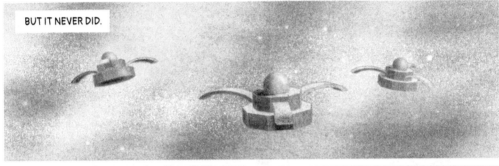

BUT IT NEVER DID.

IT HOVERED A MOMENT...

...THEN LEFT FOR THE STARS.

I LOST MY PEOPLE.

I WAS ALONE.

I HELPED LIFE FLOURISH ON THE WORLD, AT LAST.

SHE WAS A NEW ORGANISM, ONE THAT I CREATED.

I DIDN'T MAKE HER IN THE IMAGE OF MY PEOPLE.

SHE HAD NUMEROUS LIMBS, LIKE A MILLIPEDE, LIKE ME.

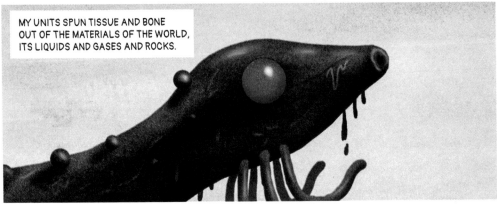

MY UNITS SPUN TISSUE AND BONE OUT OF THE MATERIALS OF THE WORLD, ITS LIQUIDS AND GASES AND ROCKS.

THOUGHT WAS MORE DIFFICULT.

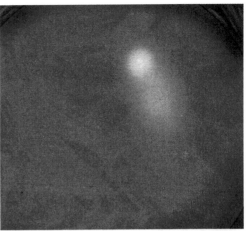

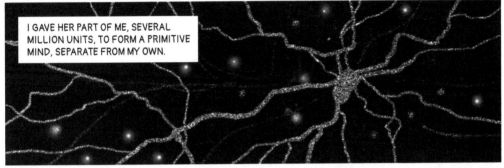

I GAVE HER PART OF ME, SEVERAL MILLION UNITS, TO FORM A PRIMITIVE MIND, SEPARATE FROM MY OWN.

MY REMAINING NUMBERS STUCK CLOSE TO MY CREATION.

OUR UNITS WERE NO LONGER NETWORKED, BUT I WONDERED IF SHE FELT MY PRESENCE.

THE ERUPTIONS CAME AGAIN. BUT IT WAS NO MATTER.

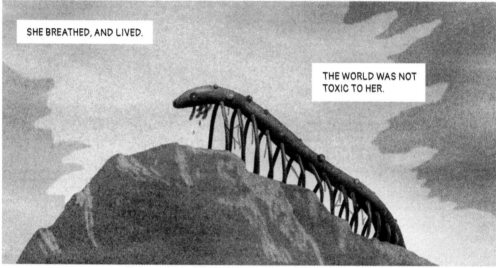

SHE BREATHED, AND LIVED.

THE WORLD WAS NOT TOXIC TO HER.

SHE WAS PART OF THE WORLD, MADE FROM THE WORLD.

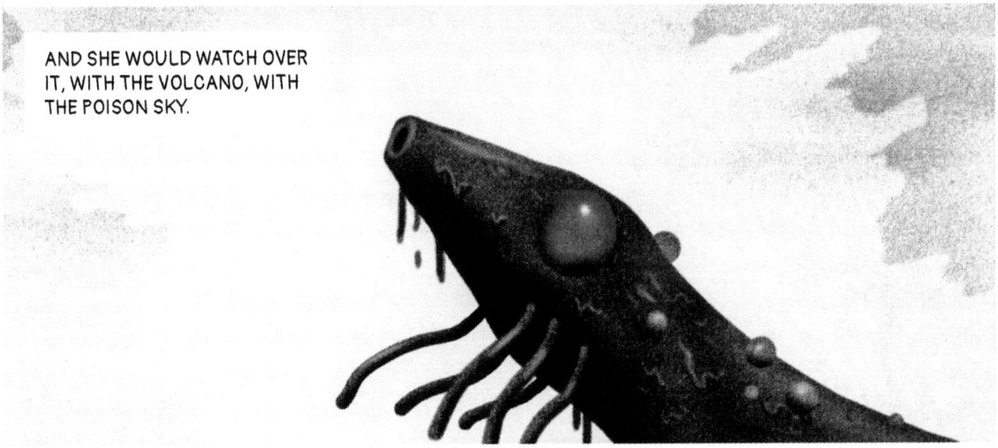
AND SHE WOULD WATCH OVER IT, WITH THE VOLCANO, WITH THE POISON SKY.

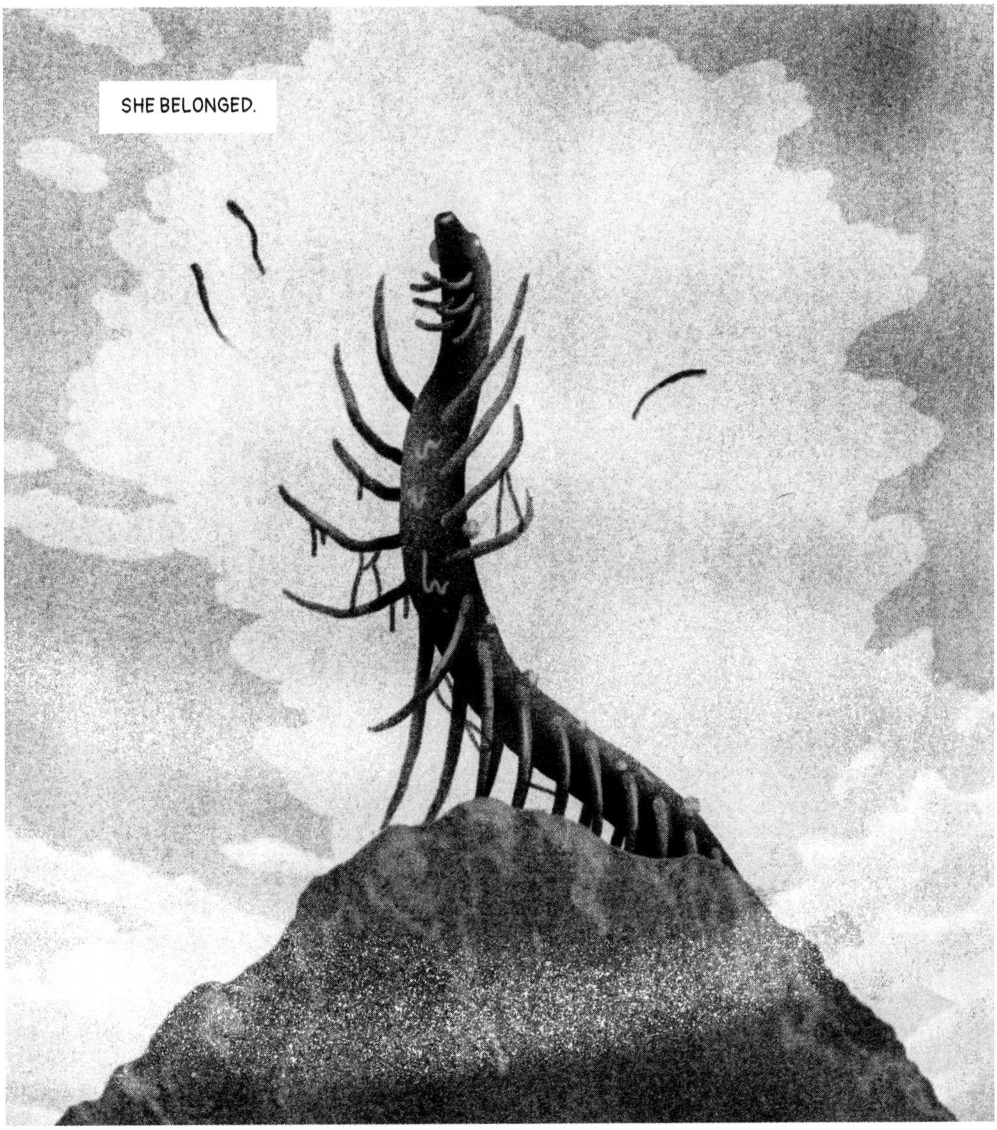
SHE BELONGED.

Snow Day for Mr. Good Guy

NISHANT SALDANHA

originally published on

instagram.com/nishantsaldanha
SELF-PUBLISHED
DIGITAL

Biography

Nishant Saldanha graduated from the California Institute of the Arts in 2016, with a BFA in Character Animation, and a grounding in filmmaking. After working as a freelance animator in Los Angeles, he now pursues an independent practice that focuses on short films, books, illustration, and photography. He lives and works in Goa, his ancestral homeland and India's smallest state, from where he self-publishes his comic series *Mr. Good Guy* online.
instagram.com/nishantsaldanha

Statement

My comic-making got an unusual start with six full episodes for an animated TV show called *Heartlands* that I wrote in 2016. Its ensemble of characters included an unconventional antagonist, who quickly grew to fill up most of my stories, and always drew the most laughs at my screenplay workshops in college. Later, I made comics with this material as a way to get out of animator's block on a film. I find limiting myself to a single-panel format is immensely liberating, and an expressive way to explore some of the more abstract ideas in my head. *Snow Day For Mr. Good Guy* is one of very few multi-panel comics in a predominately single-panel collection, which revolves around the misadventures of the blundering antihero.

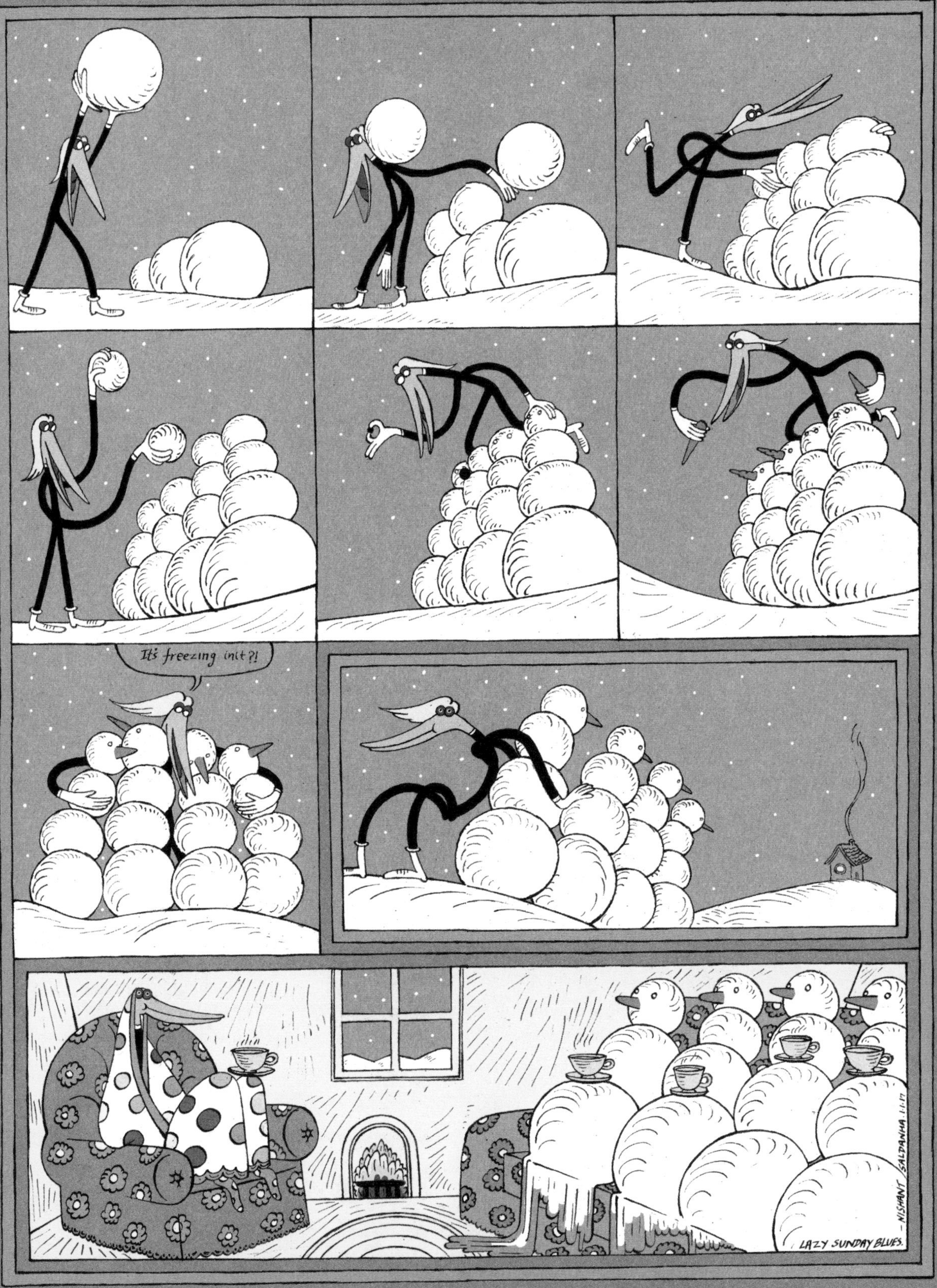
It's freezing init?!
LAZY SUNDAY BLUES.
– NISHANT SALDANHA. 1.1.17

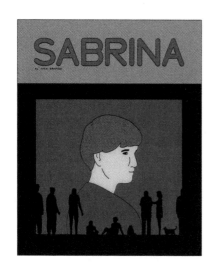

Sabrina (*Excerpt*)

NICK DRNASO

originally published in

Sabrina
DRAWN AND QUARTERLY
7.8 x 9.5 inches • 204 pages

Biography

Nick Drnaso was born in Palos Hills, Illinois, and now lives in Chicago with his wife and three cats. He is the author of *Beverly* (2016) and *Sabrina* (2018), both of which were published by Drawn and Quarterly.

Statement

This excerpt is from around the halfway point of the book, and seems to be a good representation of what the rest of the story is about.

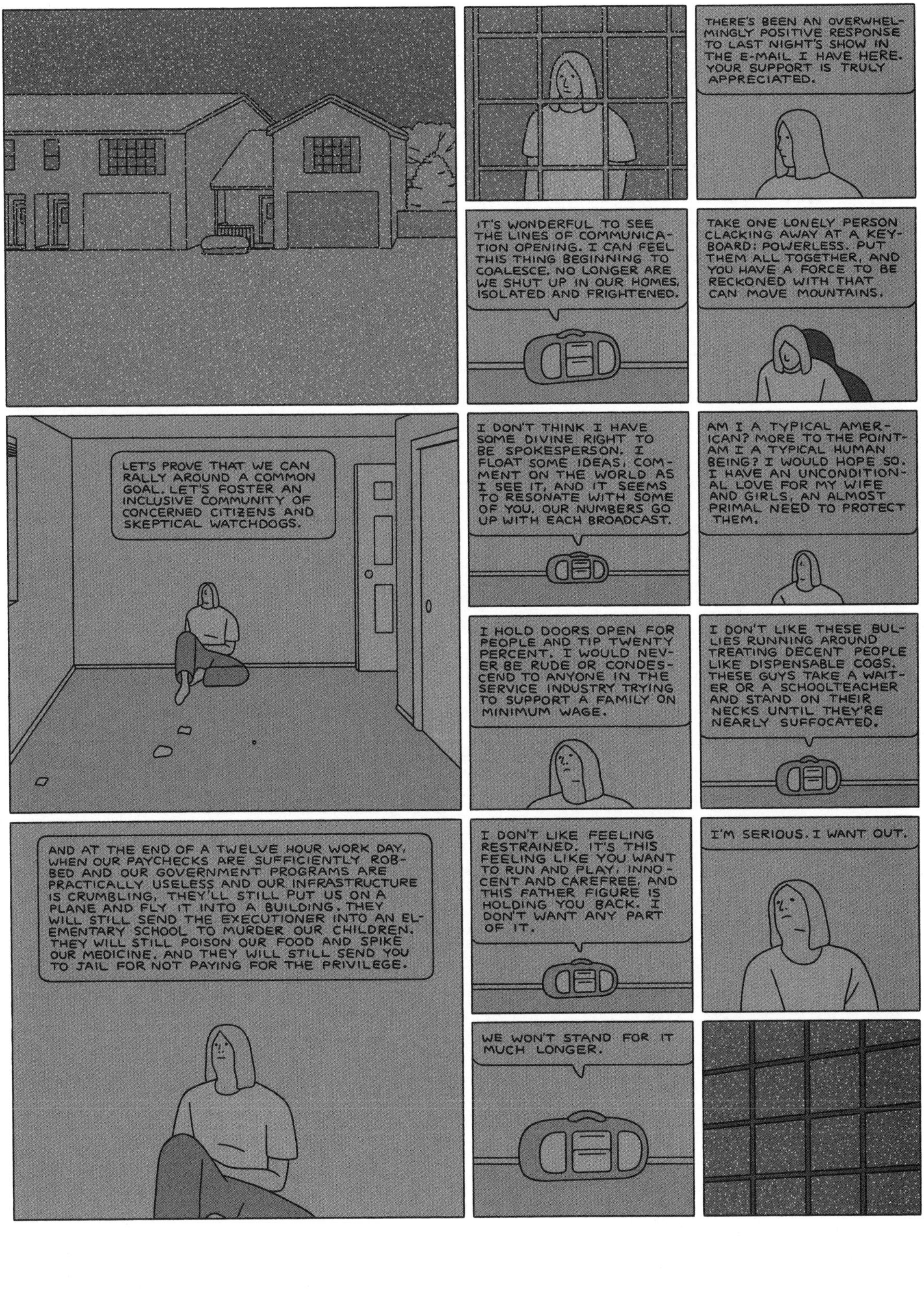
THERE'S BEEN AN OVERWHELMINGLY POSITIVE RESPONSE TO LAST NIGHT'S SHOW IN THE E-MAIL I HAVE HERE. YOUR SUPPORT IS TRULY APPRECIATED.
IT'S WONDERFUL TO SEE THE LINES OF COMMUNICATION OPENING. I CAN FEEL THIS THING BEGINNING TO COALESCE. NO LONGER ARE WE SHUT UP IN OUR HOMES, ISOLATED AND FRIGHTENED.
TAKE ONE LONELY PERSON CLACKING AWAY AT A KEYBOARD: POWERLESS. PUT THEM ALL TOGETHER, AND YOU HAVE A FORCE TO BE RECKONED WITH THAT CAN MOVE MOUNTAINS.
LET'S PROVE THAT WE CAN RALLY AROUND A COMMON GOAL. LET'S FOSTER AN INCLUSIVE COMMUNITY OF CONCERNED CITIZENS AND SKEPTICAL WATCHDOGS.
I DON'T THINK I HAVE SOME DIVINE RIGHT TO BE SPOKESPERSON. I FLOAT SOME IDEAS, COMMENT ON THE WORLD AS I SEE IT, AND IT SEEMS TO RESONATE WITH SOME OF YOU. OUR NUMBERS GO UP WITH EACH BROADCAST.
AM I A TYPICAL AMERICAN? MORE TO THE POINT-AM I A TYPICAL HUMAN BEING? I WOULD HOPE SO. I HAVE AN UNCONDITIONAL LOVE FOR MY WIFE AND GIRLS, AN ALMOST PRIMAL NEED TO PROTECT THEM.
I HOLD DOORS OPEN FOR PEOPLE AND TIP TWENTY PERCENT. I WOULD NEVER BE RUDE OR CONDESCEND TO ANYONE IN THE SERVICE INDUSTRY TRYING TO SUPPORT A FAMILY ON MINIMUM WAGE.
I DON'T LIKE THESE BULLIES RUNNING AROUND TREATING DECENT PEOPLE LIKE DISPENSABLE COGS. THESE GUYS TAKE A WAITER OR A SCHOOLTEACHER AND STAND ON THEIR NECKS UNTIL THEY'RE NEARLY SUFFOCATED.
AND AT THE END OF A TWELVE HOUR WORK DAY, WHEN OUR PAYCHECKS ARE SUFFICIENTLY ROBBED AND OUR GOVERNMENT PROGRAMS ARE PRACTICALLY USELESS AND OUR INFRASTRUCTURE IS CRUMBLING, THEY'LL STILL PUT US ON A PLANE AND FLY IT INTO A BUILDING. THEY WILL STILL SEND THE EXECUTIONER INTO AN ELEMENTARY SCHOOL TO MURDER OUR CHILDREN. THEY WILL STILL POISON OUR FOOD AND SPIKE OUR MEDICINE, AND THEY WILL STILL SEND YOU TO JAIL FOR NOT PAYING FOR THE PRIVILEGE.
I DON'T LIKE FEELING RESTRAINED. IT'S THIS FEELING LIKE YOU WANT TO RUN AND PLAY, INNOCENT AND CAREFREE, AND THIS FATHER FIGURE IS HOLDING YOU BACK. I DON'T WANT ANY PART OF IT.
I'M SERIOUS. I WANT OUT.
WE WON'T STAND FOR IT MUCH LONGER.

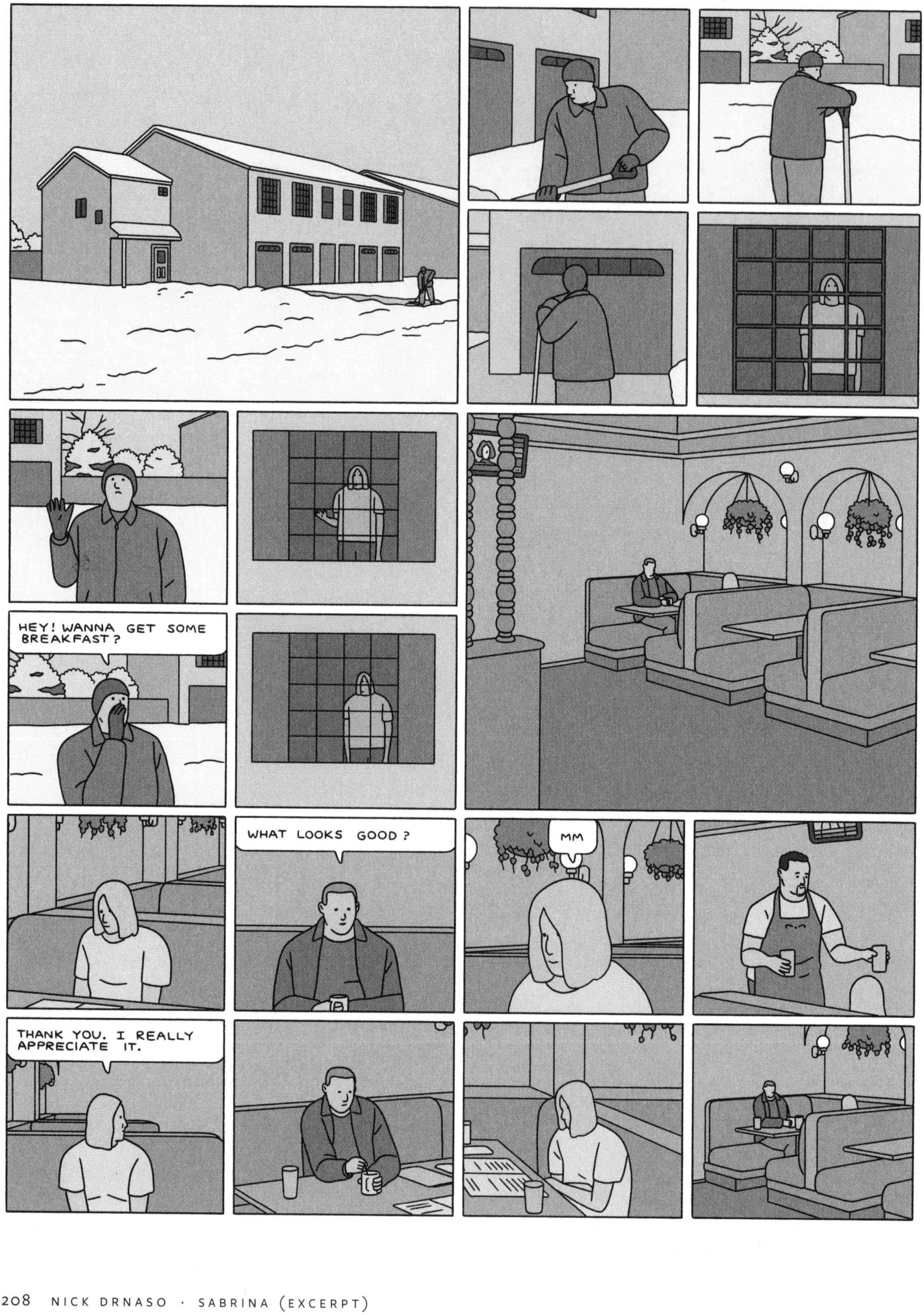
HEY! WANNA GET SOME BREAKFAST?
WHAT LOOKS GOOD?
MM
THANK YOU. I REALLY APPRECIATE IT.

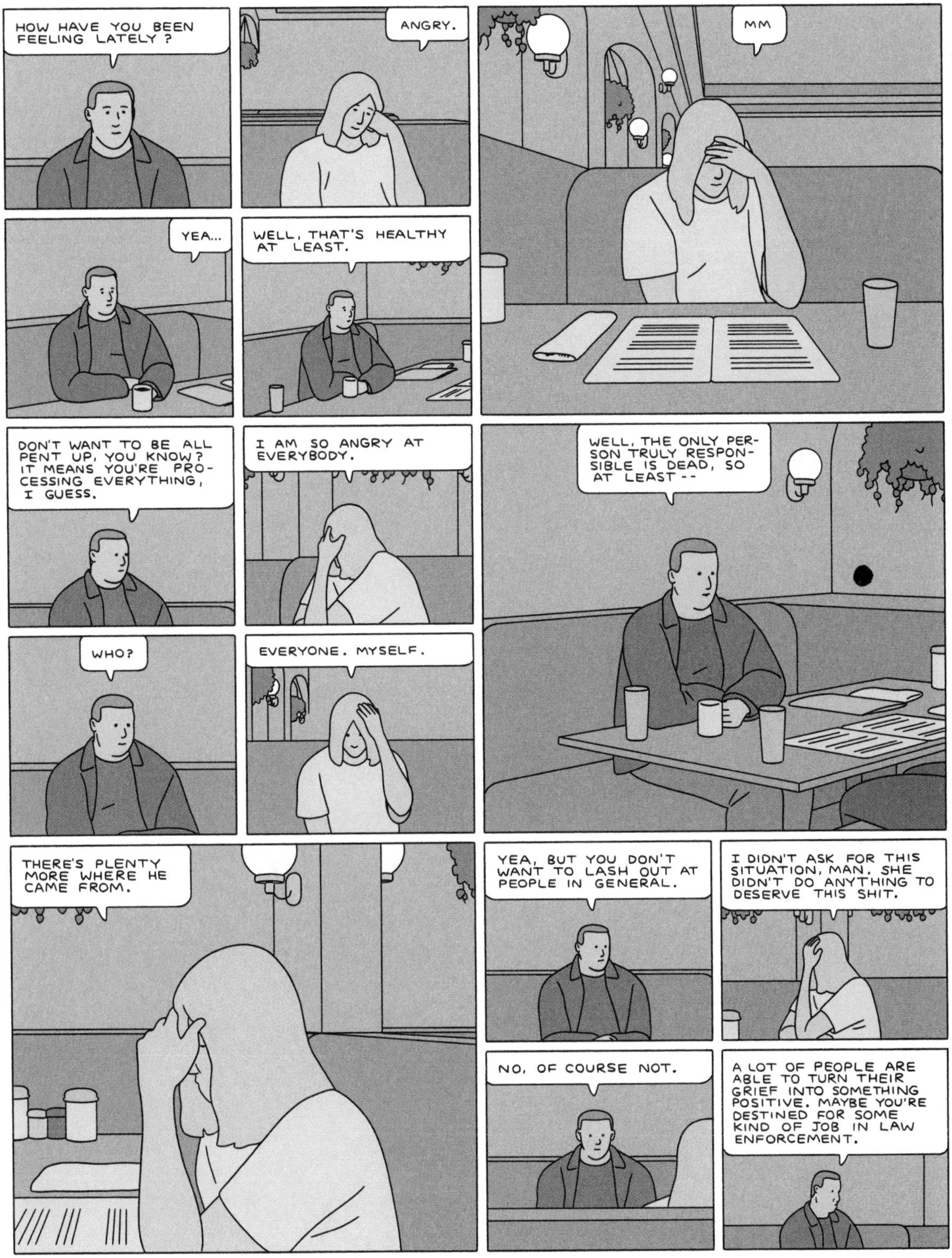
HOW HAVE YOU BEEN FEELING LATELY ?
ANGRY.
MM
YEA...
WELL, THAT'S HEALTHY AT LEAST.
DON'T WANT TO BE ALL PENT UP, YOU KNOW? IT MEANS YOU'RE PRO-CESSING EVERYTHING, I GUESS.
I AM SO ANGRY AT EVERYBODY.
WELL, THE ONLY PER-SON TRULY RESPON-SIBLE IS DEAD, SO AT LEAST --
WHO?
EVERYONE. MYSELF.
THERE'S PLENTY MORE WHERE HE CAME FROM.
YEA, BUT YOU DON'T WANT TO LASH OUT AT PEOPLE IN GENERAL.
I DIDN'T ASK FOR THIS SITUATION, MAN. SHE DIDN'T DO ANYTHING TO DESERVE THIS SHIT.
NO, OF COURSE NOT.
A LOT OF PEOPLE ARE ABLE TO TURN THEIR GRIEF INTO SOMETHING POSITIVE. MAYBE YOU'RE DESTINED FOR SOME KIND OF JOB IN LAW ENFORCEMENT.

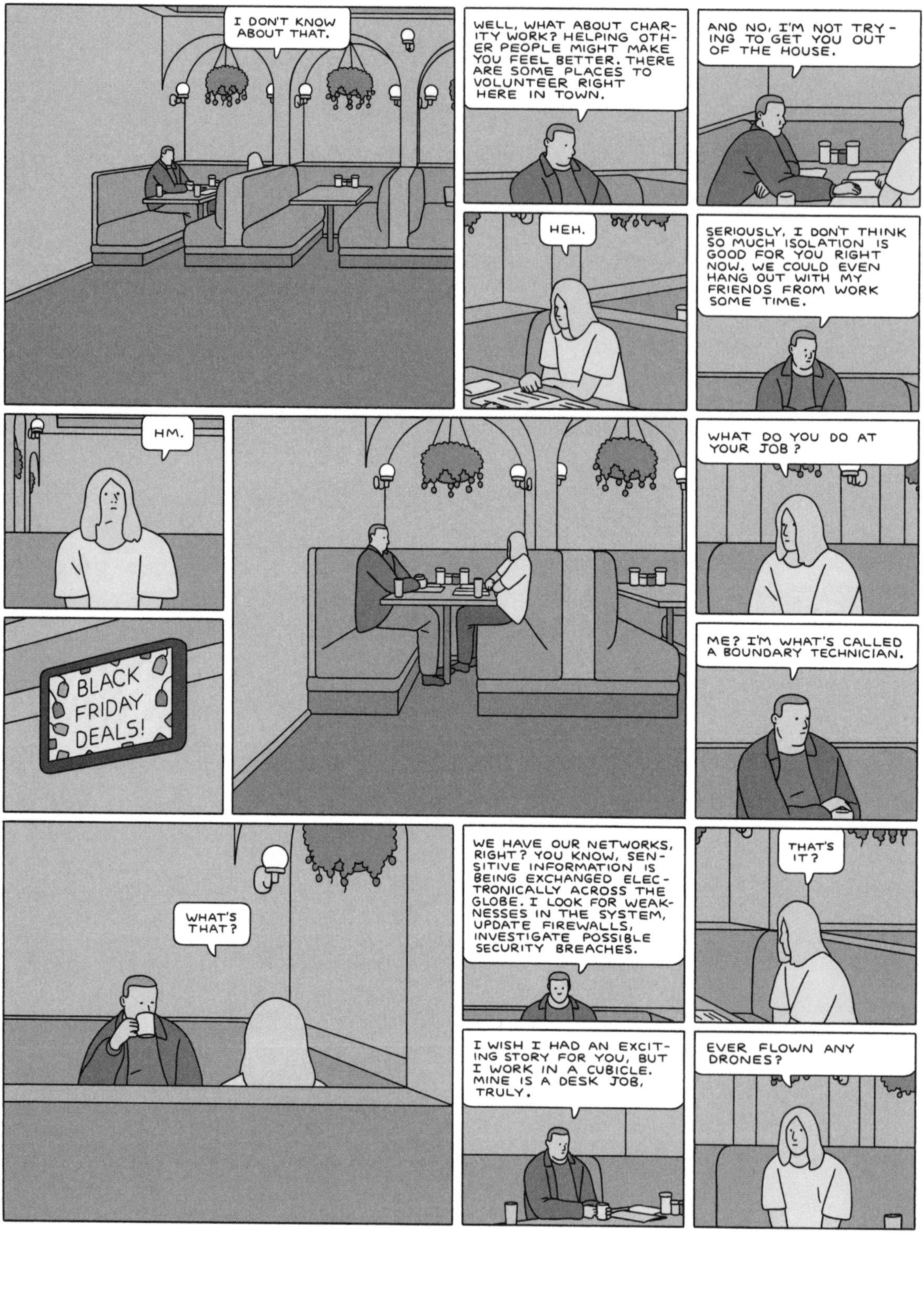
I DON'T KNOW ABOUT THAT.
WELL, WHAT ABOUT CHARITY WORK? HELPING OTHER PEOPLE MIGHT MAKE YOU FEEL BETTER. THERE ARE SOME PLACES TO VOLUNTEER RIGHT HERE IN TOWN.
AND NO, I'M NOT TRYING TO GET YOU OUT OF THE HOUSE.
HEH.
SERIOUSLY, I DON'T THINK SO MUCH ISOLATION IS GOOD FOR YOU RIGHT NOW. WE COULD EVEN HANG OUT WITH MY FRIENDS FROM WORK SOME TIME.
HM.
BLACK FRIDAY DEALS!
WHAT DO YOU DO AT YOUR JOB?
ME? I'M WHAT'S CALLED A BOUNDARY TECHNICIAN.
WHAT'S THAT?
WE HAVE OUR NETWORKS, RIGHT? YOU KNOW, SENSITIVE INFORMATION IS BEING EXCHANGED ELECTRONICALLY ACROSS THE GLOBE. I LOOK FOR WEAKNESSES IN THE SYSTEM, UPDATE FIREWALLS, INVESTIGATE POSSIBLE SECURITY BREACHES.
THAT'S IT?
I WISH I HAD AN EXCITING STORY FOR YOU, BUT I WORK IN A CUBICLE. MINE IS A DESK JOB, TRULY.
EVER FLOWN ANY DRONES?

ME? NO, NOTHING LIKE THAT.

YOU KNOW, IT'S CALLED THE DEPARTMENT OF DEFENSE, NOT THE DE-PARTMENT OF OFFENSE. MOST OF OUR EFFORTS ARE DEVOTED TO SECUR-ITY AND SURVEILLANCE.

WE ALL MAKE FUN OF THOSE COMMERCIALS THAT MAKE THE AIR FORCE LOOK LIKE AN ACTION MOVIE.

--THE VOTE IS SCHED-ULED TO GO BEFORE CONGRESS THIS EVENING.

YEP.

DO YOU WANT TO KNOW WHY THIS RESTAURANT IS EMPTY?

--SIGNIFICANT CUTS TO SOCIAL PROGRAMS AND AN INCREASE IN--

YEA.

THIS USED TO BE A CLAS-SIC, GREASY SPOON, ALL-AMERICAN KIND OF DINER.

UNTIL LAST YEAR, WHEN THE HEALTH INSPECTOR CAME IN AND NEARLY SHUT THE PLACE DOWN. THEY HAD TO REPLACE THEIR KITCHEN EQUIPMENT, CLEAN ALL THE GREASE OFF THE WALLS, REPLACE THE VENTILATION.

NOW, FOR SOME REASON, THE FOOD JUST DOESN'T TASTE AS GOOD. PEOPLE REALLY WANTED IT TO STAY THE SAME, BUT THEY COULDN'T RECRE-ATE THE TASTE.

MY FRIEND CONNOR CALLED IT A CASUALTY OF PROGRESS. HEH...

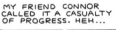

I ONLY COME BACK BE-CAUSE JACKIE AND I USED TO EAT HERE WITH CICI ALL THE TIME.

I SHOULD TAKE PIC-TURES OF THIS PLACE BEFORE IT SHUTS DOWN. WOULD THAT BE WEIRD?

I DON'T THINK SO.

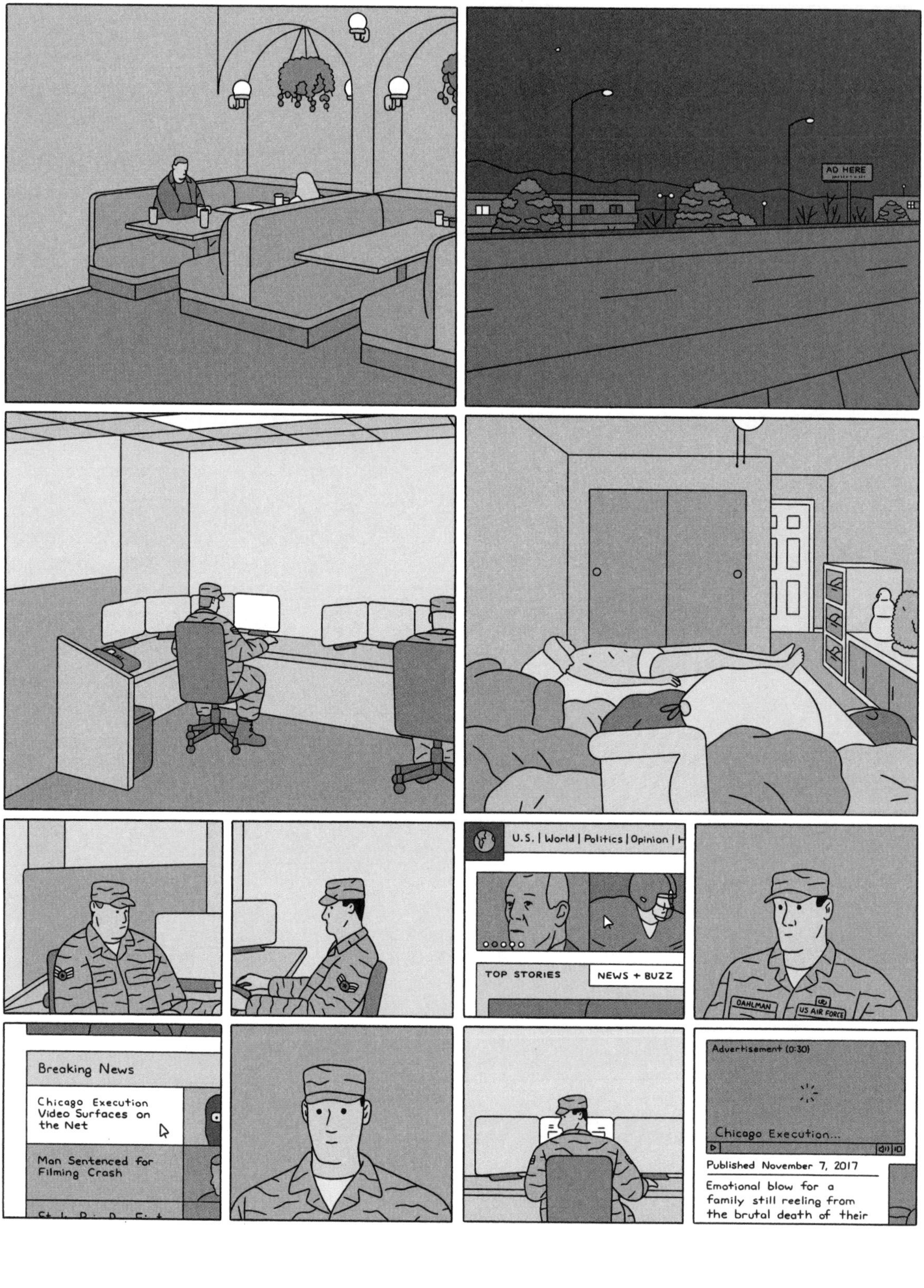
AD HERE
U.S. | World | Politics | Opinion |
TOP STORIES
NEWS + BUZZ
DAHLMAN
US AIR FORCE
Breaking News
Chicago Execution Video Surfaces on the Net
Man Sentenced for Filming Crash
Advertisement (0:30)
Chicago Execution...
Published November 7, 2017
Emotional blow for a family still reeling from the brutal death of their

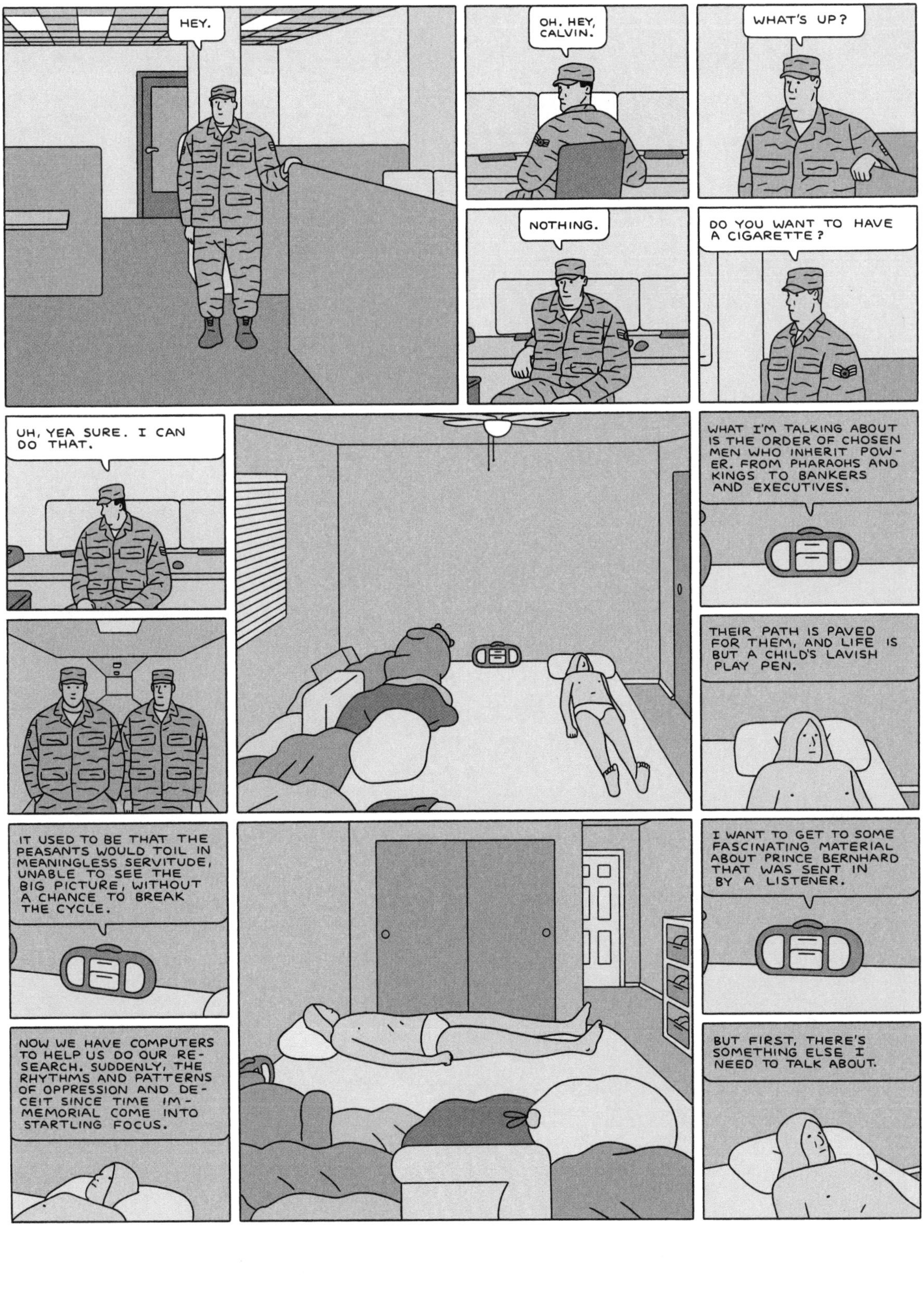
HEY.
OH. HEY, CALVIN.
WHAT'S UP?
NOTHING.
DO YOU WANT TO HAVE A CIGARETTE?
UH, YEA SURE. I CAN DO THAT.
WHAT I'M TALKING ABOUT IS THE ORDER OF CHOSEN MEN WHO INHERIT POW-ER. FROM PHARAOHS AND KINGS TO BANKERS AND EXECUTIVES.
THEIR PATH IS PAVED FOR THEM, AND LIFE IS BUT A CHILD'S LAVISH PLAY PEN.
IT USED TO BE THAT THE PEASANTS WOULD TOIL IN MEANINGLESS SERVITUDE, UNABLE TO SEE THE BIG PICTURE, WITHOUT A CHANCE TO BREAK THE CYCLE.
NOW WE HAVE COMPUTERS TO HELP US DO OUR RE-SEARCH. SUDDENLY, THE RHYTHMS AND PATTERNS OF OPPRESSION AND DE-CEIT SINCE TIME IM-MEMORIAL COME INTO STARTLING FOCUS.
I WANT TO GET TO SOME FASCINATING MATERIAL ABOUT PRINCE BERNHARD THAT WAS SENT IN BY A LISTENER.
BUT FIRST, THERE'S SOMETHING ELSE I NEED TO TALK ABOUT.

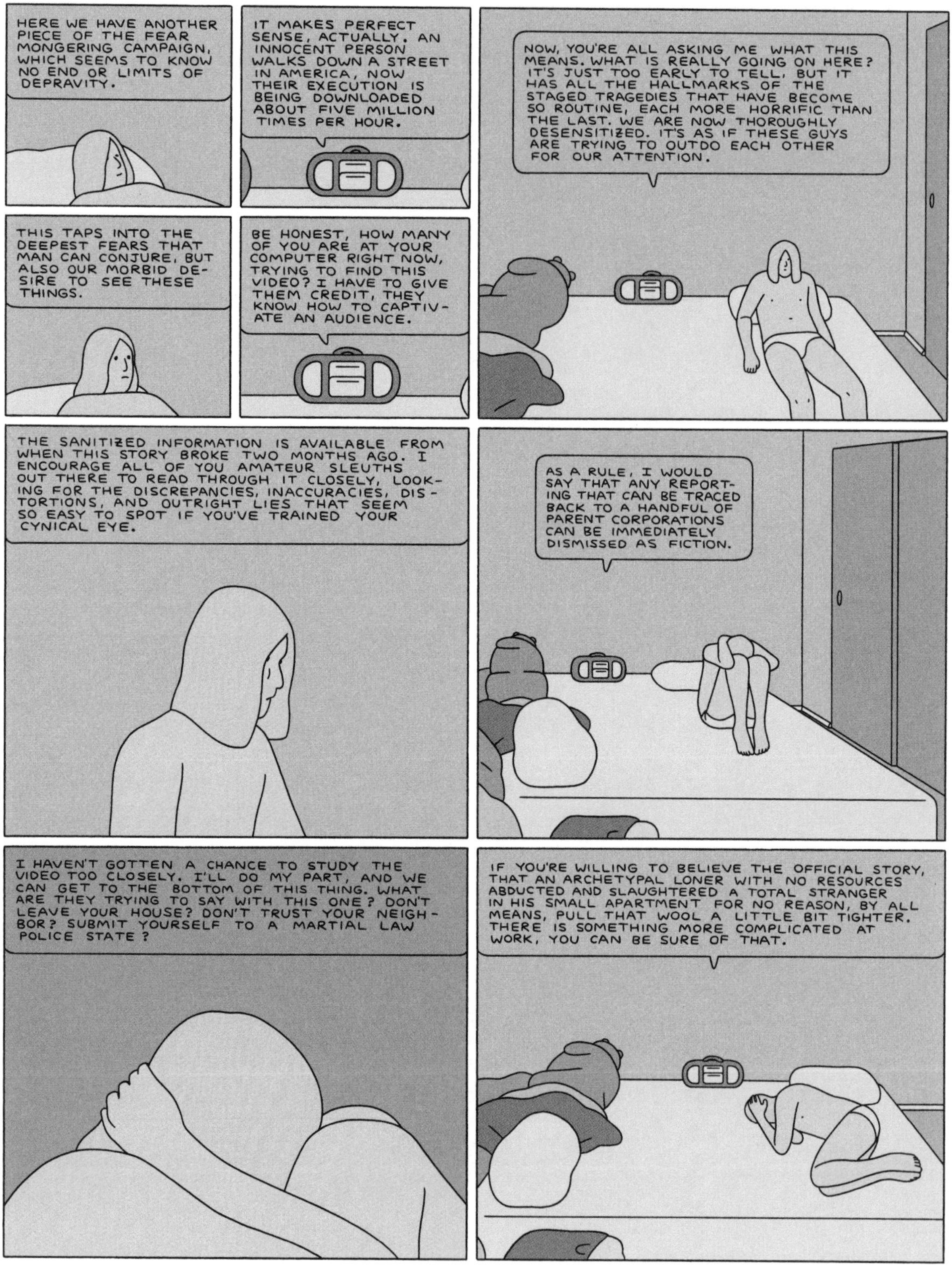
HERE WE HAVE ANOTHER PIECE OF THE FEAR MONGERING CAMPAIGN, WHICH SEEMS TO KNOW NO END OR LIMITS OF DEPRAVITY.
IT MAKES PERFECT SENSE, ACTUALLY. AN INNOCENT PERSON WALKS DOWN A STREET IN AMERICA, NOW THEIR EXECUTION IS BEING DOWNLOADED ABOUT FIVE MILLION TIMES PER HOUR.
THIS TAPS INTO THE DEEPEST FEARS THAT MAN CAN CONJURE, BUT ALSO OUR MORBID DESIRE TO SEE THESE THINGS.
BE HONEST, HOW MANY OF YOU ARE AT YOUR COMPUTER RIGHT NOW, TRYING TO FIND THIS VIDEO? I HAVE TO GIVE THEM CREDIT, THEY KNOW HOW TO CAPTIVATE AN AUDIENCE.
NOW, YOU'RE ALL ASKING ME WHAT THIS MEANS. WHAT IS REALLY GOING ON HERE? IT'S JUST TOO EARLY TO TELL, BUT IT HAS ALL THE HALLMARKS OF THE STAGED TRAGEDIES THAT HAVE BECOME SO ROUTINE, EACH MORE HORRIFIC THAN THE LAST. WE ARE NOW THOROUGHLY DESENSITIZED. IT'S AS IF THESE GUYS ARE TRYING TO OUTDO EACH OTHER FOR OUR ATTENTION.
THE SANITIZED INFORMATION IS AVAILABLE FROM WHEN THIS STORY BROKE TWO MONTHS AGO. I ENCOURAGE ALL OF YOU AMATEUR SLEUTHS OUT THERE TO READ THROUGH IT CLOSELY, LOOKING FOR THE DISCREPANCIES, INACCURACIES, DISTORTIONS, AND OUTRIGHT LIES THAT SEEM SO EASY TO SPOT IF YOU'VE TRAINED YOUR CYNICAL EYE.
AS A RULE, I WOULD SAY THAT ANY REPORTING THAT CAN BE TRACED BACK TO A HANDFUL OF PARENT CORPORATIONS CAN BE IMMEDIATELY DISMISSED AS FICTION.
I HAVEN'T GOTTEN A CHANCE TO STUDY THE VIDEO TOO CLOSELY. I'LL DO MY PART, AND WE CAN GET TO THE BOTTOM OF THIS THING. WHAT ARE THEY TRYING TO SAY WITH THIS ONE? DON'T LEAVE YOUR HOUSE? DON'T TRUST YOUR NEIGHBOR? SUBMIT YOURSELF TO A MARTIAL LAW POLICE STATE?
IF YOU'RE WILLING TO BELIEVE THE OFFICIAL STORY, THAT AN ARCHETYPAL LONER WITH NO RESOURCES ABDUCTED AND SLAUGHTERED A TOTAL STRANGER IN HIS SMALL APARTMENT FOR NO REASON, BY ALL MEANS, PULL THAT WOOL A LITTLE BIT TIGHTER. THERE IS SOMETHING MORE COMPLICATED AT WORK, YOU CAN BE SURE OF THAT.

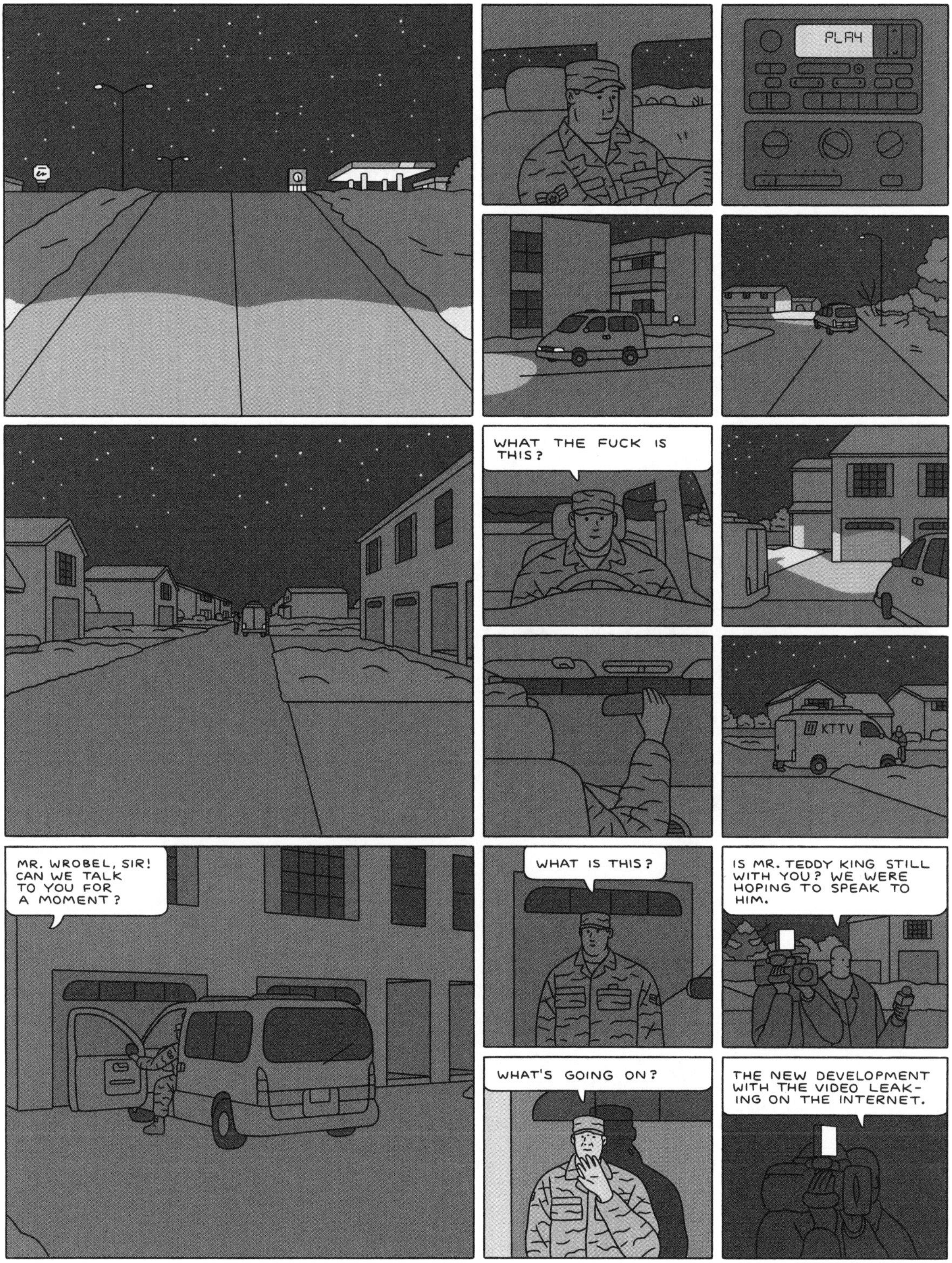
PLAY
WHAT THE FUCK IS THIS?
KTTV
MR. WROBEL, SIR! CAN WE TALK TO YOU FOR A MOMENT?
WHAT IS THIS?
IS MR. TEDDY KING STILL WITH YOU? WE WERE HOPING TO SPEAK TO HIM.
WHAT'S GOING ON?
THE NEW DEVELOPMENT WITH THE VIDEO LEAKING ON THE INTERNET.

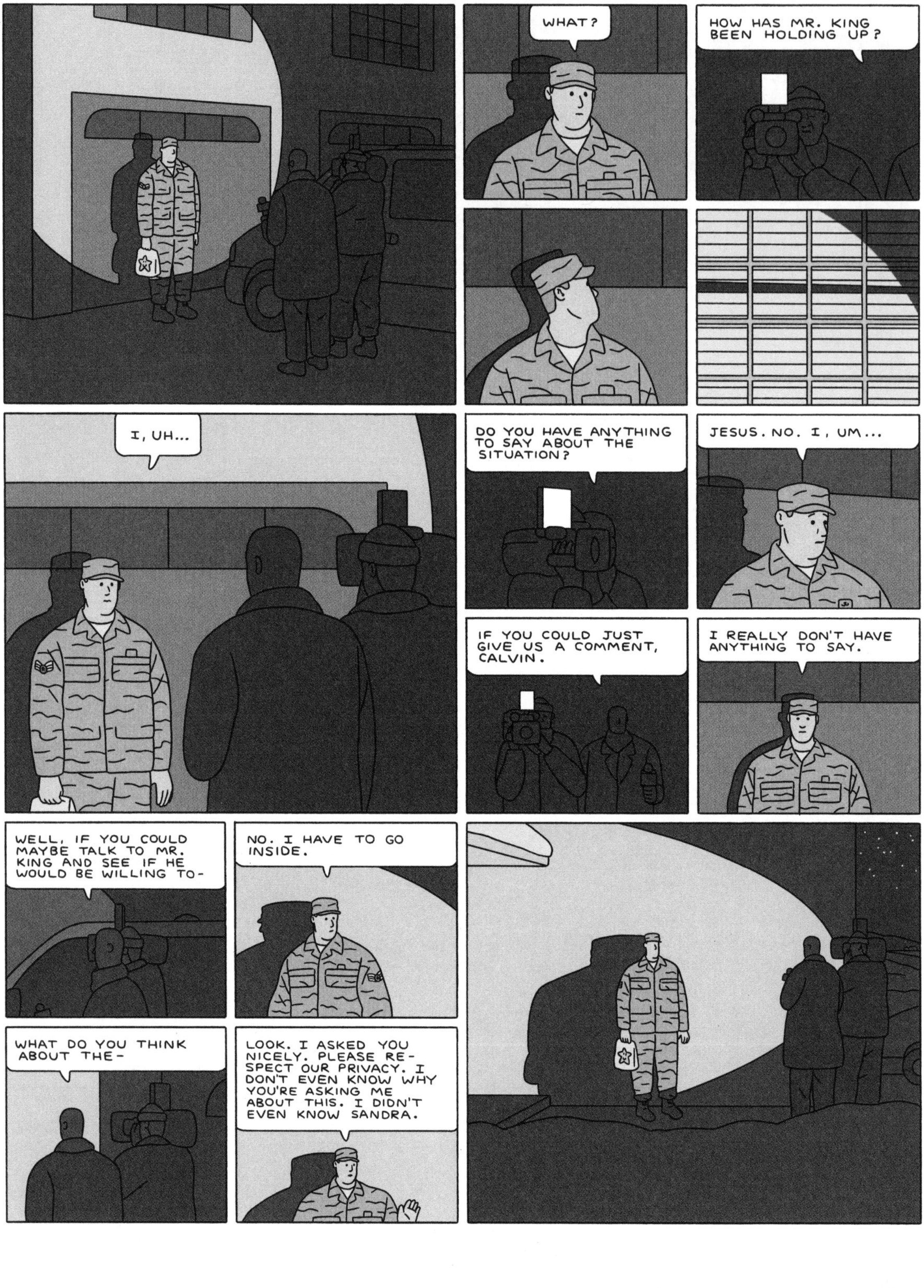
WHAT?
HOW HAS MR. KING BEEN HOLDING UP?
I, UH...
DO YOU HAVE ANYTHING TO SAY ABOUT THE SITUATION?
JESUS. NO. I, UM...
IF YOU COULD JUST GIVE US A COMMENT, CALVIN.
I REALLY DON'T HAVE ANYTHING TO SAY.
WELL, IF YOU COULD MAYBE TALK TO MR. KING AND SEE IF HE WOULD BE WILLING TO-
NO. I HAVE TO GO INSIDE.
WHAT DO YOU THINK ABOUT THE-
LOOK. I ASKED YOU NICELY. PLEASE RE-SPECT OUR PRIVACY. I DON'T EVEN KNOW WHY YOU'RE ASKING ME ABOUT THIS. I DIDN'T EVEN KNOW SANDRA.

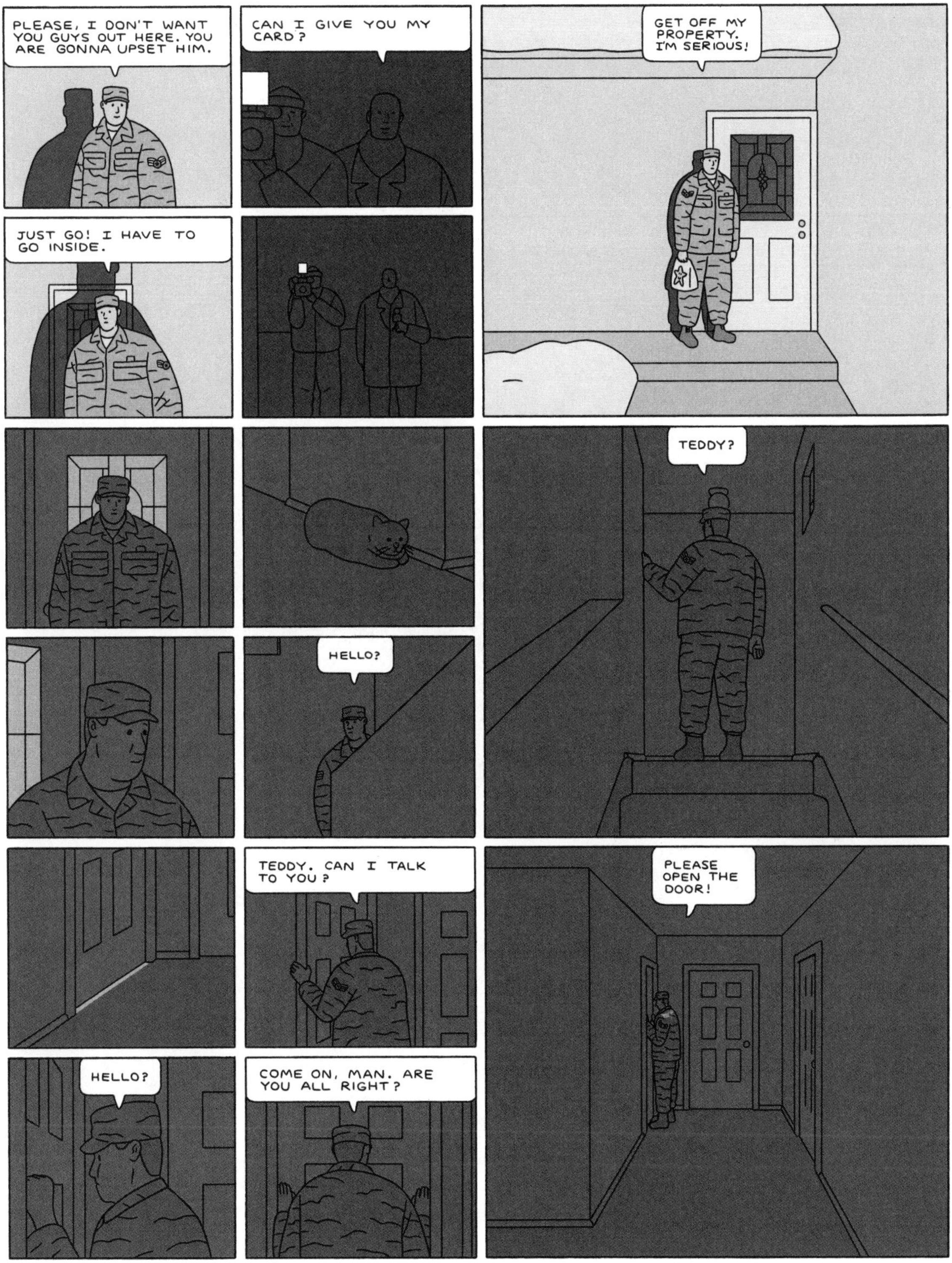
PLEASE, I DON'T WANT YOU GUYS OUT HERE. YOU ARE GONNA UPSET HIM.
CAN I GIVE YOU MY CARD?
GET OFF MY PROPERTY. I'M SERIOUS!
JUST GO! I HAVE TO GO INSIDE.
TEDDY?
HELLO?
TEDDY. CAN I TALK TO YOU?
PLEASE OPEN THE DOOR!
HELLO?
COME ON, MAN. ARE YOU ALL RIGHT?

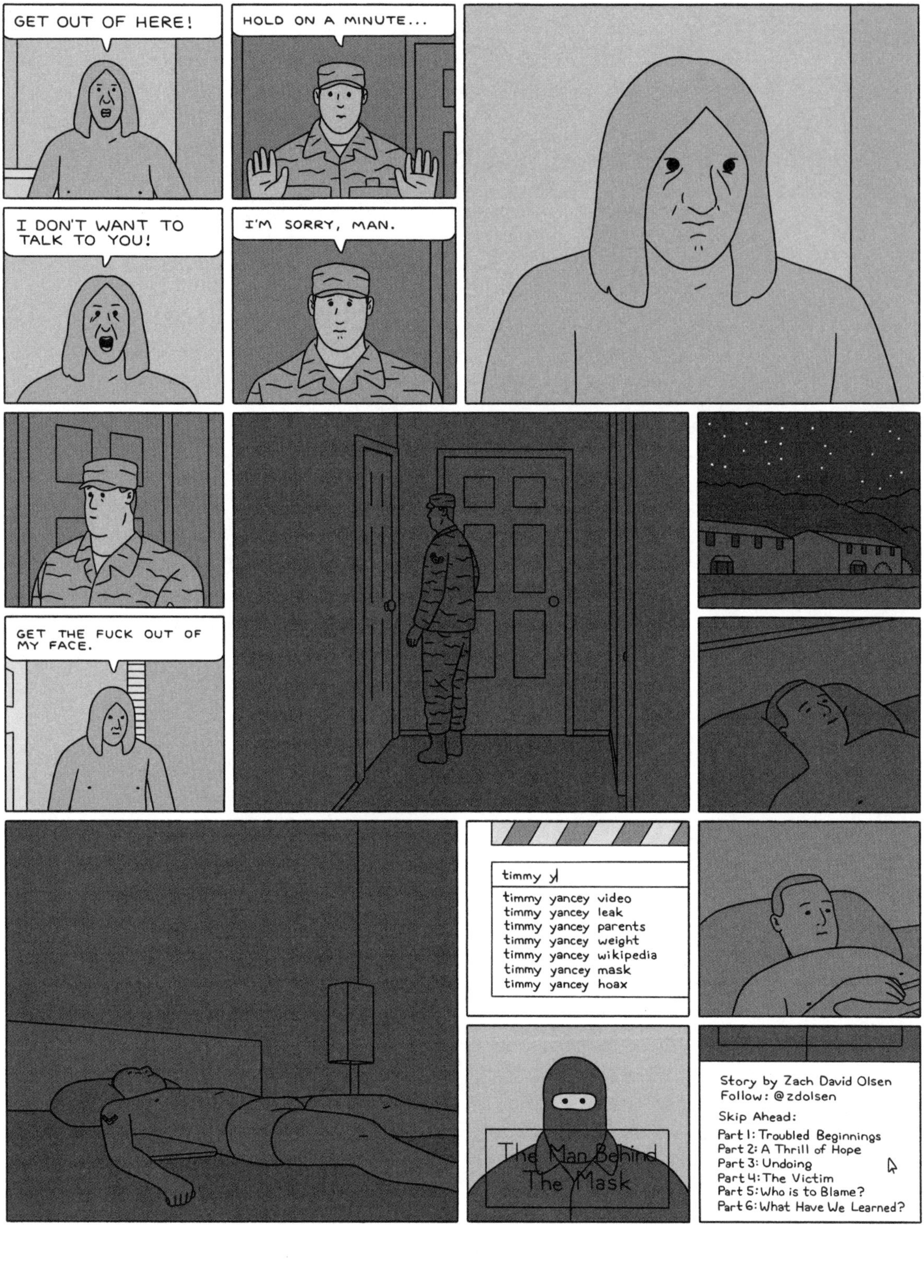
GET OUT OF HERE!
HOLD ON A MINUTE...
I DON'T WANT TO TALK TO YOU!
I'M SORRY, MAN.
GET THE FUCK OUT OF MY FACE.
timmy y
timmy yancey video
timmy yancey leak
timmy yancey parents
timmy yancey weight
timmy yancey wikipedia
timmy yancey mask
timmy yancey hoax
The Man Behind The Mask
Story by Zach David Olsen
Follow: @zdolsen
Skip Ahead:
Part 1: Troubled Beginnings
Part 2: A Thrill of Hope
Part 3: Undoing
Part 4: The Victim
Part 5: Who is to Blame?
Part 6: What Have We Learned?

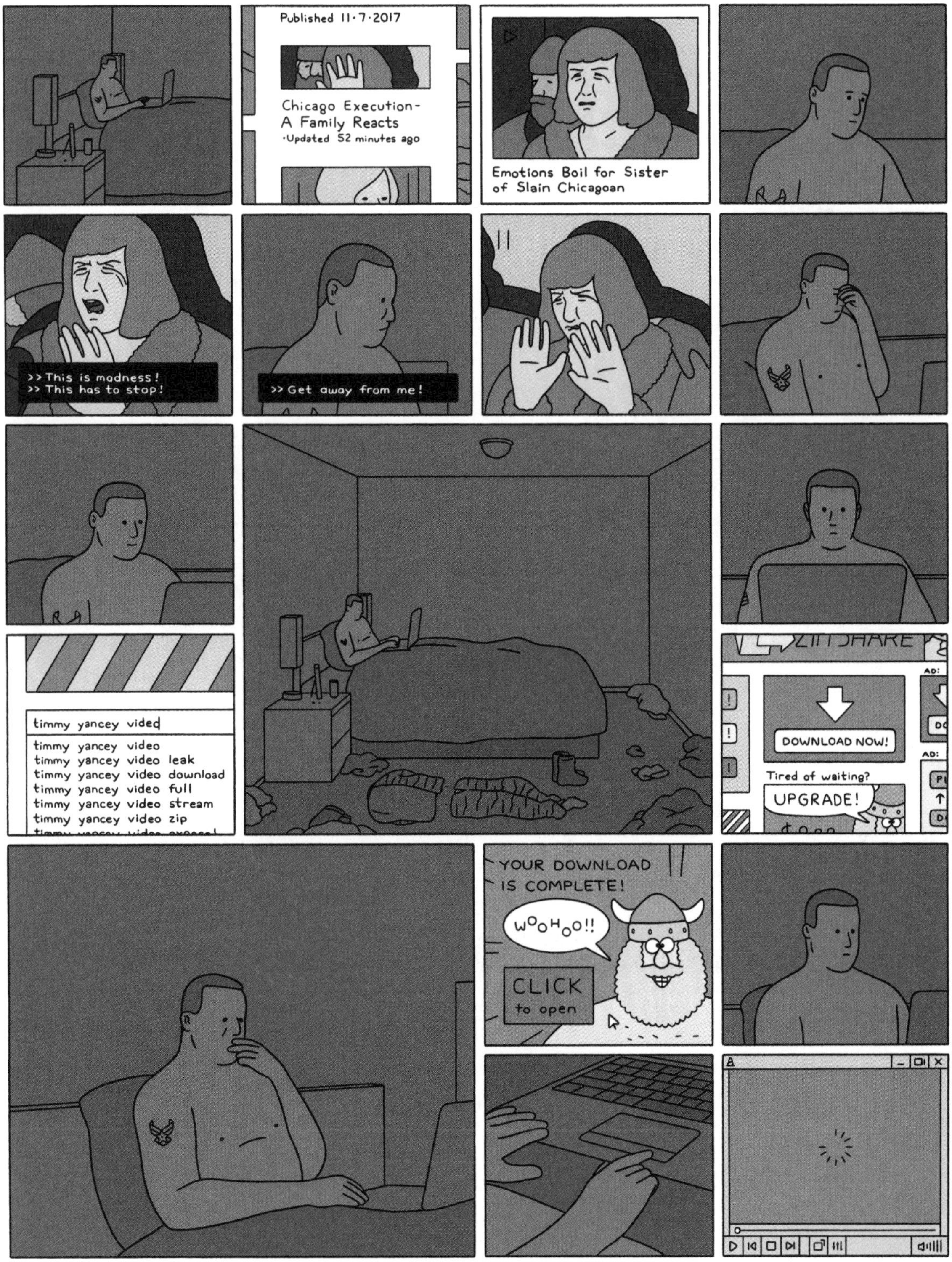
Published 11·7·2017
Chicago Execution-
A Family Reacts
·Updated 52 minutes ago
Emotions Boil for Sister
of Slain Chicagoan
>> This is madness!
>> This has to stop!
>> Get away from me!
timmy yancey vided
timmy yancey video
timmy yancey video leak
timmy yancey video download
timmy yancey video full
timmy yancey video stream
timmy yancey video zip
AD:
DOWNLOAD NOW!
AD:
Tired of waiting?
UPGRADE!
YOUR DOWNLOAD
IS COMPLETE!
WOOHOO!!
CLICK
to open

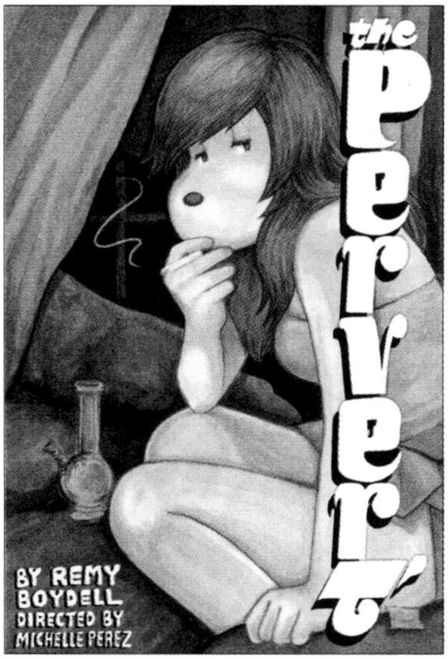
the Pervert
BY REMY BOYDELL
DIRECTED BY MICHELLE PEREZ

Sex Positive (*Excerpt*)

REMY BOYDELL AND
MICHELLE PEREZ

originally published in

The Pervert
IMAGE COMICS
6.5 x 10 inches • 160 pages

Biography

Remy Boydell currently lives in Vancouver, working as a cartoonist and managing @nervanaofficial. *The Pervert* was painted when Boydell was 22.
slimgiltsoul.com

Michelle Perez is a writer, originally from the state of Michigan. She is a severe depressive Marxist dumbass who posts nudes online at a ballpark at 3 pm.

She's written in *Five Out of Ten, Medium Difficulty, Women Write About Comics,* and *The Rainbow Hub*. Her debut comic *The Pervert,* co-created with Remy Boydell, has been featured in *Autostraddle, Paste Magazine,* the *Huffington Post, Publishers Weekly,* and the *Comics Journal,* and was listed among *Vulture/NY Magazine*'s Best Comics of 2018, listed among Barnes and Noble's Favorite Comics & Graphic Novels of 2018, and number one on *AiPTcomics* top ten LGBTQ comics of 2018.
twitter.com/mperezwritesirl

Statement

Hey what's up guys—REMY BOYDELL

This excerpt is a pivotal segment of our graphic novel, *The Pervert*. Our story is told in connecting vignettes that we tried to design to work as a self-contained story that can connect to a greater narrative. Near the end of our work, we had a more defined ending arc. This is "Sex Positive," which is one of many scenes where we use the character of Felina to sorta go through experiences that I've had personally, as well as other folks I've known.—MICHELLE PEREZ

SEX POSITIVE

6pm client

Snooze   OK

SEATTLE IS OK FOR THIS LINE OF WORK GIVEN THE PREVAILING ATTITUDES.

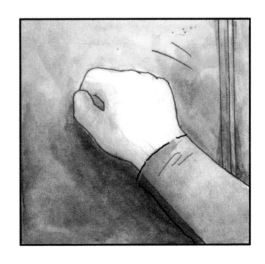

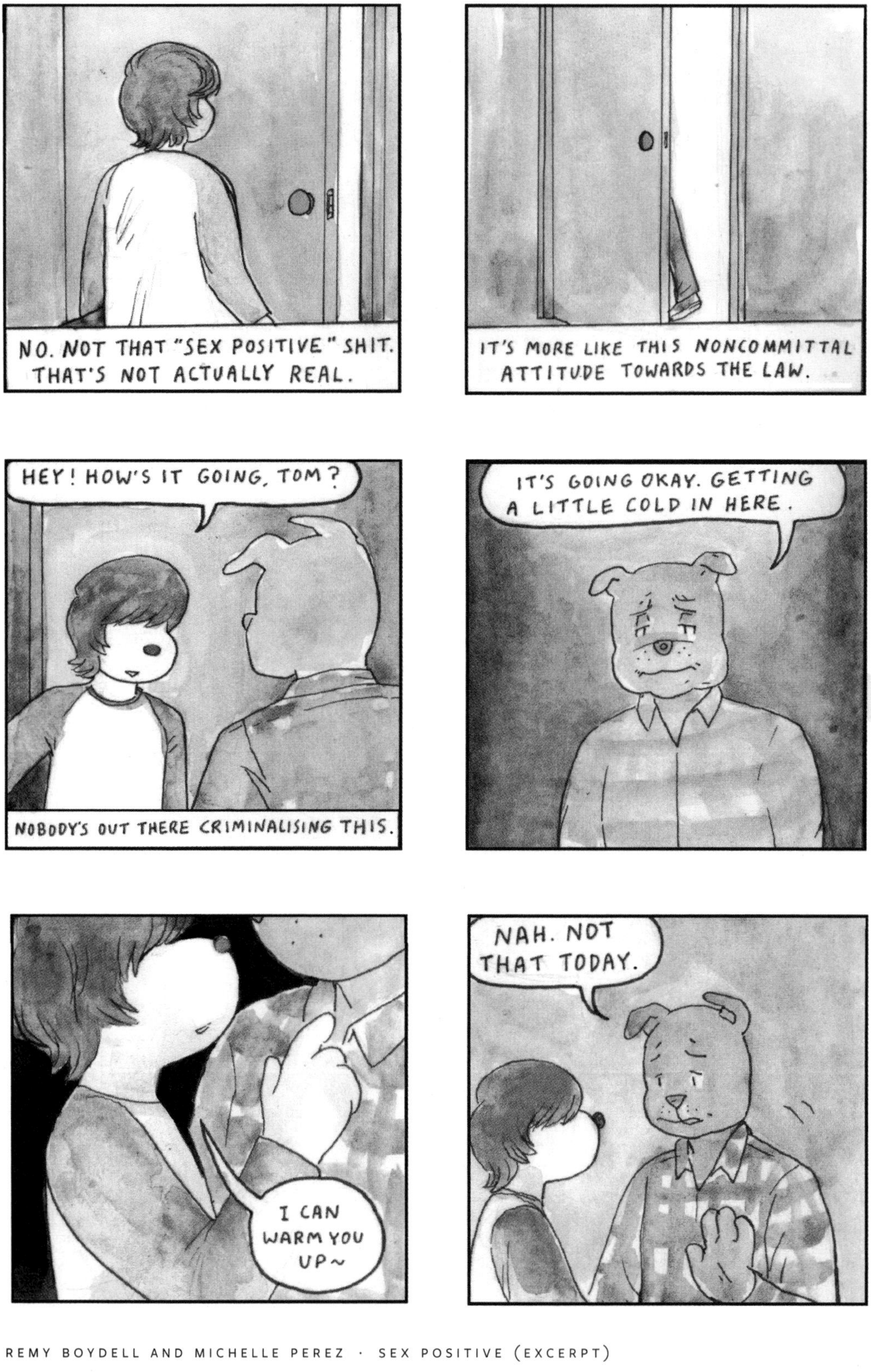
NO. NOT THAT "SEX POSITIVE" SHIT. THAT'S NOT ACTUALLY REAL.
IT'S MORE LIKE THIS NONCOMMITTAL ATTITUDE TOWARDS THE LAW.
HEY! HOW'S IT GOING, TOM?
NOBODY'S OUT THERE CRIMINALISING THIS.
IT'S GOING OKAY. GETTING A LITTLE COLD IN HERE.
I CAN WARM YOU UP~
NAH. NOT THAT TODAY.

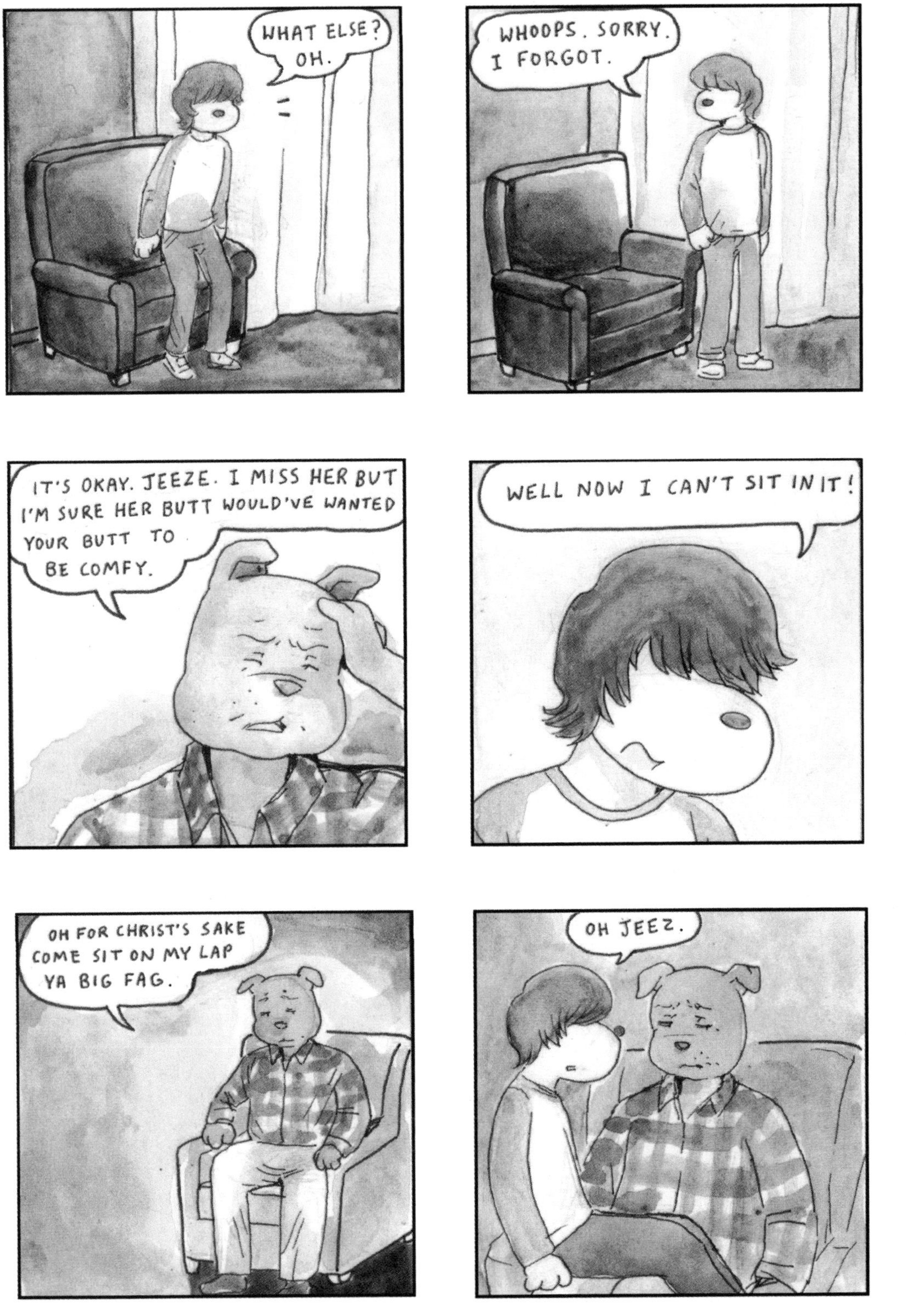
WHAT ELSE? OH.
WHOOPS. SORRY. I FORGOT.
IT'S OKAY. JEEZE. I MISS HER BUT I'M SURE HER BUTT WOULD'VE WANTED YOUR BUTT TO BE COMFY.
WELL NOW I CAN'T SIT IN IT!
OH FOR CHRIST'S SAKE COME SIT ON MY LAP YA BIG FAG.
OH JEEZ.

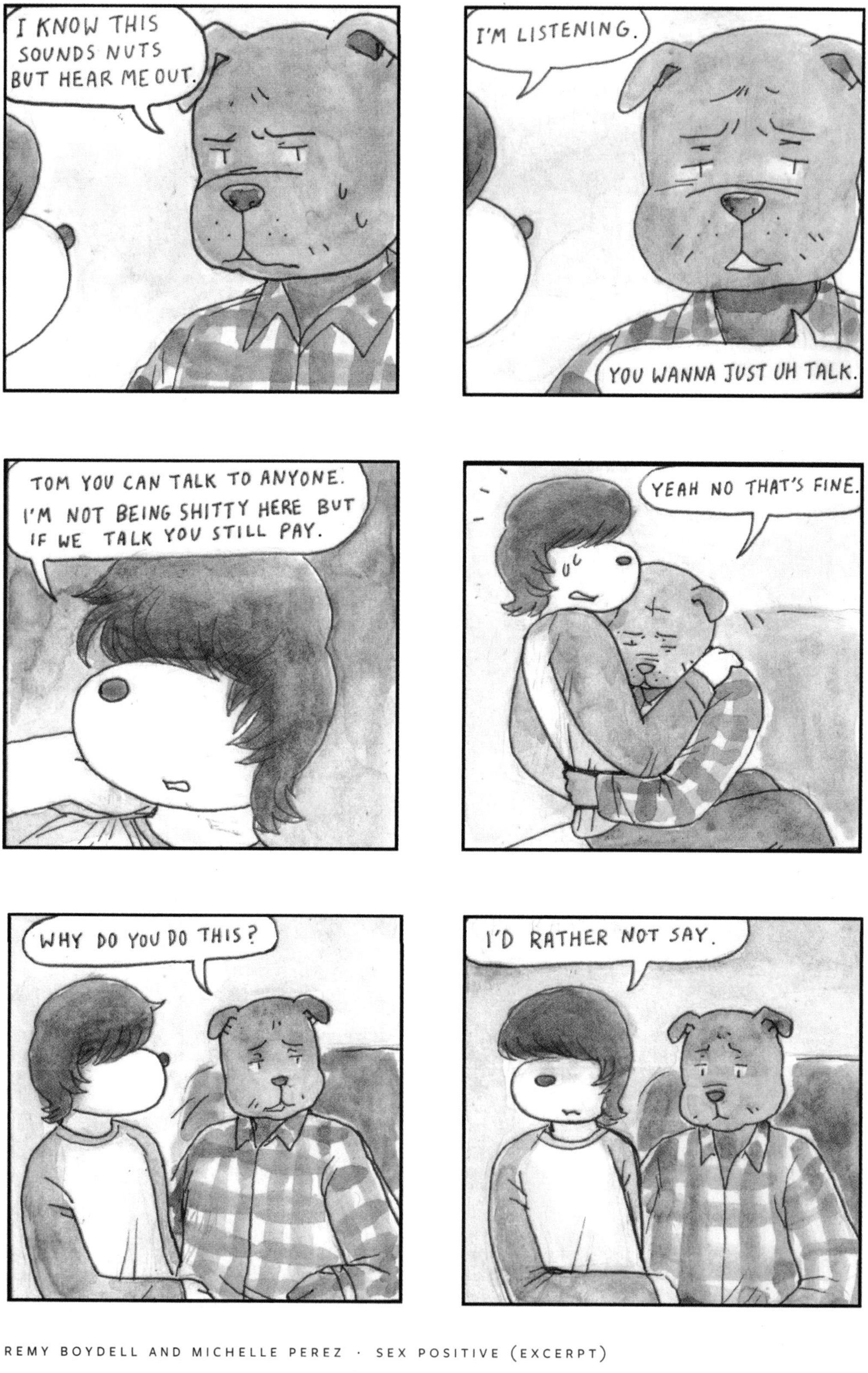
I KNOW THIS SOUNDS NUTS BUT HEAR ME OUT.
I'M LISTENING.
YOU WANNA JUST UH TALK.
TOM YOU CAN TALK TO ANYONE. I'M NOT BEING SHITTY HERE BUT IF WE TALK YOU STILL PAY.
YEAH NO THAT'S FINE.
WHY DO YOU DO THIS?
I'D RATHER NOT SAY.

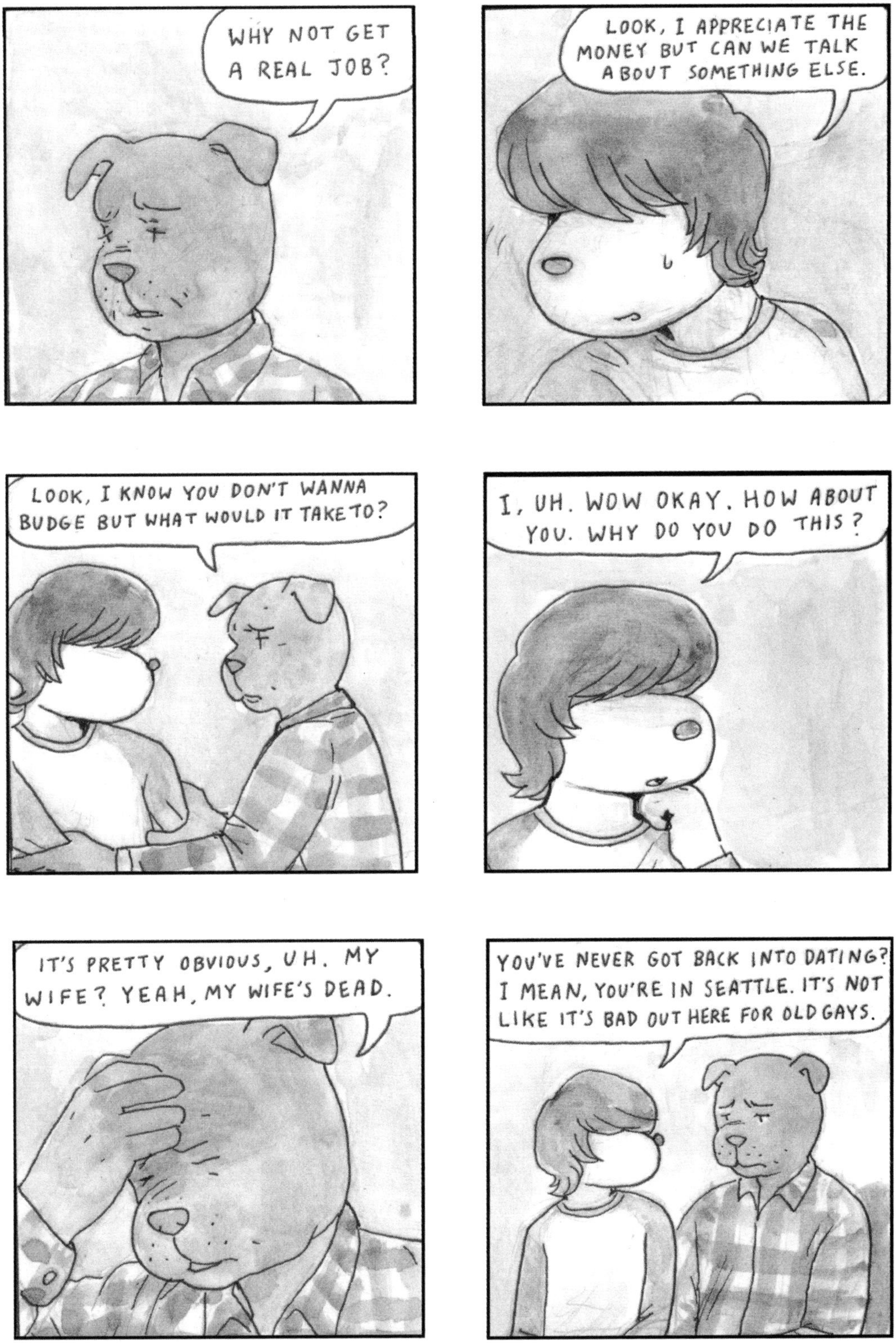
WHY NOT GET A REAL JOB?
LOOK, I APPRECIATE THE MONEY BUT CAN WE TALK ABOUT SOMETHING ELSE.
LOOK, I KNOW YOU DON'T WANNA BUDGE BUT WHAT WOULD IT TAKE TO?
I, UH. WOW OKAY. HOW ABOUT YOU. WHY DO YOU DO THIS?
IT'S PRETTY OBVIOUS, UH. MY WIFE? YEAH, MY WIFE'S DEAD.
YOU'VE NEVER GOT BACK INTO DATING? I MEAN, YOU'RE IN SEATTLE. IT'S NOT LIKE IT'S BAD OUT HERE FOR OLD GAYS.

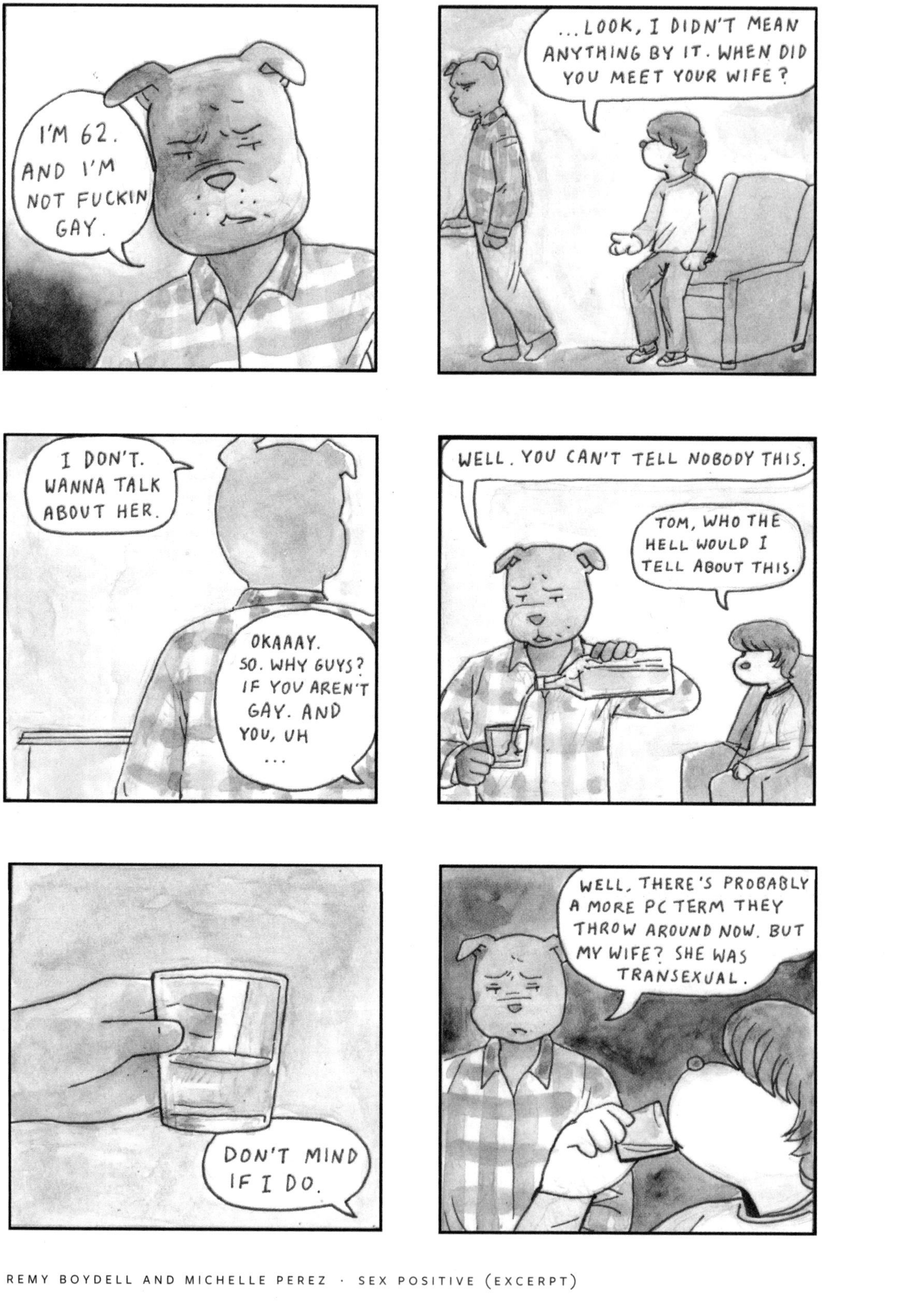
I'M 62. AND I'M NOT FUCKIN GAY.
...LOOK, I DIDN'T MEAN ANYTHING BY IT. WHEN DID YOU MEET YOUR WIFE?
I DON'T. WANNA TALK ABOUT HER.
OKAAAY. SO. WHY GUYS? IF YOU AREN'T GAY. AND YOU, UH ...
WELL. YOU CAN'T TELL NOBODY THIS.
TOM, WHO THE HELL WOULD I TELL ABOUT THIS.
DON'T MIND IF I DO.
WELL, THERE'S PROBABLY A MORE PC TERM THEY THROW AROUND NOW. BUT MY WIFE? SHE WAS TRANSEXUAL.

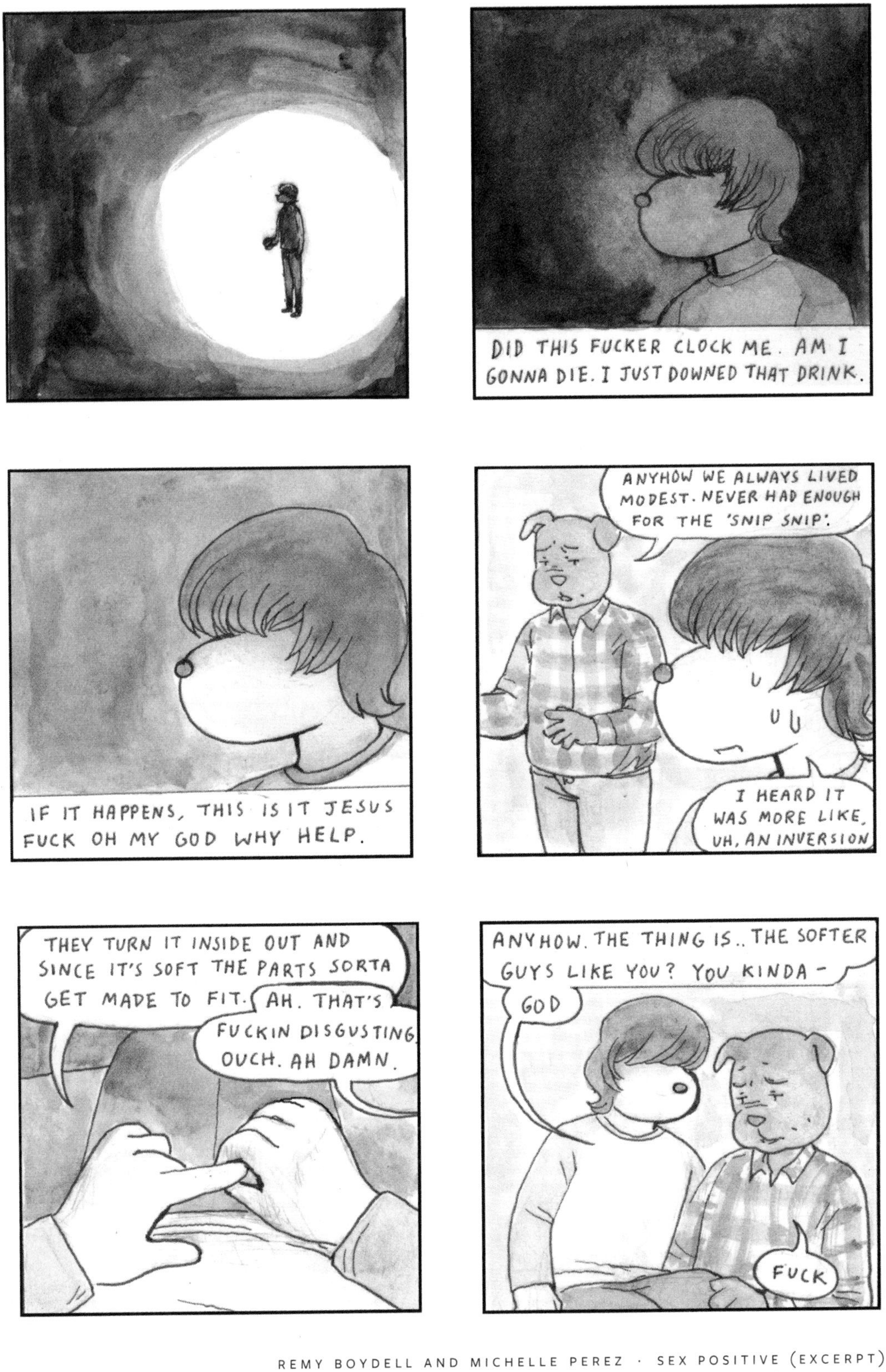
DID THIS FUCKER CLOCK ME. AM I GONNA DIE. I JUST DOWNED THAT DRINK.
IF IT HAPPENS, THIS IS IT JESUS FUCK OH MY GOD WHY HELP.
ANYHOW WE ALWAYS LIVED MODEST. NEVER HAD ENOUGH FOR THE 'SNIP SNIP'.
I HEARD IT WAS MORE LIKE, UH, AN INVERSION
THEY TURN IT INSIDE OUT AND SINCE IT'S SOFT THE PARTS SORTA GET MADE TO FIT.
AH. THAT'S FUCKIN DISGUSTING. OUCH. AH DAMN.
ANYHOW. THE THING IS.. THE SOFTER GUYS LIKE YOU? YOU KINDA -
GOD
FUCK

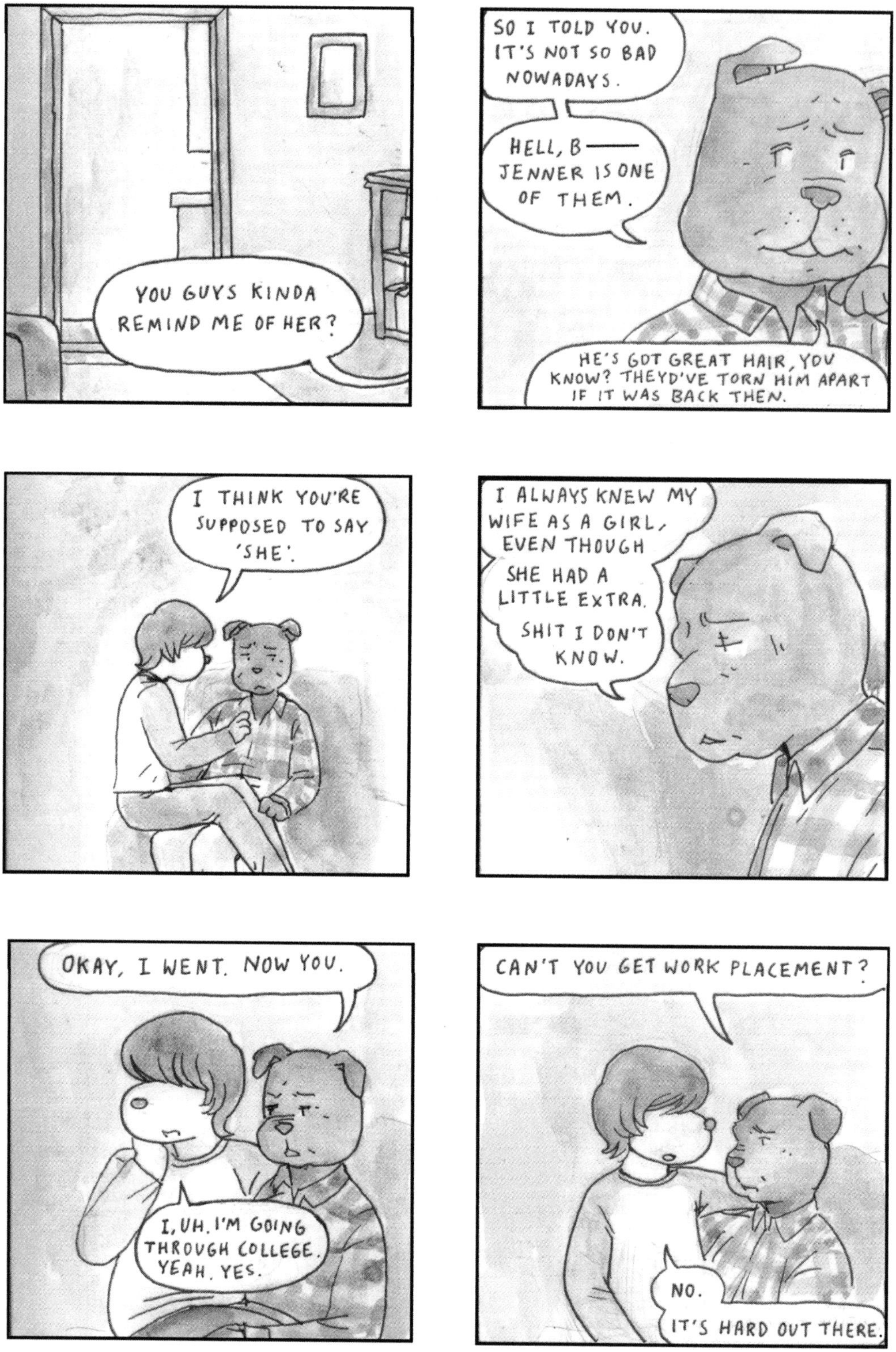
YOU GUYS KINDA REMIND ME OF HER?
SO I TOLD YOU. IT'S NOT SO BAD NOWADAYS.
HELL, B—— JENNER IS ONE OF THEM.
HE'S GOT GREAT HAIR, YOU KNOW? THEYD'VE TORN HIM APART IF IT WAS BACK THEN.
I THINK YOU'RE SUPPOSED TO SAY 'SHE'.
I ALWAYS KNEW MY WIFE AS A GIRL, EVEN THOUGH
SHE HAD A LITTLE EXTRA.
SHIT I DON'T KNOW.
OKAY, I WENT. NOW YOU.
I, UH. I'M GOING THROUGH COLLEGE. YEAH. YES.
CAN'T YOU GET WORK PLACEMENT?
NO.
IT'S HARD OUT THERE.

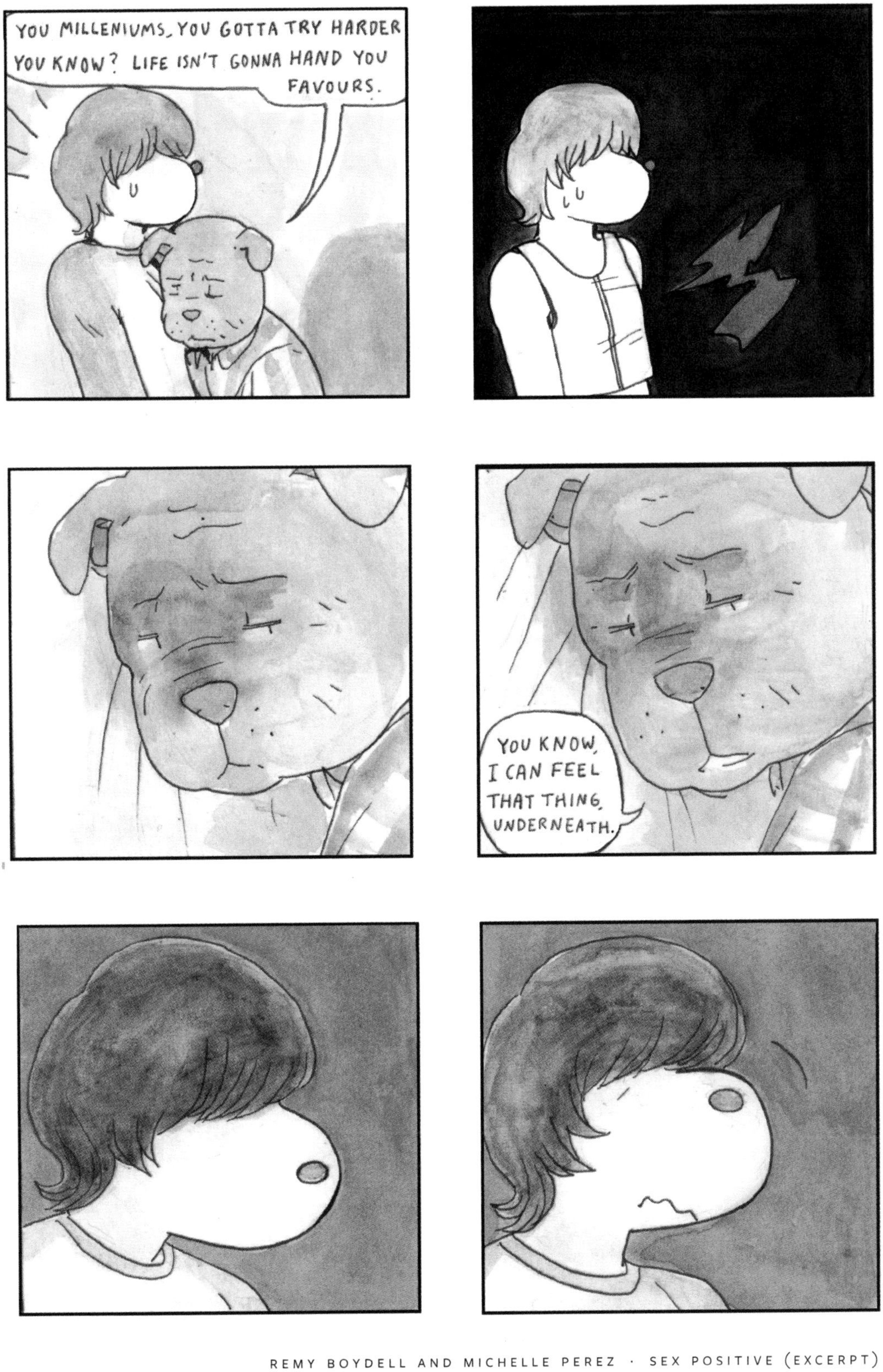
YOU MILLENIUMS, YOU GOTTA TRY HARDER YOU KNOW? LIFE ISN'T GONNA HAND YOU FAVOURS.
YOU KNOW, I CAN FEEL THAT THING UNDERNEATH.

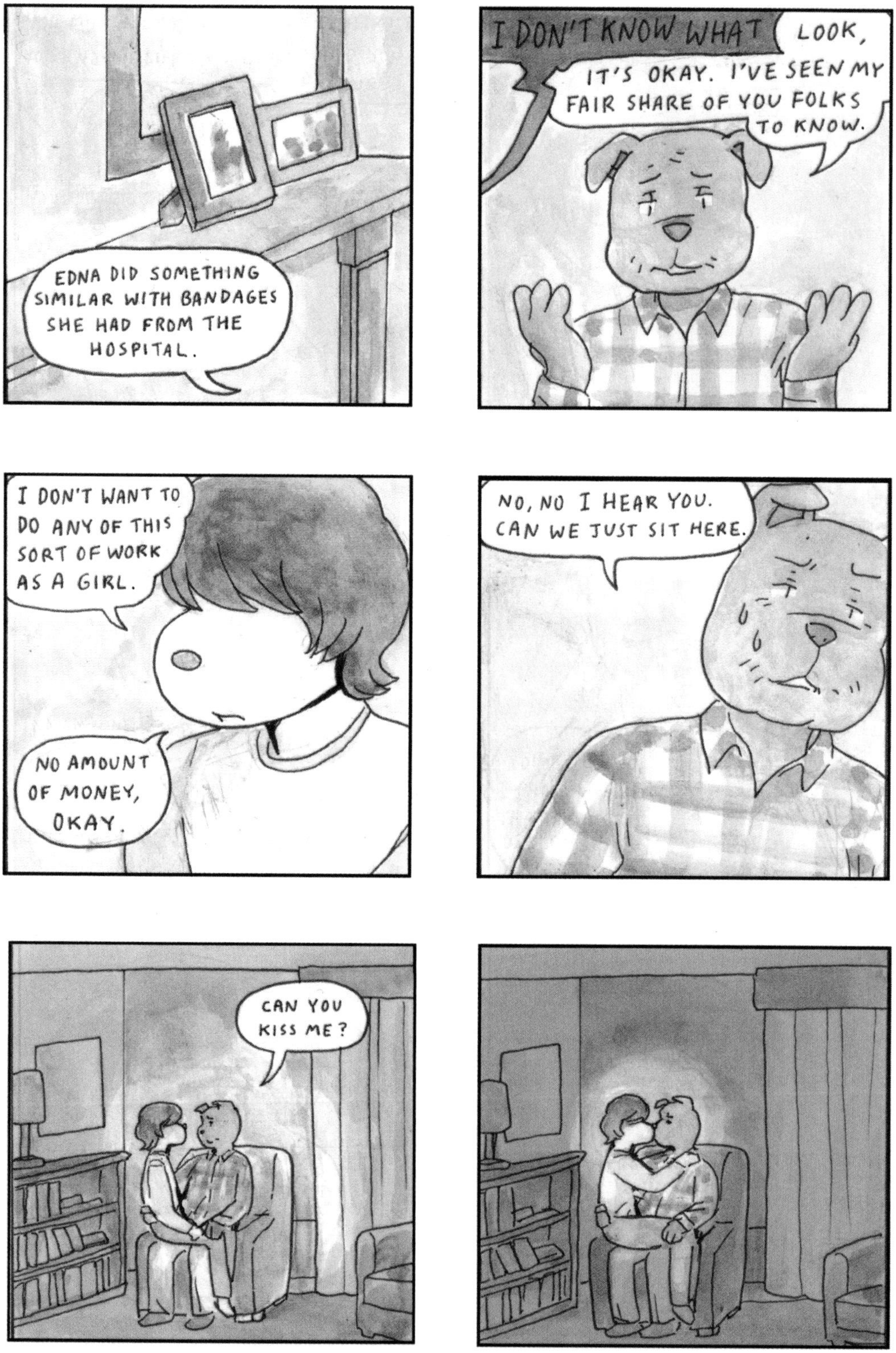
EDNA DID SOMETHING SIMILAR WITH BANDAGES SHE HAD FROM THE HOSPITAL.
I DON'T KNOW WHAT
LOOK, IT'S OKAY. I'VE SEEN MY FAIR SHARE OF YOU FOLKS TO KNOW.
I DON'T WANT TO DO ANY OF THIS SORT OF WORK AS A GIRL.
NO AMOUNT OF MONEY, OKAY.
NO, NO I HEAR YOU. CAN WE JUST SIT HERE.
CAN YOU KISS ME?

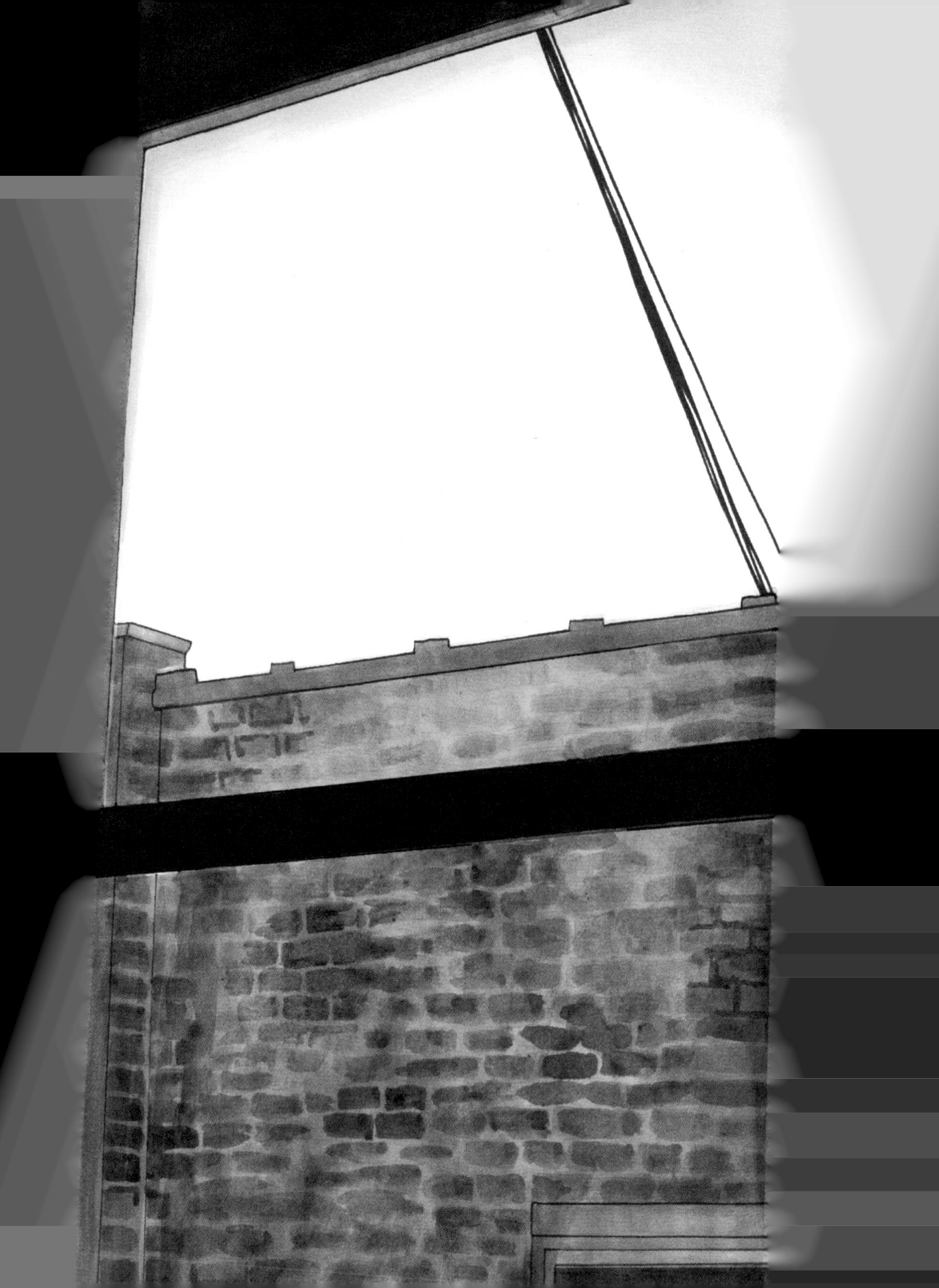

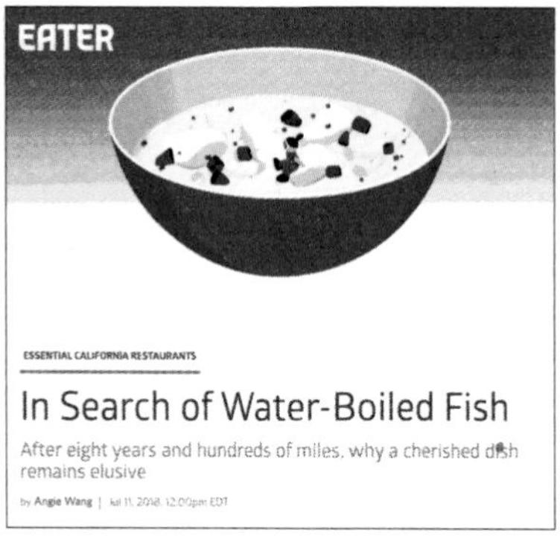
EATER
ESSENTIAL CALIFORNIA RESTAURANTS
In Search of Water-Boiled Fish
After eight years and hundreds of miles, why a cherished dish remains elusive

In Search of Water-Boiled Fish

ANGIE WANG

originally published on

Eater

EATER.COM

DIGITAL

Biography

Angie Wang is a James Beard Award–winning illustrator, cartoonist, animator, poet, game developer, prop/FX designer on *Steven Universe,* and co-founder of Comic Arts Los Angeles.
okchickadee.com

Statement

It's hard to articulate the feeling that drives this comic, even now. I went through several revisions trying to understand my obsession with water-boiled fish—I actually feel the same way about fish and chips from Manchester, which is where I lived for a good part of my childhood, so it's not *strictly* about being Chinese and having some claim to authentic Chinese cuisine, and more about a lived, deeply personal relationship with food. But a communal immigrant nostalgia about the home country's food—which, though shared, is not exactly the same for each of us—is another part of the story. In either case, it felt appropriate for all the dishes to be enormous, monumental in my imagination, compared to me. This piece, which was originally published online in an "infinite canvas" continuous vertical scroll and was reformatted for publication here, wound up winning a James Beard Award for innovative storytelling.

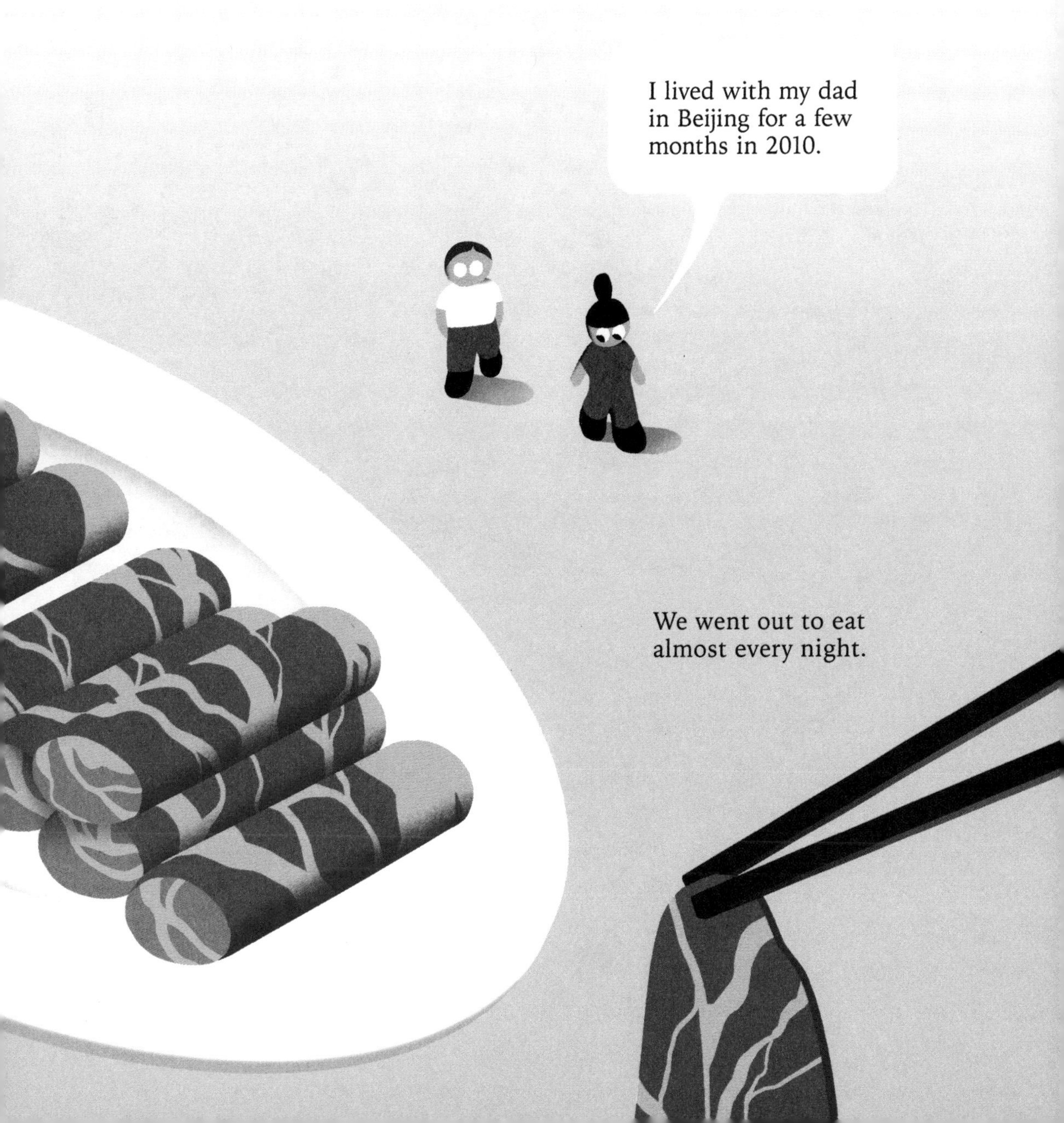
I lived with my dad in Beijing for a few months in 2010.
We went out to eat almost every night.

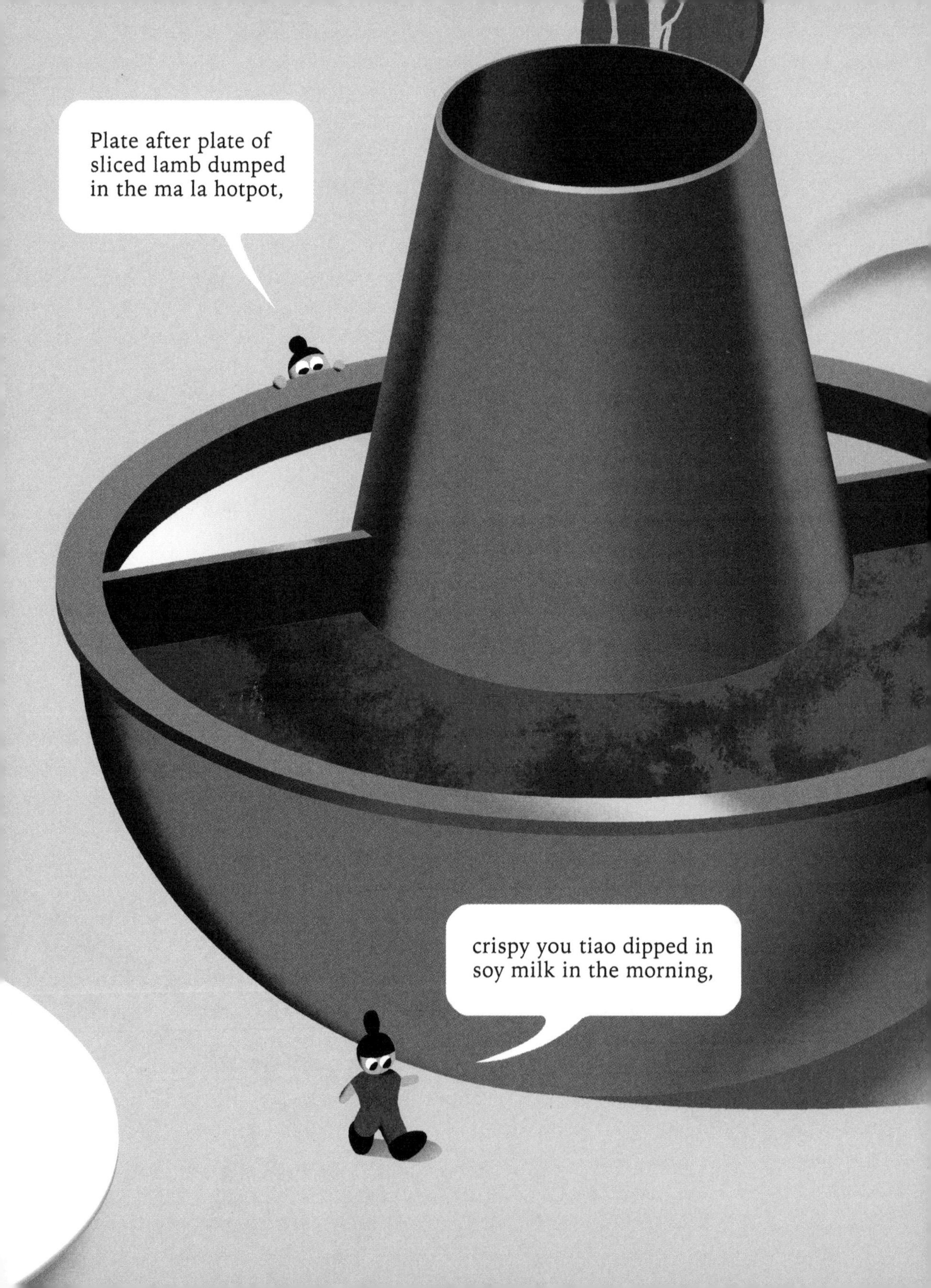
Plate after plate of sliced lamb dumped in the ma la hotpot,
crispy you tiao dipped in soy milk in the morning,

jars of Beijing
yogurt in the fridge,

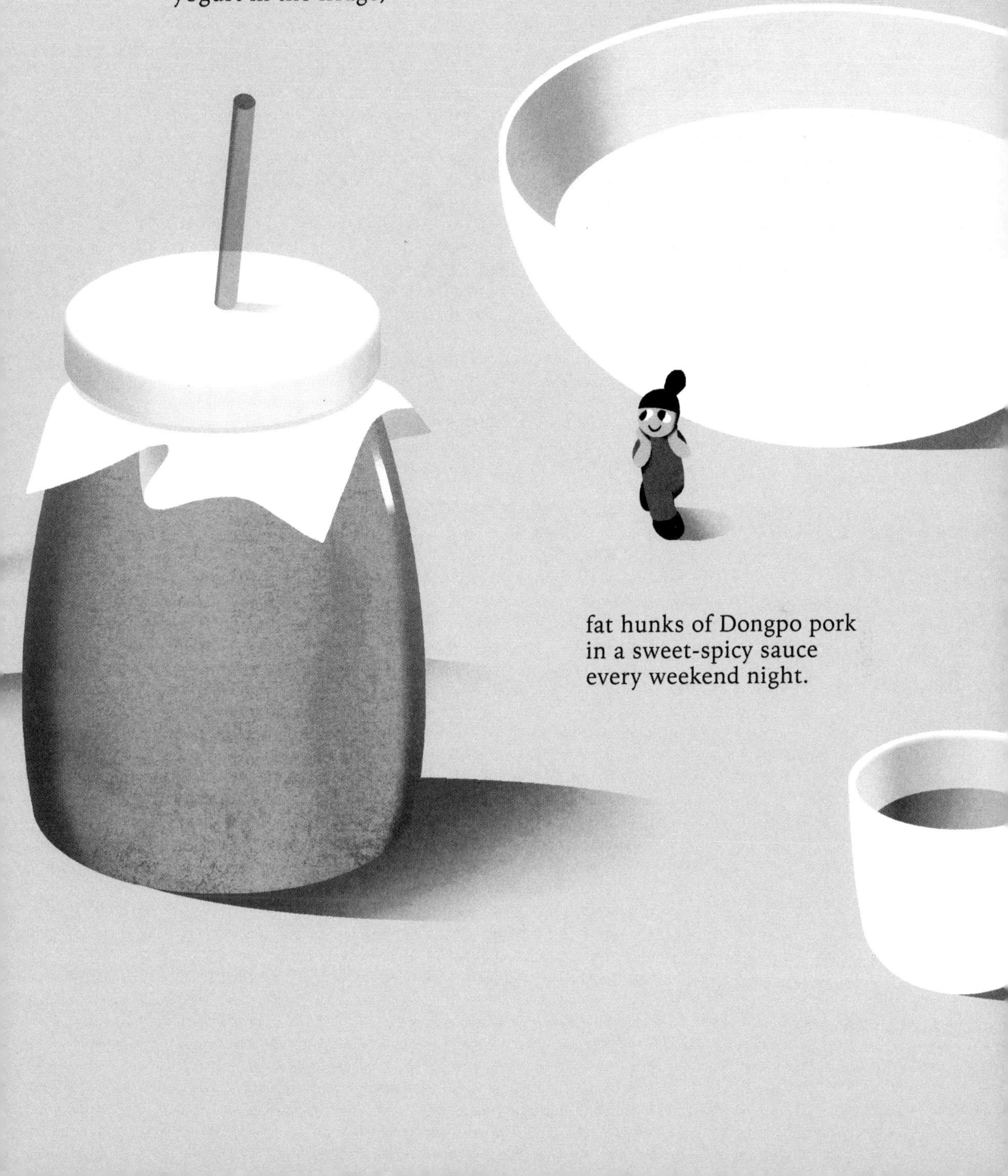

fat hunks of Dongpo pork
in a sweet-spicy sauce
every weekend night.

But eight years later—

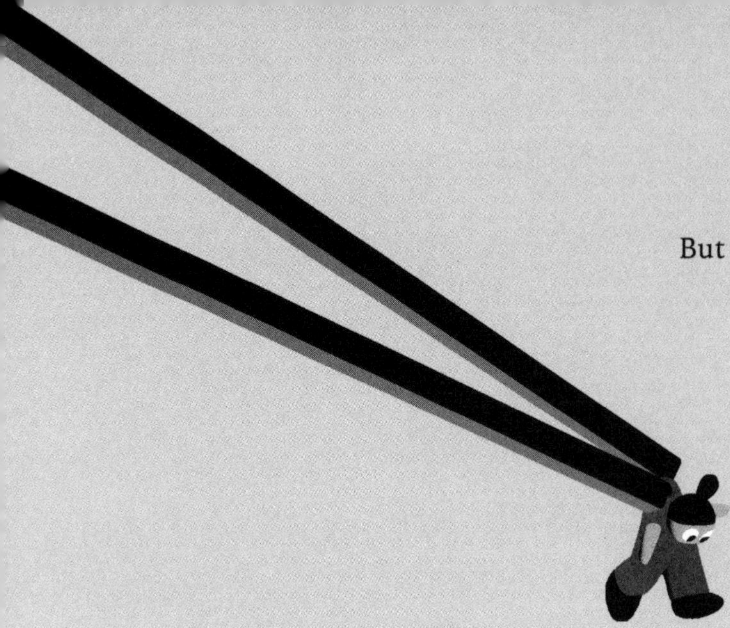

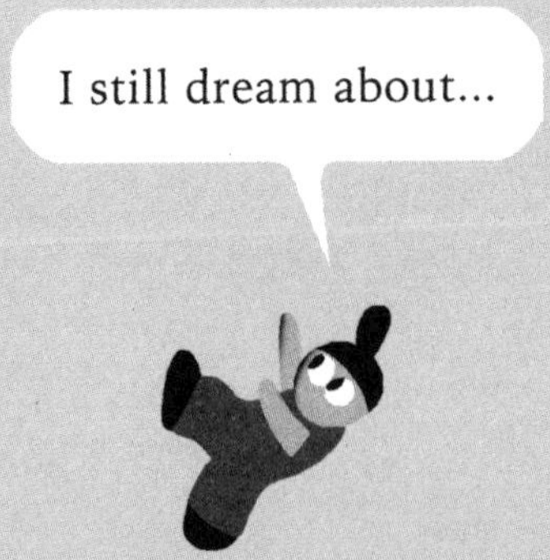
I still dream about...

shui zhu yu

水煮鱼

(water boiled fish)

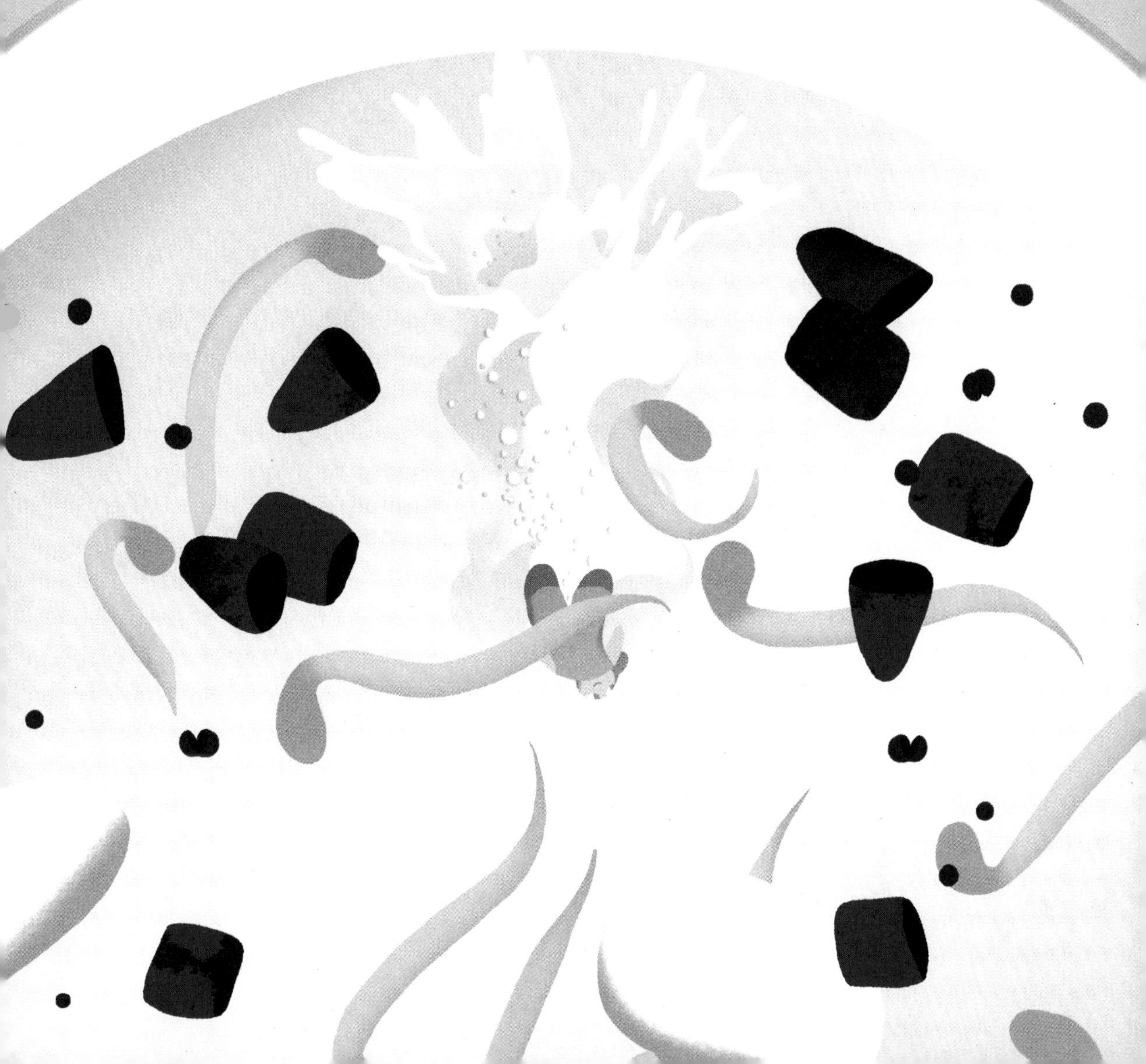

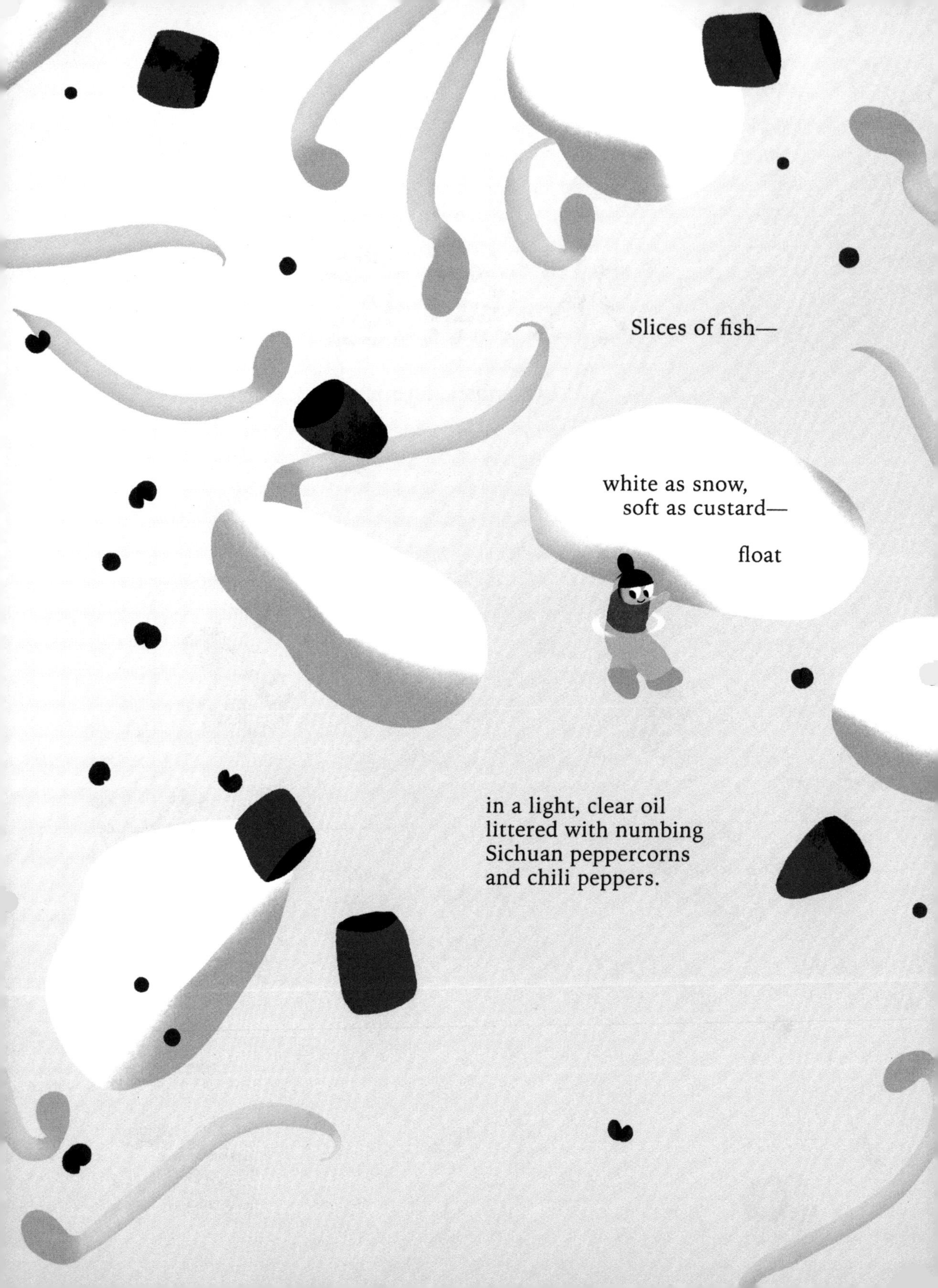

Slices of fish—

white as snow,
soft as custard—

float

in a light, clear oil
littered with numbing
Sichuan peppercorns
and chili peppers.

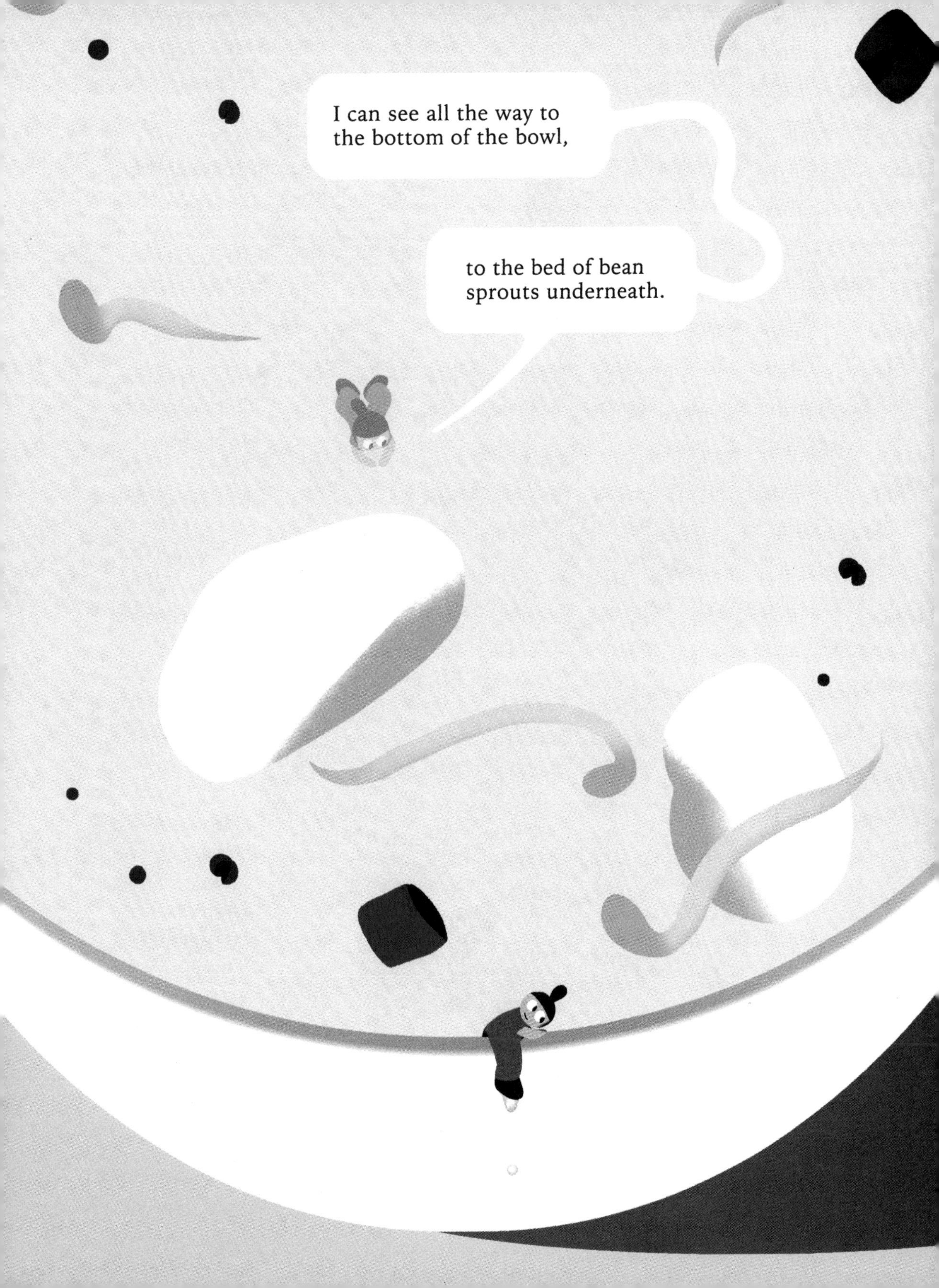
I can see all the way to the bottom of the bowl,
to the bed of bean sprouts underneath.

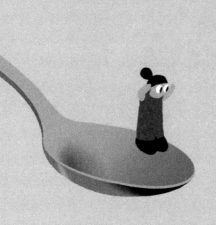

The day I flew back to Oregon, I looked up a restaurant that served shui zhu yu.

Beautiful white fish fillets—

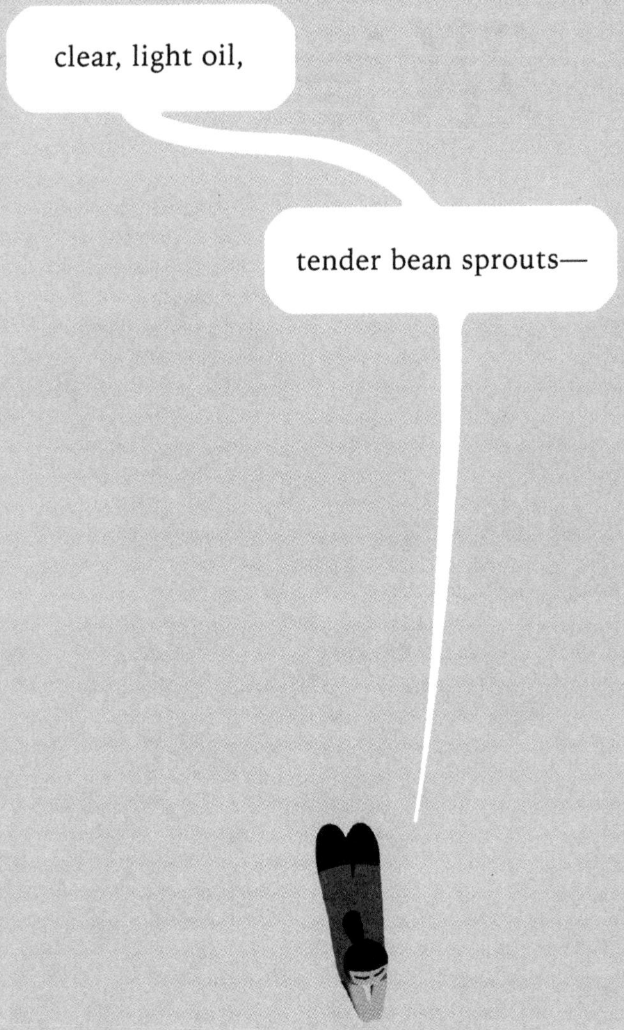
clear, light oil,
tender bean sprouts—

shui zhu yu

水煮鱼

(water boiled fish)

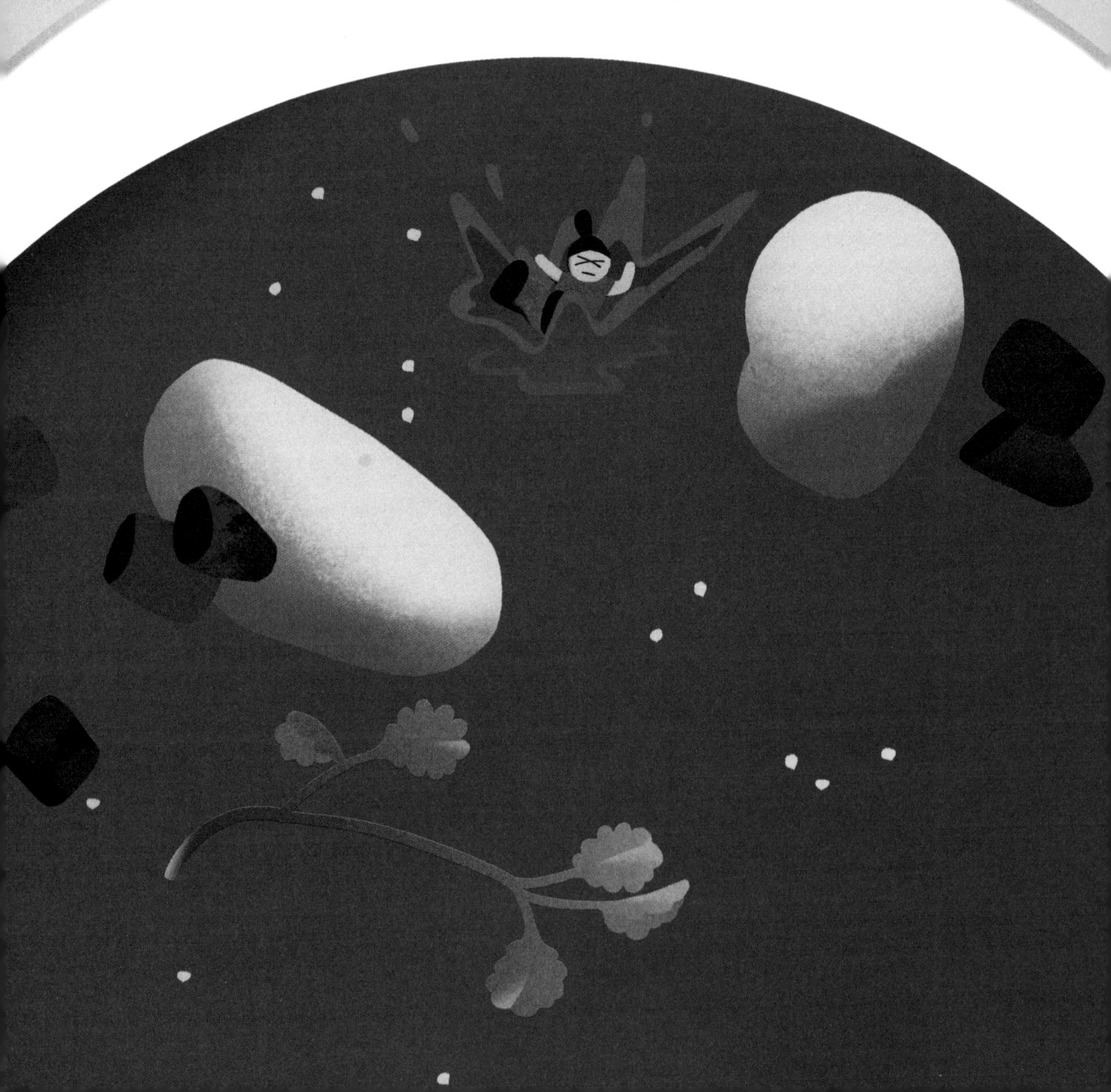

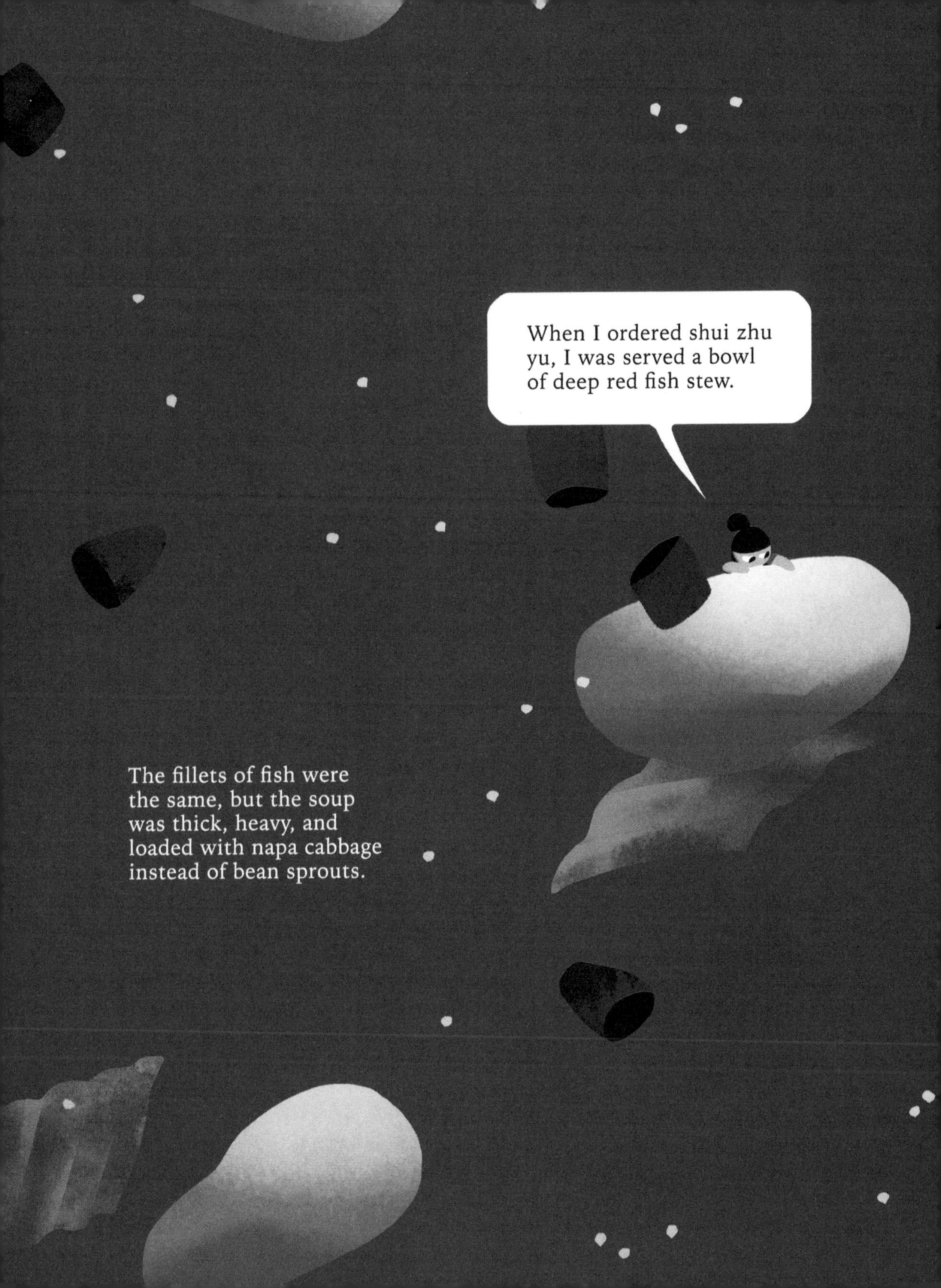
When I ordered shui zhu yu, I was served a bowl of deep red fish stew.
The fillets of fish were the same, but the soup was thick, heavy, and loaded with napa cabbage instead of bean sprouts.

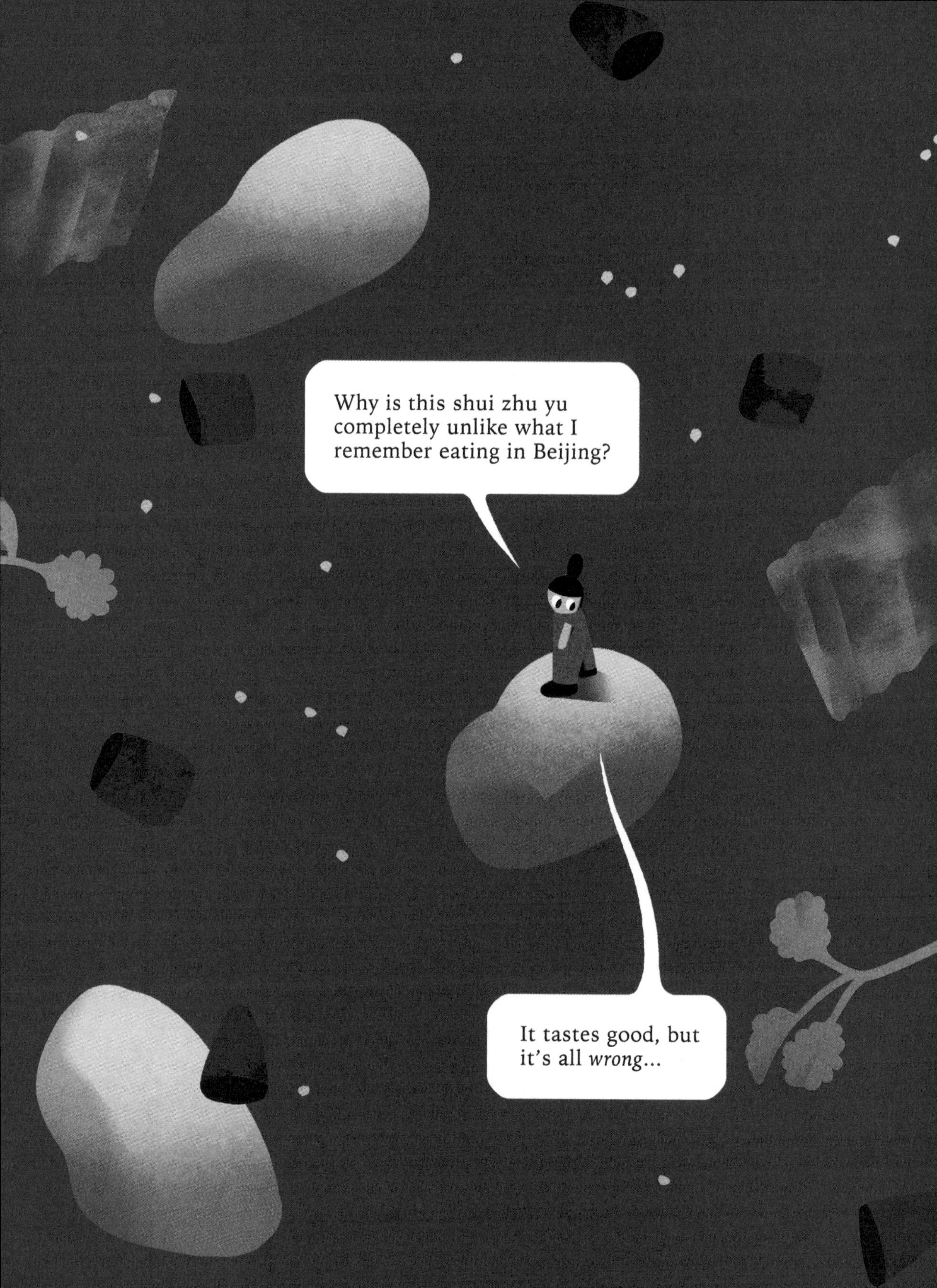
Why is this shui zhu yu completely unlike what I remember eating in Beijing?
It tastes good, but it's all *wrong*...

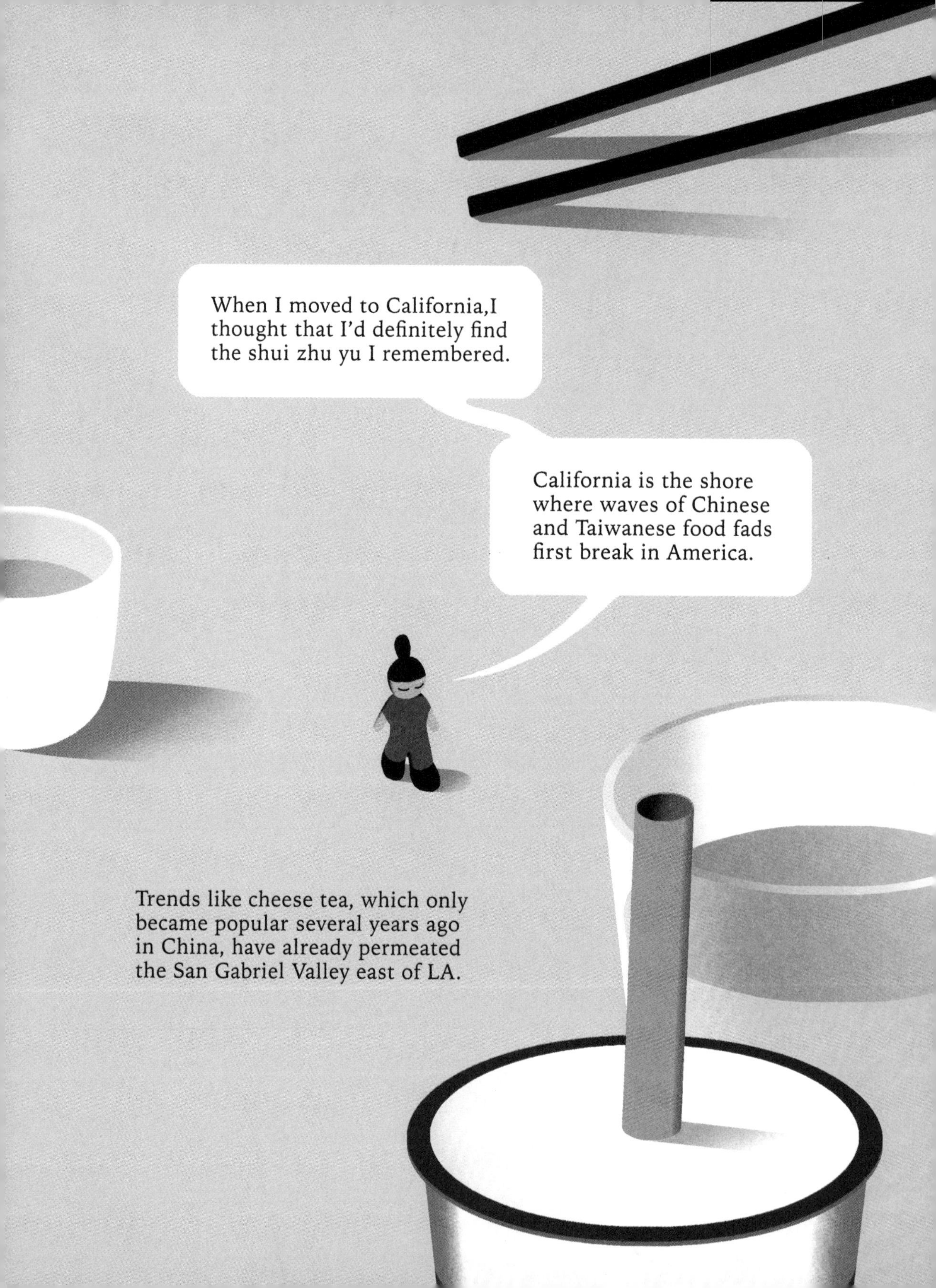
When I moved to California,I thought that I'd definitely find the shui zhu yu I remembered.
California is the shore where waves of Chinese and Taiwanese food fads first break in America.
Trends like cheese tea, which only became popular several years ago in China, have already permeated the San Gabriel Valley east of LA.

The San Gabriel Valley is home to some of the most regionally specific Chinese food you'll find in the States.

A little from Southern China, a little from the North...

Sichuan, Hunan, Shanghainese, Cantonese

and so on.

When I still lived in Portland, my friends and I used to make regular pilgrimages to California for the most satisfying Chinese food in the U.S.

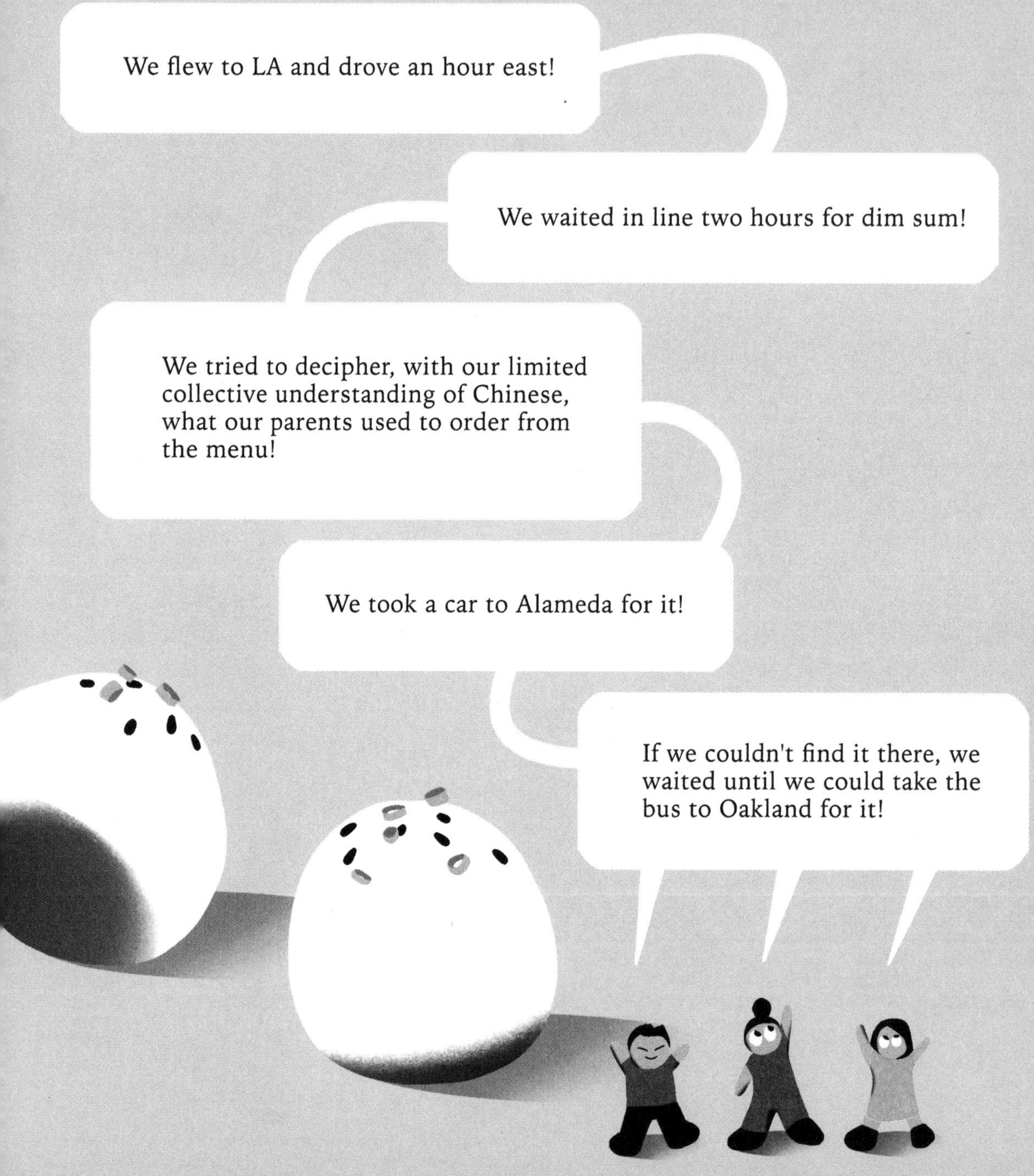
We flew to LA and drove an hour east!
We waited in line two hours for dim sum!
We tried to decipher, with our limited collective understanding of Chinese, what our parents used to order from the menu!
We took a car to Alameda for it!
If we couldn't find it there, we waited until we could take the bus to Oakland for it!

We took it back on the plane in three Tupperware boxes wrapped in a plastic bag and then another plastic bag so it didn't leak.

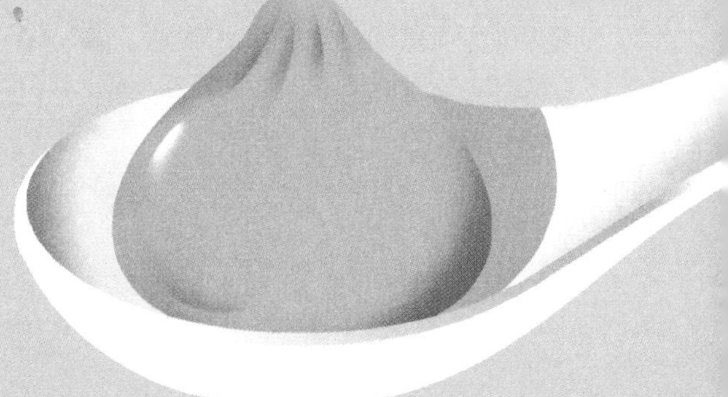

And when the TSA asked us, "What kind of meat is *that*?" we'd answer

Braised oxtail!

with some embarrassment.

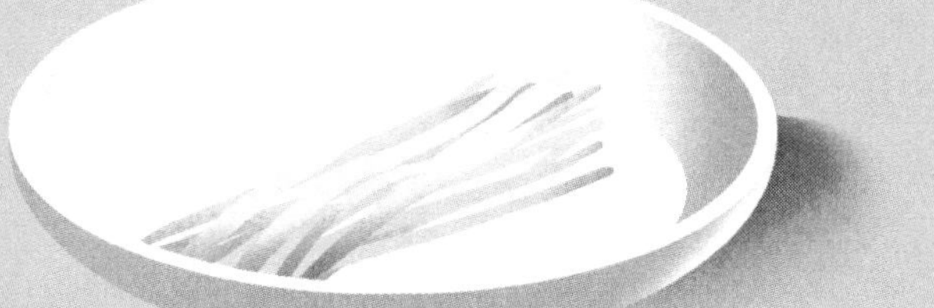

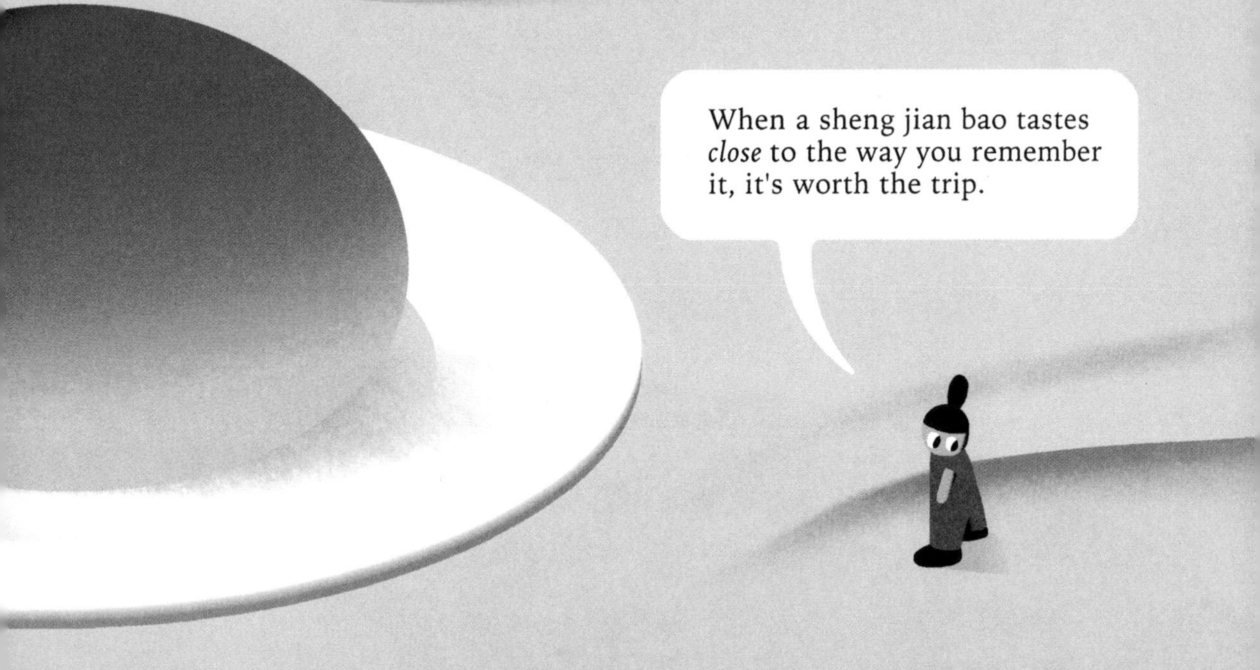
When a sheng jian bao tastes *close* to the way you remember it, it's worth the trip.

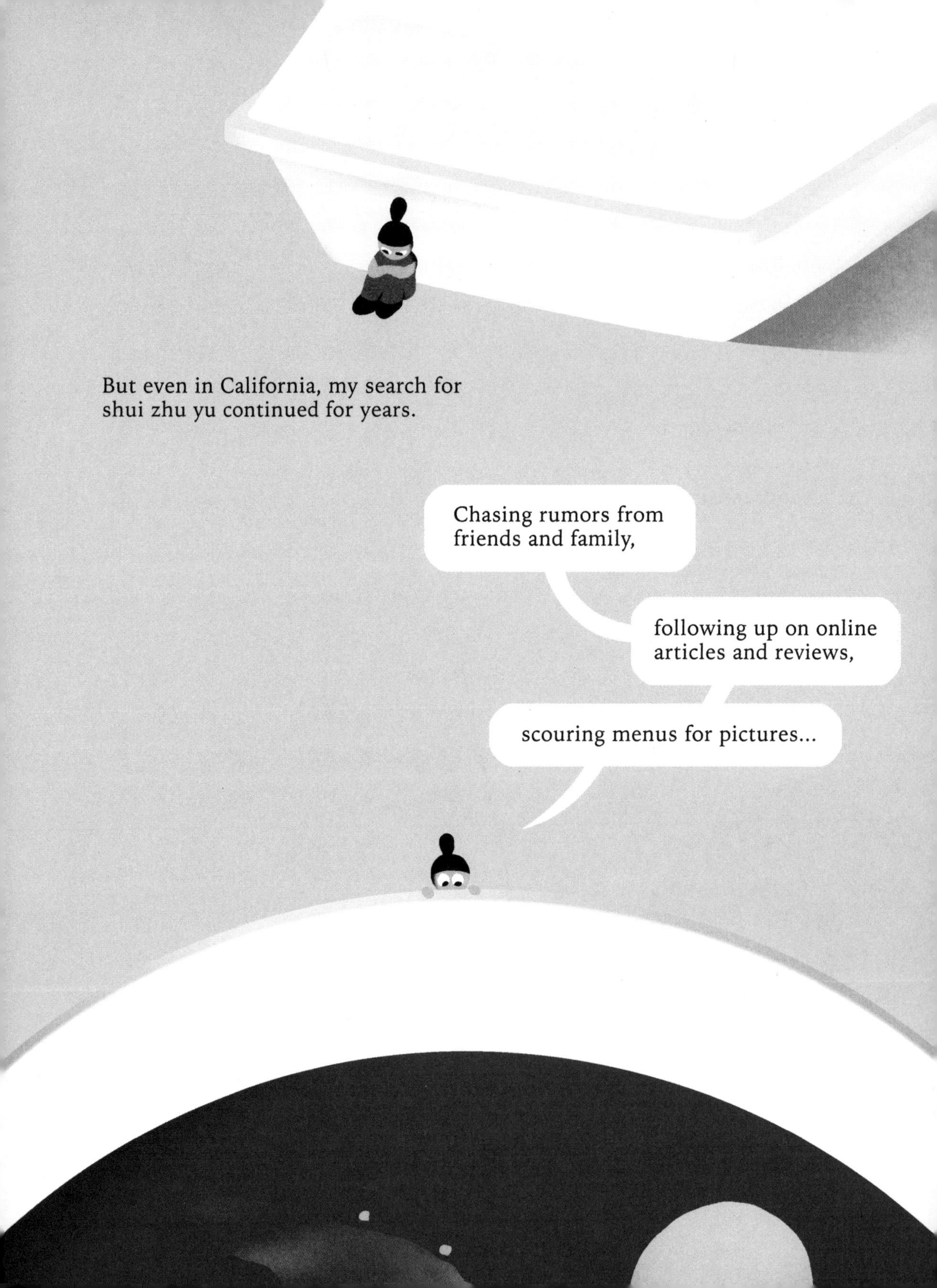
But even in California, my search for shui zhu yu continued for years.
Chasing rumors from friends and family,
following up on online articles and reviews,
scouring menus for pictures...

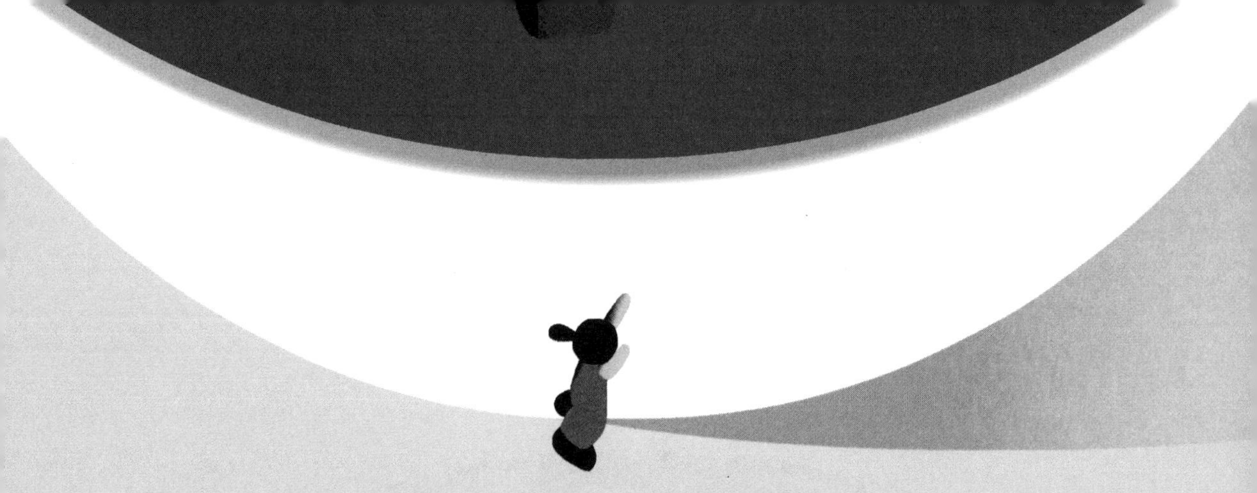

In fact, you'll find the red variety of shui zhu yu at most Sichuan restaurants in California.

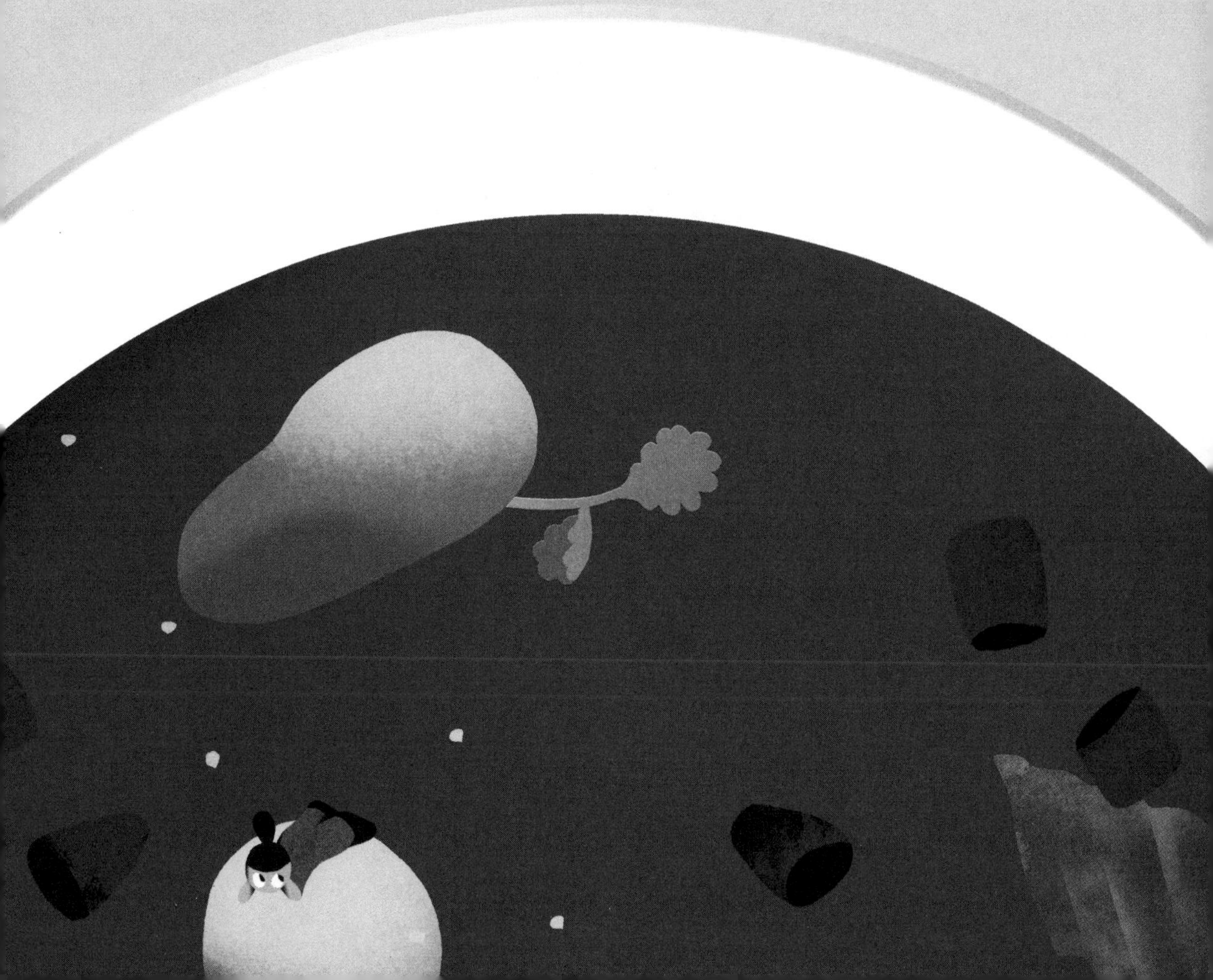

It has close cousins in shui zhu beef and shui zhu pork, all of which involve poaching meat and serving it in a fiery stew.

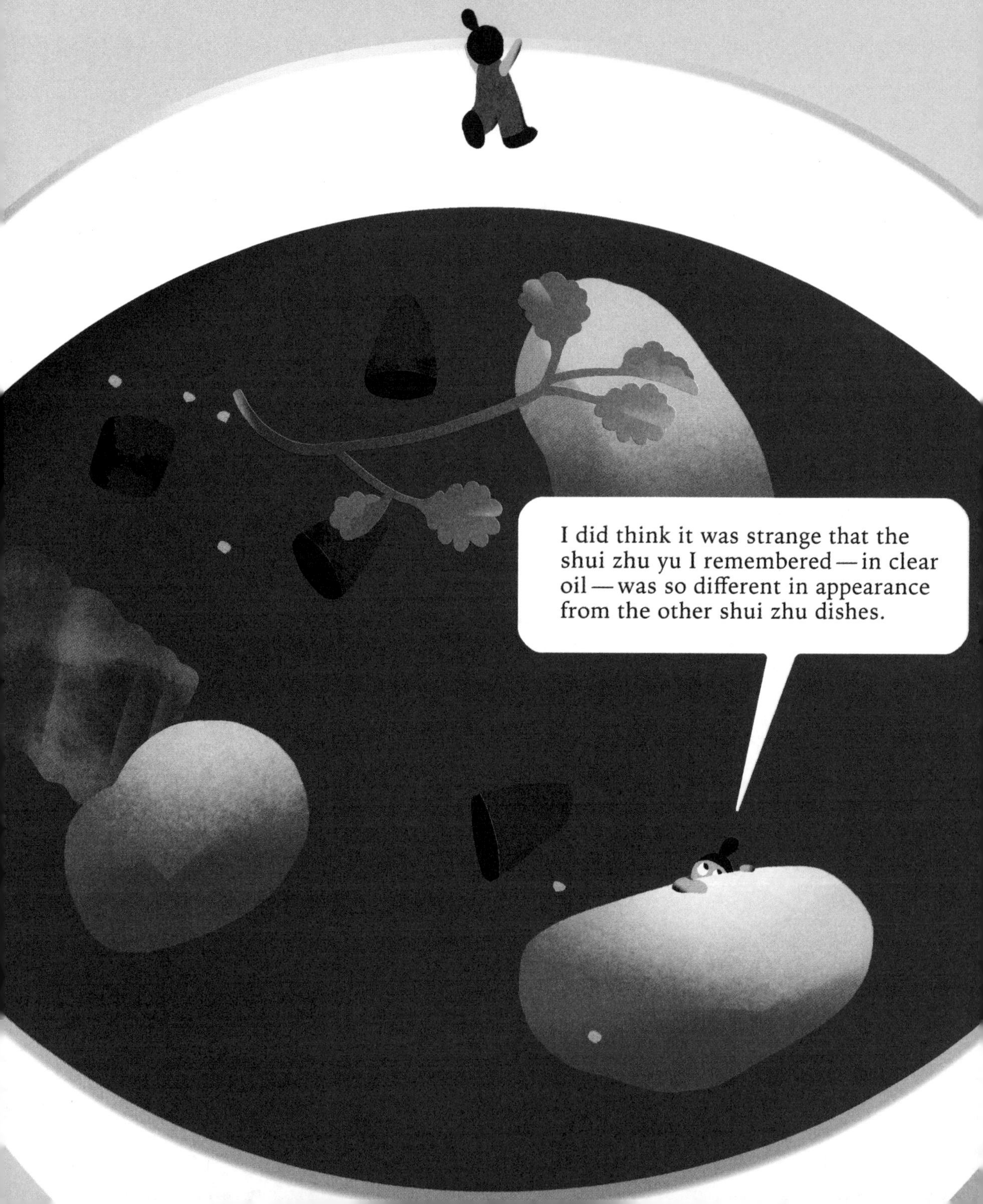
I did think it was strange that the shui zhu yu I remembered—in clear oil—was so different in appearance from the other shui zhu dishes.

But I just kept searching,

ordering,

eating,

being disappointed—

searching,

ordering,

being disappointed—

eating,

eating,

searching,

ordering,

being disappointed—

searching,

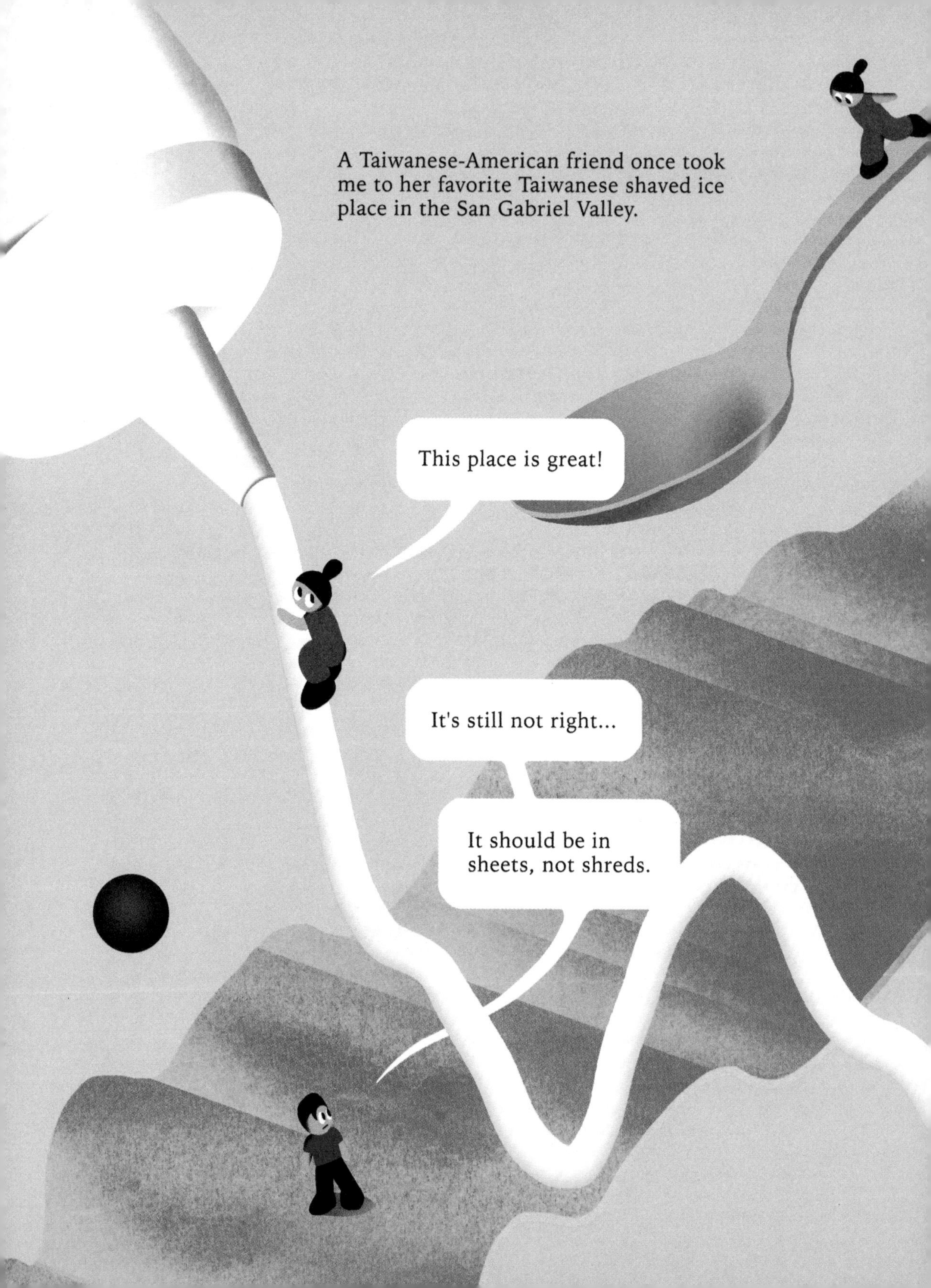
A Taiwanese-American friend once took me to her favorite Taiwanese shaved ice place in the San Gabriel Valley.
This place is great!
It's still not right...
It should be in sheets, not shreds.

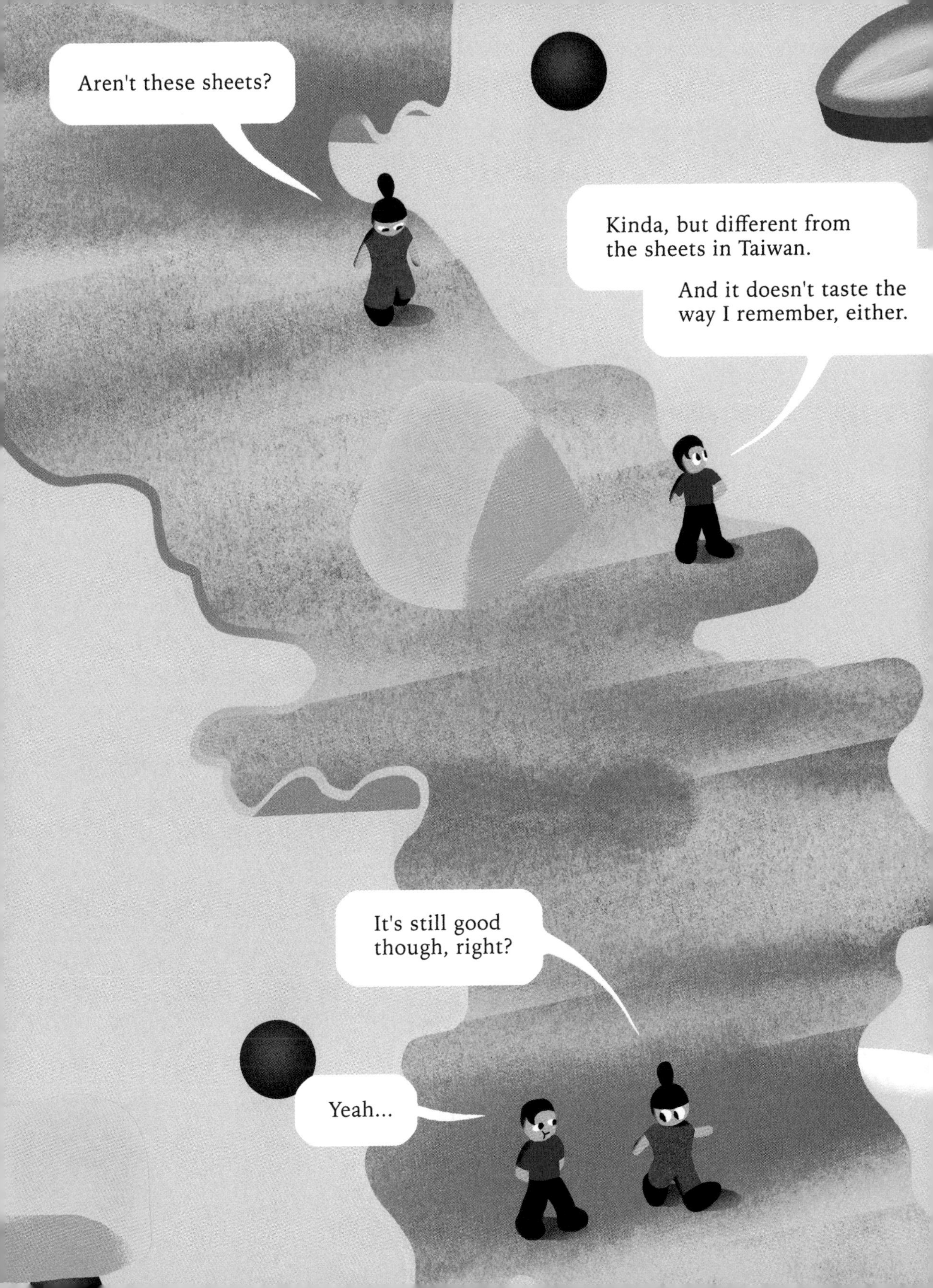
Aren't these sheets?
Kinda, but different from the sheets in Taiwan.
And it doesn't taste the way I remember, either.
It's still good though, right?
Yeah...

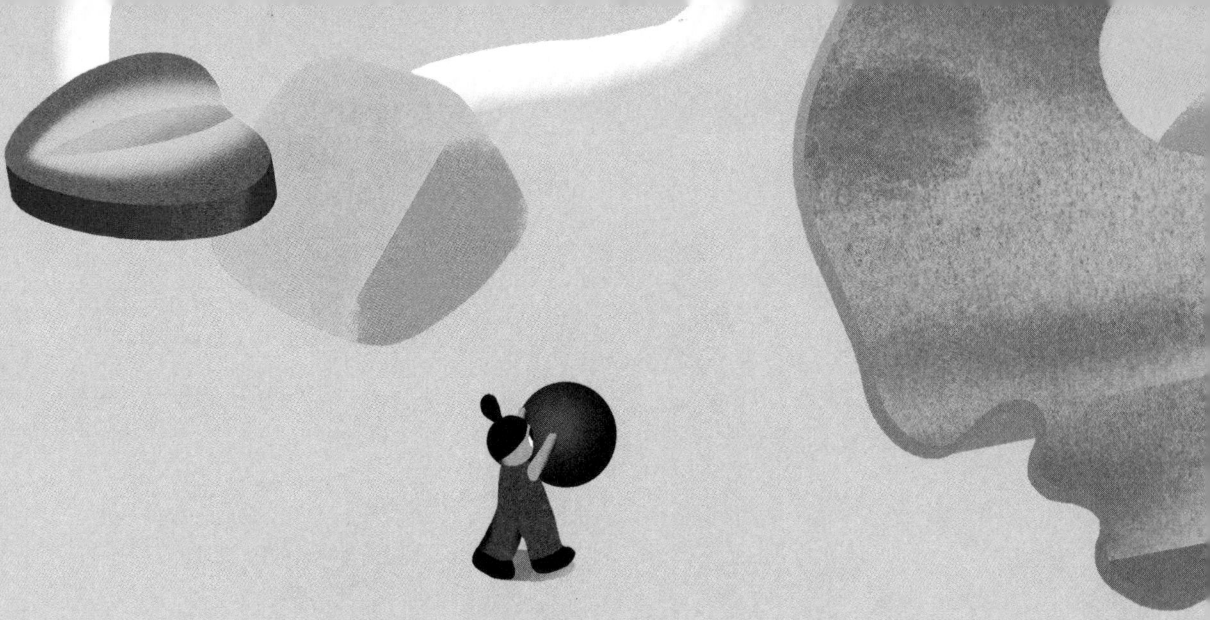

As someone who has never been to Taiwan, it tasted like every other Taiwanese shaved ice I've had.

But we're each the authorities of our own food memories.

Besides, what else are you going to do?

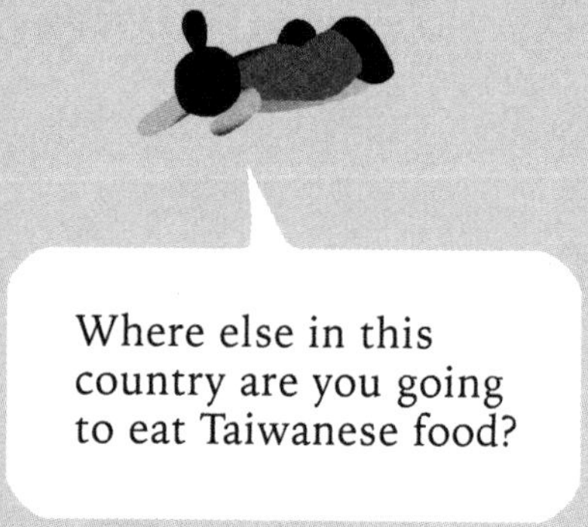
Where else in this country are you going to eat Taiwanese food?

I still think about the you tiao I had as a child in Shanghai.

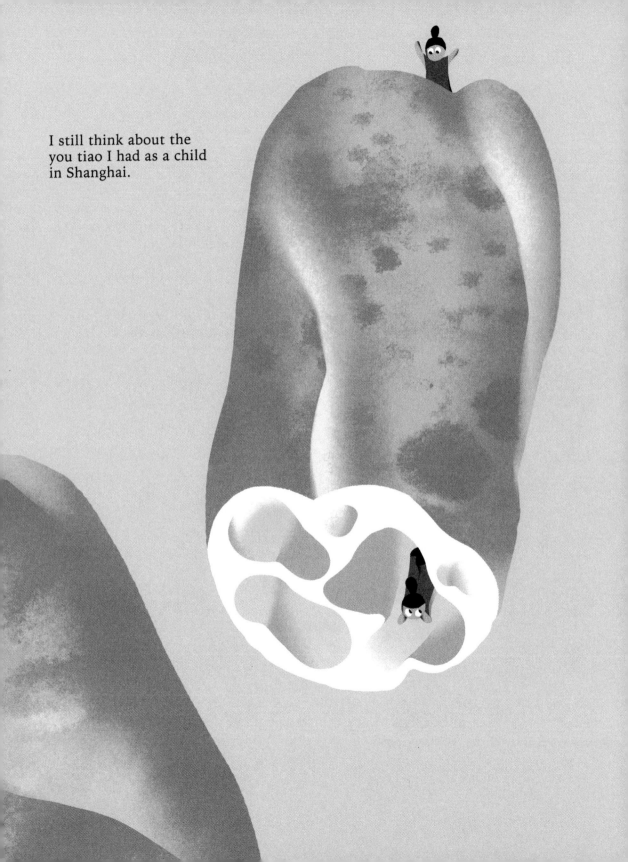

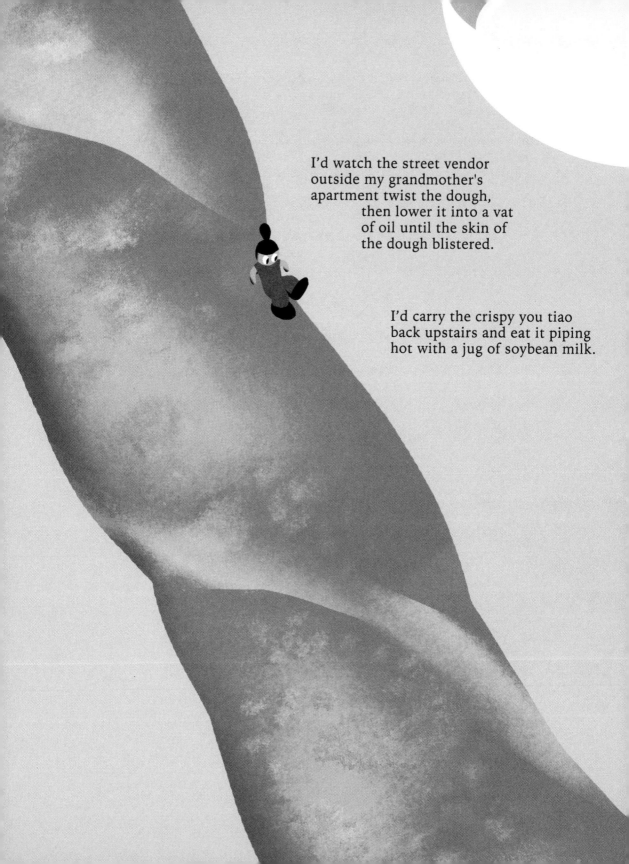

I'd watch the street vendor
outside my grandmother's
apartment twist the dough,
then lower it into a vat
of oil until the skin of
the dough blistered.

I'd carry the crispy you tiao
back upstairs and eat it piping
hot with a jug of soybean milk.

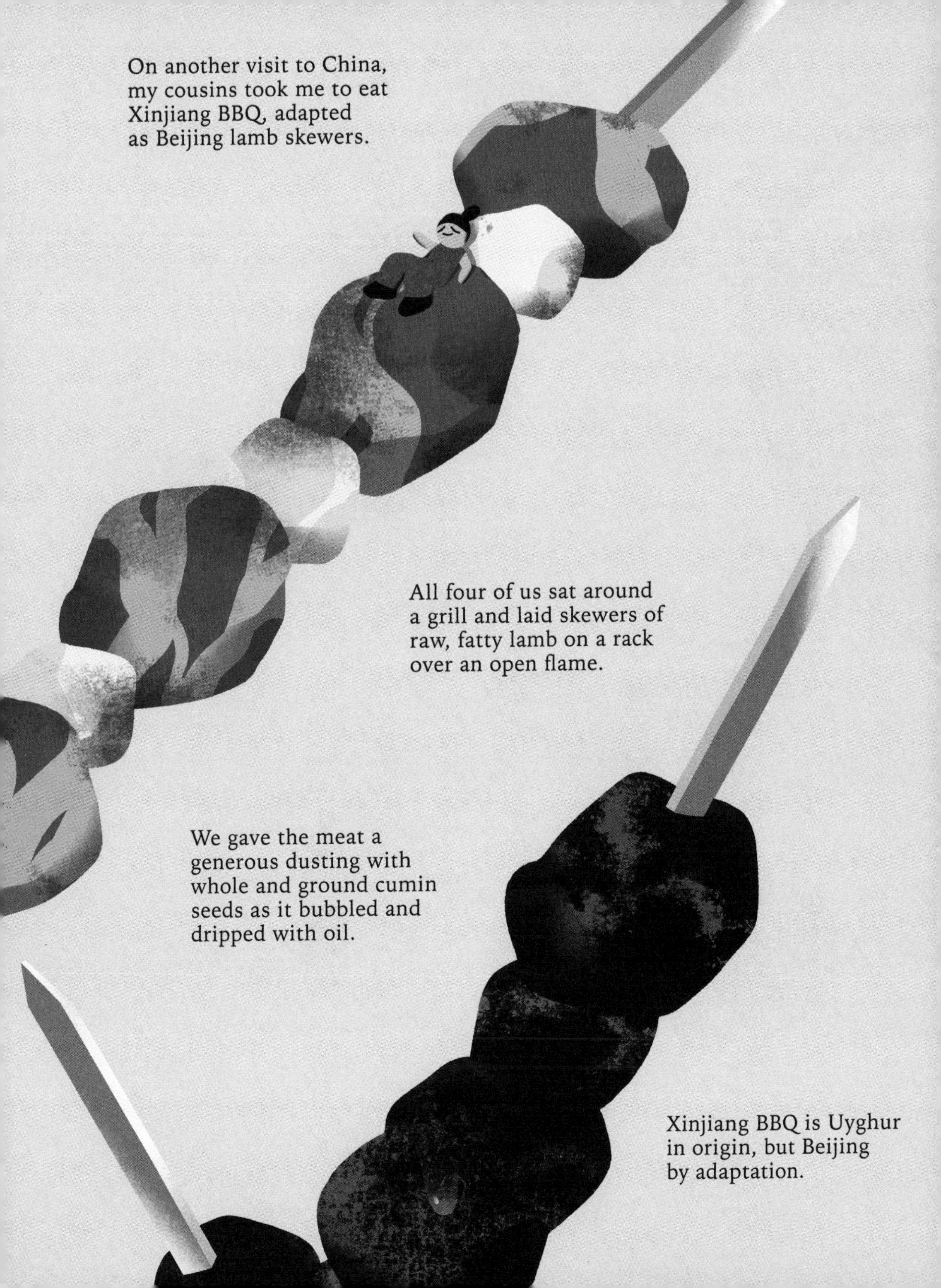

On another visit to China, my cousins took me to eat Xinjiang BBQ, adapted as Beijing lamb skewers.

All four of us sat around a grill and laid skewers of raw, fatty lamb on a rack over an open flame.

We gave the meat a generous dusting with whole and ground cumin seeds as it bubbled and dripped with oil.

Xinjiang BBQ is Uyghur in origin, but Beijing by adaptation.

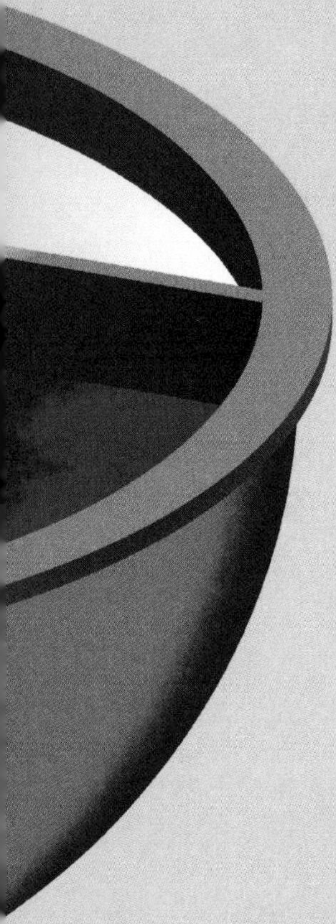

I'm still searching for a perfect replica of the ma la hotpot I ordered every other night in Beijing.

Yang mei, a stonefruit I bought in bags off the street in Shanghai, has proven impossible to find here in California.

But there's rumored to be a yang mei tree near a dumpster behind a Trader Joe's in El Cerrito.

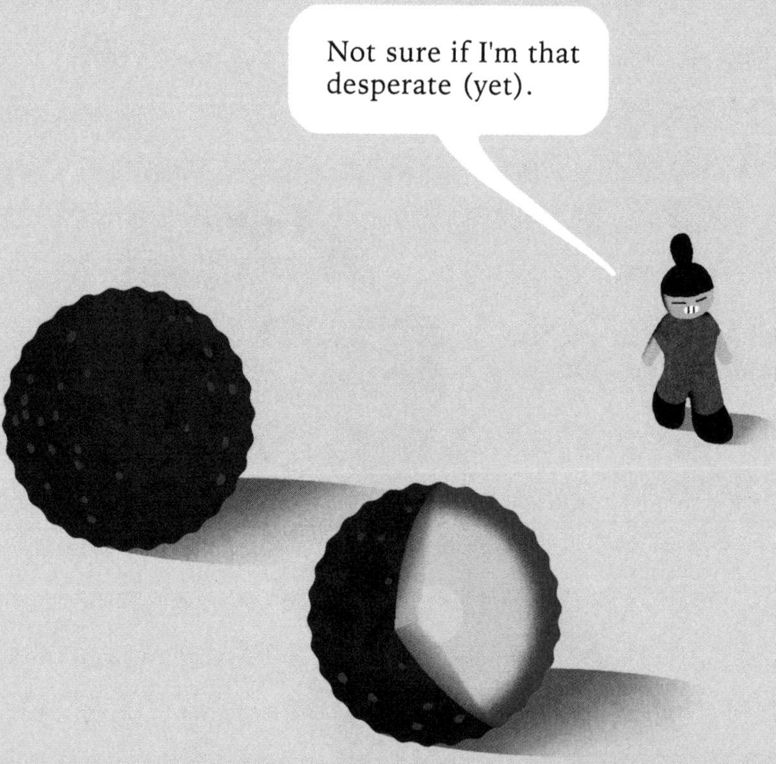
Not sure if I'm that desperate (yet).

It turns out that shui zhu dishes were first
created 35 years ago in the city of Chongqing.

The original version, which won a local
cooking contest, was a fiery red stew
with meat and an assortment of vegetables.

In 1999, the first shui zhu yu
restaurant opened a thousand
miles away in Beijing.

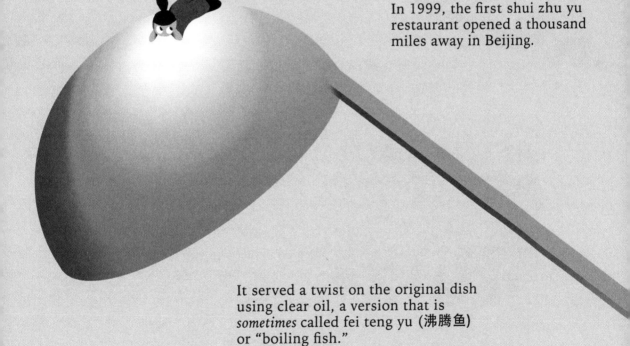

It served a twist on the original dish
using clear oil, a version that is
sometimes called fei teng yu (沸腾鱼)
or "boiling fish."

—which is what I got used to eating.

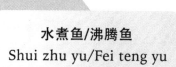

水煮鱼
Shui zhu yu

Vegetables, red chilis, Sichuan pepper, fish in heavily spiced red oil. The original.

水煮鱼/沸腾鱼
Shui zhu yu/Fei teng yu

Bean sprouts, red chilis, Sichuan pepper, fish floating in clear oil. The remix.

Sichuan restauranteurs in the States hew closer to the original dish, but the version most popular in Beijing is the remix.

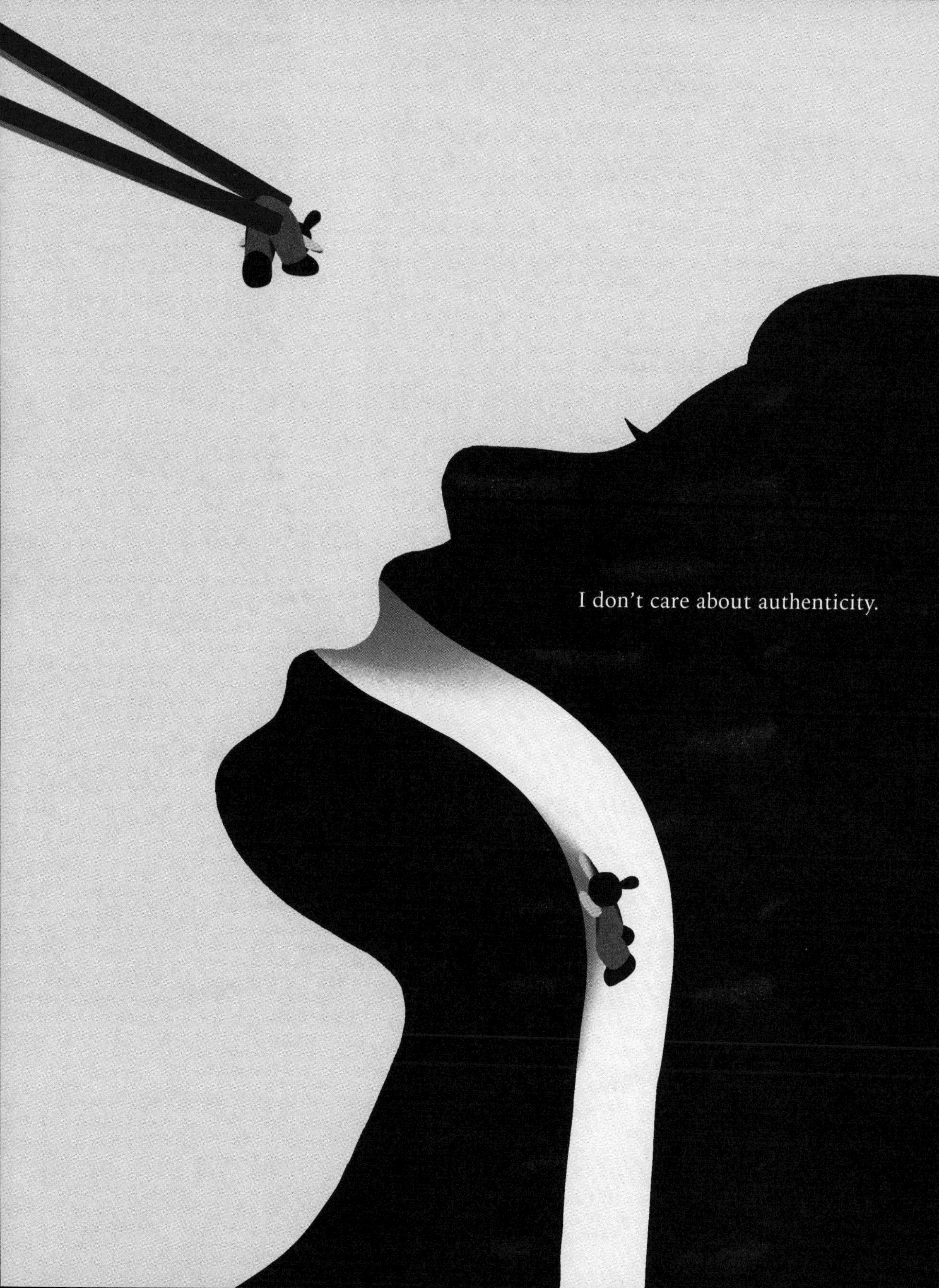
I don’t care about authenticity.

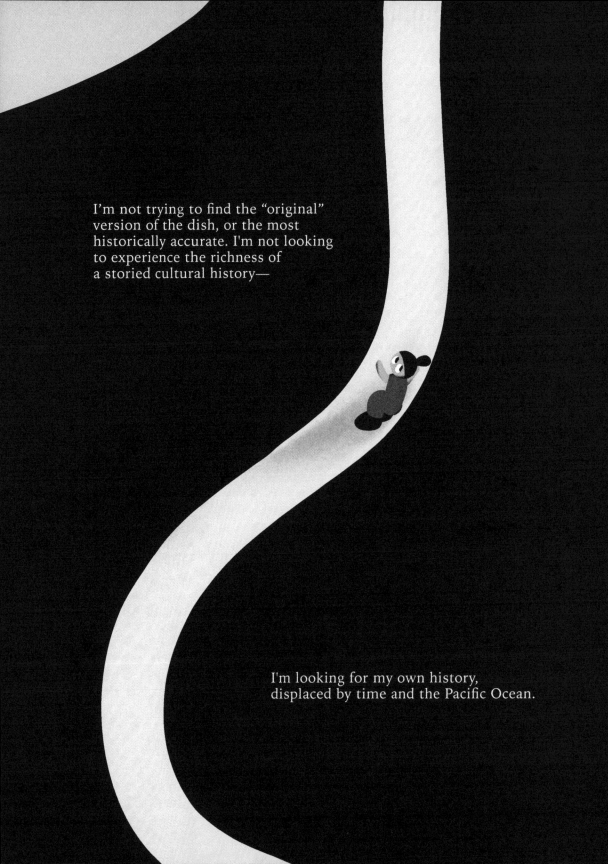

I'm not trying to find the "original"
version of the dish, or the most
historically accurate. I'm not looking
to experience the richness of
a storied cultural history—

I'm looking for my own history,
displaced by time and the Pacific Ocean.

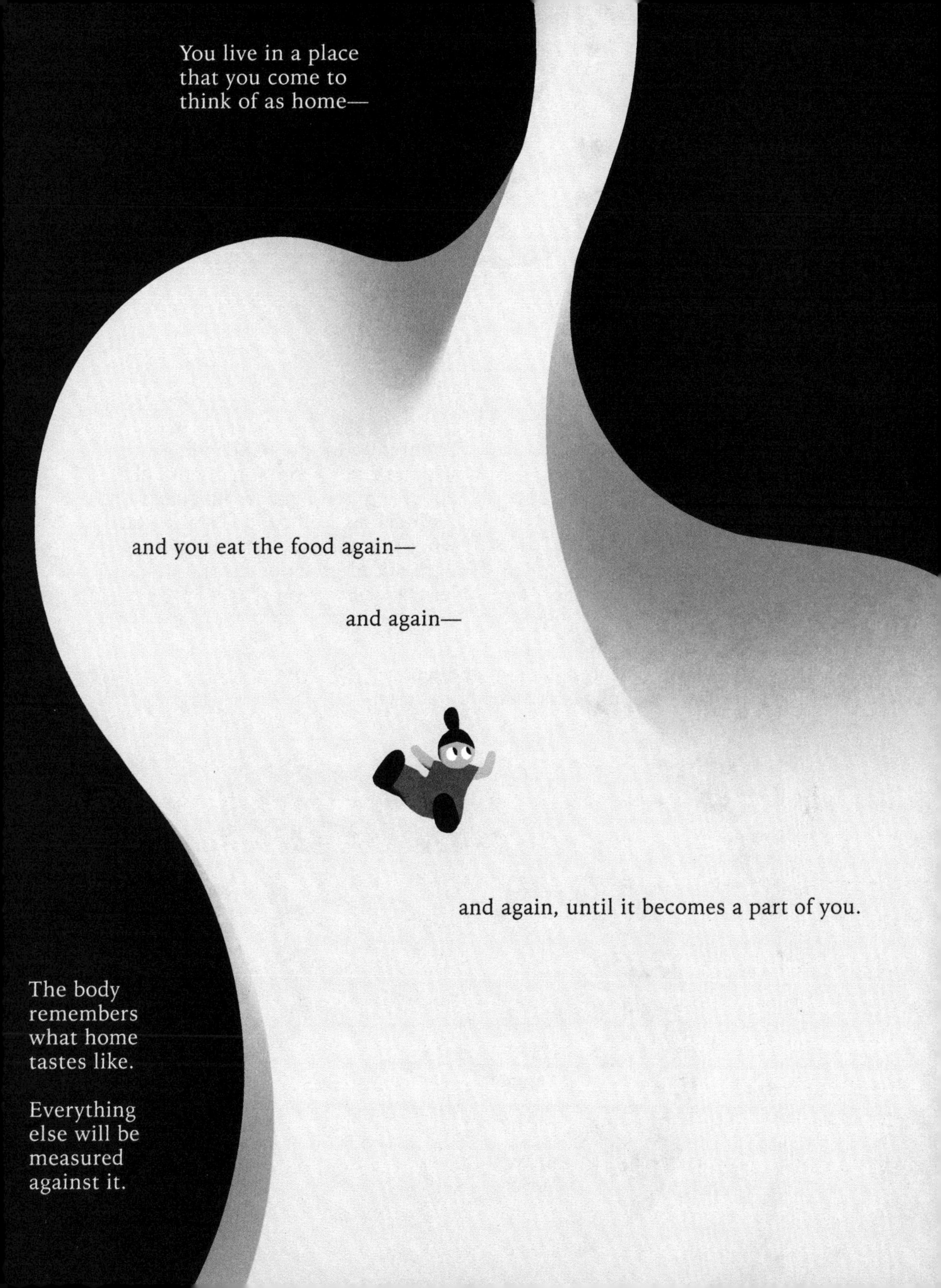

You live in a place
that you come to
think of as home—

and you eat the food again—

and again—

and again, until it becomes a part of you.

The body
remembers
what home
tastes like.

Everything
else will be
measured
against it.

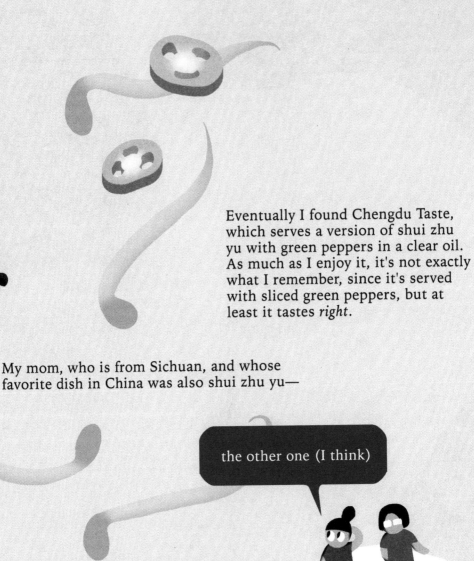

Eventually I found Chengdu Taste, which serves a version of shui zhu yu with green peppers in a clear oil. As much as I enjoy it, it's not exactly what I remember, since it's served with sliced green peppers, but at least it tastes *right*.

My mom, who is from Sichuan, and whose favorite dish in China was also shui zhu yu—

the other one (I think)

always asks if I want to go to Chengdu Taste for lunch.

California is her home now, so she's had me learn the taste of all of her hometown faves from restaurants in Alhambra.

I'm fond of la zi ji, a stir-fried spicy chicken dish, but I suspect that if I went back to China, the actual Sichuan version would taste... a little strange to me.

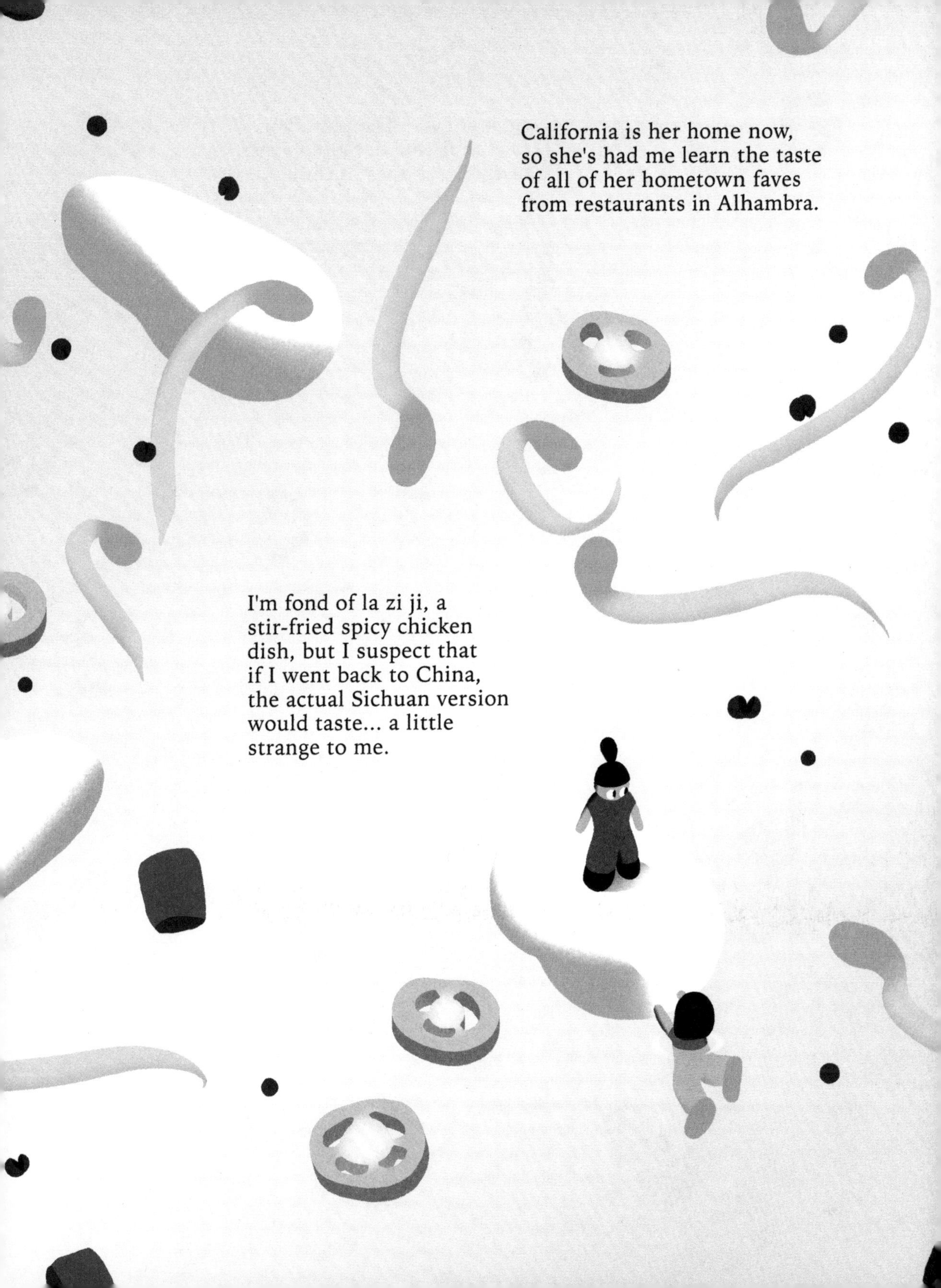

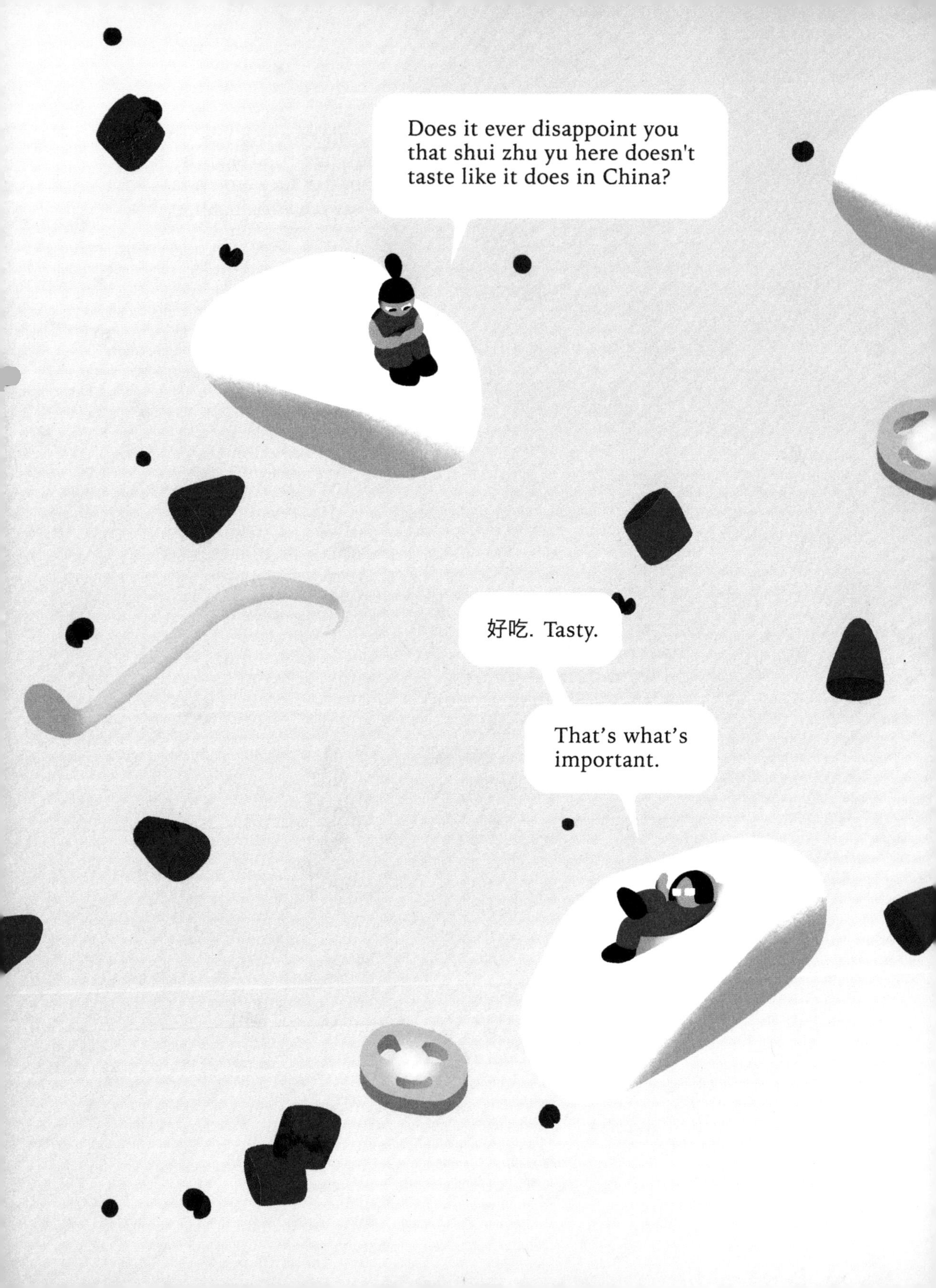
Does it ever disappoint you that shui zhu yu here doesn't taste like it does in China?
好吃. Tasty.
That’s what’s important.

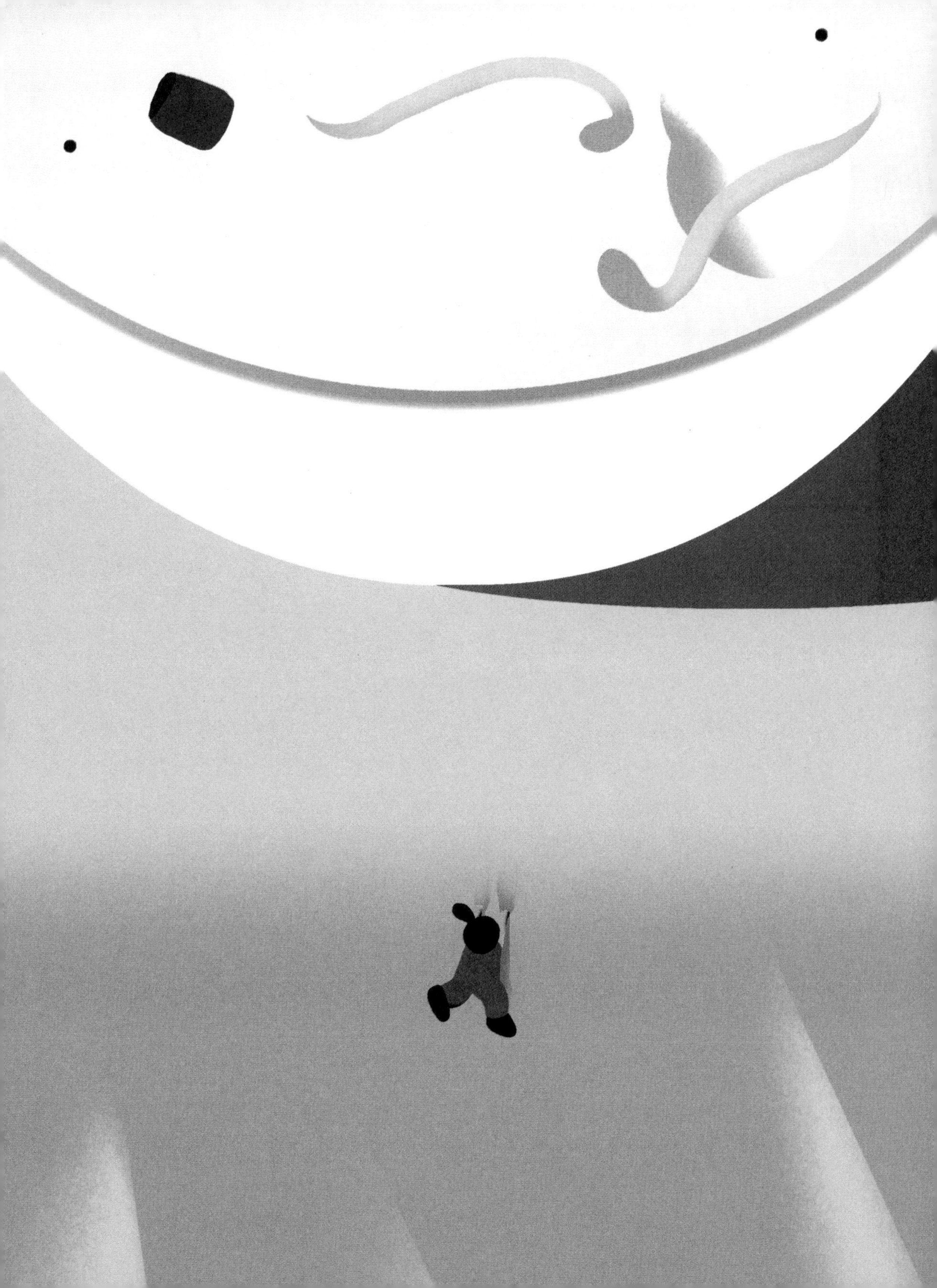

Anti-Gone (*Excerpt*)

CONNOR WILLUMSEN

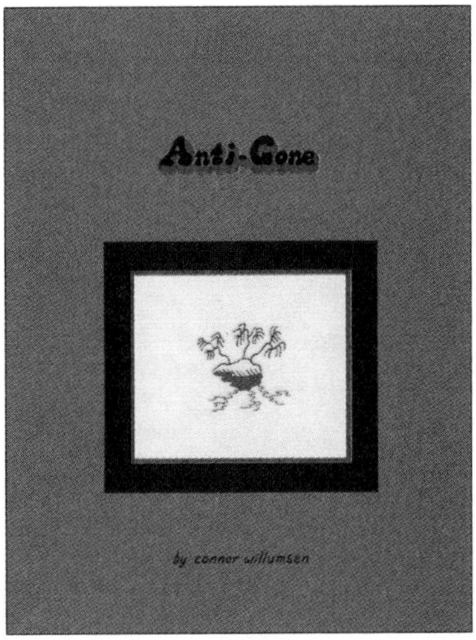
Anti-Gone
by connor willumsen

originally published in

Anti-Gone

KOYAMA PRESS

8.5 x 11 inches • 120 pages

Biography

Connor Willumsen is a Montreal-based multidisciplinary artist with varied experience in art, design, and publishing. He has designed and illustrated covers for the Criterion Collection and illustrated books for Marvel Comics, while his main body of work, self-authored printed comics, has received various awards, honors, and academic scholarships, including a fellowship at the Center for Cartoon Studies. His work is regularly published by Breakdown Press and Koyama Press, the latter having published his first major book, *Anti-Gone,* which has been a finalist for an *LA Time*s Book Prize, a Doug Wright Award, a Pingprizen Award, and an Ignatz Award.
connorwillumsen.com

Statement

Anti-Gone is a vague and expansive ocean world in which every comfort is available to those willing to kill their time searching for it. To this point, Spyda and Lynxa have have been doing so in a half-submerged contemporary metropolis wrung by tropical flora, fauna, and various fine retail outlets by going shopping and purchasing designer drugs that affect visual perception, memory, and emotional conditions with hyper specificity. Their goal is to use the tickets secured by a mysterious Jet Ski–traveling merchant to engender the most ideal movie-viewing experience at the most prominent theater, the Galleria. *Anti-Gone* is a book designed to chart an outline around the invisible territory that gratification excludes.

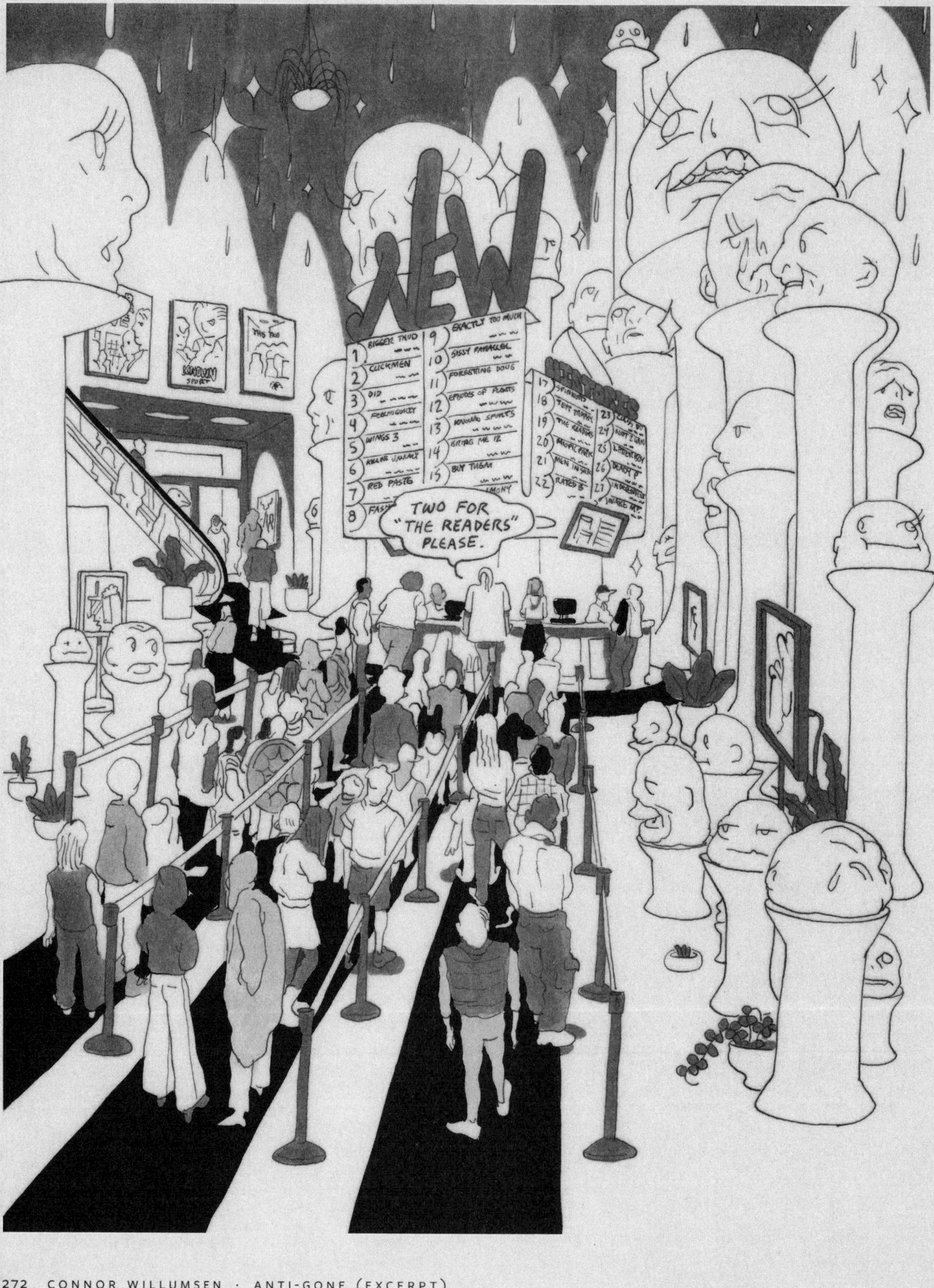
NEW
1 BIGGER TRUD
2 CLICKMEN
3 DID
5 WINGS 3
7 RED PASTE
9 EXACTLY TOO MUCH
11 FORGETTING DOUG
12 EPISODES OF FLOATS
19 THE READERS
TWO FOR "THE READERS" PLEASE.

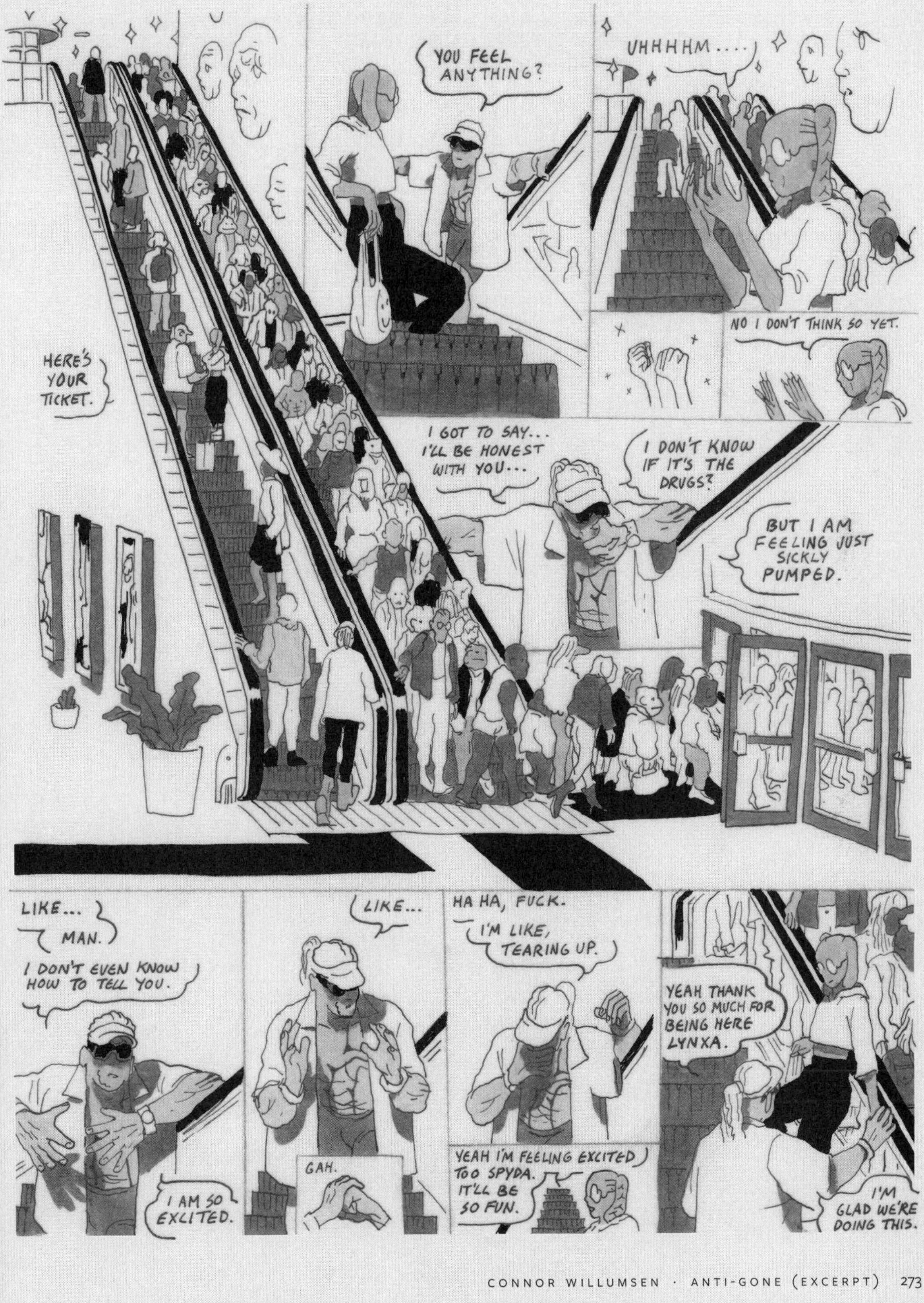

HERE'S YOUR TICKET.
YOU FEEL ANYTHING?
UHHHHM....
NO I DON'T THINK SO YET.
I GOT TO SAY... I'LL BE HONEST WITH YOU...
I DON'T KNOW IF IT'S THE DRUGS?
BUT I AM FEELING JUST SICKLY PUMPED.
LIKE...
MAN.
I DON'T EVEN KNOW HOW TO TELL YOU.
I AM SO EXCITED.
LIKE...
GAH.
HA HA, FUCK.
I'M LIKE, TEARING UP.
YEAH I'M FEELING EXCITED TOO SPYDA. IT'LL BE SO FUN.
YEAH THANK YOU SO MUCH FOR BEING HERE LYNXA.
I'M GLAD WE'RE DOING THIS.

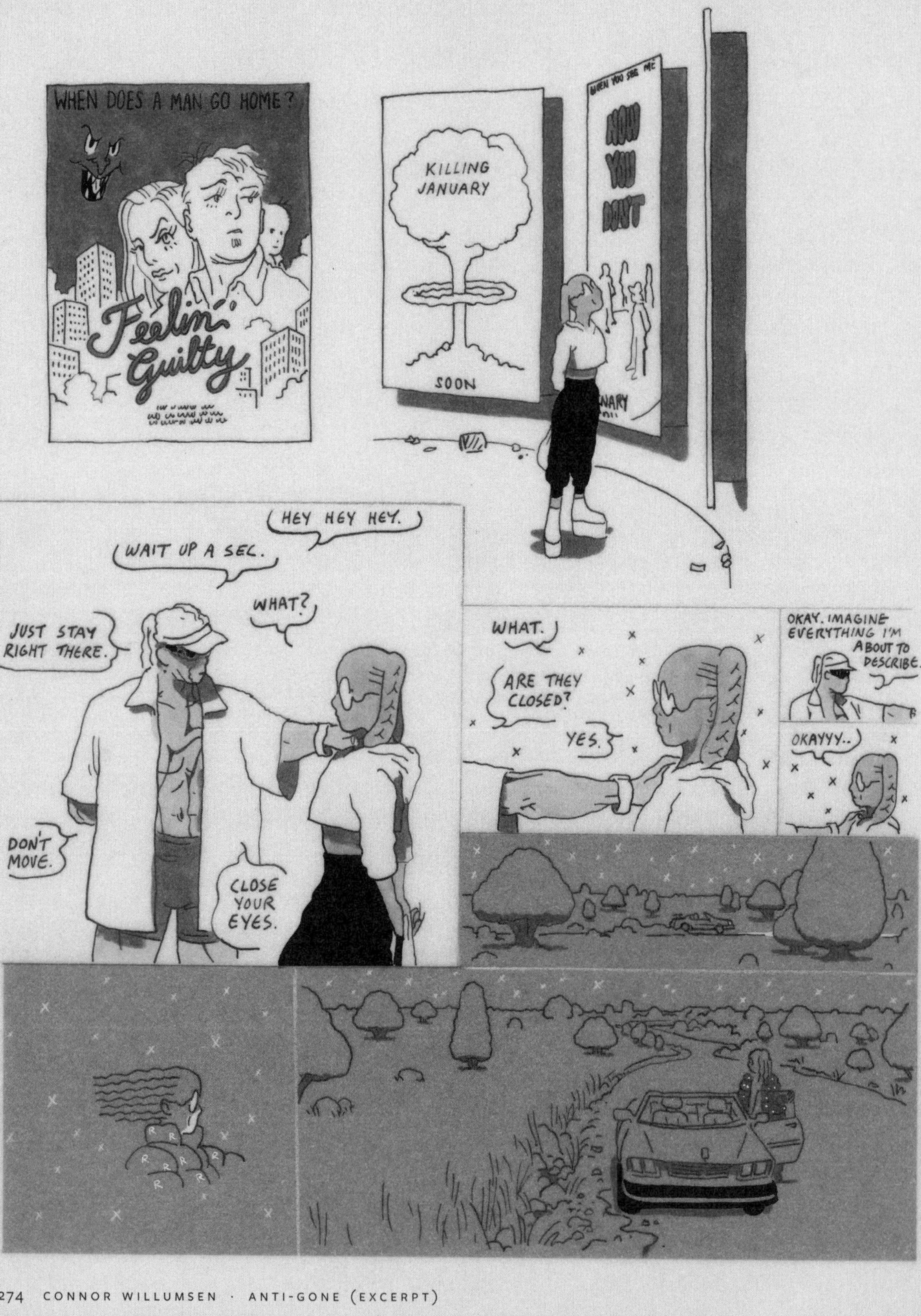
WHEN DOES A MAN GO HOME?
Feelin' Guilty
KILLING JANUARY
SOON
WHEN YOU SEE ME
NOW YOU DON'T
HEY HEY HEY.
WAIT UP A SEC.
JUST STAY RIGHT THERE.
WHAT?
DON'T MOVE.
CLOSE YOUR EYES.
WHAT.
ARE THEY CLOSED?
YES.
OKAY. IMAGINE EVERYTHING I'M ABOUT TO DESCRIBE.
OKAYYY..

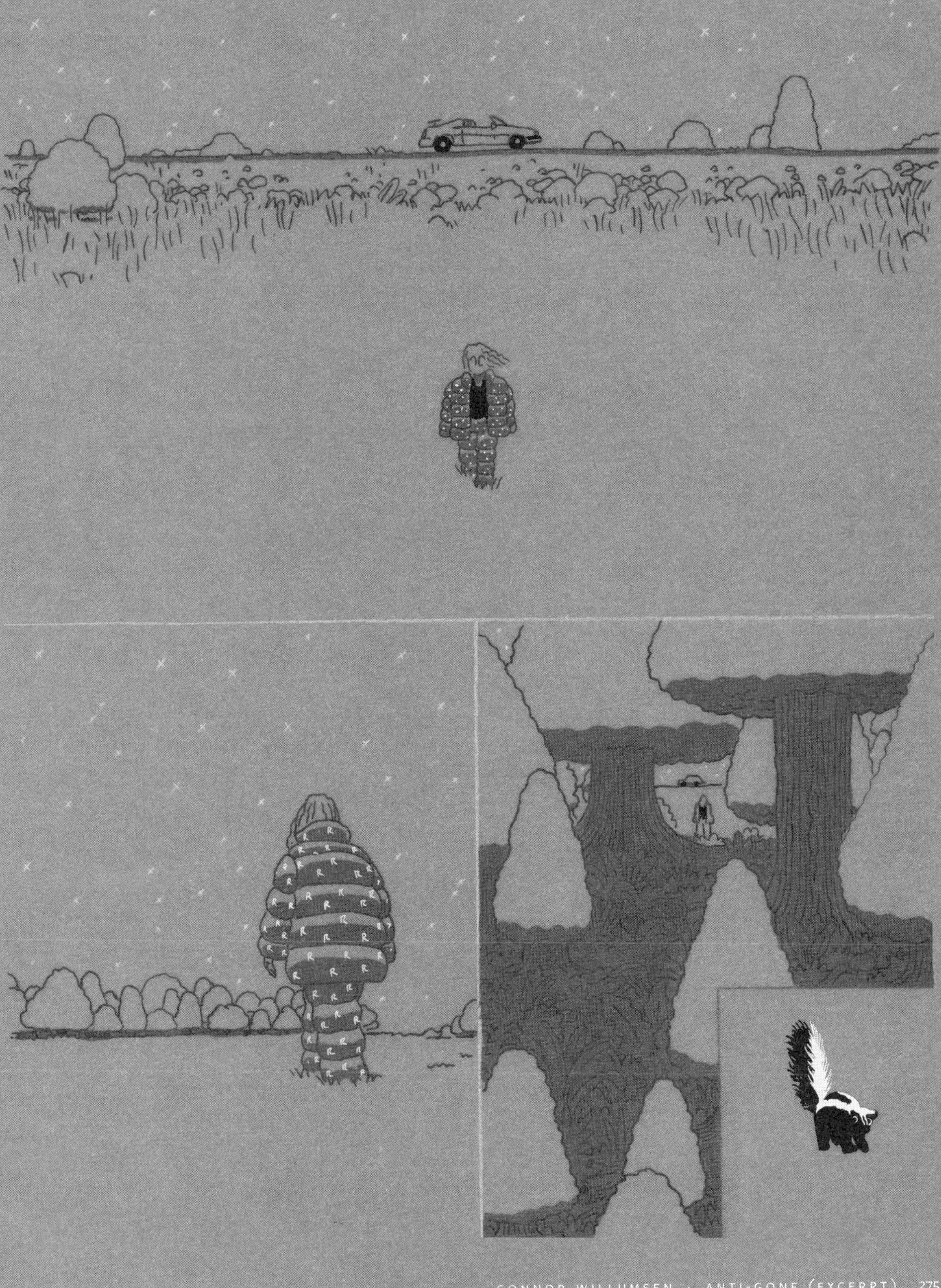

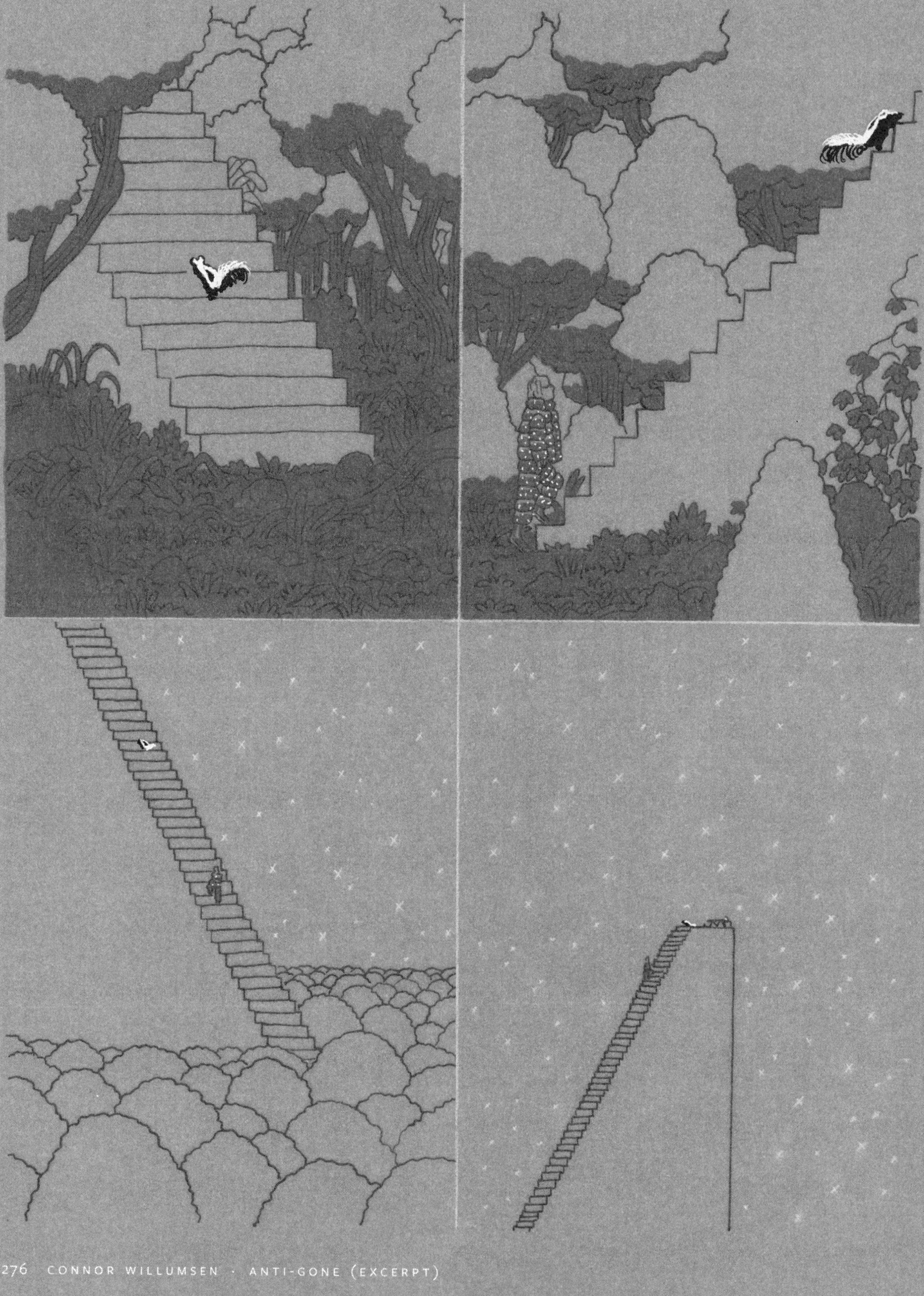

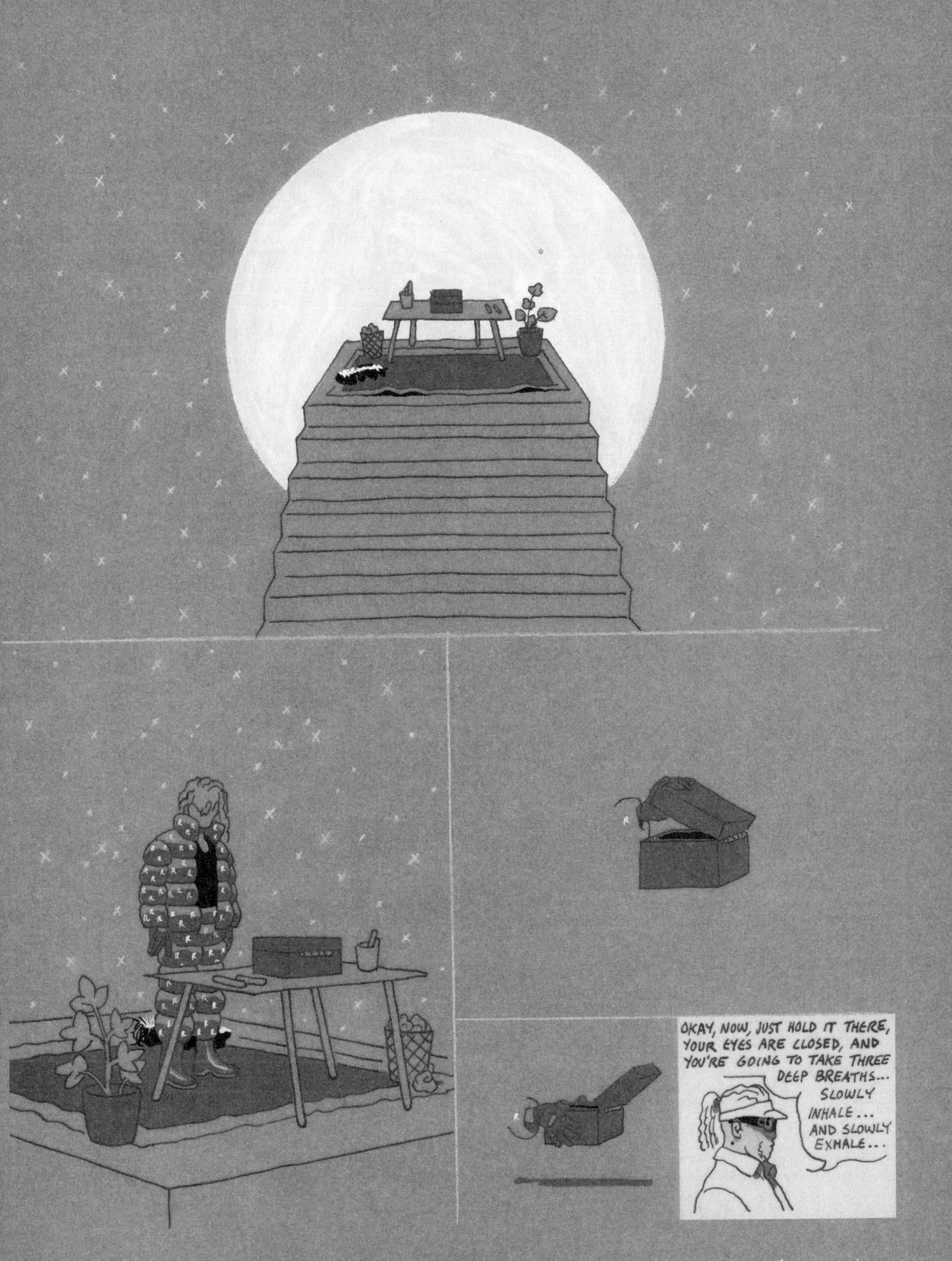
OKAY, NOW, JUST HOLD IT THERE, YOUR EYES ARE CLOSED, AND YOU'RE GOING TO TAKE THREE DEEP BREATHS...
SLOWLY INHALE... AND SLOWLY EXHALE...

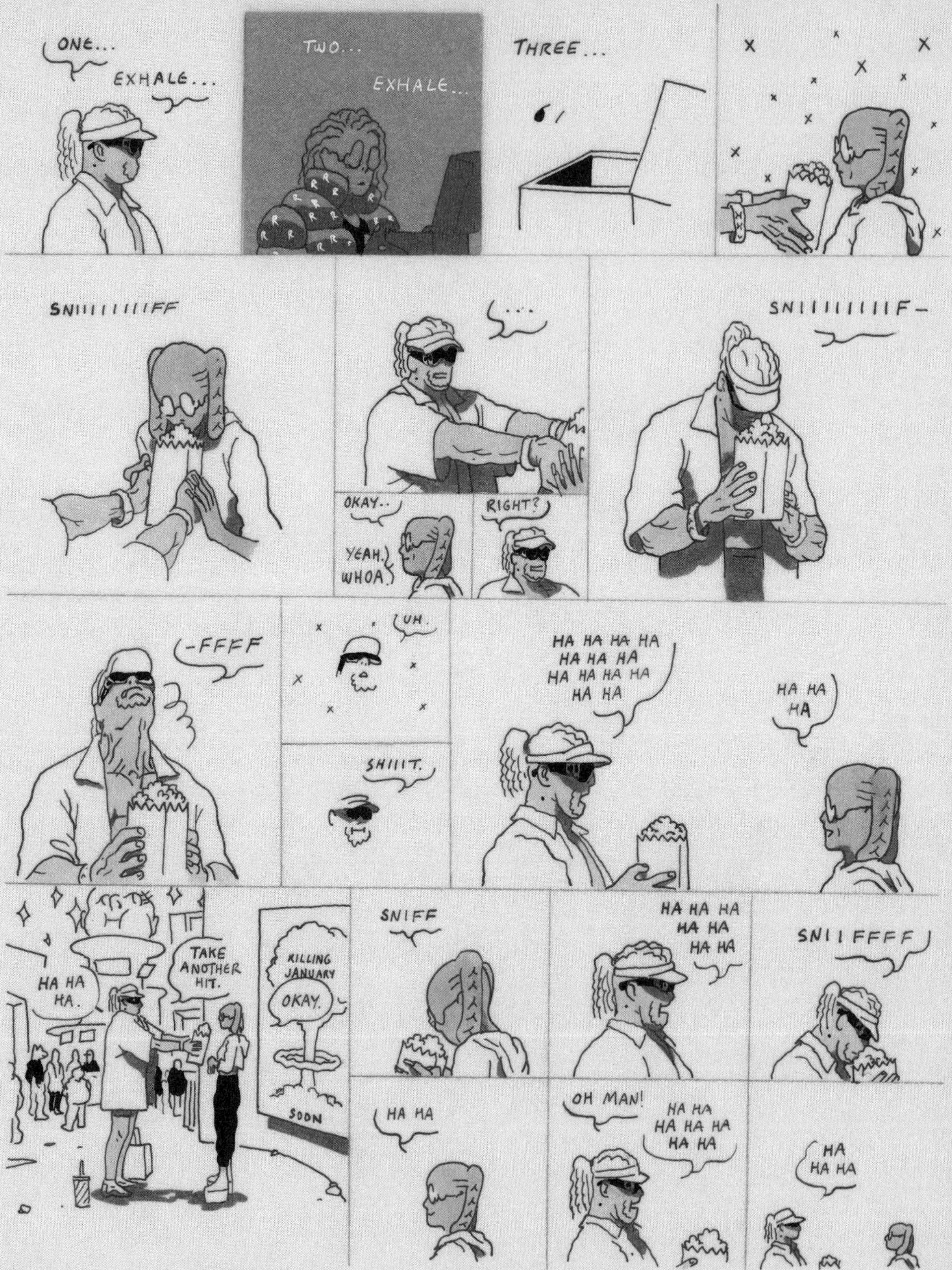
ONE...
EXHALE...
TWO...
EXHALE...
THREE...
SNIIIIIIIFF
...
SNIIIIIIIIF–
OKAY..
YEAH.
WHOA.
RIGHT?
-FFFF
UH.
SHIIIT.
HA HA HA HA
HA HA HA
HA HA HA HA
HA HA
HA HA
HA
HA HA
HA.
TAKE ANOTHER HIT.
KILLING JANUARY
OKAY.
SOON
SNIFF
HA HA HA
HA HA
HA HA
SNIIFFFF
HA HA
OH MAN!
HA HA
HA HA HA
HA HA
HA
HA HA

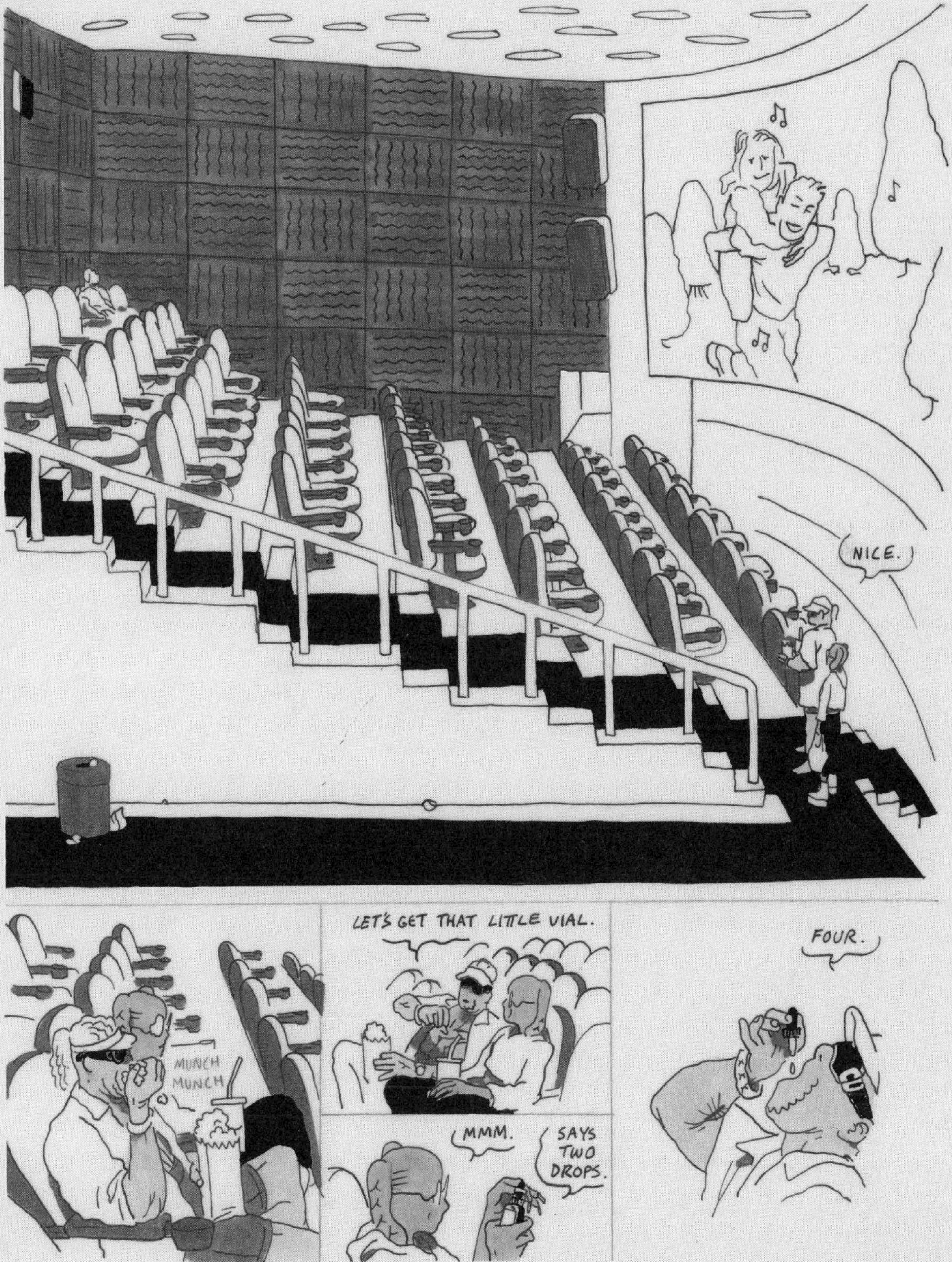
NICE.
MUNCH MUNCH
LET'S GET THAT LITTLE VIAL.
MMM.
SAYS TWO DROPS.
FOUR.

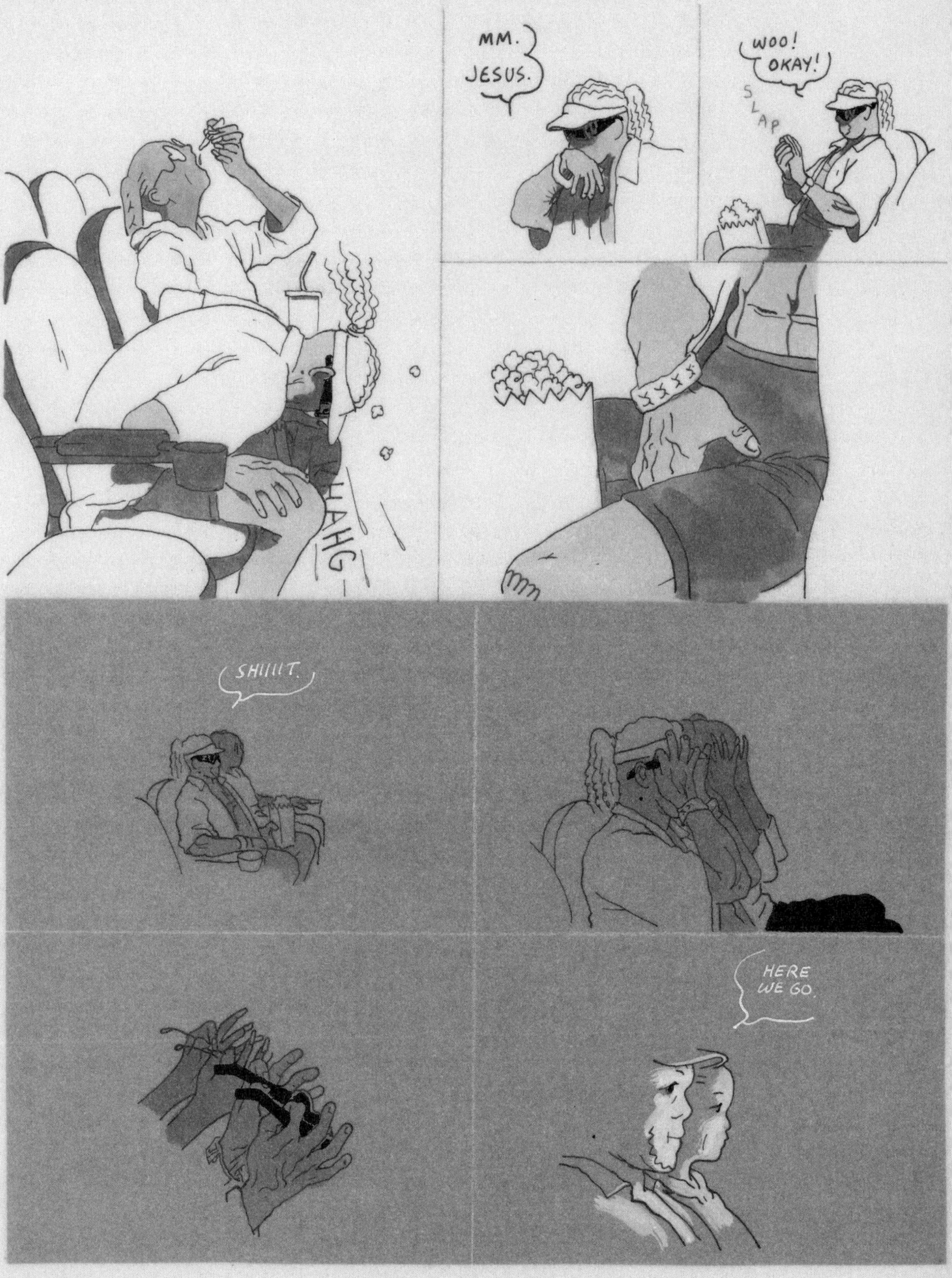
HAHG
MM.
JESUS.
WOO!
OKAY!
SLAP
SHIIIIT.
HERE
WE GO.

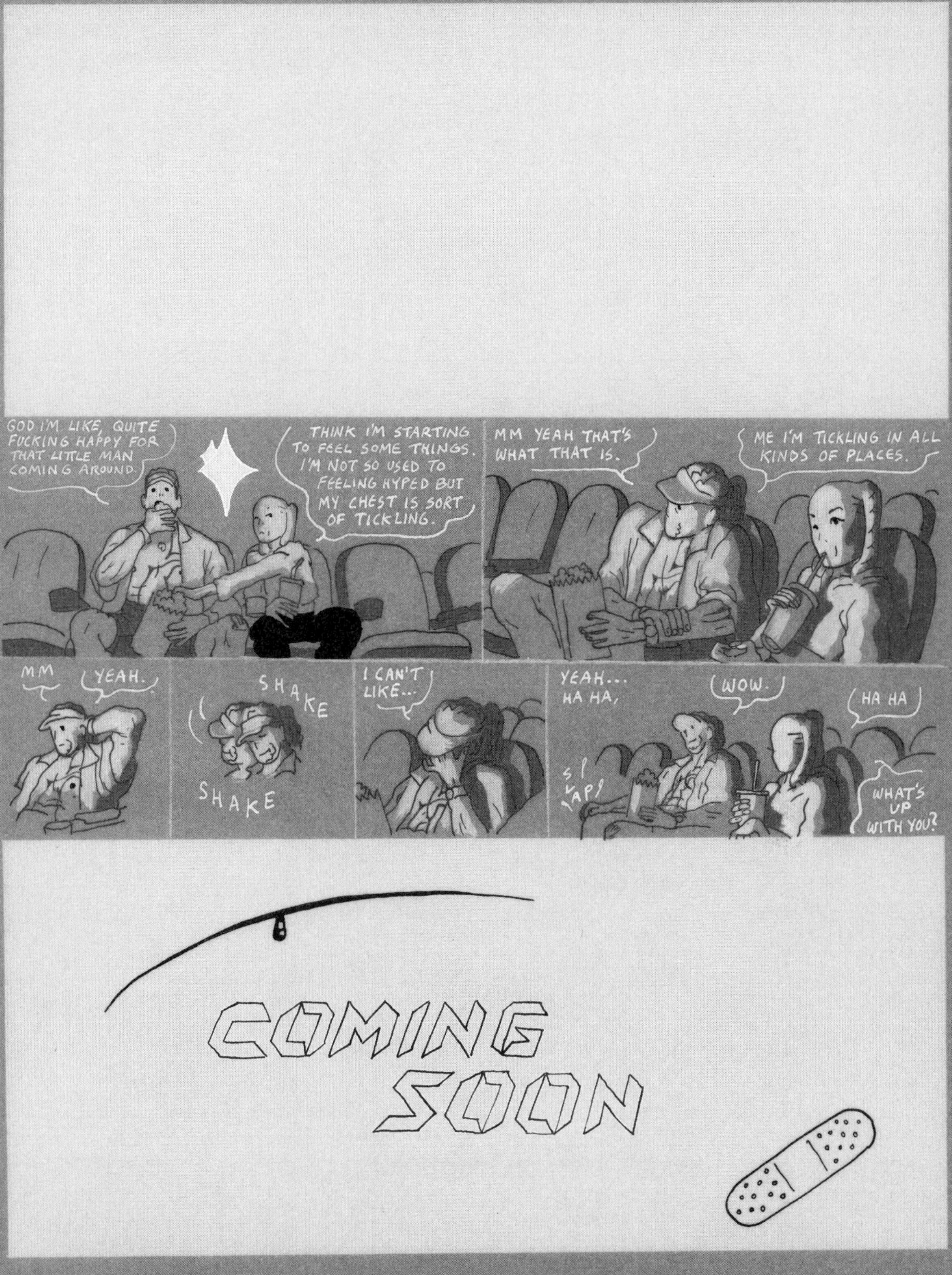
GOD I'M LIKE, QUITE FUCKING HAPPY FOR THAT LITTLE MAN COMING AROUND.
THINK I'M STARTING TO FEEL SOME THINGS. I'M NOT SO USED TO FEELING HYPED BUT MY CHEST IS SORT OF TICKLING.
MM YEAH THAT'S WHAT THAT IS.
ME I'M TICKLING IN ALL KINDS OF PLACES.
MM
YEAH.
SHAKE
SHAKE
I CAN'T LIKE...
YEAH... HA HA,
WOW.
HA HA
SLAP!
WHAT'S UP WITH YOU?
COMING SOON

IT'S JUST LIKE...
THIS IS THE FIRST
TIME, YOU KNOW?
LIKE THE FIRST,
NUMBER ONE
TIME.

LIKE YEAH,
NORMALLY I'D BE
EXCITED. BUT THIS
FEELING OF ....NOT
KNOWING? IT'S LIKE
PRIMAL. LIKE I'M
WAITING TO BE
DELIVERED.

MMM
OKAY.

WELL, THIS IN FACT
REALLY IS MY FIRST
TIME, SO...

NO NO, LISTEN.
I FEEL LIKE I'VE
BEEN BUILDING UP
TO SEE THIS MY
ENTIRE LIFE.

HA HA.
I DON'T FEEL LIKE
I'VE BEEN WAITING
QUITE AS LONG BUT
I SORT OF HEAR YOU.

NAH
LIKE..

HMPH

HYMPH

OH MY GOD, SPYDA—
ARE YOU OKAY?

SNIFF

YES!

HA HA, IT'S OKAY!

IT'S JUST FUNNY YOU KNOW?
I FEEL SO INNOCENT.
AND PURE.
AND GOOD.

EXPECTING...
THE FIRST TIME.

SNIFF

I FEEL
LIKE A
VIRGIN.

LIKE UH...I JUST CAN'T BELIEVE I
GET TO SEE THIS... IT'S LIKE
A PRIVILEGE.

UHK?

SORRY.

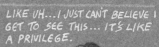

YOU LOOK LIKE A
VIRGIN.

HEY, CAN I EXPECT YOU TWO TO BE TALKING OVER THE ENTIRE MOVIE?
OH MY GOD. IS THIS GUY BEING SERIOUS?
RIGHT NOW?
IT'S ALRIGHT. JUST CHILL.
YEAH WE'RE PLANNING ON HAVING A GENUINE EMOTIONAL RESPONSE ACTUALLY.
IF THAT'S ALL RIGHT WITH YOU?
YEAH START SOME SHIT MAN.
HEY.
JUST ASKIN'.
KID'S DREAMING HE THINKS HE'S GOING TO KEEP ME FROM ENJOYING WHAT I CAME HERE FOR.
NO FORGET ALL THAT. EYES ON THE SCREEN.
YO SHIT THE LOGOS!
YEH,
FOR REAL THIS IS THE BEST PART.
FUCK FEEL MY ARM I GOT GOOSEBUMPS.
KRÏSIS
ENTRTNMT

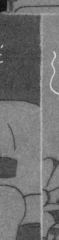

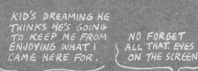

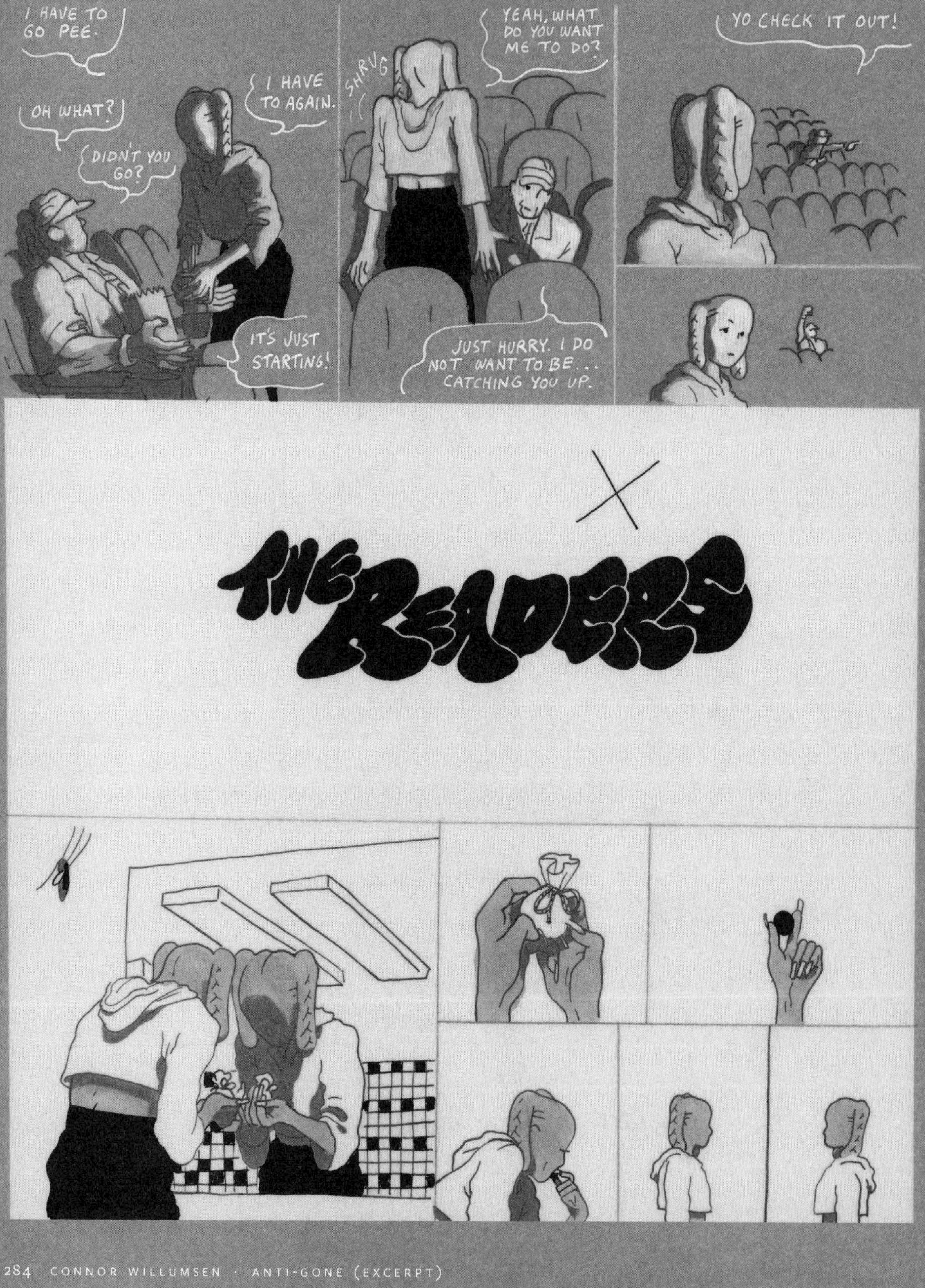

I HAVE TO GO PEE.
OH WHAT?
I HAVE TO AGAIN.
DIDN'T YOU GO?
IT'S JUST STARTING!
SHRUG
YEAH, WHAT DO YOU WANT ME TO DO?
JUST HURRY. I DO NOT WANT TO BE... CATCHING YOU UP.
YO CHECK IT OUT!
THE READERS

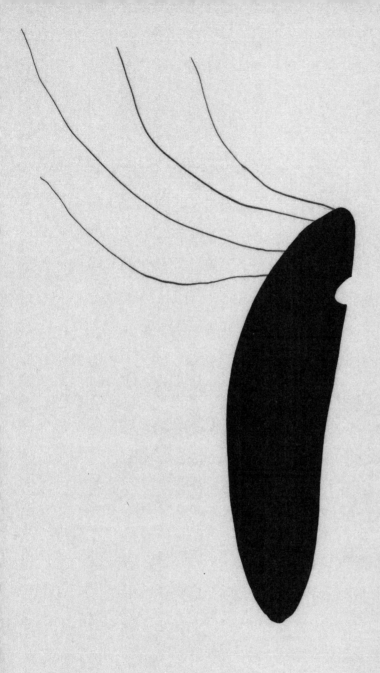

Old Ground
Noel
Freibert

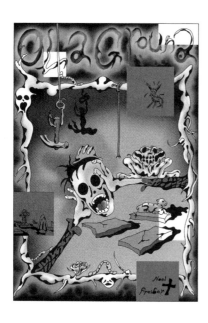

Old Ground (*Excerpt*)

NOEL FREIBERT

originally published in

Old Ground

KOYAMA PRESS

7 x 10 inches • 224 pages

Biography

Kentucky-born multidisciplinary artist Noel Freibert is best known for his comics, sculptures, and works on fabric. Noel's work has been shown internationally and is featured in the book collections of the Museum of Modern Art NYC and the Baltimore Museum of Art. Recent projects include "Memories from the Emptied Out Field" with Leon Sadler at Calm and Punk Gallery, Tokyo, Japan, and "From Ewe" presented at the Women's History Museum Biennale: Poupées Gonflabes at Springsteen Gallery, Baltimore, Maryland. Noel's work has been published in *Kramers Ergot, Mould Map,* and *Lagon Revue.*
cutcross.storenvy.com

Statement

I first began work on a project called *Old Ground* in 2012; the children and frog developed as a tangent in the first attempt. Soon the project fell to the wayside when my energy went to shorter deadlines. After two years of focusing on one-page comics, I realized I needed to make a longer work in order to move forward. Initially, I thought the project would be serialized in self-published installments. "Old Ground #1" was released at Comic Arts Brooklyn in 2014; the self-published volume contained the first 48 pages of the narrative. Not long after, Anne Koyama contacted me to do a book for Koyama Press. That book was published in late 2017, an excerpt of which is reprinted in this volume. *Old Ground* is like a printed time capsule, drawings collected over a stretch of years bundled into a crawling narrative. When I look back through it, I can see how the pacing reflects my indulgences, experiences, and faults. It is a sprawling record of my ideas. I feel grateful that it exists.

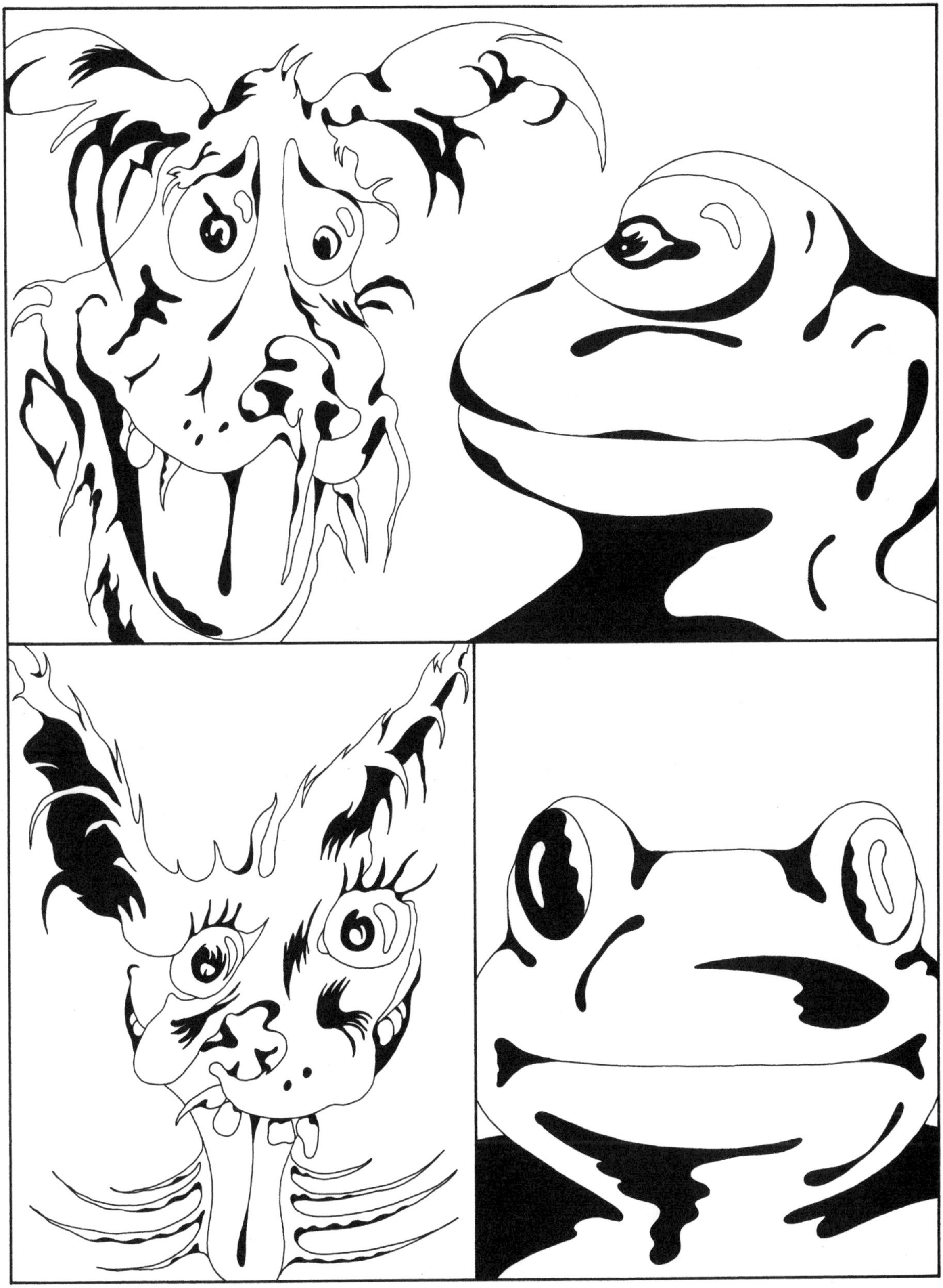

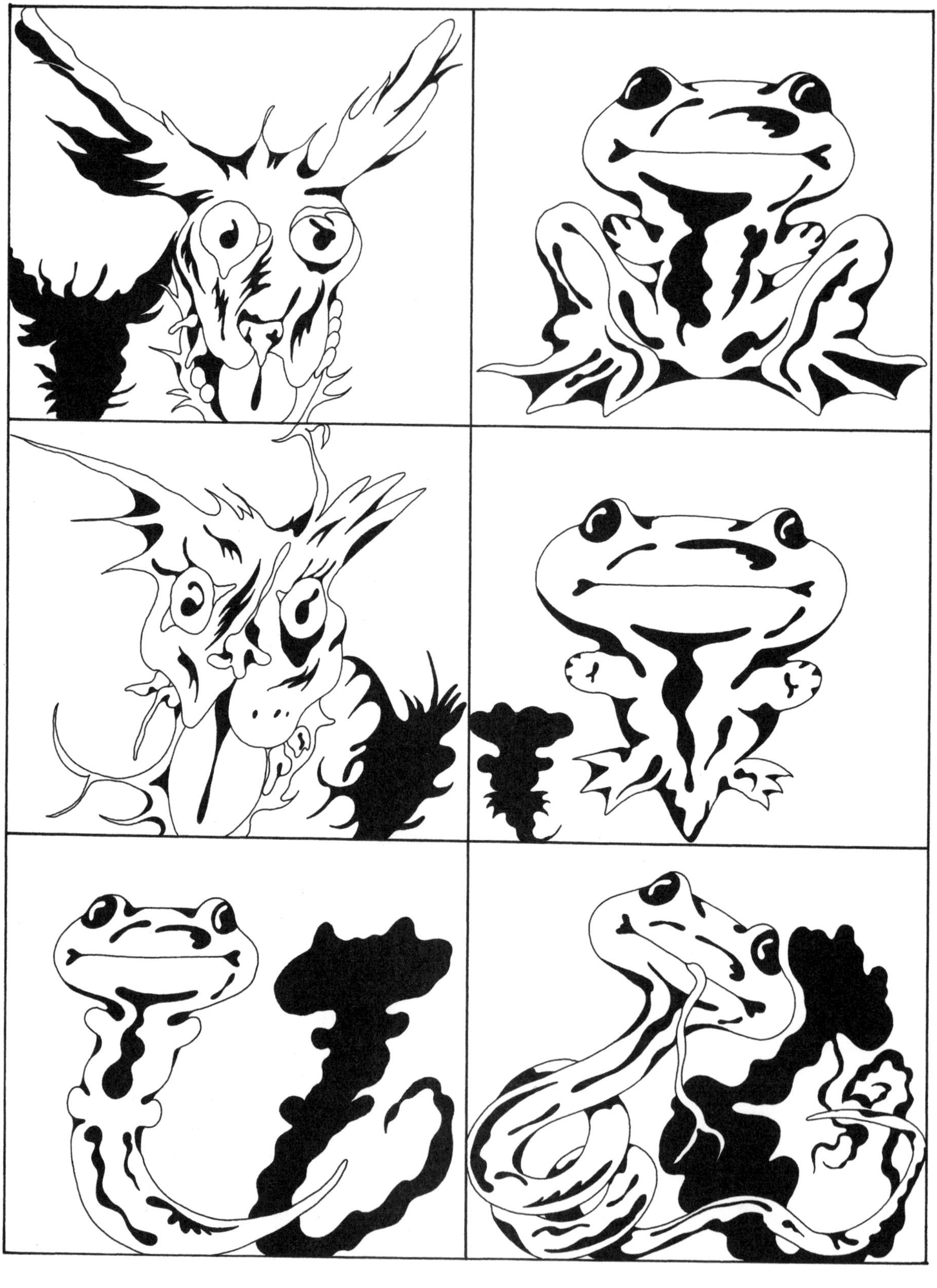

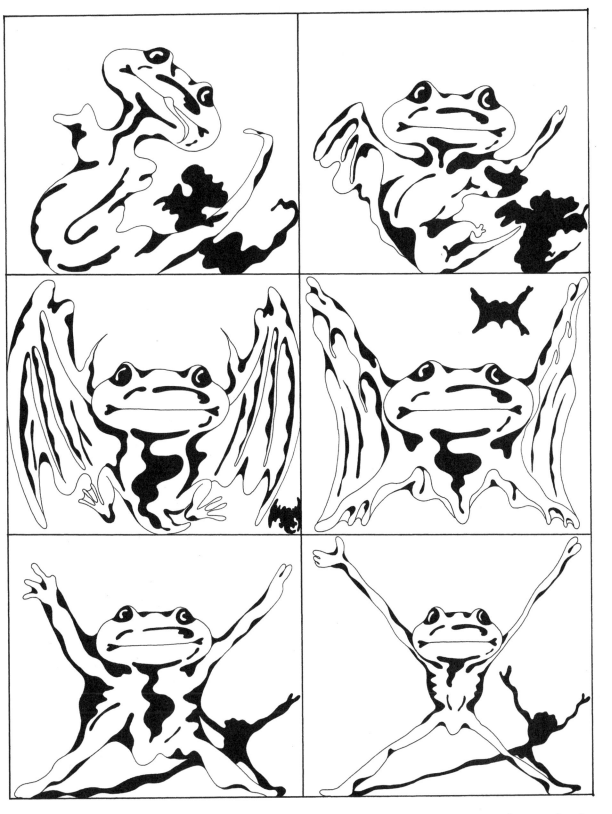

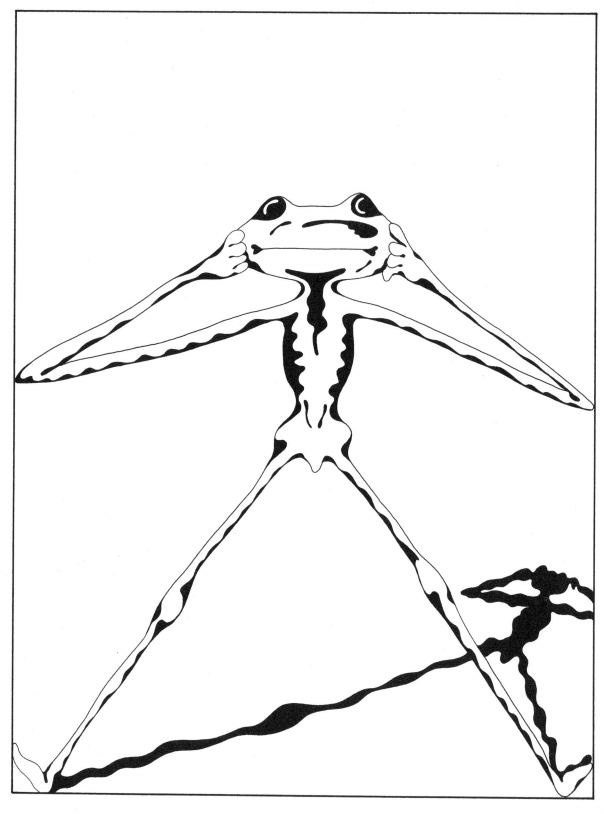

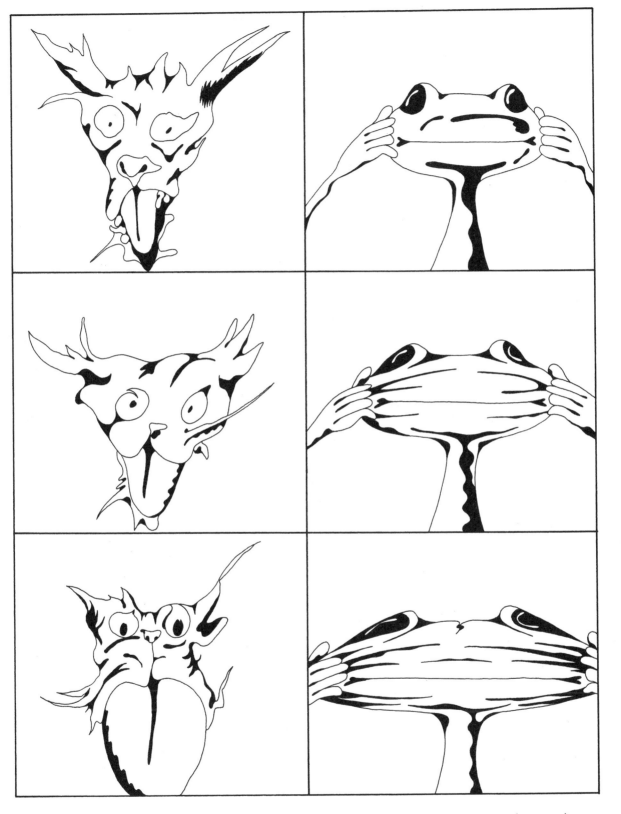

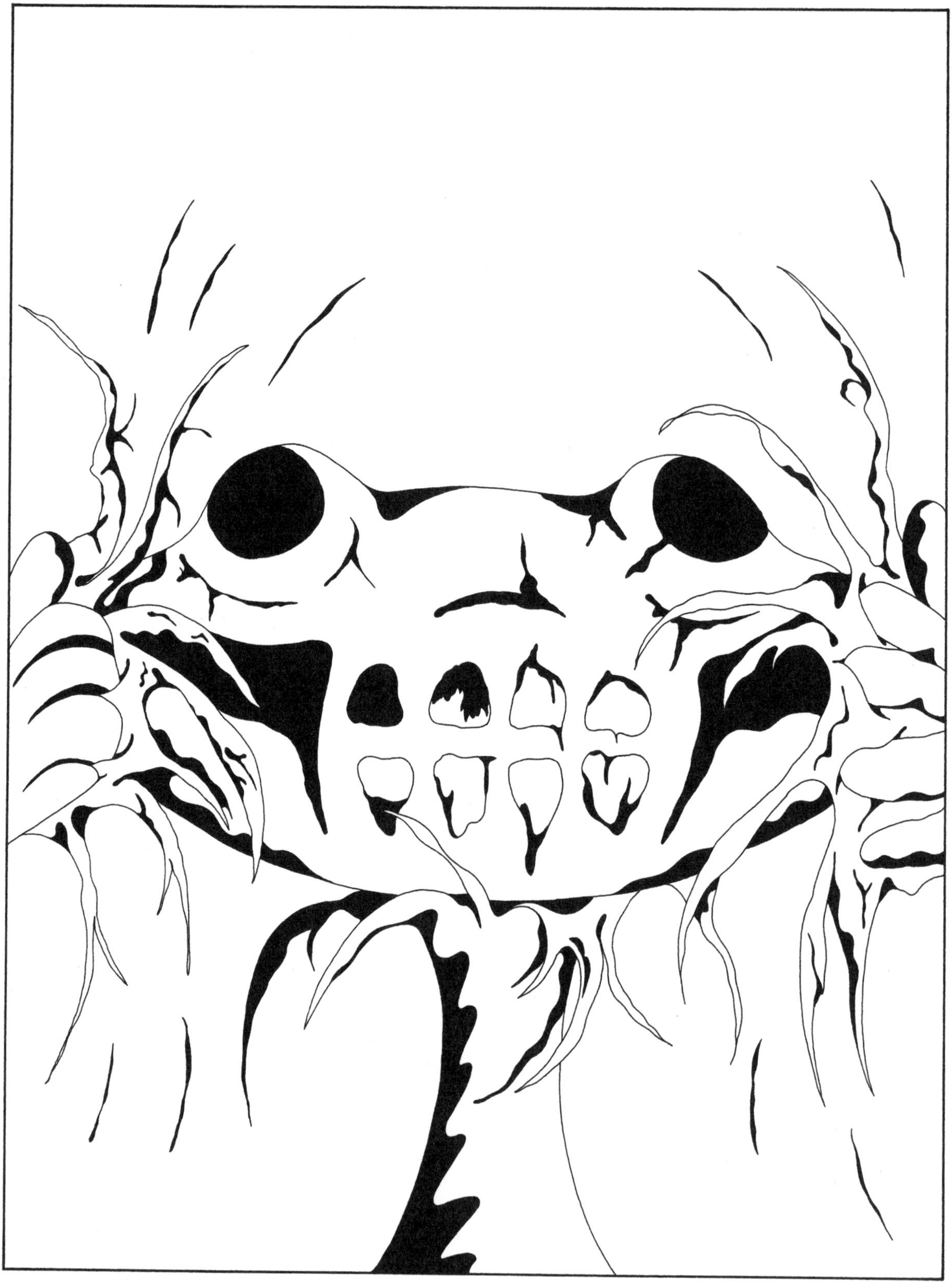

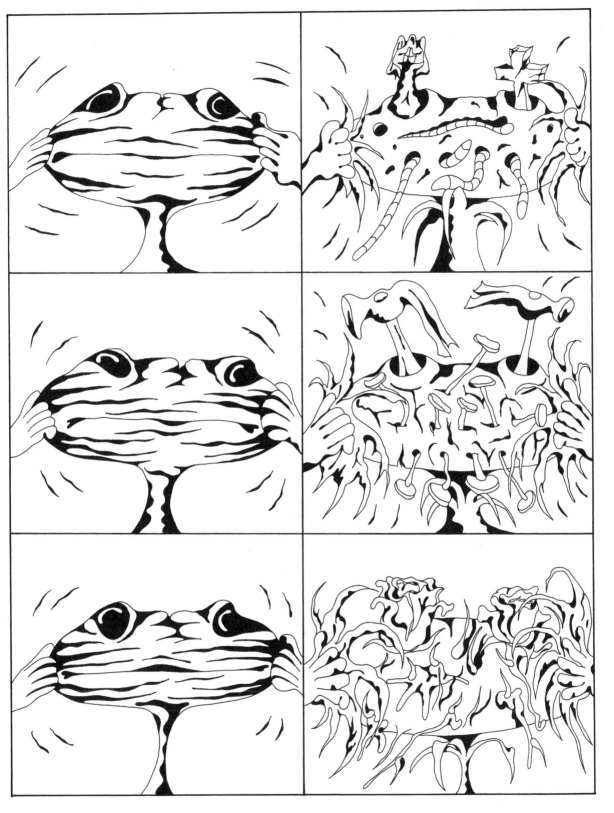

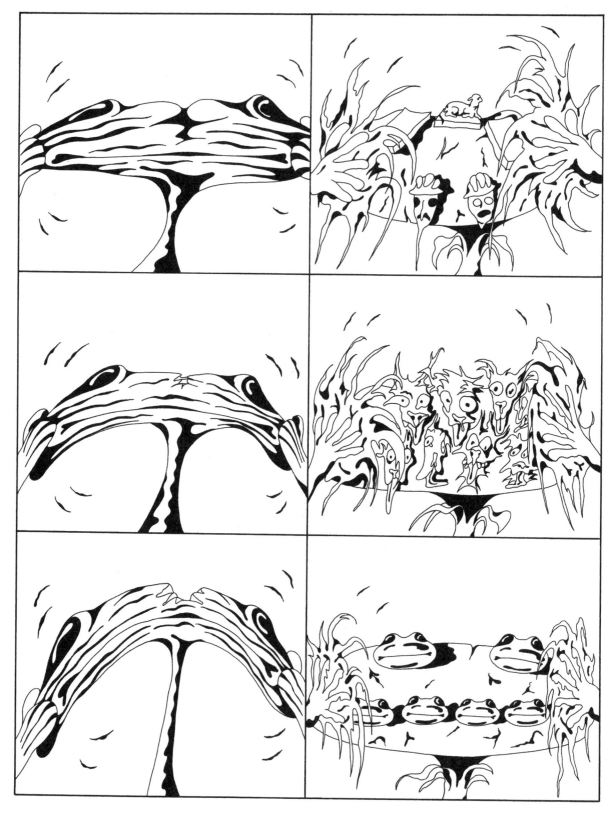

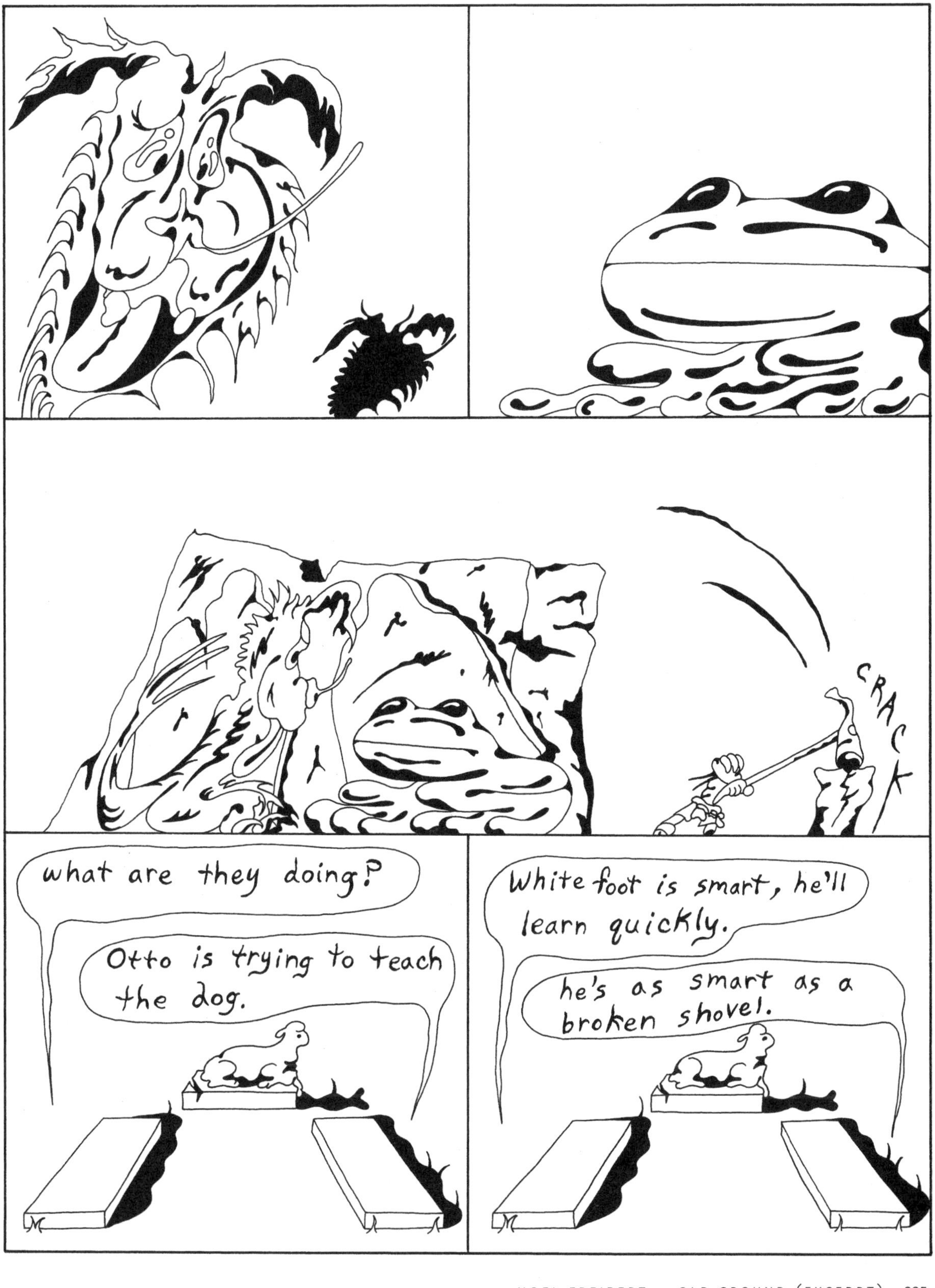
CRACK
what are they doing?
Otto is trying to teach the dog.
White foot is smart, he'll learn quickly.
he's as smart as a broken shovel.

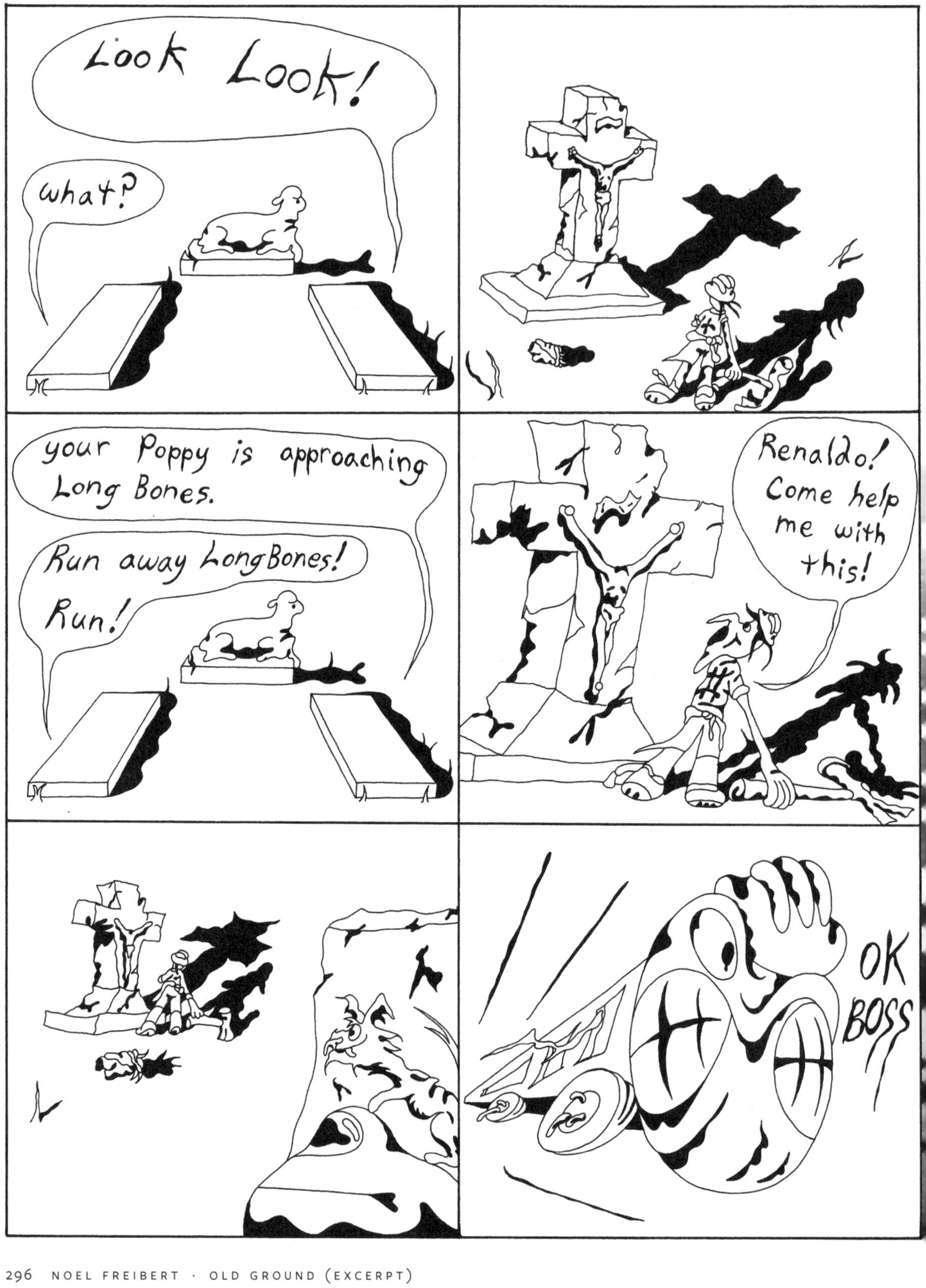
Look Look!
what?
your Poppy is approaching Long Bones.
Run away LongBones! Run!
Renaldo! Come help me with this!
OK BOSS

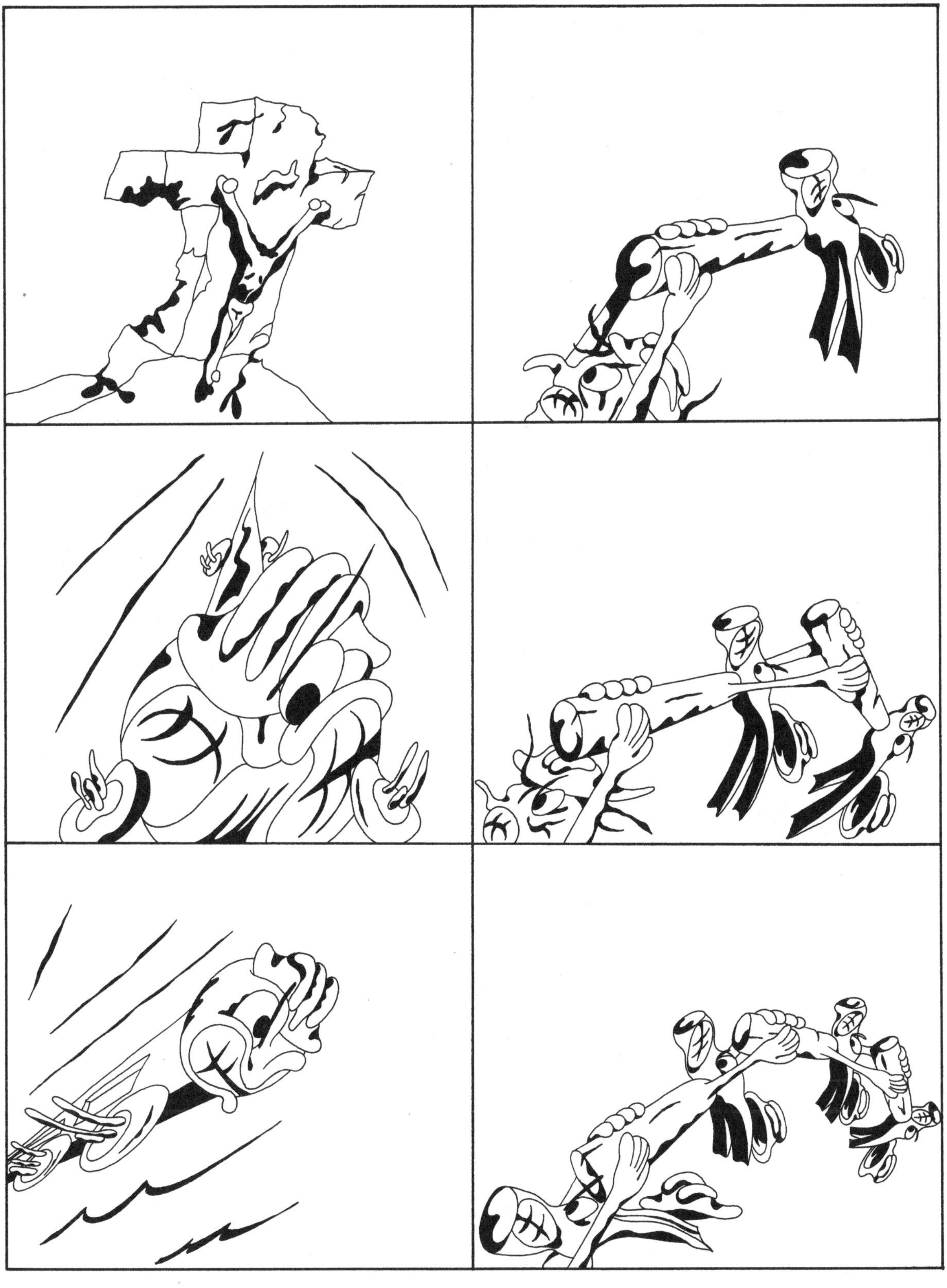

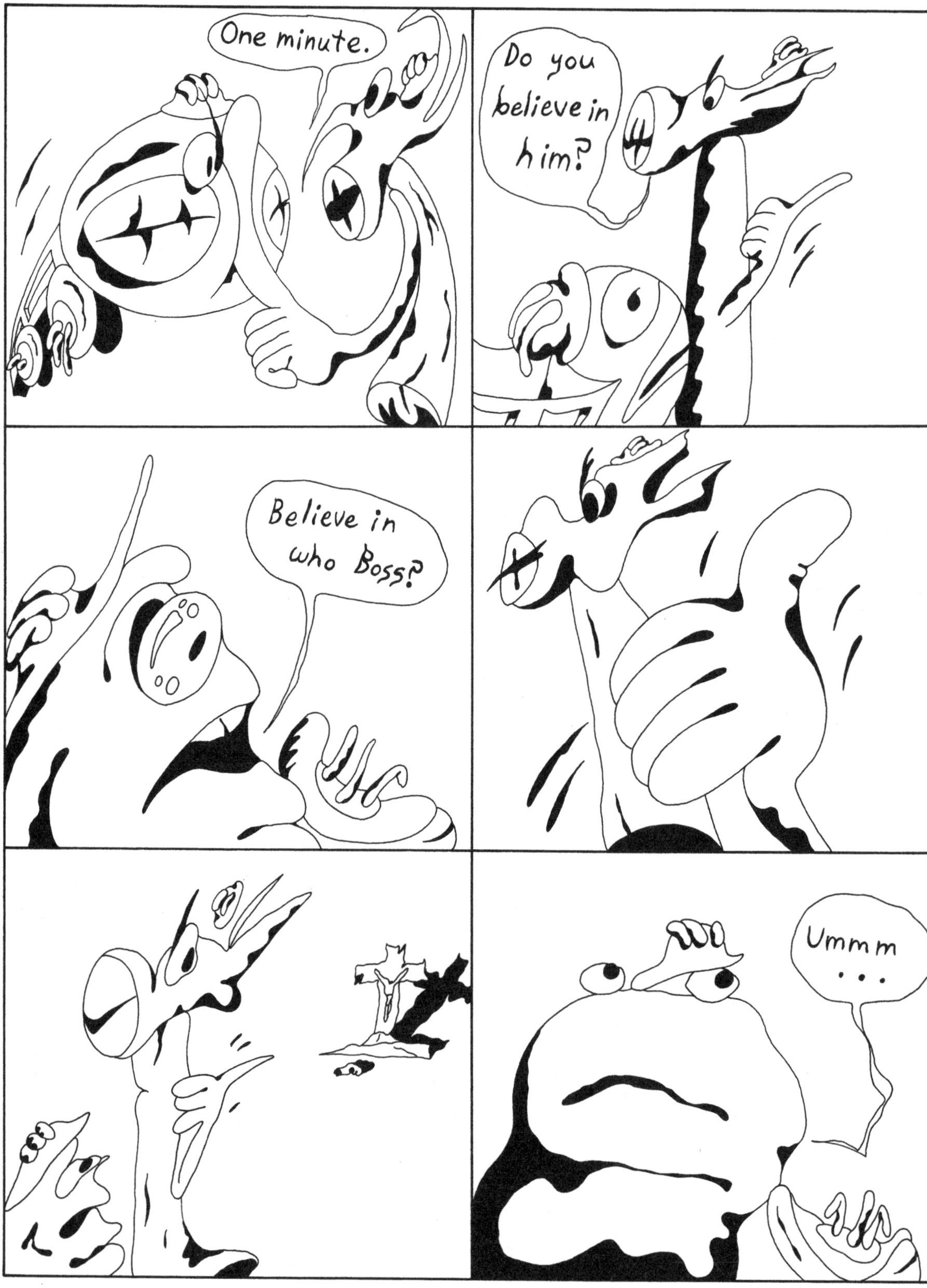
One minute.
Do you believe in him?
Believe in who Boss?
Ummm ...

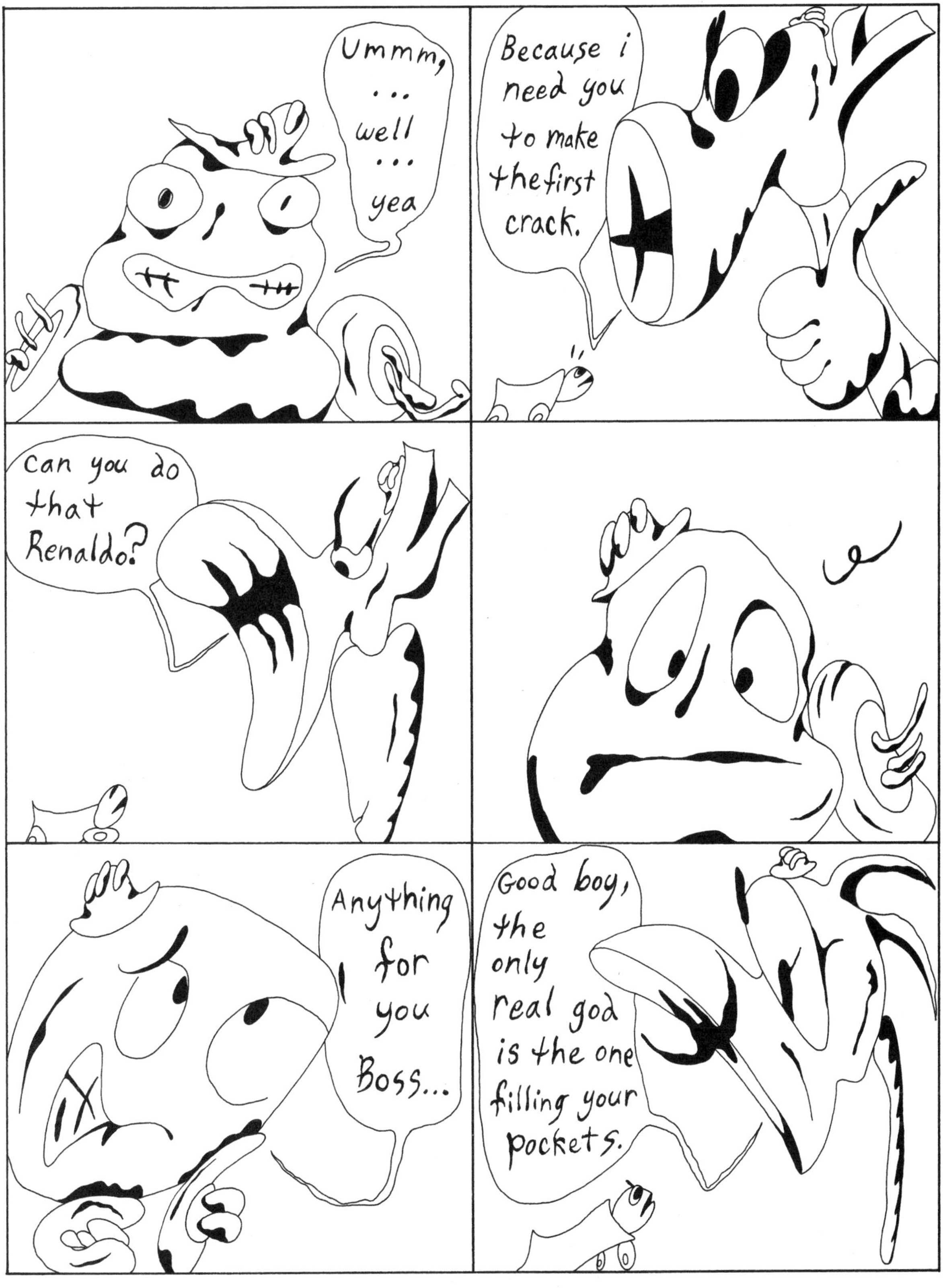
Ummm, ... well ... yea
Because i need you to make the first crack.
Can you do that Renaldo?
Anything for you Boss...
Good boy, the only real god is the one filling your pockets.

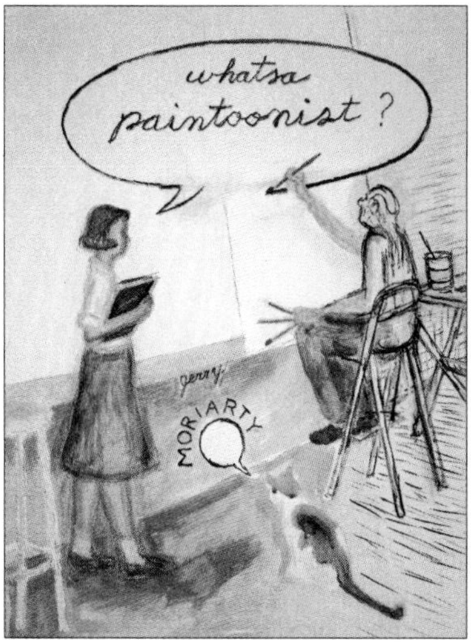
whatsa paintoonist ?
jerry
MORIARTY

whatsa paintoonist? (*Excerpt*)

JERRY MORIARTY

originally published in

whatsa paintoonist?

FANTAGRAPHICS BOOKS

10 x 13 inches • 88 pages

Biography

I am 81. Born in Binghamton. Went to Pratt. Was a magazine illustrator (girlie mags mostly), painter, got an NEA. Taught at SVA for fifty years. First comic was *Jack Survives,* published by RAW in 1984. Buenaventura Press published *The Complete Jack Survives* in 2010. Got fired by SVA in 2014. Moved back to Binghamton in 2014. *whatsa paintoonist?* was published by Fantagraphics in 2017. Working on *Visual Crime* for Fantagraphics right now.

Statement

In *whatsa paintoonist?* I painted with acrylic and drew with a Papermate pen.

My intention was to challenge my "male" assumptions. Glad I did. Sally is my avatar. Mom, Dad, and Pat are real and in situations they never were in. The places are my childhood home and my NYC artist's loft that I lived and worked in for fifty years. In 2013 I was able to buy my childhood home in Binghamton and live and work here now.

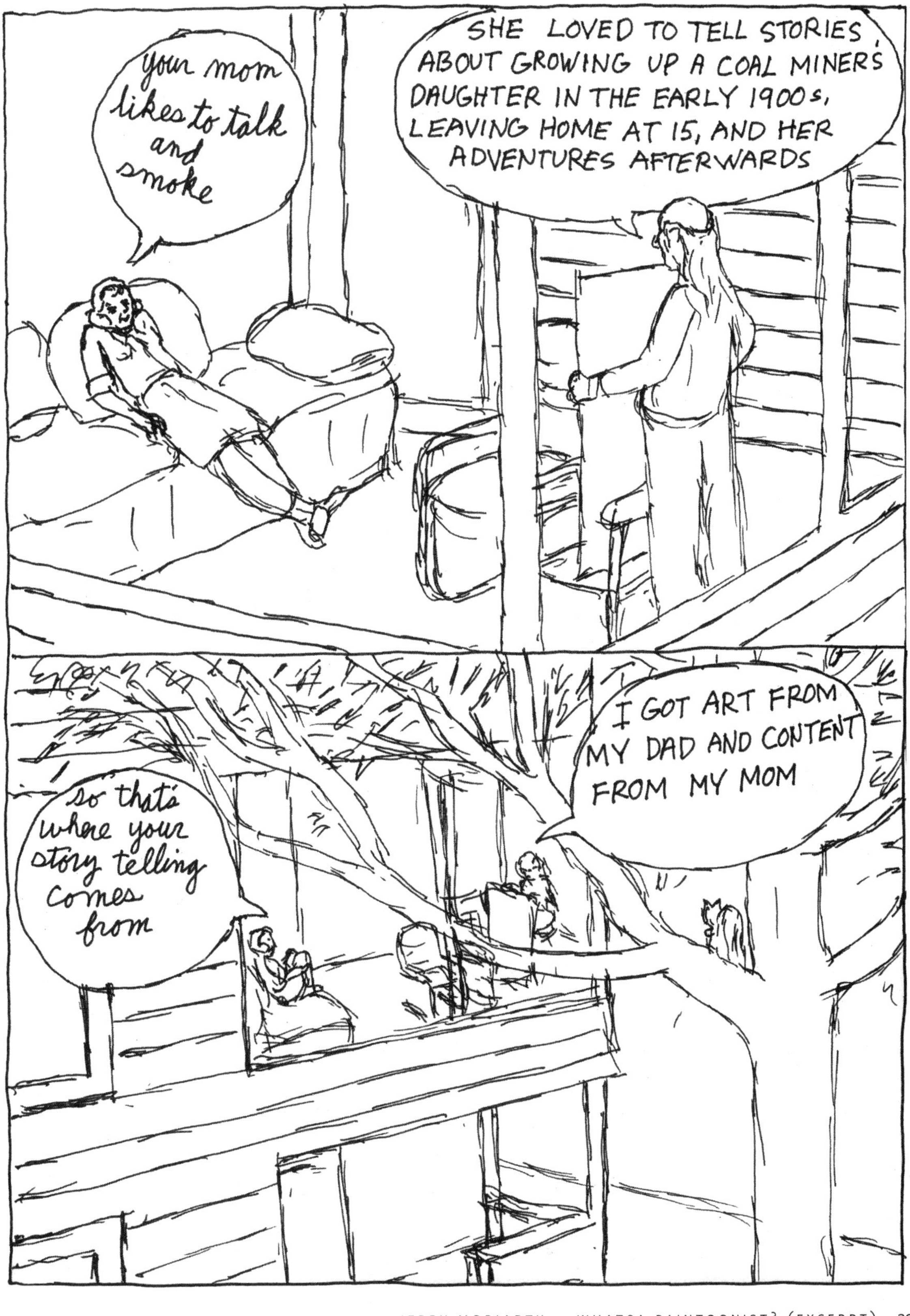
your mom likes to talk and smoke
SHE LOVED TO TELL STORIES, ABOUT GROWING UP A COAL MINER'S DAUGHTER IN THE EARLY 1900s, LEAVING HOME AT 15, AND HER ADVENTURES AFTERWARDS
so that's where your story telling comes from
I GOT ART FROM MY DAD AND CONTENT FROM MY MOM

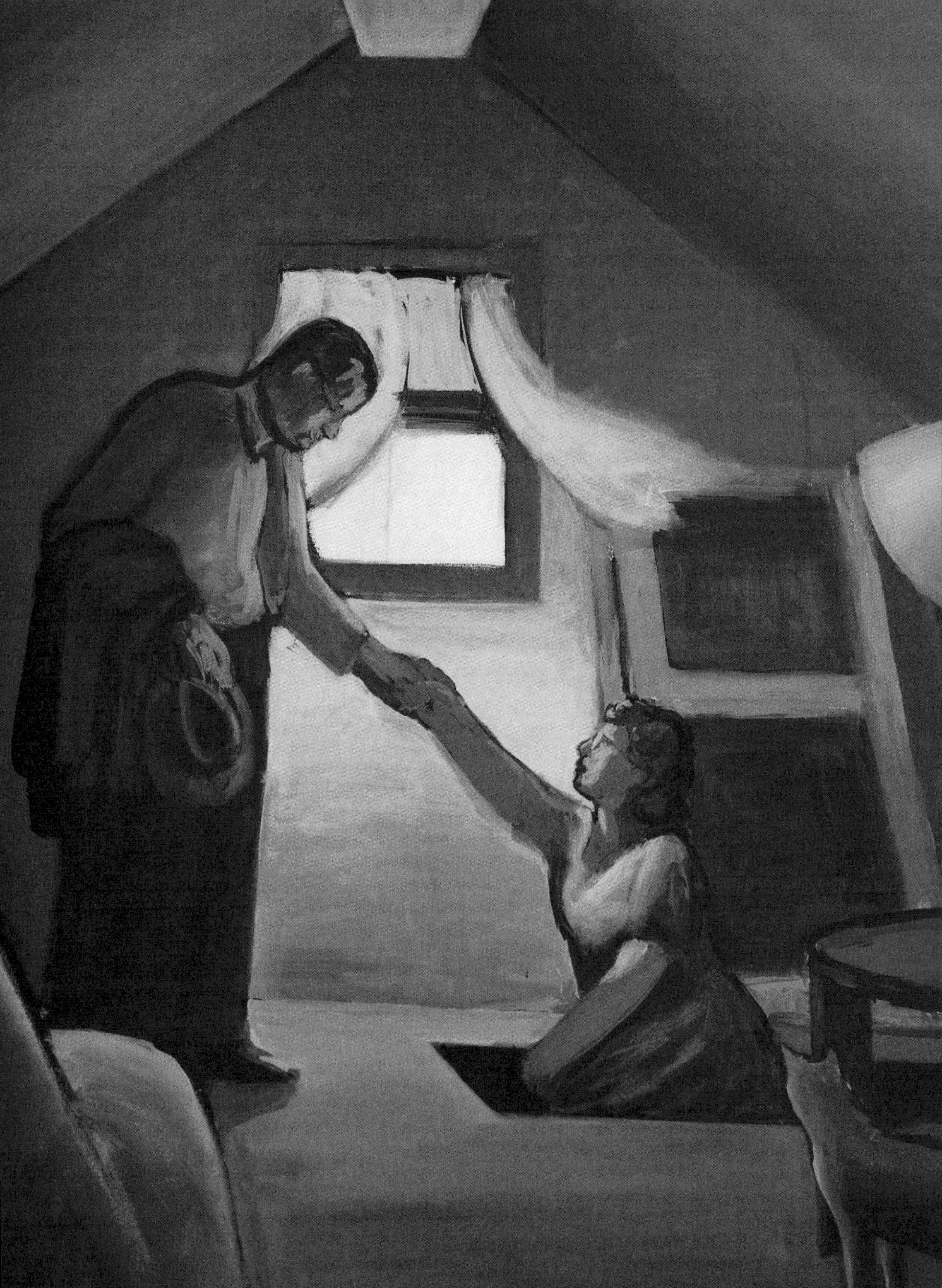

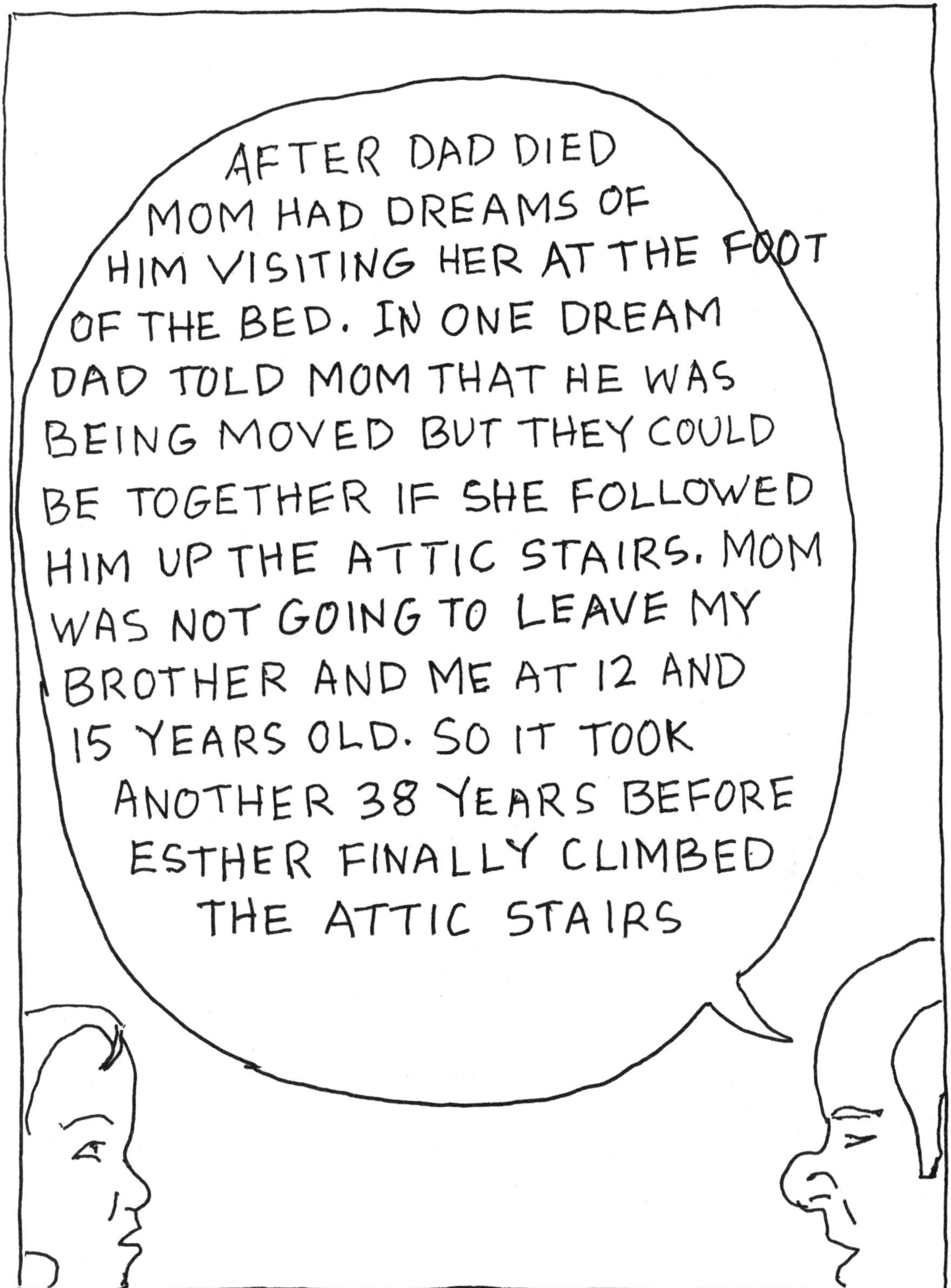
AFTER DAD DIED MOM HAD DREAMS OF HIM VISITING HER AT THE FOOT OF THE BED. IN ONE DREAM DAD TOLD MOM THAT HE WAS BEING MOVED BUT THEY COULD BE TOGETHER IF SHE FOLLOWED HIM UP THE ATTIC STAIRS. MOM WAS NOT GOING TO LEAVE MY BROTHER AND ME AT 12 AND 15 YEARS OLD. SO IT TOOK ANOTHER 38 YEARS BEFORE ESTHER FINALLY CLIMBED THE ATTIC STAIRS

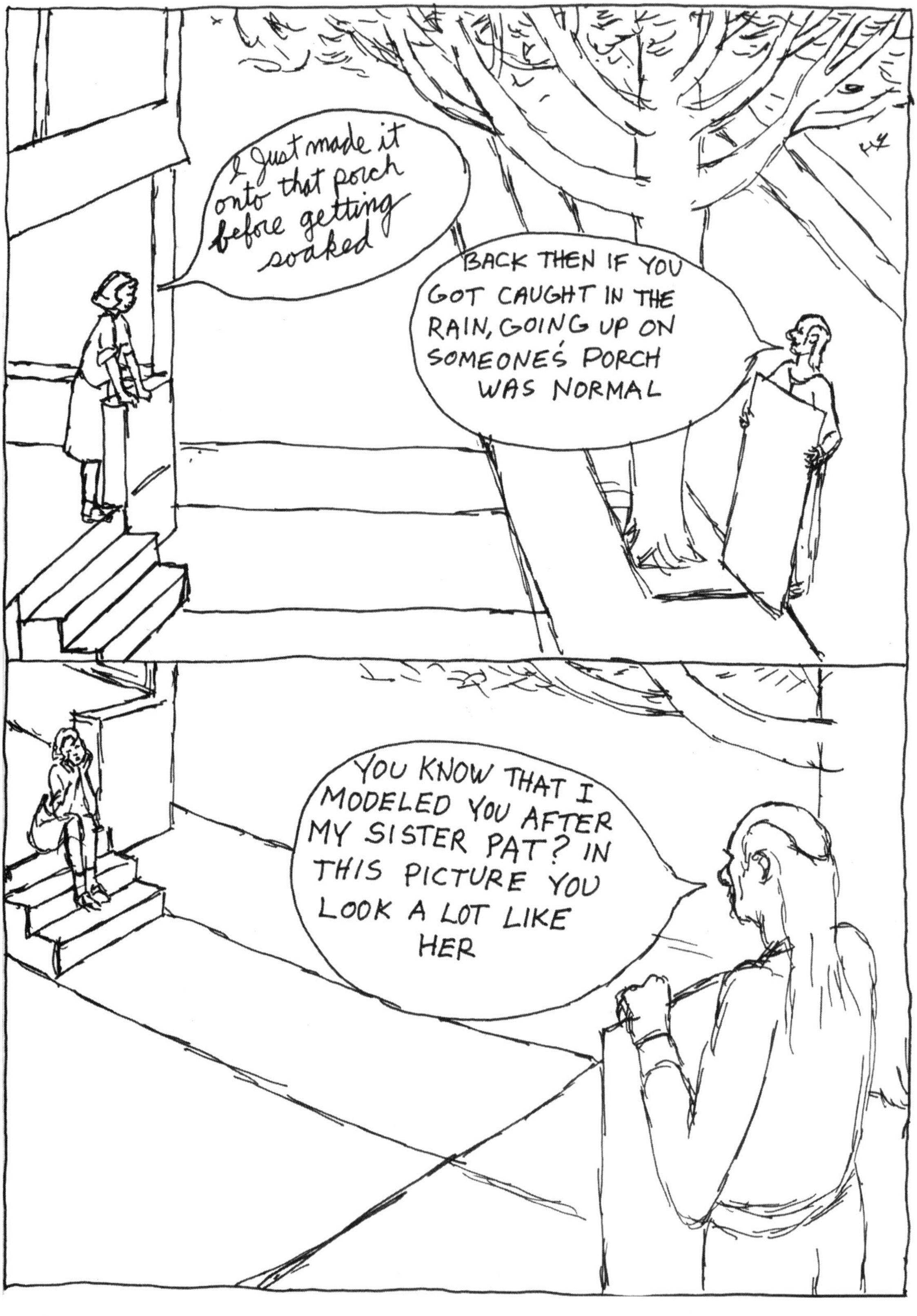
I just made it onto that porch before getting soaked
BACK THEN IF YOU GOT CAUGHT IN THE RAIN, GOING UP ON SOMEONE'S PORCH WAS NORMAL
YOU KNOW THAT I MODELED YOU AFTER MY SISTER PAT? IN THIS PICTURE YOU LOOK A LOT LIKE HER

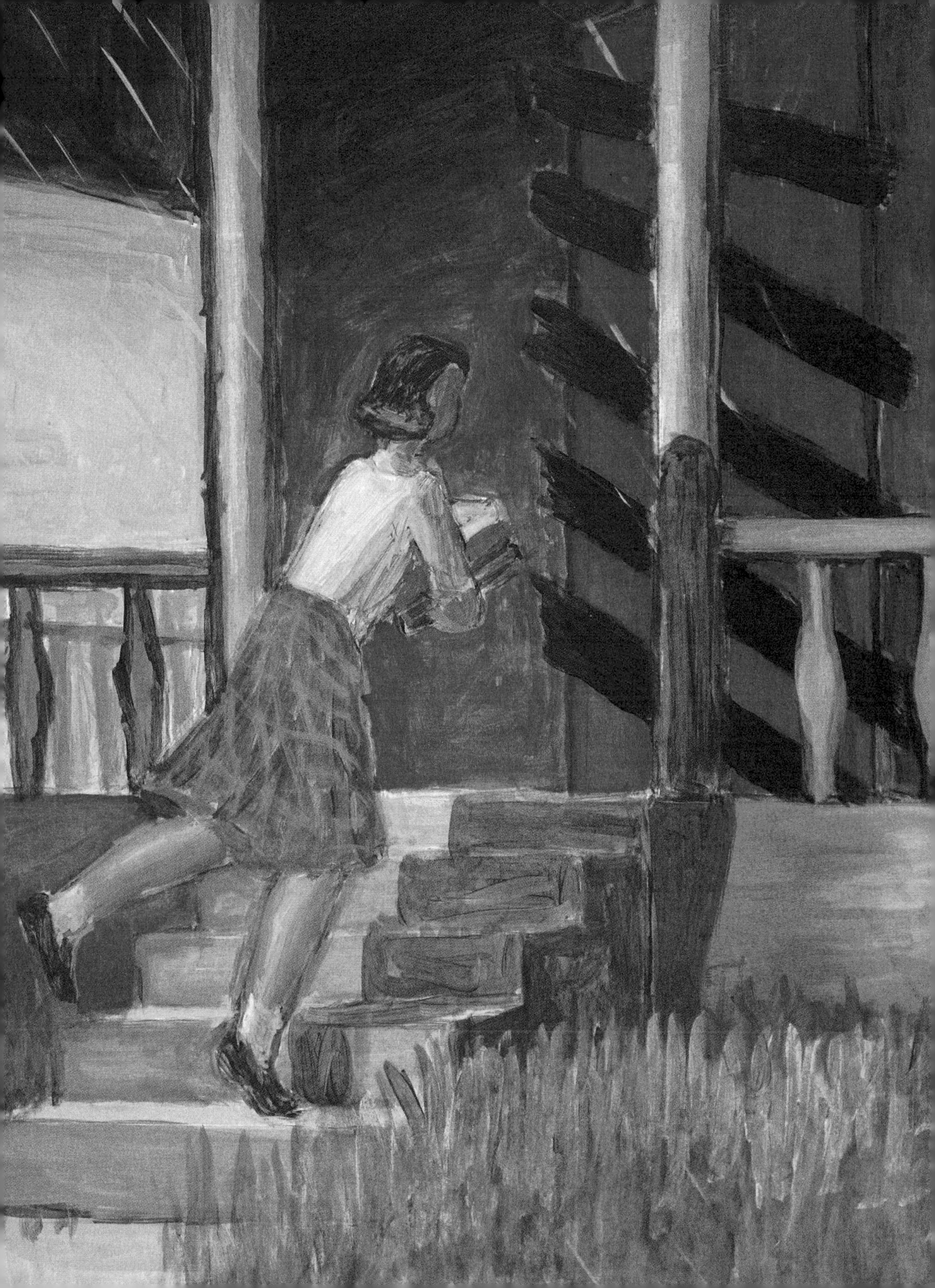

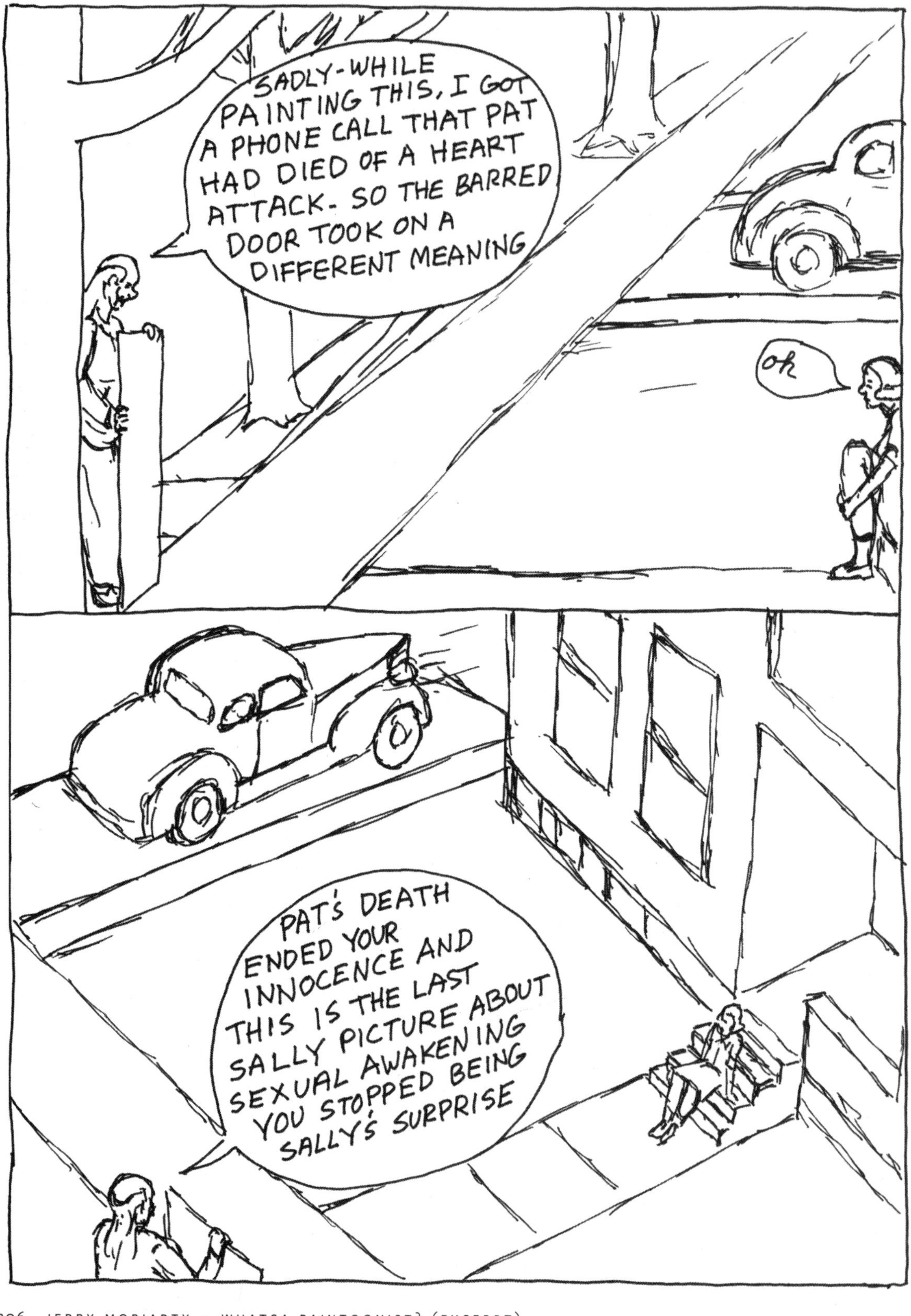
SADLY-WHILE PAINTING THIS, I GOT A PHONE CALL THAT PAT HAD DIED OF A HEART ATTACK- SO THE BARRED DOOR TOOK ON A DIFFERENT MEANING
oh
PAT'S DEATH ENDED YOUR INNOCENCE AND THIS IS THE LAST SALLY PICTURE ABOUT SEXUAL AWAKENING YOU STOPPED BEING SALLY'S SURPRISE

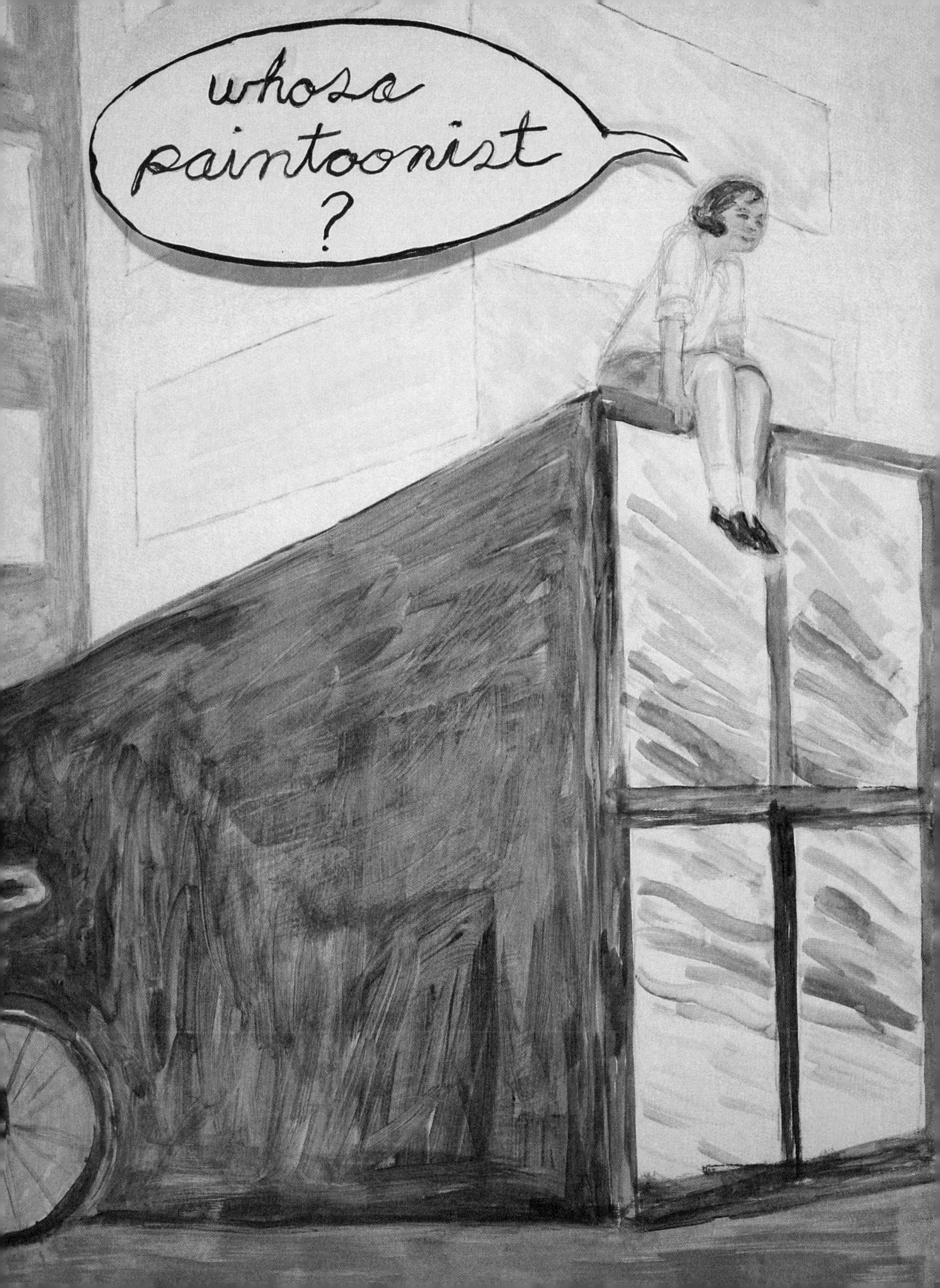
whosa paintoonist ?

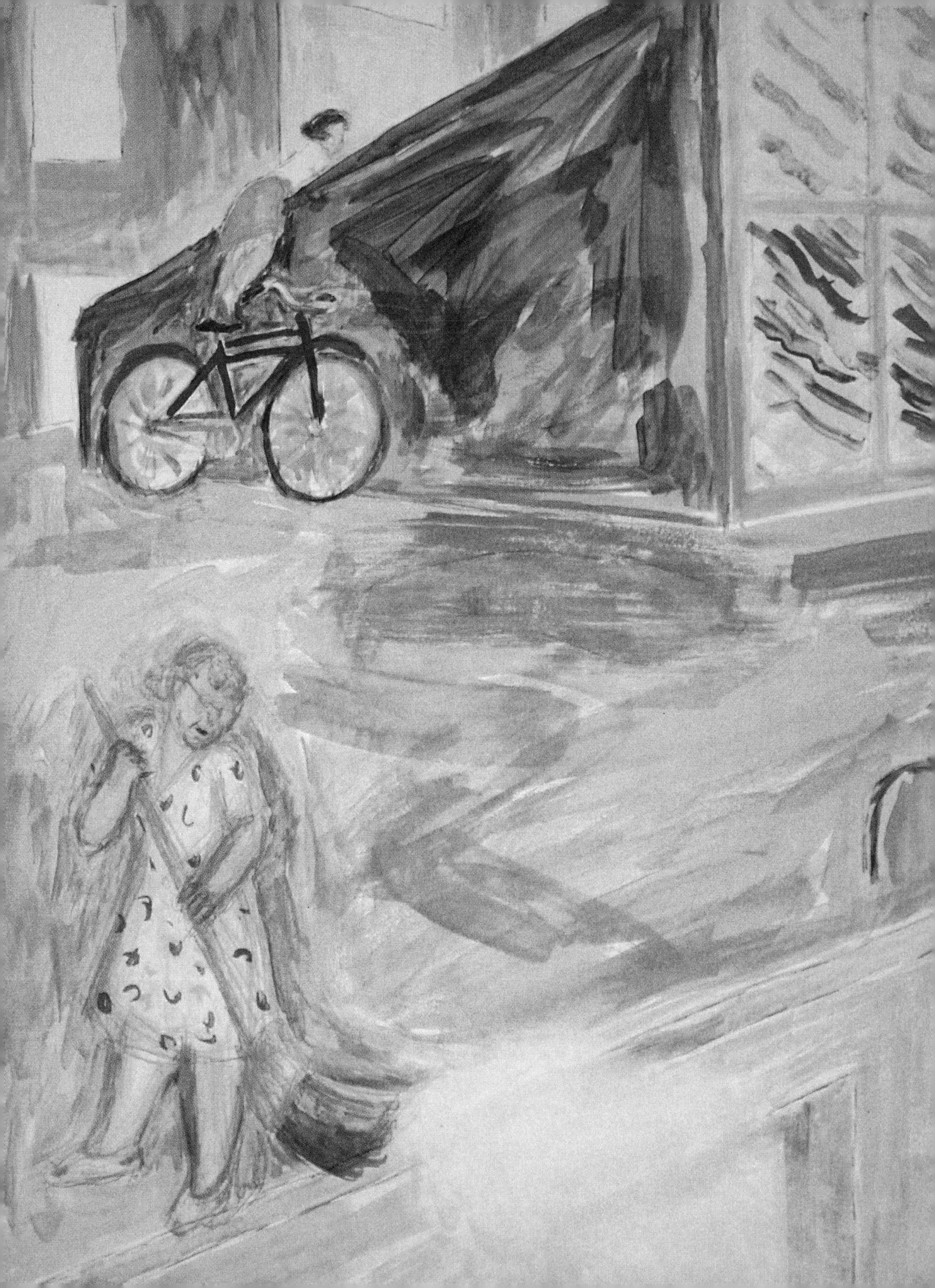

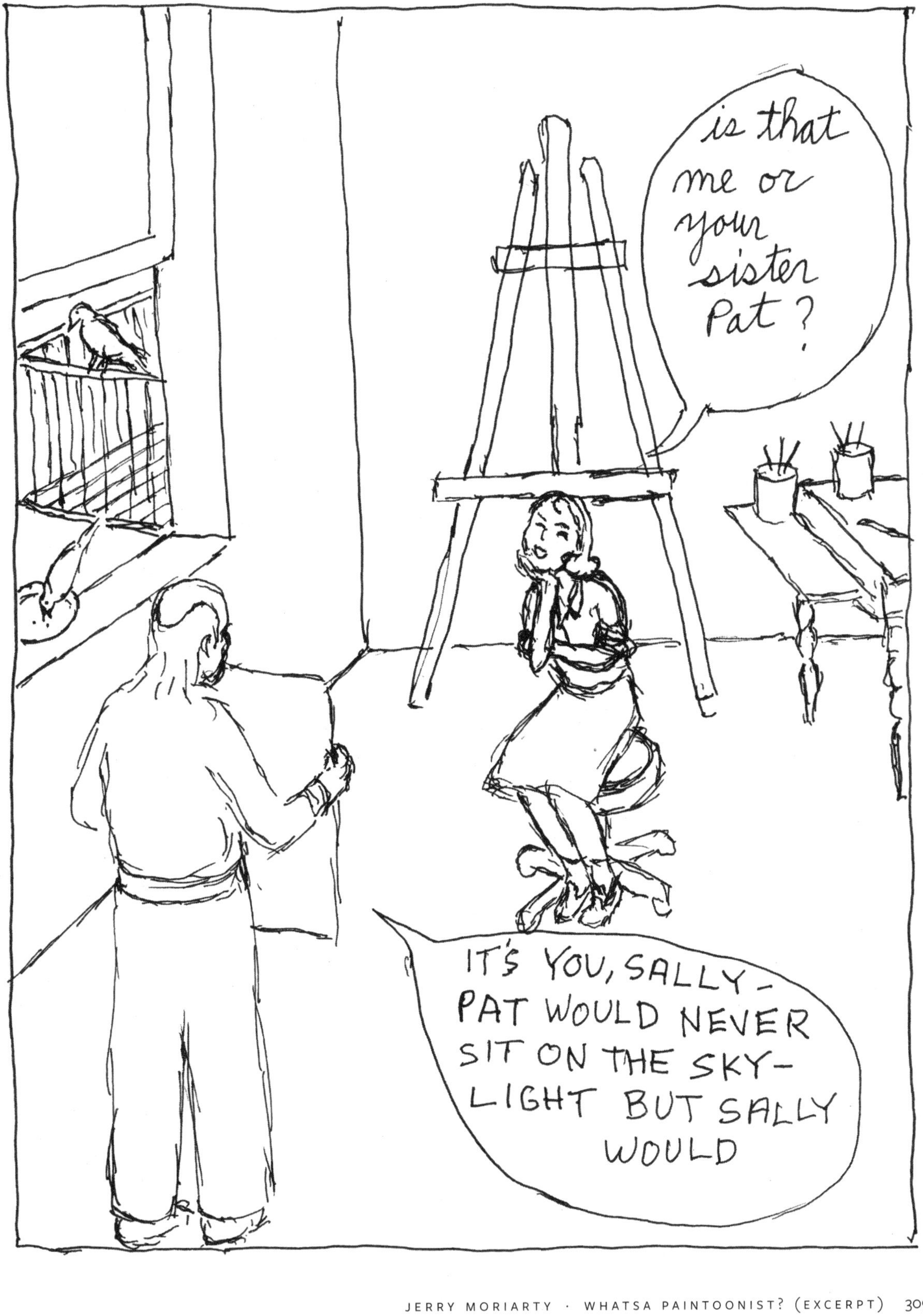
is that me or your sister Pat?
IT'S YOU, SALLY- PAT WOULD NEVER SIT ON THE SKY-LIGHT BUT SALLY WOULD

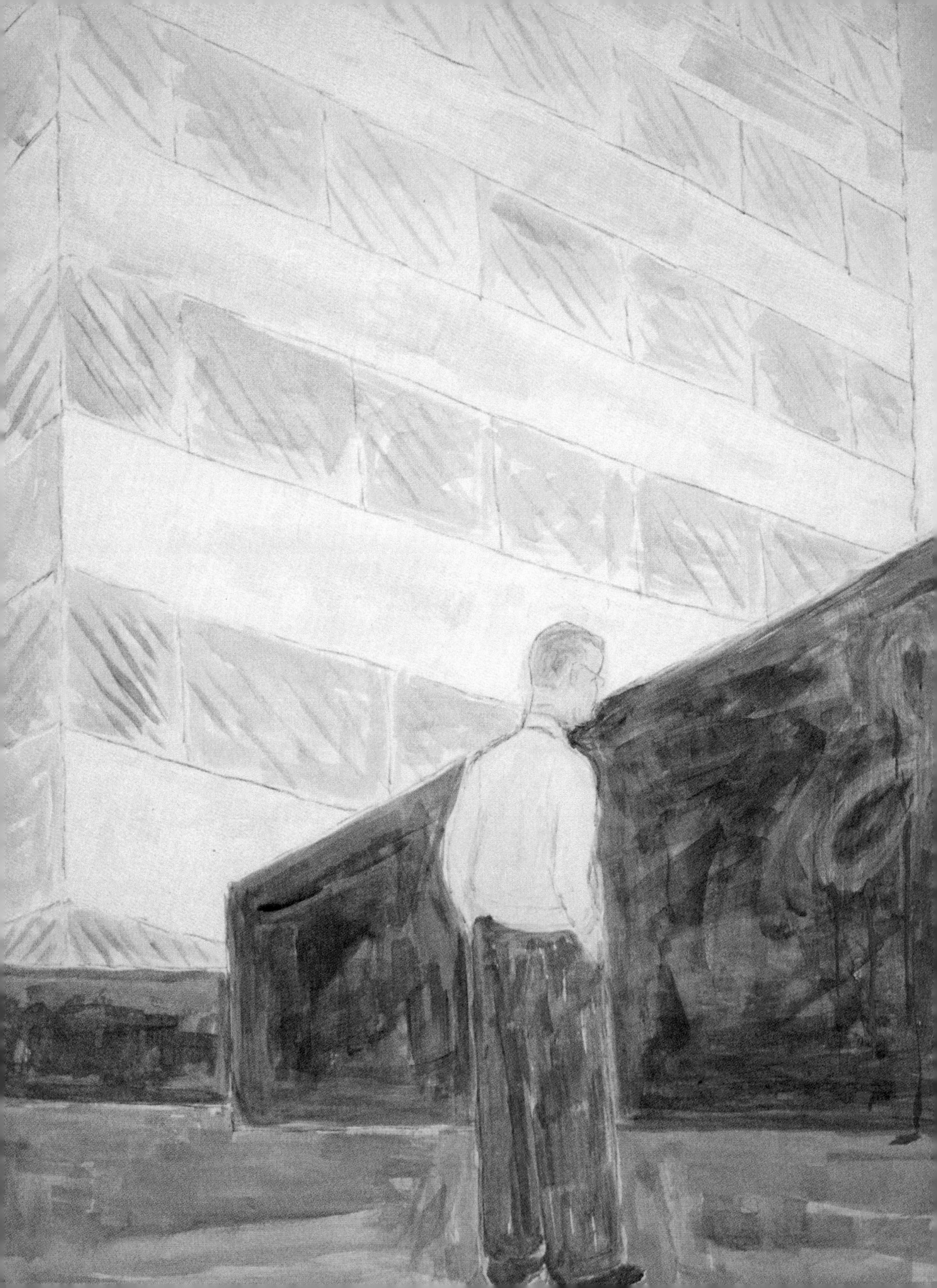

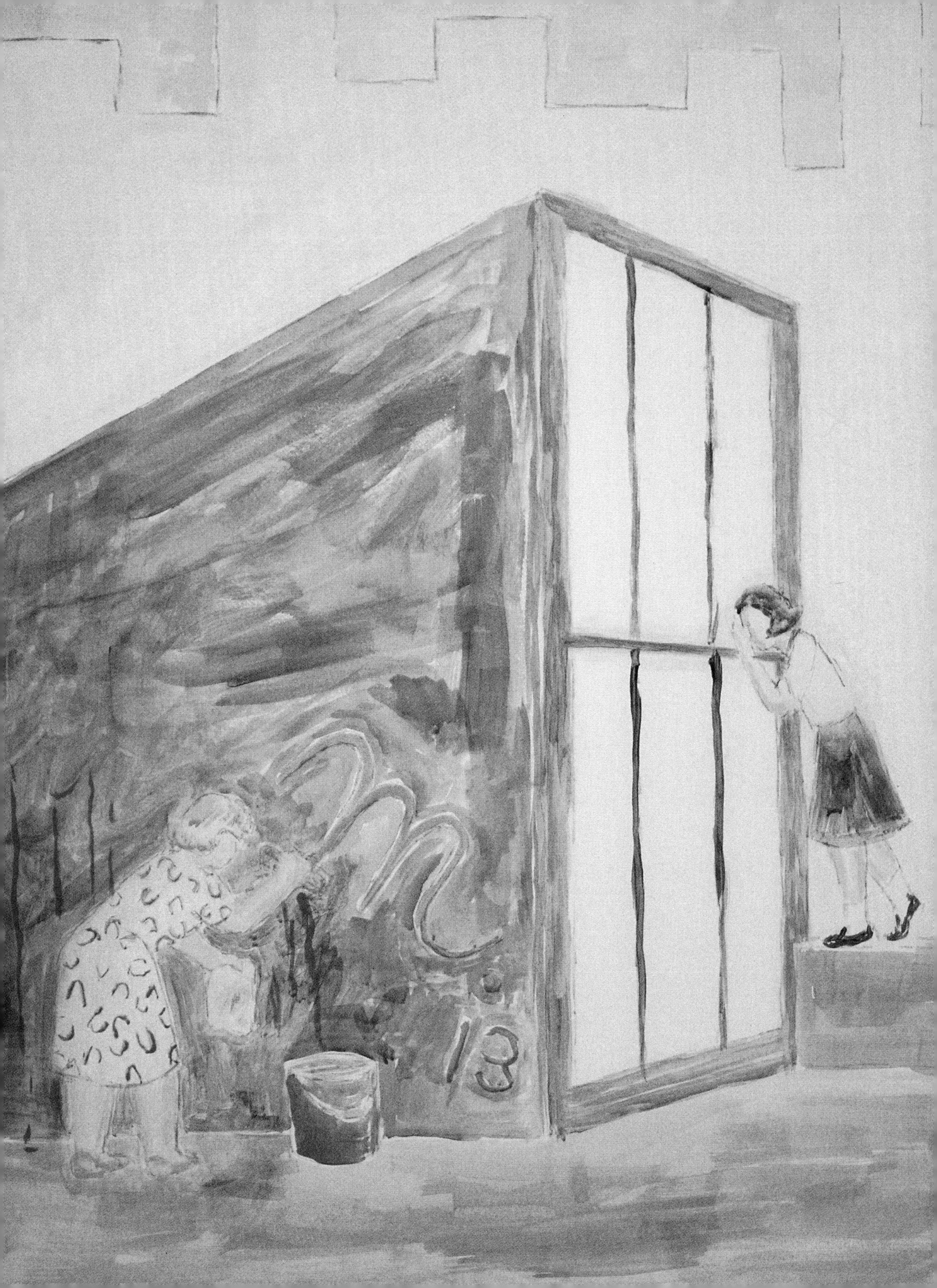

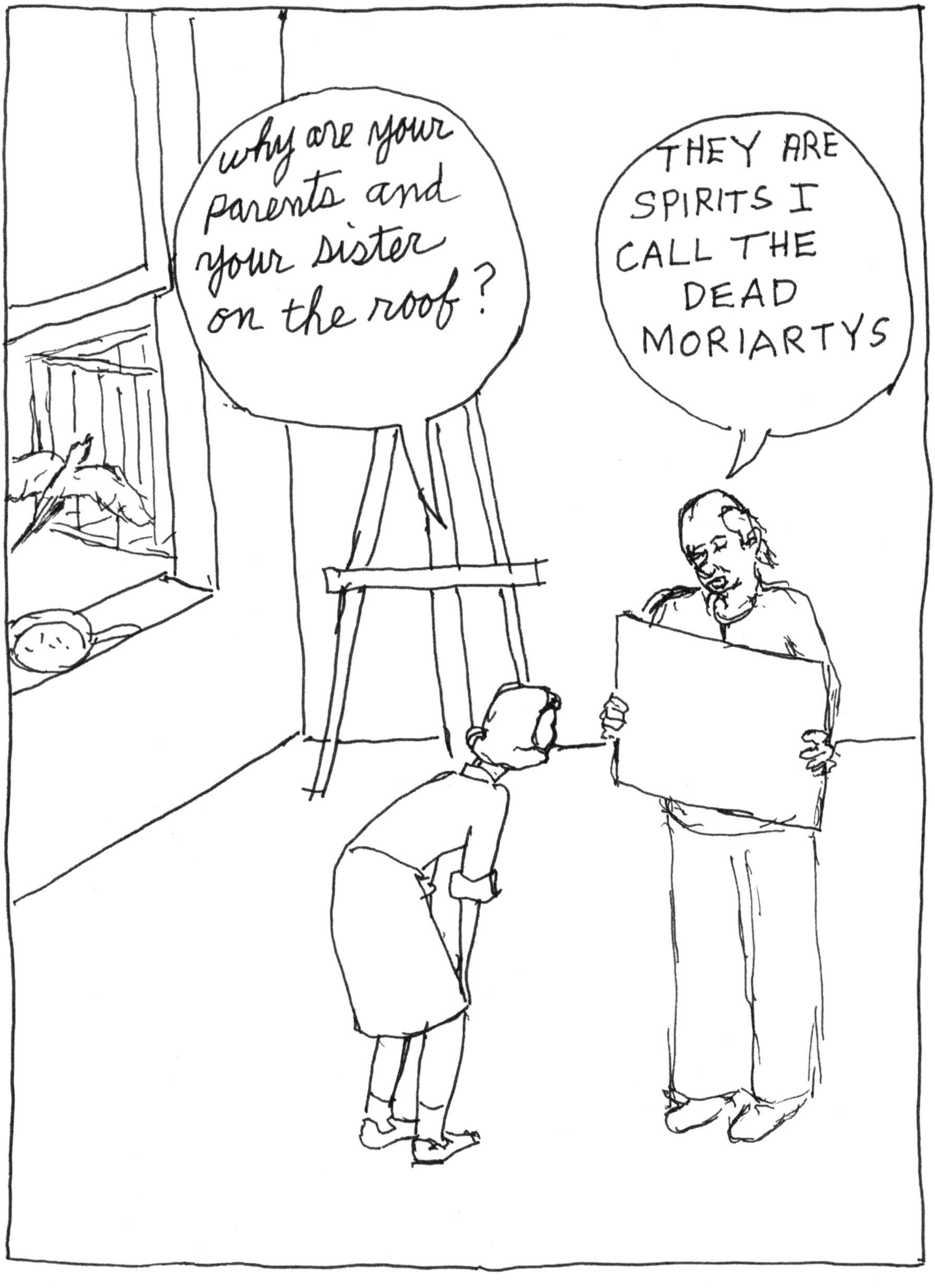
why are your parents and your sister on the roof?
THEY ARE SPIRITS I CALL THE DEAD MORIARTYS

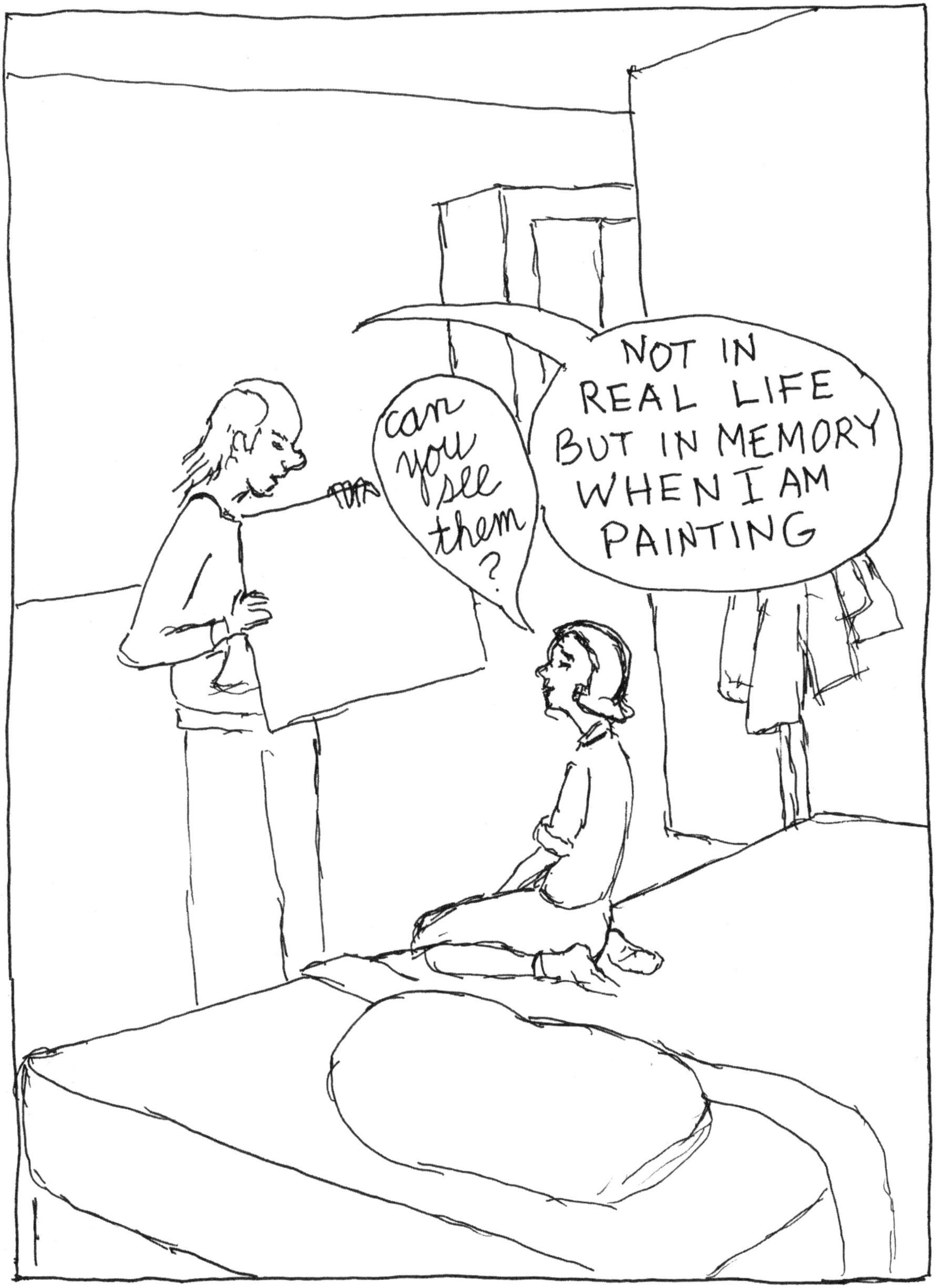
can you see them?
NOT IN REAL LIFE BUT IN MEMORY WHEN I AM PAINTING

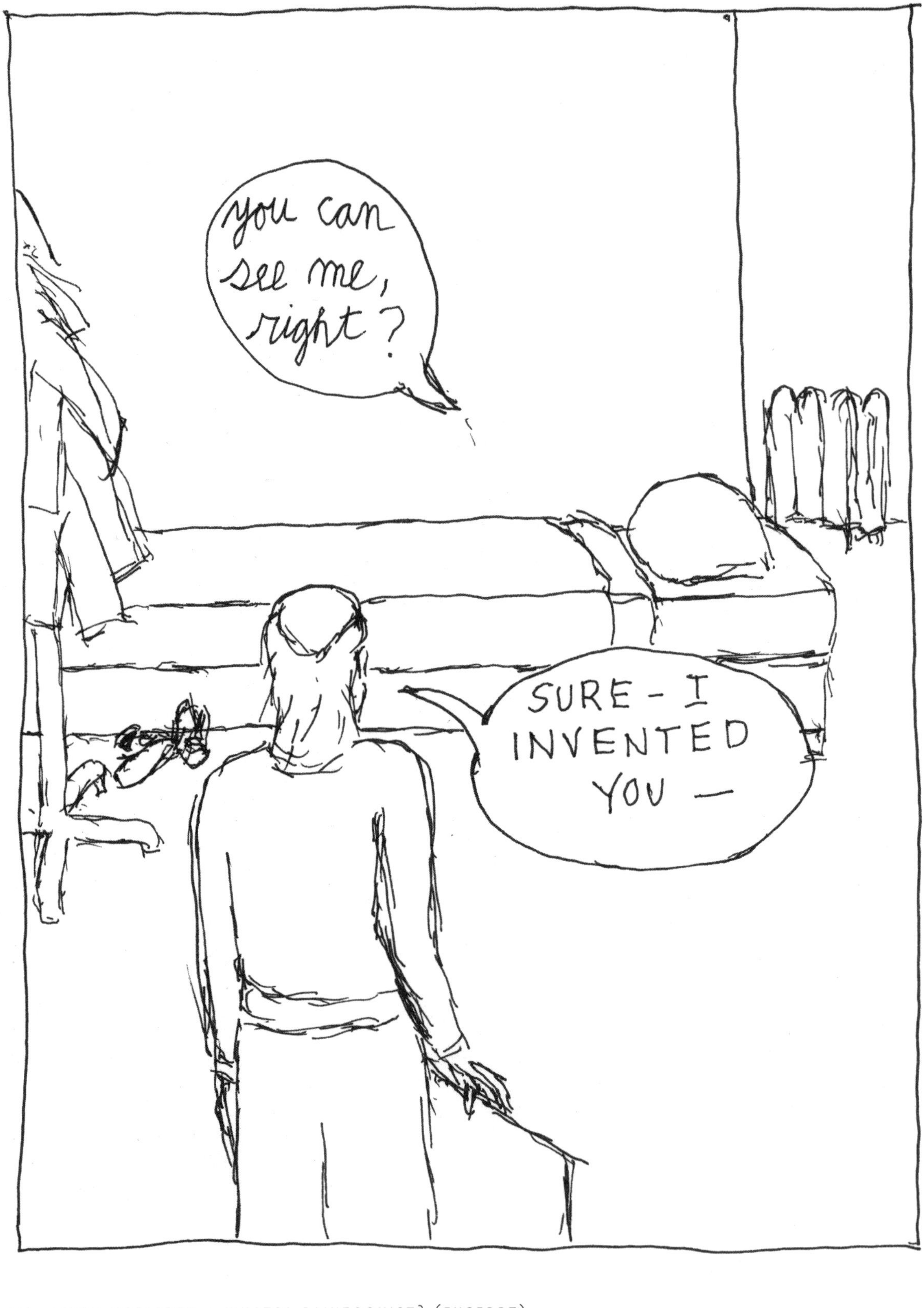
you can see me, right?
SURE - I INVENTED YOU —

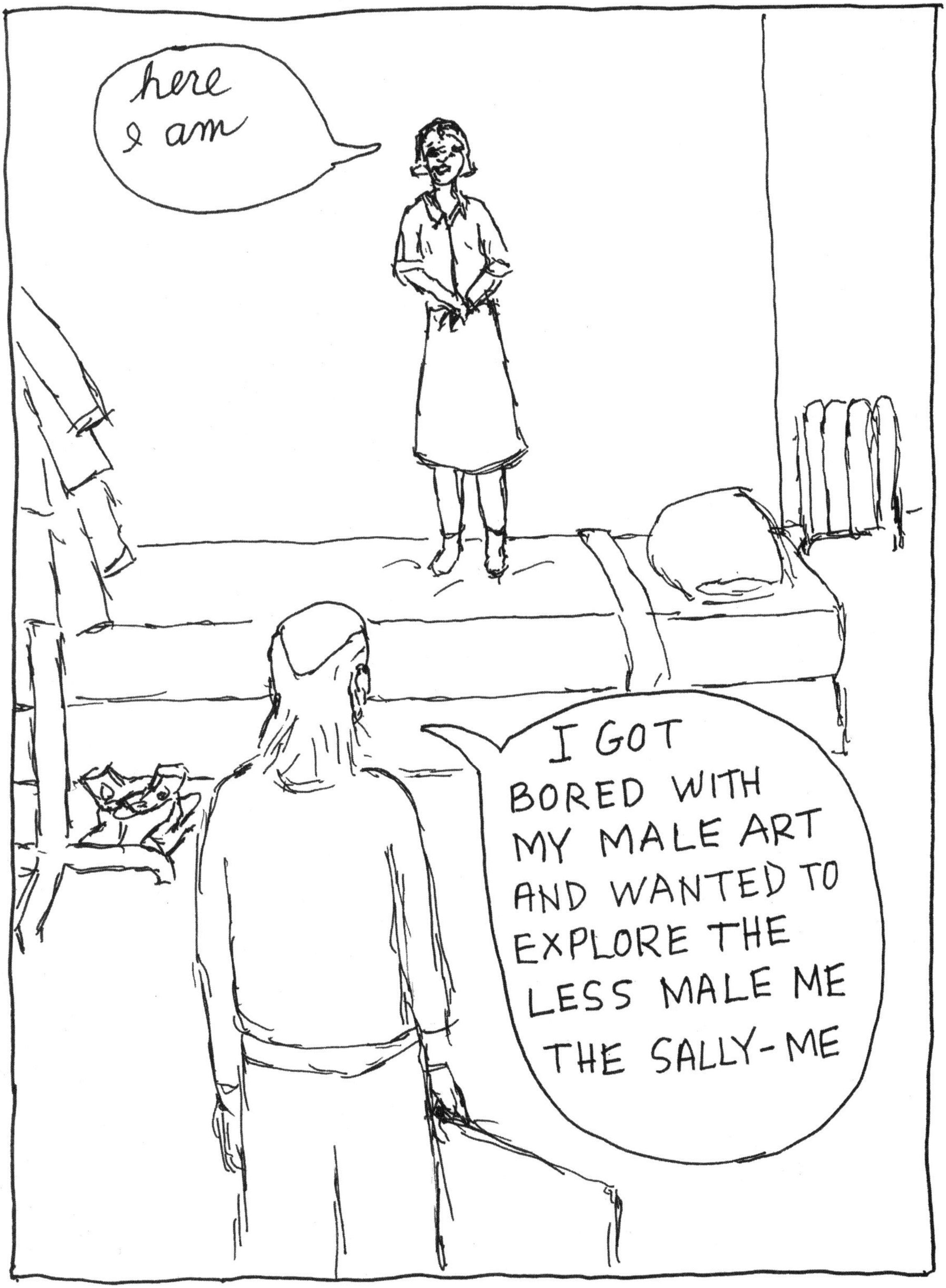
here i am
I GOT BORED WITH MY MALE ART AND WANTED TO EXPLORE THE LESS MALE ME THE SALLY-ME

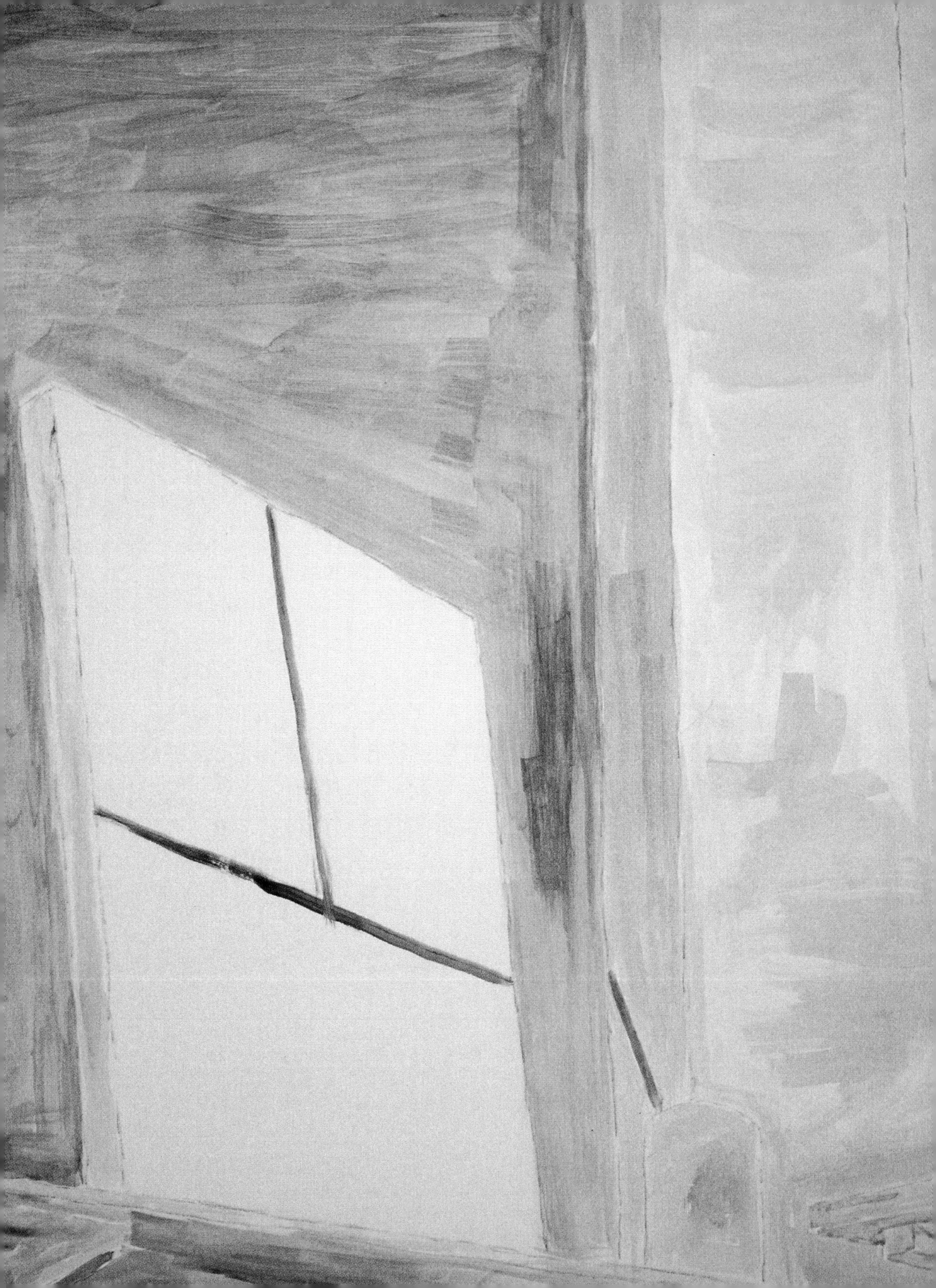

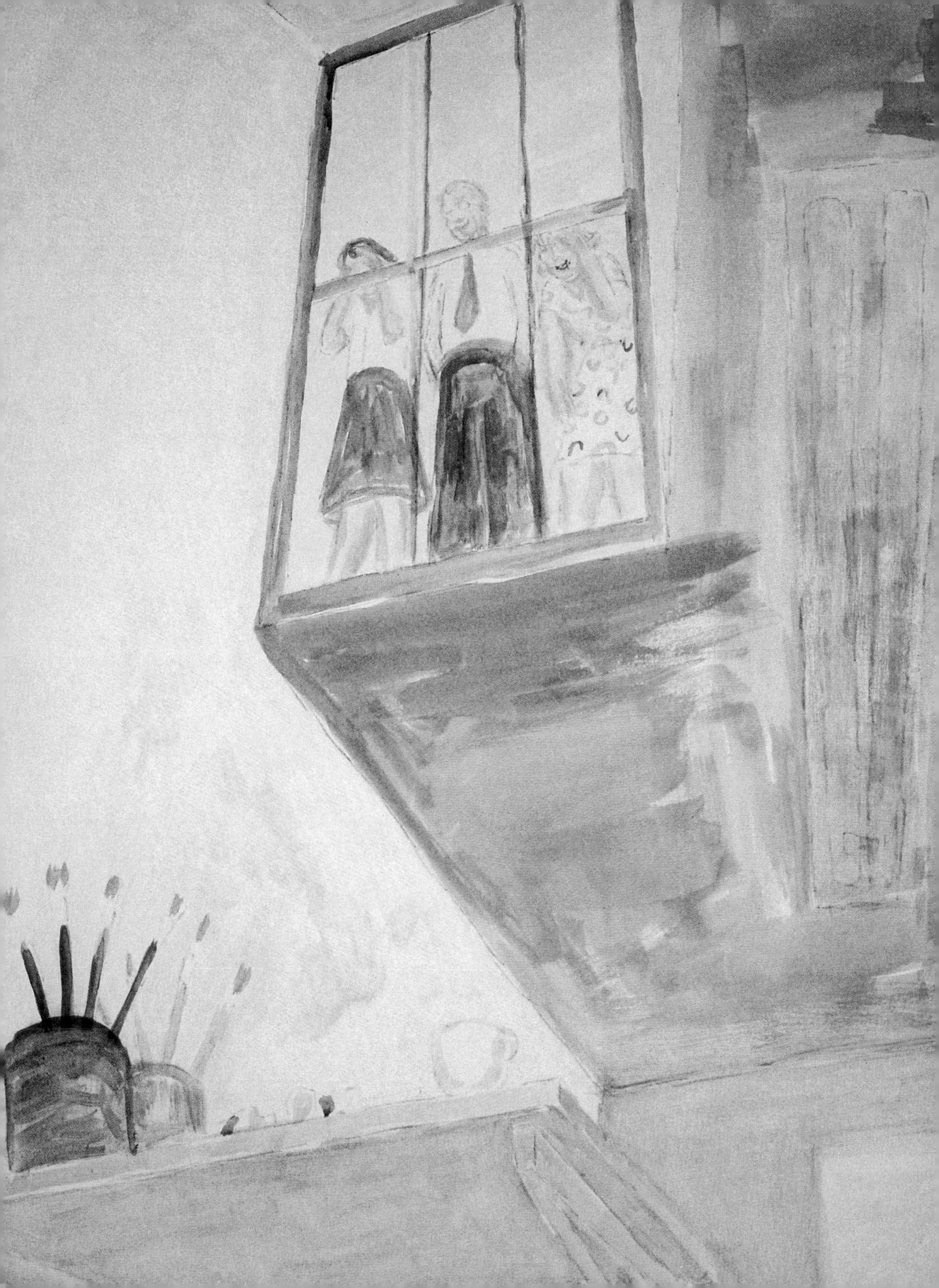

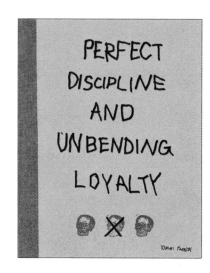

PERFECT
DISCIPLINE
AND
UNBENDING
LOYALTY
TOMMI PARRISH

Perfect Discipline (*Excerpt*)

TOMMI PARRISH

originally published in

Perfect Discipline and Unbending Loyalty
PERFECTLY ACCEPTABLE PRESS
8 x 10 inches • 36 pages, 12-page interior booklet

Biography

Tommi Parrish is an Australian cartoonist living in between Montreal and Western Massachusetts. They have books published by Fantagraphics, 2dcloud, and Perfectly Acceptable Press. Tommi's work was featured as the most recent cover of *Granta* magazine and *The Best American Nonrequired Reading,* and their comics have been translated into French, Spanish, and Dutch.
instagram.com/tommi_pg/

Statement

This piece is a short excerpt from a story about an adult child returning home to care for her estranged ailing mother. The story was beautifully printed by Matt Davis at Perfectly Acceptable Press.

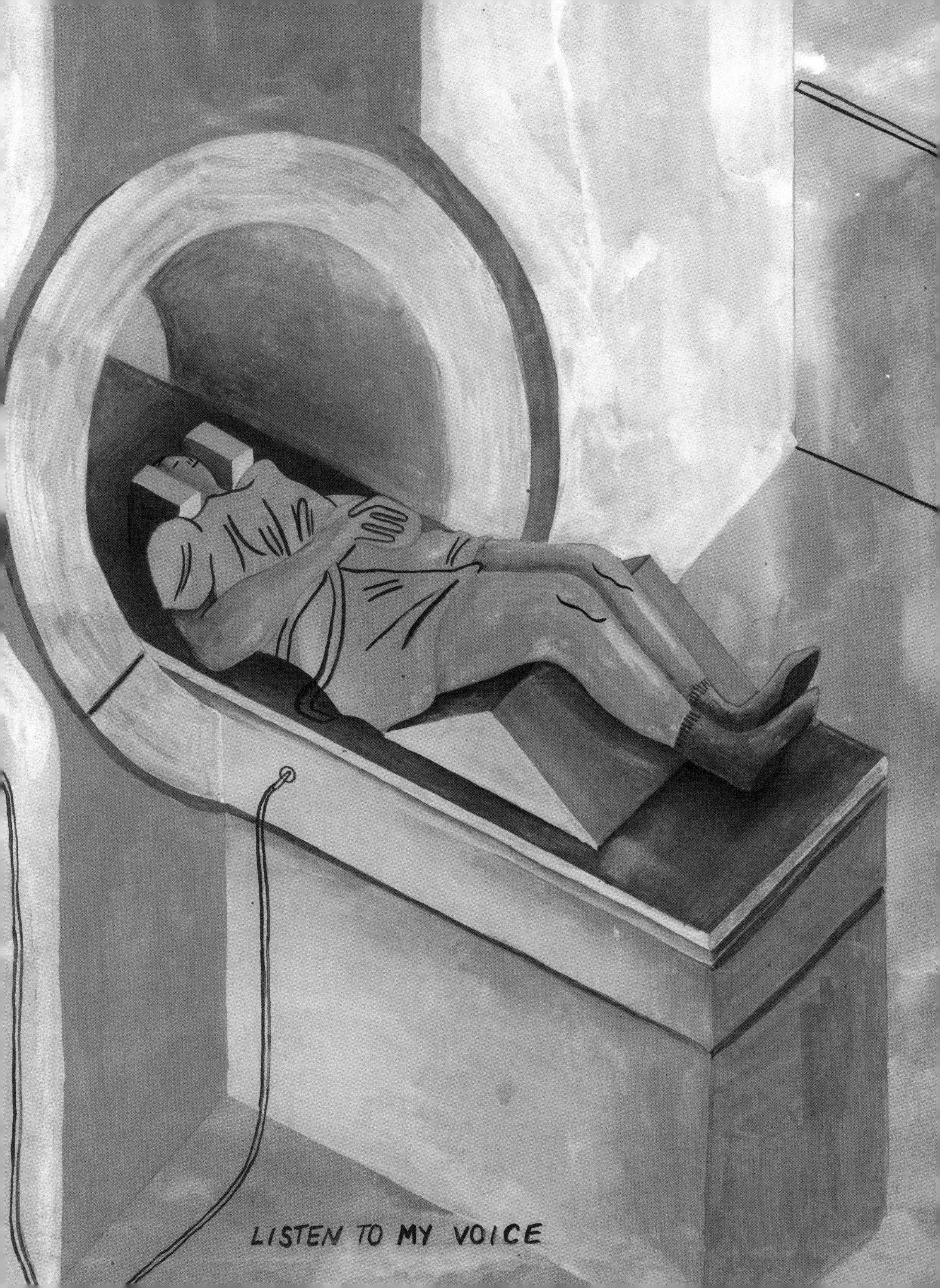
LISTEN TO MY VOICE

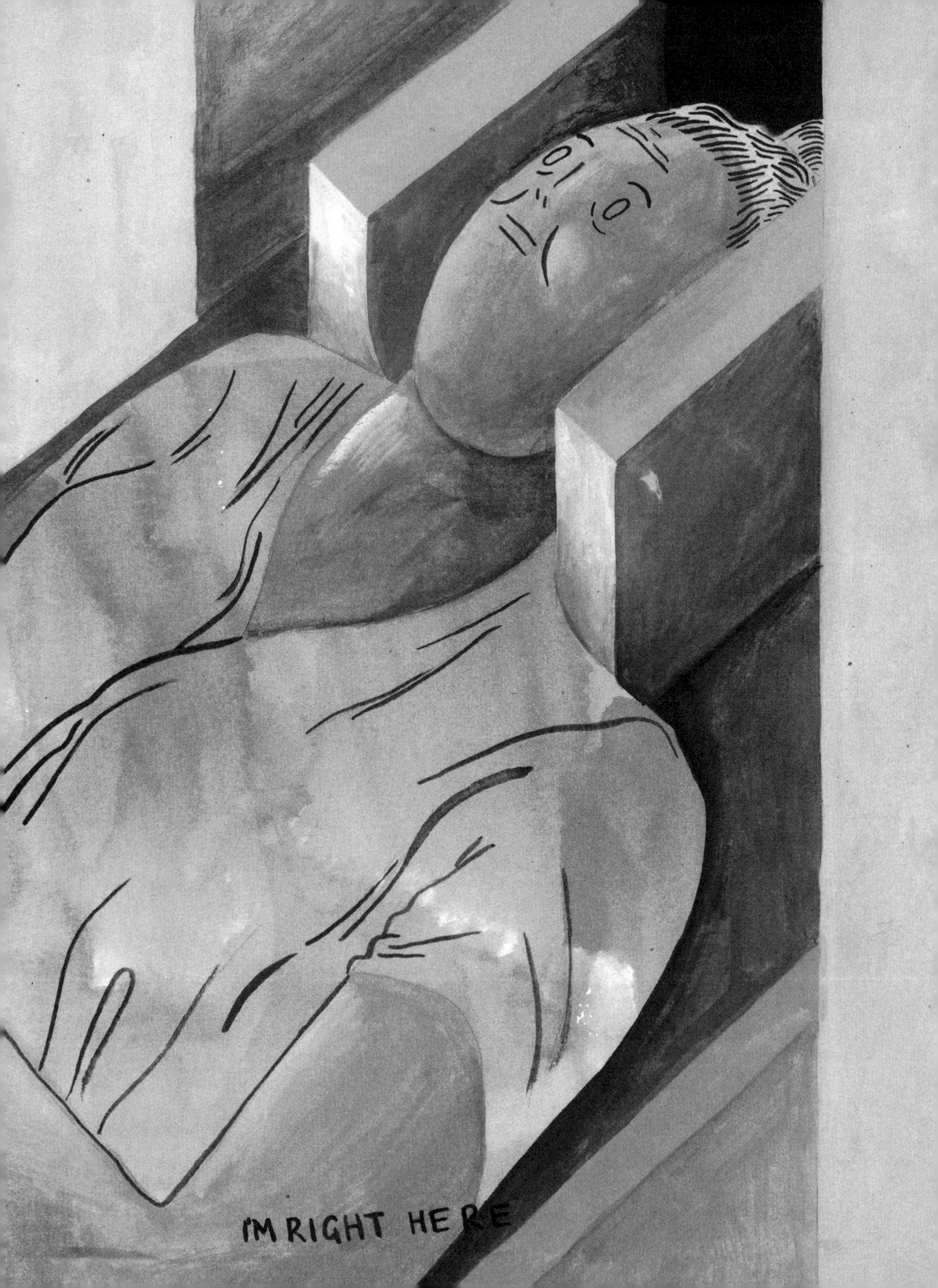
I'M RIGHT HERE

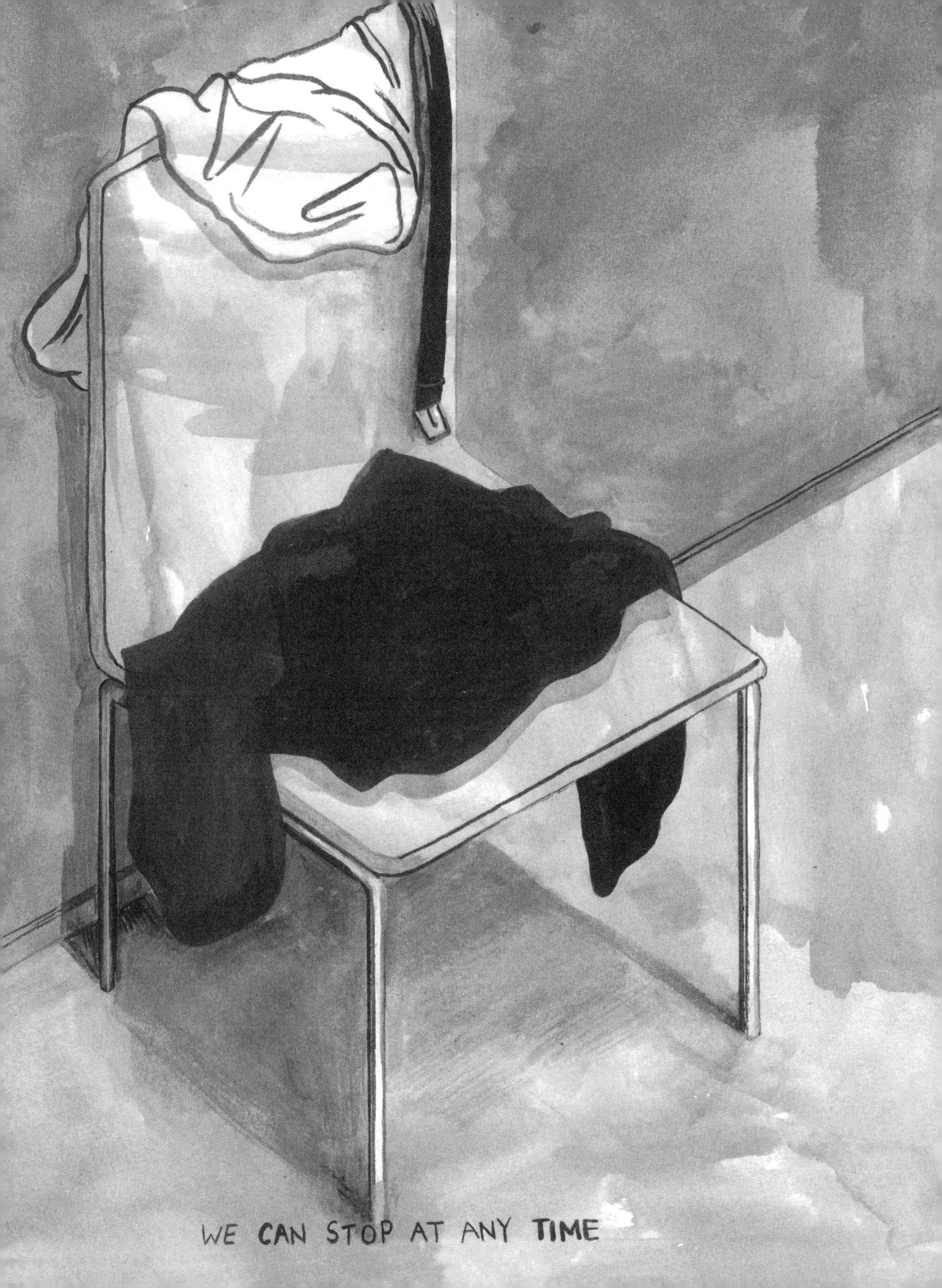
WE CAN STOP AT ANY TIME

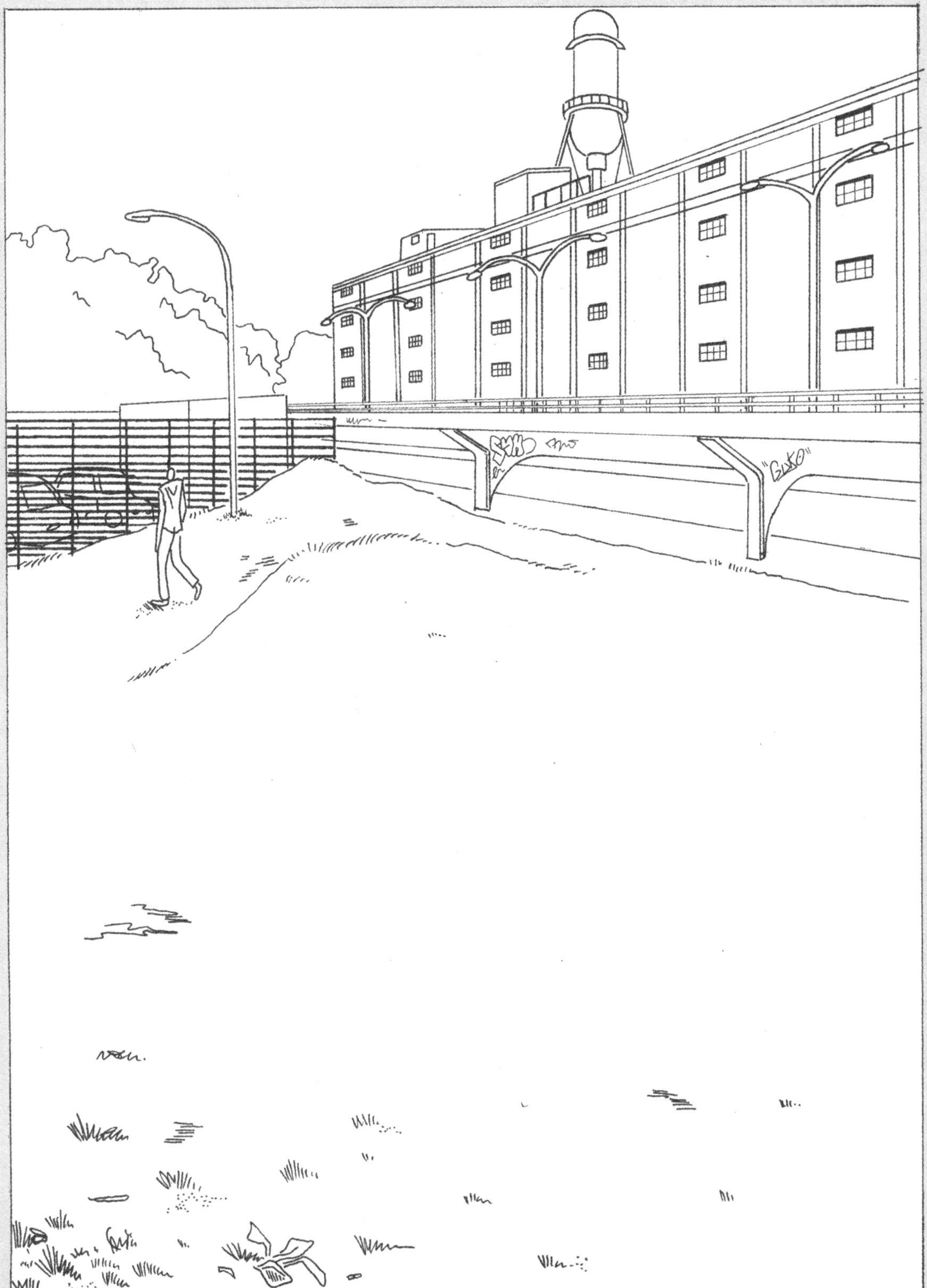

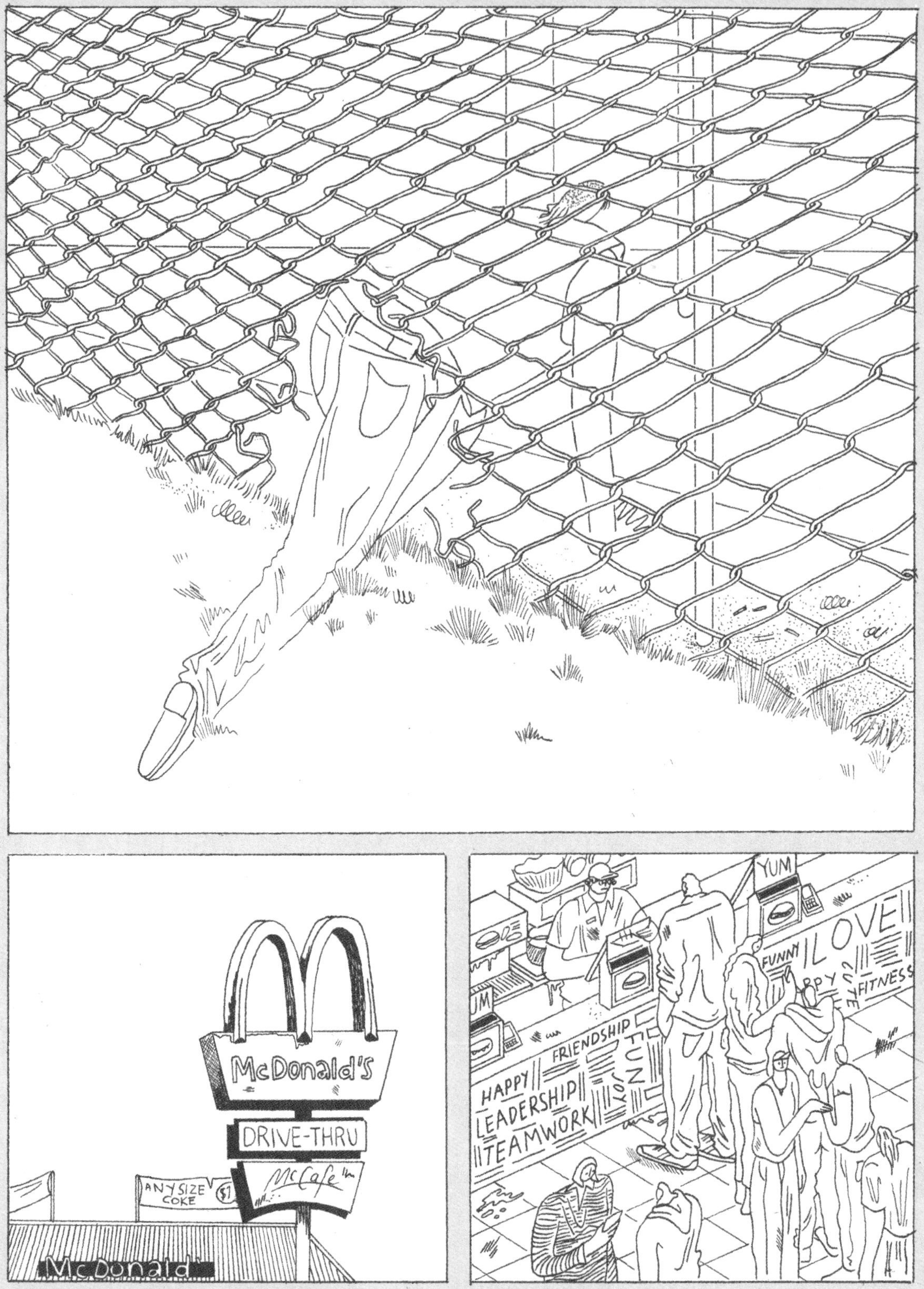
McDonald's
DRIVE-THRU
McCafe
ANY SIZE COKE
YUM
YUM
YUM
LOVE
FUNNY
FITNESS
FRIENDSHIP
HAPPY
LEADERSHIP
TEAMWORK
FUN

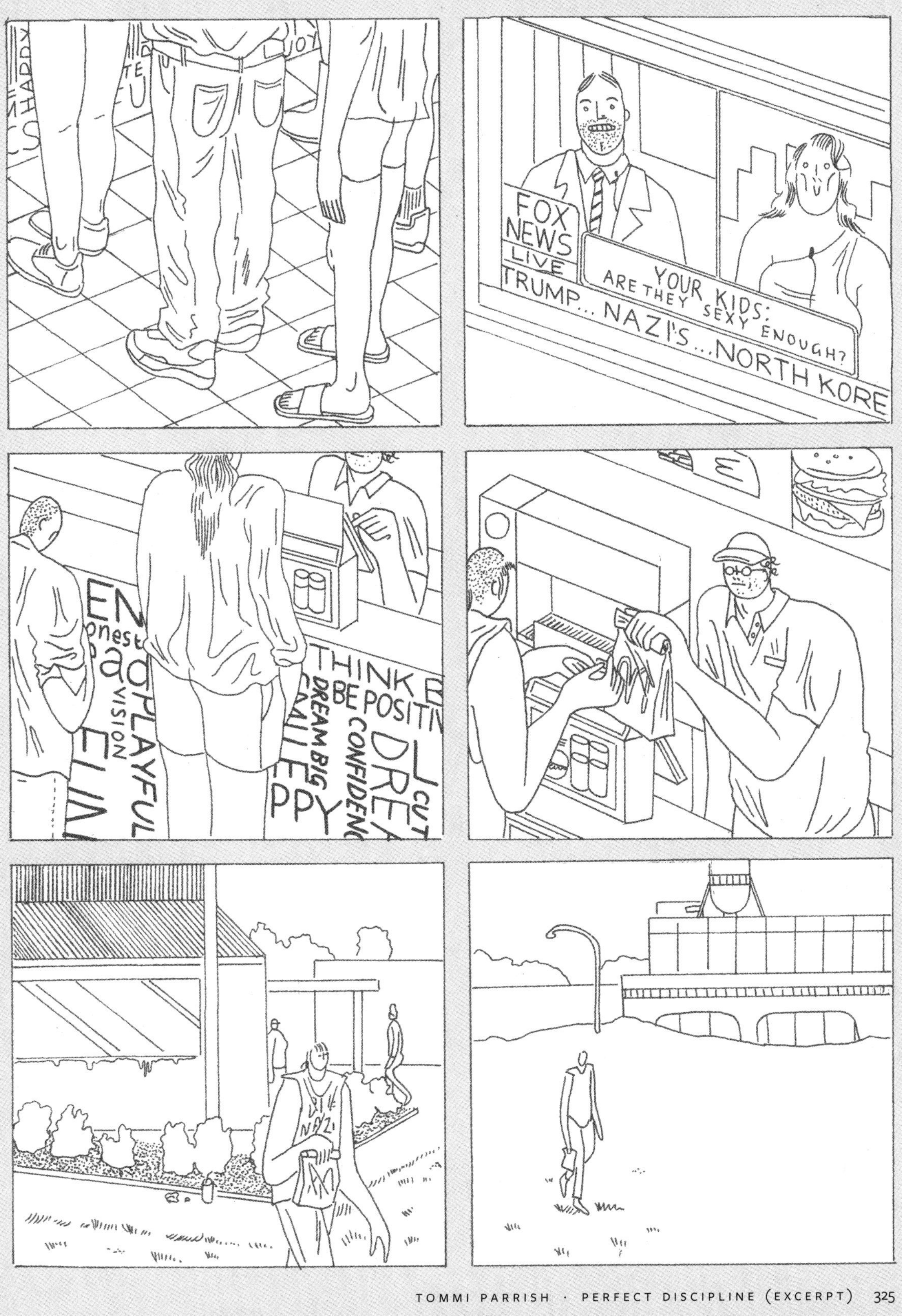
FOX NEWS LIVE
YOUR KIDS: ARE THEY SEXY ENOUGH?
TRUMP... NAZI'S...NORTH KORE
THINK
BE POSITIV
DREAM BIG
CONFIDEN
PLAYFUL
VISION

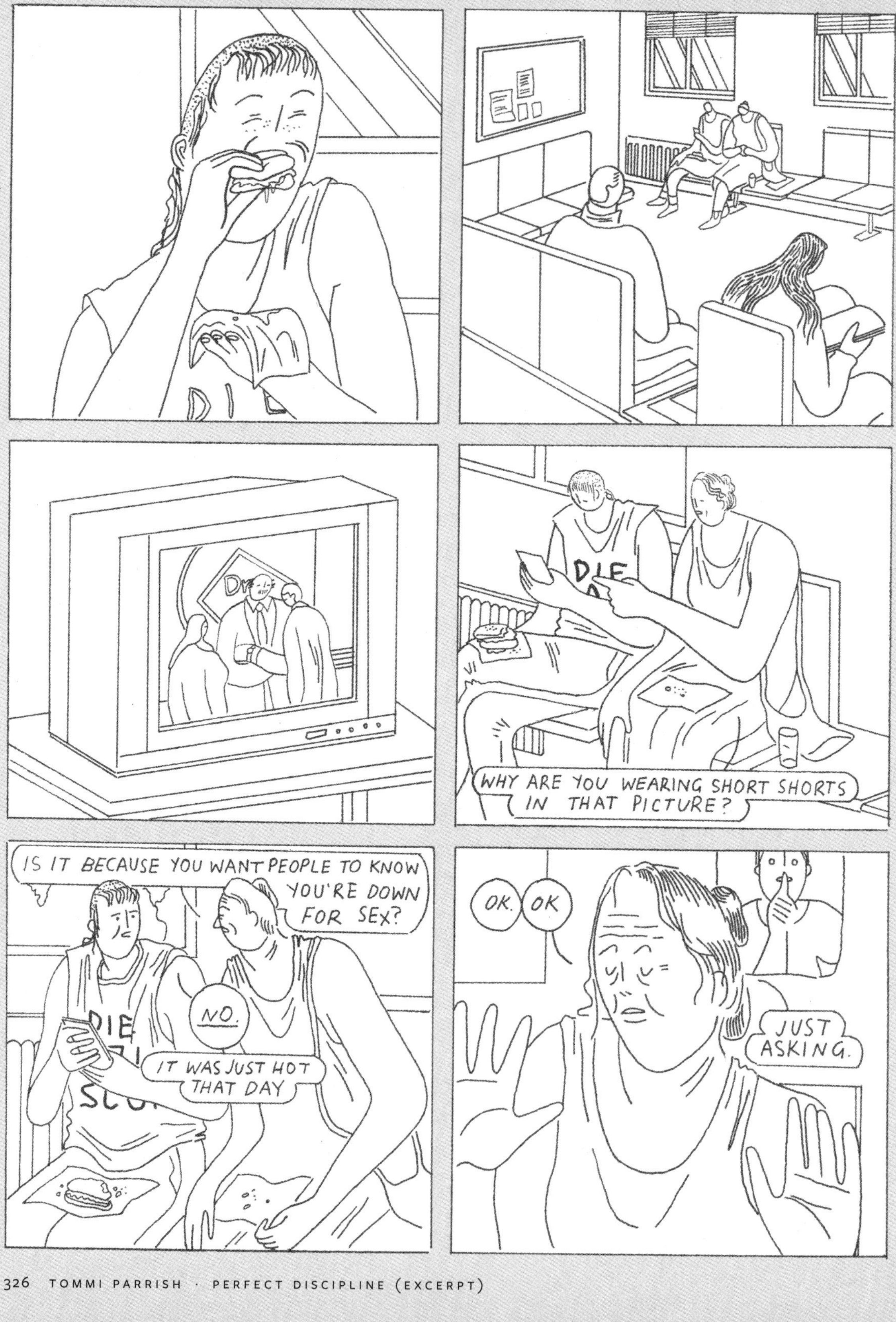
DIE
WHY ARE YOU WEARING SHORT SHORTS IN THAT PICTURE?
IS IT BECAUSE YOU WANT PEOPLE TO KNOW YOU'RE DOWN FOR SEX?
NO.
IT WAS JUST HOT THAT DAY
OK.
OK
JUST ASKING.

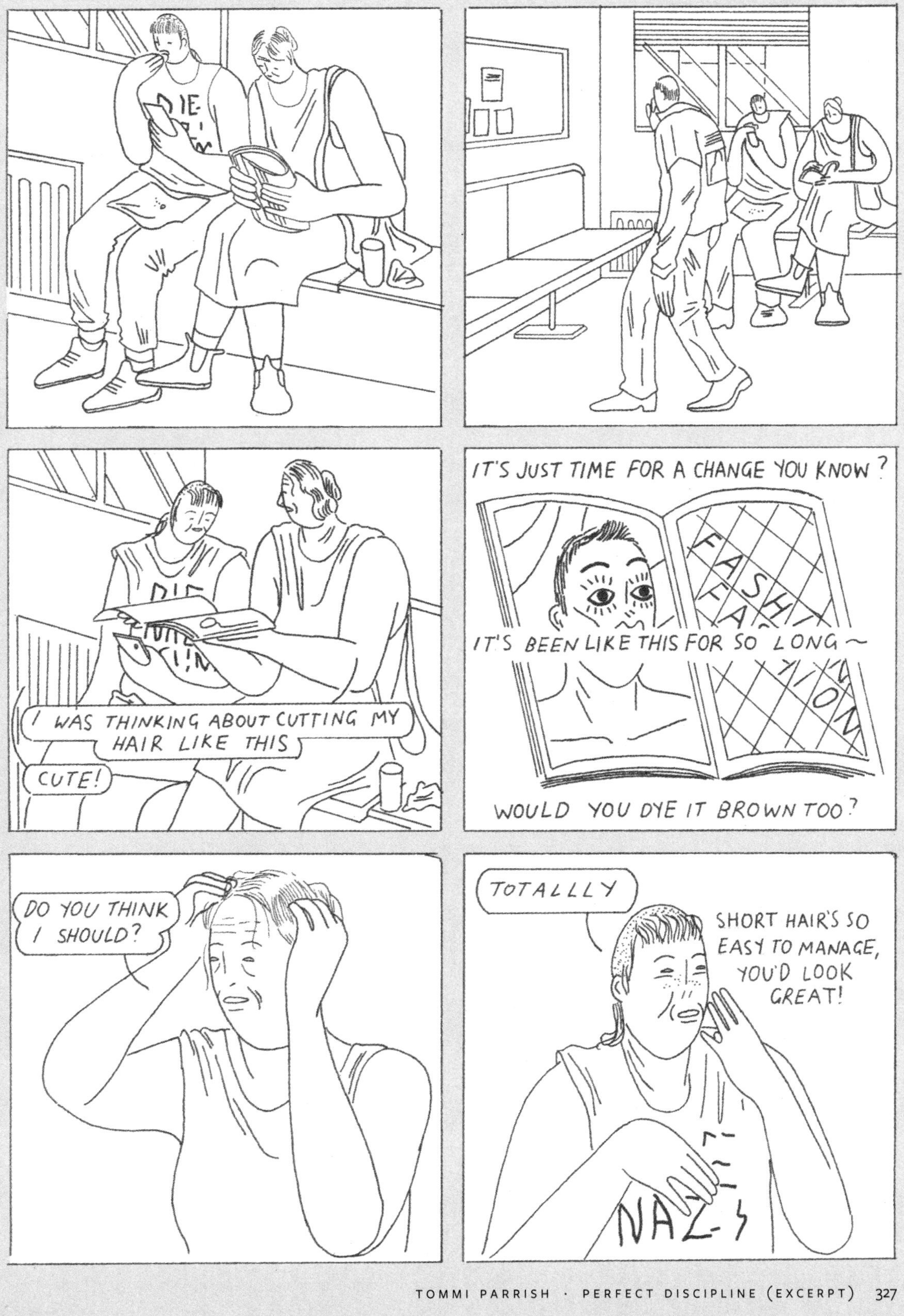
I WAS THINKING ABOUT CUTTING MY HAIR LIKE THIS
CUTE!
IT'S JUST TIME FOR A CHANGE YOU KNOW?
IT'S BEEN LIKE THIS FOR SO LONG~
WOULD YOU DYE IT BROWN TOO?
DO YOU THINK I SHOULD?
TOTALLLY
SHORT HAIR'S SO EASY TO MANAGE, YOU'D LOOK GREAT!

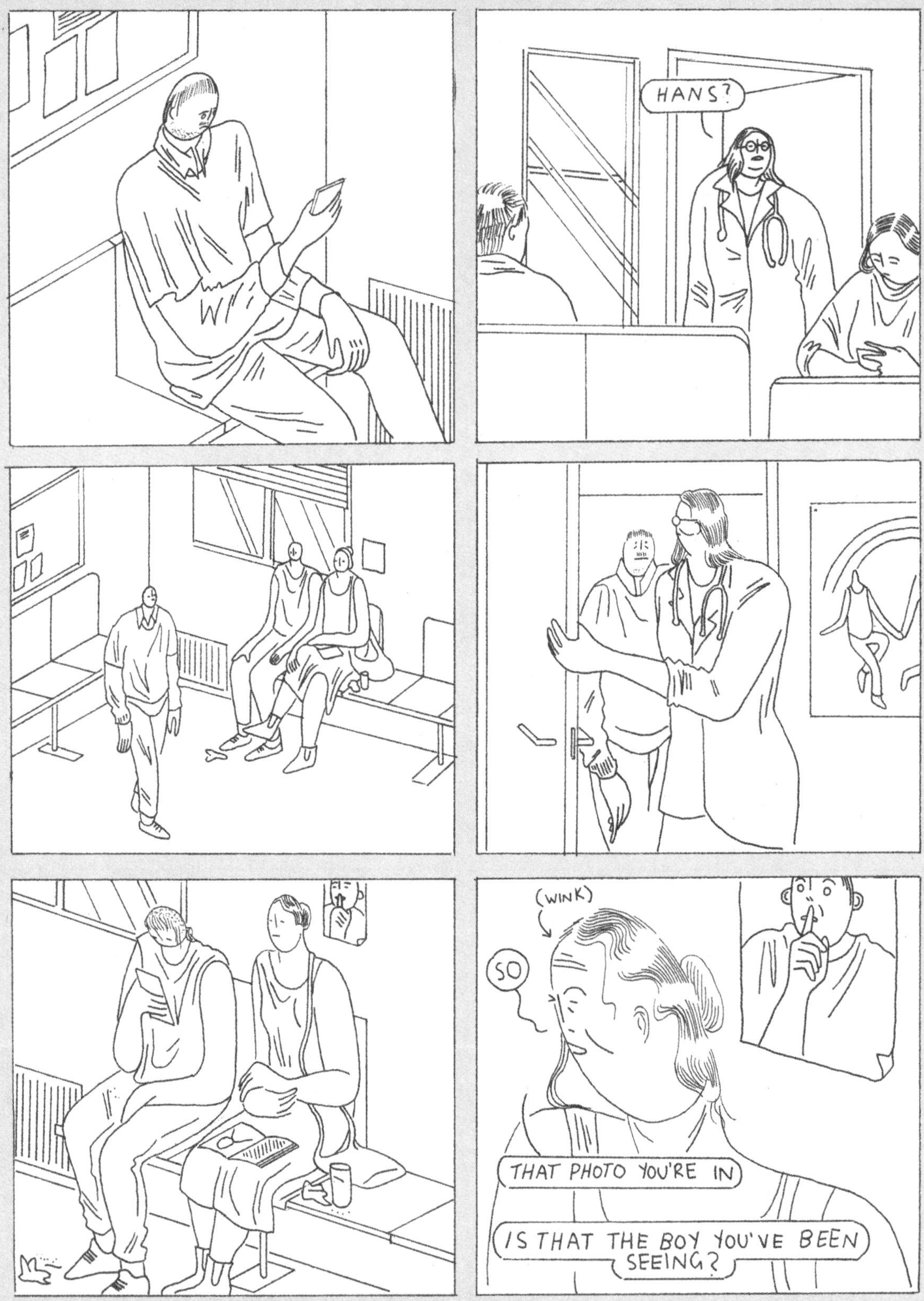
HANS?
(WINK)
SO
THAT PHOTO YOU'RE IN
IS THAT THE BOY YOU'VE BEEN SEEING?

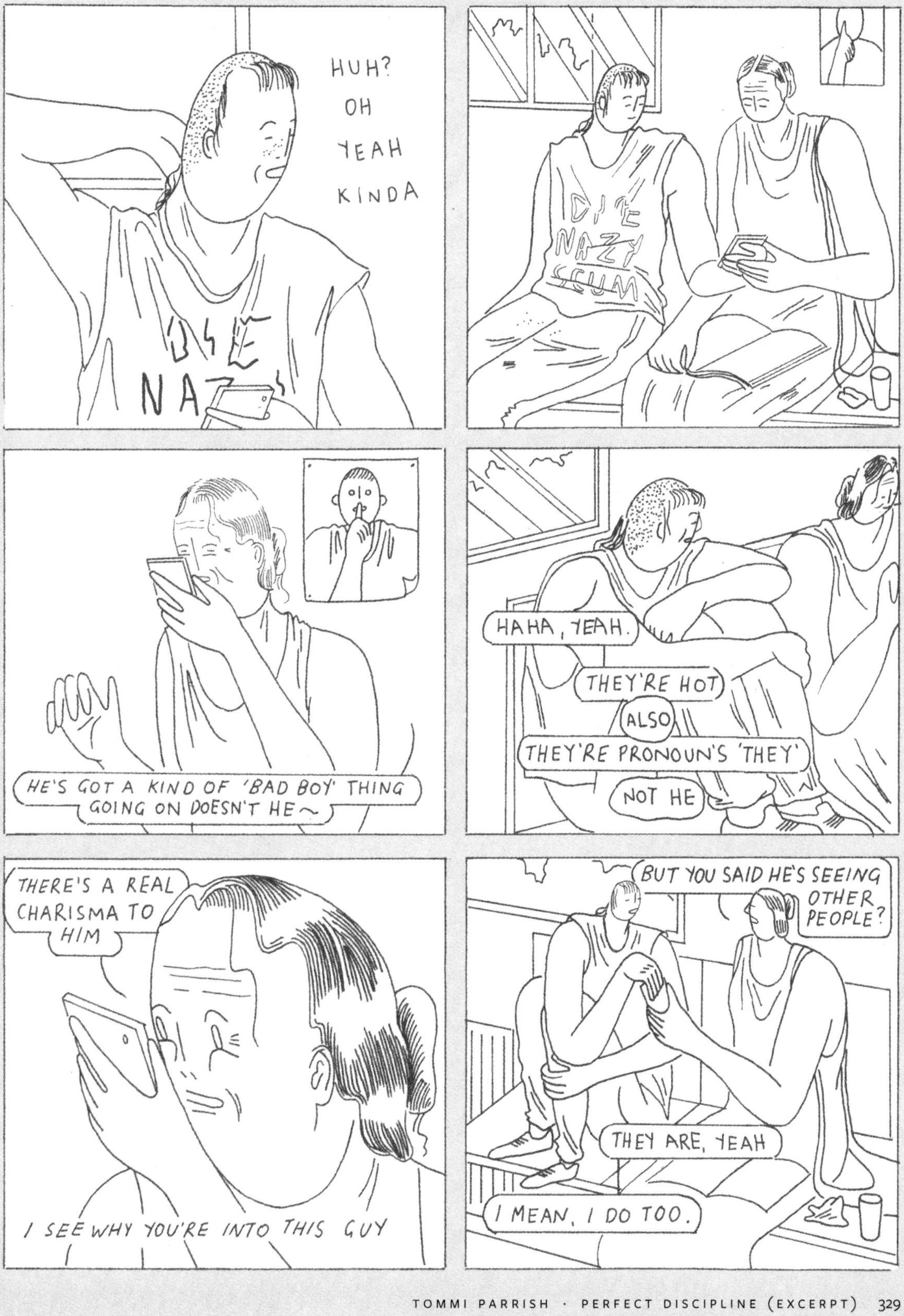
HUH? OH YEAH KINDA
DIE NAZI SCUM
HE'S GOT A KIND OF 'BAD BOY' THING GOING ON DOESN'T HE~
HAHA, YEAH.
THEY'RE HOT
ALSO
THEY'RE PRONOUN'S 'THEY'
NOT HE
THERE'S A REAL CHARISMA TO HIM
I SEE WHY YOU'RE INTO THIS GUY
BUT YOU SAID HE'S SEEING OTHER PEOPLE?
THEY ARE, YEAH
I MEAN, I DO TOO.

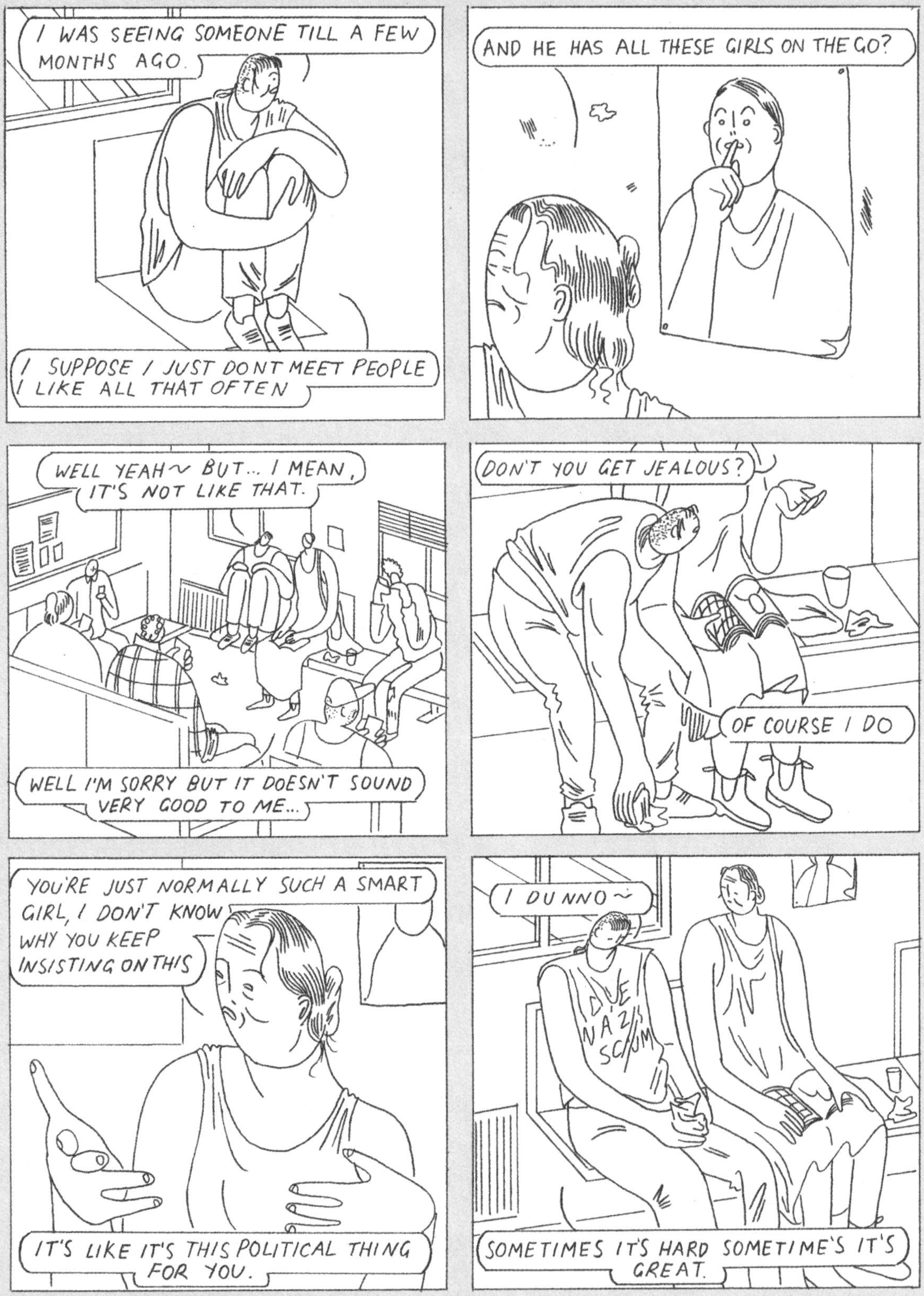
I WAS SEEING SOMEONE TILL A FEW MONTHS AGO.
I SUPPOSE I JUST DONT MEET PEOPLE I LIKE ALL THAT OFTEN
AND HE HAS ALL THESE GIRLS ON THE GO?
WELL YEAH~ BUT... I MEAN, IT'S NOT LIKE THAT.
WELL I'M SORRY BUT IT DOESN'T SOUND VERY GOOD TO ME...
DON'T YOU GET JEALOUS?
OF COURSE I DO
YOU'RE JUST NORMALLY SUCH A SMART GIRL, I DON'T KNOW WHY YOU KEEP INSISTING ON THIS
IT'S LIKE IT'S THIS POLITICAL THING FOR YOU.
I DUNNO~
DIE NAZI SCUM
SOMETIMES IT'S HARD SOMETIME'S IT'S GREAT.

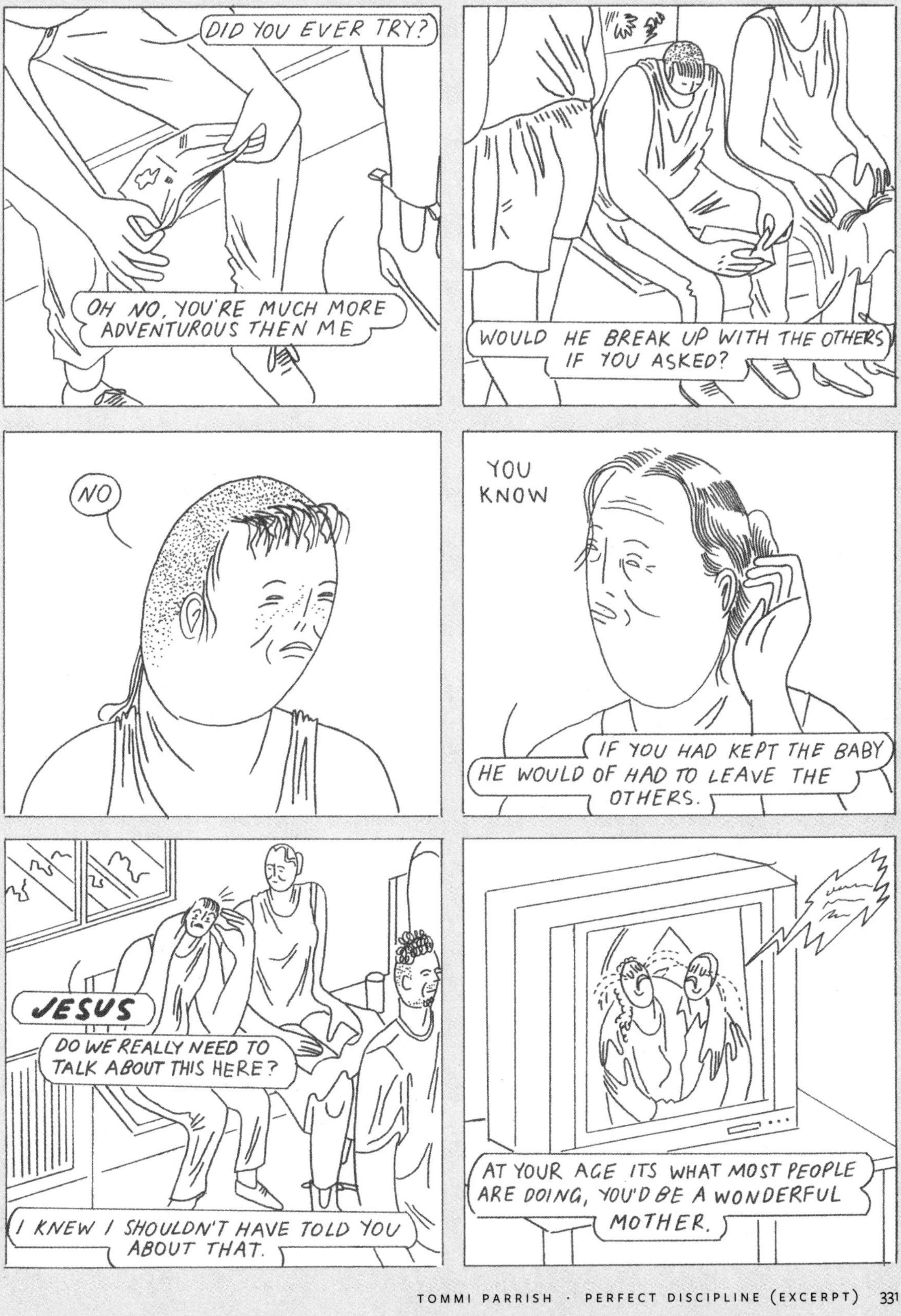
DID YOU EVER TRY?
OH NO, YOU'RE MUCH MORE ADVENTUROUS THEN ME
WOULD HE BREAK UP WITH THE OTHERS IF YOU ASKED?
NO
YOU KNOW
IF YOU HAD KEPT THE BABY HE WOULD OF HAD TO LEAVE THE OTHERS.
JESUS
DO WE REALLY NEED TO TALK ABOUT THIS HERE?
I KNEW I SHOULDN'T HAVE TOLD YOU ABOUT THAT.
AT YOUR AGE ITS WHAT MOST PEOPLE ARE DOING, YOU'D BE A WONDERFUL MOTHER.

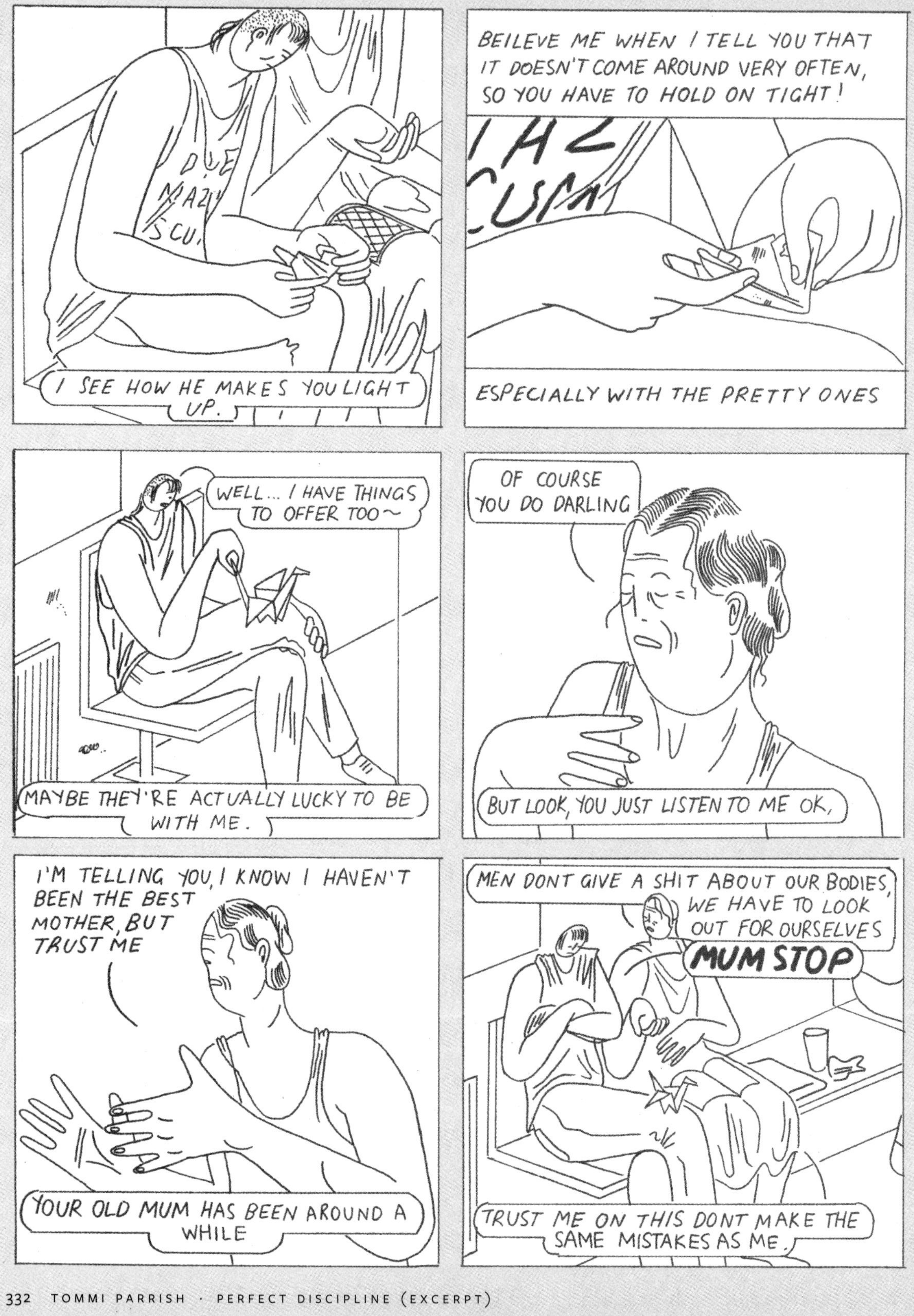
I SEE HOW HE MAKES YOU LIGHT UP.
BEILEVE ME WHEN I TELL YOU THAT IT DOESN'T COME AROUND VERY OFTEN, SO YOU HAVE TO HOLD ON TIGHT!
ESPECIALLY WITH THE PRETTY ONES
WELL... I HAVE THINGS TO OFFER TOO~
MAYBE THEY'RE ACTUALLY LUCKY TO BE WITH ME.
OF COURSE YOU DO DARLING
BUT LOOK, YOU JUST LISTEN TO ME OK,
I'M TELLING YOU, I KNOW I HAVEN'T BEEN THE BEST MOTHER, BUT TRUST ME
YOUR OLD MUM HAS BEEN AROUND A WHILE
MEN DONT GIVE A SHIT ABOUT OUR BODIES, WE HAVE TO LOOK OUT FOR OURSELVES
MUM STOP
TRUST ME ON THIS DONT MAKE THE SAME MISTAKES AS ME.

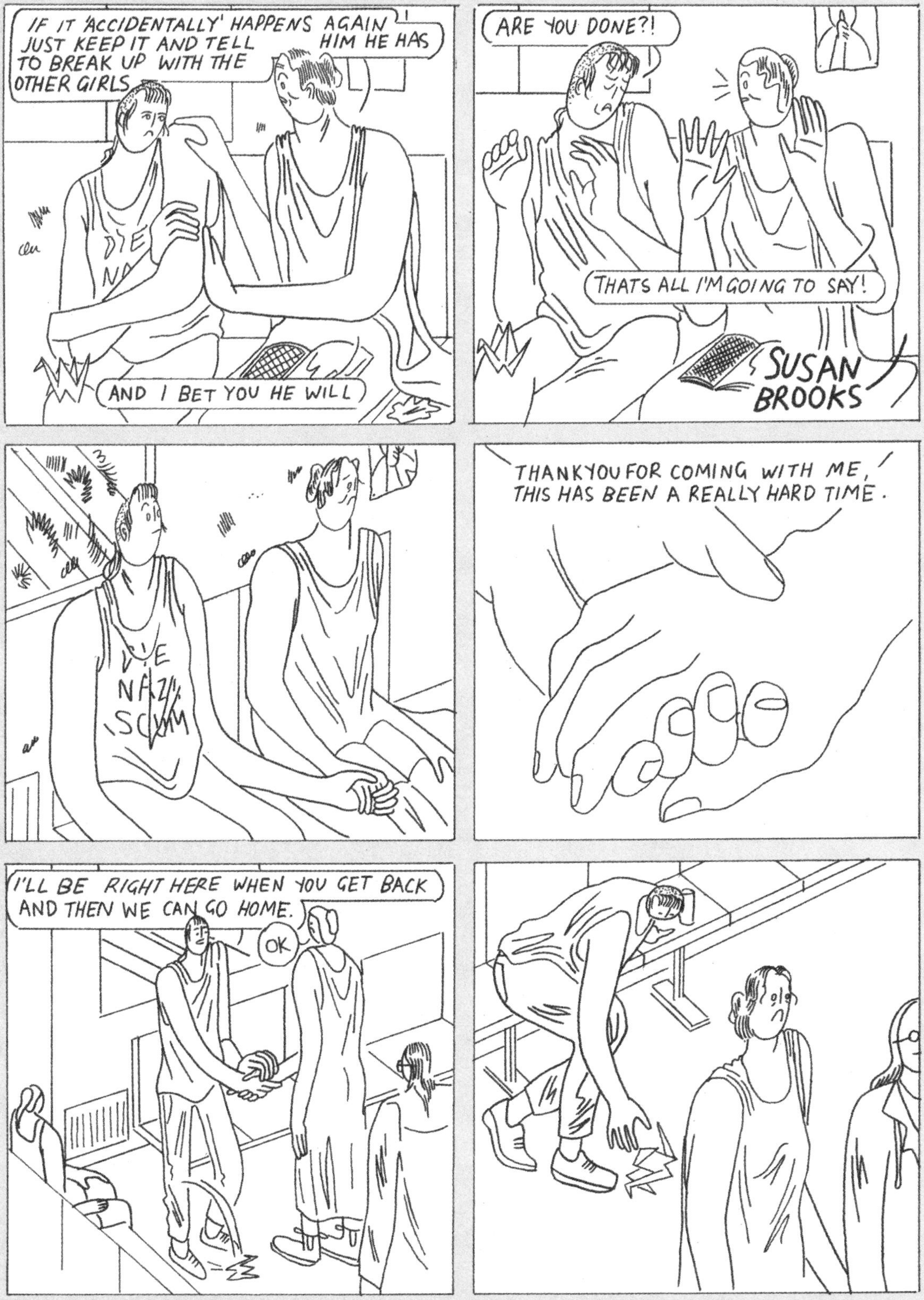
IF IT 'ACCIDENTALLY' HAPPENS AGAIN JUST KEEP IT AND TELL HIM HE HAS TO BREAK UP WITH THE OTHER GIRLS
AND I BET YOU HE WILL
ARE YOU DONE?!
THATS ALL I'M GOING TO SAY!
SUSAN BROOKS
THANKYOU FOR COMING WITH ME, THIS HAS BEEN A REALLY HARD TIME.
I'LL BE RIGHT HERE WHEN YOU GET BACK AND THEN WE CAN GO HOME.
OK

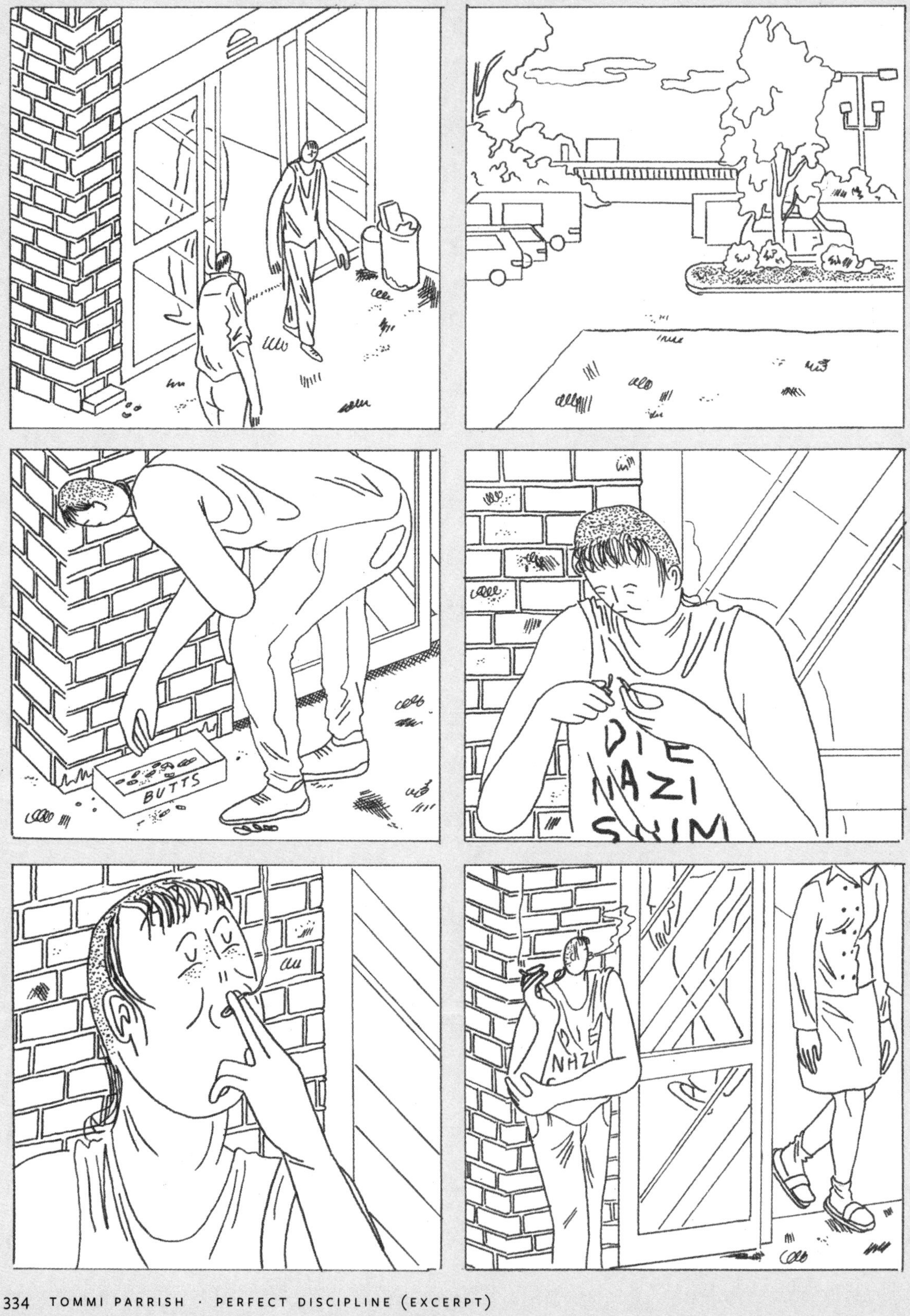
BUTTS
DIE
NAZI

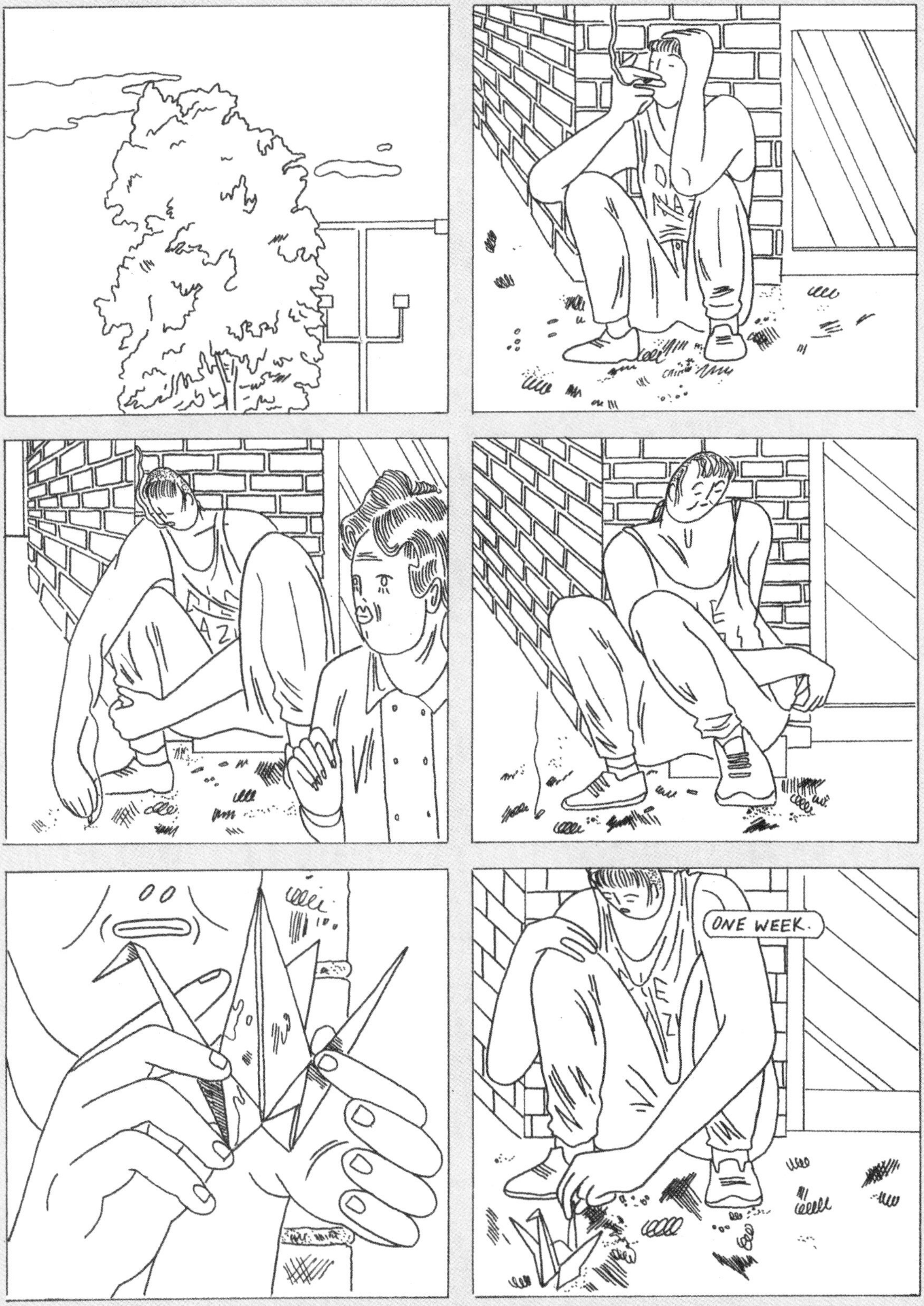
ONE WEEK.

By Monday I'll Be Floating in the Hudson with the Other Garbage (*Excerpt*)

LAURA LANNES

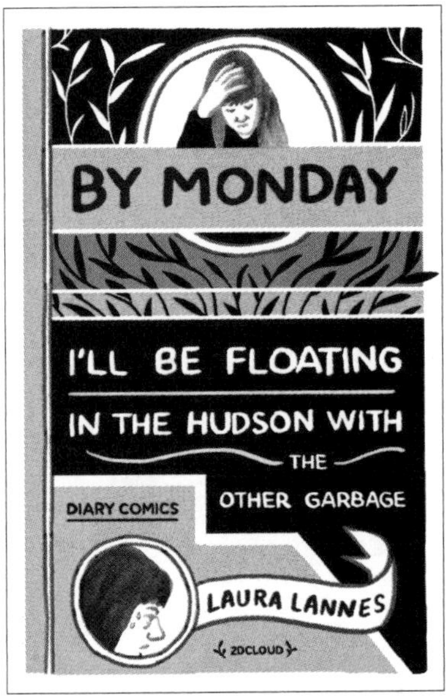
BY MONDAY
I'LL BE FLOATING
IN THE HUDSON WITH
THE
OTHER GARBAGE
DIARY COMICS
LAURA LANNES
2DCLOUD

originally published in

By Monday I'll Be Floating in the Hudson with the Other Garbage

2DCLOUD

8.5 x 13 inches • 30 pages

Biography

Laura Lannes is an illustrator and cartoonist from Rio de Janeiro, Brazil, living in New York City.

lauralannes.com

Statement

In 2017 I briefly dated a man who was in an open relationship. His girlfriend had recently moved to a different city. I was making daily diary comics and posting them online; they were later collected in a book called *By Monday I'll Be Floating in the Hudson with the Other Garbage*. This is an excerpt from that book.

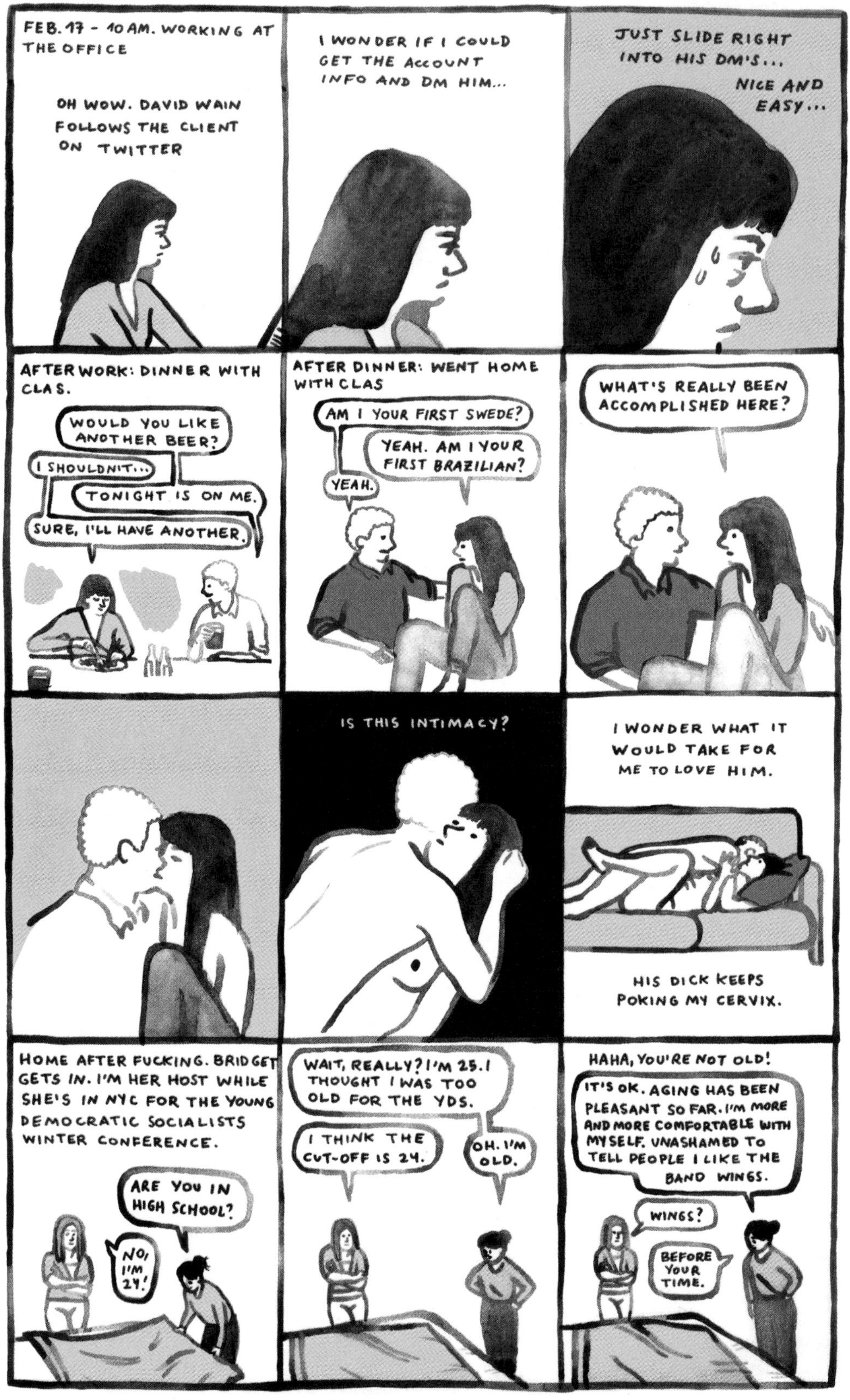
FEB. 17 - 10 AM. WORKING AT THE OFFICE
OH WOW. DAVID WAIN FOLLOWS THE CLIENT ON TWITTER
I WONDER IF I COULD GET THE ACCOUNT INFO AND DM HIM...
JUST SLIDE RIGHT INTO HIS DM'S...
NICE AND EASY...
AFTER WORK: DINNER WITH CLAS.
WOULD YOU LIKE ANOTHER BEER?
I SHOULDN'T...
TONIGHT IS ON ME.
SURE, I'LL HAVE ANOTHER.
AFTER DINNER: WENT HOME WITH CLAS
AM I YOUR FIRST SWEDE?
YEAH.
YEAH. AM I YOUR FIRST BRAZILIAN?
WHAT'S REALLY BEEN ACCOMPLISHED HERE?
IS THIS INTIMACY?
I WONDER WHAT IT WOULD TAKE FOR ME TO LOVE HIM.
HIS DICK KEEPS POKING MY CERVIX.
HOME AFTER FUCKING. BRIDGET GETS IN. I'M HER HOST WHILE SHE'S IN NYC FOR THE YOUNG DEMOCRATIC SOCIALISTS WINTER CONFERENCE.
ARE YOU IN HIGH SCHOOL?
NO, I'M 24!
WAIT, REALLY? I'M 25. I THOUGHT I WAS TOO OLD FOR THE YDS.
I THINK THE CUT-OFF IS 24.
OH. I'M OLD.
HAHA, YOU'RE NOT OLD!
IT'S OK. AGING HAS BEEN PLEASANT SO FAR. I'M MORE AND MORE COMFORTABLE WITH MYSELF. UNASHAMED TO TELL PEOPLE I LIKE THE BAND WINGS.
WINGS?
BEFORE YOUR TIME.

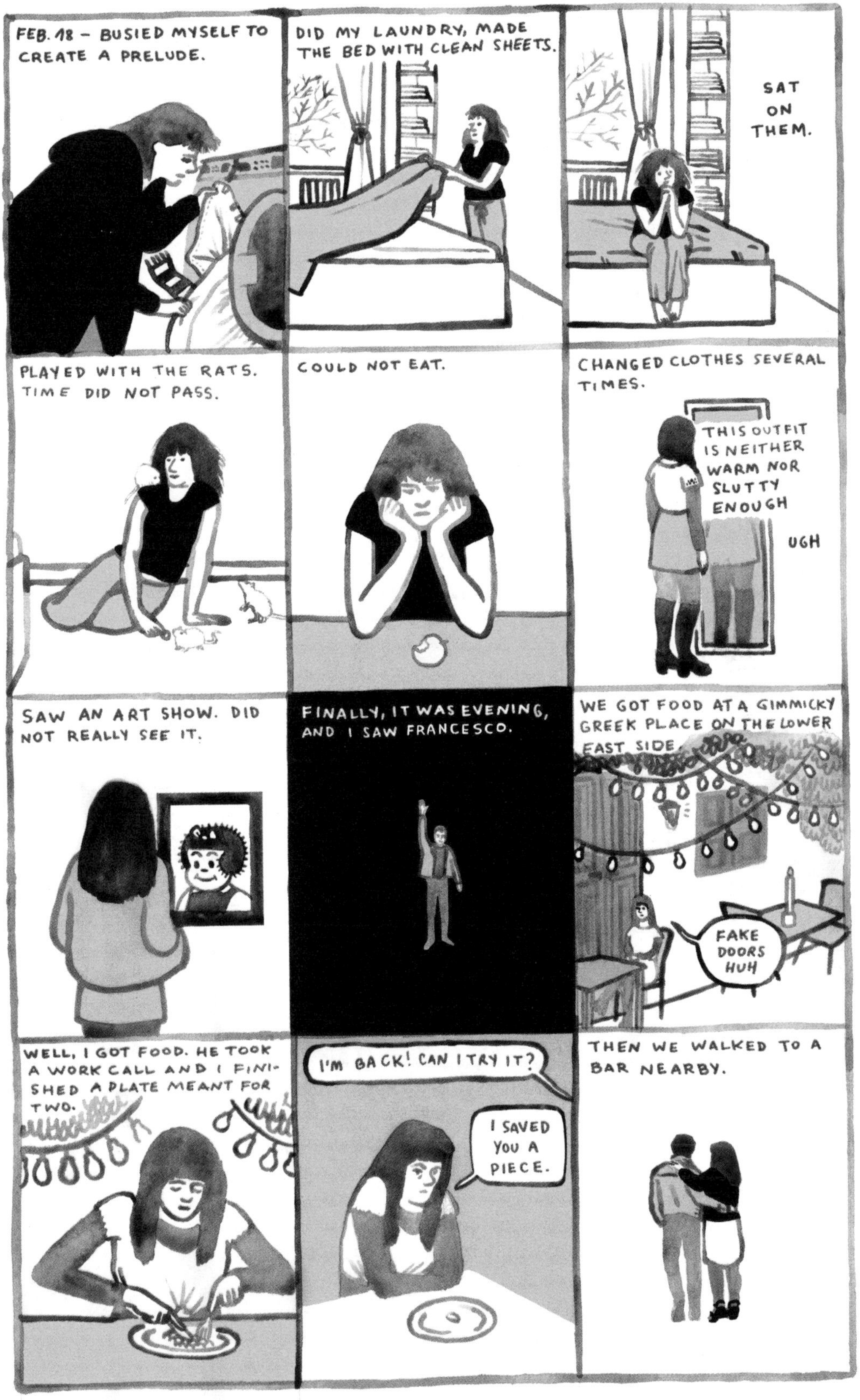
FEB. 18 – BUSIED MYSELF TO CREATE A PRELUDE.
DID MY LAUNDRY, MADE THE BED WITH CLEAN SHEETS.
SAT ON THEM.
PLAYED WITH THE RATS. TIME DID NOT PASS.
COULD NOT EAT.
CHANGED CLOTHES SEVERAL TIMES.
THIS OUTFIT IS NEITHER WARM NOR SLUTTY ENOUGH
UGH
SAW AN ART SHOW. DID NOT REALLY SEE IT.
FINALLY, IT WAS EVENING, AND I SAW FRANCESCO.
WE GOT FOOD AT A GIMMICKY GREEK PLACE ON THE LOWER EAST SIDE.
FAKE DOORS HUH
WELL, I GOT FOOD. HE TOOK A WORK CALL AND I FINI-SHED A PLATE MEANT FOR TWO.
I'M BACK! CAN I TRY IT?
I SAVED YOU A PIECE.
THEN WE WALKED TO A BAR NEARBY.

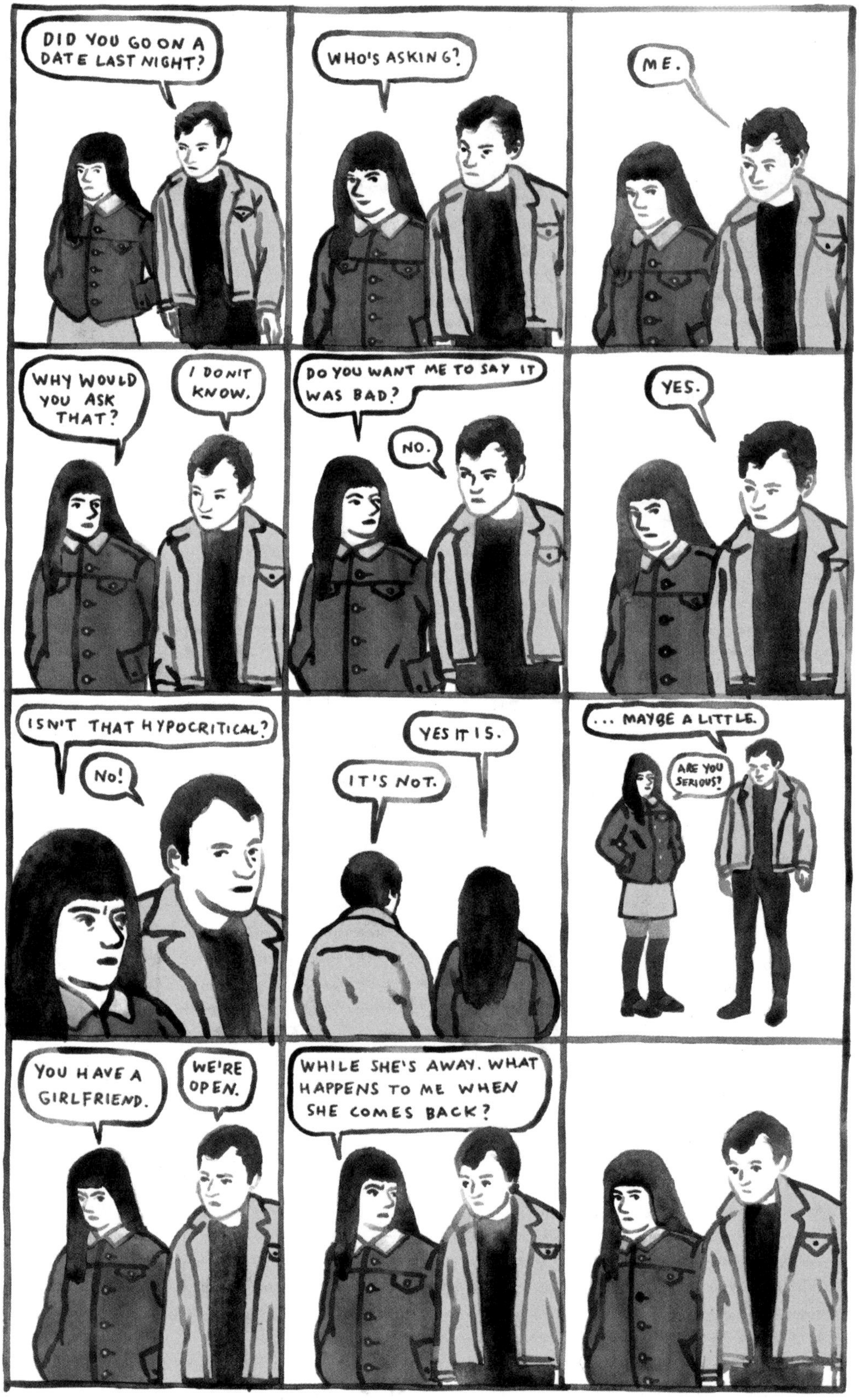
DID YOU GO ON A DATE LAST NIGHT?
WHO'S ASKING?
ME.
WHY WOULD YOU ASK THAT?
I DON'T KNOW.
DO YOU WANT ME TO SAY IT WAS BAD?
NO.
YES.
ISN'T THAT HYPOCRITICAL?
NO!
YES IT IS.
IT'S NOT.
... MAYBE A LITTLE.
ARE YOU SERIOUS?
YOU HAVE A GIRLFRIEND.
WE'RE OPEN.
WHILE SHE'S AWAY. WHAT HAPPENS TO ME WHEN SHE COMES BACK?

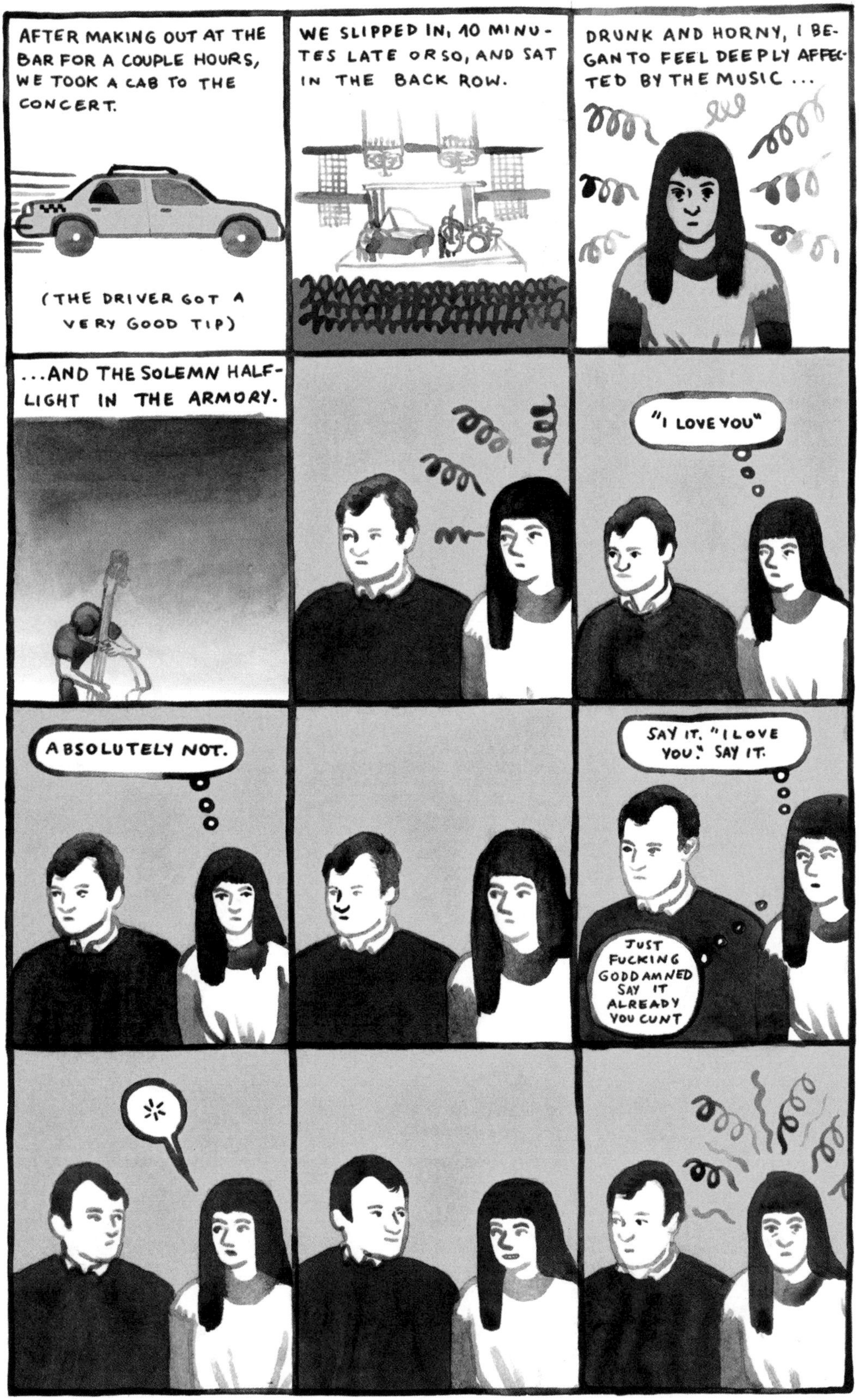
AFTER MAKING OUT AT THE BAR FOR A COUPLE HOURS, WE TOOK A CAB TO THE CONCERT.
(THE DRIVER GOT A VERY GOOD TIP)
WE SLIPPED IN, 10 MINUTES LATE OR SO, AND SAT IN THE BACK ROW.
DRUNK AND HORNY, I BEGAN TO FEEL DEEPLY AFFECTED BY THE MUSIC ...
...AND THE SOLEMN HALF-LIGHT IN THE ARMORY.
"I LOVE YOU"
ABSOLUTELY NOT.
SAY IT. "I LOVE YOU." SAY IT.
JUST FUCKING GODDAMNED SAY IT ALREADY YOU CUNT

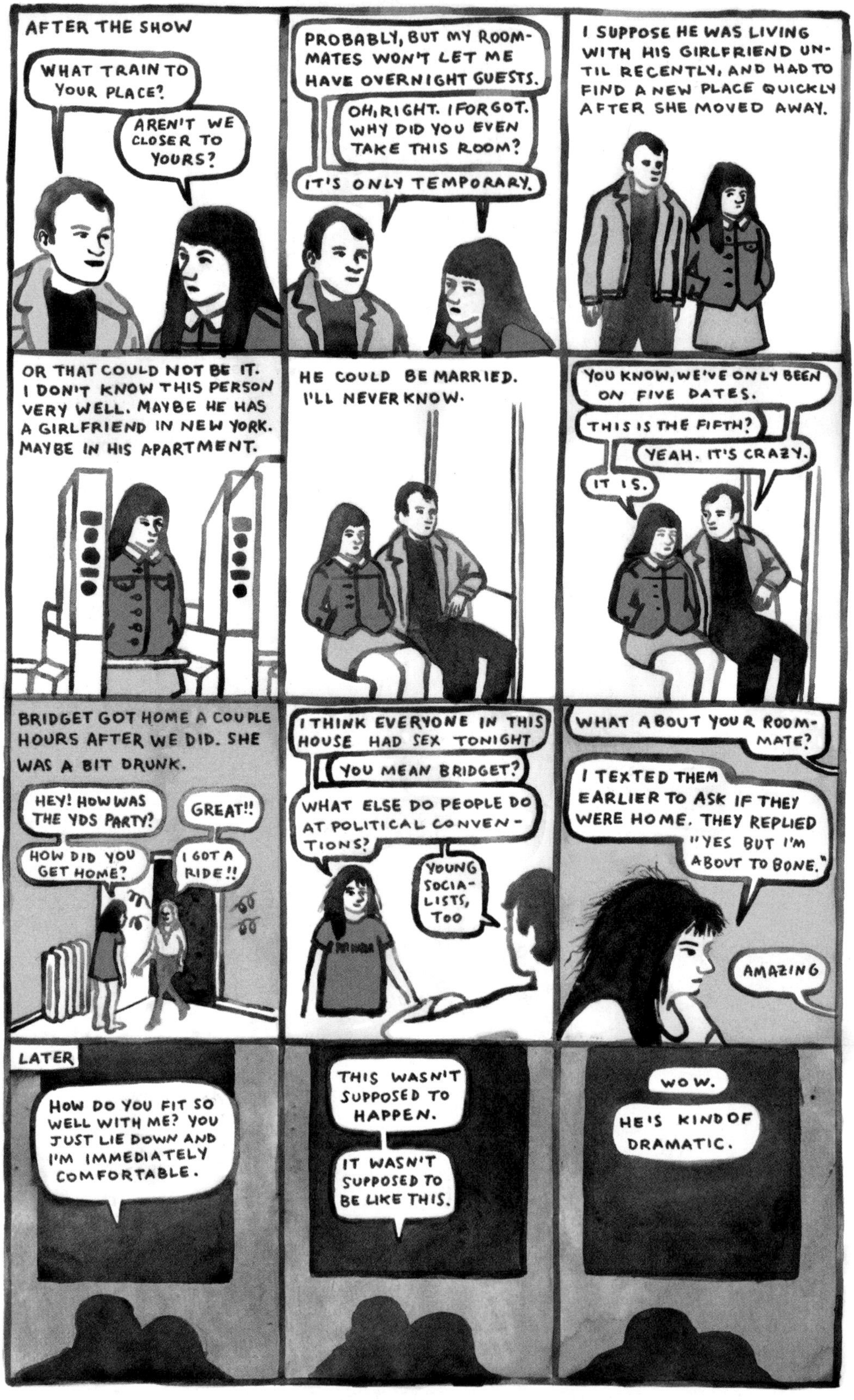

AFTER THE SHOW
WHAT TRAIN TO YOUR PLACE?
AREN'T WE CLOSER TO YOURS?
PROBABLY, BUT MY ROOMMATES WON'T LET ME HAVE OVERNIGHT GUESTS.
OH, RIGHT. I FORGOT. WHY DID YOU EVEN TAKE THIS ROOM?
IT'S ONLY TEMPORARY.
I SUPPOSE HE WAS LIVING WITH HIS GIRLFRIEND UNTIL RECENTLY, AND HAD TO FIND A NEW PLACE QUICKLY AFTER SHE MOVED AWAY.
OR THAT COULD NOT BE IT. I DON'T KNOW THIS PERSON VERY WELL. MAYBE HE HAS A GIRLFRIEND IN NEW YORK. MAYBE IN HIS APARTMENT.
HE COULD BE MARRIED. I'LL NEVER KNOW.
YOU KNOW, WE'VE ONLY BEEN ON FIVE DATES.
THIS IS THE FIFTH?
YEAH. IT'S CRAZY.
IT IS.
BRIDGET GOT HOME A COUPLE HOURS AFTER WE DID. SHE WAS A BIT DRUNK.
HEY! HOW WAS THE YDS PARTY?
GREAT!!
HOW DID YOU GET HOME?
I GOT A RIDE!!
I THINK EVERYONE IN THIS HOUSE HAD SEX TONIGHT
YOU MEAN BRIDGET?
WHAT ELSE DO PEOPLE DO AT POLITICAL CONVENTIONS?
YOUNG SOCIALISTS, TOO
WHAT ABOUT YOUR ROOMMATE?
I TEXTED THEM EARLIER TO ASK IF THEY WERE HOME. THEY REPLIED "YES BUT I'M ABOUT TO BONE."
AMAZING
LATER
HOW DO YOU FIT SO WELL WITH ME? YOU JUST LIE DOWN AND I'M IMMEDIATELY COMFORTABLE.
THIS WASN'T SUPPOSED TO HAPPEN.
IT WASN'T SUPPOSED TO BE LIKE THIS.
WOW.
HE'S KIND OF DRAMATIC.

Hurt or Fuck

ELEANOR DAVIS

originally published in

Now #1
FANTAGRAPHICS BOOKS
7.25 x 10.125 inches • 128 pages

Biography

Eleanor Davis is a cartoonist and illustrator. Her books include *How to Be Happy* (Fantagraphics, 2014), *You and a Bike and a Road* (Koyama Press, 2017), *Why Art?* (Fantagraphics, 2018), and the upcoming *The Hard Tomorrow* (Drawn and Quarterly, Fall 2019). She lives in Athens, Georgia, with her husband, fellow cartoonist Drew Weing.
doing-fine.com

Statement

I wrote this comic while brainstorming what to say in a keynote speech I had been invited to give at ICON, an illustration conference. I was thinking about some of the reasons people make art, and the risks inherent in making art, and in making human connections. It turned into a love story because most of my comics turn into love stories. (The final keynote speech I wound up giving at ICON turned into my small book *Why Art?*)

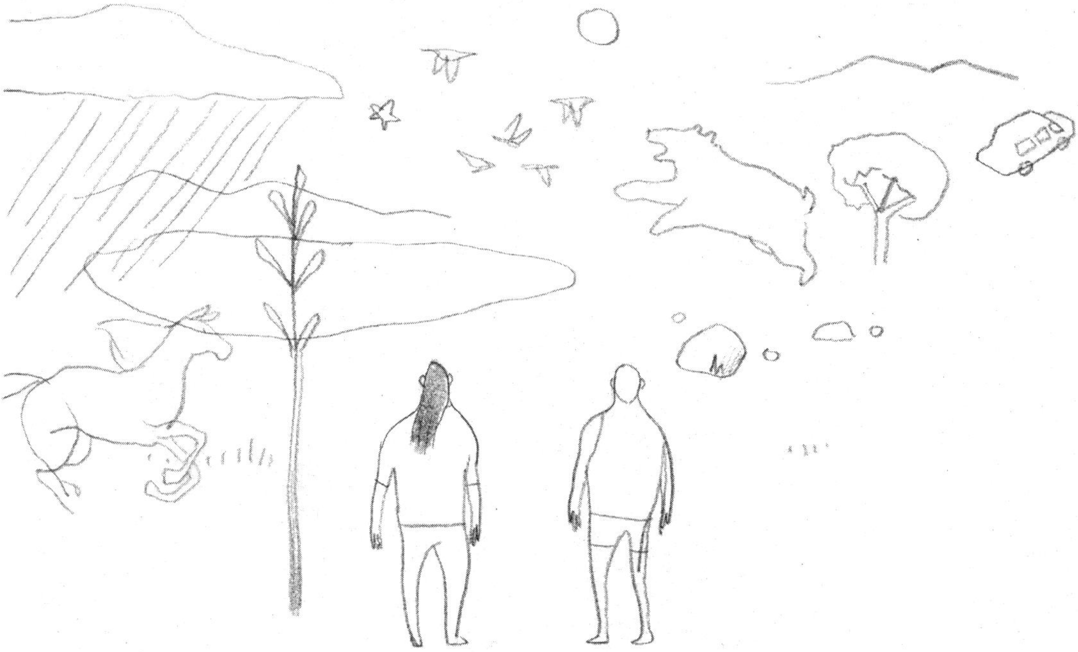

HURT OR FUCK

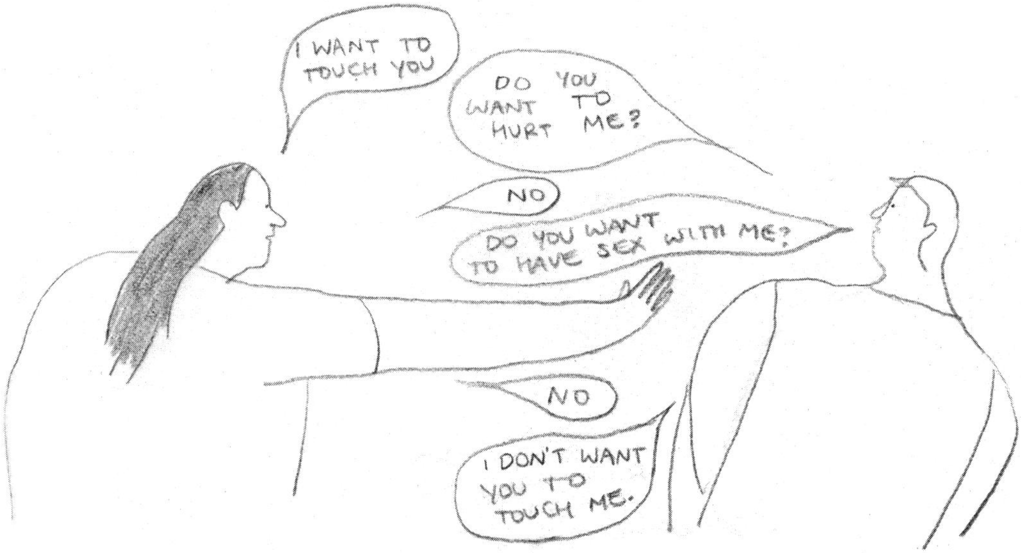
I WANT TO TOUCH YOU
DO YOU WANT TO HURT ME?
NO
DO YOU WANT TO HAVE SEX WITH ME?
NO
I DON'T WANT YOU TO TOUCH ME.

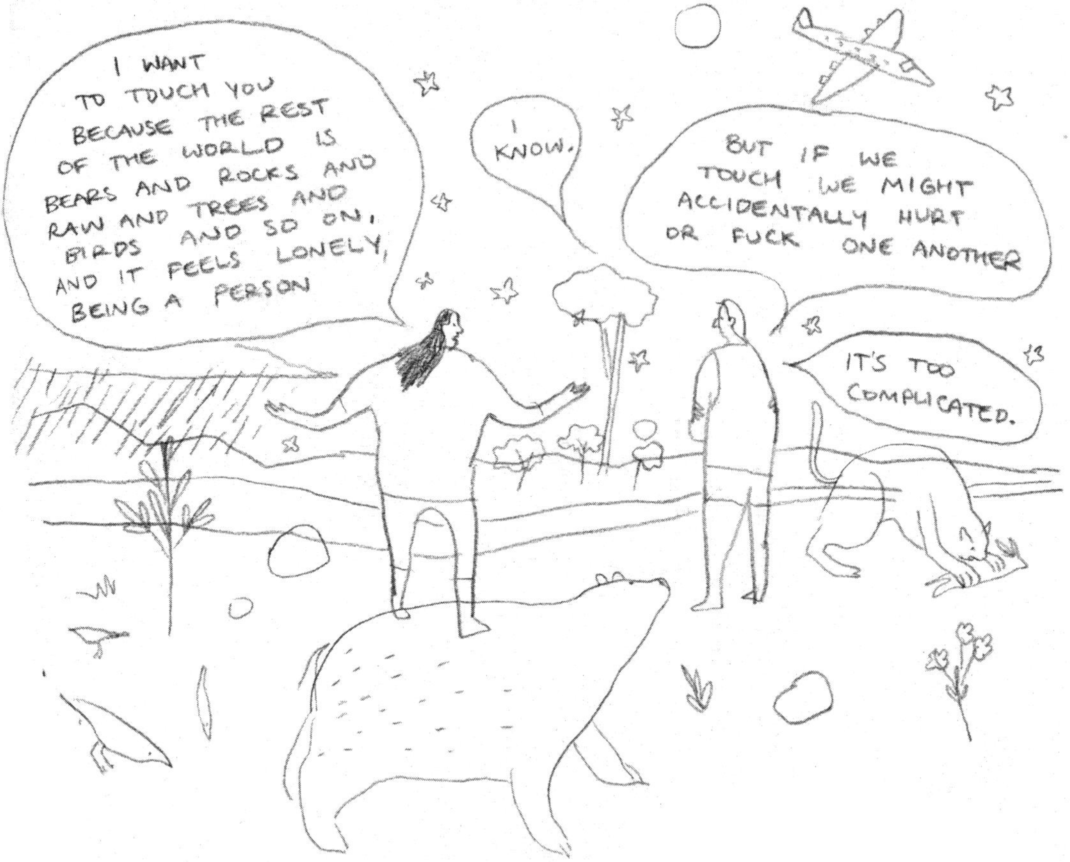
I WANT TO TOUCH YOU BECAUSE THE REST OF THE WORLD IS BEARS AND ROCKS AND RAIN AND TREES AND BIRDS AND SO ON, AND IT FEELS LONELY, BEING A PERSON
I KNOW.
BUT IF WE TOUCH WE MIGHT ACCIDENTALLY HURT OR FUCK ONE ANOTHER
IT'S TOO COMPLICATED.

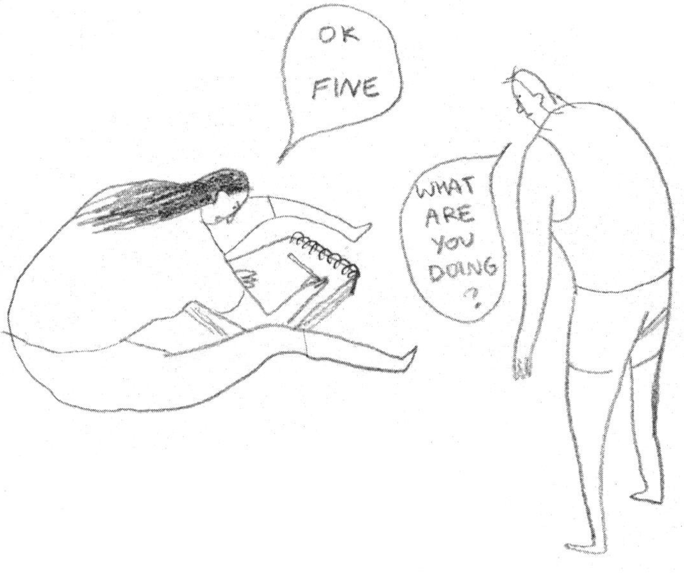
OK FINE
WHAT ARE YOU DOING ?

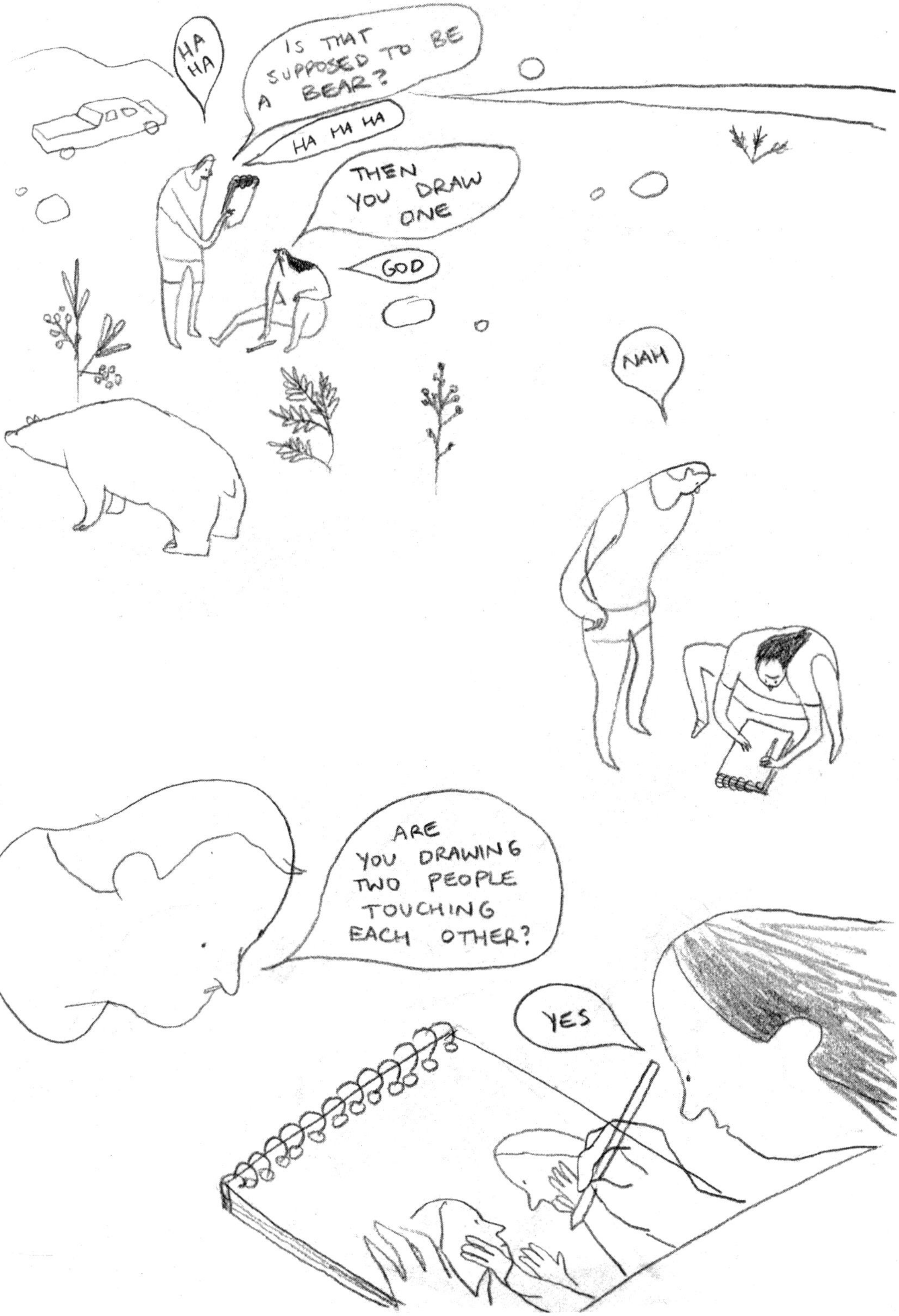
HA HA
IS THAT SUPPOSED TO BE A BEAR?
HA HA HA
THEN YOU DRAW ONE
GOD
NAH
ARE YOU DRAWING TWO PEOPLE TOUCHING EACH OTHER?
YES

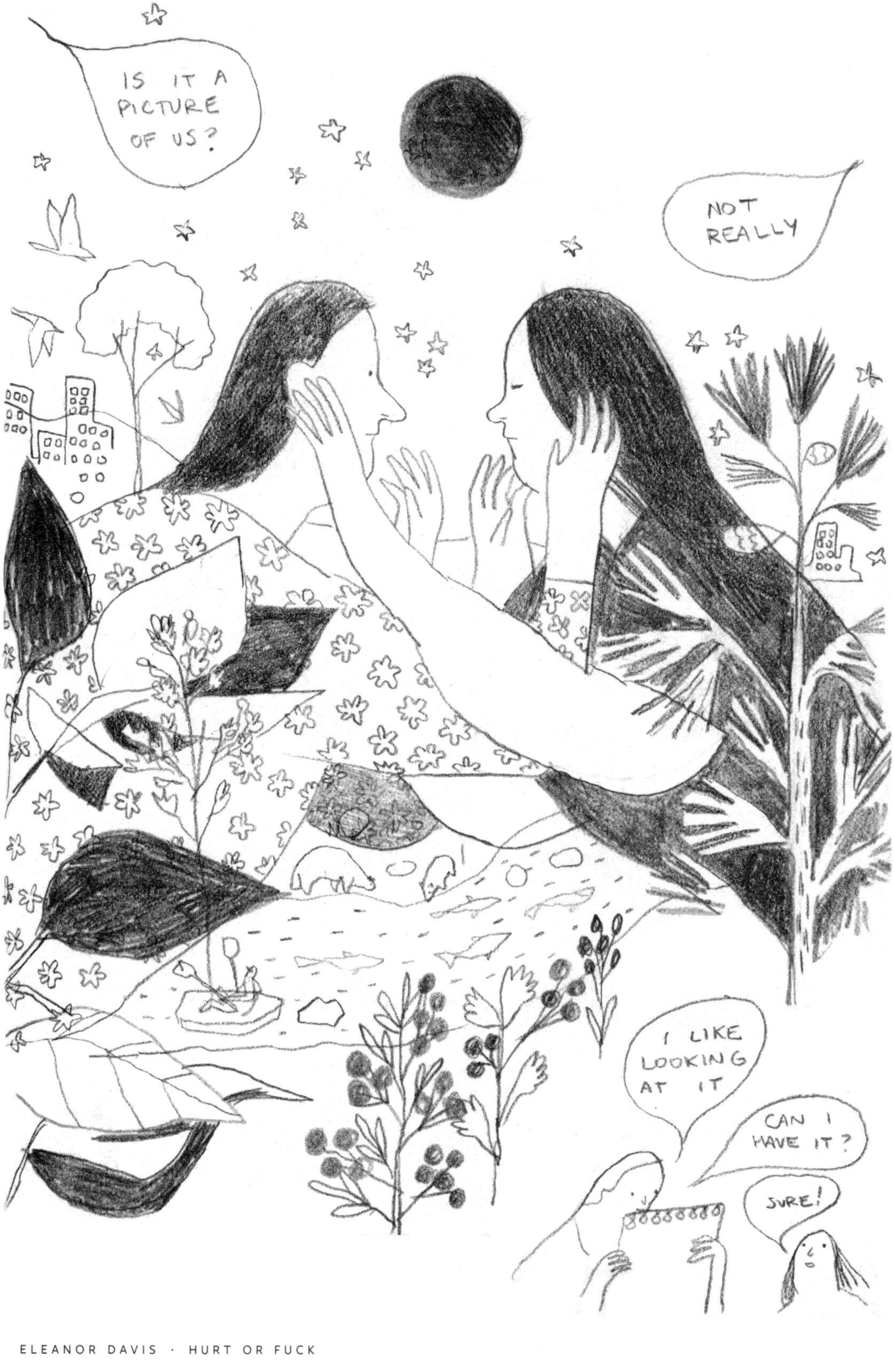
IS IT A PICTURE OF US?
NOT REALLY
I LIKE LOOKING AT IT
CAN I HAVE IT?
SURE!

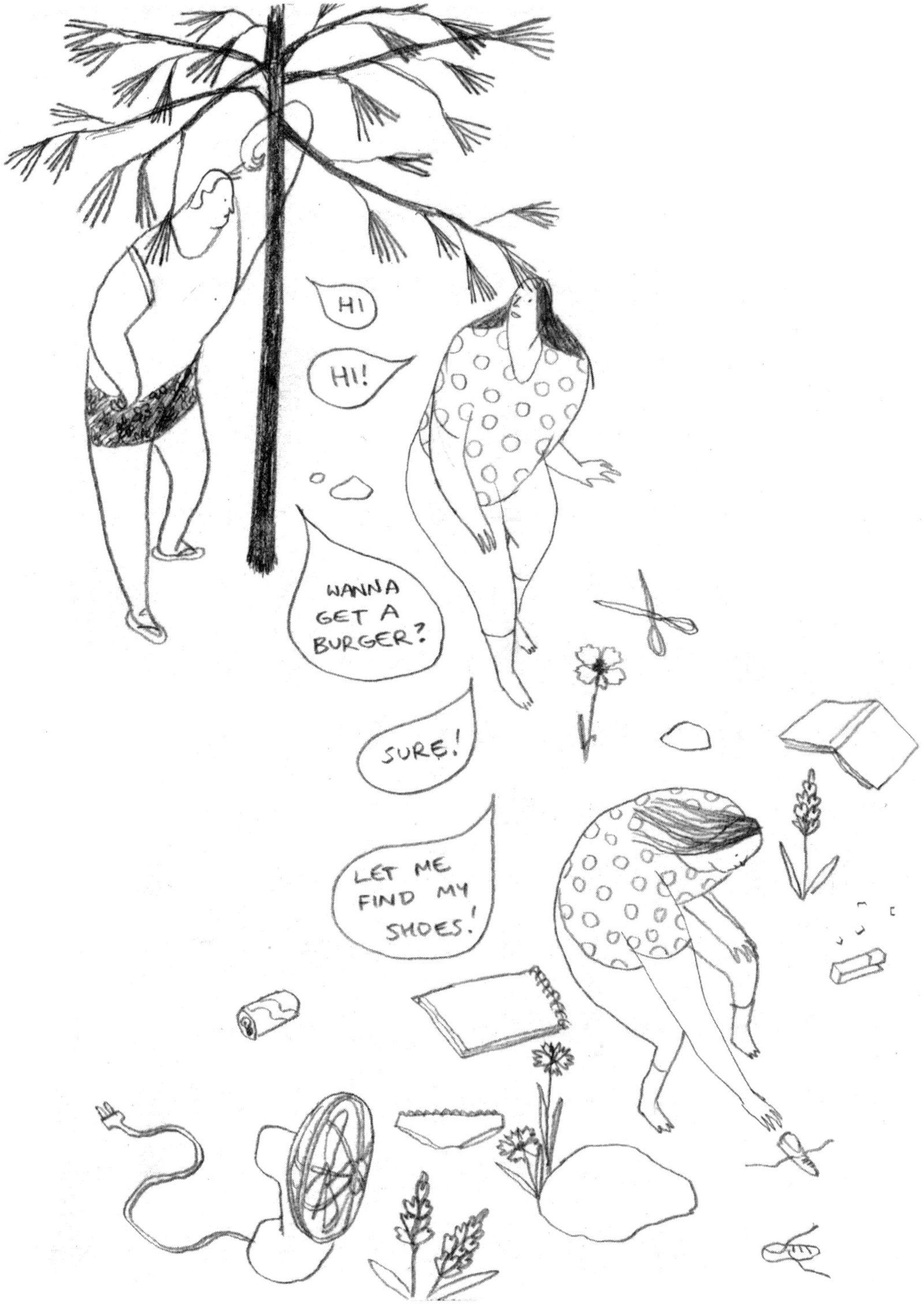
HI
HI!
WANNA GET A BURGER?
SURE!
LET ME FIND MY SHOES!

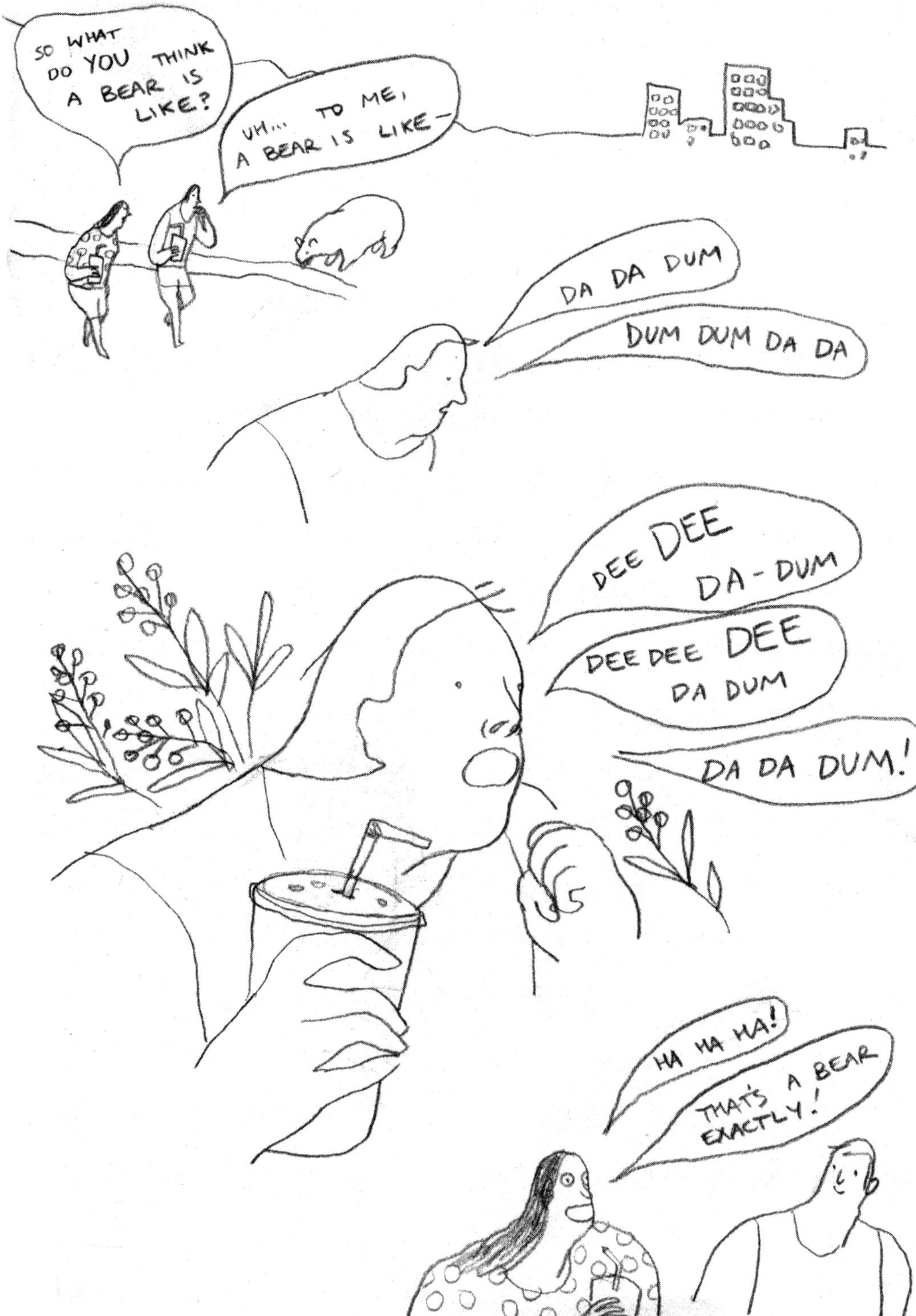
SO WHAT DO YOU THINK A BEAR IS LIKE?
UH... TO ME, A BEAR IS LIKE—
DA DA DUM
DUM DUM DA DA
DEE DEE DA-DUM
DEE DEE DEE DA DUM
DA DA DUM!
HA HA HA!
THAT'S A BEAR EXACTLY!

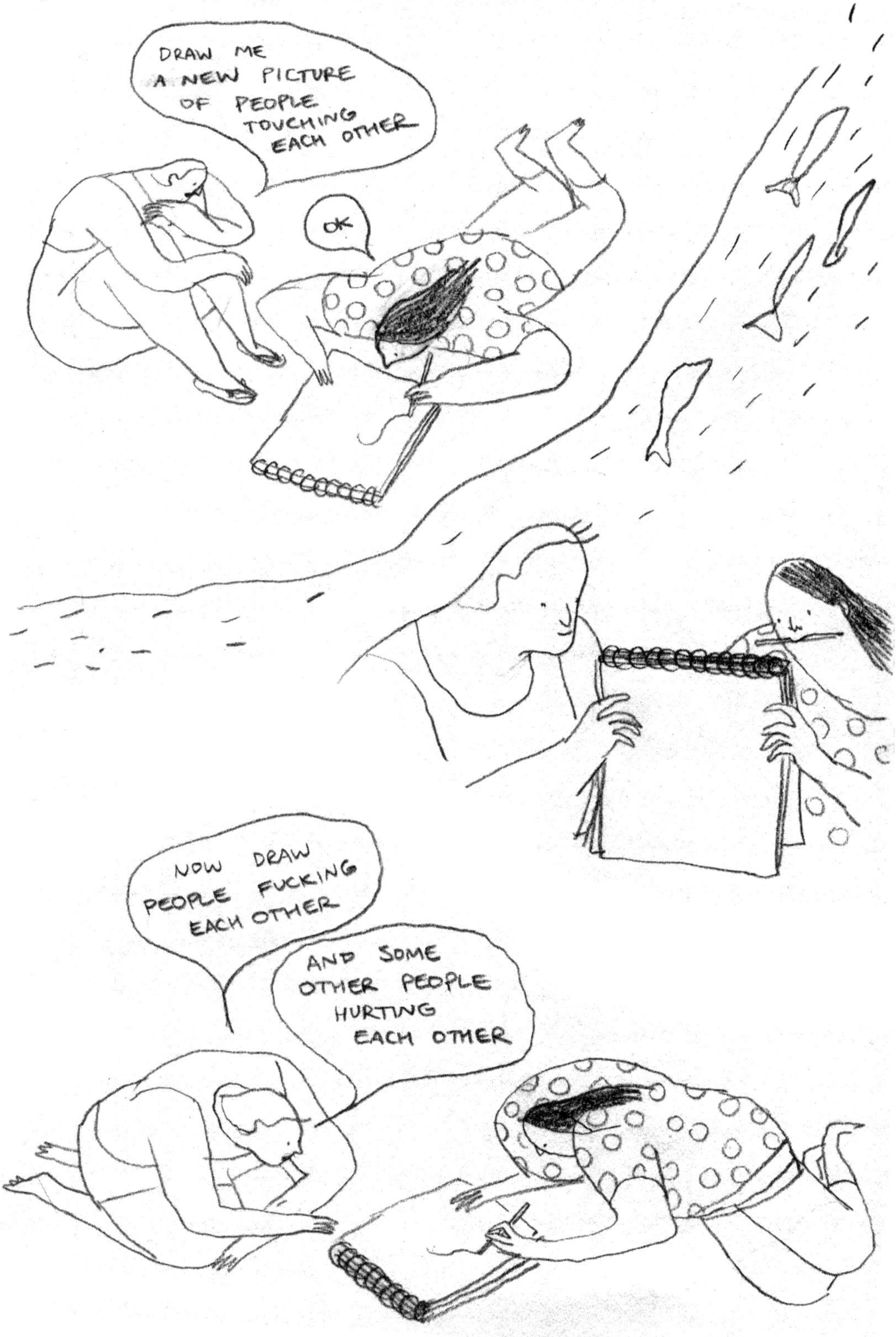
DRAW ME
A NEW PICTURE
OF PEOPLE
TOUCHING
EACH OTHER
OK
NOW DRAW
PEOPLE FUCKING
EACH OTHER
AND SOME
OTHER PEOPLE
HURTING
EACH OTHER

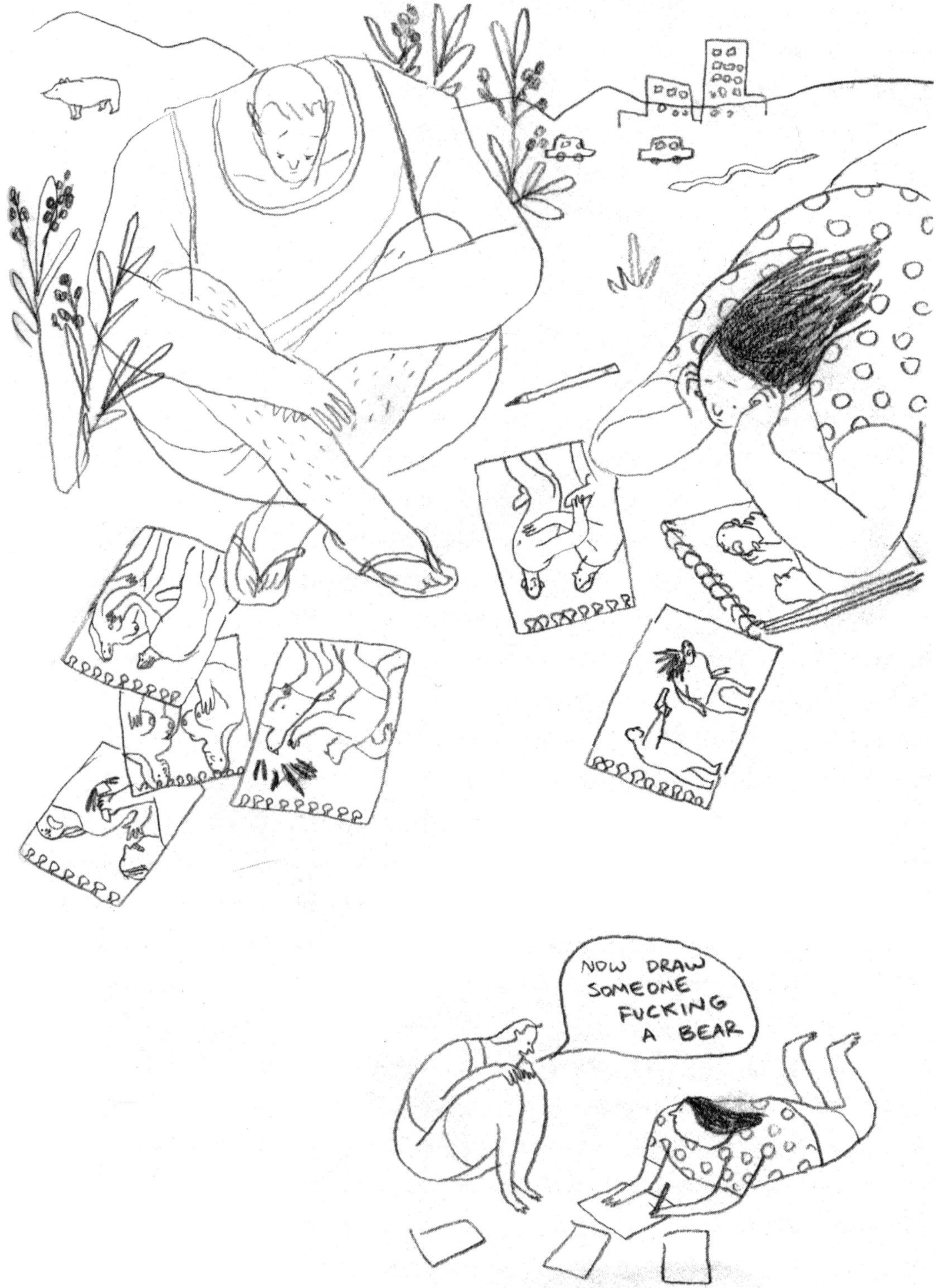
NOW DRAW SOMEONE FUCKING A BEAR

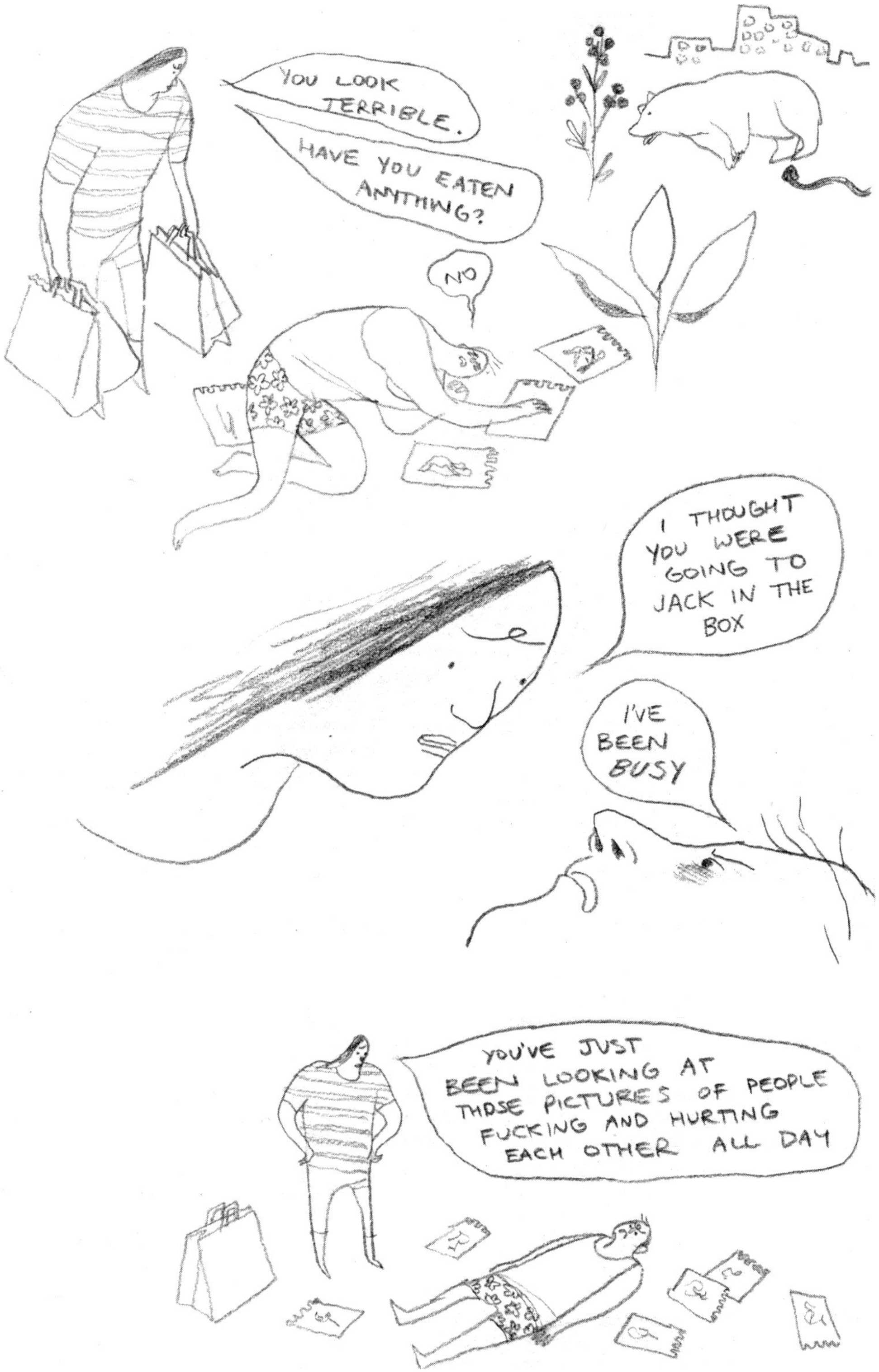
YOU LOOK TERRIBLE.
HAVE YOU EATEN ANYTHING?
NO
I THOUGHT YOU WERE GOING TO JACK IN THE BOX
I'VE BEEN BUSY
YOU'VE JUST BEEN LOOKING AT THOSE PICTURES OF PEOPLE FUCKING AND HURTING EACH OTHER ALL DAY

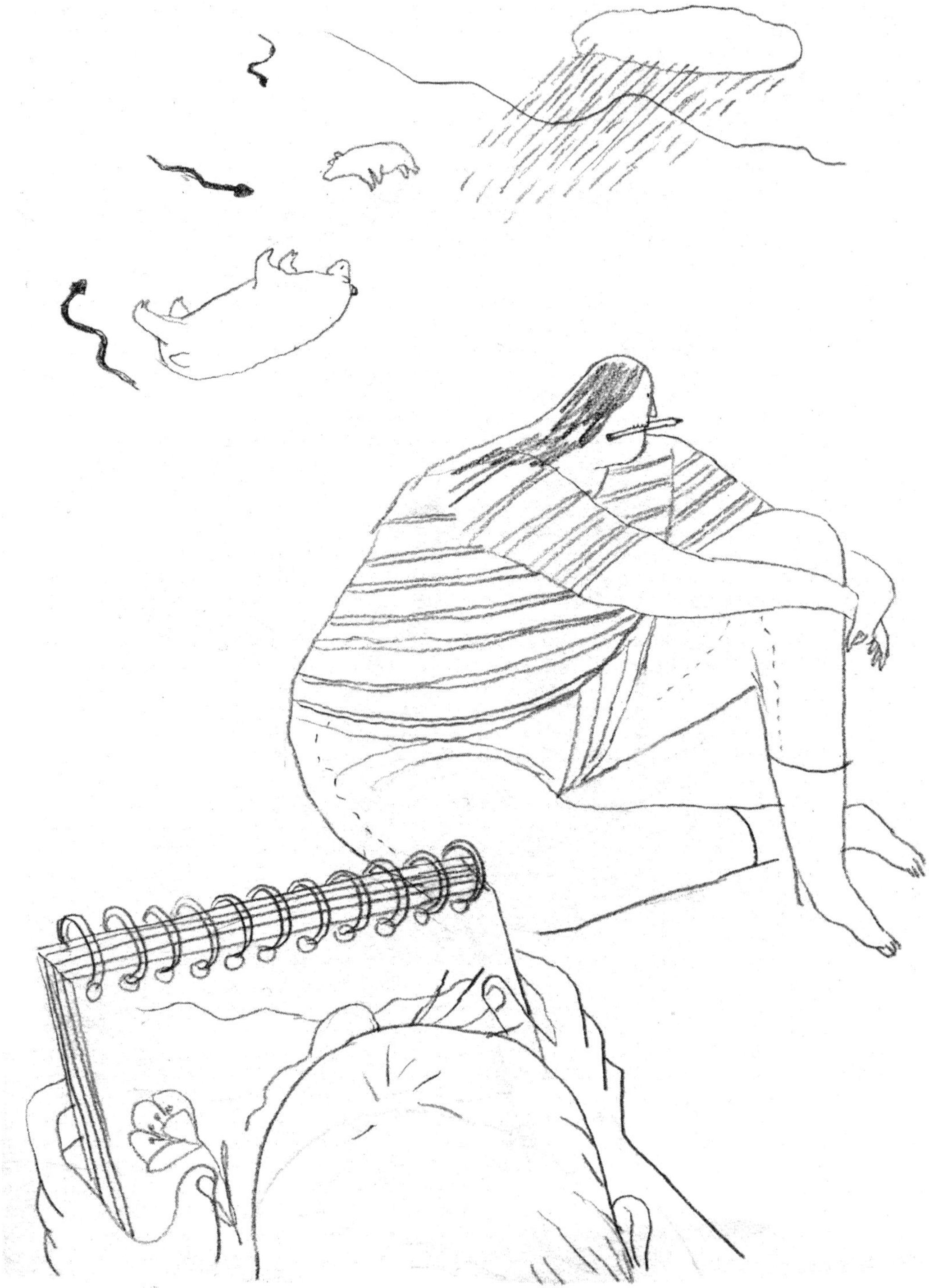

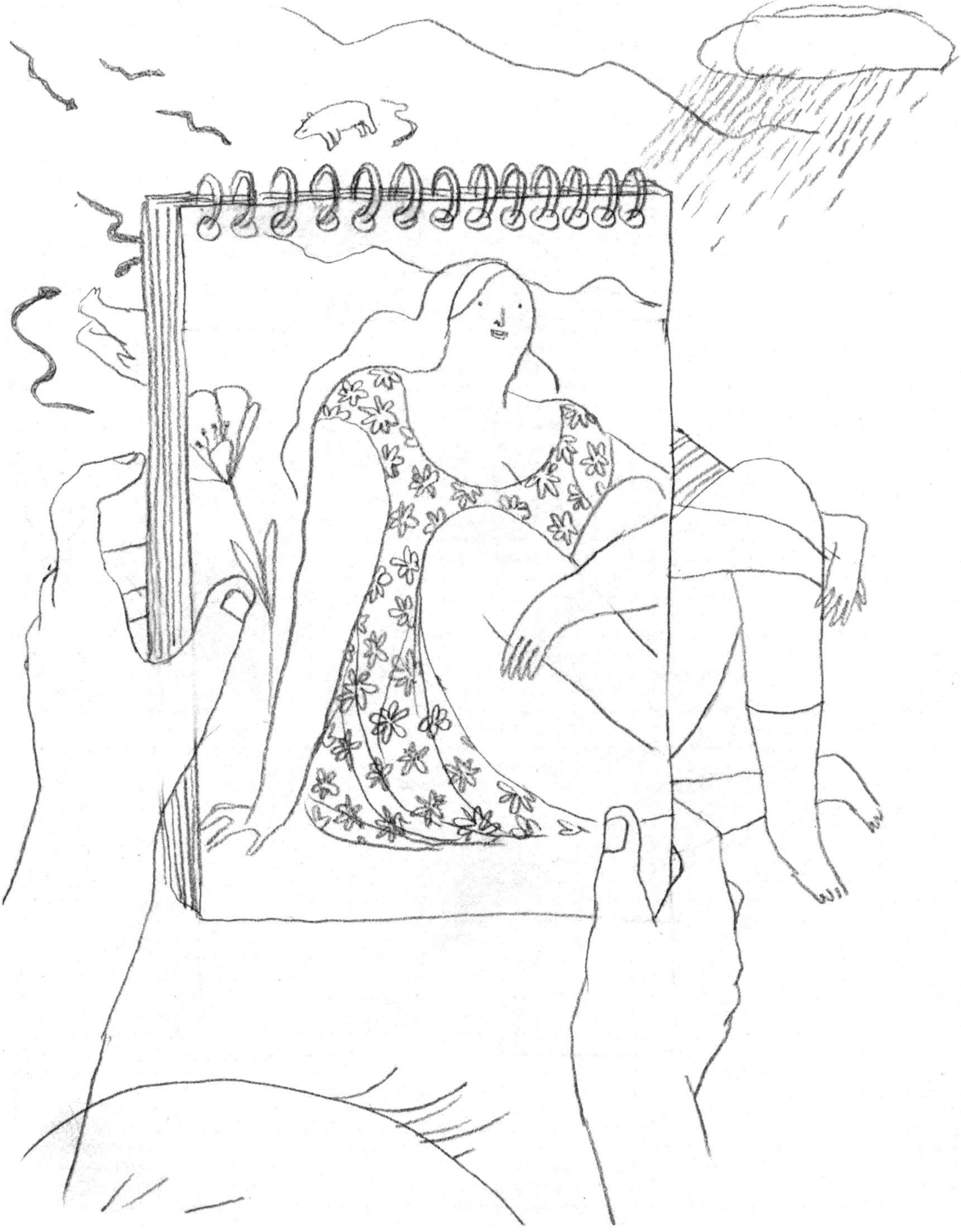

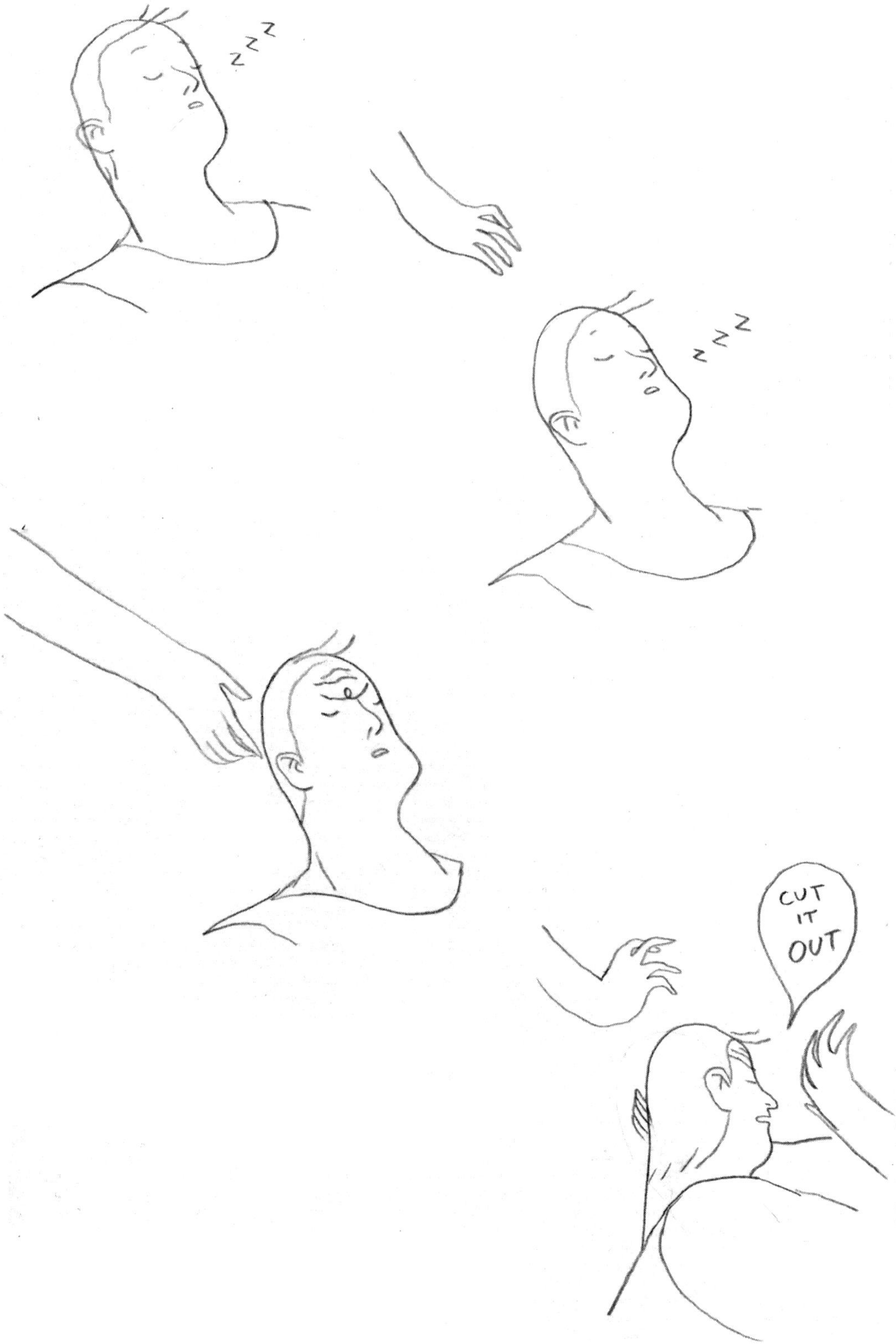
Z Z Z
Z Z Z
CUT IT OUT

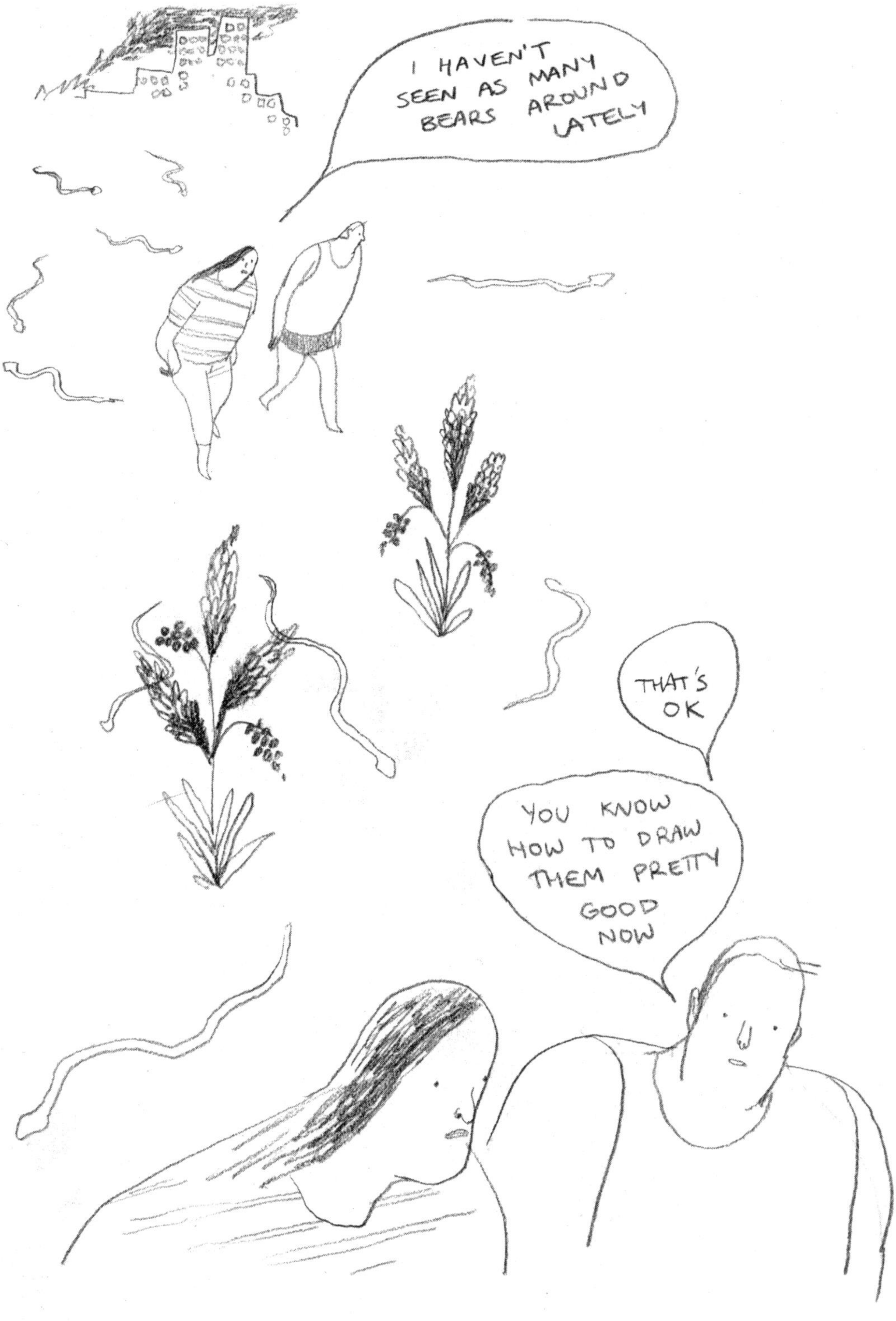
I HAVEN'T SEEN AS MANY BEARS AROUND LATELY
THAT'S OK
YOU KNOW HOW TO DRAW THEM PRETTY GOOD NOW

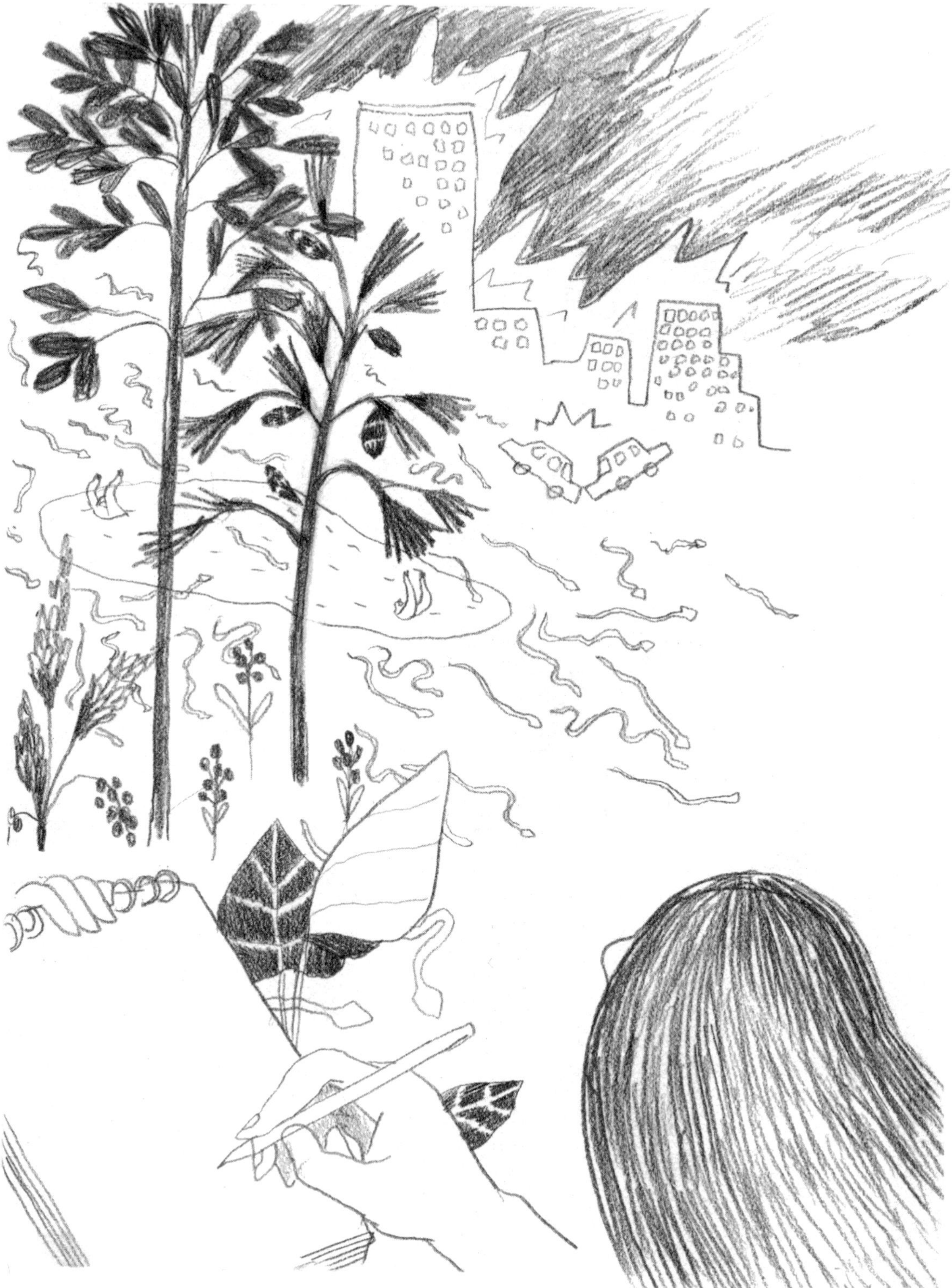

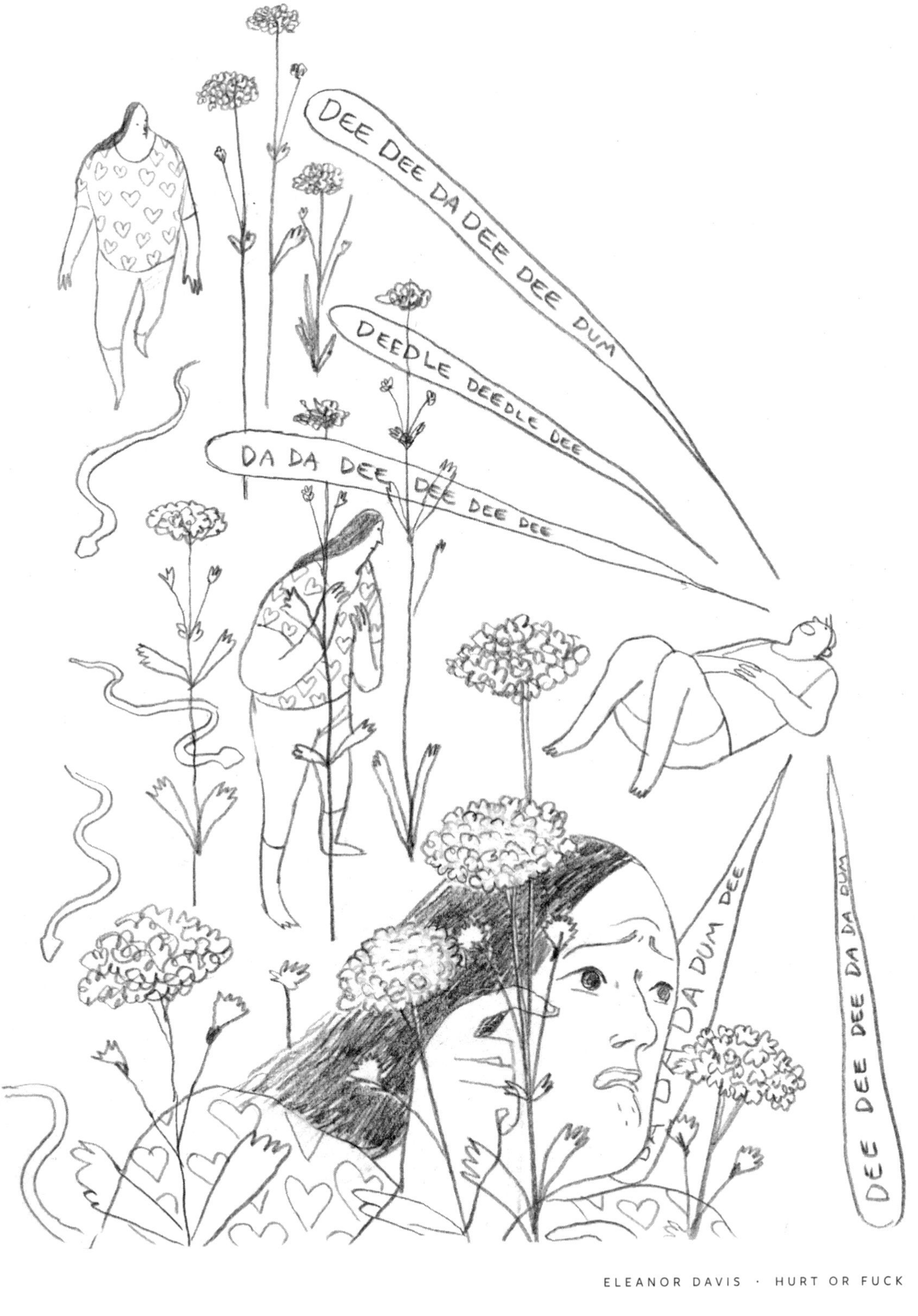
DEE DEE DA DEE DEE DEE DUM
DEEDLE DEEDLE DEE
DA DA DEE DEE DEE DEE
DA DA DUM DEE
DEE DEE DEE DEE DA DA DUM

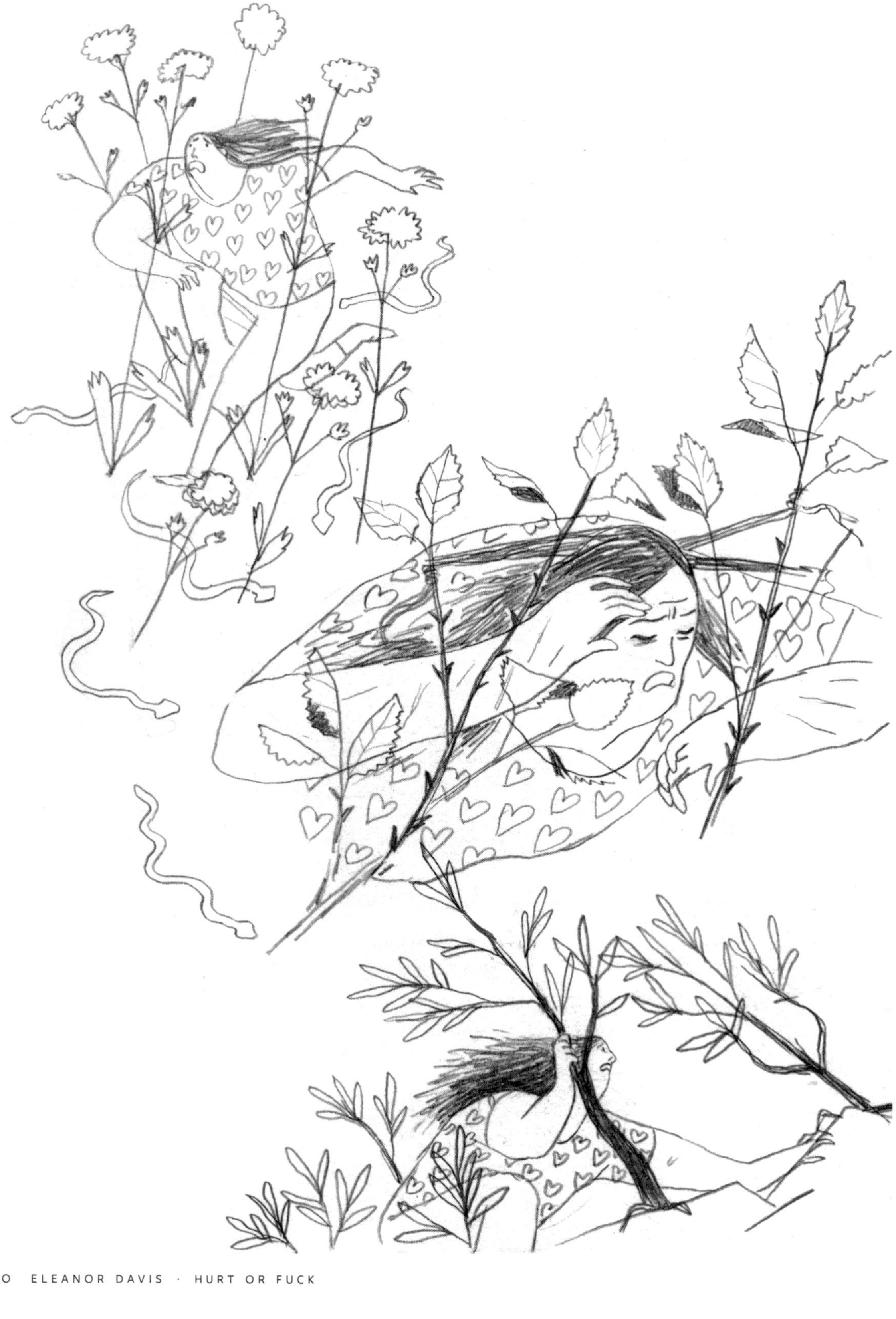

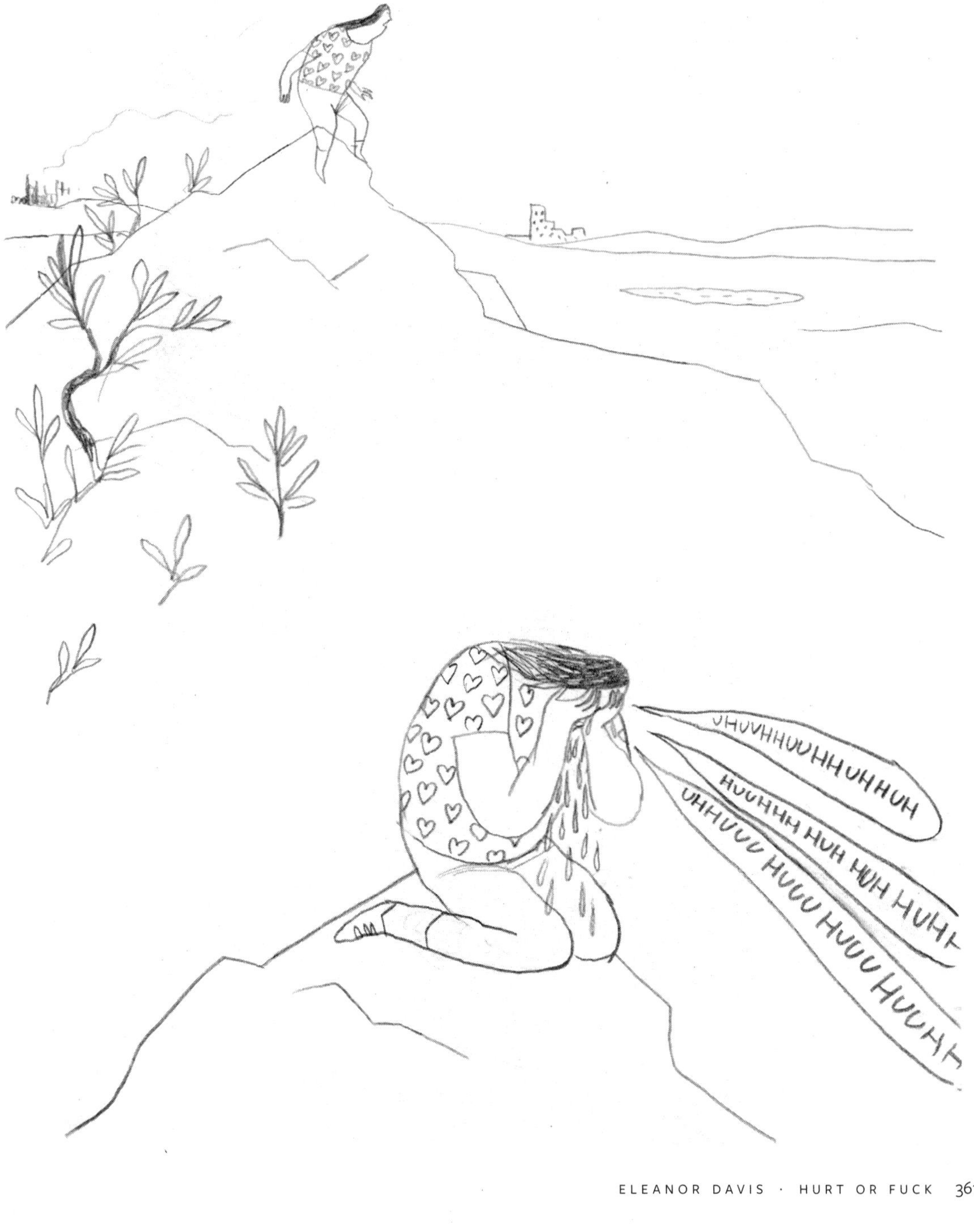
UHUVHHUUHHUHHUH
HUUHHH HUH HUH HUH
UHHUUU HUUU HUUU HUUH

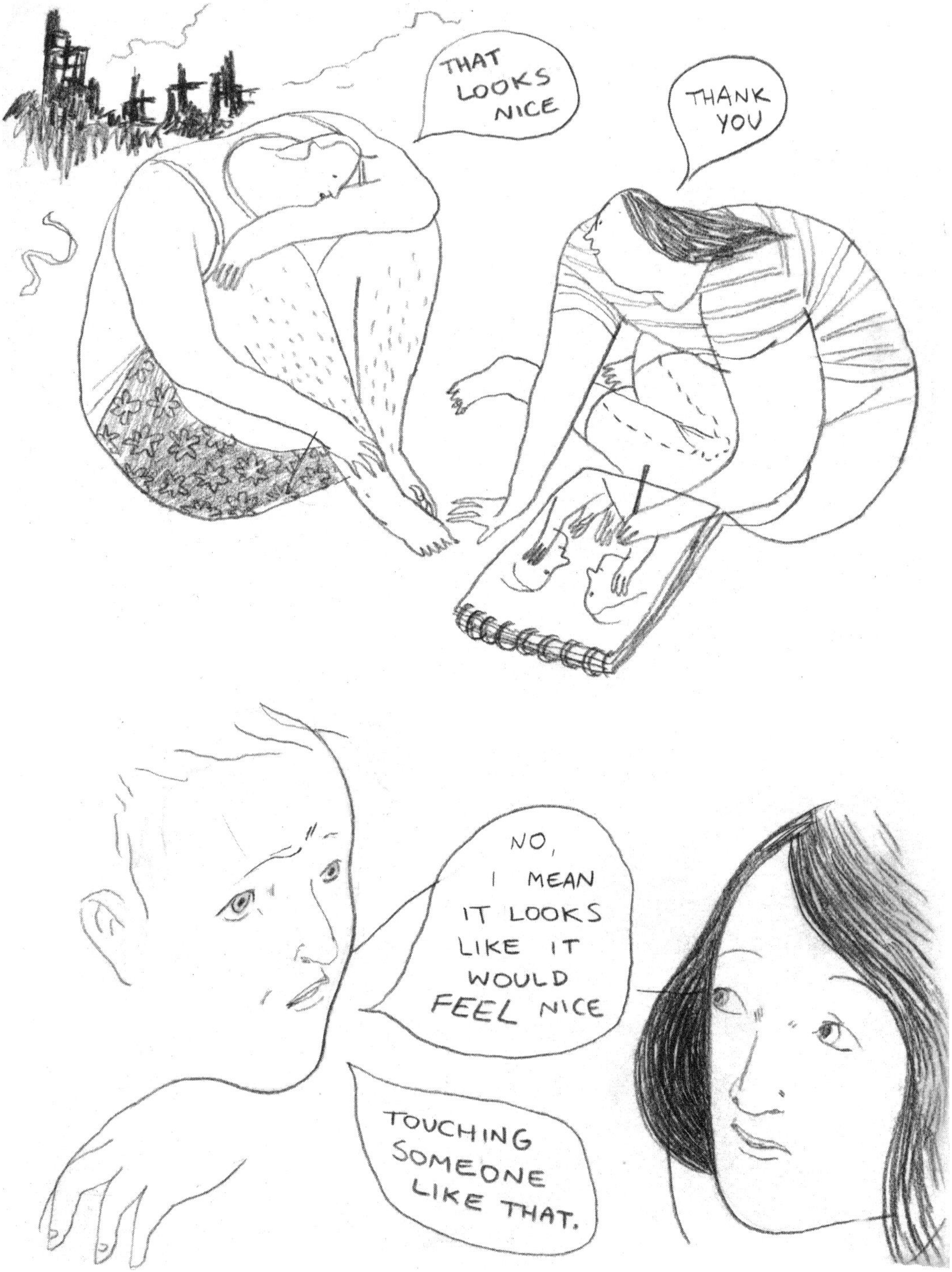
THAT LOOKS NICE
THANK YOU
NO, I MEAN IT LOOKS LIKE IT WOULD FEEL NICE
TOUCHING SOMEONE LIKE THAT.

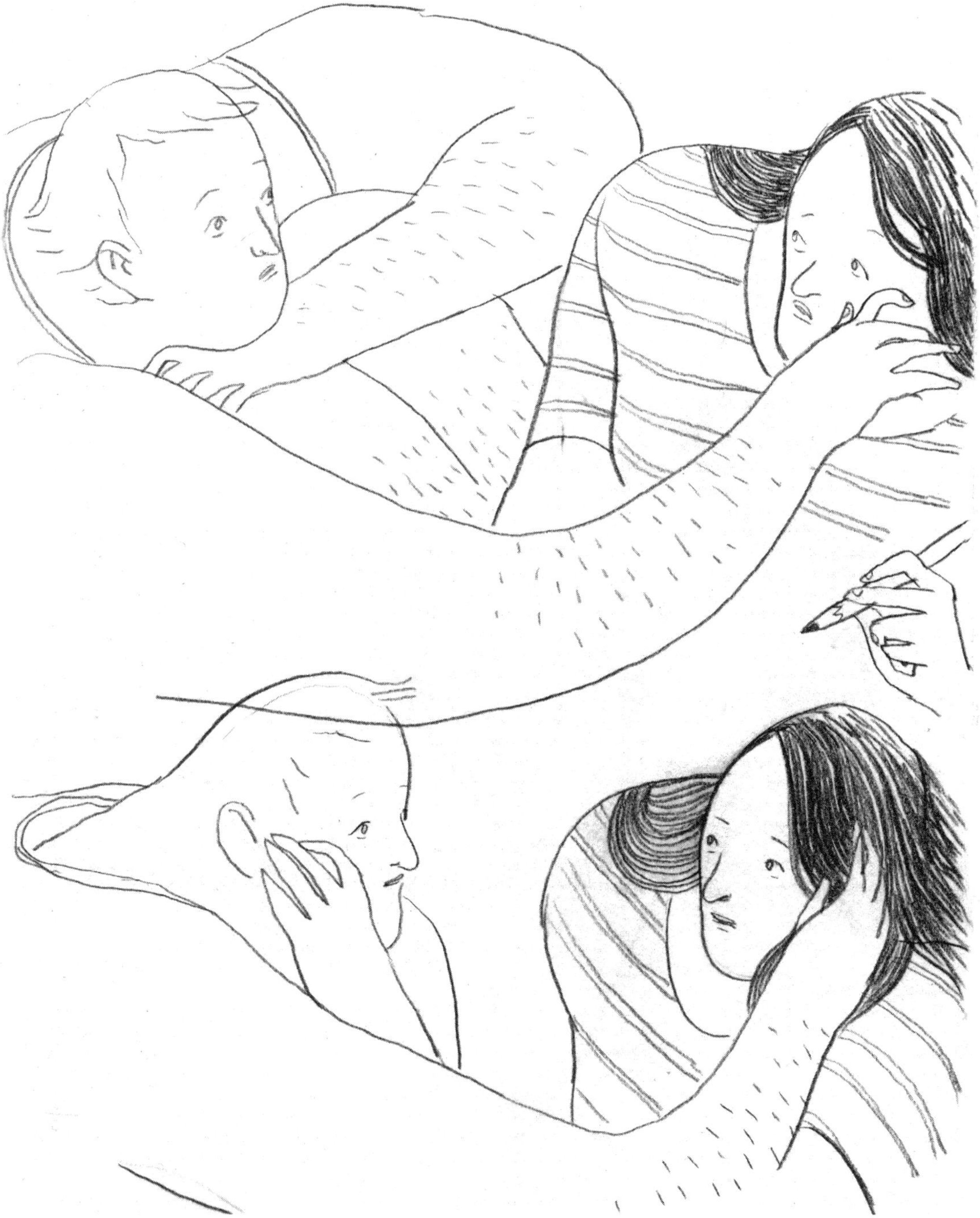

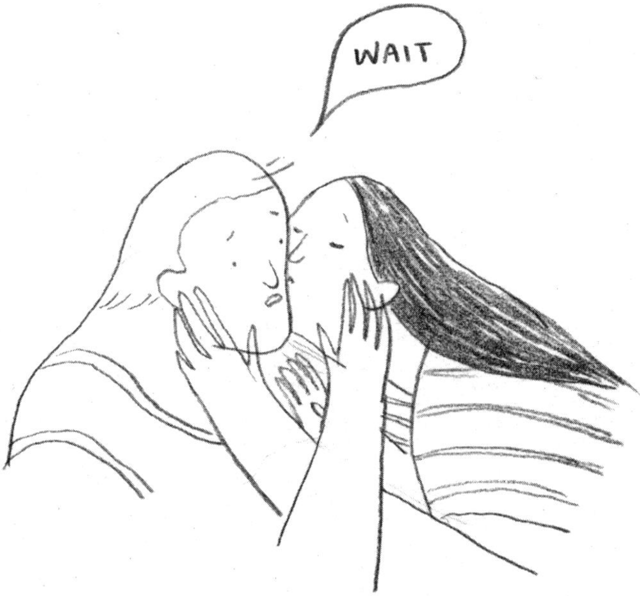
WAIT

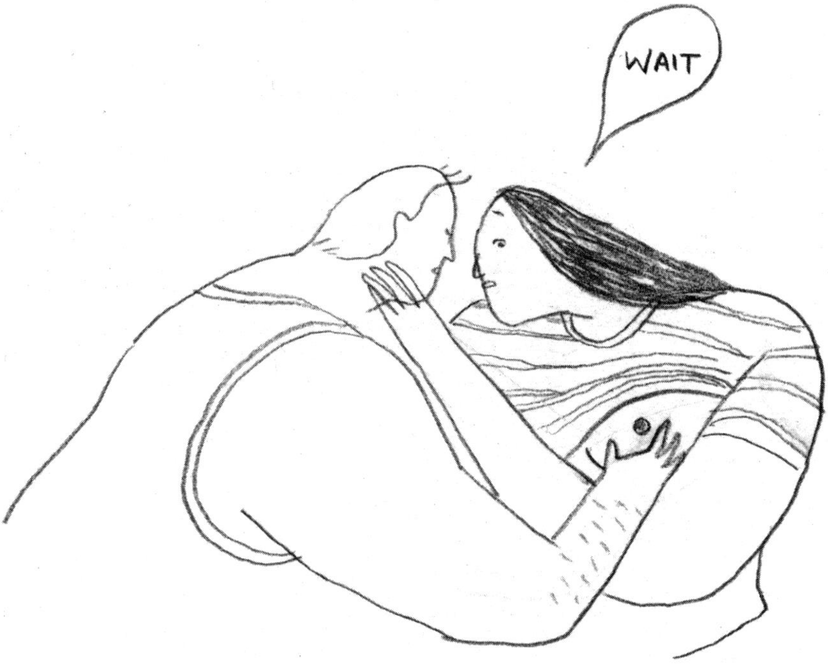
WAIT

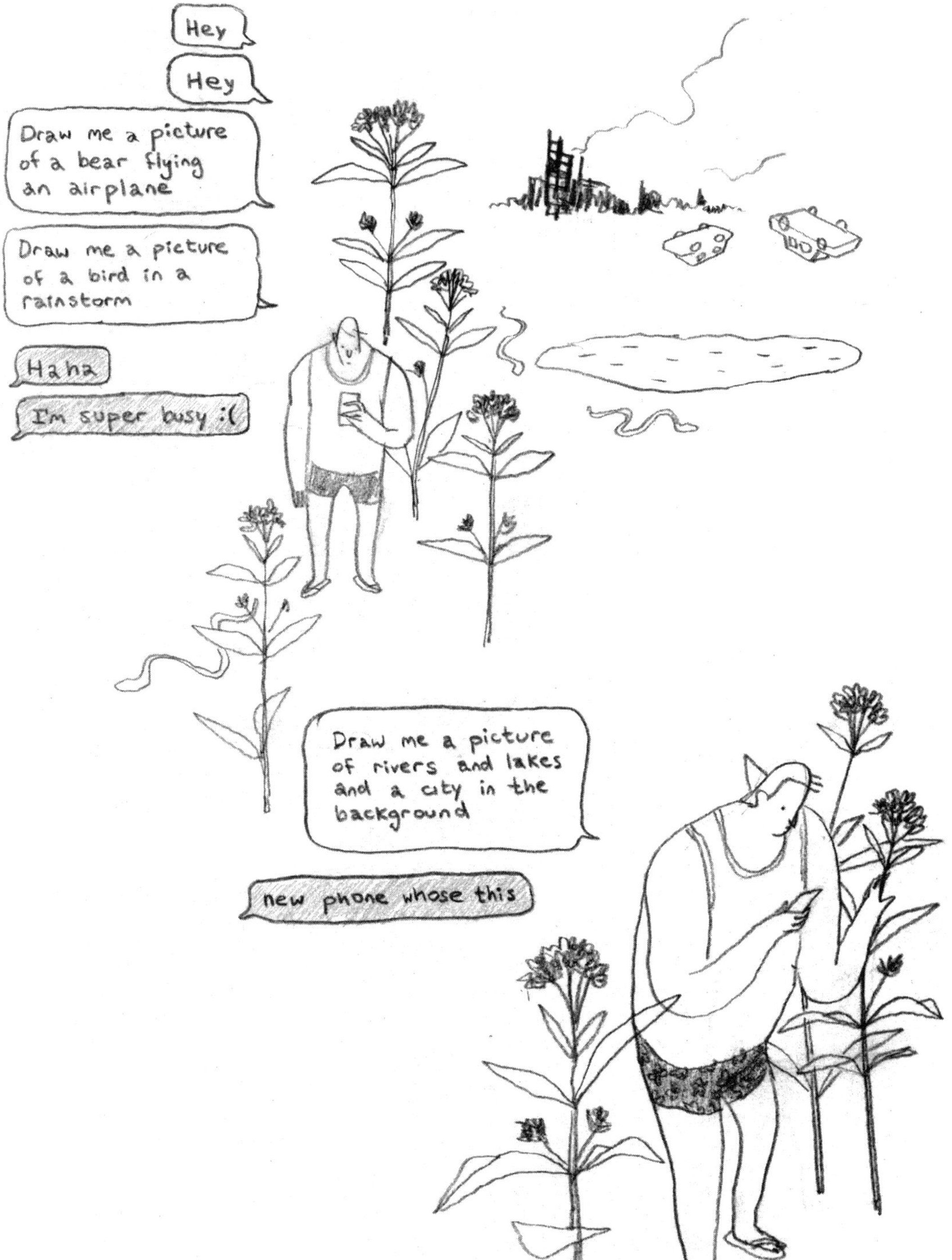
Hey
Hey
Draw me a picture of a bear flying an airplane
Draw me a picture of a bird in a rainstorm
Haha
I'm super busy :(
Draw me a picture of rivers and lakes and a city in the background
new phone whose this

With people swimming
in the rivers

I want to look at
your picture of that

wrong number sorry

Notable Comics

from September 1, 2017, to August 31, 2018

Selected by Bill Kartalopoulos

CHRISTOPHER ADAMS
  Gustave Flaubert: Trois Contes.

AEON MUTE
  Untitled.
  The Beginning.

DEREK M. BALLARD
  Choreograph, Volume One.

JOSH BAYER
  RM.

GABRIELLE BELL
  Were We Dating?
  medium.com/spiralbound

ALYSSA BERG
  No Man Is an Island.

BRIAN BLOMERTH
  Alphabet Junction.
  vice.com

JENNIFER CAMPER
  Boys Will Be Boys.
  The Believer #118.

EMILY CARROLL &
LAURIE HALSE ANDERSON
  Speak.

GENEVIÈVE CASTRÉE
  A Bubble.

ANGELA CHEN
  Diary comics.
  instagram.com/angelafanche2

CHRIS CILLA
  Blue Onion #1.

JORDAN CRANE
  Keeping Two, Part Six.

FAREL DALRYMPLE
  Proxima Centauri #1–3.

MICHAEL DEFORGE
  Rhode Island Me.
  A Western World.

A. DEGEN
  Soft X-Ray / Mindhunters.

ABRAHAM DÍAZ
  Nausea.

STEVE DITKO
  #26.

D.R.T.
  Qoberious, Vol. 1.

G. W. DUNCANSON
  Yaffingale Iditarod.
  Freaker Unltd #5.

DW
  Mountebank.

JESSICA EARHART
  Khloris, Issue 3.

THEO ELLSWORTH
  The Murders in the Rue Morgue.
  The Graphic Canon of Crime & Mystery, Vol. 1.

AUSTIN ENGLISH
  The Enemy from Within.

INES ESTRADA
  Alienation #6.

EDIE FAKE
  Gaylord Phoenix, Issue 8.

JULES FEIFFER
  The Ghost Script.

GG
  I'm Not Here.

ROLANDE GLICENSTEIN
  Uncovering Walter Benjamin, Vols. I & II.

LEIF GOLDBERG
  Lost in the Fun Zone.

ALEX GRAHAM
  Cosmic BE-ING #6.

VERONICA GRAHAM
  Cold Snaps: Weather Reports, Vol. 2.

JAIME HERNANDEZ
The Dragon Slayer:
Folktales from Latin America.

JENNIFER L. HOLM & MATTHEW HOLM
Swing It, Sunny.

KEVIN HOOYMAN
Mr. Meow.
š! #30.

SARA L. JACKSON
The Woman Minotaur.

SEAN KAREMAKER
Feast of Fields.

AIDAN KOCH
Daughter.

ALINE KOMINSKY-CRUMB
My Very Own Dream House.
Love That Bunch.

JEFFREY ODELL KORGEN &
KEVIN C. PYLE
Migrant.

MICHAEL KUPPERMAN
All the Answers.

PATRICK KYLE
The Death of the Master, Part One.

KATE LACOUR
Vivisectionary III.

BLAISE LARMEE
2001.

HANNAH K. LEE
Hey Beautiful.
Language Barrier.

AUGUST LIPP
Roopert.

MITA MAHATO
In Between.

SACHA MARDOU
Someday, My Witch Will Come.
muthamagazine.com

RICHARD MCGUIRE
My Things.

JESSE MCMANUS
The Whistling Factory.

BEN MENDELEWICZ
Renovator.
š! #30.

ADAM MEUSE
Taking Up Space.

HAYLEY DAWN MUIR
one is all, all is one.
The Beginning.

ROMAN MURADOV
Resident Lover.

JASON MURPHY
Cecil's Riddles.

MUSHBUH
310,310.

ALEX NALL
Lawns.

L. NICHOLS
Recapitulation.
Ley Lines #16.

NICK NORMAN
Peggy.

NOU
A Hidden Pleasure.
Freaker Unltd #5.

LAURA PALLMALL
Sporgo #2 & 3.

RON REGÉ, JR.
The Weaver Festival Phenomenon.

KEVIN REILLY
A Thousand Times.

DAVID SANDLIN
Belfaust: A Love Story.
Strapazin #129.

ROBERT SERGEL
TSA Cares.
September 12th and Other Stories.

FIONA SMYTH
Oneirology.
Somnambulance.

CONOR STECHSCHULTE
Generous Bosom 3.

KARL STEVENS
The Winner.

BRENNA THUMMLER
Sheets.

SETH TOBOCMAN
A New America AND Rex R Us.
World War 3 Illustrated #48.

TOM VAN DEUSEN
The Big Me Book.

SARA VARON
New Shoes.

JEE-SHAUN WANG
Paper Mountain.

CHRIS WARE
Pedantry & Pedagogy.

LINDSAY WATSON
Those Eyebeams.
Cold Cube 003.

COOPER WHITTLESEY
Omens of Normal Living.

DAVID WIESNER & DONNA JO NAPOLI
Fish Girl.

ERIC KOSTIUK WILLIAMS
Bathhouse at the End of the World.
Phile Magazine #2.

MADELEINE WITT
House Fires.

JIM WOODRING
Poochytown.

GEORGE WYLESOL
Ghosts, Etc.

GINA WYNBRANDT
Thank You.

MICKEY ZACCHILLI
L.I.B.W.I.W.D. (or, Lay Off My Earthly Vessel).
Lovers Only #2.

CREDITS

"Bit Rot" by E. A. Bethea. First published in *All Killer No Filler.* Copyright © 2018 by Elizabeth Bethea. Reprinted by permission of Elizabeth Bethea.

Excerpt from *Louis Undercover* by Fanny Britt and Isabelle Arsenault. First published in *Louis Undercover*. Copyright © 2018 by Fanny Britt and Isabellel Arsenault. Reprinted by permission of Groundwood Books/House of Anansi Press, Toronto. www.groundwoodbooks.com

Excerpt from "Sex Positive" from *The Pervert* by Remy Boydell and Michelle Perez. First published in *The Pervert.* Copyright © 2018 by Remy Boydell and Michelle Perez. Reprinted by permission of Remy Boydell and Michelle Perez.

Excerpt from "Welcome to O.R.R.A." from *Be Prepared* by Vera Brosgol © 2018 by Vera Brosgol. Reprinted by permission of First Second, an imprint of Roaring Brook Press, a division of Holtzbrinck Publishing Holdings Limited Partnership. All Rights Reserved.

"Hurt or Fuck" by Eleanor Davis. First published in *NOW* #1, Fantagraphics Books. Copyright © 2018 by Eleanor Davis. Reprinted by permission of Eleanor Davis.

Excerpt from *Sabrina* by Nick Drnaso. First published in *Sabrina.* Copyright © 2018 by Nick Drnaso. Images courtesy of Drawn & Quarterly.

Excerpt from *Dognurse* by Margot Ferrick. First published in *Dognurse,* Perfectly Acceptable Press. Copyright © 2018 by Sarah Ferrick. Reprinted by permission of Sarah Ferrick.

"Small Mistakes Make Big Problems" by Sophia Foster-Dimino. First published in *Comics for Choice.* Copyright © 2018 by Sophia Foster-Dimino. Reprinted by permission of Sophia Foster-Dimino.

Excerpt from *Old Ground* by Noel Freibert. First published in *Old Ground.* Copyright © 2018 by Noel Freibert. Reprinted with permission from Koyama Press.

Excerpt from *Kindling* by Xia Gordon. First published in *Kindling.* Copyright © 2018 by Xia Gordon. Reprinted by permission of Xia Gordon.

"Self-Love-Cycle" by Anatola Howard. First published in *What Are You Thinking About?,* Shortbox. Copyright © 2018 by Anatola Howard. Reprinted by permission of Anatola Howard.

Excerpt from *By Monday I'll Be Floating in the Hudson with the Other Garbage* by Laura Lannes. First published in *By Monday I'll Be Floating in the Hudson with the Other Garbage.* Copyright © 2018 by Laura Lannes. Reprinted by permission of Laura Lannes.

Uninhabitable by Jed McGowan. First published in *Uninhabitable.* Copyright © 2018 by Jed McGowan. Reprinted by permission of Jed McGowan.

Excerpt from *whatsa paintoonist?* by Jerry Moriarty. First published in *whatsa paintoonist?* Copyright © 2018 by Jerry Moriarty. Reprinted by permission of Jerry Moriarty.

Excerpt from *Why Don't We Come Together* by Erik Nebel. First published in *4PANEL2*. Copyright © 2018 by Erik Nebel. Reprinted by permission of Erik Nebel.

"Perfect Discipline" from *Perfect Discipline and Unbending Loyalty* by Tommi Parrish. First published in *Perfect Discipline and Unbending Loyalty*. Copyright © 2018 by Tommi Parrish. Reprinted by permission of Kate Parrish Gandrabur.

"Martin Luther King Jr. Was More Radical Than You Think" by Ben Passmore. First published in *The Nib*. Copyright © 2018 by Benjamin Scott Passmore. Reprinted by permission of Benjamin Scott Passmore.

Selections from *King-Cat #78* by John Porcellino. First published in *King-Cat Comics and Stories #78*. Copyright © 2018 by John Porcellino. Reprinted by permission of the author.

"Bitumen or Bust" by Joe Sacco. First published in *Global Warming and the Sweetness of Life*, The MIT Press, 2018. Copyright © 2018 by Joe Sacco. Reprinted by permission of Joe Sacco.

Snow Day for Mr. Good Guy by Nishant Saldanha. First published in Tumblr and Instagram. Copyright © 2018 by Nishant Saldanha. Reprinted by permission of Nishant Saldanha.

"Vanguard" by Leslie Stein. First published in *Present*. Copyright © 2018 by Leslie Stein. Images courtesy of Drawn & Quarterly.

"In Search of Water-Boiled Fish" by Angie Wang. First published in *Eater*. Copyright © 2018 by Vox Media, Inc. Reprinted by permission of Vox Media, Inc.

"Being an Artist and a Mother" by Lauren Weinstein. First published in *The New Yorker*. Copyright © 2018 by Lauren R. Weinstein. Reprinted by permission by permission of Lauren R. Weinstein.

Excerpt from *Grip, Vol. 1*, by Lale Westvind. First published as *Grip, Vol. 1*, Perfectly Acceptable Press, 2018. Copyright © 2018 by Lale Westvind. Reprinted by permission of Lale Westvind.

Excerpt from *Anti-Gone* by Connor Willumsen. First published in *Anti-Gone*. Copyright © 2018 by Connor Willumsen. Reprinted with permission from Koyama Press.

THE BEST AMERICAN SERIES®

FIRST, BEST, AND BEST-SELLING

The Best American Comics

The Best American Essays

The Best American Food Writing

The Best American Mystery Stories

The Best American Nonrequired Reading

The Best American Science and Nature Writing

The Best American Science Fiction and Fantasy

The Best American Short Stories

The Best American Sports Writing

The Best American Travel Writing

Available in print and e-book wherever books are sold.

Visit our website: *hmhbooks.com/series/best-american*

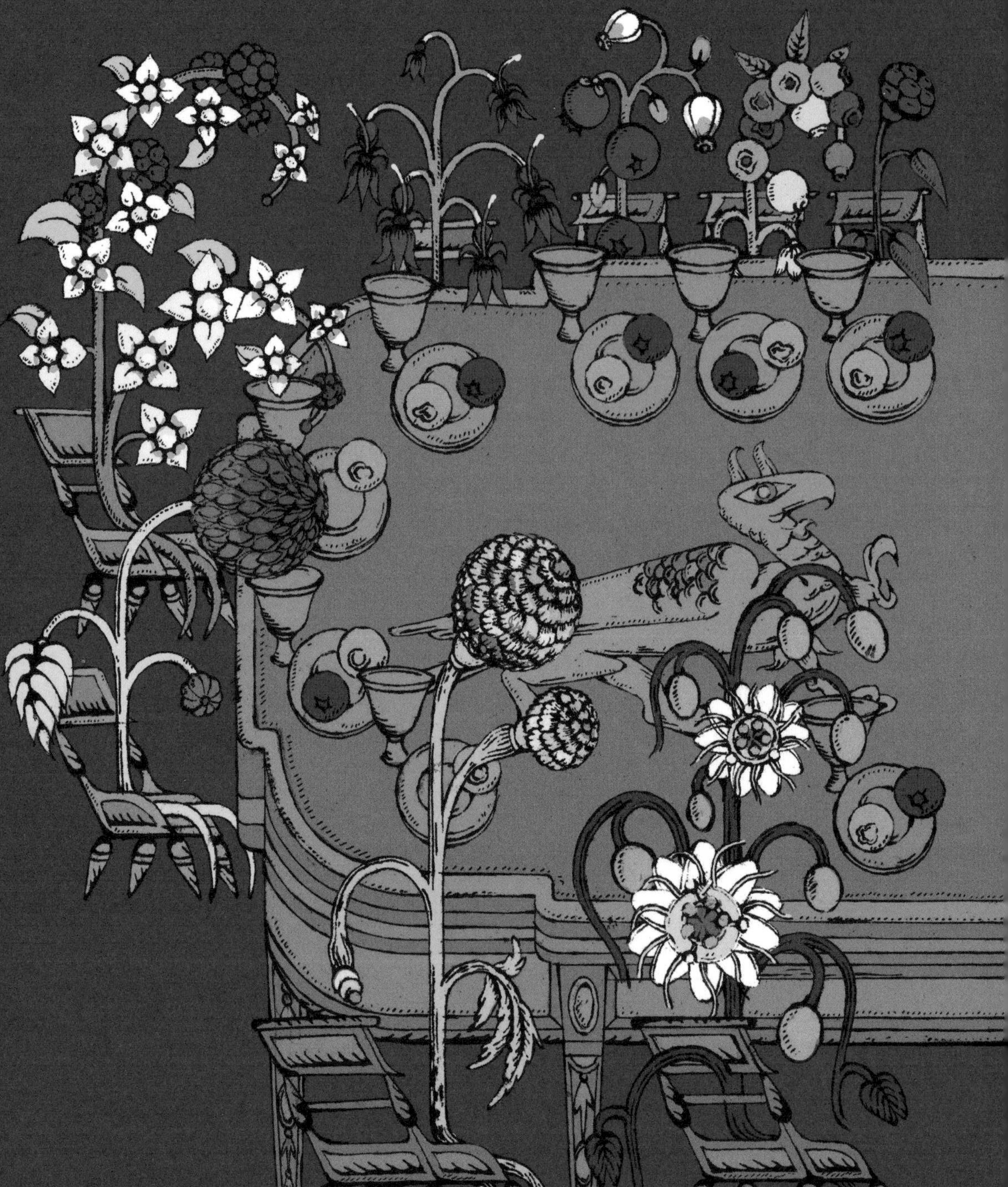